Marshall Cavendish

CONTENTS

Editor: Mary Lambert

Designer: Eljay Crompton

Published by
Marshall Cavendish Books Limited,
58 Old Compton Street,
London W1V 5PA.

Printed and bound in Milan,
Italy by New Interlitho

ISBN 0 86307 271 2

Electricity—the law and you
In the UK, regulations covering wiring are compiled by the Institute of Electrical Engineers. Anyone may do his own wiring, but the IEE regulations must be complied with. These require that major electrical installations should be inspected, tested and certified by a 'competent person' such as a qualified electrician or your local electricity board. Minor improvements do not need to be certified, provided they follow the IEE regulations.
If in doubt, consult a qualified electrician
Electrical regulations stated apply to the UK only and for 240 volt single phase supply.

While every care has been taken to ensure that the information in *Home Handyman* is accurate, individual circumstances may vary greatly. So proceed with caution when following instructions, especially where electrical, plumbing or structural work is involved.

INTRODUCTION

Improving and altering your home can be fun but all too often a project is not attempted because it is too difficult or you just don't have the necessary skills. *Home Handyman* is a comprehensive DIY book which has all the information you need to learn how to keep your home in tip-top condition without spending a fortune.

The book is divided into six sections for easy reference. You can bring to life those neglected rooms by painting or wallpapering them in exciting new colours. All those fiddly repair and installation problems are covered in detail; learn how to plumb-in your washing machine or install a burglar alarm in the electrics section. Insulating your home can save a lot of money in years to come, so why not attempt the double-glazing project in the heating section? Improvement and building projects are also included: you can acquire carpentry skills by designing your own shelf systems or find out how to knock a hole in a brick wall and perhaps fit a serving hatch.

The text is clear and easy to follow and all the projects are illustrated with full colour step-by-steps and comprehensive diagrams. With *Home Handyman* to help, you can really transform your home and also keep it in smooth running order.

PAINTING AND DECORATING

Making good

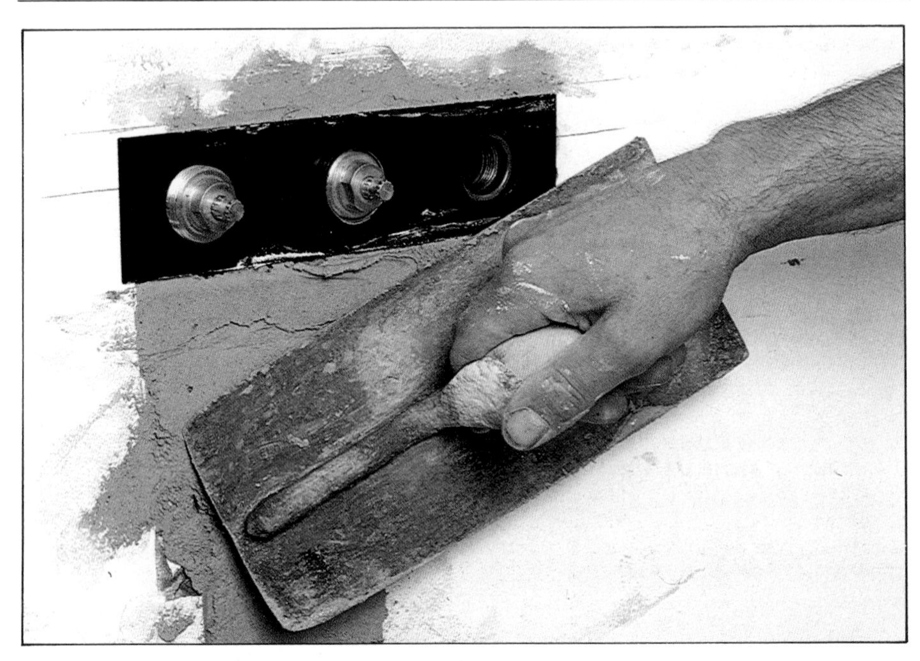

Above: Installing new fittings—like this mixer tap—is only part of the process of home improvements. You must be prepared to take time and trouble to make good any damage to the surrounding surface afterwards or the whole effect could be ruined

However impressive your home improvements, they will not look good until you have repaired the damage inevitably created in the process: this is called *making good.*

Making good is really the cosmetic finish to all the structural, building, plumbing and electrical work that has gone on before. But this does not mean that it is an excuse for hiding bodged or slipshod work. Quite the contrary: making good can be a skilled task and one that often requires care and patience if the work is to be completed neatly and unobtrusively. Not only do you have to make quite certain that the filler and paints that you are using are suitable, but also that the background material—the substrate—is in sound condition.

Correct preparation

No matter what sort of job you are tackling there is no substitute for thorough preparation of the surface beforehand. Remember too that making good—especially the final sanding—is a messy job: always clear the work area of furnishings and lay dust sheets on the floor before starting.

Holes, cracks and indents

Under this classification come all the minor surface imperfections that inevitably accumulate on plastered walls over the years. There are now plenty of products on the market for dealing with them, but which you choose depends a great deal on the extent of the damage and also on how good the finished surface has to be.

For example, a few widely spaced cracks in a wall to be papered are simple to make good using proprietary filler. But a wall which is to be painted and which contains blemishes over more or less the entire surface demands more comprehensive treatment or it will end up looking blotchy and pitted.

Small cracks: These are best filled with ready mixed fine surface filler—a thin, smooth compound which is normally sold with its own plastic spreader. Press the filler hard into the crack and feather off against the surrounding surface. If a slight depression remains, let the first application dry for about half an hour before adding more. You should be able to get the surface perfectly smooth with the spreader alone provided you avoid applying too much filler in one go.

Large cracks and holes: These call for something more robust—it is best to use either ready mixed or powder-form cellulose filler.

The golden rule with all fillers is to work in stages, never applying too much in one go. Applied thinly, they dry quickly so the job is unlikely to take much longer. Traditionally they are applied with a filling knife or palette knife, but many people find a plastic spreader much easier to handle.

Large cracks are unlikely to be the same size along their length, so your first job here is to open them out slightly to provide a sound key for the filler. With holes, trim the edges to a regular shape and make sure there is enough depth for the filler to grip. On both holes and cracks, brush out any dust and flaking material and then dampen the area so that the filler dries consistently.

Extensive damage

Extensive surface damage is best dealt with by resurfacing the whole area with a 'skim' coat of either repair plaster or ready mixed plaster. Before this is done, however, any really deep holes must be made good with cellulose filler to within 3–5mm of the final surface. Holes which extend back as far as the brick or blockwork are best filled with sand and cement mixed with PVA adhesive.

Repair plaster: This is available in small quantities from stores and is a good filler; however, it requires good plastering skill and has an open time of only about 15 minutes.

Ready mixed plaster: This is available in large 10kg tubs. Its great advantage over repair plaster is that it sticks well and it has a long open time—normally quite a few hours.

Repairs to wood

Repairs to wooden surfaces can be tackled in a number of ways. Minor dents and cracks can be easily filled with a proprietary filler either in paste or powder form. With bare wood, however, it is best to treat the timber first using a wood preservative or suitable primer before carrying out the actual repair.

Redecorating

The final job in any making good work is redecoration. If the wall or woodwork is in need of this anyway, there is no problem, as the whole surface can be painted or wallpapered.

If, however, you have made a repair in an otherwise sound surface, you will want to try to minimize the amount of redecoration that is necessary. It is of course quite possible to paint a plastered repair, using the same paint as the rest of the wall, but you may find that the plaster varies in absorbency from the remainder of the surface and so the paint will dry to a slightly different tone. Before repainting therefore, use a proprietary stabilizing solution which will obviate such problems.

If you can still buy the same product, or if you kept some offcuts of wallpaper when the rest of the wall was covered, it is comparatively easy to strip in a new piece to cover up a repair that has been made on the wall.

1 Ready mixed skimming plaster for making good comes in large tubs and is ideal for this larger type of repair job. Stir it well before you use it. Clear the area to be repaired of any tiles, wallpaper or other wallcoverings. Remove stubborn bits of paper carefully with a scraper and use plenty of water

2 The preparation of the surface to be repaired is extremely important as a bodged job will be immediately apparent. Make sure that you take all loose deposits off the wall with the scraper. Then remove any obvious bumps with a piece of glasspaper wrapped firmly round a block of wood

5 When you are plastering larger areas of wall, you may find that it is just not practicable to use a plastic applicator to get it smooth. If this is the case use a plasterer's float, remembering to wet it frequently as the plaster dries off. You can then achieve a really smooth, and very professional-looking finish

6 The plaster has then to be left to dry for quite a long time—normally about six hours. The actual timing very much depends on the depth of the plaster used and the type of drying conditions available. The surface should then be carefully rubbed down with glasspaper wrapped round a block of wood

3 Putting on the plaster is a careful art and it should be applied to the wall using a large paintbrush or distemper brush. Try to get an even amount over the whole area to be covered. Do not use wide strokes at this stage or make it too smooth but rather 'dab' the plaster on in small amounts

4 The long open time of this type of plaster allows you to 'play' with the surface until you get it really smooth. But it is only when it starts to dry—it gets lighter in colour—that you can perfect the surface using the applicator. Keep the strokes light to get it really smooth, feathering off at the edges

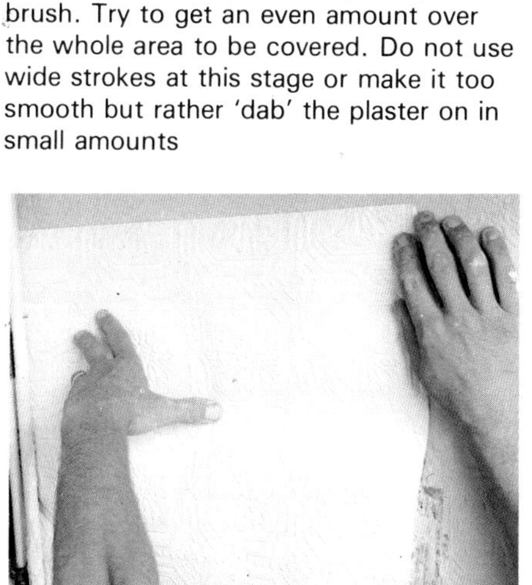

7 Now the damaged area is ready to be repainted or to have a patch of wallpaper. You can often still buy the same wallpaper or possibly use an offcut which you have kept. Tear, not cut, the patch to overlap the hole and then match the pattern. Paste in position and then repaint in the appropriate shade

8 A very deep indent should not be filled with ready mixed plaster. The hole should either be filled out with mortar (made with 1:3 sand and cement) first or conventional plaster. This comes in powder form and needs to be mixed with water, but it has much better filling qualities than ready mixed plaster

Painting walls and ceilings

When you are painting walls and ceilings, bear in mind the preparation of surfaces for paint is the most important part of the process. Without a smooth, clean and dry surface, no amount of care in applying the paint is going to give a professional finish.

New plaster

Make sure that new plaster is absolutely dry before applying paint to it: water trapped in the plaster weakens the adhesion of the paint and may cause blistering.

After preparation, the plaster must be sealed. If you are using emulsion paint, a coat of emulsion thinned with water is sufficient. With oil-based paint use alkali-resisting primer.

Wallpapered surfaces

It is advisable to remove existing wallpaper before painting, as it is never possible to know how well the paper is adhering to the surface and the finished work can be spoiled later. Stripping the wallpaper can be quite a difficult and time-consuming job. If you have a large area, hiring a steam stripper will save a lot of time.

After stripping the old wallpaper, it is important to remove any trace of paste and size left on the surface as these can cause newly applied paint to flake.

Existing painted surface

Painted surfaces must be washed down to remove dirt and grease. In bedrooms and halls, a mixture of washing powder and warm water should be sufficient to remove it. But in kitchens, where the grease is often thick, stronger cleaning agents such as a washing soda solution may be required.

Paints

Emulsion paints dry by the evaporation of their water content, so when you are applying emulsion, keep the windows closed to stop it from drying too quickly. Open the windows as soon as the work is completed to remove moisture from the atmosphere. Emulsion can be applied to central heating radiators, but light shades will discolour easily.

Oil paints are generally more durable than emulsion paints and are well suited to kitchens and bathrooms, where there is a lot of moisture and hard wear.

Oil paint is available in gloss or eggshell (semigloss) finish. Although gloss requires an undercoat if used on an unpainted surface, most brands of eggshell specify that two coats of the finish paint gives sufficient coverage.

Some brands of oil paint are supplied in jelly-like, *thixotropic* form. These are designed to produce thicker coatings and—if applied correctly—present fewer problems with drips and splashes.

When oil paint begins to dry, the thinners base evaporates into the atmosphere and oxygen then combines with the oil in the coating to form a hard film. Because of this, you must complete each coat as quickly as possible.

Painting ceilings and walls

The most important consideration when painting ceilings is to have a suitable scaffold arrangement to avoid the temptation to over-reach and to ensure that there is sufficient light to show up the wet edge between the applied paint

1 If you are repapering a wall it is always advisable to completely remove the old paper first. Try to pull off any loose wallpaper, then brush water liberally on to the remainder of the paper which cannot easily be removed by hand. Use large sweeping strokes with the brush to thoroughly soak the paper

2 Allow the water to thoroughly soak in for a few minutes, then using a paint scraper start to remove the wallpaper. Use the scraper carefully or you will damage the plaster underneath and the wall will then have to be patched. Also remove any old paste and size that is still on the wall

3 Old varnishes can sometimes be difficult to remove, so use a stiff wire brush to really bite into the surface of the paper. When you have removed all the varnish you can with the scraper and firmly scratched the surface, brush more water on the paper and then repeat the process again

4 Stripping large surfaces of wallpaper can be very hard work and takes a lot of time. If you have a large area of paper to remove, hiring a steam stripper from a local hire shop can be a very good idea. Work the stripper in straight lines from the bottom of the wall and let the steam rise up the wallpaper

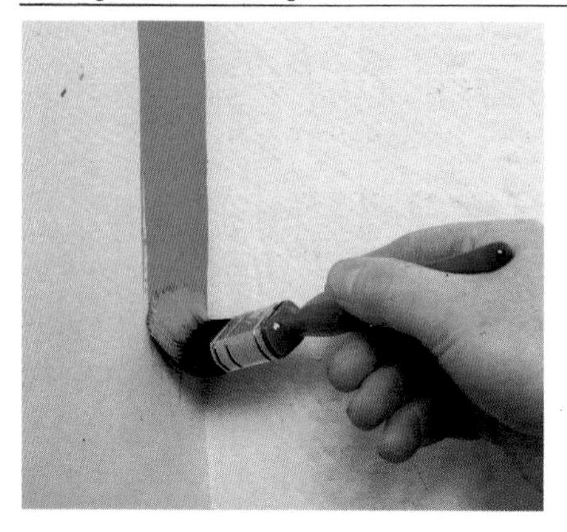

5 When you are using a roller to paint the wall, use a small paint brush to cut in at the corners before painting the main area of wall

6 When you have cut in the line at the edges, paint the first strip. Make sure the handle join of the roller is not right against the corner

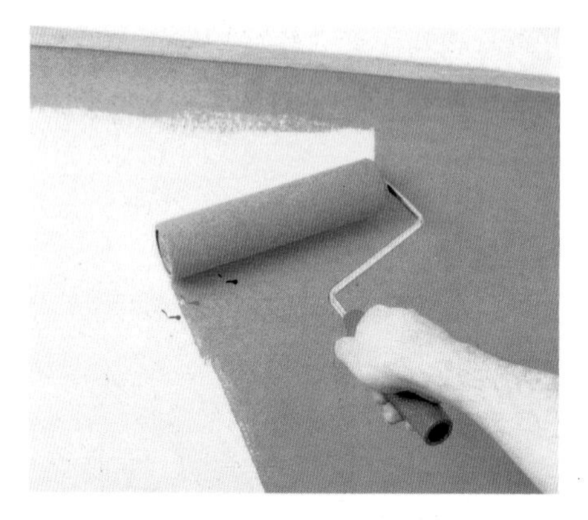

7 It is best to paint only a small area of wall at a time, working from the corners where you have cut in and over-lapping and crossing the strips

8 Extend the strokes of the roller out from each completed area and get a smooth, even coat by criss-crossing each strip of paint you have done

and the unpainted surface which is left.

As with ceilings, it is most important that the wet edge is not allowed to set before more paint is applied. If this happens, the paint does not flow together and thick ridges appear.

Unless the walls are very high, a pair of stepladders should be sufficient.

Recommended equipment

Brushes should be as large as you can handle—130mm or 150mm are the most suitable sizes for emulsion paints, while 75mm or 100mm brushes are better for applying the more viscous oil paints.

If you use a roller, mohair or short-pile synthetic coverings are suitable for smooth surfaces. For heavily textured surfaces such as plastic texture paints or heavily embossed papers, lambswool or medium-pile synthetic covers are much more suitable.

Applying the paint

Apply brushed-on emulsion in all directions, using long sweeping strokes to give a full, level coat of the paint. Use a smaller brush of about 25mm to apply the paint behind pipes and awkward areas.

A similar method is used for applying emulsion paint with a roller. Coat the roller evenly with paint and roll in all directions, making the final strokes lighter to cut down the texture imprint.

Brush on oil paints with much firmer strokes, making sure that there is not too much paint on the brush. Oil paints are more viscous and without good, firm strokes they will run or sag. Apply the thixotropic type paints firmly in all directions and leave them to flow out smoothly of their own accord.

Below: Painting a mural in a child's room can be a fun thing to do and can make the room much more interesting

Drying

Most water-based paints can be given a further coat after approximately four hours, depending both on the temperature and humidity of the room and on the porosity of the surface.

Oil paints may appear dry after about three hours, but if further coats are applied at this time, you will find that the existing coat starts to soften and pull off on to the brush. This is due to the action of the thinner in the paint which is being applied. If you are not certain that the coating is sufficiently hard to paint over, leave it until the next day.

Cleaning equipment

Remember that paint dries on rollers and brushes just as easily as on walls or ceilings, and is difficult to remove once it has dried. So, if you have to pause while painting do not let the brushes dry out completely.

Maintaining brushes and rollers

With the right painting equipment, decorating takes less time and effort and good results are more easily attained.

Choosing a brush

Brushes for painting normally come in widths from 12mm up to 150mm. Small brushes are often known as 'varnish brushes'. Large ones are called 'wall brushes'.

A brush has four parts: a handle, of wood or plastic; the metal heel or *ferrule*, which contains the bristles; the bristles themselves; and filler strips within the ferrule which plump out the bristles. Some brushes have the bristles set into rubber, which is intended to prevent them from working loose from the ferrule.

Using brushes

When using a varnish brush you should hold it almost completely by the ferrule, with four fingers to one side and the thumb on the other. This will give you close control and enable you to flex your wrist in fine movements. On larger areas apply the paint first in one direction, then at right-angles, and finally lay off in gentle strokes with the brush barely charged. Make the final strokes follow one direction to get the best finish.

Maintaining brushes

In general you must try to keep paint away from the ferrule and the top end of the bristles. When cleaning brushes, scrape off any excess paint that has gathered there with a blunt blade. Always remember to clean brushes thoroughly before storing them.

After emulsion painting: Emulsion paint dries very quickly, and if you take a break of more than 20 minutes you must scrape off any excess paint and put the brush, wrapped in a damp rag, inside a sealed polythene bag. At the end of a painting session, wash the brush clean in some warm water with detergent.

After gloss painting: Although brushes which have been used for most oil-based paint are in fact harder to clean, they take longer to dry out and can be stored temporarily without being cleaned immediately.

To store a gloss-polluted brush, suspend the bristles (but not the ferrule) in water. Do not allow the brush to rest on the bristles. Purpose-made racks are available, but alternatively you can drill a small hole near the base of the handle and insert through this a short length of wire. Suspend the brush from the wire in a suitable jar of water and when you restart, shake off the excess.

To clean a brush that has been used with gloss paint, soak it in turps, white spirit or a proprietary paint cleaner. Then, when the brush is clean, wash the solvent out of it with soapy water.

To store a brush for any length of time, first spin it in your hand and rub it on a clean rag to remove excess water. Then smooth the bristles flat, wrap the brush in newspaper and lay it flat or hang it up—keeping the paper in place with a rubber band.

Choosing a roller

Rollers consist of a wooden or plastic handle attached to a metal frame, around which the painting sleeve is fixed. Most of them come with a special tray to hold the paint with which the sleeve is charged.

The sleeves are available with either a short, dense pile or a long, looser pile. The shorter piles are usually made of

Brushes below: **(A)** 12mm synthetic brush—these are very hard wearing **(B)** 12mm pure bristle 'cutting in' brush—the slant allows accurate straight line painting **(C)** 25mm pure bristle brush **(D)** 50mm pure bristle paint brush—an ideal medium-sized brush for general-purpose work **(E)** 75mm pure bristle flat paint brush—the largest brush for fine work **(F)** 175mm bristle flat wall brush, used to apply emulsion paints to large areas and adhesives to surface coverings **(G)** Pure bristle two-knot brush—the knots are usually bound in copper and the brush is suitable for applying emulsion paints to large areas and adhesives to surface coverings **(H)** 100mm pure bristle flat paint brush, suitable for applying most types of paint and varnish to a wide variety of surfaces including doors, sashes, frames and wall areas **(I & J)** Bristle brushes, but **(I)** is a cheaper one

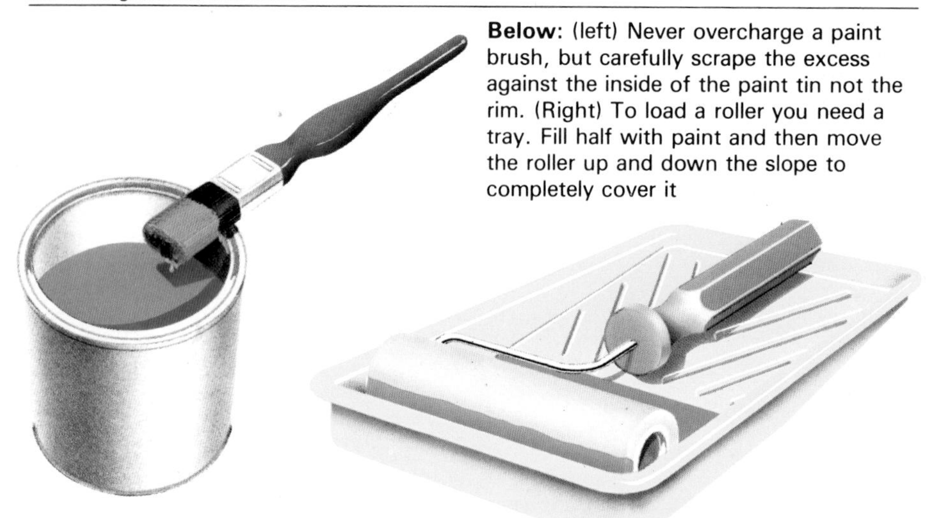

Below: (left) Never overcharge a paint brush, but carefully scrape the excess against the inside of the paint tin not the rim. (Right) To load a roller you need a tray. Fill half with paint and then move the roller up and down the slope to completely cover it

mohair, plastic foam, or felt. The long-pile types may be wool, sheepskin, or a synthetic imitation material.

When you are using oil-based paints, short-pile rollers are best, but still not as good as brushes. Mohair pile is expensive, but is very effective with any type of paint, provided the pile is in good condition.

Sleeves, which are available in 180mm, 229mm and 305mm sizes, are always the major consideration when choosing a roller. But you should check also how easy it is to remove the sleeve—they have to be taken from the frame to clean them.

Using a roller

Start by filling the tray with paint, but leave at least half of the sloping portion uncovered. Dip the roller into the deep part then work it up and down on the slope so that you really distribute the paint evenly.

Make the first run upwards on a wall, or away from you on a horizontal surface. Roll steadily until an area is covered but do not apply excessive pressure in the hope of squeezing more paint out of the roller. Criss-cross the area to get the paint on evenly and smoothly, but make the finishing strokes in only one direction.

Maintaining rollers

Cleaning roller sleeves generally presents a much more daunting prospect than cleaning brushes. If you stop work temporarily, you can seal the roller in a plastic bag to stop the paint from hardening. But first remove the excess paint, and then wrap the sleeve carefully in a wet rag.

Below: To store a roller cover for a long period of time, it is enough simply to place it upright on a shelf so that the pile is not crushed

Special effects painting

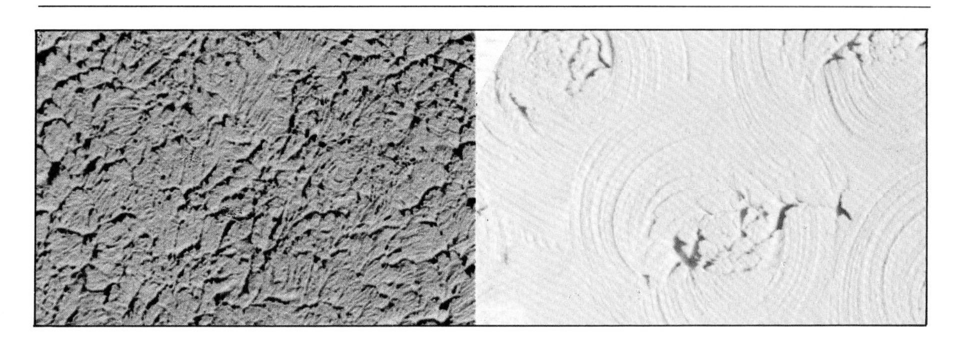

Above: You need only a few tools—many of which can be homemade—to create a variety of patterns using texture paints. Try doing the stipple and swirl above

Texture painting involves brushing a thick compound on to a wall or ceiling and then rippling the surface with a special tool to the pattern of your choice. This form of decoration was very popular in the 1920s and 30s in cinemas, restaurants and private homes and is now enjoying a decorative revival in the UK.

It has the advantage that you can use it on both internal and external walls, to improve the look of plain surfaces as well as filling small cracks and faults.

Another positive benefit is that it is cheap and easy to apply to a wide variety of different surfaces. For instance, you can easily and neatly coat plasterboard ceilings with texture paint. This should be cheaper than plastering all over, and better-looking than dry walling (where you fill just the joints). The technique can also be carried out on many types of building board.

However, bear in mind that texture paints become semi-permanent when fully hardened, and that removing them is often difficult and may damage the underlying surface. So make sure whether texture paint is the finish you require before decorating.

Exterior finishes

You can apply texture paint to a wide variety of exterior surfaces—such as concrete, cement rendering, brick, plasterboard, asbestos cement panels and plaster—where the dense finish will help to cover small cracks and discoloured backgrounds. Most exterior-grade texture paints have a ready built-in fungicide which resists the growth of mould and you can apply them with a brush, synthetic roller, trowel or spray gun.

Before you start painting, clean all the surfaces thoroughly and remove any grease by washing them down with detergent. Any loose paint and dust should be removed with a wire brush and if there is any sign of mould on the walls, make sure that this too is brushed away. All large cracks or splits need to be raked out and made good. Also, this is a good time to repair all the defective gutters,

1 A stipple texture can be achieved by applying the compound with a brush then dabbing the wet surface gently but firmly, with the stippler

2 You can also get a stipple finish by applying the compound with a synthetic roller and working vigorously from side to side

5 By pushing the edge of a caulking blade right into the material, a wide variety of fan and circle patterns can be created easily

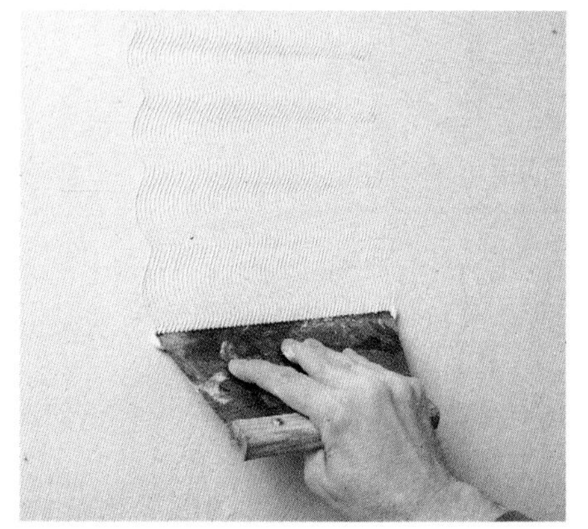

6 A distinct variety of comb effects can be created by gently drawing a notched blade right across the surface of the compound

downpipes and brickwork.

Exterior texture paint is usually supplied ready for use and only one coat is needed.

Preparing interior surfaces

It is well worth taking extra care when you are texture painting inside the house, since a good finish is particularly important. Meticulously preparing surfaces before you paint is time well spent and may prevent long-term problems such as splits and cracks in the drying paint.

Bare wooden surfaces: Prime these with a suitable sealer and fill any gaps between joints with a creamy mixture of the paint compound.

Paint and emulsion: Remove any dirt and grease and scrape off flaking paint

3 The tree bark type of effect is made with a hard rubber roller criss-crossed with rubber bands to achieve a deeper relief

4 Draw a piece of plastic across the surface of a deep texture before it dries to remove any high or sharp edges that might have occurred

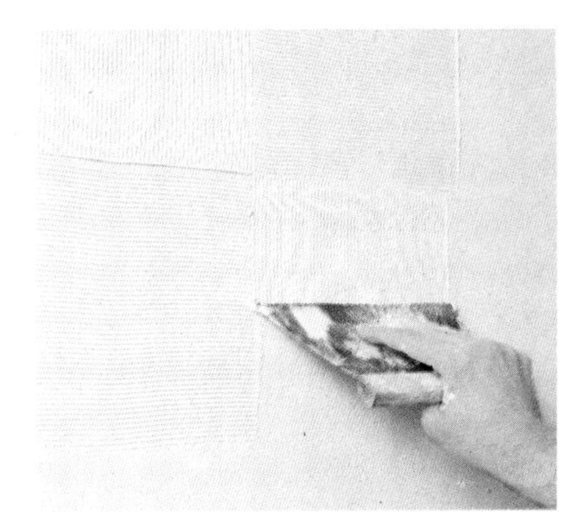

7 This patchwork pattern effect is made by combing alternate lines at right-angles to one another across the actual face of the wall

8 By using a brush with hard rubber bristles, you can inscribe a whole variety of deep-relief patterns on to the surface of the wall

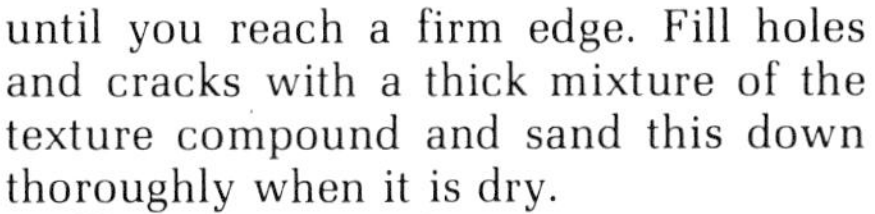

until you reach a firm edge. Fill holes and cracks with a thick mixture of the texture compound and sand this down thoroughly when it is dry.

Wallpaper: Even though your existing wallpaper appears to be securely fixed to the wall, it should be removed—it may come loose after some time, and may well take a great deal of the texture paint along with it.

Applying the paint

Apply the paint to the surface thick enough to allow for some depth of patterning, using a 200mm distemper brush, roller or spray gun. Apply it with a long, stroking action—working from top to bottom in the case of a wall. Be careful not to paint too large an area in one go or you may find that the paint has completely dried out before you have a

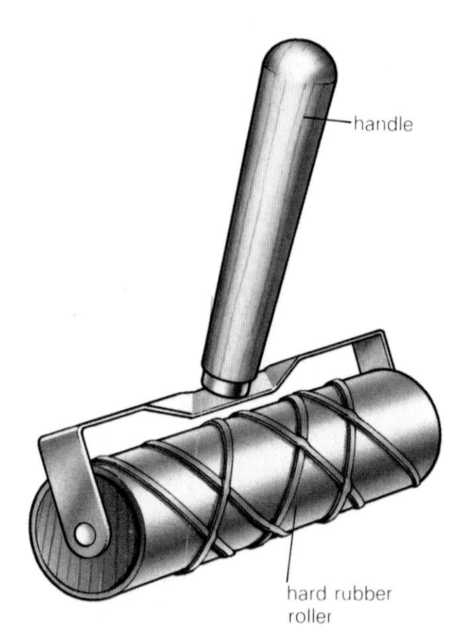

Above: A hard rubber roller—as wide as you can get it—criss-crossed with rubber bands is used to create the popular and attractive tree bark effect

chance to texture it properly.

Ashlar: This effect gives the appearance of stone slabs or blocks with mortar joints. Before you paint it, divide the edge of the area to be textured into brick or block widths and mark these clearly. Then texture the surface in a stipple finish, taking care not to obscure the marks.

While the paint is still wet, hold a wooden straightedge against the marks with small blocks at each end to stop it touching the surface. Draw a thin piece of wood through the wet coating to produce the joint effect horizontally and vertically, then, when the material is dry, remove any high points with a sanding block.

Tree bark effect: For this you need a hard rubber or wooden roller in as wide a size as you can get. Cover this with rubber bands arranged so that they criss-cross one another. After you have applied the paint, wet the roller slightly and roll it lightly over the surface until the whole area is textured, making sure that you do not go over any areas twice. When set, scrape the surface to remove any sharp high points (fig. 4).

Stippled texture: This is perhaps the most popular texture and can produce striking results.

When you have applied the paint, dab the stippler against the wet surface with an irregular action to avoid straight lines (fig. 1). Again, never go back over previously textured areas.

To avoid the sharp points produced by this type of texturing, especially on wall areas, draw a piece of plastic sheet lightly across the surface before it hardens—a process known as *lacing*—to flatten the stipples.

Swirl effect: To make this, start by painting and stippling the surface as above, then hold the stippler against the surface and twist it in a clockwise direction (fig. 8). The swirl formed by each twist should overlap the previous one to give an overall, random effect.

Comb patterns

Several different effects can be produced by drawing notched blades or *combs* through the wet coating. Make these yourself from sheets of plastic, metal or hardboard, cut to the pattern of your choice.

Repairs and painting

Though texture paints are available already coloured, it is possible to paint the plain white type with both emulsion and oil-based paints: simply make sure that the surface has dried properly before painting in the normal way.

Despite good preparation of base surfaces, repairs often have to be made to textured finishes. It may be that water has leaked through a ceiling to damage the coating or that the existing texture has extended to another area. Before carrying out this type of work, prepare sample boards 500mm square to practise matching textures.

Interior woodwork

Above: A light upward stroke of the brush will ensure that your painted surface is free from unsightly streaks and noticeable ridges

Repainting the woodwork around the house will give your decoration a facelift for very little cost. And if you set about it the right way, you can be sure of a really professional finish.

Preparing the surface

Whether painting over new woodwork or a surface that has been painted previously, it is vital to make sure that the surface is sound, clean and dry.

With new woodwork, smooth the surface down with glasspaper, slightly rounding off any sharp edges. Treat knots or resinous patches with a knotting compound to prevent them from leaking sap through to the new paint. Fill cracks and open joints with a cellulose filler such as Polyfilla.

To ensure that the paint adheres to the surface, new wood should be given a coat of primer. Primer also partially seals the wood surfaces, preventing leaking sap from spoiling the final coat of paint.

In most cases, previously painted woodwork needs no more than cleaning and lightly rubbing down to prepare it. Remove all dirt and grease by washing the surface with warm water and detergent or sugar soap, paying particular attention to areas on doors that are handled often and to wax polished surfaces.

To key the surface for the new paint, old gloss must be abraded to remove its shine. Although glasspaper can be used for this, better results are obtained with wet and dry paper, used wet.

Dealing with damaged surfaces

Unless a damaged surface is thoroughly prepared beforehand, flaws such as blisters and bubbles will be accentuated and may spoil the finish.

Large or resinous knots and small resinous patches in woodwork should be treated with a knotting compound.

Flaking paint is most likely to be found on window frames which have been affected by the weather and by condensation. Remove as much of the

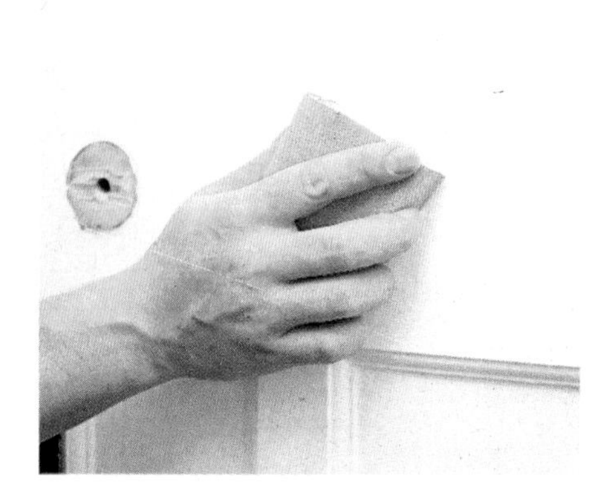

1 When treating woodwork that has been previously painted, sand down the old surface with glasspaper slightly rounded at the edges. This removes the shine and gives a good key for the new paint. After sanding the old paintwork, wash the surface with warm water and detergent to remove all traces of dust and grease. Use white spirit where there are heavy deposits of grease

2 Remove loose paint and any flaws on the surface of old paintwork, such as badly flaking paint around door fittings, with a paint scraper or a sharp knife. Paint on the area around window frames and glass panels is particularly bad for flaking. Scrape off as much of the old paint as possible, paying particular attention to all the corners where dirt has a habit of collecting

3 Where cracks have occurred in the woodwork, clean them and widen with a sharp knife and then apply a coat of primer. This then seals the surface and prevents sap leaking from new wood. Always check that the primer you buy is suitable for the particular type of wood to be painted. Highly resinous wood should be treated with aluminium wood primer, which has very effective sealing qualities

4 Fill the cracks and dents with cellulose filler so that the damaged areas are brought up level with the existing paintwork. Allow the cellulose filler to completely dry out and then carefully smooth the area with some glasspaper wrapped around a wood or cork block. Make sure you smooth the filled area so that it is completely flat and then prime the wood again

5 Use a special paint-stripping head when stripping paint with a blowlamp. Carefully play the flame from side to side to avoid charring the wood. Keep a waste tin nearby to catch the pieces of hot paint as they fall. When working on stripping paint off mouldings, use a shave hook. To avoid shreds of melting paint falling on to your hand and burning you, keep the tool at an angle

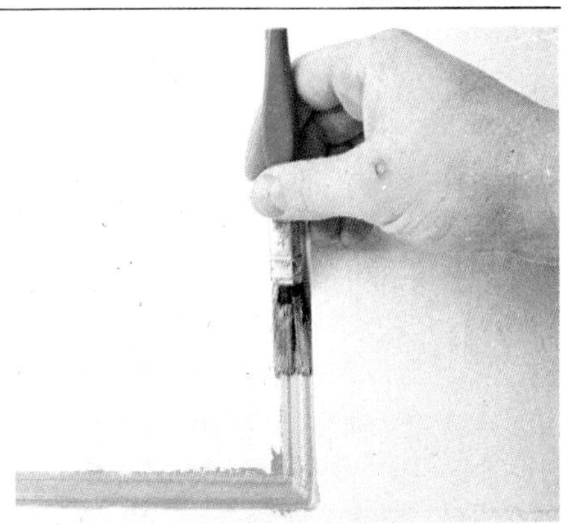

6 When painting mouldings or panel doors, use a 12mm brush. Apply the paint sparingly so that it does not accumulate in ugly ridges and use quick and smooth strokes. When actually painting the main panel, start the brush strokes from the moulding edges and work in towards the middle. Always blend the edges together so that you completely eliminate any overlap marks

7 A handy gadget to keep paint off glass when painting doors or windows is a paint shield. It is obtainable from do-it-yourself shops and comes in either aluminium or plastic. You can also use masking tape round all the edges of the glass. However, if paint still gets through on to the glass, leave it to dry completely and then scrape it off with either a paint scraper or a sharp knife

loose paint as possible with a paint scraper or sharp knife (fig. 2). Smooth down the area with glasspaper until all the remaining paint is quite sound. Any knots that have been exposed in this process should be dealt with as described above.

Cracks occur when wood joints have dried out or split. The most common problem areas are window frames, architraves—the mouldings around doors and windows—and the corner joints in skirtings. Start by widening the cracks with a sharp knife, raking out any dust and dirt as you go. Prime the enlarged cracks and plug them with adequate cellulose filler (fig. 4). When dry, smooth with glasspaper and prime with a multipurpose primer.

Stripping paint

If a painted surface is particularly badly damaged, strip the paint off completely. Although paint can be stripped using just a paint scraper, this can become tiring

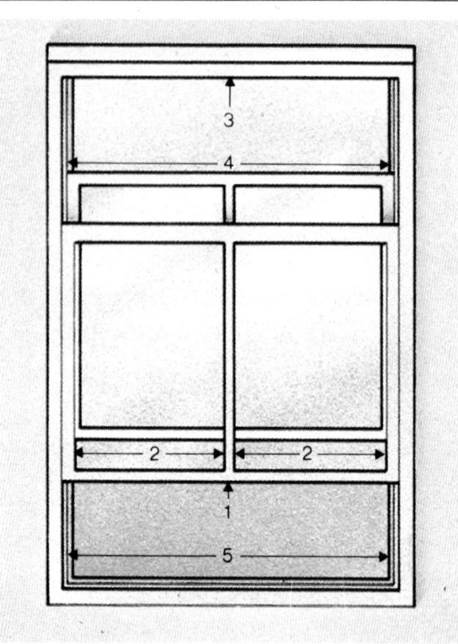

A. The painting sequence for a double-hung window. Finish off in the order shown for casement windows

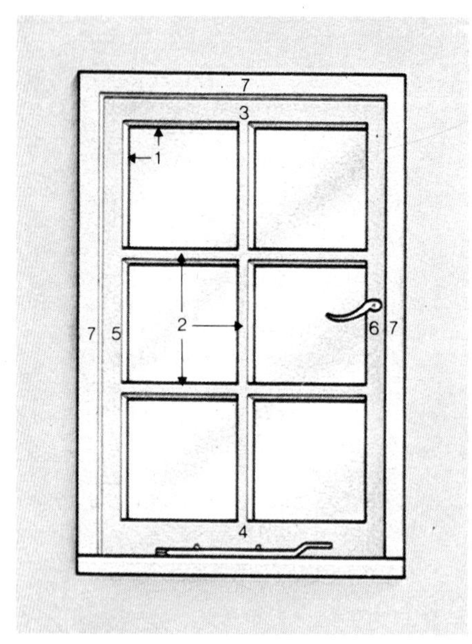

B. Casement windows should be painted in sequence. Make sure you paint all edges of the frame

over large areas. More efficient methods are chemical stripping or heat stripping with a blowlamp and scraper. However, use a low flame—and extra caution—when stripping window frames with a blowlamp as the very strong heat may crack the glass.

Begin stripping at the bottom of an area and work upwards, covering only a small area at a time. Play the flame from side to side to avoid burning the paint and charring the wood. As the paint melts, scrape it off holding the scraper at an angle so that shreds of hot paint do not fall on to your hand. For stripping mouldings, use a shave hook. When all the paint has been completely stripped, prime the bare wood.

Undercoats

If you are painting new wood that has only been primed, or over paintwork of a different colour, it is advisable to apply an undercoat to provide a good key for the final coat of gloss. Check the paint charts when buying gloss and undercoat to ensure they are compatible.

Gloss paint

Interior woodwork is traditionally painted with gloss or semi-gloss paint. Doors, skirtings and window frames all take quite a few knocks and gloss paint stands up to hard wear better than flat paints—as well as being easier to clean with a damp cloth.

Traditional gloss paint is oil based and includes resin to give it hard-wearing qualities. Acrylic paint is a water-based gloss which is jelly-like in consistency and does not drip. It should never be stirred, however, as this will reduce its non-drip qualities. If applied incorrectly, gloss shows up blemishes and brush marks more than any other type of paint. So you must use proper brush strokes.

In large areas, brushing in three different directions will help you obtain a smoother finish. Start by applying the paint in a random way, criss-crossing the brush: when a section has been covered, draw the brush over the paint horizontally. Finally, lay off the paint by running the brush upwards over the paint very lightly so that no mark is left.

Painting doors

Doors are not as easy to paint as you might think. To make the job easier, start by wedging the door base against the floor with a wedge or screwdriver. This will stop it from swinging shut, and perhaps ruining a wet edge. Remove as much metalwork as you can, including handles, knobs and key escutcheons.

When painting flush doors, start at the top and work down in sections using a 75mm brush. Work quickly so that the paint does not harden before you have completed an adjoining section.

Apply the paint by making two or three separate downward strokes. Without reloading the brush, fill in any gaps by cross brushing, then gently lay off the paintwork. When you are painting the edge of the door, use a brush slightly narrower than the width of the edge. If you use a wider brush, paint is likely to run down the door.

Panel doors should be painted in a strict sequence (fig. C) and as quickly as possible—any pauses will result in the formation of a hard edge which is almost impossible to remove.

C. The painting sequence for a panel door. Panel doors should be painted in one session without pauses

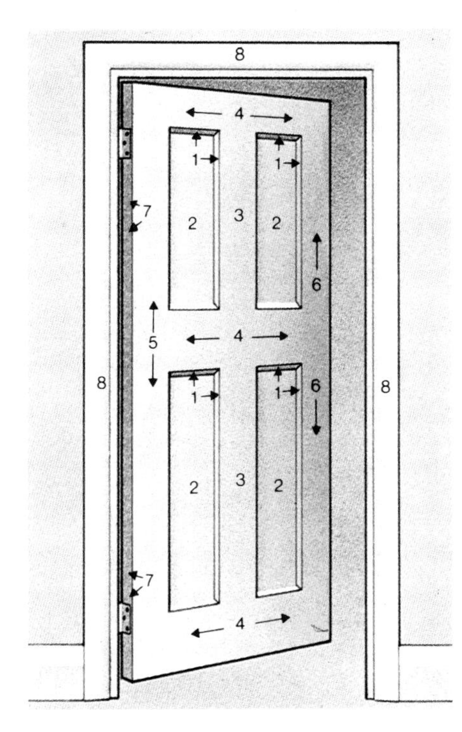

Skirting and architraves

Start painting skirtings at the top edge and architraves at the edge where they meet the wall.

To brush up, or 'cut in' to the wall at this point, use a cutting-in tool—a specially angled brush—or a 25mm brush on its side. Avoid overloading the brush, dipping it only about 13mm into the paint. Cut in with one, continuous stroke, supporting your 'painting' hand with the other hand to steady it.

Windows

The paintwork on wooden windows must be kept in good condition if the frames are to be prevented from rotting.

Remove any window fittings such as sash fasteners and make sure that the surface is clean and sound. Clean the glass, to prevent any dust or dirt on it from falling on to the wet paint.

To keep paint off the glass, you can if you wish mask up each pane. This is best done with an aluminium or plastic paint shield (fig. 7)—obtainable from do-it-yourself shops—or masking tape. If paint still penetrates on to the glass, wait until it is dry then scrape it off with a paint scraper or a sharp knife.

Casement windows, like panel doors, should be painted in sequence (fig. B).

To paint a double-hung window, begin by pulling the bottom sash up and the top sash down to expose the meeting rail. When the bottom parts of the top sash have been painted, almost close the window then paint the remaining areas (fig. A). Finish off in the order shown for casement windows.

Outside walls

As with all painting, the quality and integrity of the finish depends to a large extent on the preparation of the surface before you even open a tin of paint. And the preparation differs according to the surface to be painted.

New brick

Concrete, cement rendering and pebbledash should be treated in the same way as new brick.

To start with, remove any dust or loose material using a stiff brush, and scrape off any splashes of cement or concrete. Look out for any patches of white fluffy crystals; these are a result of efflorescence, and indicate that moisture is coming to the surface of the wall. If you paint over the patches the moisture will tend to lift the paint off. Clean the efflorescent debris off the walls with a stiff brush and wait about two weeks to make sure that no more patches emerge. Finally, make good deep cracks or holes in the surface with sand and cement.

Previously painted masonry

It is always advisable to prepare painted surfaces before repainting, and in the case of exterior work it is essential if the new coatings are to protect the building in the way they are designed to.

Oil paints: Wash with a strong cleaning agent such as washing soda, then rinse with clean water.

Emulsion paints: Wash with a detergent, then rinse with clean water. Again, scrape off loose and flaking paint and then repair cracks.

Cement-based paints: These and other non-washable types of paint have been used extensively in the past on large areas of exterior masonry, mainly because they are fairly cheap. However, most cement paints tend to become very powdery with age, and washing, which only softens them further, must be avoided. You must, therefore, thoroughly brush, and if necessary scrape, the walls until you have a firm surface. Finally, you must apply a masonry sealer or stabilizing solution to the cleaned walls. This will soak into the existing material, binding it into a solid film not soluble in water and resistant to it.

Above: Painting outside walls can be a straightforward task, provided the necessary preparation has been done

Wood

Preparing large areas of wood—eg weatherboard or clapboard siding—for painting is dealt with in the next section. The amount of work needed depends mainly on the condition of the already existing paintwork.

Damp surfaces

Walls which display signs of either damp or mould growth must be treated before you can paint.

Where surfaces are prone to damp, such as basement walls or garden walls, you must apply a coat of bituminous emulsion sealer and allow it to dry thoroughly.

Masonry paints

Masonry paint is a water-based paint similar to emulsion but with the addition of other materials such as granulated quartz, mica, and in some instances fine strands of glass fibre. These additives render it highly durable, moisture resistant and give it the ability to resist cracks in the surface, while providing a very attractive fine texture.

Applying masonry paint

Masonry paint may be applied by brush or roller. A roller is much faster than a brush, but for inaccessible corners a brush is unbeatable. On heavily textured surfaces such as pebbledash or rough brickwork a long-pile roller, which can penetrate into all the crevices, is most suitable.

Brushes, if you decide to use them, must be as large as possible—100-150mm wide. Nylon or bristle and fibre brushes will stand up to the abrasive nature of exterior surfaces much better than pure bristle.

Access for application

In most cases exterior surfaces are larger and higher than interior surfaces. Consequently some form of scaffolding may be required, and a method of working which will result in even coverage after a number of sessions.

Unless you have to contend with a large expanse of wall, a ladder will probably suffice. Use a ladder stay when working at heights; it will make the ladder more stable and make it easier to hang a bucket or roller scuttle on the underside with easy access for the brush or roller. Extend the ladder so that you can reach the top of the wall. But remember that it is unsafe to leave less than four rungs above your feet; this will allow you a safe hand hold. Position the ladder so that you can reach the extreme right-hand side—or left-hand side if you are left-handed—of the wall.

Painting

Try to plan exterior painting for warm, dry days. Extreme cold or frost can affect the water content of the paint, causing a complete breakdown in the film. Rain on the surface before the paint is dry can thin it disastrously.

The first coat on porous surfaces can be thinned—but follow manufacturer's instructions carefully.

Charge the brush or roller with plenty of paint, and lay it or roll it in all directions. Do not apply the material too far, however, because correct covering and protection requires that it be twice as thick as ordinary liquid paints. Any spots and splashes must be washed off immediately with water because exterior-grade paint sets rapidly.

When you have completed a session of work immediately clean all the equipment in detergent and water. But take care not to block sink wastes with the fine granulated quartz, or scratch enamel or stainless steel sinks.

Painting wood surfaces

On the wood that is already painted, or if you prefer a painted finish, then ordinary oil-based gloss paint can be used. Apply this using a brush rather than a roller. On horizontal, overlapping siding, paint the underneath projections before painting the vertical surfaces, making sure they are completely covered—areas that you miss will be very obvious from ground level. Try not to break a painting session in the middle of a length of siding—make your breaks between adjacent boards.

Exterior wood stains and coloured wood preservatives can also be used, especially on shingles and shakes. But check manufacturer's instructions first: most products are applied to new wood.

1 Before you can start painting your property outside, you must remove all wall decorations such as shutters and tie trellis-trained plants so that they are well out of harm's way. It is also advisable to cover all nearby plants and tile steps or thresholds so that you avoid spoiling them with ugly and defacing splashes of paint

2 The next stage is to brush away any heavy deposits of dirt that have accumulated with a stiff brush. Do not use a wire brush, however, because stray strands, that might be left behind, will cause rust marks. Also be on the lookout for patches of white fluffy crystals—these indicate that moisture is coming to the surface of the wall

5 To get the walls really clean before you start painting, make up a strong bleach solution and apply it sparingly with a brush to all visible mould and plant growth in order to destroy it. When you have thoroughly treated the whole area, carefully wash off the bleach with plenty of cold water

6 Damaged pointing or surface defects will show up badly if painted over, so before you start you should examine the surface closely. Any defects which are found should be raked out and then made good using sand and cement. Apply the mixture smoothly and evenly in small amounts using a small trowel

3 It is advisable in most cases to apply a coat of masonry sealer or stabilizing solution to the brickwork. Brush it on liberally, allowing it to soak well into the bricks. This will give the wall much more protection because the solution binds with the existing material making an overall covering film that is completely water resistant

4 As you do not want to go up and down a ladder constantly to get more paint, mix a sufficient quantity to complete the job before you start, filling a paint bucket with the mixture. This will avoid changes in colour. Also remember when you stop painting for a while to put the brush in a polythene bag to keep it moist and pliable

7 When you are working at heights, a ladder stay is a very useful accessory as it makes the ladder much more stable. You can also hang a bucket or roller scuttle from it, making it easier to paint. Remember that you must always leave four rungs of ladder above your feet to give you a safe hand hold

8 Always work from one side of the ladder only. Trying to cover both sides will result in difficulties because the ladder is in the way. It is also not possible to use the roller when painting inaccessible or awkward areas. In these cases it is far easier to resort to using a small distemper brush

Exterior wood and metal

Painting the outside of your house is by far the most demanding and time-consuming type of decoration you can do. It is obviously not work you want to repeat often so careful planning, the right tools and materials, and an extremely methodical approach are important. This way, you can be sure of an attractive and durable finish.

When to paint

Although spring is the traditional time to paint the outside it is not necessarily the best time. If the exterior wood and metal need painting in the spring, no doubt they needed it in the autumn; and the ravages of winter can worsen the condition of the paintwork and make your job far harder.

Early autumn is a good time for painting, provided you can be sure of finishing before winter sets in.

Checking for damage

Check all surfaces very carefully before starting preparations: the paint film which appears firm can often hide a decaying substrate. Usually, flaking paint indicates that the surface is wet, rotting or rusting.

Scrape the paintwork and prod the timber surfaces to ensure that there is good adhesion and sound material underneath. If the timber is rotten, it must be removed and replaced with sound, seasoned wood. Paint does not halt corrosion or wood rot and to ignore such defects will result in very expensive repairs in later years.

Investigate the sources of damp around affected timber and put them right before starting to paint.

Above: Before painting plastic gutters clean them with a piece of steel wool and a bucket of water

Where to start

Always start work at the top of the house so that at no time are you painting, or preparing, above finished work. Your main objective is to avoid having to move the ladder or tower scaffold more often than is absolutely necessary. Plan your sitings carefully before starting so that you can safely reach as large an area as possible and carry out as many processes as you can in that position.

Priming or undercoating can usually be carried out as soon as the surface has been prepared, so avoiding a scaffold move between preparation and painting.

Metal gutters and pipes

Cast-iron or mild steel gutters and cast-iron drainpipes rust if they are not properly protected. Always take the opportunity to clean out and paint the inside of gutters when you paint the outside.

Sequence for Exterior Painting

Start all preparation and painting work on a house exterior at the top and work downwards.

1 Gutters: Start at one end of the roof and work around the house
2 Eaves: Prepare and paint the eaves working from one end
3 Fascia and barge boards: Begin at the ridge and work down the board
4 Downpipes: Prepare and paint these working from top to bottom
5 Brickwork: This should be cleaned and pointed before painting
6 Rendering: Fill in any cracks and render walls where necessary
7 Doors and windows: Complete the sequence by painting any wooden walls, front and garage doors and windows as well as wooden railings

Scour the surfaces of both sides of the gutters with a wire brush. If rust is left on the surface it will continue to form under the paint film and eventually cause flaking.

When you have cleaned the surfaces, dry them thoroughly with rags or *carefully* pass a blowlamp over them. The bare metal areas are then ready for immediate priming.

When the primer on the bare area is dry—after 24 to 48 hours—wash all the surfaces with a detergent solution to remove accumulated grime and dry them with a rag or chamois leather. You can then apply an oil-based undercoat to the primed areas.

After the patches of undercoat are dry—at least eight hours later—apply undercoat to the entire surface. When this is dry follow it with a coat of gloss paint. For gutters, 25mm is the handiest size of brush.

Although you can paint the insides of gutters in the same way as the outsides, it is cheaper to use either black bitumastic paint or a thick coat of any gloss paint left over from previous jobs (fig. 2). Be

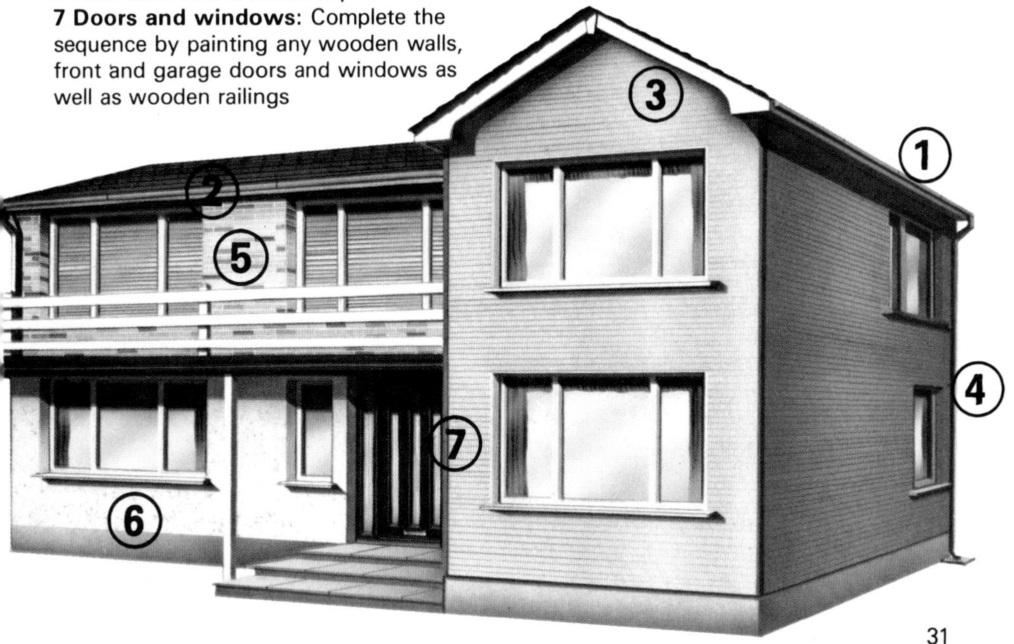

1 Clean out all the accumulated dirt and debris from the inside of the gutter. Make sure that the downpipes are free of any blockages. Then use a wire brush to ensure that all rust deposits are removed from the inside of the guttering. Try to make sure that you clean right down to the bare metal

2 The next stage is to wash out the inside of the gutter and dry it thoroughly with a cloth or with the flame from a blowlamp. Prime the bare metal. When it is dry—about 24 hours later—apply the undercoat and finish off about eight hours later with a top coat of black bitumastic paint

sure to prime all bare areas before applying either paints.

Treat all downpipes as for gutters. If the pipes are black, check first if they are painted with bitumastic either by rubbing with white spirit, which will quickly dissolve bitumastic, or by applying a white undercoat to a small section to see if it becomes stained.

Pipes painted with bitumastic will not take an oil-based finish unless you seal them first with stop-tar knotting or aluminium paint. Do this after the surface has been derusted, primed and washed with detergent.

You can also paint plastic gutters and downpipes. These need to be cleaned thoroughly with strong detergent solution, scoured with fine steel wool, dried, and painted with two coats of gloss paint. Gutters painted in this way then match metal ones.

Windows

Metal windows are usually made from galvanized steel and do not rust. But if they are very old and badly maintained, the zinc coating may fracture allowing the metal underneath to rust. In such cases remove the rust with medium-grade steel wool or a flap-wheel drill attachment and prime immediately with a calcium plumbate or a proprietary zinc chromate metal primer.

If paint is flaking but the galvanized metal underneath is in good condition, this indicates that there is poor adhesion and all the paint should be removed. You can do this easily by dry scraping with a 25mm stripping knife.

If there are no signs of rusting or flaking, wet abrade the old paint film with a grade 240 wet-and-dry paper. Put detergent in the water to make the rubbing down easier. When the surface is rinsed and dried, it is ready for undercoating.

Primed or washed and abraded surfaces need only one coat of undercoat and one coat of gloss.

Aluminium garage doors

If flaking is considerable—about 20 percent of the total area—strip off all the paint and start from scratch. Use a spirit paint remover. Then, after washing and

3 Downpipes and their fittings should first be cleaned with a wire brush. This is also a good opportunity to check how secure the fixings are. Then make sure that any areas of bare metal around the fixings are liberally painted with primer as these are the areas which are particularly prone to corrosion

4 Begin working on windows by cleaning out old putty and flaking paint. A blowlamp and scraper can be used to make the task easier, but be careful of the heat near the glass. Metal window frames should be cleaned with a wire brush. With the window open you can clean right underneath the frame

drying, prime the aluminium with zinc chromate—calcium plumbate is not suitable for aluminium.

If the paint is in good condition, use grade 240 wet-and-dry paper with detergent in the water to prepare the surface. Keep rubbing until the gloss of the old paint has all gone: the new paint will then key well.

One coat of undercoat and one of gloss is quite sufficient over primed or wet-abraded aluminium.

Timber surfaces

Severe flaking: This usually leaves large areas of the substrate exposed so you need to remove the old coatings completely. You will get rid of most of the paint by dry scraping it with a 75mm stripping knife. Remove the tricky areas with spirit paint remover.

Wash off the paint remover with medium-grade steel wool and detergent, rubbing in the direction of the grain.

When the surface is dry, dry abrade it with grade M2 glasspaper.

Isolated areas of flaking: These are to be found most often around edges and joints. Scrape away the flaking paint with a stripping knife, shave hook or paint scraper until a hard, firmly adhered edge of paint is left. Then use M2 or F2 glasspaper to dry abrade the exposed wood. Dust off and prime the wood, pushing the paint as deep as possible into the joints and overlapping the old paint by about 5mm all round.

Good condition: Paint in this state needs only to be wet abraded.

When the priming paint is dry, fill any holes or open joints so that no moisture can penetrate the wood and cause rotting. You could use linseed oil putty (mixed with a little undercoat to make it dry faster and be more flexible), mastic or caulking compound, or a proprietary filler.

Press the filler into the gaps, and rub down smooth when hard.

Give timber surfaces which have been stripped at least three coats of paint over the primer to ensure good protection. This can be one undercoat and two coats of gloss or two undercoats and one coat of gloss.

Surfaces which have a covering of old

5 Primer should be applied to all areas of the frame which are later to be covered with filler or filled with putty. Press the putty in the rebate, first using your fingers and then a putty knife. Then flatten the putty so that it forms a smooth bevelled edge, then leave for a while so that it can set

6 All cracks in the surface should be covered with filler. Press in firmly and when it has hardened smooth down the whole frame with glasspaper which has been mounted on a block. Then paint the frame with undercoat and top coat. Paint on to the glass, over the putty, for a few millimetres to prevent leaks

paint in good condition need only one coat of undercoat and one of gloss.

Doors

Unless you require a special finish, you can treat and paint front and rear doors in the same way as timber windows.

Because they are less exposed, doors rarely get into such a bad state that they need stripping.

You may have to strip your door completely if it is severely blistering or flaking, or if the paint coats already on it are too thick, making the door difficult to shut.

Whatever method of preparation you use, always remove all fittings.

The easiest, quickest and cheapest method of stripping the door is to burn off the paint with a blowlamp. Start on the mouldings, using a combination head shave hook to scrape away the peeling debris. Strip the flat areas with a 50 or 75mm stripping knife, working behind the flame torch and always pushing the knife in the direction of the grain. When the paint is completely stripped, prepare and paint the wood in the same way as you would timber window frames.

If the paint is not to be stripped, you should wet abrade the door. For paint coatings with very coarse brush-marks and deep chippings use a grade 180 wet-and-dry paper. If the paint has a reasonable finish, a 240 grade paper will be sufficient.

Keep the surface wet and clean with a sponge dipped in the detergent water, rubbing the paintwork until all the gloss is removed and all the hard edges are erased.

Apply the undercoat. When the undercoat is dry, abrade with a grade 1 glasspaper to remove any unevenness.

Before applying the gloss paint, wipe over the surface with a tacky duster and lay clean newspapers under the door.

Remember to include the top edge of the door and, if possible, the bottom edge. If the door opens into the hall, paint the hinge end in the same colour as the outside. To achieve a glass-like finish, apply a second coat of gloss as soon as the first is completely hard.

Easy wallpapering

Wallpapering may look simple, but it is all too easy to get into a mess unless you know the right way to do it. Most of the techniques involved are easily mastered and will help give your walls a professional touch.

Preparing the surface

Painted walls: Unless the paint is flaking or the surface is uneven, painted walls do not have to be stripped. However, make sure that the surfaces are completely free of grease and dirt.

Bare walls: Freshly plastered or rendered walls and walls that have been stripped to the plaster can be papered over with little trouble, providing they are free of damp. Your first task is to make good any chips or cracks in the surface with filler and to sand down bumps and bulges.

Sizing, or painting the wall with a suitable compound, evens out the absorbent qualities of the plaster or plasterboard and creates a smooth surface on which to wallpaper. If you are using a cellulose wallpaper paste, use this as your sizing compound. Leave the wall to dry thoroughly before you start hanging your paper.

Walls already papered: In most cases, it is inadvisable to lay fresh paper over an already papered wall—over-papering causes the paste between layers to interact, giving rise to additional problems such as unsightly peeling, staining and possible blistering.

Below: Wallpapering borders are an inexpensive way of finishing off a semi-papered wall which has no picture rail. They can be pasted up in the same way as wallpaper and add a particular style and elegance to a room

1 A steam stripping machine is extremely useful when you have to strip heavier papers. Easy to use, it can be readily obtained from most hire shops

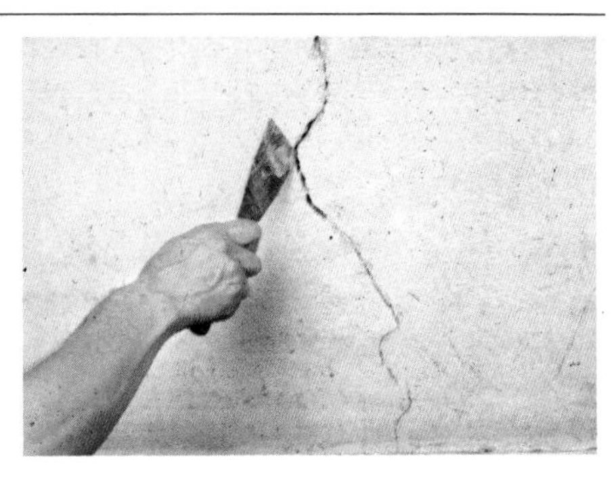

2 Taking the trouble to fill cracks in the wall before you paper over it will improve the overall finish. Build up the filler in layers and smooth when dry

5 Next, to give some paper overlap at the starting point, measure back 25mm from the mark. Repeat this procedure again at the base of the wall

6 Now hang a chalked plumbline over the mark nearer the corner. Secure the line at top and bottom, and 'snap' it so that it leaves a marked line on the wall

9 When pasting a strip, paste the edges of the strip completely off the table. This will help to avoid accidentally getting unwanted paste on the other side of the wallpaper

10 Folding strips of paper so that they are all 'paste to paste', as shown, makes them far easier to handle. The end you paste last will go right up at the top of the wall

3 Sizing a plastered wall before you paper over it will stop the paste from soaking in too quickly. It will also prevent the paper from peeling later

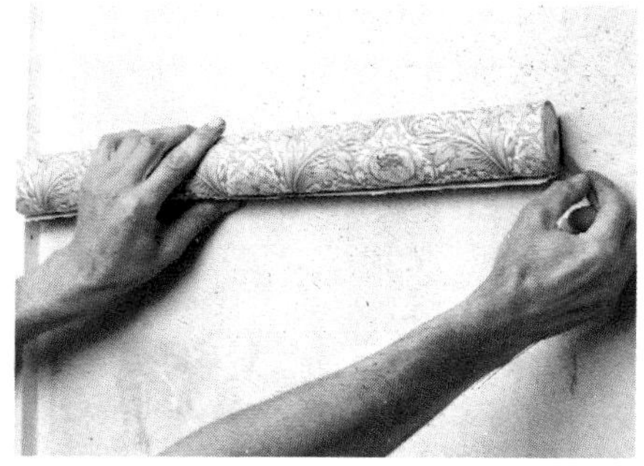

4 To mark up the wall for the first strip, measure the width of your roll along the wall from your chosen starting point and make a mark with a pencil

7 Carefully align your first strip of wall-paper against the chalk mark. Do not forget to allow for sufficient overlap of paper top and bottom

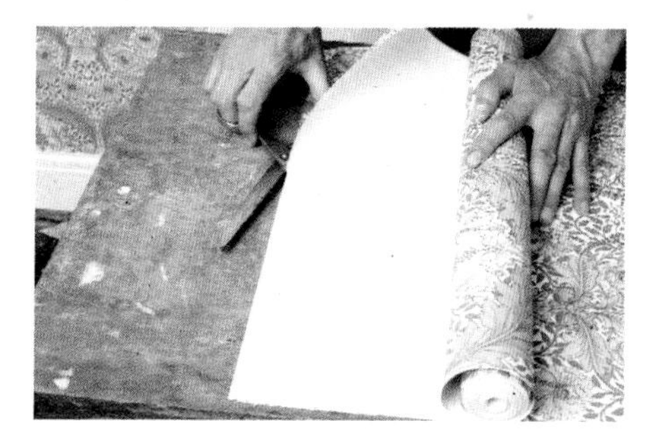

8 When you are cutting strips of wallpaper, take the overlap on to match the pattern. Fold the paper back on itself so that you keep the cut square

11 Cutting strips lengthways is always easier if you remember to paste and fold them first. Mark cutting lines clearly in pencil and then slice them neatly with the shears

12 When you have positioned a strip correctly on the wall, firmly crease the overlaps, then peel away the paper around them and trim with the shears in a neat and accurate line

13 Where the paper goes over a switch or a socket, crease an impression of the outline then make V-shaped cuts to the corners. Trim away the flaps with a sharp knife

14 When you are measuring strips before corners, take measurements at both the top and bottom of the wall. Butt a strip of paper next to the previous strip, then crease into the corner

15 Always plumb a fresh line after turning a corner to keep straight. As you hang the next strip, run the overlap into the corner, crease and trim it carefully with your shears

16 On small sections of wall, there is no real need to plumb a straight line. Align one side of the strip of wallpaper on the edge with the other left overlapping at the side

However, with vinyl-laminated paper, it is sometimes possible to peel away the vinyl layer from its paper backing strip. If the backing paper remains firmly and evenly pasted to the wall, you can paper directly on to it.

Stripping wallpaper

There are two methods of stripping wallpaper in general use: soaking and scraping—with or without a proprietary stripping compound—and steam-stripping, using a special tool.

Soaking and scraping tends to be a messy job and if just water is used to soften the paper it can also be hard work. So where medium and heavyweight papers are concerned, you can add either proprietary stripping compound or some vinegar or acetic acid—available from chemists—to the water.

Normally, the mix is simply painted on with a distemper brush. But if you are dealing with PVA-coated washable paper, you may need to score the surface with a wire brush so that the stripper can penetrate through to the wall. Leave the stripper to soak for a few minutes, then use a stripping knife to scrape it away from the wall.

Steam stripping is about as fast as using water but requires much less effort, creates less mess and minimizes the chances of damaging the wall. You can hire a steam stripper quite cheaply from hire shops and, if your old wallpaper is particularly heavy, it is worth the cost.

To use the tool, you simply press the steam-generating pad against the wall with one hand (fig. 1) and scrape off the loosened paper with the other. These operations soon become continuous with practice, although thick layers of paper may require more than one application.

Preparing to paper

A good working surface on which to cut and paste the wallpaper is essential. Ideally, you should use a pasting board about 25mm narrower than the paper you are hanging. Alternatively, use a sheet of chipboard or a flush-faced door—laid over a pair of trestles or the kitchen table.

Arrange the equipment so that you can work on it comfortably and safely, not forgetting that you will often need both hands free to hang the wallpaper. At the same time, gather together all the other tools necessary for the job.

One final preparatory step is to compare the shades of each separate roll of wallpaper. Where the batch numbers on the outer packing are the same, there should be no problem. But especially if the numbers differ, check the colour of each roll and arrange them so that similar shades run next to each other when you come to paste them up on the wall.

Where to start

Where you start papering depends to a large extent on whether your wallpaper is subdued, or bold and striking. In the former case, follow the general rule that you should paper away from the light—otherwise any overlaps between strips will cast shadows.

Start at the end of a wall, or against a window or door frame, where you will have a straight run before tackling the more intricate bits.

Where the wallpaper you have chosen has a bold pattern, start with a feature wall or chimney breast which immediately catches the eye. Centre up the pattern so it is symmetrical, then work on from either side.

Measuring and cutting

The simplest way of measuring and cutting wallpaper is to offer each strip up to the wall as you go along. But use a plumbline to make sure that the first strip is straight or you will run into difficulties later on.

Having chosen your starting point, which should be in a corner or against a door frame, measure from this along the top of the wall 25mm less than the width of your roll and mark the spot with a pencil.

Secure a plumbline running from the top of the wall and through this point, rub it with chalk, then snap it against the wall as shown in fig. 6. This leaves a vertical chalk line down the wall which in turn acts as a guide to help you position the side edge of the first strip.

Cut your first strip of paper about 50mm longer than the height from the ceiling to the actual skirting board. When measuring the next strip, use the edge of the first as a guide. Allow a 50mm overlap for trimming top and bottom, then mark and cut it as described before. If your wallpaper is patterned, make sure that you match the design from strip to strip—*before* you allow for your top overlap.

Pasting and folding

When pasting wallpaper it is important to stop the paste from getting on the table (fig. 9). Note that edges are pasted only when they overhang the table. Brush on the paste in a cross-cross 'herringbone' fashion, ensuring not only an even coverage but also that the edges receive plenty of paste. Work from the middle of the strip outwards.

When you have pasted about two-thirds of the strip, take the top edge in your fingers and thumbs and fold the strip down on itself. Make sure that the edges line up then slide the rest of the strip on to the table and paste it. Fold this back on itself as well, so that you are left with two folds—a large one at the top of the strip and a small one at the bottom of the strip (fig. 10).

Hanging and trimming

Lift the folded strip off the pasting table, take the top edge in your fingers and thumbs and allow the top fold to drop. Lay the strip against the wall, in line with your chalk line at the side and with about 25mm of trimming overlap at the top. Brush down the middle of the strip with the paperhanger's brush and unfurl the bottom fold.

Next, use the brush to form trimming creases at the top and bottom. Mark off the waste by running along the creases with the back of your shears, then pull the edges slowly and carefully away from the wall again.

Cut along each crease mark in turn, pressing the finished edges down as you go. Run over the finished job with the brush to remove air bubbles—working from the centre of the strip out towards the edges and using short, light but even strokes.

But, subsequent strips up against each other so the side edges touch, but do not overlap. Make sure that the pattern matches at the top of the wall before you start trimming.

Switches and sockets

First offer up the pasted strip in the normal way, lining it up with your plumbed line or an adjacent strip. Brush the top part of the strip down against the wall to hold it in place, but leave the rest of the paper hanging freely over the obstruction.

Now press the strip lightly over the obstruction so that its outline is left indented on the paper. Pull the strip out from the wall again and pierce it with the shears, roughly in the middle of the indentations. Gently snip out to the four corners of the indented mark so you are left with four triangular flaps (fig. 13).

Papering around corners

When you come to an internal corner, paper into the corner with one piece and out again with another. As you paper in, allow about 25mm overlap and crease the paper into the corner with the back of the shears.

Whenever you paper out, plumb a fresh line on the adjoining wall first. As you hang the paper, align it with the plumbed line and make sure it goes well into the corner to cover the overlap on the previous strip.

Folding paper around an external corner is possible only if the corner is vertical and cleanly finished. If you have any doubts, treat the corner in the same way as for an internal one.

Below: A wallpaper border can be used for dramatic effect to frame a doorway to a room. It can then be continued across the wall at a lower level

Papering ceilings

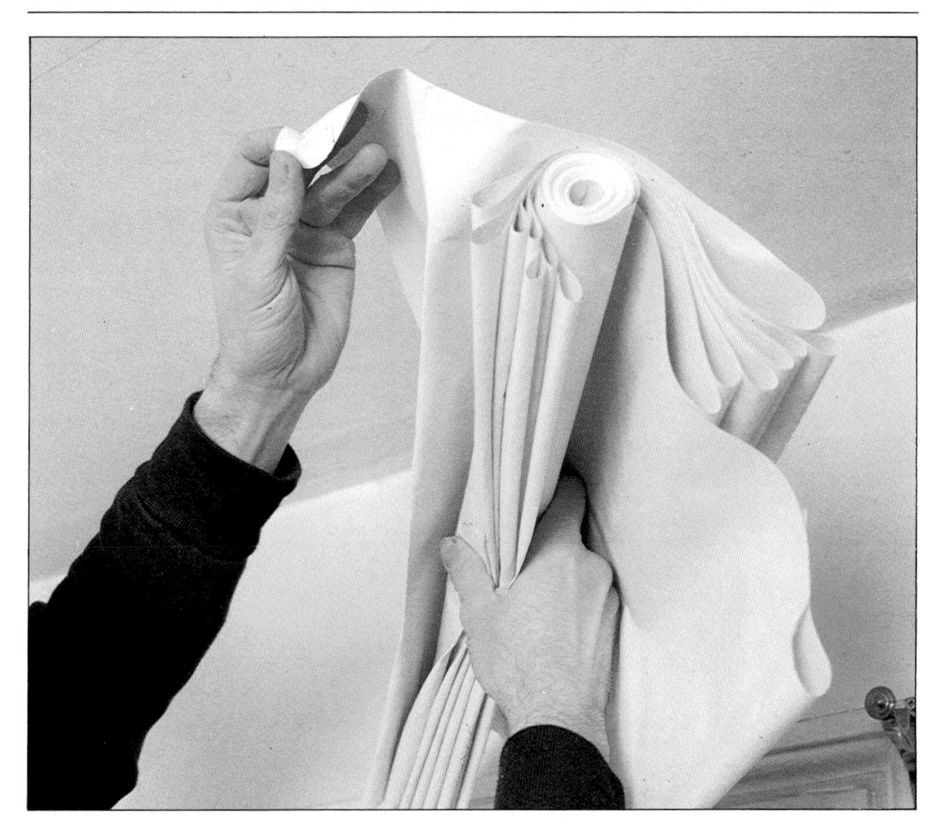

Above: The ceiling paper must be supported with a cardboard tube and folded concertina-style so that it can be applied to the ceiling in manageable sections

Papering a ceiling is not as difficult as it looks. With a sensible scaffolding arrangement and the right technique, the job is no harder than papering an ordinary wall.

How much paper?

First decide which way the paper is to be hung, as this determines how many lengths of paper can be obtained from one roll. A standard British roll of wallpaper measures about 10m long, is between 500mm and 550mm wide and covers an area of around 5.3m^2.

To estimate the number of rolls required for your ceiling, measure the length of each wall (ignoring any protrusions such as chimney breasts), add the measurements together and match the total against the chart.

Other materials

All papers suitable for walls can also be used on ceilings. Heavily embossed ones such as Anaglypta usually need two coats of paint for a good and even finish.

How many rolls?

British measurements

Distance around the room in metres	No of rolls required
10.0–12.0	2
12.5–14.5	3
15.0–17.5	4
18.0–20.0	5
20.5–21.5	6
21.5–22.5	7

The ceiling must be sized, or lined with lining paper, to make it less porous before you start hanging.

Lining paper

Lining a ceiling with lining paper is not essential but gives a more lasting finish —providing you hang it at right-angles to the direction which the top paper will eventually take.

Where to start

Make sure the ceiling is completely clean before you start. Where possible, all papering should start and work away from the natural daylight source. This system prevents shadows from obscuring the joints as you hang the paper. Obviously if there are windows at both ends of the room, either one may be used as the starting point. Where a bay window is involved, the first length should be hung across the opening of the bay. Then work back towards the top of the window.

Makeshift scaffolding is extremely dangerous. To be safe you need two pairs of sturdy stepladders and a wide scaffold plank.

Marking a guideline

The scaffolding should be set up under a chalked guideline which marks the outside edge of the first strip. To work out where this line should run, measure the width of the paper and deduct 10mm. The deduction allows for bumps and other imperfections at the junction of the ceiling and the wall. Measuring out from the wall, mark off this measurement on the ceiling at either end of the first run of paper (fig. 2).

Next, fix a steel drawing pin into the ceiling at one of the measured points and tie a length of twine around it. Thoroughly rub the twine with coloured chalk then pull it taut across the ceiling to the other measured point and fix it securely. Pull the centre of the twine down from the ceiling, letting it snap back into place (fig. 3). This leaves an accurate guideline by which you can hang the first length of paper with just the right amount of overlap at the side wall.

Pasting

To paste a length of paper evenly, slide it across the board so that it overhangs the edge furthest from you (the back edge) by about 10mm. This prevents the paste from being deposited on the board or on the other lengths of paper.

Apply a full brush of paste down the centre of the paper—the larger the brush the quicker the paste can be applied, thus avoiding the risk of drying before the paper is hung.

Folding

When you are sure that the length of paper has been completely coated in paste, fold it ready for hanging. Fold over the first 300mm paste to paste, lift the fold and place it on top of the next 300mm (fig. 4). Continue this pattern down the whole length to obtain a concertina-type series of folds. This enables you to release the paper in manageable lengths on the ceiling.

Hanging the paper

Place a part roll of paper or cardboard tube under the concertina-folds of the pasted length—this supports the paper and should be held parallel and close to the ceiling at all times (fig. 5). If you are

1 Scaffolding set up between two sturdy stepladders is the ideal arrangement for hanging wallpaper on ceilings. Carefully adjust the position of the plank until you can comfortably touch the ceiling with the palm of your hand. Then the scaffolding has been positioned in just the right place to start papering

2 Before you start papering it is essential to measure up where the first strip should be hung. Deduct 10mm from the width of the wallpaper to find the right measurement for marking off the position of the guideline. This allows for imperfections where the ceiling actually meets the wall

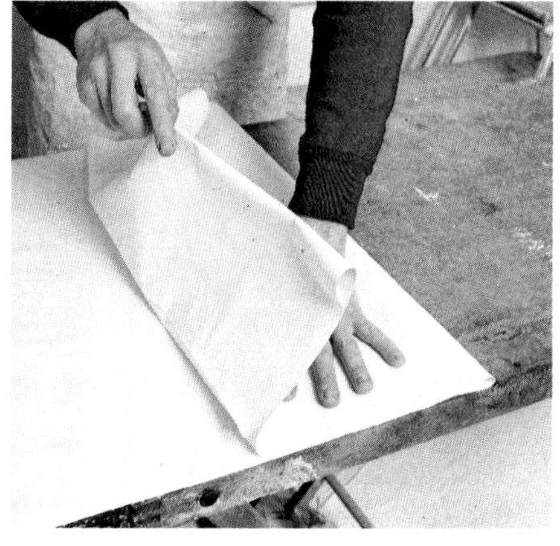

3 To achieve your chalked line, fix a steel drawing pin into the ceiling at one measured point and tie a length of twine around it, then cover the twine in coloured chalk. Secure firmly at the other measured point and then snap the twine against the ceiling to leave the necessary chalked mark

4 When you have completely covered the length of paper in paste, fold in neatly ready for hanging. Turn in the first 300mm of paper, paste to paste, then lift this fold and put it on top of the next 300mm. Continue in this way down the whole length to make a complete concertina of the sheet of wallpaper

5 Thread string through the loops of the paste bucket and rest the brush on it. This keeps it free of excess paste while you are hanging the paper. Firmly support the folded, pasted paper with a roll of paper leaving the top fold ready to lay down

6 Lay the first fold of paper against the chalked line and smooth it out before applying the second and subsequent folds. Keep smoothing the paper as you go along the ceiling, expelling air bubbles and keeping parallel and near the ceiling

right-handed, take the roll, with its folded, pasted paper on top, in your right hand and hold the paper in place with your thumb—leaving the top fold free.

Pull this top fold open and lay it on to the ceiling against one end of the chalk line. Taking the brush, smooth down the centre of the section then to the edges to expel any air bubbles under the surface (fig. 6).

Make sure this first fold is running true to the line and then release the next fold and smooth it out in the same way.

When you have applied a few folds of paper, you can move around so that you are facing the roller and the folded paper. Walk along the platform, slowly releasing the folds and brushing them into place.

Continue hanging the paper in this way until the whole length has been pasted up. The surplus paper can now be trimmed off allowing 5–10mm to remain hanging down the wall. This makes for a cleaner finish when the walls are papered.

Paste and fold subsequent strips in the same way as the first, applying them to the ceiling and using the edge of the previous strip as the guideline. Take care not to overlap the strips—they should only butt tightly up against each other.

Use a seam or angle roller to smooth out the joints, but the full face of the roller should not be used on embossed paper as the pressure will flatten out its design. Instead, use the edge of the roller directly on the joints.

Lights and chimney breasts

The paper will need to be cut so that it fits round obstructions such as light fittings. If the fitting is near the edge of a strip, you can cut from the edge of the paper inwards to the centre of the fitting (fig. 7). Make a few cuts outward to form a star pattern and press the paper over the fitting. Thread the loose electrical flex through the hole and smooth down the rest of the strip. Trim off the excess paper with a sharp knife.

How you paper around a chimney breast depends on whether it is parallel or at right-angles to the direction of the ceiling paper.

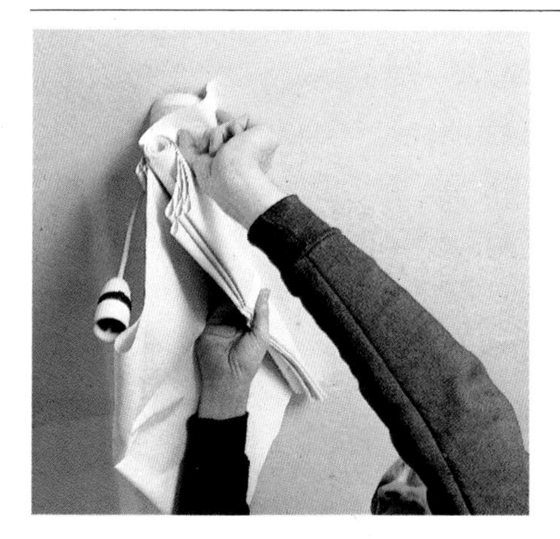

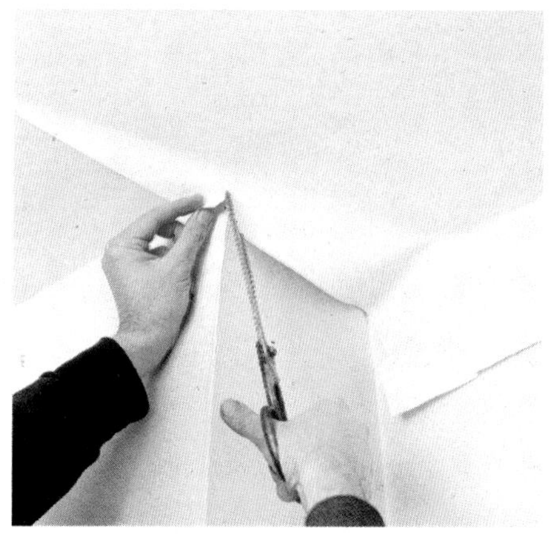

7 Mark the position of the light fitting with your fingers and then if near the edge of the paper cut in towards the centre of the fitting. Or make a few cuts outwards with the shears to form a star pattern, and then press into place round the fitting

8 When you get to the corner of a chimney breast, press the paper into place to make a mark and then peel it back so that it can be cut. The last cut should form a 'V' shape up to the mark, to enable the paper to be pasted down the chimney breast

When the chimney breast is at right-angles, make a cut along the length of the strip—equal to the depth of the breast minus the usual 10–15mm overlap—and smooth the paper into the corner. Repeat the procedure on the other side of the chimney breast.

If the chimney breast is parallel to the direction of the ceiling paper, smooth the paper right into the corner. This makes a crease mark indicating the depth of the chimney breast on that strip of paper. Crease another mark at the point where the side wall of the chimney breast and the ceiling meet.

Next, gently peel the strip back from the ceiling and cut down a line connecting the two creases. Replace the strip, checking as you carefully smooth it down that the other side is lined up with your chalk line or that it is correctly butted against the adjacent strip further out in the room.

Below: Ceilings need not be the boring aspect of a room. Imaginative use of borders and bold patterns can liven up even the most bland ceilings. Diminishing squares can be made with coloured paints or borders

The final strip

The final strip of paper will almost certainly be narrower than a standard width. If this is the case, you will find it easier to hang and trim if the piece is measured and cut to size. Allow about 50mm extra then paste and hang.

Papering awkward corners

Wallpapering on straight, uncluttered walls can be great fun and sometimes almost therapeutic. But papering walls that have many things fitted to them, or which are sloping, recessed or out of true, can have the opposite effect. They are always difficult and often very frustrating.

Types of paper

Your first job is to make a simple test on the walls to determine whether or not they are true. Hold a wooden straightedge against the wall and see whether it touches right along its length. Provided the end of the straightedge is cut square, you can hold it also to the corner angles of window and door reveals and alcove recesses.

Use a good quality paper in a room where there are a great many awkward features. A cheap, soft paper quickly absorbs the paste and in such a wet state, easily tears or becomes marked. Cutting round reveals, arches or radiators means that you have to handle the paper more, and for longer periods, than on flat areas.

Paste

Paste is another important consideration: it must be a thick or stout solution which sticks readily to the surface without the need for continuous or heavy brushing. Thick pastes also stay wet longer—important when you need time to cut the paper carefully to fit an awkward shape.

Window and door reveals

There are several practical ways of papering reveals. Where reveal and soffit (the top internal wall surface) are narrower than the width of wallpaper you are using, the method shown in figs 1 to 5 may be appropriate. The step-by-step photographs show also how to paper around pipes and cables and deal with the sloping walls found in an attic.

Arches and alcoves

When you come up against the problem of papering arched openings, make sure you do not use heavily patterned paper. When you come to cut the strip to fit the reveal, the pattern will be upside down on one side of the arch if you use the wrong paper. If you need to cut the reveal filling strip, do so where the arch soffit meets the strip or at the top of the arch.

An alcove in the form of an arched recess in the wall is another feature that is often difficult to paper.

Start, as you would for an arched opening, by cutting around the shape, making small cuts in the overlap and

Papering an attic room: Wallpapering a room with a sloping ceiling and walls poses problems, and it is important that you start in the right way and paper in the correct sequence. Start at wall **A** under the window working towards wall **B**. An awkward-shaped wall like **B**, which sharply narrows at one end, needs particular care. Continue from **A** and work towards the sloping end. Wrap the paper about 100mm around the edge of the ceiling where it meets **D**. Later when you paper the ceiling this will result in a neat edge where it joins the wall. If you are using a matching wallpaper, try to continue the design around the corner between **B** and **C**. Begin wall **C** at the edge with **B** and then paper towards the door. Where the wall begins to slope upwards accurately trim the paper so that it runs about 100mm on to the actual ceiling. The final ceiling section **D** is the most difficult and has to be completed most carefully since it is usually a different pattern from the walls. Start at the edge between **C** and **D**, working from the bottom and brushing the paper upwards, expelling all the air bubbles as you go. Continue along until you reach the sloping edge with **B**. Mark and then trim the paper carefully with the shears so that you can achieve a really neat finish that you will be proud of

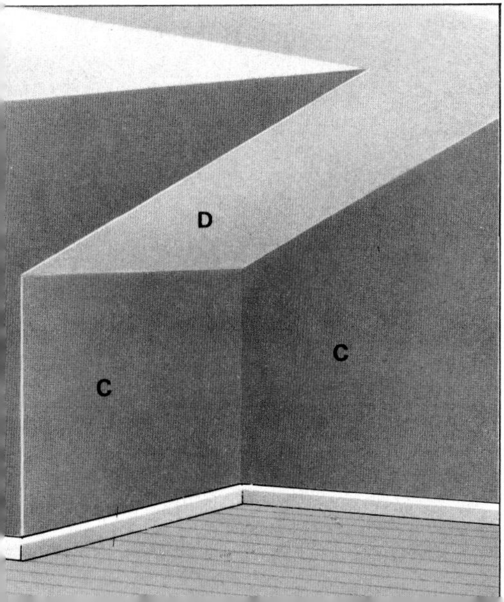

D

C

C

smoothing down the lapping piece into the soffit and reveals to form a smooth line along the edge of the arch.

Next, match a length of paper to go on the wall inside the recess. Do this by holding the roll up against the wall and lining up the edge of it with the edge of the paper stuck to the wall outside the recess.

Take the paper away and cut a piece out about 10–15mm bigger than your pencil marks. Paste this and carefully apply it to the wall, pushing the paper into the angle with the aid of a paper-hanging brush.

It will be necessary to make a few cuts at the top of the piece to the shape of the arch in order to get it to fit the angle. To do this, mark the position of the internal angle with the back of the shears, pull the paper a little way from the wall and cut it about 10mm bigger than the shape you have marked. Make a number of small cuts along the overlap on the arch section and brush it back into position.

If the alcove is wider than the width of the paper, hang to a centre line marked down the back wall of the recess with a plumbline.

Curved ceilings

In some older properties the ceiling curves into the wall so that there is no line at which to stop the wallpaper. You must get round this by deciding on the line you want and marking it before you cut the paper.

The curves are very seldom true so it is probably best to select a line at a point where the wall starts to curve. Measure up the height you have decided upon at each end of the wall and stretch a piece of fine string, which you have thoroughly rubbed with coloured chalk, between these two points. When the string is pulled taut and snapped against the surface, you will have a chalked guideline to work from.

You need a very sharp craft knife—preferably with a curved blade—and a straightedge for this job in addition to the other wallpaper hanging tools.

1 When papering round a window, hang the wallpaper matching the previous piece, push the paper close against the line of the soffit, then cut into the corner with a sharp knife. Cut a small piece of wallpaper to fit at the end of the soffit overlapping on to the reveal in the corner and on to the main wall

2 Carefully brush the overlap of the main piece so that it fits snugly into the reveal, then neatly cut off the excess paper at the edge. Match the next piece of paper above the window allowing for an overlap at the bottom and then carefully brush the hanging piece into the soffit, making sure you remove all creases

5 When you have to wallpaper up to a pipe in an awkward corner, fold back the paper and indent it neatly with the shears where it meets the pipe's brackets. Then cut neatly down to the mark and make an upward and downward angle cut from a point which is roughly about 15mm before the initial mark

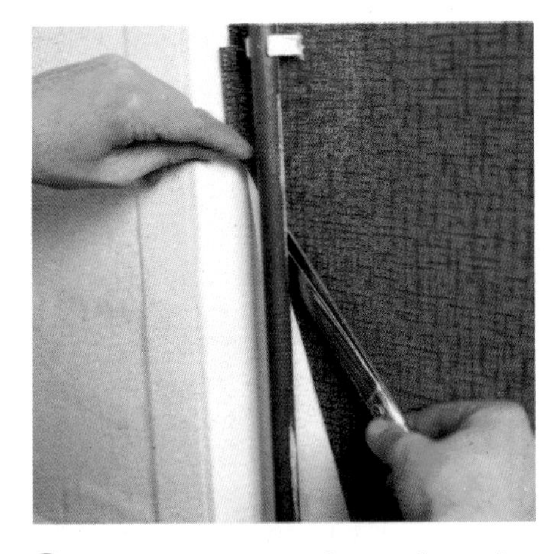

6 When you have made cuts for each bracket, push the paper behind the pipe with closed shears so that the paper easily slips over each bracket. Snip the paper behind the bracket so that it lies very flat to the wall, then carefully cut off all the waste bits of paper with a sharp handyman's knife

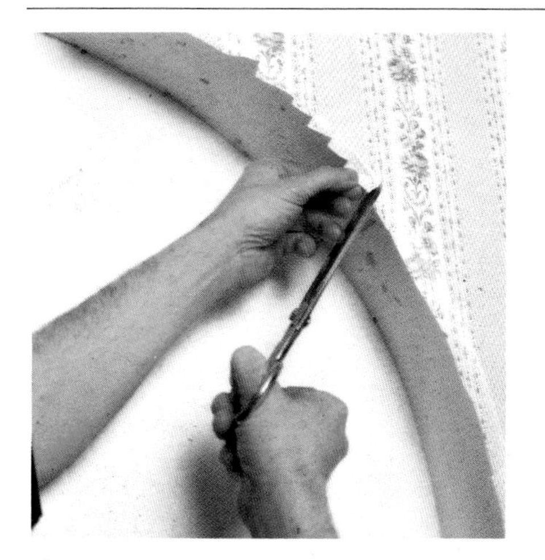

3 When you come to an arched alcove, hang the first piece in line with the last one, then press the wallpaper to the edge of the arch and cut off the waste area about 25mm inside the edge of the arch. Snip the wallpaper that overlaps the arch at about 50mm apart and 25mm apart at the most curved point

4 Brush the overlapping paper on to the reveal and then match up the adjoining piece above the arch. Stand in front of the arch and match the piece for the back of the recess, then press the edges into the corner. Cut the waste and fold the overlap on to the reveal. Then cut the reveal width and press in place

Cut the paper so that it will overlap the chalked line by at least 30mm, then hang the paper. Place the straightedge carefully on the paper so that each end is touching the chalk line and cut along it with one sweeping cut. Remove the cut piece and wipe the curved area free of paste.

When you hang the next piece, cut from the edge of the first length to the chalk line on the other side of the paper. Continue in this fashion, hanging and cutting a piece at a time.

Wall-mounted radiators

You will get the neatest results if you can take radiators off a wall before trying to paper behind them. But this is difficult with radiators connected to a 'wet' central heating system; you will probably have to drain the whole system first.

If the radiator cannot be moved, you need to make a simple tool to help get behind it and smooth the paper down so that it is completely flat.

A flat piece of wood about 500mm long is suitable for the job, though you should wrap a piece of rag around it to avoid tearing the paper. A wire coat hanger is another possibility: straighten the hook out to act as a handle and then wrap a piece of soft fabric around the cross bar.

To hang a length of wallpaper behind a radiator start by pasting half the length and hanging from the wall in the normal way. Take the free bottom half, fold it back on itself face side to face side, and slide it behind the radiator. Adjust the fold to coincide with the tops of any brackets, crease the paper then mark the bracket positions in pencil.

Make vertical cuts from the bottom of the length up to the marks, fold the paper back against the wall and paste.

Finally, slip the pasted length down behind the radiator so that the brackets run in the slits you have just made. Smooth the paper as thoroughly as you can with the special tool.

Hanging wall fabrics

Wall fabrics have a surface covering of natural textured material—grasscloth, silkcloth, cork or hessian—and they are usually laminated to a cardboard or paper backing so that they hold together without breaking.

Although they are generally more expensive than printed wallpapers, wall fabrics give a dramatic finish to any wall or ceiling and are worth the extra cost. However, it is essential to take care when working with them since mistakes are expensive and likely to be more obvious than with printed wallcoverings.

Above: Hanging fabric wallpaper needs more care and attention than ordinary wallpaper but the finished effect can be extremely striking

Lining paper

Wall fabrics, more than any other type of wall covering, need to be laid on top of lining paper. This helps to even out areas of uneven porosity on the wall—often due to patches of bare plaster mixed with areas that have been painted.

Lining paper should be 'cross hung' in the opposite direction to the final wall-covering so that none of the joints on the two covering materials coincide and spring open. Hang it so that the joints overlap by a few millimetres: this will prevent the underlying wall surface from showing through.

Tools and equipment

As well as the usual paper-hanging tools and brushes, some more specialized equipment is needed to hang wall fabrics successfully.

Felt and rubber roller: Most wall fabrics have delicate surfaces which are easily damaged. Using a normal wallpaper smoothing brush is likely to mark the material, so it is best to use a felt or rubber roller. The felt roller should be used on fragile fabrics, while the rubber roller is best where extra pressure is needed.

Scraper and trimmer: This is a rigid plastic tool which measures approximately 200mm × 120mm. One edge is angled so that it can be used for cutting the edges of the fabric and for fitting it tightly around corners. The scraper edge of the tool is used to smooth out heavy fabrics such as vinyls, glass fibre and the smoother varieties of hessian.

Steel edge and zinc strip: These are for cutting the waste off the edge of the fabric and trimming irregular ends. They can also be used to cut wide rolls into narrow widths. Never use scissors to do this.

To use the tools, first place the zinc

strip under the material to be cut so that you avoid damaging the surface underneath. Then place the steel edge along the line to be cut and use a trimming knife to carefully cut the material to size.

You will find that it is impossible to cut all the way across in one go, especially if you are cutting along the edge, so make a number of cuts.

Mohair roller: Most of the adhesives used to hang wall fabrics are thick and viscous, so the best way of applying them is to use a mohair roller together with a paint tray to hold the adhesive.

Adhesives

As a general rule, the adhesive should be applied to the back of the fabric when this has a paper backing and to the wall surface where there is no backing at all. Make sure, therefore, that you get the correct type of adhesive for the fabric you are hanging.

Hotwater starch: This is suitable for delicate materials—such as grass cloths, paper-backed silks and lightweight corks —but needs very careful preparation.

Starch adhesive: Suitable for heavy relief materials, this is a strong adhesive which is bought as powder and mixed with cold water to form a smooth paste.

PVA adhesive: This is the most common type of adhesive used to hang a variety of wall fabrics and is available ready mixed in 1-litre and 5-litre containers.

Estimating quantities

Wall fabrics are obtainable in a wide variety of widths and lengths, so measuring the quantities needed must be done with care. The best method is to start by measuring the total length of the walls and then divide this by the width of the material you are using to find the number of lengths needed overall.

Setting out

The texture produced by wall fabrics often leaves noticeable joins between the lengths of material once these are applied to the wall. And since this is an unavoidable feature, it is best to plan carefully where each length is to hang so the joins are less obvious.

Hanging fabrics

Since fabrics vary greatly in type and texture it is essential to tackle each variety in the correct way.

Paper-backed hessian: Normally sold in widths of 530mm, 910mm widths are available which are more difficult to handle but leave fewer joins.

The hessian is hung in a similar way to ordinary wallpaper. To balance the joints, start from the centre of the wall to be covered and hang a plumbline so that the first length can be hung square. Apply the fabric by smoothing it from the centre towards each diagonal, using a rubber roller or a plastic scraper (fig. 4).

To give a perfect butt joint between each roll of paper, allow an overlap of 25mm on each joint. Then, before the paste has had a chance to harden, use a sharp knife to make a cut down the centre of the overlap, from top to bottom, and peel away the excess fabric from both lengths.

Grasscloth: This consists of hand-dyed grasses, reeds or split canes which are woven together with fine cotton warp and laminated on to a coloured paper backing.

Use a stiff adhesive and spread this evenly to avoid delaminating the backing; again, only a little soaking time is required. Hang the material as described above but cut tops, bottoms and around obstacles with shears to avoid tearing.

Silkcloth: This expensive but attractive material consists of a dyed silk yarn with an extremely fine denier warp and a thicker horizontal weft. When laminated on to a coloured paper backing, it produces a material with the natural shimmer of silk but with interesting irregularities in the woven pattern.

Silkcloth should be hung using hot-water starch or a heavy-duty paste but there is no need to soak it. Hang the fabric in the normal way, using butt joints. Use the shears for trimming and

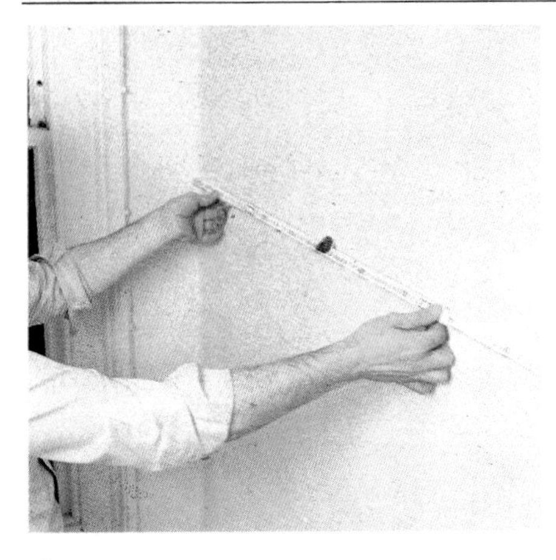

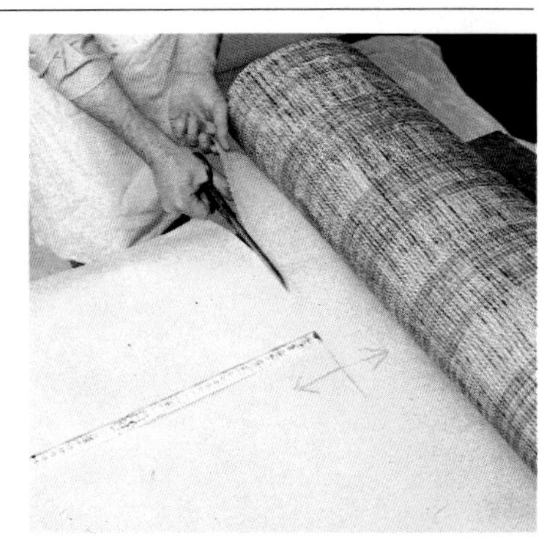

1 To create a balanced finish, find the centre of the largest wall and mark out the position of the first length of fabric. Hang this, aided by a plumbline, so that the first length is square. Then clearly mark the fabric top and bottom so that each alternate length can be reversed when hung if this is recommended

2 To ensure that each length of wall fabric is hung exactly the right way up, mark up the adjoining lengths with care before actually cutting to size. Then pour a small amount of PVA adhesive into the bottom of a clean paint tray where you can then use just a little of it on the roller at a time

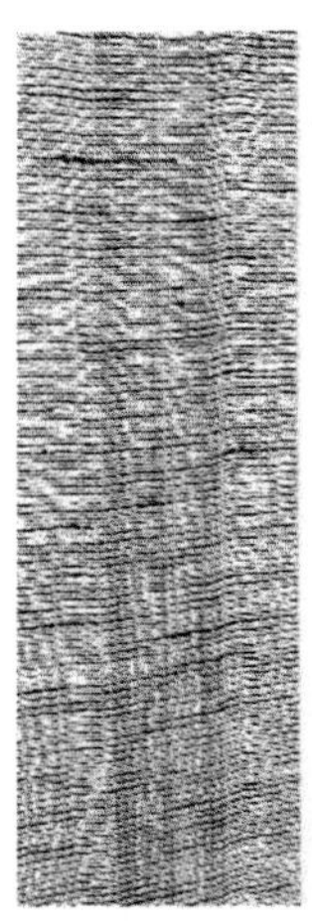

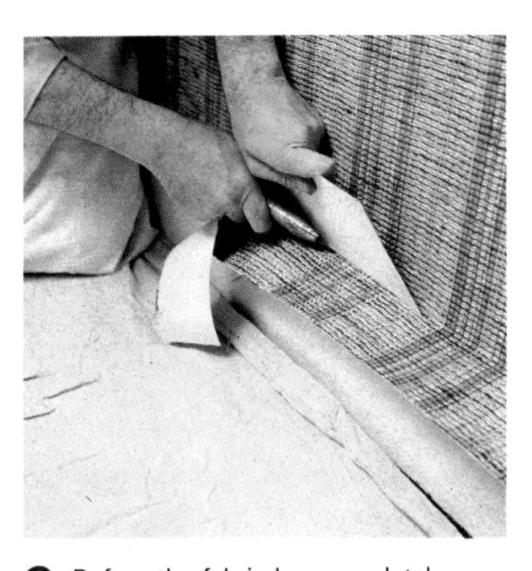

5 All air bubbles should be removed by slowly peeling back the material, applying extra adhesive and then rolling the fabric back into place. Most fabrics can either be butt jointed or made to overlap each other by 25mm. A perfect, hardly noticeable, join can then be made by careful trimming of the fabric

6 Before the fabric has completely dried out, use a steel edge or alternatively a template and a sharp knife to trim the material neatly at the top and bottom. The same technique should be used when you have to trim all the way around light switches, power points and perhaps door or window frames

3 Dip the short-pile mohair roller into the paint tray and coat in the adhesive. Then apply enough to the wall to stick just one length of fabric at a time. Next thoroughly coat the back of the fabric, rolling rigorously until each part of the material has a thin, but adequate, covering of adhesive

4 So that it can be easily picked up, fold each end of the length of wall fabric over on itself, the sticky side inwards, trying, at the same time, not to crease the fabric. Having positioned each length, start from the centre and smooth it into place with a rubber roller, working towards the diagonals

7 To fit the fabric around angles and still make a neat and tidy join, cut the last length fractionally long so that it continues on around the corner. Transfer this measurement on to the fabric backing and then carefully mark the amount which has to be removed using a pencil and steel straightedge

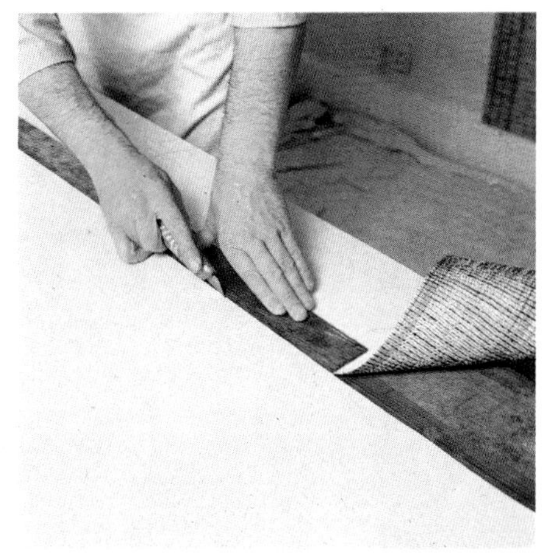

8 Cutting the material lengthways is best done with a steel edge, trimming knife and also a zinc strip to protect the actual pasting table. If you find these tools are not available, an alternative method is to cut very carefully along the marked line using a pair of very sharp and clean shears

9 Apply the shortened length to the wall and allow it to run right around the corner, then push it firmly and neatly into place with a plastic template

10 Once the next length is firmly in place, trim down the centre of both sheets and slowly remove the excess fabric to leave a neat butt joint

make sure that you avoid leaving ragged edges on the fabric.

Paper-backed suede: This is made from a thick blanket of dyed wool fibres laid in random directions. The fibres are specially treated to give the effect of crushed suede.

Apply the adhesive to the backing paper and hang the fabric lengths as described above. Make butt joints where lengths meet then roll them lightly with a felt roller to avoid crushing the suede. Trim with a sharp knife, steel edge and zinc strip. Dirty marks can be removed by sponging with warm, clean water.

Textured wallcoverings

A. Grasscloth is a unique and eye-catching fabric which is both decorative and natural

B. Most hessians are self-coloured but they can easily be renovated with a coat of emulsion

C. The subtle sheen of silkcloth adds an air of sophistication to almost any wall or ceiling

D. Imitation suede fabrics made from processed felt are very realistic and easy to keep clean

E. This warm-looking hessian is only one of a number of alternating patterns

Decorating with tiles

As coverings for walls, tables and working surfaces, ceramic tiles have several distinct advantages over other materials. As well as offering a superb range of colours, patterns and glaze finishes, they make a hard-wearing, easy to clean, practical surface.

Types of tile

Ceramic tiles come in a wide variety of plain colours, patterns and shapes. The three most common sizes are 108mm square by 4mm thick, 152mm square × 6mm, and 152mm × 76mm × 6mm. Mosaic tiles—group arrangements of tiny tiles on a backing sheet—are also available.

The field tile used for most tiling usually has lugs around the edges which butt against adjacent tiles and ensure an equal 2mm gap all round.

When tiling food preparation surfaces in the kitchen, you should always check with the manufacturer or retailer that the tiles are suitable for the purpose—some have a potentially toxic heavy lead glaze. Tiles used near heat sources such as cookers and fireplaces should be heat resistant or at least 9.5mm thick.

The basic tool kit

Cutting tools, adhesive and grout are readily available from any do-it-yourself shop.

You will need a simple wheel cutter or a scriber with a tungsten-carbide tip. A wheel cutter with breaker wings, for scoring and breaking in one action, costs a little more. A carborundum file is useful for smoothing down the edges of cut tiles.

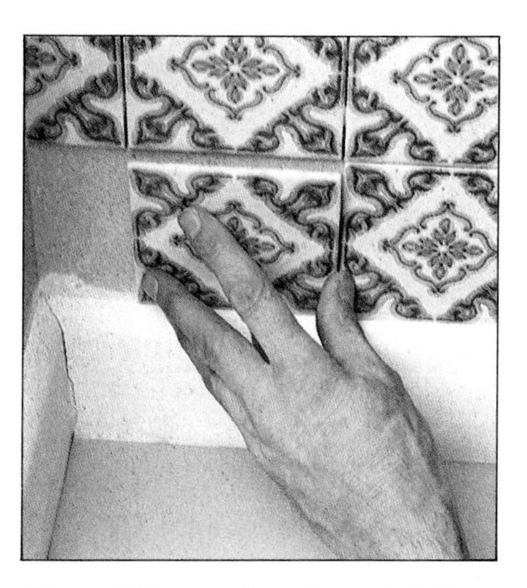

Above: Tiling a wall can be a straightforward and easy task provided you follow the set guidelines

Materials

Tile adhesive is available either in powder form, to which water is added, or else ready-prepared in cans: 5 litres will cover about 6m^2 on a good surface.

However, use a water-resistant adhesive for areas around sinks, baths and showers and one which is heat resistant where temperatures are likely to be high, such as around cookers and fires.

Grout is a cement-based paste which is rubbed into the gaps between tiles to provide a neat finish. As a rough guide 500g of the powder, mixed with water to a fairly stiff consistency, will grout about 2m^2 of small tiles or 4m^2 of larger ones.

A non-toxic grout should always be used on tiled food preparation surfaces

How many tiles?

To estimate how many tiles you will need for a wall or worksurface, measure the length and height in metres then use our formula

108mm square tiles: Length × Height × 86 = No. of tiles
152mm square tiles: Length × Height × 43 = No. of tiles
152mm × 76mm tiles: Length × Height × 86 = No. of tiles

If necessary, add on the required number of special border tiles or subtract tiles to allow for fittings. Add on an extra 5 or 6 tiles to cover breakages.

1 Make a pencil mark a tile's height from the top edge of the skirting board. This will show you exactly where to draw the necessary baseline

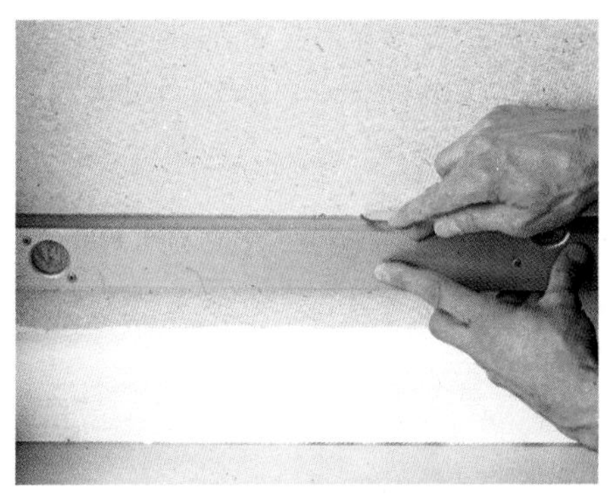

2 Drawing the baseline. The spirit level ensures that the baseline is exactly level and acts as a straightedge for marking the line all the way across

3 Pin the batten along the bottom of the line to provide a level base for the tiling. The bottom row will be filled in when you have finished the rest

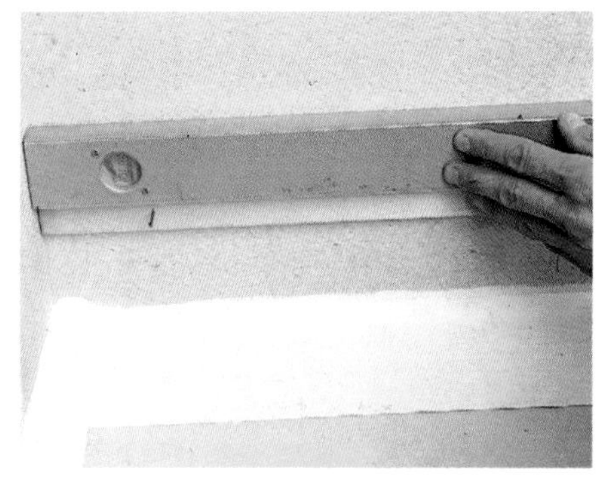

4 Check the batten with the spirit level to make sure it is horizontal. If it is not quite right, it will have to be unpinned and re-adjusted

5 Mark tile widths all the way along the batten to give an even cut at each end of the wall. This ensures the proper symmetry of the tiled wall

6 Use the spirit level to draw the vertical line at the last tile mark. The line then acts as a guide to keep all the tiling square and even

and a water-resistant grout around sinks, baths and showers.

Preparing the surface

The quality of any tiling job is largely dependent on the surface to which the tiles are fixed. This should be firm, level, clean and dry.

Plaster: Minor bumps and cracks can be filled with a proprietary plaster filler. The entire surface should then be given a coat of plaster primer, to provide a non-porous base for the adhesive. If the surface is very uneven, it should be replastered and left for a month before being sealed and tiled.

Wallpaper: On no account should tiles be laid on to wallpaper. Strip the wall back to the bare plaster or wallboard, then fill and level in the same way as described above.

Painted walls: Provided these are smooth and firm, tiles may be applied direct. But flaking or rough paint should be partially stripped with medium glasspaper and brushed clean.

Timber walls: These must be sanded or planed level and treated with wood primer before the tiles are applied.

Existing ceramic tiles: The ideal tiling surface, providing the tiles are clean, firmly fixed and not chipped.

Constructing a baseline

Before you start tiling you will need a horizontal baseline from which to work—floors and skirting boards are not suitable, as they are seldom completely level and can throw the tiling out of true.

To draw a baseline, measure the height of a tile from the floor or skirting board and make a mark (fig. 1). Using the spirit level as a straightedge, check for level and draw a line through this mark (fig. 2).

Pin the top edge of a batten along the line so it forms a level base, right along the length of the surface to be tiled. Later, when you have tiled above it, you can remove the batten and fill in the space below (fig. 9). The tiles here may have to be cut or trimmed.

Marking a side line

To keep the tiles exactly square to the baseline, you will also need a vertical line at one side of the surface. Find the centre point of the batten and mark out the tile widths along either side of it. Draw your line where the last full tile ends on the left-hand side, using the spirit level—or a plumbline—to give you an accurate vertical line (fig. 6).

Fixing the tiles

Begin tiling at the intersection of the

7 With the adhesive spread over about $1m^2$ of the wall, fix the first tile at the intersection of the batten and the vertical line. Press the tile home

8 When you are fitting cut tiles into corners and other awkward areas, it is often easier to apply the adhesive to the backs of the tiles

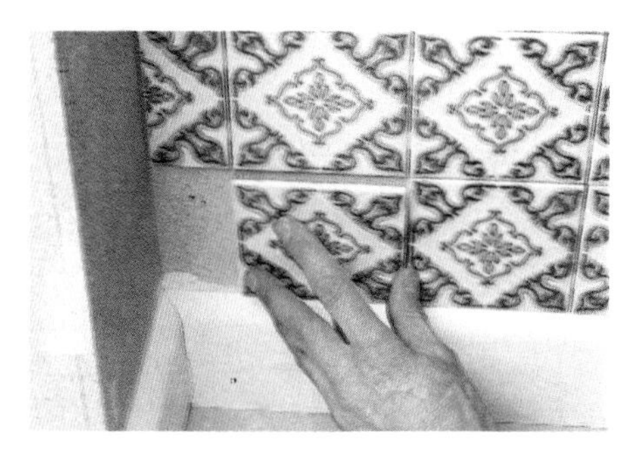

9 Once you have tiled the rest of the wall you can remove the batten and fix the bottom row, carefully scribing each tile to fit the space left

10 Use a tile cutter to score neatly through the glazed surface of a tile. The try square ensures that the score mark is straight and even

11 Place a matchstick under the score mark on the tile. Exert strong downward pressure and the tile should snap cleanly along the mark

12 An alternative method of cutting tiles is with the Oporto cutter. The tile itself is actually snapped in half by the breaker wings

13 For a shaped cut, score the area that is to be removed then carefully nibble out small pieces of the tile with a pair of pincers

14 When the shape has been nibbled out of the tile, smooth off any unevenness that is left on the cut edges with a carborundum file

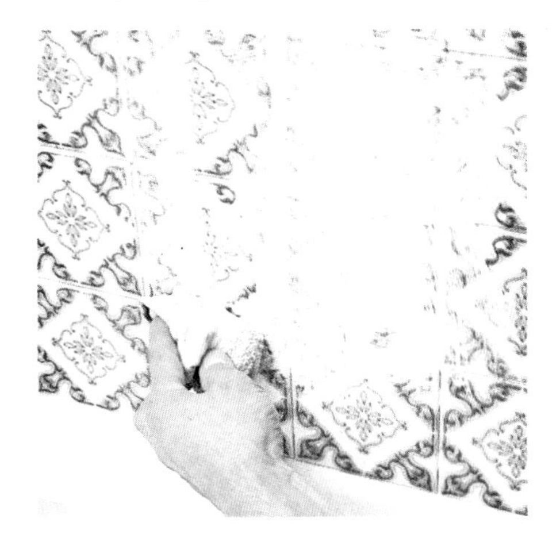

15 Once the tiling has been completed and the adhesive has set, rub grout firmly into the joints, ideally with a sponge or a piece of rag

16 When the grout is almost dry, draw a stick with a rounded point along the joints to give a neat and tidy appearance to the finished tiling

horizontal batten and the vertical line (fig. 7), filling in the bottom row and working upwards.

Adhesives should be applied thinly to the wall over an area of not more than $1m^2$ at a time.

If adhesive is applied over a greater area, some may dry before it has been tiled over. Draw the serrated edge of the spreader over the adhesive, forming ridges to provide good suction and adhesion.

Press the tiles firmly into place without sliding them, wiping away any adhesive that squeezes on to the surface of the tiles with a damp cloth. The alignment of the tiles should be checked with the spirit level on completion of every three or four rows.

When the tiles have set, the corner tiles may be fixed and the batten removed before filling in the bottom row—butter their backs with adhesive and fit them firmly home. Always fit cut tiles so that the spacer lugs—that is the uncut sides—face those of the adjacent tile (fig. 9).

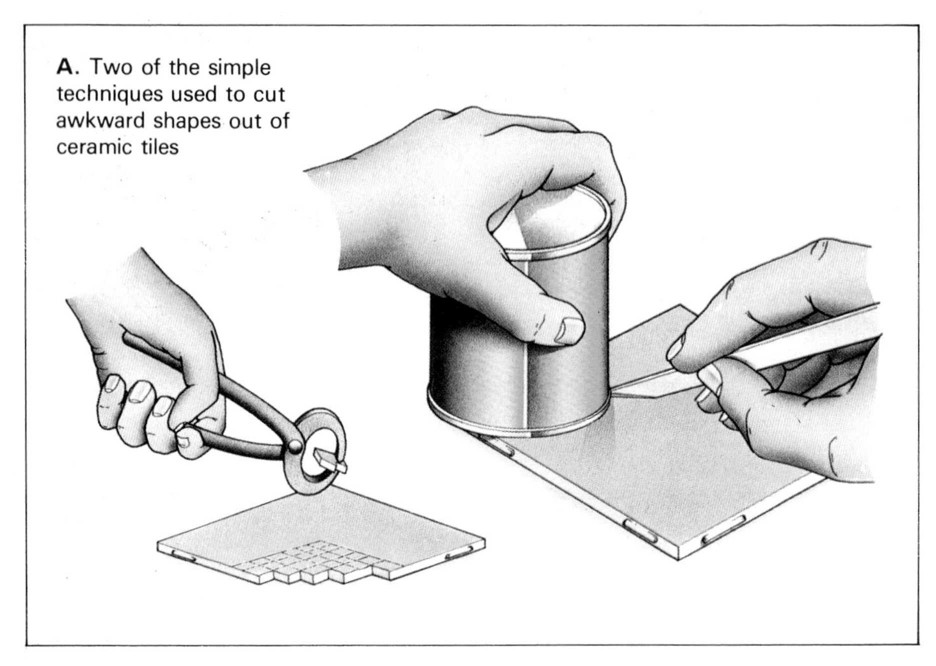

A. Two of the simple techniques used to cut awkward shapes out of ceramic tiles

Butt the spacer lugs of the tiles on the adjacent wall against the surface of the cut corner tile at right-angles to it—thus allowing a grout line to run down the junction of the two walls.

Cutting and shaping tiles

Straight cuts in ceramic tiles can be made either by scoring and snapping with a standard tile cutter (figs 10 and 11) or by scoring and breaking with an Oporto tile cutter (fig. 12).

Notches and curved cuts must be 'nibbled' by hand with a pair of pincers (fig. 13). In the case of curved cuts, make a straight cut first as near to the curve as possible—be very careful how you work, the tile will snap if you attempt to pincer out larger areas.

The guidelines for curved cuts can be drawn in either by eye, or—more satisfactorily—with a cardboard template. Trim the template to the required shape in situ then carefully transfer it to the tile and then draw around it in felt-tip pen.

Pipes present some of the trickiest tiling problems. The safest way to tile around them is to cut the relevant tile in two and to cut a semi-circle out of each half.

All cuts in ceramic tiles can look neater and much more professional looking if they are smoothed thoroughly afterwards with a carborundum file or block (fig. 14).

Right: A tile-topped table, like this one with medallion tiles, can, if carefully made, look superb in any setting. You do not need a new table, you can use a second-hand or even a cut-down kitchen table if you find that its proportions are completely right.

Before buying tiles, take home some samples and make a test pattern on your table top, check that:

1 You will not need to cut square tiles; on a table cut ones are unsightly.

2 In a pattern using two or more colours, you will finish up with the same colour in all four corners.

When tiling, always work from the centre following a grid.

Tiling around fitments

Where the fitment runs the length of a wall—a bath or kitchen unit for example—treat the top edge as you would a floor or skirting board. Fix a horizontal batten along this edge and leave it in place while you tile the wall above. When the tiles are dry, remove the batten and tile down to the edge with tiles cut to fit.

Tiling around windows

When tiling window reveals and sills, arrange the tiles to achieve a good visual balance, with cut tiles of equal size on each side of the window. Fit any cut tiles at the back and in the corners where they are not so obvious. Ensure the patterns are kept continuous, and the finished surfaces smooth, by placing the spacer lugs of any cut tile by those of the next.

Grouting

When the tiling is finished, leave it to set for 12 to 24 hours, then rub grout firmly into the tile joints with an old sponge, squeegee or cloth (fig. 15). Remove excess grout with a damp sponge: when it has almost set, run a blunt stick across the joints to leave a neat finish (fig. 16). Allow the grout to dry and then give the tiles a final polish with a soft, dry cloth.

Mosaic tiling

Above: Mosaic is a tough and durable form of decoration which has many uses, both inside and outside the house

Mosaic is a spectacular art form and an excellent decorative and durable surface finish for walls and floors. Its use was widespread during Roman times.

Mosaic

Mosaic work can be made up of any small pieces—chips—of oven-fired clay tiles (glazed or unglazed), coloured or plain glass, polished or natural pebbles, plastic or metal.

Commercially produced chips are becoming more varied: the 'standard' chip is square in shape and comes in assorted sizes from 25mm × 25mm upwards, with 50mm × 50mm as the most usual size. Rectangular tiles are also popular, while circular, octagonal and multi-faceted shapes are now becoming widely available. These all come in a variety of colours and textures, some of them bearing decorative motifs.

Creating a mosaic floor or wall in a house using the 'piece by piece' technique is a lengthy and difficult job. Most manufacturers therefore supply mosaic chips in large sheets 305mm or 515mm square, which can be laid complete. In addition to the variety of materials normally used there are a number of slip-resistant finishes for use in areas such as bathrooms and outside patios, while some types are suitable mainly for wall use, others for external use, and some for indoor use only.

Preparation

To lay a mosaic floor you will first have

1 Before laying mosaic tiles, you must make sure the floor is completely clean and dry or the final surface will be uneven and the adhesive may not adhere properly. If the floor is uneven, you should lay hardboard all over it—rough side up, to provide an adequate key for the tiling adhesive to be applied later

2 Before finally nailing down the hardboard, condition it to the atmosphere in the room so that it does not buckle once the mosaic tiling has been laid. When you have firmly fixed the hardboard, arrange guidelines at right-angles in the centre of the room using a chalked line or lengths of string

3 Using a sheet of mosaic chips as a guide, cut a measuring strip from an offcut of spare timber. Remember to allow adequate space for the necessary gaps between sheets. Then accurately mark off the floor with the strip and mark the points on the lines where the last complete sheets fall before they actually reach the walls

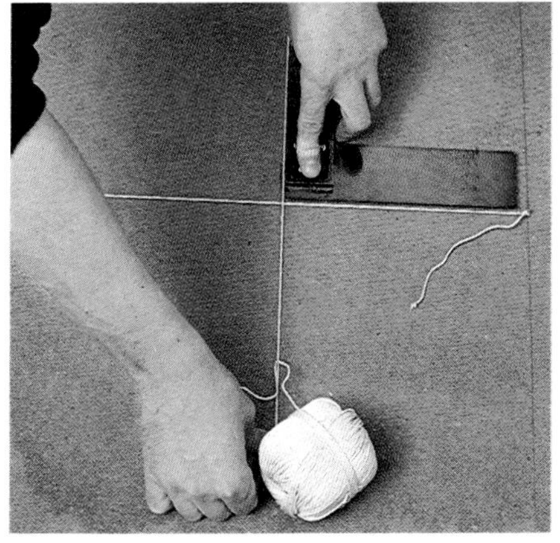

4 Taking one of these measured points, fix a length of string or alternatively a wooden batten to run across it at right-angles to the original guideline. Then repeat this procedure at the point marked on the other original line so that you have two new guidelines which then cross each other in one particular corner of the room

5 Start spreading the adhesive in the angle made by the two guidelines and then lay the mosaic sheets, tamping them down

6 In the gaps between the covered area and the wall, lay a sheet of chips backing side upwards and mark a cutting line

7 Free the chips which need to be cut from their backing, then cleanly and neatly score or cut them with a tile cutter or pincers

8 Lay the small pieces in place, trying to match the pattern and making sure there are no unsightly gaps that are visible between them

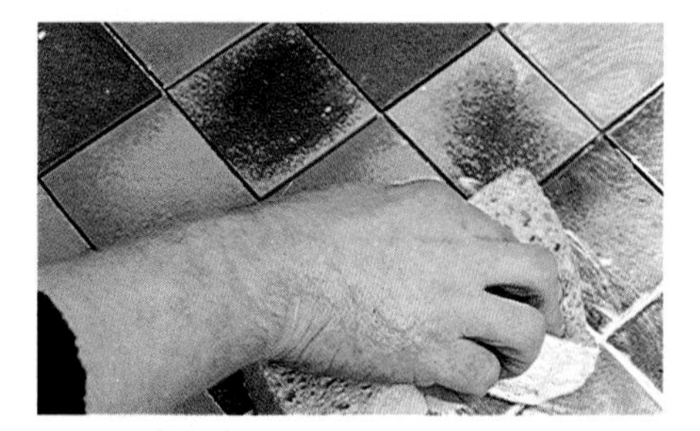

9 When the adhesive has completely set, apply the grout with a sponge and work it well into the joints. Then carefully wipe away the surplus

10 Finally, before the grout has dried, draw a rounded stick between the joints to finish them off and then carefully wipe off the excess

to prepare the surface. Concrete provides the best base for any kind of tiling work, though for mosaic tiling it must be absolutely level. If the existing base is uneven, it should be levelled with a new mortar screed or a suitable self-levelling compound.

While mosaic can usually be laid directly on to wet mortar, this can cause problems for the amateur, and it is best to allow the screed to dry completely and then use adhesive to secure the mosaic.

Floorboards—unless they are extremely firm and even—are best covered with hardboard before tiling. Nail any loose boards securely and punch down any protruding nails. Lay the hardboard rough side up to provide a good key for the adhesive and then secure it with screw nails to prevent any movement once the mosaic has been laid. Make sure that the hardboard has been conditioned to the climate in the room first.

Once the surface is ready the floor should be marked up to ensure that the mosaic will be square in relation to the door. Though the process is rather time-consuming it is essential for a satisfactory result.

Start by arranging a guideline across

A. Below: Marking up walls and floors for mosaic is quite a simple task but the necessary preparation must be meticulously done. Also great care should be taken with the actual cutting and laying of the tiles to get a really professional and neat finish.

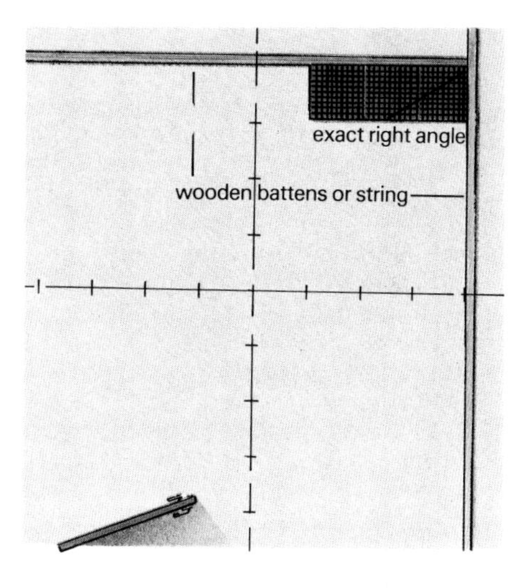

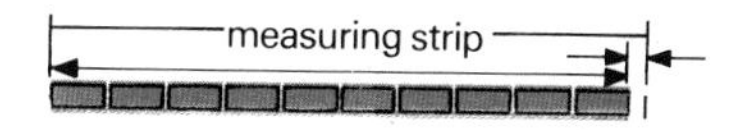

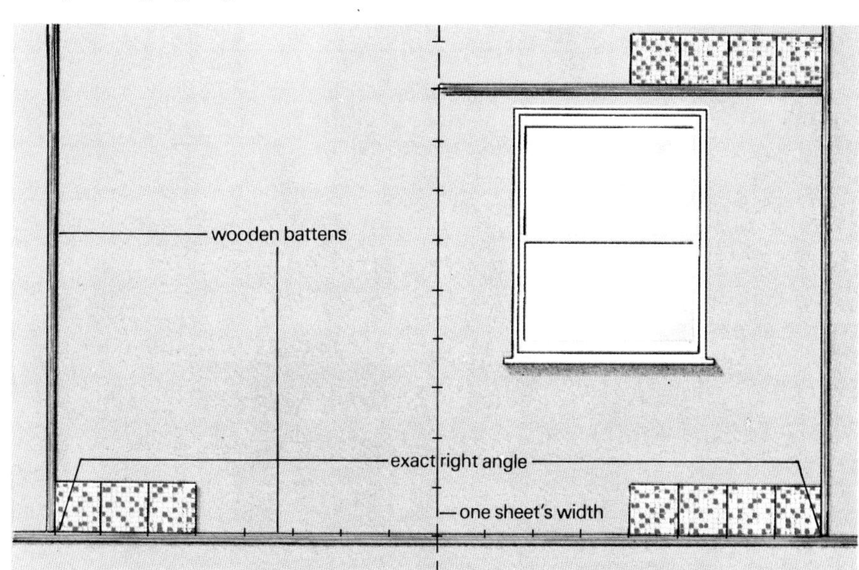

the room at right-angles to the door, and then another at right-angles to this. Make a measuring strip the width of a mosaic sheet from a length of scrap timber. Use it to transfer the dimension of the sheets to the lines on the floor, so that these are divided into sheet-sized sections along their full length.

Mark the points on the guidelines where the last full sheets fall, then prepare lengths of batten or string to stretch the length and breadth of the room. Arrange these to pass through the marked points, at right-angles to the original guidelines, so that they cross in one corner of the room (fig. A).

This should leave you with a regular shaped area calculated from the middle of the room and visually in line with the doorway. This area is tiled first, starting from the angle between the two border battens or strings. Afterwards, the guidelines should be removed and the remaining edge spaces should be filled in with mosaic sheets cut carefully to size.

Laying the tiles

Aim to lay three or four sheets of mosaic at a time, no more. Start by spreading adhesive in the angle of the two corner battens or strings, following any instructions that come with the adhesive or the sheets. Prepare the sheets for laying by grouting the underside; mix a fairly dry grout, or the water in the mixture will soak the paper holding the chips together and may dislodge them. Work the grout well into the gaps between the chips and wipe away any surplus before laying the sheets.

Patterned mosaics will have a direction arrow printed on the paper to help you lay the sheet correctly: make sure that this is lined up as instructed by the manufacturer when you lay each sheet.

Once they have been accurately positioned, the sheets must be tamped firmly in place to ensure that each individual mosaic chip comes into contact with the adhesive.

Repeat this process until the marked-out area is completely covered. The guides may then be removed. This will leave a narrow strip around the edge of the room which must be filled.

Lay a sheet of chips backing side upwards and butt it against the wall, trying to match any pattern in the rest of the floor. Mark the exposed underside of the mosaic to correspond with the edge of the sheet already laid, allowing for the standard gap between sheets.

If the infill sheet does not divide naturally between a row of chips, remove from backing and score along the line with a tile cutter, tear off the unwanted portion of the sheet, and break individual chips along the scored line using pliers or combination glass/tile cutter pincers.

Continue this process until infill sheets have been prepared for the entire area, and mark each one with a pencil so that they do not get mixed up. Grout, lay and tamp them into place. Complete the job by filling any gaps between sheets with grout, carefully wiping away any surplus.

Mosaic walls

The techniques described above can easily be applied to walls as well. If the entire wall is to be covered, nail a horizontal batten across the wall, positioned one sheet width above the skirting board using a level to ensure that it is perfectly horizontal.

Use a measuring strip to plan the job—ensuring that you work outwards from

B. Below: A striking floral pattern can be created with pre-cut mosaic chips

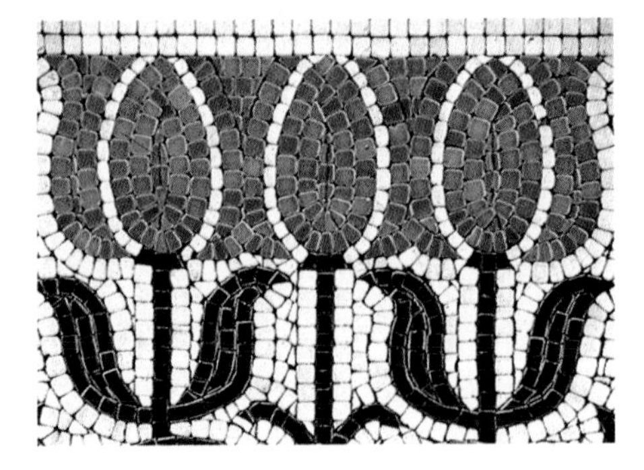

Above: This attractive heat-proof stand can be made from left-over mosaic tiles. It is made from one sheet of tiles — cut a piece of chipboard to this size and fix your tiles to it. Edge the board with hardwood and cover the bottom with felt

the centre of the wall so that any cut sheets finish in the vertical corners of the room. Nail a vertical batten where the last complete sheet will fall, using a plumbline to ensure that a perfect right-angle is formed where the two battens meet. This is where you start laying the sheets, and you proceed as for a floor.

It is possible to tile a bare brick wall by covering it with sheets of hardboard before you apply the sheets of mosaic. The hardboard should be fixed to a timber framework with horizontal and vertical battens at 300mm intervals to ensure that the boards are rigidly fixed.

The tops of baths, sinks and windows are rarely true: when you reach these, use an extra horizontal batten to ensure that the work remains level. Position it to line up with the first complete row of sheets above the fixture.

Other effects

It is possible to drop mosaic 'panels' into ceramic tiling, provided that you can find suitable mosaic sheets that will fit exactly into the gap left by omitting, say, four standard tiles. The mosaic material may be thinner than the main tiles so complete the tiling first and then pack the gap with a 1:3 mortar mix.

Mosaic can be used to cover such things as work surfaces and tables. There are even heat-resistant chips available for fireplaces and hearths. Individual mosaic designs can be created for decorative purposes, rather like pictures. It is first necessary to establish what loose mosaic chips you can obtain—the better the selection of shapes and colours, the greater your design flexibility.

Preparing a floor for tiling

Above: Dry laying of tiles, against marks which you have already measured, ensures accurate and neat tiling

A tiled floor can transform the appearance of any room, and for the most part the job is straightforward and quick. Badly laid tiled floors can be an eyesore, but you can prevent this by taking a little extra care at the planning and preparation stages.

Vinyl floor coverings are by far the most popular choice, especially for kitchens and bathrooms, and it is not difficult to see why.

Cork has some splendid characteristics which make it well suited for use as a flooring material, and is almost as easy to lay and finish. And of course there is nothing to match the quality and durability of quarry or ceramic tiles.

You can tile a floor only if the surface is sound, firm and level. Loose floorboards, damp or uneven concrete, old linoleum and pitted asphalt are typical floor conditions that need to be checked and corrected before laying vinyl or any other form of tiling. Bumps and high points quickly cause wear or cracks in floor coverings.

Preparing wood floors

Nail or screw down any loose boards and drive in or remove insecure nails and screws. Wood floors should be covered with plywood or hardboard.

Vinyl flooring may be laid directly on chipboard used in place of floorboarding provided the chipboard is of flooring grade and has a minimum thickness of 18mm. Be sure to remove any existing floor covering first.

Preparing concrete floors

Provided concrete floors are dry, clean, level and free from anything which could conceivably react with the overlay (particularly grease and solvents which can have a marked effect on vinyl), they form an ideal base for flooring.

The most common problem is dampness, particularly on concrete floors laid directly on top of earth that have not been provided with a permanent damp-proof membrane. Even if a concrete floor looks dry, try a simple test to check whether or not it is so. Place a rubber mat, piece of cooking foil or plastic sheet on the concrete and tape the edges down as best as possible. Turn on the heating at a setting a little higher than normal, then, after 24 hours, peel off the test sheet. The presence of any moisture underneath indicates a damp floor.

If the floor is damp, it must be treated with waterproofer before being overlaid with flooring of timber, cork or any other material that could be affected by moisture. A wet floor may have to have its surface relaid and a waterproof membrane inserted (regardless of the floor covering used).

Pitting and general unevenness can be rectified using what is known as a self-levelling compound. Pour this over the floor area to a minimum depth of about 4mm, following the maker's instructions closely as these may vary. You cannot, however, lay sheet material over some damp-proofing compounds—so check this point with your floor covering dealer.

Floors with a surface which is powdery but otherwise sound can be coated with a latex-based sealer before being overlaid by tiling.

Other floors

It is possible to lay vinyl and cork flooring over existing quarry or ceramic tiling provided that the gaps between the original tiles are filled with self-levelling compound. This is to prevent the old tile pattern from working through—a particular problem near doorways and other areas subject to continuous wear.

Also, take particular care to remove grease, dirt and grit: perhaps harmless to the original tiling but often damaging to vinyl and cork. A good wash with household detergent and hot water is normally sufficient.

You can also lay some types of vinyl and cork tile over existing linoleum and vinyl flooring where removal poses problems. Again, make sure the surface is clean and that all edges on the old tiling are stuck down properly.

Laying hardboard

On an old, rough wooden floor, laying hardboard or plywood over the entire surface is often the only way of easily achieving a smooth surface on which to lay tiles.

Standard-sized hardboard comes in sheets 2400mm×1200mm, and for this job select the 6.4mm thickness.

Hardboard sheets have to be conditioned prior to use otherwise buckling may occur through localized shrinkage or expansion after they have been laid. Temper the boards by brushing the rough side with water and lay the sheets flat, smooth sides together, overnight or longer so the moisture is fully absorbed. The idea is that the sheets will dry out after being laid, in the process shrinking slightly to form a very tight, level surface.

The hardboard is laid rough side upwards as this gives a better key for any tile adhesive used. Stagger the joints to reduce the likelihood of strain at any particular point—which could lead to cracks or wear in flooring placed above—and, similarly, avoid coinciding the hardboard joins with those of floorboarding.

On a wooden floor, use 25mm hardboard pins to nail the board at 150mm spacings over the entire surface and at 100mm spacings along the edges. On a

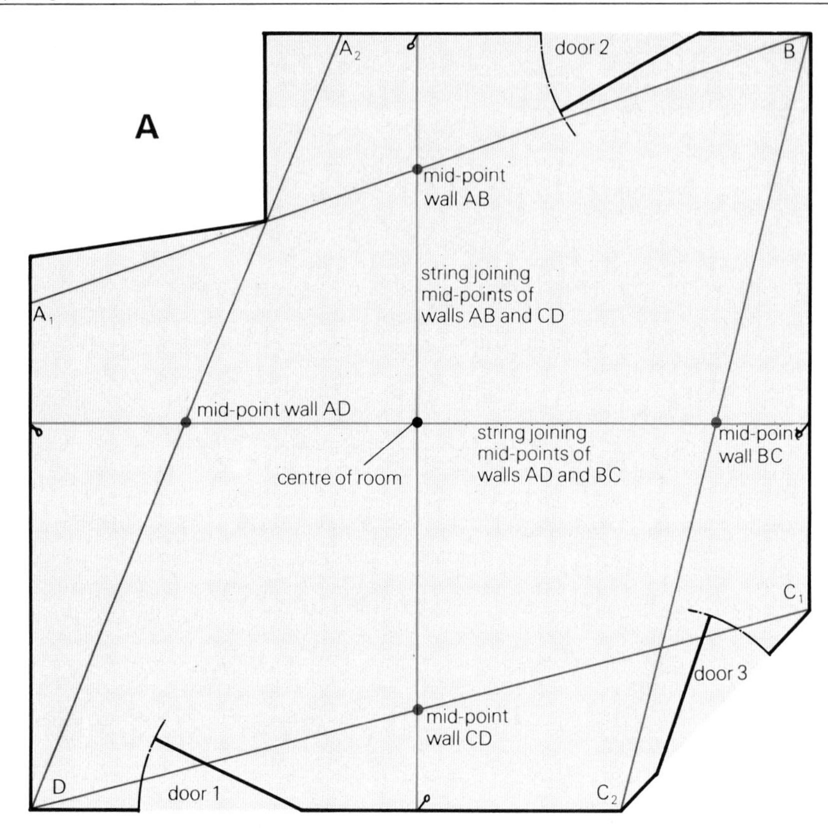

concrete or cement floor you have to glue the board in place using a suitable adhesive such as neoprene thixotropic. When sticking anything to concrete, check whether or not an initial coat of primer is required as concrete can very easily absorb some other types of adhesive.

When you have laid the boards, allow them to dry out before overlaying vinyl tiles or sheet—a day or so is normally long enough. Spend the time correcting any tight-fitting doors which open into the room. Normally the gap between the base of the door and the floor is sufficiently large enough to accommodate a layer of thick floor covering or a layer of plywood or hardboard.

Laying plan

Once the floor preparations have been completed, some idea of the lie of the room is necessary for planning a design and for choosing tiles or tile sheeting.

In theory, all designs should radiate or progress from the centre of the room. Find this by measuring off the centre line of two opposing walls. Stretch a chalked string between the two and snap this against the boards on the floor. Repeat this for the two remaining walls so that another chalk mark is made: where they cross is the centre point of the room.

Border walls

Although any design is based on the centre of the room, border walls must be considered if an even pattern is to be achieved. Also, the tile direction should be square, or perfectly symmetrical, to the main doorway of the room. So in figure A you would base the tile pattern

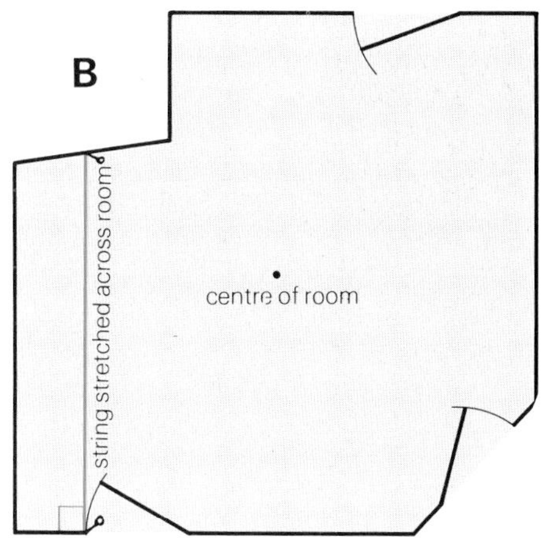

on either door 1 or door 2 in preference to door 3 even though the tile pattern falls at 45° to this, which is visually acceptable.

To mark out guidelines for laying, produce a chalked mark at right-angles to the doorway (fig. B), far enough for another chalked mark to be made across the room and coinciding with the centre point (fig. C).

Make another chalked line at right-angles to the second line, again passing through the centre point. This line is of course parallel with the first. The resulting cross you have chalked on the floor is now used for the exact planning of a pattern, and also provides a guide for the tile-laying sequence which follows.

When, later, you have chosen your tiles and have designed a pattern for these follow the cross-lines in a 'dry laying' sequence to check how the tiles finish off at the edges. Ideally the border round the room should be even and although this is not always possible as far as the pattern is concerned, it is certainly possible to rearrange the position of the chalked cross so that tile widths are even on each pair of opposing walls.

It is not always possible to make sure that you get an even finish all the way round the outside. If not, try to restrict awkward cuts to sides of the room which are not so noticeable.

Above: To find the centre point of a perfectly square or rectangular room presents no problems, but awkwardly shaped floors need a different approach (A). Instead of totting up individual parts of each wall, measure across the room to take in the obstruction (shown by red line A_1B) and find the mid-point of this. Repeat the procedure for each of the three remaining sides of the room (red lines A_2D, DC_1, C_2B) and find the mid-point of each of these.

Mark the floor at these points. Now stretch strings across the room in such a way as to join up each pair of opposing mid-points (green lines). Where the two strings end up crossing is the mid-point of your room.

Your laying plan must be based both on the centre point and on the main doorway (taken here to be door 1) if the tile pattern is to look regular and symmetrical. To do this, first stretch a string at right-angles to the doorway to a point on the facing wall (B). Follow this with another string, at right-angles to the first and coinciding with the room centre point (C). A third string line, which is fixed parallel to the first, completes the cross. By thoroughly rubbing the strings with chalk, a chalked cross can be snapped on the floor to act as your final tiling guide. The strings can then be removed before you start tiling.

1 Measure up the room to be tiled and decide how best to use standard hardboard sheet sizes. Remember to allow adequate space for cuts around difficult obstacles. When actually cutting the hardboard to fit round a corner, pull the sheet as close as possible to this so that direct and accurate measurements can easily be made

2 The next step is to carefully measure back the corner depth on the hardboard and then use a tool like a straightedge to mark the necessary cutting line. Do this in brightly coloured chalk or alternatively make a strong pencil mark. Allow a cut which is slightly at an angle if the shape is such that it warrants cutting in this way

5 Nail the board down at 100mm spacings at the board edges and at 150mm spacings over the entire surface of the hardboard sheet. When you are working on a concrete or cement floor you have to fix the board in place with a good adhesive. Something like neoprene thixotropic would be particularly suitable. Otherwise, use masonry nails

6 All floor tile designs should start or progess from the actual centre of the room you want to tile. So you will need to find this before you start. Use a tape measure or steel rule to find the mid-point of each wall. By joining up the opposing mid-points you will now be able to find the centre of the room. Recheck your measurements before you progress

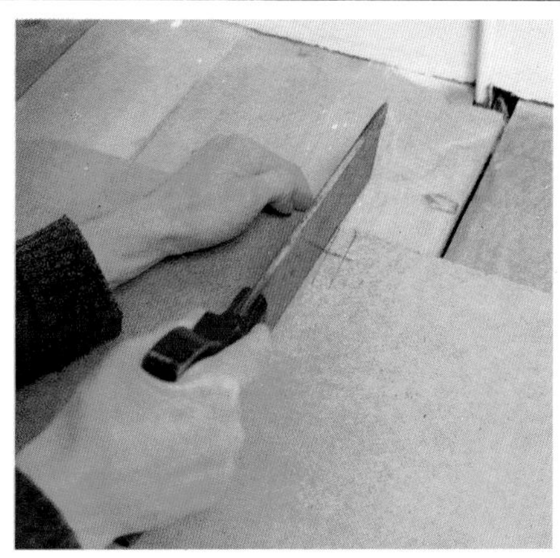

3 You will find it much easier to cut the hardboard at floor level if you make sure you prop up the edges as best as possible to enable sawing. When the board has been completely cut to shape, push it firmly in position and then use fixings like hardboard pins or possibly screw-thread nails to secure it in place permanently

4 Obviously in a normal room you are still going to come across minor obstructions. These should be dealt with as they are encountered, but be careful that you remove only as much of the board as is necessary for a neat and tight fit. Be especially careful with the intricate fitting around items like pipes, for instance

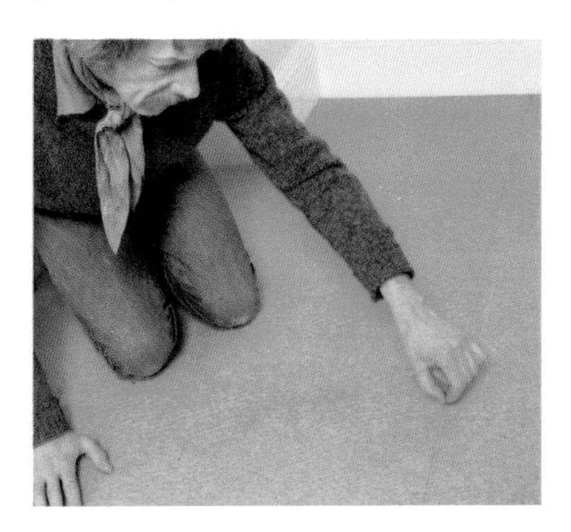

7 To give yourself an accurate laying pattern for the tiles, stretch a chalked string between opposing walls. When this is snapped against the floor the necessary mark is left. Repeat this method for the two remaining walls in the room, so that you get another clear chalk mark. The point where the lines cross over is the room centre

8 These marks are now your main guideline for your tiling. Use them for the necessary trial 'dry run' where you lay out all the tiles and discover where they need cutting down and trimming around doorways. When you have established the way the pattern works, use the chalk marks again for the permanent fixing of the tiles

Laying floor tiles and sheet vinyl

Laying vinyl or cork floor tiles is one of the best ways of providing a room with a good-looking and tough floor covering. And provided that the floor preparation and design stages have not been skimped, the job is quick and uncomplicated. Laying hardboard on a wood, cement or concrete floor to provide a smooth and level base for all forms of tiling is covered in the previous section.

The centre of the room is also used as the starting point for tile laying. This ensures that the tiles are laid evenly and squarely in what is the most conspicuous part of the room and means that you end up by trimming and cutting tiles to fit. Even in small rooms or hallways, always start tiling in the middle.

Before tiling, do a 'dry run' to check for problems in laying and also that your design works. Tile fit can be checked across the length and the breadth of a room, in alcoves, and anywhere else where the basic shape of the room alters.

Arrange two lengths of string to cross the centre of the room and to act as guides for tile laying. Fixed carefully to the skirting and stretched taut a little above the floor, these can then be chalked and snapped against the floor to produce the final laying marks.

Having finally established the laying guides, chalk these on the support flooring. Remove the strings but leave the skirting pins in place so that chalked marks can be remade.

Laying individual tiles

Individual tiles are laid starting from the centre of the room outwards. If tile adhesive is required, spread a little of this along the chalked cross lines. Always use the adhesive recommended by the tile manufacturer, and follow the specified instructions for applying this. With cork tiles, for example, you may have to apply adhesive to the underside of the tile as well as to the floor, perhaps leaving an interval for drying before bringing both together.

The important rule for tiling is to cover only a small part of the floor at a time. Lay the centre four tiles against each other to coincide with the crossed chalked marks at the centre of the room.

Work outwards from the centre four tiles once these have set, applying only as much adhesive as is necessary for each small area before you tile. Deal with one quadrant of the floor before moving on to the next.

Cutting tiles to fit

Eventually you will come to the border where, unless the fit is arranged to be perfect, the tiles need cutting to shape and width.

Place a tile squarely on top of the last one before the border. Take another and place this partly on top but firmly butted against the wall. The inner edge is then used to mark a cutting line on the middle tile.

Even on what looks to be a straight and even border, mark up tiles for cutting individually so that you take care of any irregularities.

You can also use a shape-tracing tool or template former with metal teeth similar to a comb. These teeth take the form of any firm object against which they are

1 In a small room there is no particular need to mark the floor for tile laying, but do go through a dry lay routine to see how the tiles do fit

2 Use the recommended adhesive and fix a small area of tile at a time. Remove adhesive squeezed up between tiles before this sets

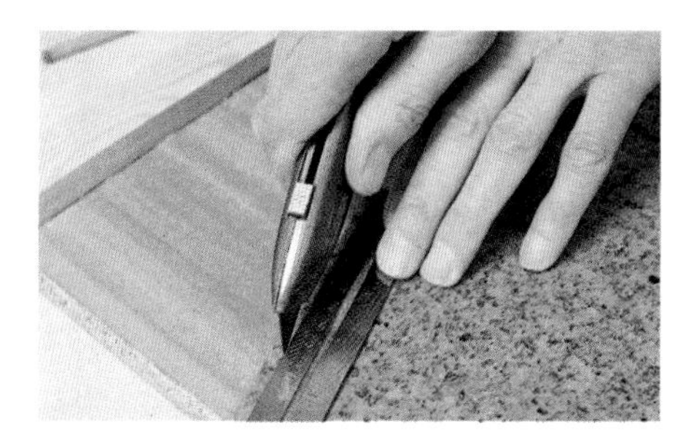

3 Use a steel rule, heavy-duty handyman's knife and a cutting board to trim tiles. Take special care when cutting tiles to fit round door frames or awkward obstacles. A special tool or card template is also useful

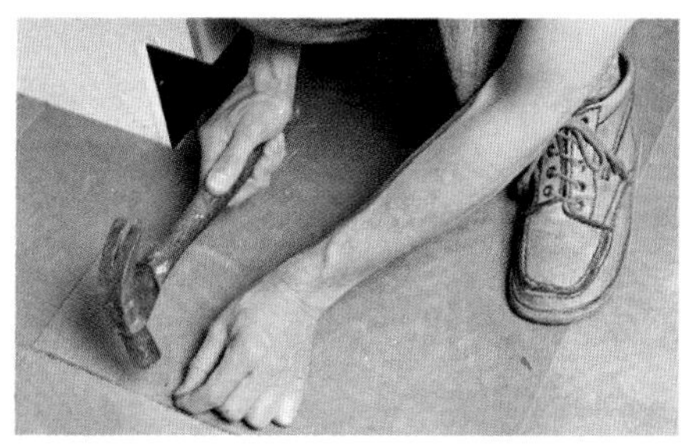

4 Mix different packs of tiles so that colour differences become less noticeable when the tiles are laid. With sheet vinyl tiling do not forget to first lay down hardboard sheeting (see the previous section) on uneven floors

5 Cut vinyl sheeting to fit into every nook and cranny as the whole sheet is laid down. Use a cutting board and handyman's knife. Slit the sheet edges so that a good fit is achieved around obstacles and fittings

6 After settling and shrinkage the vinyl sheet can be properly trimmed. Use a straightedge as a cutting guide. Then use suitable adhesive to fix edge joins and elsewhere that may cause problems if curling occurs

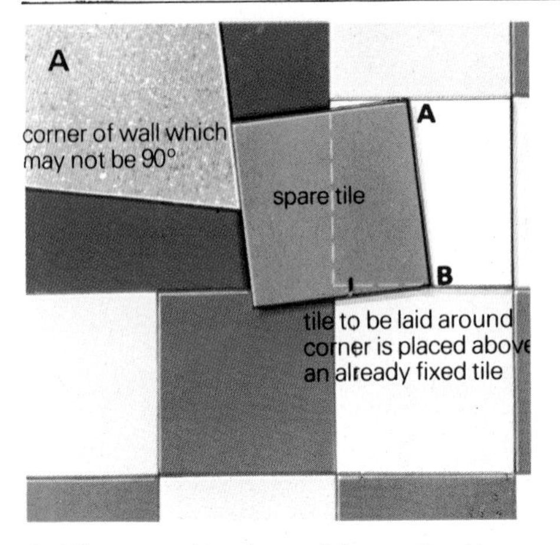

A. The procedure for scribing a tile. Use a matching tile as the transfer ruler, and then neatly pencil in an accurate mark for cutting

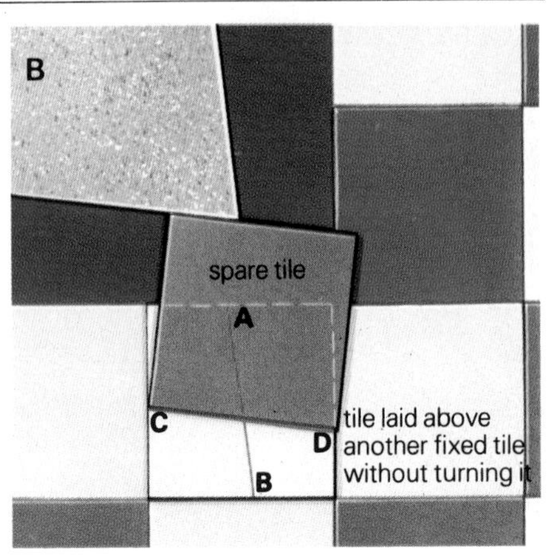

B. Without twisting the tile, carefully scribe the second mark and then remove the waste corner with a handyman's knife and rule

pushed and once tightened in place, the outer ends can be used as a cutting guide.

Sealing the tiles

Vinyl tiles do not require any surface treatment after laying. Some cork tiles are pre-finished with a vinyl coating and also need no further work. Untreated tiles can be treated with oleo-resinous and polyurethane varnishes which are available in eggshell, matt or gloss finishes.

Fitting sheet vinyl

Sheet vinyl is the modern answer to the once popular linoleum flooring and is warmer, if not quite so hard wearing. It provides a simple solution to those who require a good-looking floor covering—possibly highly patterned—but cannot be bothered with the planning that laying individual tiles involves.

Vinyl sheet flooring can sometimes shrink, so the makers usually advise cutting oversize when the material is first laid: follow these cutting instructions closely. After about two or three weeks of use, final trimming can take place at join overlaps and edges.

The possibility of shrinkage must always be considered when planning and laying down cuts and joins.

You will need a scribing tool for marking cutting lines at the sheet edges and ends. Make this by driving a nail partly through a wooden batten, 50mm from the end, so that the point protrudes about 3mm (fig. C).

Allowing a little extra for shrinkage and trimming, cut a length of sheet from your supply roll. Lay the sheet to allow an overlap of up to 150mm at sides and ends. Follow the scribing techniques outlined for final trimming. Use the same procedure for trimming sheet edges as you lay. To do this, make a pencil mark on the edge of the vinyl sheet 250mm from the wall (fig. D) and draw the sheet back from the wall so that it lays flat.

Now measure back 250mm towards the wall and make another mark (fig. E). By carefully sliding the sheet, arrange it so that the point of your scribing tool coincides with the second mark when the batten end is held against the skirting board (fig. E). Take care not to twist the sheet out of alignment in the process. Finally, scribe along the sheet as described above, cut off the waste and push the sheet tight against the skirting.

C. A scribing tool which has been made from a square-ended piece of spare battening. Drive a nail partly through so that the point protrudes about 3mm. Cover the end with cloth or felt

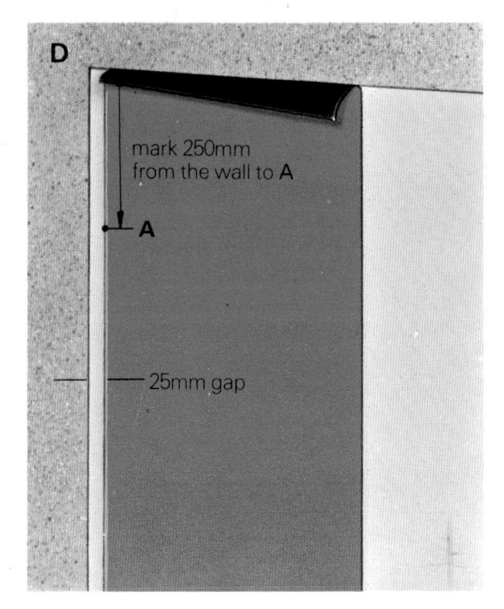

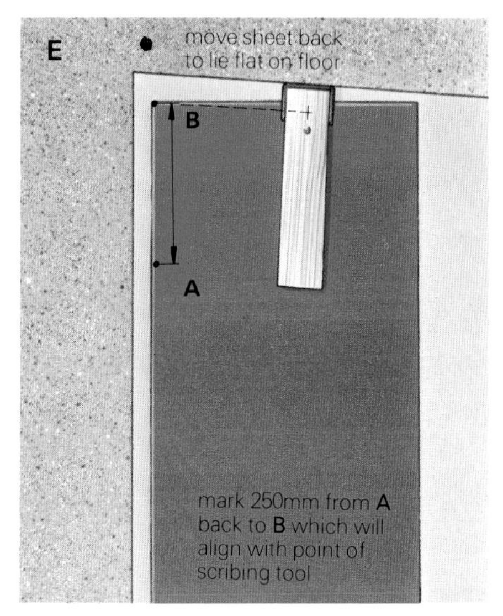

Start the sequence for cutting sheet vinyl by measuring back from the wall, marking a point on the edge of the sheet (D). Pull the sheet back enough to back-mark the edge by the same distance and place the scribing nail neatly on this (E). Scribe the necessary cutting line and remove the waste. Where two sheets of vinyl overlap, cut between the edges carefully

Lay the end of your scribing tool at right-angles against the skirting and mark the sheet along the length of the wall. Take your time over the job, and try not to scrape the skirting board paintwork in the process. Slit the sheeting but do not nibble away any more of the sheet than is necessary for fitting—trimming is best left until much later (fig. 6).

Cut the sheet edge to shape using a handyman's knife, steel rule and cutting board, then push it against the wall.

The alignment of the second sheet should of course match that of the first. Also check that trimming to fit the wall still leaves an overlap of at least 30mm with the first. This may mean a bit of calculating before keying the second sheet.

Trimming sheet vinyl

After the two-week ageing period, final trimming can take place. Use a metal straightedge to force the sheet firmly against skirting boards and fittings before making the trimming cuts (fig. 6).

After the final trimming, vinyl sheet that needs to be glued in place can be raised and the adhesive applied.

At corners, or on awkward shapes, you need to ease the vinyl into place by slitting the waste. If the shape is particularly awkward, a series of slits will help you to trim the sheet more accurately. On small, round obstructions like pipes, slit the vinyl to the centre of where the pipe will pass through. Then make a circle of small cuts out from this point.

With modern, 'lay flat' vinyl sheet, gluing is not normally necessary.

Laying wood flooring

The beauty of wood as a flooring material is not just skin deep—it has many other, more practical, advantages. As well as being one of the hardest wearing floorcoverings, it is reasonably comfortable to walk on and sit on; and when it starts to look a bit shabby, the surface can be refurbished to give it a new lease of life.

Using the exising floor

If you want a wood floor, the cheapest solution is to sand and lacquer an existing timber floor. Floorboards and chipboard can both be easily treated—the latter producing a cork-like finish—using a hired floor sander. Before using the sander, you must first go over the floor punching down protruding nails and securing loose boards, preferably with screws.

Hardwood flooring

The 'proper' wood floorings are all hardwoods. There is a bewildering range—not only of species of timber, but in the form in which the flooring comes and in laying methods. Confusingly, most of the different forms are called 'parquet' and this term is no guide to what you are getting.

Types of wood flooring

Of the various forms of wood floor, mosaic panels—mostly 460mm or 290mm square—are made up from small tongues of hardwood laid in a basket-weave pattern and bonded to a felt or fabric backing (fig. 2). The panels are stuck to a smooth, solid or wood sub-floor, using a spirit-based or bitumen adhesive, in a procedure much the same as for laying cork or vinyl tiles. And as they are often pre-sanded, they need only to be sealed after laying.

Another form of wood floor, particularly suited to large rooms, is strip overlay. This consists of long, narrow strips of solid hardwood—about 10mm thick—which, when laid, look like very smart, narrow floorboards. The strips are tongued-and-grooved, and are laid—to wood sub-floors only—by 'secret nailing' through the tongue. To prevent creaking, the strips can also be glued and the strips should be laid at 45° or 90° to existing floorboards. Strip overlay usually needs sanding before it can be sealed or polished; some types are pre-finished.

Although similar in appearance to mosaic panelling, pre-finished laminated wood panels consist of two or three layers of plywood faced with a relatively thin layer of hardwood—oak, mahogany and maple are commonly used—which acts as a 'wear layer'. The wear layer is about 4mm thick, and is therefore unlikely to wear through with normal domestic use.

The panels—normally 305mm square—are tongued-and-grooved and are loose-laid over a special underlay material.

Floor blocks are what most people would think of as 'parquet flooring'. The solid blocks—about 75mm × 225mm and 18mm to 25mm thick—are traditionally laid in a herringbone pattern, but there are other interesting possibilities (figs A to D). They are usually tongued-and-grooved, and are glued to an asphalt or concrete sub-floor with a bitumen adhesive. They are normally of oak or, perhaps, pine—but other different woods are also available. More than one wood

A. Herringbone

B. Double Herringbone

C. Basket

D. Basketweave

Above: Individual floor blocks can be laid in a variety of ways, but determine which one beforehand, as many makes are tongued-and-grooved to a specific pattern

can be used to create interesting colour and grain effects.

Preparing to lay

It is essential that the sub-floor is sound and in good condition before flooring is laid. No flooring lasts long or looks good on a sub-floor which is bumpy, damp or sagging.

If you have a concrete sub-floor, remember that some types of wood flooring—such as the strip overlays—cannot be laid on it. All concrete in direct contact with the ground must contain some form of damp-proof course.

In the case of downstairs suspended floors, check that there is plenty of ventilation beneath the floor so that rot and dampness are not encouraged. Any gaps between the floorboards—which you are about to cover up—may be providing most of the ventilation at present. Check that there are plenty of air bricks around the base of the outside walls, and that they are not covered over or otherwise blocked.

Check the position of any electric cables or pipes running underneath the floor. These are going to be much more difficult to get to after the flooring has been laid. It is important to arrange that part of the flooring can be lifted for access unless you can reach piping and

1 Before laying any form of wood flooring, make sure the sub-floor is level and dirt-free. Lay hardboard if the floor is particularly uneven. Dry lay the flooring, in this case mosaic panelling, to check the fit. Mark clear cutting lines, making sure you allow about a 12mm gap at the wall

2 Cutting wood flooring can be more difficult to do than, say, cork or vinyl, so short cuts should be taken where possible. Try to arrange the actual laying so that the panels can be trimmed to length at the edge of one of the 'fingers'. Cut completely through the felt or fabric backing of the flooring

5 Follow the manufacturer's own instructions for applying the adhesive, covering only about panel-sized areas as individual tiles are laid. Carefully lay the first panel, remembering to leave a small gap right next to the walls. Always leave some adhesive overlap in readiness for the laying of the next panel. Take care not to get bitumen on the tile surfaces

6 Inevitably with this type of flooring, there will be unsightly gaps at the edges which you will have to fill in. Quadrant or other similar forms of moulding will neatly, and attractively, conceal the gap between panelling and the walls. Use the handy mitre block to make it easier for sawing the necessary corner cuts

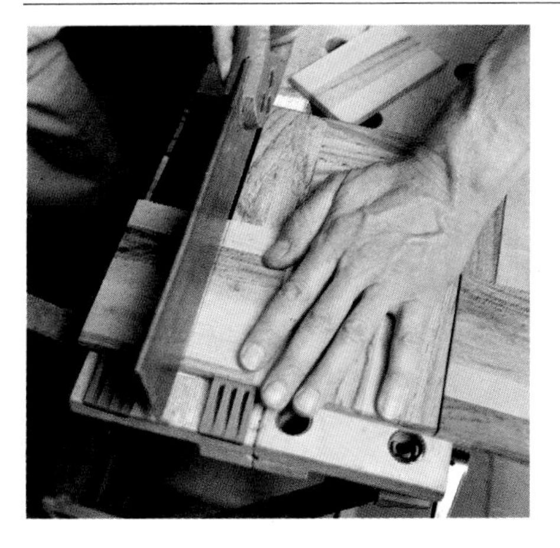

3 When you are not cutting on one of the edges of the 'fingers' but need to cut an awkward opening to allow for some obstruction, use a tenon saw to make it easier. If you have to cut apertures for pipework, a flexible-blade framed saw is much more suitable for this type of task

4 For semi-permanent fixing of some forms of wood flooring, you may be able to just use special double-sided tape. For permanent fixing of flooring, use the recommended adhesive which will probably be a latex-bitumen compound. Make sure you buy enough, initially, for the job in hand

7 To complete the wood flooring, your chosen moulding should then be fitted neatly against the edge of the already fixed panels. A close fit is essential for the perfect finished effect. Suitable fixing pins should then be hammered in at close intervals to firmly nail the moulding close into the existing skirting board

8 Unfinished board should be sanded. If necessary hire a floor sander for doing large areas. Remove glue from the surface in this way. Then use the recommended floor lacquer/sealer. Three or more coats will be necessary for best results. Be careful to always keep the floor completely dust-free or you will spoil the finished appearance

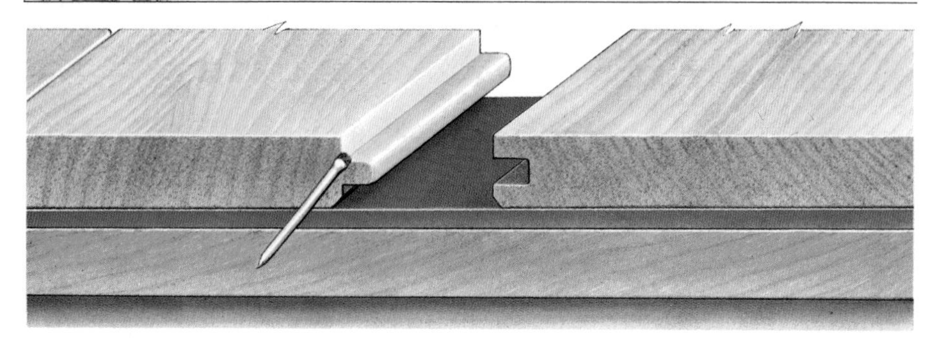

Above: 'Secret nailing' can be used to fix tongued-and-grooved forms of wood flooring. Knock the nail heads well in, using a nail punch

wiring from below.

Inspect floorboards for looseness and protruding nails. If boards have loosened, it is likely that the nail holes will have enlarged, so to get the board to stay down firmly replace the nails by screws.

Unless all this work has produced a perfectly level floor, with not the sign of a gap, bump or hollow, it is a good idea to now cover the floorboards with hardboard.

If you are laying strip overlay, laminated boards, or loose-lay mosaic panels which have their own underlay, it may be possible to lay flooring on a less than perfect sub-floor without using a hardboard underlay.

Condition the hardboard before laying by leaving it stacked flat for a week or two in the room where it is to be laid. Acclimatize the wood flooring in the same way.

Unless the flooring manufacturer recommends otherwise, lay the hardboard rough side up, nailed all over at centres of about 150mm, starting from the middle of each sheet. Use ring-shank or screw nails if you can get them, otherwise use ordinary panel pins or hardboard pins.

Lay the sheets brickwork fashion, so that the joints are staggered, and make sure that none coincide with gaps between floorboards. Screw down separate pieces of hardboard over boards that you may want to lift for access later on.

Laying the flooring

The setting-out procedure for mosaic panels and the tricks used for cutting them accurately at edges and around obstructions are exactly the same as for vinyl or cork tiles.

Except for the loose-lay interlocking

types, panels are glued to the sub-floor and most manufacturers sell an adhesive suitable for the purpose. In some cases, you may need to prime the surface first with a diluted coat of glue. Glue the panels down, butting up the edges tightly against one another; leave those around the edges—which may need trimming—until last.

At least one manufacturer also sells double-sided adhesive tape for laying mosaic panels: you could use this over the whole floor, or just for panels which you need to be able to lift.

Cutting panels presents few problems. If the cut coincides with the edge of one of the 'fingers' (fig. 2), the panel can be cut with a handyman's knife. Otherwise, cut the fingers with a fine-toothed tenon or coping saw.

Leave a gap of about 12mm at the edges of the floor to allow for movement. On solid sub-floors, this gap can be filled with a cork strip; on wooden sub-floors, it can be easily concealed with a strip of wooden scotia or quadrant.

Loose-lay mosaic panels are particularly easy to lay: the interlocking tongues and grooves are simply knocked together.

Strip overlay is laid at an angle to the floorboards or sub-floor. Start by snapping a chalk line parallel to one wall, a few millimetres less than the width of a strip away from it. Lay the first row of strips along this line, with their tongues pointing towards the centre of the room. Then 'secret nail' them to the floor, carefully nailing at about 250mm intervals, and at the end of each strip.

Lay the next row of strips against the first, but this time stagger the joints. As you hammer the tongues and grooves together, protect the tongue of the strip you are hammering with an offcut of strip, its groove against the tongue. Lay subsequent rows in the same way.

The first and last strips have to be accurately cut to size. These cannot be secret nailed, so nail through the surface, punching the nail heads well down, and cover the hole with filler.

Pre-finished panels and boards are usually tongued-and-grooved, and are laid in the same way as strip overlay. Most types are glued to a solid sub-floor, or nailed to a timber one.

Floor blocks are probably the most difficult of all types of wood flooring to lay. Blocks are relatively small, and are usually laid in a fairly complicated pattern which demands a lot of careful cutting at edges and corners.

They are glued to the sub-floor, often using a bitumen-based adhesive. Better quality blocks are tongued-and-grooved to simplify laying, but as these are machined for a specific pattern (the tongues and grooves provide accurate location) be sure you buy the correct type.

As well as following the procedure recommended by the manufacturers, bear in mind that most designs

Left: Individual floor blocks laid in the traditional herringbone pattern

incorporate a border layer of two blocks or so, and that laying is based on this. Work normally starts at the room centre, or along the centre line of the room, depending on the type of pattern.

Finishing the floor

Much wood mosaic is pre-sanded, and does not require much work apart from smoothing off the odd proud corner, or sanding down a patch of excess glue. The easiest way to finish them is by applying a lacquer/sealer. Most manufacturers recommend a suitable product, many preferring those with an oleo-resinous base—rather than polyurethane—for use on new wood floors. Three or more coats of the sealer will be needed.

Strip overlay floorings, and some other types, will need sanding first. Hire a proper floor sander for this, and sand until the boards are smooth and flat.

Maintenance

A well-sealed hardwood floor needs little maintenance, though you should wipe up spills immediately to prevent stains and accidents. Dust the floor with a slightly damp, clean cotton mop—so that you buff up the surface at the same time. Rewax or reseal sparingly.

Below: Wood floor coverings are quite easy to lay and transform any room, although they are particularly effective when used in living and dining areas

PLUMBING AND DRAINAGE

Understanding your water system

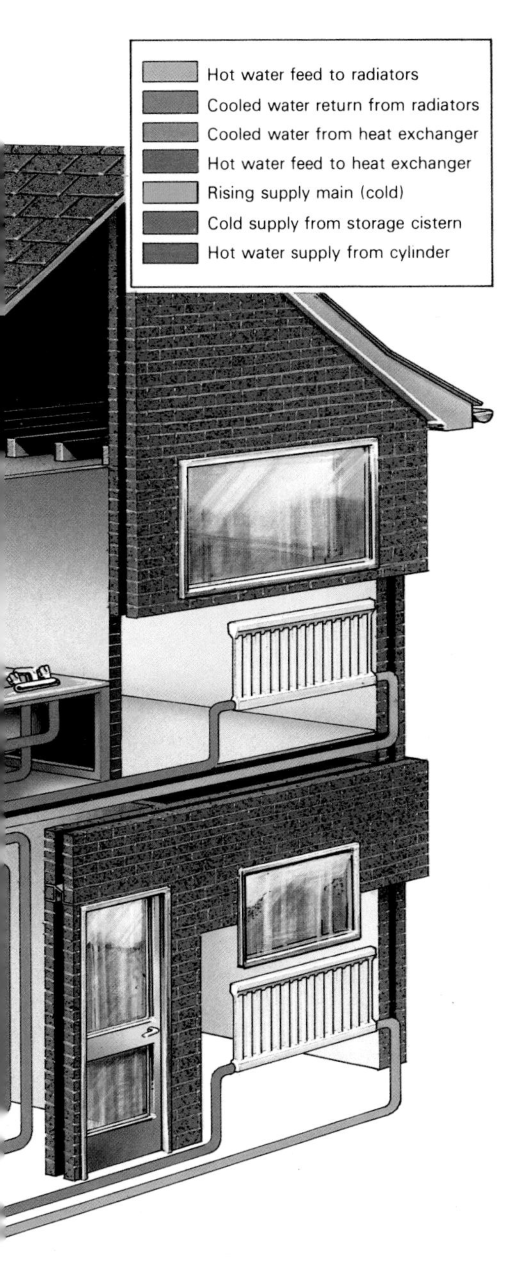

Domestic water systems come in two main types:

High-pressure systems, in which water at 'mains pressure' is supplied directly to all the taps and other water-using appliances.

Low-pressure systems, in which the water supply to most taps and appliances is via a cold-water storage cistern in the attic, only the kitchen tap(s) being supplied directly from the mains.

This section deals with low-pressure systems, which are common in the UK.

Where the water comes from

Cold water comes to your house from the water authority mains via a smaller, service pipe. This pipe may have been installed specifically to serve your house or you many share it with a neighbour. Either way, it will be controlled by a water authority stopcock somewhere on the edge of your, or your neighbour's, property. The stopcock is sunk below ground (usually about a metre) and is encased in brickwork, concrete, or a stoneware pipe to provide access. To mark the site, a small cast-iron casing is usually fitted at ground level.

From here, the service pipe runs to your house and becomes known as the rising main. At the point where it enters, a further stopcock—known as the consumer's, or house, stopcock—is fitted. This one is your own personal property and, because it controls all the water entering the house, it is as well to know exactly where you can locate it.

The most common place is under the kitchen sink, where a branch of the rising main directly supplies the kitchen cold tap with drinking water. The other most likely locations are under the stairs, or maybe situated below the floorboards immediately inside the front door.

Left: A typical modern plumbing system incorporates two hot water loops for the hot water cylinder and radiators. The water enters the house via the rising main and then feeds the heating system from the supply tank

The cold storage tank

After the branch to the kitchen cold tap, the rising main runs to a cold storage tank or cistern, normally in the roof space. Older storage tanks are made of galvanized iron, which is both heavy and prone to rust. These have now been replaced by the lighter, more hygienic, plastic tanks.

The storage tank helps to iron out irregularities in the mains supply and also provides an emergency reservoir if the supply is cut off.

The rising main's supply of water to the top of the tank is controlled by a ball-valve similar to the one in a WC cistern. At the base of the storage tank you will find the main water outlet. The stored water flows through here under the pressure of gravity and then branches off to supply the rest of your house's water requirements. These will include the WC, the bathroom cold taps and the hot water cylinder.

A stopcock is normally fitted somewhere near the outlet, so that you can turn off most of the water but still leave your kitchen cold tap in operation to supply the family's needs while you are working.

The hot water supply

In household plumbing, cold water is converted to hot either directly or indirectly. Direct heating means that the cold water comes into direct contact with a heater—normally a boiler or an electric immersion heater—then flows straight to the taps.

With indirect heating—usually combined with central heating—the water heated by the boiler is itself used to heat up fresh cold water. In this system, the two hot water circuits are separate and heat is transferred from one to the other by means of a heat exchanger.

The hot water cylinder, a copper tank heavily insulated to guard against heat loss, is common to most hot water installations.

In direct systems, it houses the electric immersion heaters—if fitted—and acts as a storage tank to keep your hot water supply as constant as possible. In an indirect system, the cylinder has the additional function of housing the heat exchanger.

The direct flow

The flow of water in both direct and indirect systems relies on the principle that hot water always rises above the cold water around it. So, in a direct system, the flow starts with cold water running to the base of the hot water cylinder.

If a boiler is fitted then the flow continues from the cylinder down to the base of the boiler. As the water is heated it rises out through the top of the boiler, up to the top of the hot water cylinder and then on to the hot taps.

If immersion heaters are fitted instead of a boiler, the flow is greatly simplified. The water runs from the storage tank to the base of the hot water cylinder and is heated: it then rises straight out of the cylinder and on to the hot taps.

The great disadvantage of direct systems is that water, when it is heated above 60°C (140°F)—or 80°C (176°F) in soft water areas—deposits scale similar to kettle fur.

The scale can block up pipework and boilers alike unless adequate precautions are taken. These include keeping the water temperature down below the 'scaling point' and using scale-inhibiting additives in your cold storage tank.

The indirect flow

The easiest way of understanding an indirect hot water flow is to visualize two independent 'loops' of water. The first loop consists of the water used to feed the hot taps.

This flows from the cold storage tank to the base of the hot water cylinder, where it comes into thermal contact with hot water on the other loop (via the heat exchanger). As the water is heated, it rises out of the cylinder and on to supply the taps.

The other loop supplies the boiler, heat

exchanger and—if fitted—the radiators. Here, fresh water flows to the base of the boiler from either the storage tank or from another separate tank, which is known as the 'expansion tank'.

Once in the boiler, the water is heated and then rises out to feed the heat exchanger and radiators. After the water has given up its heat, it flows directly back to the boiler again for re-heating.

Because the water in this loop is hardly ever changed, the problems of scaling are greatly reduced. The first time it is heated, the water gives up its scale; from then on, it is unable to do further damage.

The expansion tank

The indirect arrangement works best when an expansion tank is fitted to supply the boiler loop. This makes the loop almost completely independent of the one supplying the hot taps.

The tank is supplied with water from the rising main via another ball-valve. So, if the loop needs topping up with water because of evaporation, the process is automatic. In practice, however, you will find changes in the water level inside the expansion tank are barely noticeable.

To guard against the build-up of high pressures in the hot water system, safety overflows or vents are fitted.

In a direct system, only one pipe is needed. This runs to the top of the cold storage tank, either from the crown of the hot water cylinder or from a branch which is off the hot water service pipe.

In an indirect system, an additional vent is installed at the top point of the primary circuit.

Turning off the hot water

Whatever your hot water system, the hot water which reaches the taps comes from the top of your hot water cylinder. It does so because of the pressure of the cold water entering the cylinder beneath.

So, if you cut off the cold water supply at the base of the cylinder, no further hot water will rise from the top. Most hot water cylinders have a stopcock for this purpose, fitted at the cold water inlet. Those that do not, invariably have a stopcock somewhere on the pipe between the inlet and the cold storage tank. Before touching this stopcock make sure that all heating apparatus is turned off.

Wet central heating

Wet central heating, in which hot water is used to heat the house via a system of radiators, adds an additional complication to plumbing installations. But if you can imagine the radiators and their pipes as being part of the boiler 'loop' in a basic hot water system, the whole thing becomes easier to understand.

Some older installations work on the direct principle in which hot water heated by the boiler flows to the radiators as well as to the hot taps. Because this system is uneconomical and causes scaling, it has been replaced by indirect installations.

Here, the water which flows to the radiators is on a pump-driven loop like the one used to supply the heat exchanger. Consequently it is always fairly hot and requires less heating, which in turn makes it far more economical and efficient than a direct system.

In some indirect systems, the water which supplies the boiler loop is drawn direct from the storage tank. But most incorporate a separate expansion tank to keep the loop independent of the rest of the water supply.

Radiator systems

The pipework used to supply the radiators may take one of two forms. In the simpler, one-pipe system, hot water flows from the boiler to each radiator in turn and then back to the boiler again. Although this cuts down the amount of pipework needed, it allows hot and cooled water to mix near the end of the run. Consequently, the last radiator in the run often remains rather cool however hard the boiler itself is working.

In the two-pipe system, the pipework is

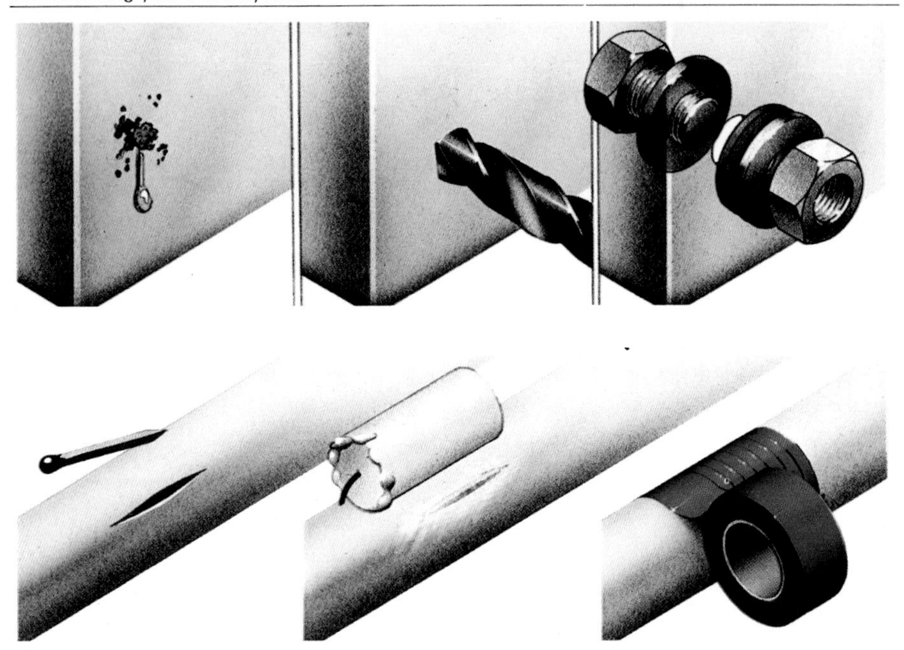

Above: If you are unlucky enough to have a leak or burst pipe, your first step must be to cut off the water supply. Do this as near to the damage as possible so that inconvenience is minimal. When it is a hot water pipe or tap look for a stopcock on the pipe which runs into the base of the hot water cylinder or boiler. Before you turn it, make sure that all heating apparatus is off. With a cold water pipe or tap you should trace back along the pipe until you come to a stopcock. If there is none between the burst and the cold storage tank you will have to block the tank outlet. To do this, nail a cork slightly larger than the outlet hole to a piece of timber. By feel, you can now insert the cork into the outlet to block it. A leak in the tank (top) can often be fixed by plugging the hole with a bolt. Use a soft washer between the two metal rings for a close fit. Temporary repairs (bottom) can be made to a split lead pipe by plugging the crack with a bit of matchstick, waxing the plug, then taping it together firmly

arranged so that cooled water leaving the radiators cannot mix with the hot water entering them. The radiators therefore heat up faster, as well as remaining at the same temperature.

Sizing of inward and outward piping in the radiator circuit is matched to the given radiator load—so pipe sizes can vary quite a lot throughout the different systems.

Water is forced around the circuit by means of an electrically driven pump, placed either in the flow or return pipe, close to, or in, the boiler.

Even without the use of a pump, water can flow around the circuit by natural circulation—this method of gravity flow is widely used for heating domestic hot water. It is rarely used for central heating because it requires large-diameter pipes with relatively short and simple pipe runs. Even so, most central heating systems will circulate by gravity to some extent when the pump is switched off, unless a control valve has been fitted to the system.

Controlling the water flow

In any domestic water system the flow of water through the pipes can be carefully regulated by taps, shut-off valves and stopcocks. When closed any of these devices should shut off the flow completely—and when open they should not obstruct the flow at all. Inefficient or damaged taps can lead to problems and leaks elsewhere in the system. And a leaky tap in the hot water circuit can be costly, letting expensively heated water dribble away. So a smooth uninterrupted flow of water is essential and can only be guaranteed by the correct choice and placement of fittings.

Three parts of the domestic system have an important bearing on the flow of water through the pipes. The main stopcock or valve controls the flow of water into the system from the outside water supply. As it proceeds around the pipes, the water flow is regulated by a number of subsidiary valves.

Turning a stopcock

Probably the most important fitting in any domestic system is the mains stopcock, since it is this that allows water to enter the system from the outside supply. If you are unlucky enough to have a leak or want to carry out major repairs to the system, the water must be turned off at this stopcock before work can begin.

Make sure you know exactly where this stopcock is located—otherwise a sudden leak will find you unprepared. In the UK it is usually to be found under a key-hole-shaped metal cover near the front boundary of the house.

When the cover is open the stopcock handle should be visible about 600mm (in the UK) below ground level. Quite often it is covered in soil; clear this away by hand, or with a stick if the hole is too narrow.

If you cannot reach the handle, use a turning key to grasp the stopcock. Make a key by cutting a wide V-shaped notch from the bottom of a long piece of waste wood (fig. 5).

Many main stopcocks do not have a cross-head handle like a tap, but are fitted with a four-sided shank, over which a special turnkey must be fitted to operate the valve. The local water authority needs to be contacted before the supply is turned off as they can supply the key.

Many modern houses have a second stopcock or valve situated just inside the house, and cutting off the water at this point is usually far easier. Look for this stopcock under the kitchen sink.

Relining a stopcock

The drain recess surrounding a mains stopcock is usually strong enough to last for some time, but often it becomes damaged by ground movement—or pressure from the paving stones above—and the pipe surrounding the drain splits. When this occurs a new stopcock pit needs to be constructed in its place.

A 150mm diameter stoneware pipe should be cut to length to make the new liner and placed with the belled end uppermost, to enable a new lid to be fitted on top.

Fitting valves

If you want to carry out repair work on a small part of the water system it is very disruptive to turn off the whole supply at the main. This means that all of the water

1 To turn the mains stopcock, find the key-hole-shaped cover—it is usually on the edge of your property

2 If the cover has become jammed or is at all difficult to raise, bend a piece of wire and insert it into the drain hole

3 Use the wire to lever the cover upwards and over to one side to expose the drain and the stopcock

4 Often the stopcock handle is covered with dirt and needs to be cleared before turning with a piece of stick

5 Many drains are too narrow to accommodate your hand, so cut a 'V' shape out of a spare piece of wood

6 The notch can then be fitted comfortably around the tap handle and the stopcock turned gently on or off

system is out of action while the work is being done.

It is far easier to install valves at various points which can be used to isolate particular sections of pipework. There are two types of valves which are in general use—*gate valves* and *isolating valves*. To be effective great care must be taken in positioning them correctly.

Gate valves: These usually have wheel-type handles and are fitted within lengths of pipework. Their main use is in UK cistern-fed supplies, where they are fitted in pipes leading out from the cold water cistern—either to the hot water cylinder, or to cold taps (usually just those upstairs) and for fittings such as WCs.

When fitting gate valves, position them where they are clearly visible and can be reached in an emergency. The best places are in the airing cupboard for the supply to the hot water tank and on the outlet from the cold water cistern in the loft for the supply to the cold taps.

Special care needs to be taken when cutting off the supply to the hot water tank. Once the valve is shut off water is prevented from entering the tank and so the immersion heater should immediately be switched off.

Isolating valves: These are neat inline fittings used to isolate individual sections of pipework. They can usefully be employed to shut off the water supply to items such as water heaters or taps.

Using draincocks

One of the simplest types of taps is the draincock which is used throughout central heating systems but also has many applications in the domestic water system. It is used to drain difficult sections of pipe.

Draincocks can be fitted to almost any length of pipework, but in most domestic water systems they are used to drain the hot water tank or the rising main. Before emptying any of these parts of the system the appropriate gate valve needs to be closed off first.

Do remember to check with your local water authority, or with your local plumbing codes, as to whether or not you need approval before starting *any* plumbing work.

A. Below: To reline a stopcock pit cut a 150mm diameter stoneware pipe to length using a hammer and bolster. Then chip out two U-shaped slots to fit around underground pipes. Turn over, fill with sand and line the bell with brown paper. Then cast a concrete lid which has a wire handle

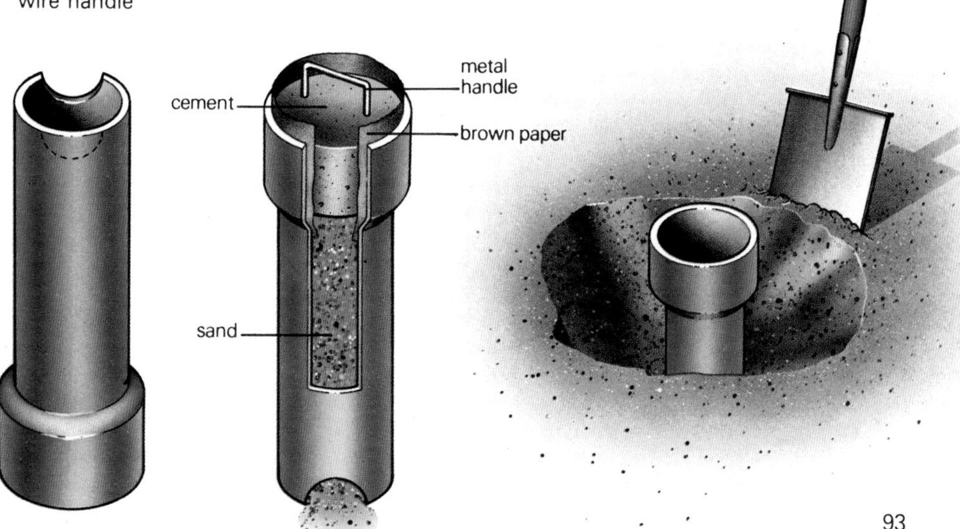

Types of taps

Fitting plain and mixer taps is a relatively simple operation if it is tackled with care. What is far more difficult is to choose the type of tap which is suitable for your needs. Practical considerations such as clear marking of hot and cold and ease of movement when turning on and off are as important as how the tap looks.

Pillar tap: This is the most popular type of tap widely used for basins and baths. It has a vertical inlet and is available in two sizes. The 15mm variety is normally fitted to sinks and wash basins while the 22mm type is more suitable for baths or extra large sinks.

Bib taps: This type of tap has a horizontal inlet and in most homes it is used to provide water for the garage or garden. Ideally it is fitted with a threaded nozzle so that a hose connector can be screwed on. Usually a bib tap is secured to an outside wall and a plate elbow needs to be used.

Supataps: These are UK taps, unlike others both in appearance and operation. Most have handles with plastic ears which do not conduct heat and are easy to grip. But their main distinctive feature is that the handle is part of the spout outlet and turns with the tap. Because of their construction Supataps can be re-washered without turning off the water supply.

Mixer taps

Mixer taps differ from plain taps—they still have two inlets but instead of having separate hot and cold taps, both are combined in one outlet.

Sink mixers: These type of taps have nozzles which contain two separate waterways—one for the hot supply and the other for cold water. It is built in this complicated way to accommodate regulations which do not allow cold water from the main to mix with hot water which has come from a storage tank. This is to avoid the risk of mains water becoming contaminated by coming into contact with the stored water.

Because of this divided flow system these type of mixers are often uncomfortable to wash your hands under—one part gets scalded, the other frozen.

In the UK, where the hot water also comes direct from the mains (via an

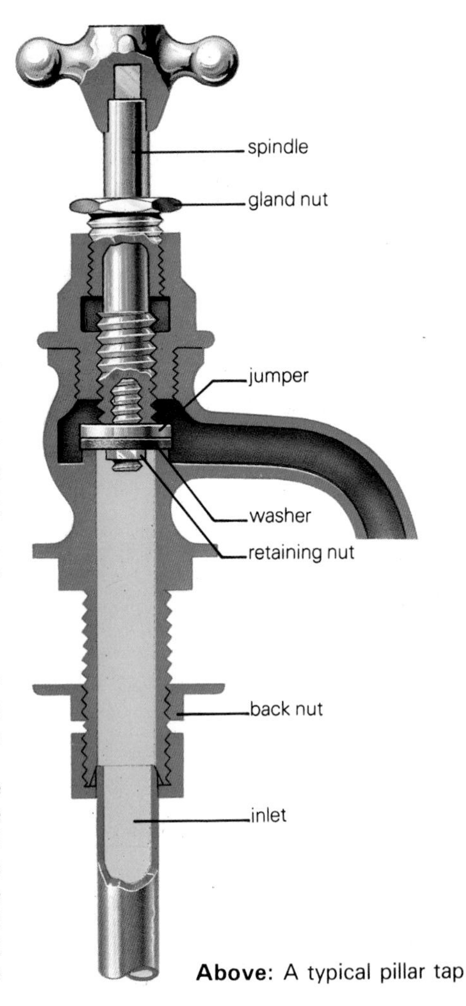

Above: A typical pillar tap

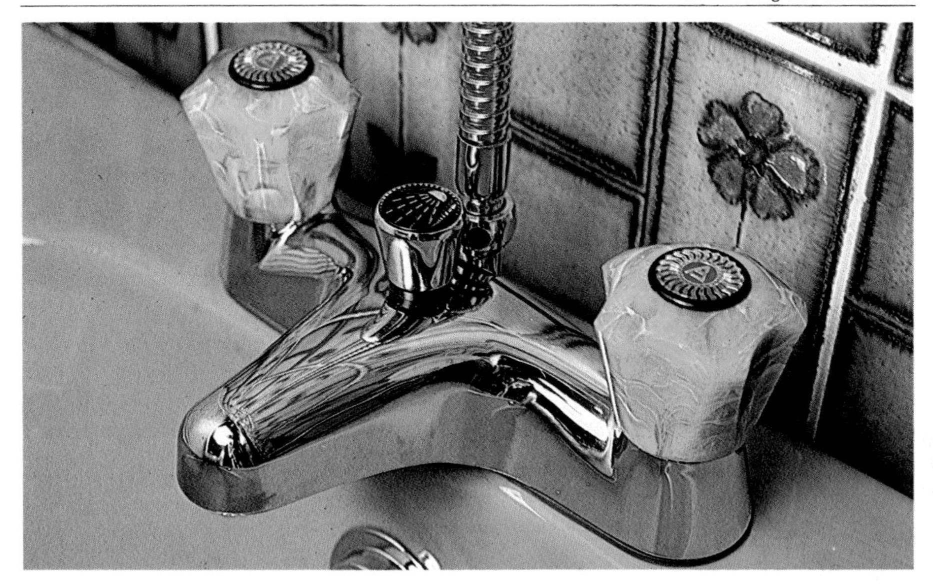

Above: This mixer tap has plastic handwheels which match the bath. It is also fitted with an outlet and automatic diverter on the spout to which it is very easy to fit a modern shower attachment

instantaneous water heater for example), divided flow mixers are not necessary.
Bath mixers: The type of mixer usually referred to by this name does not work on the divided flow principle but mixes the two water flows inside the taps themselves. These are usually permitted even in the UK, because both hot and cold water in a bathroom usually come via the cistern. But they are not allowed in areas where all the cold water is direct from the mains (unless the hot water also comes direct from the mains—again perhaps via an instantaneous heater). Check with your local water authority if in doubt.

Above: Some types of tap are fitted with both vertical and horizontal inlet fittings

Special tap attachments

There is a whole range of fittings which can be bought as attachments to taps which make them more attractive and practical.
Swivel nozzles: Many taps, particularly the mixer type can be fitted with swivelling nozzles. These move from side to side and enable the flow of water to be directed to feed both sides of a unit which is fitted with two sinks or bowls.
Shower attachments: These are normally fitted to mixer taps over baths. A separate switch usually mounted on top of the tap allows you to divert the water to the shower head which can be positioned on a rail above the bath.

Dealing with hard water

Water supplied for domestic use is purified to make it bacteria-free—and therefore fit for human consumption—by efficient filtration and storage, as well as by additives and treatments introduced by the water authorities. But even this water contains impurities, in the form of certain amounts of dissolved mineral salts that are referred to when we talk of the *hardness* or *softness* of water.

What is hard water?

Rainwater which falls in open country and on to insoluble rock such as slate or granite remains more or less mineral-free. Surface water may, however, pick up organic waste products. This water is usually *soft*.

Conversely, rainwater which falls on to sedimentary rocks tends to permeate through these to emerge as ground water which has a high dissolved mineral content. This water is relatively *hard*.

But there is another side to consider. As rainwater falls to earth it picks up quantities of gases and pollutants which acidify it slightly. The most significant of these acids generally is carbonic acid (soda water), produced by the solution of atmospheric carbon dioxide; but in heavily industrialized areas, with a far greater proportion of sulphur dioxide, rain can actually fall as a very dilute form of sulphuric acid.

The mildly acid rainwater falls on, and is absorbed by, different rock strata, during which time it reacts with minerals in the rocks themselves. It then either disgorges into rivers, lakes and reservoirs or collects underground and is pumped to the surface.

In regions where there is a high proportion of calcium and magnesium carbonate in the rock—found in limestone and chalky soil, and dolomites respectively—the carbonic acid in the rainwater reacts with the carbonates to produce bicarbonates.

It is these that make the water obviously 'hard' and pose the greatest threat to domestic water systems. At low temperatures, the bicarbonates are readily soluble in water and remain so until they reach your system. But when this water is heated, they begin to decompose into insoluble carbonates which are deposited on any surface at a temperature past the critical point.

The problem of scale and scum

Scale is the build-up of particles of the bicarbonates released from hard water when it is heated. This precipitation begins at around 60°C (140°F) and accelerates as the temperature is raised. It is for this reason that the first signs of scale are usually found in the kettle.

Much more serious is the effect of scale on hot water pipes and central heating systems: pipes become clogged, valves and pumps can jam, and boiler efficiency and life may be drastically reduced.

Testing your water

The hardness of water varies considerably. If the water is very hard, kettle furring and scummy baths are a clear sign. But if your soap lathers easily and the water feels soft to the touch, you have soft water.

Your water supply authority should be able to tell you a great deal about the water you receive, and may be able to test any water that comes into your home.

Low cost, easy-to-use *water hardness test kits* are readily available from aquarist supply shops. These employ indicator chemicals and you simply count the number of drops needed to effect a colour change in order to obtain a very accurate hardness reading.

Treatments of hard water

A number of possible options exist for the treatment of hard water. Some merely condition it, others actually soften it. The latest development is specifically intended to combat the scale caused by heating.

Chemical scale inhibitors do not actually soften water, but instead stabilize the bicarbonates so that they do not form carbonate scale. You need an indirect low-pressure plumbing system—a plastic container of crystals is suspended inside the cold water cistern.

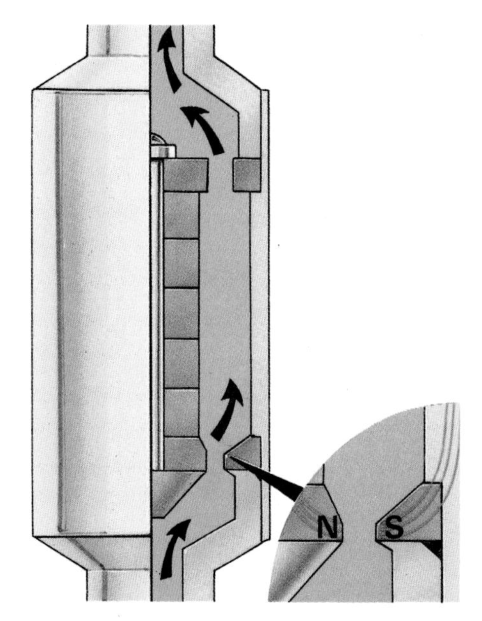

A. Above: In a magnetic conditioner, the water flows through a magnetic field. This affects the particles in the water and helps to reduce the scale

This method is cheap but the crystals do need replacing.

The same principle is applied in *descaling units*—small containers of crystals which are actually plumbed into the rising main piping. Versions of this device are available for use with chemicals specifically intended to counteract water containing too much iron or acid.

Most recent of the developments is the *magnetic conditioner* which does not actually change any of the chemical properties of the water, and therefore does not influence its taste and nutritional properties. The conditioner works by passing the water close to strong magnets. These are thought to alter the magnetic properties of the micro-particles enough to dissuade both scale and scum from forming.

Conditioners do not actually soften the water—for this you need a proper *water softener*. These work by actually removing bicarbonate salts from the water in a process known as ion exchange.

Very simply, ion exchange in a water softener takes place when the electrically-charged bicarbonate ions in the water pass over a catalyst known as the *resin bed*. Here, they change places with ions of sodium and thereafter remain attached to the resin bed while the sodium ions pass harmlessly into the water.

Eventually the resin attracts enough bicarbonate ions to become clogged and it must then be flushed clear with brine solution—which is powerful enough to overwhelm and displace the bicarbonate ions. In all makes of modern water softener this recharging takes place automatically, using salt from a built-in reservoir.

Installing a water softener

The best place to install a water softener is in a kitchen or laundry room—or wherever the rising main first emerges.

You usually need permission before doing plumbing work—check with your local authority or plumbing codes.

Specific instructions vary from make to make, but generally the work entails interrupting the rising main at a convenient point above the main stopcock and then installing inlet and outlet pipes to the softener—the latter rejoining the old rising main to restore a supply link. Between the inlet and outlet pipes, a bypass valve can be located to disconnect the softener for regular maintenance work.

Both the inlet and the outlet pipes are usually provided with shut-off valves. But check with your water authorities to see if they require the inclusion of a non-return/air-brake valve. If so, this is located between the inlet valve and the softener.

In areas with particularly high water pressure, you must guard against this exceeding the capabilities of the softener by fitting a pressure reducer between the mains stopcock and the inlet pipe junction.

Drain and overflow pipework usually take the form of hosepipes. The drain is often led to a standpipe arrangement incorporating a P-trap, based on the same principle as the drain pipework for a washing machine. The overflow pipe is led independently to the outside.

Ideally, cut the pipework to individual lengths and lay these in a dry run with fittings loosely arranged to check the plumbing-in arrangement before final assembly. Compression or capillary fittings can be used for the inlet and outlet connections to the rising main, though the latter are considerably cheaper.

Follow specific recommendations for making the electrical connections. Although most units can be connected via a fused plug to an ordinary switched socket, it is better to wire the unit to a fused spur or connection box to prevent water getting into contact with live wires and causing an accident.

After electrical connection, all that remains is to programme and start up the unit—following the manufacturer's specific instructions.

1 Before installing the new pipework for a water softener, close off the main stopcock to completely shut off the water supply and drain it down. The new pipework is inserted into the rising main at a convenient point above the main stopcock. Also cut away the old pipework at this point in the operation

2 A great deal of care should be taken when working with all forms of pipework. When joining sections of pipework, always try to remember to smear a little jointing compound around the faces of the joints. This will really help to ensure the necessary watertight seal needed when the system is working

3 When all your joints are thoroughly smeared with jointing compound, the new pipe and valve assembly, that you are constructing, should then be built up section by section. Then it should be carefully connected up, via the non-return valve, to the hard water inlet which is already in existence

4 Make sure that the cut inlet pipe is then capped off. If a separate hard water supply is required, the pipe may be connected later. In this particular type of installation, water flows to a washing machine through a completely separate pipe. This is then connected to the assembly last

5 Once the assembly is in place, make sure that all three valves are closed off, then turn the stopcock back on to renew the normal water supply. Waste water flows from this softener through an overflow and a drain hose. Arrange for these to discharge out at a suitable drainage point for your chosen location

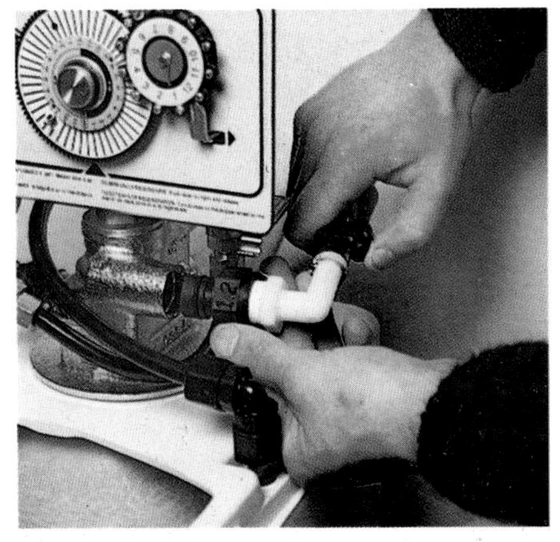

6 With the softener fitted in its correct location, secure the hoses running from it to the overflow and drain with plastic hose clips. Connect the drainage hose to the drainage outlet which is situated below the control mechanism, then firmly connect up the required overflow hose section

7 The two hoses which run from the softener to the pipe and valve assembly are joined to the machine by plastic nipple attachments. Once these nipples are firmly in place, connect up the hoses. The hard water inlet is situated at the top, with the soft water outlet featured below

8 Connect up the hose running from the inlet on the machine to the inlet valve and the hose from the outlet to the outlet valve above it. Then, next, having turned off the electricity supply at the main fuse box, wire a suitable amount of electric cable from the softener control valve to a fused spur

9 With the wiring connected, fix the old switch and the cover of the fused spur in place but do not turn on the power at this stage. Then follow the instructions for manual regeneration to flush out the cylinder. Initial dirty water will flow to the drain

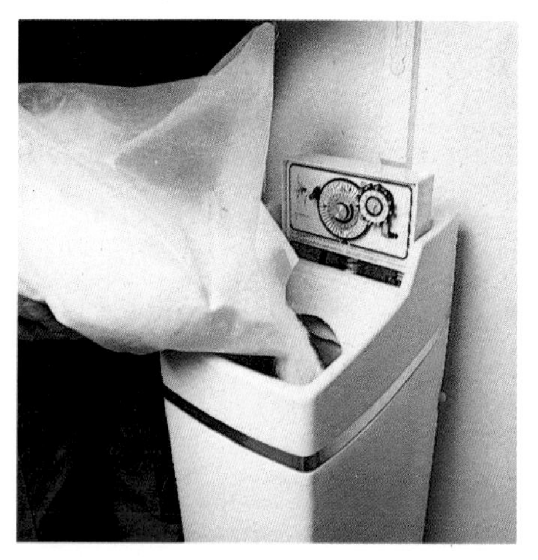

10 Replace the top cover assembly of the softener, then pour granular salt into the filling hole at the top of the machine. With the valves open, the unit programmed and the power turned on, the new softener is ready to be fully tested in operation

Plumbing with plastics

Plastic pipe is rapidly taking the place of more traditional forms of pipework in many areas of plumbing. Of the reasons why this is so, the most obvious is that plastics is an easy material to work with. But most forms are also immune to chemical attack from the ground on which they are laid and the water which they carry. And plastic piping is comparatively inexpensive and versatile in its application.

However, most forms of plastic distort when heated, so plastic plumbing pipe is usually used only for waste systems which rarely carry hot water for long, or for cold water supplies.

Note: Before carrying out any work, check your proposals with the appropriate authorities.

Plastics used in plumbing

The plastic most commonly used is PVC (*polyvinyl chloride*) available for plumbing uses in both unplasticized (uPVC or *rigid vinyl*) and in post-chlorinated forms (cPVC). Without added plasticizer, PVC is an extremely hard and rigid material. But because additional compounds such as plasticizers and hardeners can be added to it, in the process changing some of its properties, it is essential to specify exactly what you want it for when ordering materials.

Like all the plastics used for pipes, PVC is a thermoplastic. This means that it softens and then melts on heating, but unlike some plastics PVC will not support combustion. In addition, PVC is light but not weak, and rigid without being too brittle and is used for low-pressure plumbing applications.

Here, PVC is used for a wide variety of pipework including that for rainwater, soil, waste, below-ground drainage and some cold water services.

ABS (*acrylonitrile butadiene styrene*) is commonly used for fittings and some waste runs of normal diameters, but not usually for soil installations in the UK.

Polyethylene or *polythene* is perhaps the most widespread of all plastics materials, but its use in plumbing is confined mainly to fittings. In its high density form it is a tough material and one which can be used for liquids up to 100°C (212°F) but like its derivative, *polypropylene*, it has the disadvantage of melting and burning like paraffin wax when heated by a naked flame.

Polypropylene has a significantly higher softening point and can manage steam and liquids up to a temperature of 100°C (212°F).

These two materials, generically termed *polyolefins*, are used for stable-temperature cold water supplies and for drainage where there is low risk of hot waste. Another popular use is for running a water supply into the garden.

Nylon has a much better resistance to higher temperature than most other thermoplastics and is sometimes considered suitable for pressure installations—in central heating systems it can manage temperatures of between 80°C and 120°C (176°F and 248°F).

Telling the plastics apart

As this is important, not only to avoid fitting the wrong material but also to make use of the most satisfactory method of jointing, shave off a small sliver from the test pipe and see how this responds to the flame of a match when held carefully in metal tweezers. PVC will be self-extinguishing when removed from the flame, whereas ABS and nylon will continue to burn—the nylon albeit reluctantly and smelling like burnt hair.

Methods of joining plastic pipe

Two forms of joint are used for joining

together lengths of plastic pipe in the same material: the ring sealed joint and the solvent welded joint.

Ring sealed joint

This is a push-fit, semi-permanent connection, axially rigid enough for normal use, but capable of absorbing lengthways expansion. This and easy assembly explain the joint's widespread popularity.

In one half of the joint a synthetic rubber ring is housed near the mouth of the socket at the end of the pipe. The introduction of a spigot—the plain but chamfered end of the other pipe—compresses the ring within its recess to provide a firm seal which can be forced apart if and when required.

Where possible, pipes are joined with the flow in a socket-to-spigot direction to minimize the effect of the spigot if the edge of this is not fully home against the socket.

The pipe around the ring seal joint is at least as strong as a plain section of pipe and is quite capable of withstanding the same amount of pressure. This and its characteristic flexibility make it useful for most underground mains supplies and any drains.

The solvent welded joint

Also known as the solvent cement joint, this can be used for all the usual applications of PVC and ABS plastics, and is a particular favourite for the latter. Because it is a permanent joint, which cannot be accidentally knocked apart, it is usually the first choice also for water supply systems.

Unlike ring seal joints, which on underground bends and on pipework exposed to accidental knocking or external pressure must be supported on either side, solvent welded joints need no protective support.

Solvent joints cannot, however, be used with the polyolefins or nylon and a further disadvantage is that expansion joints—ring seal joints—must still be included in straight sections.

Bending plastic pipe

Although most of the plastics are elastic to some degree, only polythene is considered 'bendable' by plumbing standards. In this a temporary bend can be formed by suitably positioned pipe fixings. A permanent bend is made by heating the bend section for about ten minutes in boiling water, then bending it to the required degree and leaving it to cool in this shape.

Making a ring seal joint

To prepare the spigot end, cut the pipe end perfectly square using a fine-toothed saw—a large hacksaw with 32 teeth per 25mm is ideal. If the pipe end is not square it may strike the ring seal at an awkward angle and displace it during the course of assembly. A straight cut is not difficult on small-bore tube, but some form of template or guide is a useful aid on thicker pipe.

A quick method is to wrap a sheet of straight-edged paper around the pipe and to use the matched up edge of this as a cutting guide (fig. 5). But if you are doing much work, it is more convenient in the long run to make a template from an offcut of pipe socket. Cut a small section from this so that you form a 'C'-shape then clip it over the pipe and use its edge as a guide (fig. 1).

After you have cut the pipe end remove the internal and external burr, using a rasp for PVC and ABS and a sharp knife for polyolefins.

You then chamfer the outer edge of the pipe to enable the spigot to be easily inserted in the socket and compress the ring seal. Chamfering is especially important on larger diameter pipe and is done for both ring seal and solvent joints. A shaping tool—such as a Surform—can be used to produce a chamfer on ABS or PVC, but a special tool is required for polypropylene and this is usually supplied by the manufacturer of the pipe.

A guide line marked no less than 5mm from the pipe end helps to ensure an even, shallow-sloped (15°) bevel around the edge.

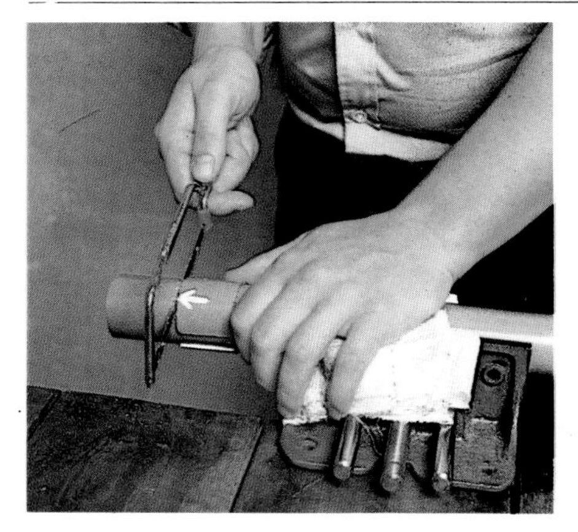

1 Use a fine-toothed hacksaw to cut plastics pipe. Make a 'C'-shaped cutting guide from an offcut to ensure that the cuts are straight

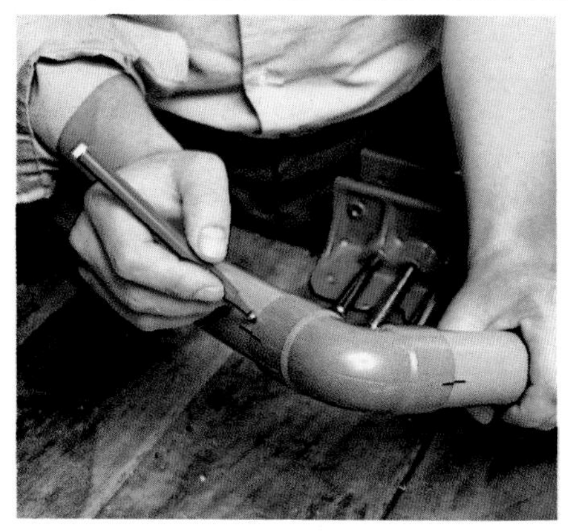

2 Dry assemble a solvent joint and make alignment marks for direction and depth as there is no other way of checking the assembly later

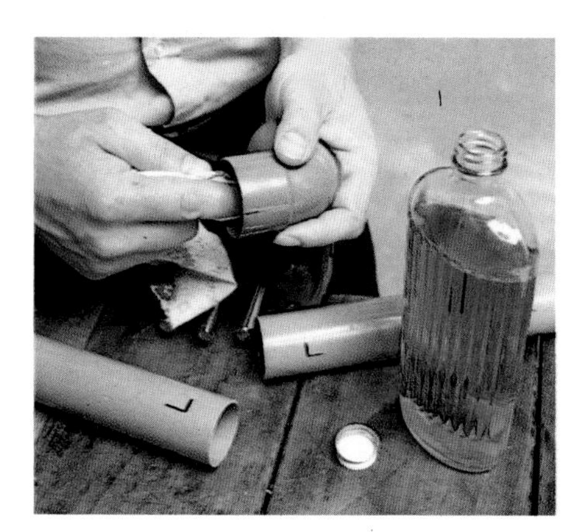

3 Clean all traces of dirt and grease from the contact areas of the spigot and socket. Then apply solvent cement to the cleaned contact areas

4 Immediately afterwards, push the spigot into the socket and hold the assembly firmly for 15 seconds. Then remove all the excess solvent

When you have done this, clean the joint area with a cloth. Small-bore pipes—15mm and below—usually have pre-fitted ring seals which are locked in position: with these, simply make sure that the seal is undamaged before you start work.

Lubricate the spigot with silicone grease just before inserting it. Do not use soap or detergent as this may become solidified near the ring seal.

A slight twisting and screwing motion makes inserting the spigot easier. Push it nearly home but leave an expansion gap between the stop of the fitting and the end of the pipe.

Special jointing clamps may have to be used for ring-seal (and solvent) joints made in pipe which is 200mm diameter and over.

Making a solvent joint

A solvent joint is normally made only in pipes and fittings of the same material and care must be taken in matching new materials to any existing pipework. However, there is a variety of adaptors that allow connection of different materials, for example uPVC to cast-iron.

The preparation stages for a solvent joint are the same as for a ring seal joint. After chamfering the spigot, remove any dust or dirt from the pipe fitting with a dry cloth then assemble the pipes and fittings in a dry run to determine the best work order. It is important that all minor problems are sorted out at this stage. Insert the spigot fully home and mark the pipe at the socket edge when it is so. During later assembly this is the only sign that assembly is correct.

Next, apply a proprietary cleaning fluid or methylated spirits to the contact area using a dry cloth. This acts as a degreasing agent and in the process removes the glossy surface of the pipe. The contact area must remain free of dirt and grease thereafter, so handle the pipe carefully during any dry run checks. On 'smooth' smaller-bore pipe, dislodged abrasive particles can become embedded in the surface of the contact area and affect the efficiency of the joint. Be especially cautious over the use of emery paper, and under no circumstances use steel wool for this job.

Immediately after cleaning, apply an even layer of solvent cement to the prepared contact area with a clean, flat brush—or a spatula in the case of thick cement. Take care not to use too much. *Note:* Solvent cement and cleaning fluid are highly volatile and should be used only in a well-ventilated room.

Push the pipe and fitting together with a slight twisting motion and hold the assembly—under pressure—for about 15 seconds, then immediately remove excess solvent with a dry cloth. Do not disturb the joint for a further two minutes. A full strength bond is achieved after several hours, but it is advisable to wait a day before using.

It is good practice and more convenient to assemble a section of pipework with dry fittings and then solvent weld several at a time. Use a pencil and rule to check alignment as each solvent weld is made.

Test pipe joins before a final connection to an existing run if you can. Fill the new run with water and leave it to stand, checking for leaks later.

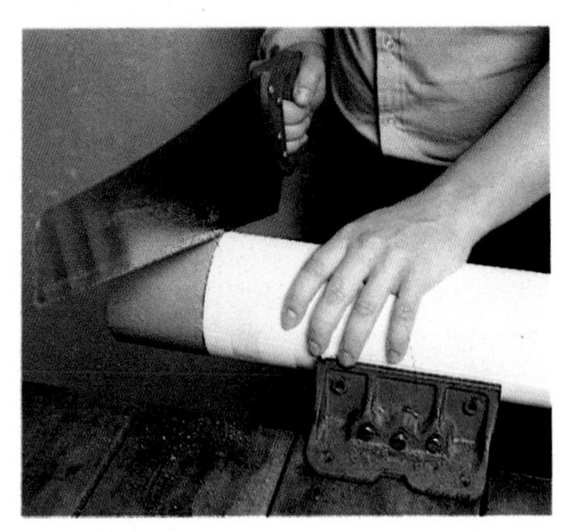

5 Use an old handsaw to cut large diameter pipe. A cutting guide can then be made by lining up the edges of a loop of paper

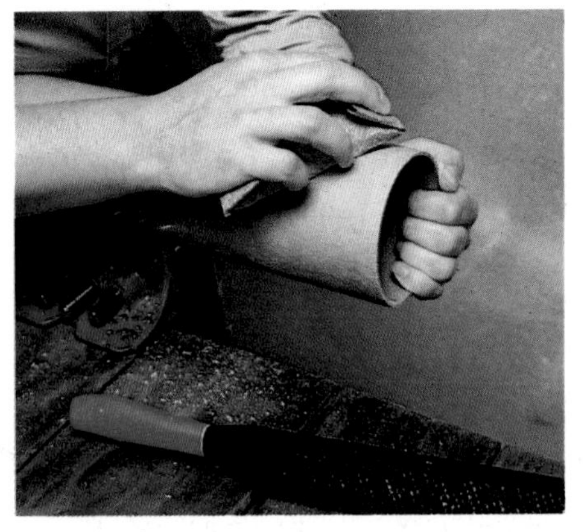

6 Roughen up the surface of large diameter pipe using a glasspaper pad. Never be tempted to use steel wool for this job—it is just too harsh

Protecting your pipework

Most substances expand when they are heated and contract as they cool. But water expands when it freezes, and this unusual property makes every part of the domestic water system a potential disaster area in a frost.

The effects of a freeze-up

Ice forming in a water supply system can have two very harmful effects. The pressure that it exerts as it expands can cause pipes to split or joints to come adrift, and it can also block vital sections of pipe so that parts of the house receive no water.

Often, the worst damage occurs when the ice in frozen pipework melts. Water leaking from cracked pipes or damaged joints can ruin decorations and make dangerous contact with electrical equipment.

Boiler explosions and cylinder implosions are, thankfully, much rarer; but both could occur during very cold weather when the house has either been left empty for a while, or allowed to cool abnormally overnight.

Most UK hot water systems operate through the circulation of water under pressure from the cold water cistern, and for this reason an expansion vent pipe is fitted between the cistern and the hot water cylinder. But if this—or any of the circulatory pipes—become blocked, pressure may build up in the system and serious problems arise.

Precautions against freezing

Insulation is your first line of defence against frost, and you should start by considering the garden.

Frost in the UK rarely penetrates more than 450mm below ground level. But to be absolutely sure they do not freeze, supply pipes should be buried between 820mm and 1000mm deep.

Make sure that your pipes are at this depth along their entire length and that garden landscaping does not reduce it. Most homes have an external, key-operated stopcock under a cover on the boundary of the property. If yours has one, check that it is operating properly and then wrap glass fibre roll around the tap to protect it. Remember that your stopcocks are the first things to tackle when a disaster occurs: they must be working properly (fig. 1).

Next check the point where the water supply enters the house. Common house renovation projects include installing damp-proof courses and excavating trenches around rooms below ground level. Make sure that you time this kind of work to avoid the worst of the winter cold and that you do not leave any pipework dangerously exposed overnight.

For a thorough lagging job you can use a length of split PVC drainpipe as insulation. Wrap glass fibre or jute lagging around the horizontal runs and then cover them with the pipe: deal with vertical runs by fitting the pipe around them and then filling the space in between with a loose-fill insulation such as polystyrene chips.

The roof space

UK houses usually have pipes and cold water storage cisterns in the roof space and, particularly if the loft is well insulated, these are prone to freezing in the winter.

Make sure, therefore, that all pipework

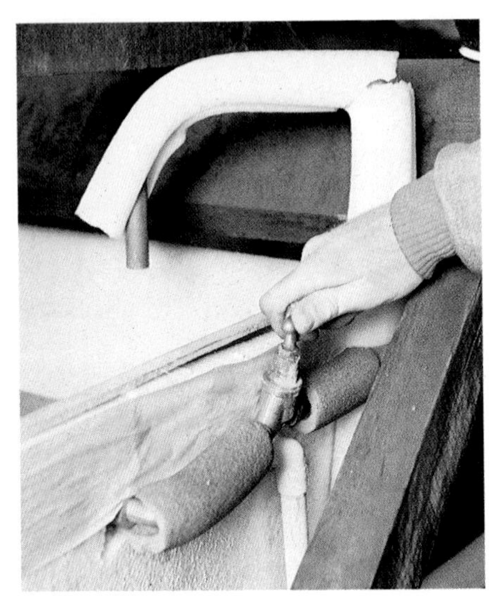

1 As well as insulating the cold water tank and pipework in the loft, thoroughly check the operation of the rising main stop valve nearby

2 Foam plastic insulation is an excellent protector for your pipework and is widely available in a variety of sizes and different thicknesses

5 However, before you actually cut the insulation to length, make sure that it does cover the entire length of the particular pipe which you are trying to protect and insulate

6 The next stage is to secure the insulation with tape at points where it could easily come adrift—such as at joints in the pipes or possibly at bends in the heating system

3 The insulation is easily split down its length for fitment, and adhesive on the split edges helps maintain a really good seal around the pipe

4 When lagging bends in a pipe, use a mitre box to cut mitred joints in the insulation. This then ensures a good fit between adjoining sections

7 If you have no frost thermostat fitted on your heating system, set your boiler thermostat to 'low' and the timer to 'constant' when you leave the house during a frosty period

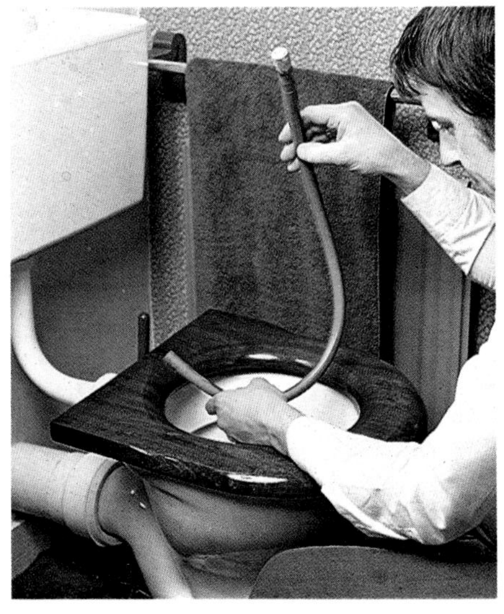

8 You can protect your WC by slipping the open end of a bunged rubber hose into the trap. If the water freezes, this will absorb the expansion that will inevitably take place

in the roof is completely lagged.

The cold water storage cistern and—if fitted—the expansion cistern serving the central heating system should be thoroughly insulated.

When insulating a cistern, make sure that the vent pipe can still discharge into it by fitting a large funnel through the top insulation.

Using lagging

Pipes can be lagged with either glass fibre blanket roll or purpose-made foam plastic pipe lagging. If you choose the blanket, wrap it horizontally around the pipe so that it covers the entire surface. Fix it in place with wire or twine tied round the pipe at intervals of about 500mm.

Start lagging the pipes as close as possible to one end of the system and fix the lagging securely at this point (fig. 1). Run the lagging right up to the point where the pipe goes through a wall or through the floor and tie or tape it in place.

To insulate a cold water cistern, you can either buy a tailor-made kit, or adapt ordinary, blanket roll loft insulation material. In the latter case you must shape lengths of blanket to suit the positions of the cistern fittings.

Other precautions

Most heating systems incorporate a spring-loaded valve close to the boiler to guard against the possibility of an explosion. If steam even starts to seep out of this valve, you will know that the system is blocked and that you should shut down the boiler, open taps to let off pressure and locate the blockage.

Central heating systems can be fitted with a frost thermostat which raises the temperature of the building slightly if there is a threat of frost (fig. 7). If you do not have one, it is wise to keep the boiler on low all night in very cold weather.

Dealing with a burst pipe

Your first sign of trouble in the plumbing may be during a thaw when water starts cascading from split pipes or dislodged fittings. This is what you should do:

- Immediately turn off the rising main stopcock, or, failing that, the key-operated stopcock outside.
- Open all the taps in the house.
- Turn the boiler to its lowest setting and do not draw off any more hot water.
- Locate the fault and try to rectify it.

Thawing out frozen pipework

If you wake up on a cold morning to find that water does not come from one of the taps, or that the boiler is overheating, the most likely cause is an ice plug somewhere in the pipework.

In this case, turn off the boiler (if it is overheating), and try to let off the pressure through the nearest hot tap or safety valve. Then, by a process of trial and error, locate the ice plug and thaw it out by one of the following methods—keeping a bowl handy in case the pipe has split.

- Wrap the pipe in a towel or rag which

A. Emergency repairs. You can cut out a section of split pipe and replace it with a length of rubber hose (1). Alternatively, you can carefully cover the split with glass fibre paste, wrap on glass fibre

has been soaked in hot water.

- Wrap a half-filled hot water bottle round the pipe.
- Warm the pipe with a hair drier or fan heater.

Emergency repairs

The long-term cure for split pipes and damaged joints is to repair the joints and fit in new sections of pipework. This is easier where the pipe and joints are copper or plastic. However, lead joints must be *wiped*.

In modern systems fitted with compression joints, a freeze-up often forces the joints apart and does not burst the pipes. In this case, simply isolate the relevant pipe, unscrew the joint and reassemble it with one or two turns of PTFE tape or a smear of jointing compound at the sealing points.

Otherwise, one of the emergency repairs described below will get you out of trouble. But do not rely on them for long.

- Isolate and cut out the damaged section of pipe, then bridge the gap with a length of hose held in place with Jubilee clips. If you cannot isolate the pipe effectively, ram two potatoes over the cut ends to prevent accidental leaks. Keep the rising main stopcock turned down to half pressure until a proper repair is completed.
- Sand the area around the damaged pipework, try to close the split by hammering it and temporarily mend the split with a two-part epoxy resin filler or proprietary pipe repair compound.
- Butter glass fibre filler paste around the crack, wrap it with glass fibre bandage, and then smear on more of the filler (fig. A).

In dire emergencies you can modify the bandage method by inserting a piece of wood—such as a matchstick—into the joint, rubbing thoroughly over the top of it with candlewax, and applying a tight bandage of the most waterproof material to hand.

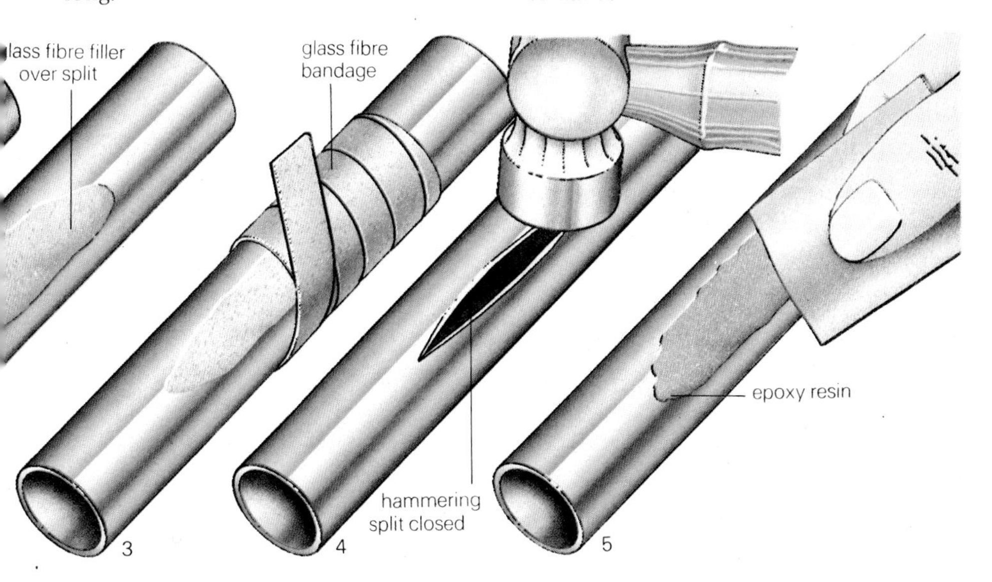

bandage, then add more of the paste (2 and 3). Where the split is only a small one, hammer it together (4) and cover it with a two-part epoxy filler (5). Allow this to completely dry before restoring the water supply. Whatever repair you use, only open the main stopcock partway afterwards to cut down the mains pressure until a more permanent repair can be effected

Plumbing in a washing machine

Though an automatic washing machine is a boon to any household, many people are discouraged from buying one because it has to be plumbed in—both to the water supply and the drains. But providing you choose the site carefully and set about the work in a logical order, the job is not half as hard as it seems.

Note: In the UK, plumbing work is strictly controlled by local water authority by-laws. You must inform your water authority of your plans at least seven days before work starts. As well as giving practical advice, they will warn you against any possible infringement of their regulations. Work on the drainage system may need building regulations consent.

Choosing a site

Your first decision here is in which room to site the machine. In the UK, the choice is normally between the kitchen and bathroom, both of which have hot and cold water supplies and drainage outlets.

You have next to consider the type of machine, the space that will be needed around it, the existing layout of the room and the design and materials used in your plumbing system.

Of these, the plumbing system must inevitably take priority. It is no use choosing the ideal space-saving site only to find that you cannot then plumb in the machine without demolishing the house.

Drainage: In the UK, for a washing machine in a ground floor kitchen, the most suitable outlet for the discharge pipe is a back inlet gully, separated from the main discharge stack and connected to the main drain by a branch underground. This is often easier to break into than the main stack and, as it is usually there to serve the kitchen sink discharge pipe, it is likely to be in the most convenient position already.

In older houses, the sink waste sometimes discharges over an open, trapped gully. You will probably be allowed to run the washing machine discharge pipe to here also, provided that the end of the pipe is below the grid.

If the pipe has to connect to the main stack, the latter will need a branch fitting. Though this is relatively easy to fit to a plastics stack, on the older, cast-iron or galvanized steel types the job is best left to an expert.

Water supply: Breaking into the hot and cold water supply generally presents less of a problem, as the final connections to the machine are usually made with flexible hose. Nevertheless, the supply must be near enough to the site to allow you to keep pipe runs as short—and as uncomplicated—as possible.

In the UK a cold-only supply might come direct from the rising main (usually the easiest arrangement if the machine is in a kitchen), though some water authorities do not allow this.

A hot and cold fill machine is best supplied via the cold water storage cistern or tank. In this case, as with some showers, low water pressure is sometimes a problem on upper floors or in flats and bungalows. Manufacturers generally specify a minimum 'head' of water—that is, the distance from the base of the storage tank to the point where the supply enters the back of the washing machine—and you should bear this is mind when choosing a site for your machine. If you cannot meet the minimum head requirement, consult both the manufacturer and your local water authority.

The pipe run must be arranged so that the branches do not cross one another, with the stop valves easily accessible. When you are planning the run, consider the best place to fit tee pieces to the supply pipes; it may be better to have a slightly longer run in order to avoid disturbing existing fixtures and fittings.

Breaking into the supply

Having chosen your supply pipes, turn off the nearest stop valves and completely drain the pipes by opening the taps at the end of them. With cistern-fed supplies, if there are no local valves, look for a cold supply stop valve on the pipe running out of the base of the storage tank and a hot supply valve on the cold supply pipe running into the base of the hot water cylinder.

If you still have no luck, you must tie up the ball valve on the storage tank and drain down the system. It is sensible to turn off the boiler or heat source before you turn off any water services. If you are taking the cold supply from the rising main, turn off at the mains.

To break into the supply, you must either cut out sections of pipe large enough to take tee fittings or remove and replace existing fittings. Opt for whichever gives the simpler pipe run.

Using the former method, measure and mark the cut sections very carefully against the tee fittings. Be sure to allow for the extra pipe taken up by the joints. If there is a joint already near a cut section, it may be easier to loosen this, make one cut and remove the pipe altogether (fig. 2). You can then trim it to the new length required on the bench. Make the cuts with a fine-toothed hacksaw, ensuring that the pipe ends are kept square.

Having prepared the pipe ends, fit the tee pieces.

Connecting to the machine

Somewhere between the tee pieces and the washing machine inlets, stop valves must be fitted so that the supply can be disconnected at any time. Some manufacturers provide these with their machines while others leave the choice of valve entirely up to you. Suitable fixing points for valves are normally the wall or the side of a unit.

1 When you find a suitable place to break into the supply, trace back along the pipes until you find the stop valves which will then isolate them

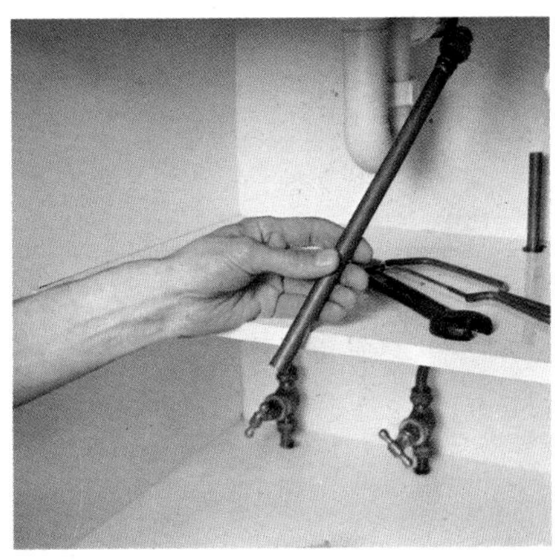

2 Having isolated and drained down the pipes, sever them with a fine-toothed hacksaw. Make sure you make the cuts as cleanly and as neatly as possible

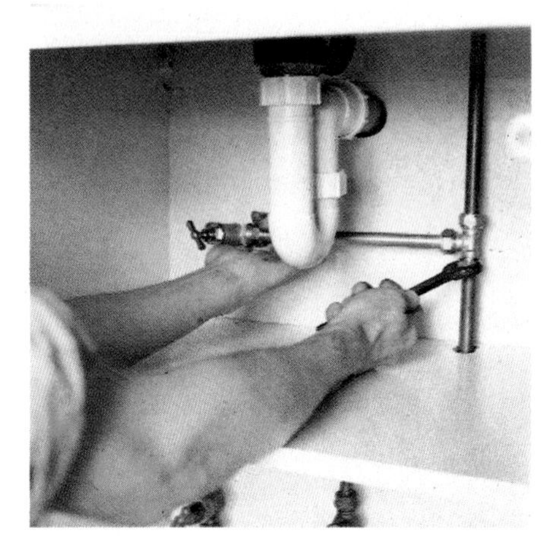

3 When you plan your new pipe run do not forget to include two extra stop valves so that you can isolate the actual supply to the machine. Then with careful planning, you can keep the run simple and the number of joints used to a minimum. Use compression or capillary joints to connect the piping

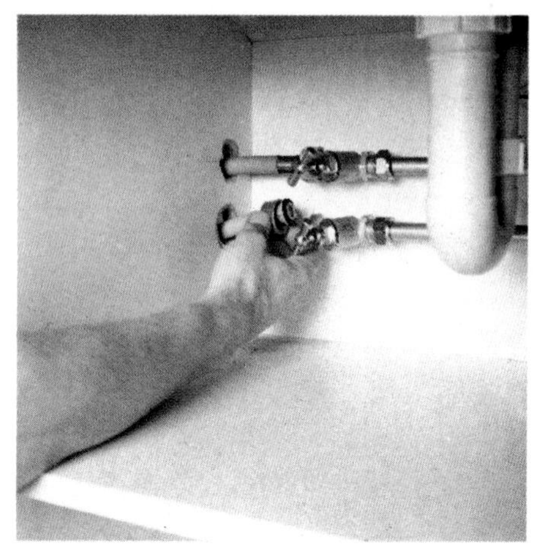

4 There are several different types of valve available and with certain types the flexible hose ends are easy to join as they can be simply screwed on, as pictured above. However, with the other types of valve available, different fixings, not always so easy to fit, will have to be used

7 Connection is then simply a matter of running the new discharge pipe down from the hole in the wall and jointing it up to the boss. Then solvent weld the joints only after you have assembled the pipes in a dry run and checked that the fall on the discharge pipe is really in the correct place

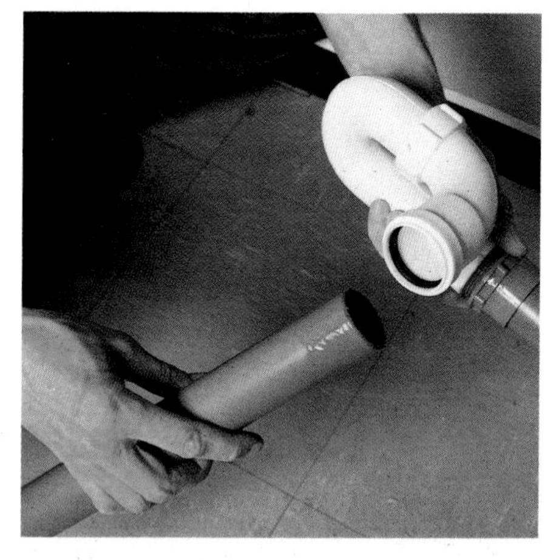

8 When the pipe run is jointed and in the right position, fit support brackets wherever necessary—either with masonry nails or plugs and screws. Back inside the house, you will need to connect the waste trap for the stand pipe at the point where the discharge pipe actually comes through the wall itself

5 The next essential task is to prepare the hole in the wall which is going to contain the discharge pipe. Make sure when you are chiselling out the hole in the wall that you make it large enough to accommodate any minor adjustments which you might find necessary to make as you go along

6 PVC drainage piping is easy to work with, but cutting it quickly blunts saw blades—it is better and more efficient to use either an old saw or medium-toothed hacksaw. Next, the discharge pipe should be connected to a stack with a spare branch outlet. The plug on the outlet is then opened up with a padsaw

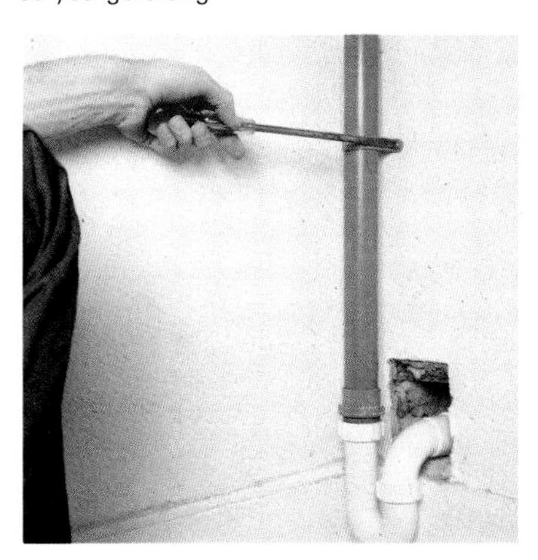

9 The next stage of the plumbing work is to cut the stand pipe to the length you require and then to screw it to the trap and fit the necessary support bracket firmly to the wall. Now is the right time for you to check all along the pipe run for any noticeable leaks appearing at the junction of the joints

10 Finally, when you are quite happy that everything is functioning as it should, make good the hole in the wall with appropriate proprietary filler. Then roll the washing machine into place, being very careful that you do not tangle the flexible hoses or maybe compress them against the wall

Mark the points clearly then measure back and fit pipe runs—using 15mm copper tube in the UK—between these and the tee pieces. Where necessary, support with wall brackets every 1.2m. Fit the valve holders to the ends of the pipe runs before you fix them to the wall.

Finally, screw the valves provided into the holders and secure the flexible connections to the machine. On no account should you attempt to shorten the flexible fittings supplied with the machine: these are designed specially to length in order to balance out irregularities in the water flow.

If you are fitting your own valves, simply fit these to the ends of your pipe runs and connect them to the flexible hoses (figs 3 to 4). But as above, make sure that the valves are so positioned that the hoses do not cross or kink.

In both cases, test the pipework and all joints for leaks at this stage. If you find any, make repairs before going on.

Installing the discharge pipe

For the pipes themselves, follow the sizes and plastics type specified in the manufacturer's handbook. Most often these will be 32mm cPVC with solvent welded joints.

A. Below: A typical completed installation. Note that in some areas of the country taking the cold supply direct from the rising main is not allowed

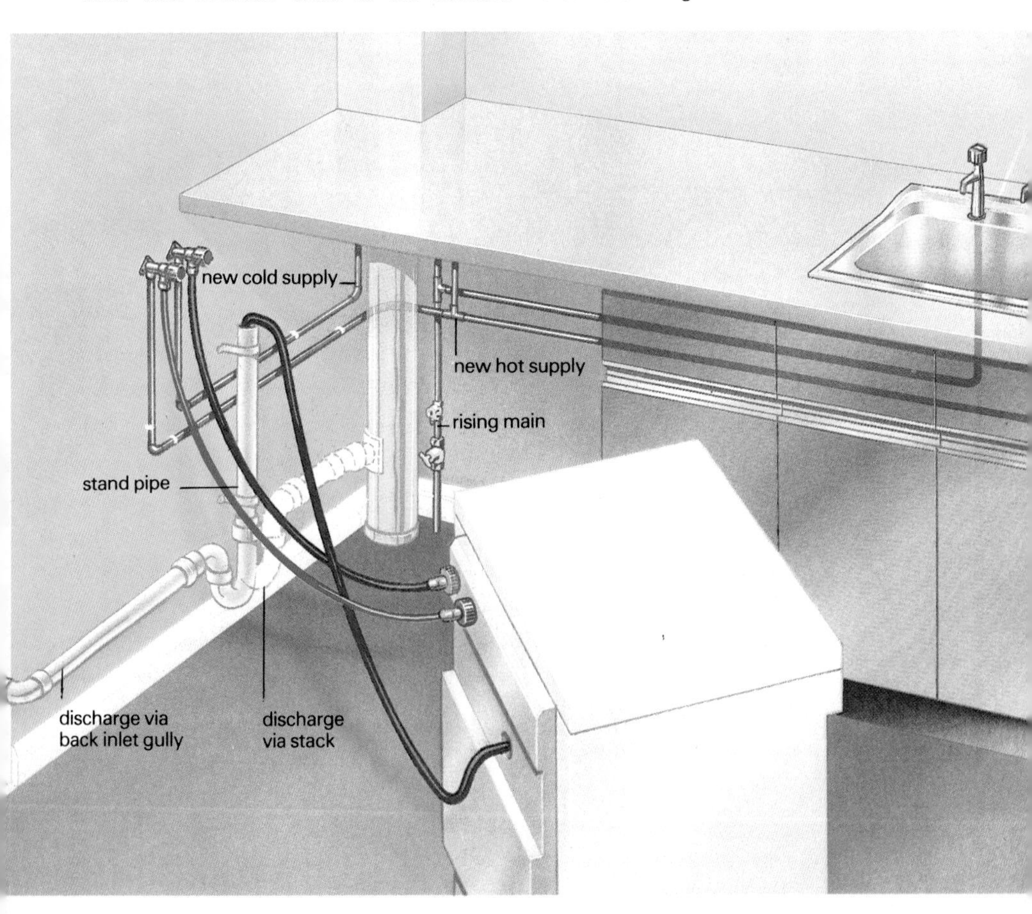

Connection to a back inlet gully: The simplest way to connect to a gully is to run the pipe just below the surface of the grid. To do this, replace the grid (if it is a metal one) with a plastic type, and cut a hole in it of the right size to take the pipe.

Alternatively, you may want to take this opportunity to replace an old gully (whether back inlet type or not) with a modern plastics back inlet gully. To do this, start by digging away the soil around the gully so that you expose the upper part. Remove the water in the trap beside it with a plunger.

Next, using a vitrified clay (V.C.) cutting tool, cut away enough of the pipe to accommodate your new PVC gully fitting. Bear in mind as you mark up for the cut that the new gully must finish above ground level and be far enough away from the wall to allow you to fit the discharge pipe (fig. A). Before you sever the pipe completely, support the gully from below to take the weight of the trap.

Remove the old gully and fittings above the cut completely. Using a V.C. chamfering tool, chamfer the remaining cut end to accept a flexible V.C.-uPVC connection. Afterwards, fit the new uPVC section and make sure that it is sited correctly in the gully trench and that the pipe is laid at a sufficient gradient to carry waste water away effectively.

You can now (at least temporarily) assemble the rest of the gully and fittings.

Connecting the discharge pipe to the back inlet may call for a little trial-and-error. Start by connecting the bend and short length of pipe P1, adjusting the length of P1 so that P2 stands out from the wall the correct distance to accommodate pipe brackets. Then fit P3 and its bends, so that the fall of the pipe is between 18mm and 45mm per metre, and so that the lower bend is vertically over the bend connected to P1. Finally, cut and fix P2.

Now continue the pipe run through the wall following the same cutting and measuring sequence. Do not permanently solvent weld the joints until you have checked the run.

After the run has been fitted as far as the wall, fill in the space between the gully and the wall with a 1:3 mortar so that the concrete gully frame is held firmly in place. Finally, solvent weld the gully hopper joint and fill in the ground around the gully with earth.

Connection to a stack: Aim to run the discharge pipe to an existing branch outlet (fig. 7). If this does not have a spare outlet, then you can either fit a new multiple connector in this position, or a boss adaptor (of the type that can be fitted to an existing stack) to a length of plain stack pipe—whichever allows the discharge pipe to have sufficient fall. If you buy new components, make sure they are compatible with the existing ones—shapes and sizes vary slightly from brand to brand.

If you are connecting to an existing spare outlet, simply cut away the blanking plug and fit the new pipe in position. A boss adaptor is almost as easy to fit: consult manufacturer's instructions. A new connector is a little more tricky: the old connector will probably have to be sawn off, and the new one may not be big enough to bridge the gap. You might have enough 'slack' in the stack to take up the gap, or you may need to fit a slightly longer piece of stack pipe.

Final connection

At this stage, you should have run the discharge pipe through the wall and almost to the site of the machine. The final connection is made as shown in fig. A with a P-trap and stand pipe fitted to the discharge pipe length. The height of the stand pipe will be specified in the machine's handbook; in most cases, the outlet hose from the machine simply hooks into the top. This provides an anti-syphonage air break in the discharge piping.

Then connect up the washing machine and test it out. Watch carefully for signs of leaks in the discharge pipe especially where the outlet hose joins it.

Planning a shower

Taking a shower is the ideal way to freshen up, much more convenient than having a bath and considerably cheaper. Among the other benefits of a shower are its constant running temperature, and the possibility of fitting it away from the bathroom to avoid early-morning congestion.

You have the choice of converting existing room space to form an enclosure or of buying one of the many prefabricated enclosures now on the market—many of which come complete with fixtures and fittings.

On the plumbing side, hot and cold water supply pipes have to be laid on as well as drainage, and these points go a long way towards influencing your choice of site.

Another alternative is to provide a shower over a bath, either by fitting combination bath/shower mixer taps or by laying on piping for an independent shower.

If it is difficult or impossible to lay on a suitable hot water supply, then an electric 'instantaneous' shower or gas heater may provide the answer, although both have disadvantages compared to a properly fitted shower. The instantaneous electric shower has a poor flow rate, and the gas shower needs ducting to the outside.

Note: You must inform your local water board of your plumbing plans at least seven days before the work starts. As well as giving practical advice, they will warn you against any possible infringement of their regulations.

Above: A shower enclosure, and other simple washing facilities, can be easily incorporated in a conversion situated under the stairs

The water supply

For proper operation of a shower, there must be sufficient water pressure at the shower rose. In many British houses, the water pressure at most taps (both hot and cold) is provided by a cold water storage cistern, mounted above the level of the water outlets. The higher the cistern above the outlet, the greater the pressure will be; the vertical distance measured from the bottom of the cistern to the outlet is called the *head*. For a shower, the head is measured to the rose and ideally should not be less than 1.5m, though in simple plumbing systems a head of 1m may be sufficient.

For heads of less than a metre, or where it is not possible to have short simple pipe runs, there are three main solutions. The first is to install a *flow booster*—a type of electrical pump which increases the pressure. Operation is automatic.

The second solution is to *increase the height* of the cold water storage cistern by raising it up on a sturdy wooden platform. Another solution is to use an *instantaneous shower* connected directly to the cold water mains.

In some areas of the UK, houses do not have cold water storage cisterns; instead, all cold taps and so on are supplied direct from the mains. Hot taps are usually supplied from a conventional hot water cylinder fed from its own small cistern.

With this arrangement it is not possible to fit a conventional mixer type shower: it would contravene water regulations. You can either fit an instantaneous shower or perhaps modify your plumbing so that the shower is fed from a suitable, conventional cold water storage cistern.

In Britain, a fully direct system like this will almost certainly use a 'multipoint' gas heater: you should consult both your gas board and your water authority about the possible problems of connecting a shower to such a supply.

Temperature fluctuations

Water starvation in either hot or cold supply pipes can cause temperature fluctuations in the shower, which could be annoying or even dangerous. It is very sensible to buy a shower that is thermostatically controlled, or at least has a temperature limiting device so that the water never gets dangerously hot.

Drainage considerations

Although deciding how to supply water to a shower can be tricky, it is usually possible to get over the problems one way or another. Leading the dirty water away, though, to a soil stack or waste water drain often presents far more constraints. PVC piping, being easy to work with, is the logical choice for this sort of job. But breaking through walling, both internal and external, is usually necessary if the discharge pipe is to remain completely hidden from view. And unlike hot and cold supply piping, the discharge branch cannot be taken under the floorboards unless the run is between, and almost parallel to, the joists underneath. The branch discharge pipe length is limited to a length of 3 metres and to a slope of between 1° and 5° (equivalent to a drop of between 18mm and 90mm per metre length).

An S trap can be employed if a pipe drop is required (fig. A), such as when underfloor drainage is possible, but otherwise a P trap is preferable. Use pipe of 42mm diameter.

If the shower base discharge pipe can be arranged to go directly through the wall and connection has to be made to an outside soil stack or waste hopper, much of the fall can be arranged externally.

Use professional help if you have to break into a cast-iron stack, though it is usually easier to replace the whole stack with the PVC equivalent so that the shower and any future additions to the system involve the minimum amount of work.

Installing a shower base

The first stage of the job is to prepare structural work—such as a timber frame for the enclosure—if this is necessary.

Thereafter the sequence is:

Run hot and cold water supply pipes to the point where a connection is made with the shower controller.

Use 15mm copper piping and T connections to connect with your existing hot and cold water pipes, keeping bends to a minimum and pipe runs as short as possible. Use either compression or capillary fittings—the latter are cheaper, and neater looking.

Remove the shower base (or tray) and its accessories from the protective wrapping, taking care not to scratch or damage these parts.

Lay the shower base on a protective groundsheet, and locate the tubular legs in the sockets welded on each side of the steel shower support frame. Fix the frame to the wooden shower support.

Secure each leg to its socket upstand using self-tapping screws.

Assemble the adjustable feet but hand tighten only as later adjustment is necessary. Place the shower base on its feet.

Fix the waste outlet to the shower base, incorporating the sealing washers

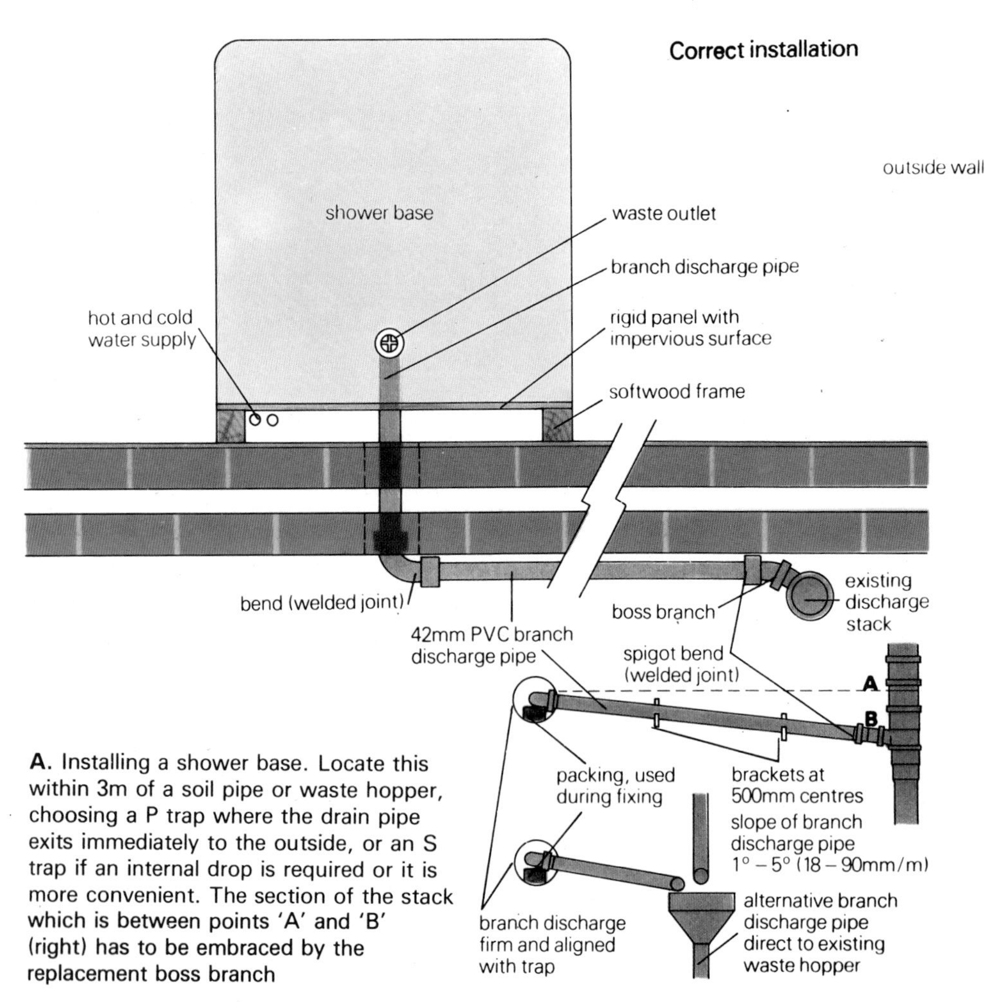

A. Installing a shower base. Locate this within 3m of a soil pipe or waste hopper, choosing a P trap where the drain pipe exits immediately to the outside, or an S trap if an internal drop is required or it is more convenient. The section of the stack which is between points 'A' and 'B' (right) has to be embraced by the replacement boss branch provided and using a waterproof mastic to complete the seal. Use a holding spanner while tightening the larger nut with an adjustable spanner.

Attach a short length of pipe to the trap and temporarily secure the trap to the waste outlet, then mark on the wall the exit position of the pipe.

Cut a hole through the wall for the discharge pipe at this point.

Reposition the shower base, then using a bradawl mark the floor fixing points of its supporting board.

Check the level of the shower base, ensuring that the trap has sufficient ground clearance, and tighten the fixing nut on each leg.

On solid floors it is difficult to drill and plug for eight screws and still have perfect alignment. It is easier to fix the support board on its own to the floor, attaching the feet later.

Temporarily link together the trap with a short length of pipe, arranged to protrude through the wall near to where it is to discharge into a hopper or stack.

If discharge is made to a soil stack, mark a point on the stack which is level with the protruding pipe and another point a little below this so that a drop of between 18 and 90mm per metre is obtained for satisfactory discharge.

Assemble a replacement triple socket, boss branch and pipe socket and then gauge the length of the piping which has to be removed from the stack in order to fit these. Transfer the measurement to the stack in such a way as to embrace points 'A' and 'B' (fig. A), with the pipe socket coinciding with the latter.

Cut out the stack length with a fine-toothed saw, taking precautions or using assistance to keep the upper and lower lengths in position afterwards.

Dismantle the triple socket from the boss branch and pipe socket. Push the triple socket into the top part of the stack as far as it will go. Then fix the boss branch and pipe branch on to the lower part of the stack. Complete the fitting by pushing the triple socket down into its final position.

Insert the spigot bend into the boss branch, attach brackets to the outside connecting length of the discharge pipe and fit this into the spigot bend. Twist the boss branch until the supporting brackets on the discharge pipe make contact with the wall.

The discharge pipe from the inside of the house should by now meet the discharge pipe attached to the stack, and the two can be marked for cutting so that you can fit a 45° bend where the inner pipe leaves the wall. Remove both pipes and cut these to final length.

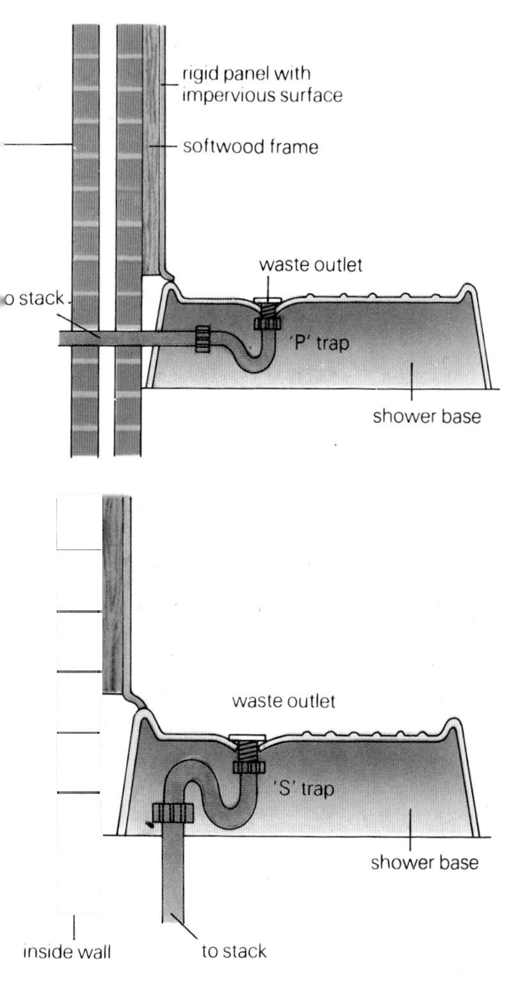

Replace all pipes, the longer (outside) one with its fixing brackets in place. The shorter (inner) length is fixed first to the trap and then to the bend. Screw the trap to the waste outlet of the shower base.

Mark and fix supporting brackets, normally required only for the outside length.

Dismantle pipework and fittings that require solvent welded joints, prepare the joints and reassemble as before.

If the discharge pipe is to be led to an outside hopper, cut the protruding pipe length to fit a slow (45°) bend. Attach this to whatever length of pipe is necessary to complete the run at a convenient point above the hopper, and provide support brackets.

Make good the hole through the wall using a proprietary filler paste. There are now aerosol foam sprays on the market which are waterproof, allow for expansion or contraction, and are easier to work with than the more traditional compounds.

Test the pipework, first for stability and then for watertightness, using a pail of water until connection is made with the supply system.

Connection of the hot and cold water supply pipes to the shower controller (or regulator) is made in the course of assembling the shower enclosure. The valve and spray piping are attached to a mounting panel attached to the wall or set into the wall along with piping. With self-contained shower enclosures, the mounting panel is attached to the rear of the cubicle with a waterproof gasket arrangement.

Completing the enclosure

Once the shower base installation is complete, you can attend to the completion of the shower enclosure. This is a relatively simple job if you are using a prefabricated kit, which often requires little more than a few minutes with a screwdriver. Built-in enclosures requiring woodwork, tiling and other jobs take much longer to make but can be matched to the room.

Install an electric shower

An instant electric shower is an attractive proposition if use cannot be made of conventional hot and cold water supplies. In most instances, connection of the heater is direct to the mains water supply. The heater needs direct and permanent connection to the electricity supply through a double-pole linked switch—the cable from the heater unit connects to one side; cable leaving the other side connects the switch to the mains. The appliance must be earthed, and protected by a 30 amp fuse. For additional safety, site the heater well away from the direct spray at the shower.

You can interrupt the rising main at any convenient point. This Deltaflow unit requires a cold water supply which has a minimum static pressure of one bar which should be available from most mains supplies.

3 When you are fitting in the instant shower, you must make sure that you safely locate the double-pole linked switch on the other side of the wall to the actual shower unit. You must also ensure that it is connected up to the heater through the necessary hole in the wall

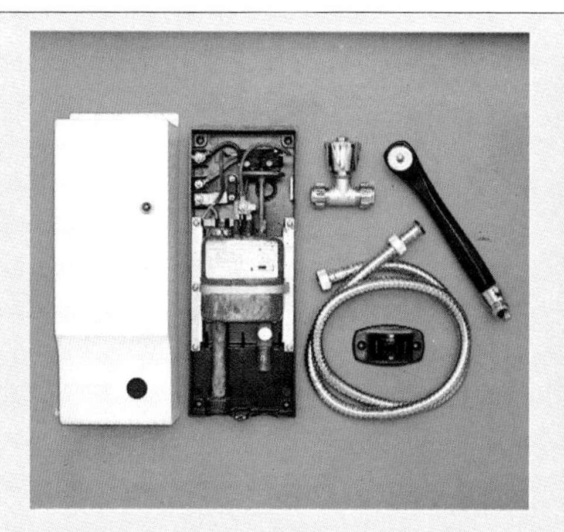

1 Installing an electric shower does require some plumbing and electrical skills so be very sure of your own abilities before you start work. Above is pictured the typical components of a shower kit which is readily available in the shops and DIY centres—the Deltaflow Showerpack instant electric shower heater

2 The first step is to remove the cover and mark the position of the fixing holes, and drill for fixings as required. Knock through for connecting wires. Cable entry to the heater is best made through the rear. Ensure this is correctly wired, tightening up the cable clamp firmly and securely afterwards

4 When making some pipe connections near to the shower heater, they should be tailor-made to fit the amount of space that is available to you in the unit. The best type of fittings to use are the capillary type up to the point that the heater fitting is used

5 The next part of the installing operation is to interrupt the cold water supply wherever is the most convenient point or junction in your supply. To do this you should use what is known as a T connector. If the pipe is in the loft you should lag it well

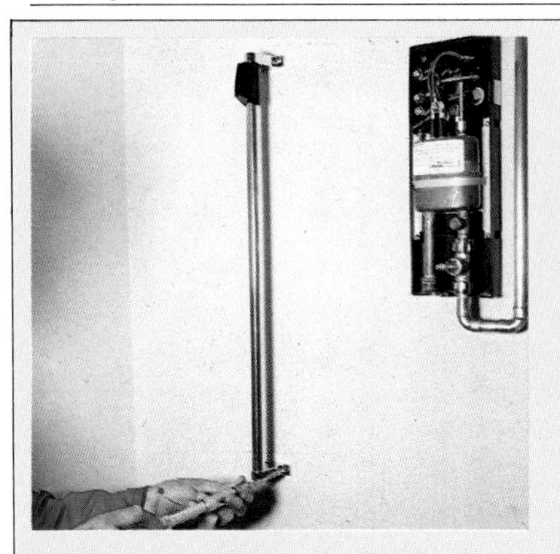

6 Now you need to go back to where the shower is going to be situated and mark the shower rail position. Then you should screw the rail firmly into place. However, before finally securing, make sure that you do not position the rail higher than the actual heater or the system will not work properly

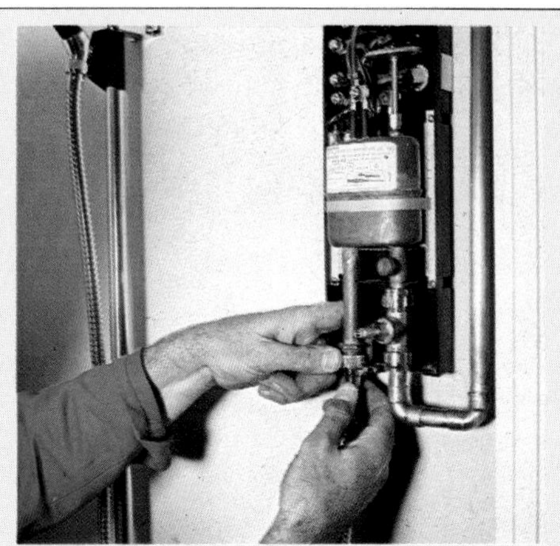

7 Now you should connect up the shower's flexible hose to the water outlet of the heater unit. Then you should turn on the water at the mains and the flow tap. Next, you should carefully check all along the length of pipework for any leaks that are visible and that need correcting

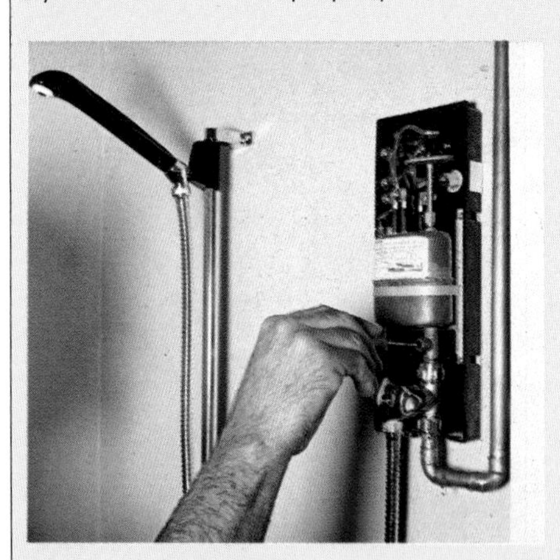

8 Carefully repeat all the checking procedures done previously but now with the heater actually switched on. Where the water pressure is just too high, the restrictor may need careful and accurate adjusting to reduce the maximum flow of water which is being given out

9 When you have carefully done all the necessary checking tests and they have all been completed to your own satisfaction, you can finally set about replacing the shower unit cover. However, you should first make sure that you have connected up the two neon spade leads

Above-ground drainage

Above-ground drainage is an important part of any house. Understanding how it works enables you to clear blockages quickly and effectively and gives a useful insight into how future additions to your plumbing can be made.

Above-ground drainage systems are governed by a variety of regulations and local by-laws. Plans of all proposed alterations to your existing system must be submitted first to the building control department of your local council. The

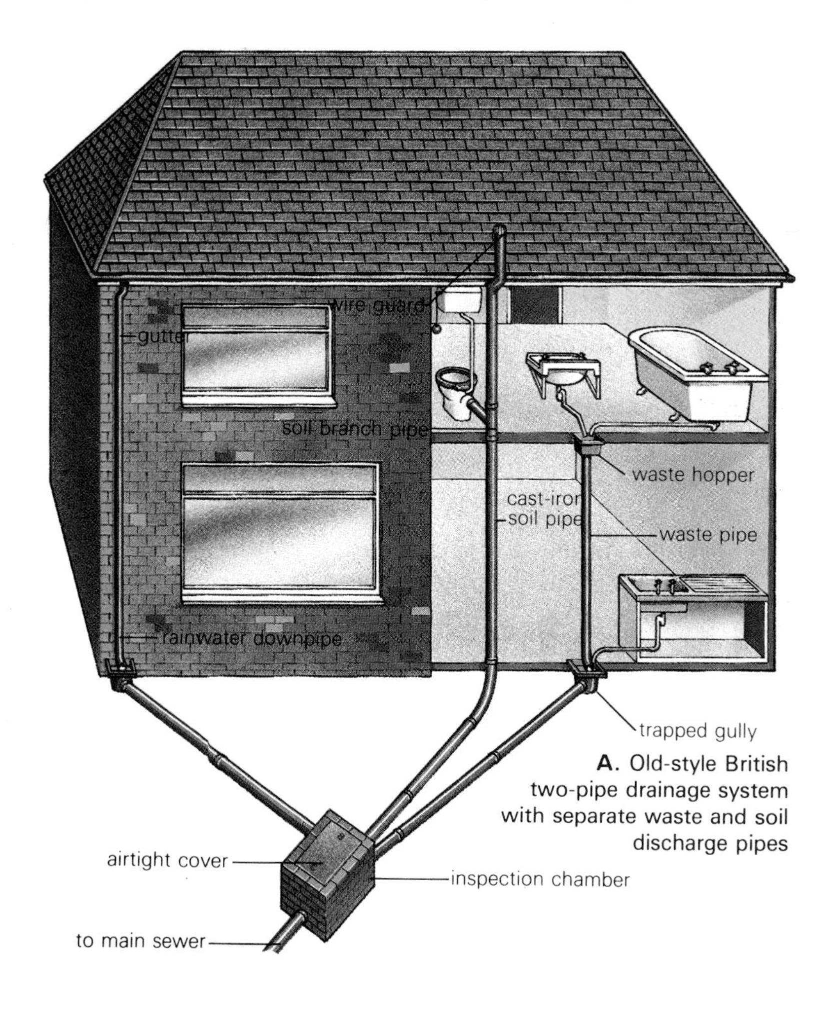

A. Old-style British two-pipe drainage system with separate waste and soil discharge pipes

inspector there will be able to authorize the plans and also give guidance and advice.

Three main types of above-ground drainage systems are in common use, although variations and modifications are frequently used.

In the *two-pipe system*, found in British homes built before the 1930s (fig. A) soil and waste discharges are piped separately to the ground drain. 'Soil' describes effluent from the WC; 'waste' describes water not contaminated by 'soil', including washwater. The two pipes may or may not be provided with some ventilation pipes to balance out pressures in the system, depending on its particular size.

A variation of the two-pipe system is still occasionally used for bungalows, but seldom on two-storey houses as the amount of pipework is considered extravagant.

The hopper head used in this system for collecting bath and basin waste at each floor can become foul-smelling in hot weather, and its waste pipe blocked by dead leaves and suchlike at other times. This causes the hopper to overspill, leaving stains on the face wall of the building.

In the *one-pipe system* (fig. B), used in

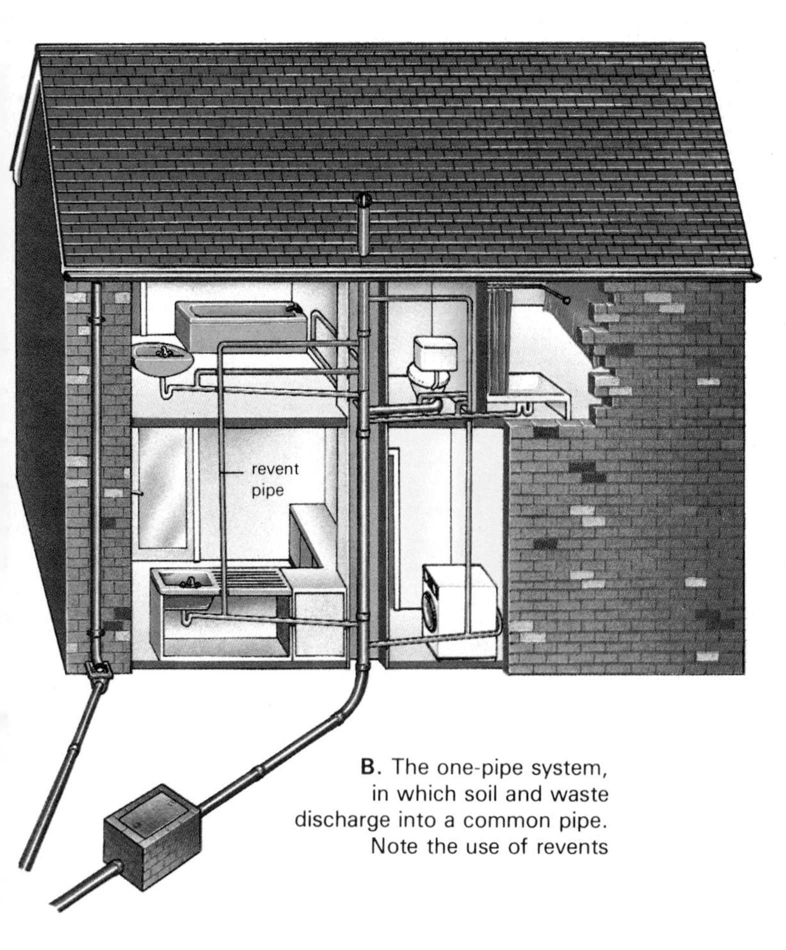

B. The one-pipe system, in which soil and waste discharge into a common pipe. Note the use of revents

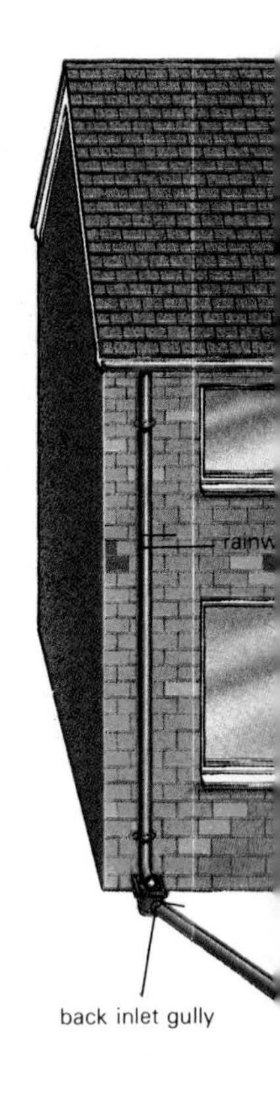

both Britain and North America, all the soil and waste water discharges into a single, common pipe which runs down an outside wall. Individual ventilating pipes from the discharge pipes, which carry the waste from the appliances, are all connected to a main ventilating pipe whose outlet is above roof level. In Britain, the one-pipe system can be seen on good-quality housing built between 1930 and 1950, but has since been superseded by the *single-stack* type of system (fig. C) for most forms of housing below five storeys.

Here, the soil and waste water discharges into a single pipe or *stack*, built into the structure of the house. The top of the stack, which rises through the roof, normally provides the sole means of ventilation.

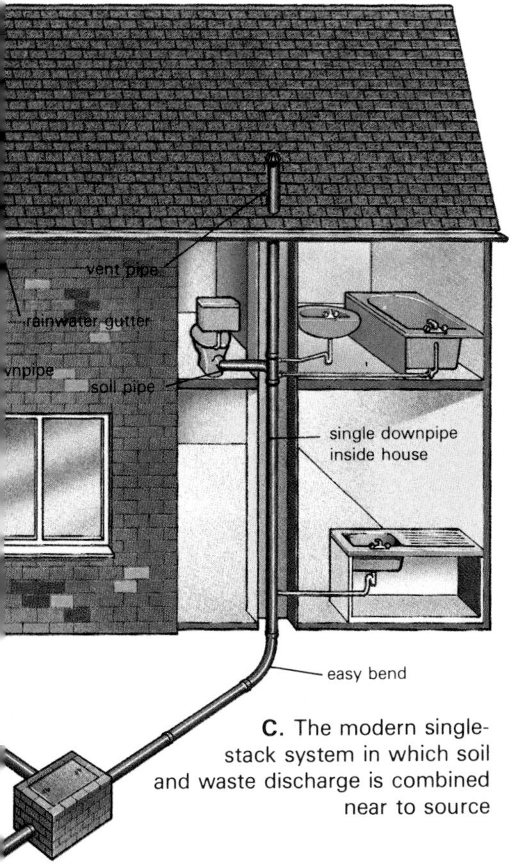

The efficient working of a single-stack system is dependent on all the branches being as short and as closely grouped on the stack as is at all possible.

Where a discharge pipe over the recommended length has to be installed, an extra vent pipe is run from the pipe near the appliance to a point at least one metre above the nearest entry to the stack. This balances out the pressures in the system which might otherwise result in the siphonage problems described below.

Because it is contained within the structure of the house, access to a single-stack system can often prove more difficult than to older systems. This is outweighed, however, by the saving on pipework and by the protection afforded against any damage caused by frost.

C. The modern single-stack system in which soil and waste discharge is combined near to source

Sub-stacks and gullies

In single-storey houses, appliances are sometimes connected to a *sub-stack*—a short stack which runs directly to the ground drain and is ventilated independently of the main stack.

In many houses, waste water discharge from the kitchen sink runs to a separate gully (fig. A) which has its own waste trap (see below) and connection to the ground drain. In houses employing a two-pipe system, the gully will be below the hopper head. In single-stacked houses, the discharge pipe from the sink is connected below the gully grid but above the level of the water in the trap. This arrangement is commonly known as a *back inlet gully*.

Some local authorities permit other waste water appliances—such as washing machines and showers—to be discharged into the gully. The rules here are the same as those governing the sink discharge pipe.

Waste traps

To prevent foul air entering the home,

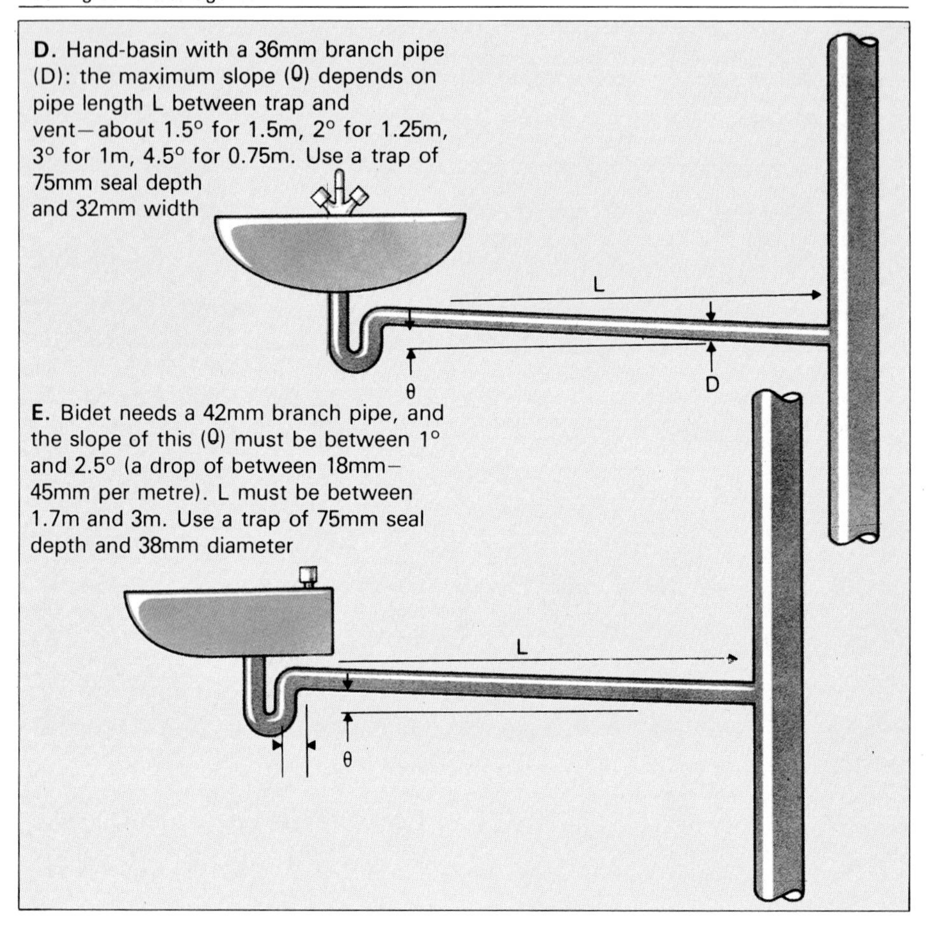

D. Hand-basin with a 36mm branch pipe (D): the maximum slope (θ) depends on pipe length L between trap and vent—about 1.5° for 1.5m, 2° for 1.25m, 3° for 1m, 4.5° for 0.75m. Use a trap of 75mm seal depth and 32mm width

E. Bidet needs a 42mm branch pipe, and the slope of this (θ) must be between 1° and 2.5° (a drop of between 18mm–45mm per metre). L must be between 1.7m and 3m. Use a trap of 75mm seal depth and 38mm diameter

simple devices known as *traps* are employed on each and every discharge pipe. A trap is little more than a depression or a bend which retains water but does not interfere with the flow of water through the pipe it serves. This *water seal* prevents air on the drain side of the bend from entering the room.

Traps come in a variety of shapes according to their function and fitting, and may in fact be incorporated within an appliance. P and S shaped traps are the most common, though they are now being superseded by the modern type of *bottle* trap. These are all used directly beneath the discharge outlet of baths, basins and sinks.

The water seal is the important part of the trap and the depth of water must be maintained. Loss of the trap through *self-siphonage*, *induced-siphonage* or *evaporation* can result in fumes or unwanted waste entering the house.

Self-siphonage occurs when a reduction of pressure occurs within the 'drain' part of a system, resulting in an individual appliance losing its seal when flushed or drained. Induced-siphonage occurs under similar conditions, but in this instance one appliance—such as a WC when flushed—sucks out the trap of another appliance where this trap is weaker or of incorrect depth.

Problems of evaporation may occur in

long hot spells if an appliance is left unused for any length of time. An outside appliance is particularly prone and the best thing that can be done to prevent the loss of water depth in the trap—hence weakening it—is to try to arrange for someone to flush the appliance from time to time.

In rare instances *blow-back* (*compression*) may occur when there is a burst of unusually high pressure in a system. A discharge high in the stack released shortly after another is nearing the bottom—and being slowed down by the bend there—causes the air between the two to become slightly compressed. Sometimes this pressure is sufficient to 'blow' the traps of lower waste appliances (bath, basin, bidet, sinks, shower) but not those of the WC.

Blow-back may also occur if discharge from one appliance (such as a WC) is allowed to force itself into a lesser discharge branch (such as that for a bath). This will occur if the centre lines of both discharge pipes meet at a common point—a mistake all too easily made when a person is considering making additions to a discharge stack.

Every type of trap has some form of access for clearing blockages. Older traps have a screw-in *eye* fitted to the lowest part. The newer, two-piece traps made of PVC are simply unscrewed if a blockage occurs. The access plate near to a WC is normally large enough to permit rodding in the event of any unexpected blockages.

Drainage requirements

The requirements governing above-ground drainage systems may seem unnecessarily complicated but failure to observe them can result in frequent blockages and the kind of siphonage problems described above.

In older houses, poor or haphazard installation of the various discharge pipes is often the most common cause of blockages.

Figures D and E show the design points to watch for when planning the drainage

Below: A plunger, ideally with a metal plate above the rubber cup, must be jerked vigorously up and down to create sufficient water pressure inside the trap to completely remove a blockage which has formed in the WC

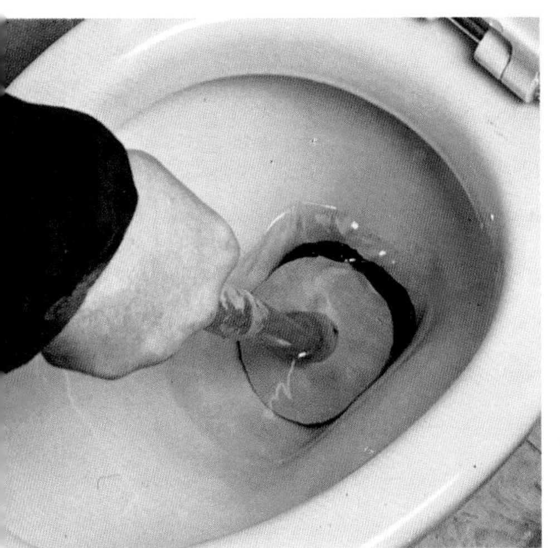

Below: When trying to unblock a sink, try a plunger before attempting to dismantle a trap. Stuff a damp rag into the overflow—or use a suitable tape and bale out all but a small depth of water before you start using the plunger

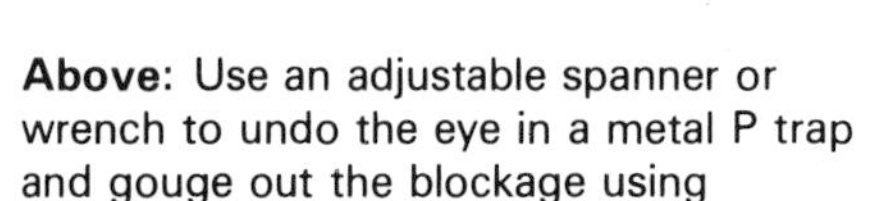

Above: Use an adjustable spanner or wrench to undo the eye in a metal P trap and gouge out the blockage using something like a screwdriver or a stick (above). Apply sealing compound before you replace the eye (right)

for a new appliance or checking on the efficiency of your existing system.

As a general rule, discharge pipes should be kept short and as free from bends as possible. Each must be connected independently to the relevant stack or pipe. In single-stack systems, the connections are best made as close together as possible.

Adding discharge pipes

When planning the run of a discharge pipe for a new appliance, bear in mind that it should follow the design recommendations in figs D and E as closely as possible—even if this restricts your choice of site.

Waste water discharges from two-pipe systems can usually run to the hopper head on the first floor, or to the gully on the ground.

Soil discharges present more of a problem as it is nearly impossible to break into old, cast-iron or earthenware soil pipes. Unless the branch fitting to the existing WC can be dismantled and replaced with a ready-made twin-branch fitting, it will generally prove easier to replace the entire soil pipe with one made of more workable PVC material.

Waste and soil discharge connections to a single stack are much more straightforward. Providing the site of the extra appliance is carefully chosen, and the run of the discharge pipe planned to join the stack close to an existing branch, then normally all you have to do is change this for a new fitting which has the extra discharge pipe socket you need. You could get this professionally fitted.

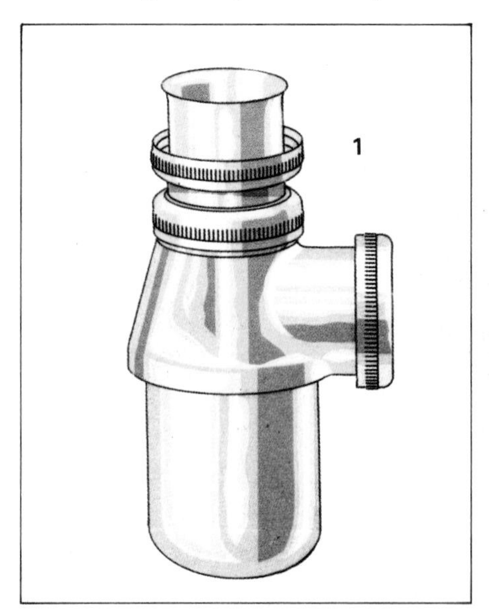

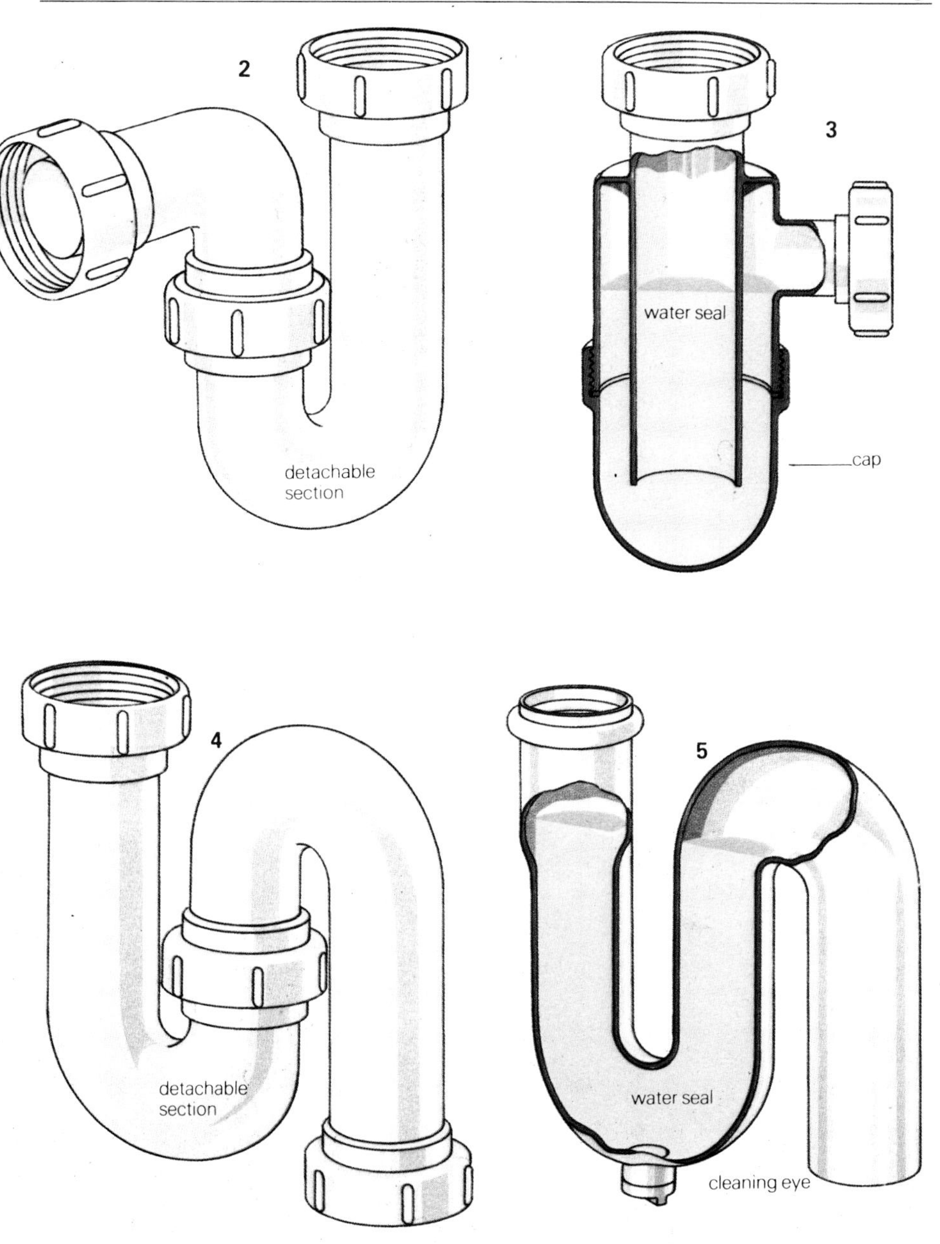

F. Left and Above: These are the different types of trap in common use in Britain today. These are fitted as close to the appliance as is possible. (1) Chrome bottle trap (2) Two-piece P trap of PVC (3) Modern bottle trap (4) Metal S trap showing seal and eye (5) Modern PVC, S trap

Dealing with damaged gullies

Domestic drainage systems consist of above-ground pipework from gutters, sinks, baths and WCs connected to below-ground systems of drains and sewers. There are variations in both above-ground and below-ground systems—but those of the above-ground system are probably more important when dealing with gullies. There are three main systems in use—the two-pipe system, found in British homes built before the 1930s; the one-pipe system used in Britain between about 1930 and 1950; and the single-stack system used on most modern British housing.

Note: You generally do not need permission simply to repair drains, but check your exact situation with your local council before starting.

Gullies

Much above-ground pipework is connected directly to the below-ground system but in the UK—particularly for rainwater downpipes, waste water pipes in the two-pipe system, and ground-floor drains with the single-stack system—the connection is made by means of a gully. All gullies have a U-bend, which forms a permanent water seal, but otherwise, the designs can vary considerably.

Below: Replacing an old gully with a new one is a straightforward job, but often is hard work and causes disruption. For this reason alone, it is well worth maintaining your gullies and protecting them from blockages or damage

Modern gullies are designed so that the waste water enters the gully by a side or back inlet while at the top is an open grid for collecting rainwater and surface water from paved areas. Older gullies are not designed for back or side entry. They collect all waste water through the grid and are consequently more prone to overflow when waste matter lodges there.

In new UK properties, the building regulations insist that all waste outlets must be through sealed gullies. Open gullies are permitted only for rainwater discharge, though they can be used to replace similar types already in existence.

Gully blockages

Blockages are the most common drainage faults and an obvious sign is an overflowing gully or inspection chamber.

Test the nature and location of the blockage by lifting the manhole cover of the inspection chamber. If the chamber is clear, but the gully is overflowing, the blockage is in either the gully or the pipe between the two.

A blockage at the gully does not necessarily mean that the gully needs replacing. Remove the grid if it is obvious that accumulated debris is causing the problem, then scrape off the dirt and scrub it with a stiff brush.

If the grid is not blocked, it may be that the trap inside the gully is blocked by grease and sediment. Remove the grid and clear the deposits by scooping them out with an old ladle or a scoop made from a piece of tin nailed to a stick. Scrub the gully with hot water and washing soda, and rinse it thoroughly. To prevent future problems, make a removable bucket to collect the debris (fig. C) and empty it regularly. Some gullies already contain such a bucket.

Damaged gullies

The oldest types of gullies, made from concrete or glazed earthenware, are difficult to handle and are fragile; they have since been superseded by plastics gullies—first low-density polythene and then polypropylene—both of which share the advantages of low weight and compactness. However, plastics gullies must not be subject to large amounts of hot water or chemicals.

Frost is the most frequent cause of damage to pipes and gullies and it is worth checking up on this possibility after each cold spell. Permanent water seals often freeze and, in expanding, the ice causes the gullies to crack or splinter. When the ice melts, the debris joins the accumulating sediment and forms a blockage.

When frost is expected, you can guard against cracking by inserting a long, partially inflated balloon into the trap (fig. A), to take up the expansion of freezing water by collapsing. Empty the gully (see below) and feed the balloon through the U-bend by hand, making sure that the end is secured to the grid with string or wire.

Gullies and pipes are especially prone to damage if they are not laid or bedded properly. If the bed is insufficient for the loads above it (such as a drive), or the ground on which they are laid is unstable, the pipes may subside or crack and the joints between them become damaged. Flexible pipe joints and adaptors are now available for most of the different pipe materials and use of these makes the likelihood of such damage remote.

Run a standard drain test if you suspect that the pipework or gully is faulty. Lift the cover from the inspection chamber and insert a drainage stopper—available from plumbers' merchants—at the appropriate inlet channel. Insert a piece of hose around the U-bend to allow trapped air to escape, then fill the gully with water. If the water level drops appreciably within an hour, you have a fault worthy of investigation.

Digging out the gully

Unless the gully receives only rainwater, most of the plumbing facilities in the house, except for the WC, will be out of use for the duration of the work, so make arrangements for washing before you begin. For short distances, you may be able to connect the waste pipes directly to the inspection chamber using wide-bore hosing, thus maintaining your facilities.

Empty the gully by pumping a mop or rag up and down to push the water seal over the bend in the trap. Where possible, remove the waste-water pipes from the mouth of the gully and keep them aside.

The gully will be bedded in concrete and granular material which has to be removed and piled up during replacement, so clear the area around the gully as much as possible—preferably by at least 2m on all sides. Inspecting the depth of the drainage pipe inlets at the inspection chamber will give you some idea of the volume of soil and rubble that has to be excavated, but always overestimate the space you think is required. Plug the inlet hole with a drainage stopper.

Mark out digging lines around the gully with chalk or by scribing with the edge of your spade. Extend them at least 1m on each side of the gully and up to 2m in the direction of the drainage pipe.

Dig out the topsoil and set it clear to one side. Make separate piles of rubble and topsoil but leave yourself enough room to work in the trench, by not depositing excavated material within half a metre of the edge of the excavation. If, for any reason, you have to dig deeper than one metre, or if space is restricted, provide yourself with planking and strutting to shore up the trench and the piles of excavated material.

Remove all the loose material around the gully to a metre on each side, and expose the drainage pipe, up to a metre beyond the joint with the gully. Work carefully and methodically, and be careful not to strike the gully or any other parts of the drainage system—especially around the drainage pipe.

When they are exposed study how the gully and pipe have been bedded, and note the nature and position of the joint and the type of pipe which has been used. The joint requires special consideration, especially if this is where the fault lies. Sometimes the most common joint—

A. When the water in a gully trap freezes, the gully cracks and must be completely renewed. But the problem can be avoided by hanging a partially inflated balloon in it, as shown, to provide the necessary expansion room for the ice

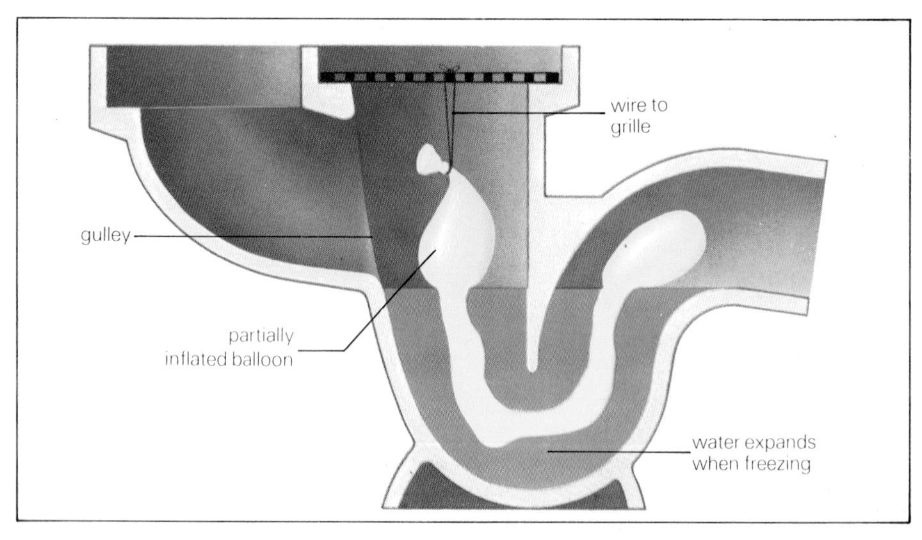

1 To remove an old gully, start by pulling away the old iron grating. Then either use a plunger or piece of cloth fitted on a pole to empty out the existing trap of water

2 Now you can also renew old pipework above the grating with new uPVC pipes. Then carefully dig away the covering around the gully with a hammer and bolster

3 Continue until you have undercut sufficient material to insert a pickaxe blade. Use the pickaxe to smash the covering, working back towards the gully

4 Once the hole is big enough, use the hammer and bolster to chip away bedding material. You can then smash the old gully into removable sections

5 Work from the grating end back towards the point at which you will joint the new gully. Try to keep disturbance of the bedding to a minimum as you remove all the gully sections that are broken

6 Here, the vitrified clay drainage pipe is being completely severed with the use of a power saw fitted with a stone-cutting blade. This will then make a clean, neat cut behind the spigot which actually joins it to the existing old gully

9 Now the new gully is fitted in position, you must run a thorough drains test to check the joints for complete water tightness before you start filling in the hole

10 Next you should shovel in the bedding material, a layer at a time, making sure that every nook and cranny visible around the gully is well and truly filled in

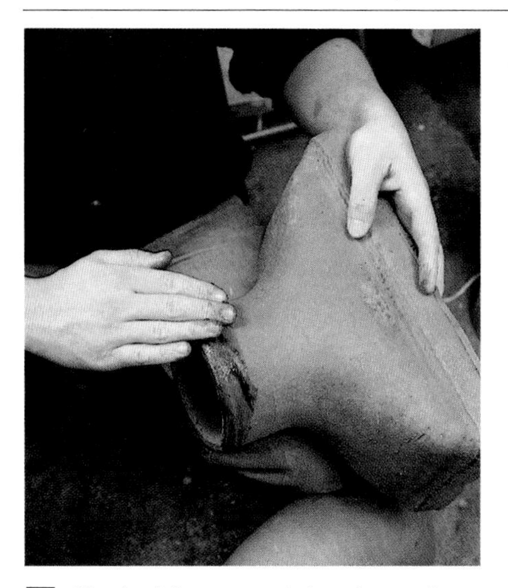

7 The bedding around the pipe end can then be cleared and the pipe stuffed with rag to keep debris out. Assemble the new gully at this stage, the one pictured is made of vitrified clay and uses joints of tar, gaskin and mortar

8 The new gully is joined to the pipe via a polypropylene sleeve. But first cut a new spigot to fit the pipe end. Fit it to the sleeve, position the gully on its bedding and join the spigot to the drainpipe with a mortar joint

11 Compress the bedding as you go, but take care not to disturb the gully itself. Bricks can be used to provide a side wall for the gully grating. Once in place you are ready to begin concreting

12 Smooth out the concrete to the edge of the grating. The final stage is to make good or renew any pipework around the gully. A good coat of paint will protect it from damage

sand and cement—is too rigid to allow settlement so that damage occurs if subsidence takes place.

Measure the dimensions of the existing gully, using a tape measure and calipers where necessary, and transfer them to paper; a standard gully has a 100mm diameter outlet connecting to a pipe of the same dimensions. Consider, too, whether the gradient of the drainage pipe affects the design as most standard gullies now have alternative designs suitable for drains with steep gradients. Based on these measurements, a builders' merchant can supply you with a suitable replacement.

The job of replacing a gully is of course much more straightforward if the replacement is a copy of the old. However, flexible joints enable you to fit modern-style gullies if these are preferred or more suitable, bearing in mind the old pipework.

Removing the gully

Remove the bedding material beneath and around the gully and pipework using a club hammer, bolster and cold chisel. When pipes, ducts, cables, mains and services are exposed, and their bedding is removed, support them temporarily with timber chocks.

Break the pipe with a hammer about 300mm from the joint, steadily striking in towards the gully until the pipe has separated all around its circumference. Then carefully tap the taped spigot until it separates from the drainpipe socket and remove the old gully. Wipe the socket clean, then stuff it with a rag to prevent fumes escaping and stop debris falling into the pipe.

In the case of a back inlet gully, remove the bedding beneath the gully so that you can move it downwards, away from the rainwater pipe. Then, in a series of twists and gentle pulls, separate the gully from the vertical pipe and remove it carefully.

Fitting the new gully

Remove the remaining concrete and screed until you have a solid bearing, then tamp the ground to make the surface flat and firm. You must now make a timber former to receive the concrete which will form the new base for the gully. The minimum thickness of this base must be 150mm over a surface area of not less than 500mm × 500mm. Make up a dry concrete mix of one part cement to three and a half of 10mm all-in ballast and shovel this into the former. Place the gully in position immediately afterwards, working it gently into the concrete and simultaneously into the drainpipe socket and rainwater pipe. Remove or add concrete until the gully is in the correct position to meet all the connections. Use a spirit level across the mouth of the gully to establish its correct upright posture.

Joints to existing pipework

Until recently, the most common way of joining vitrified clay pipes with integral sockets for the joints was with sand and cement mortar. However, this method has the limitation of being inflexible.

To prevent such damage, bed the drain-

B. Below: Building a surround and cover stops the grating from getting blocked and also provides protection for the trap

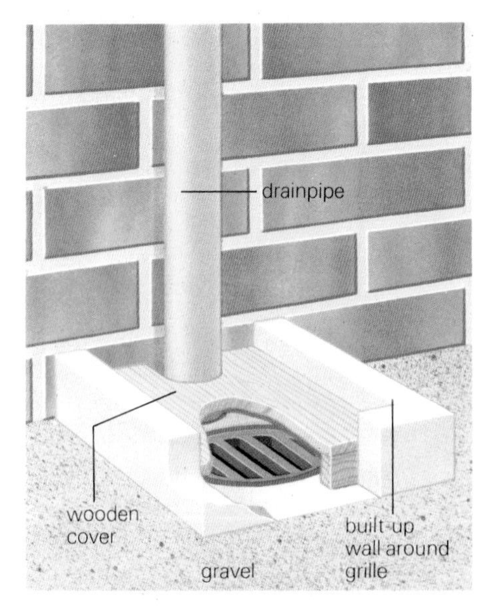

pipes on either a granular bed consisting of one part coarse sand to two parts of 10mm ballast, or on a concrete bed of 100mm or 150mm thickness. Surround rigid pipes bedded in concrete with concrete to half-way up the pipe-barrel, then fill the trench 300mm above the top of the pipe with readily compactible material.

Cement-mortar joints can only be formed on pipes with connecting sockets already built for the purpose. Sockets should face the flow of the drain, with the spigot of the last pipe fitting into them.

Form a cement mortar joint by mixing one part cement to three parts fine sand, together with a little proprietary waterproofing agent. Wrap a piece of yarn, dipped in cement grout or tar, around the spigot of the gully (or pipe), place the spigot into the socket of the drainpipe and push it on as far as possible.

Caulk the yarn against the shoulder using a blunt chisel: this ensures that the spigot is centred evenly in the socket and prevents mortar from entering the pipe.

C. Below: A home-made bucket like this makes blockages easier to remove once they occur

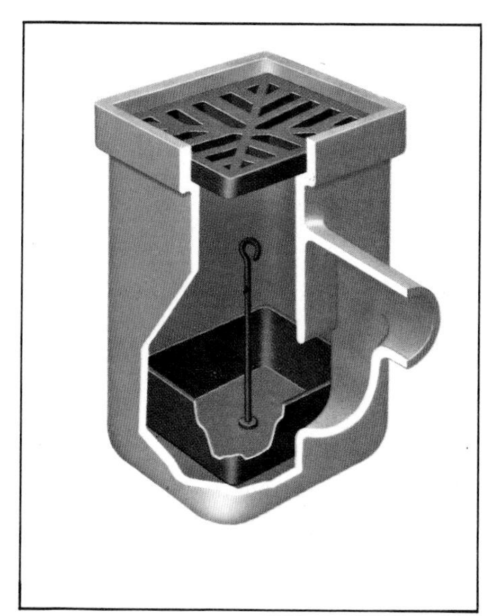

Pack the mortar into the space between spigot and socket with your fingers (wear rubber gloves) and finish the joint by trowel to an angle of about 60°.

Clay pipes with sockets can now be purchased with special polyester mouldings attached to them. Here, a rubber ring fits over the moulding on the spigot so that when it is pushed into the socket, the ring is compressed to form a watertight, yet flexible, seal.

Socketless, sleeved joints are an ideal method of dealing with clay or plastic pipes which do not have sockets. A polypropylene sleeve fits over the spigots of the butted pipes to form a flexible, watertight joint.

A new socket is then cut to make up the distance between the new gully and the drainpipe. The sleeve joins this to the gully pipe.

Each end of the sleeve contains a rubber ring which grips the walls of the pipes to form the joint. The two pipes are separated in the middle of the sleeve by a lip of polypropylene; this ensures that the two pipes do not bind against each other and that the joint therefore remains flexible.

Finishing off

When the gully is correctly positioned, and all joints have been completed, pack and tamp plenty of bedding around it and leave to dry.

Before filling in the trench, flush the gully with waste water and test the pipes and joints using the drain test.

When you are sure that the joints are watertight, remove any struts and timber left from the former. Fill in the trench to just below ground level with the rest of the excavated material, ramming it well down and removing any surplus.

Alternatively, fill the trench with medium gravel in 100mm layers, tamped well down, to a level of 100mm above the top surface of the pipe (150mm for flexible pipe). Then finish off the trench with all the previously excavated material and then lay a brand new covering of your choice.

Fixing a tap

Dripping taps can be a source of constant irritation for any household. Since the leak is usually caused by a worn-out or perished washer, one way of solving the problem is to replace the whole tap with a new one of the non-drip, washer-less type. A far cheaper way is to learn to mend the tap yourself.

Replacement parts cost only pennies and can usually be fitted in a few minutes, once you know how to take the tap apart.

How taps work

Most taps which have washers work in the same basic way: turning the handle raises or lowers a spindle with the rubber or nylon washer on the end in its seating. When the spindle is raised water flows through the seating and out of the spout; when it is lowered, the flow is cut off. But when the washer becomes worn and disintegrates, water can still creep through, irrespective of the position of the spindle. This is what usually causes the tap to drip. If the seals around the moving spindle are worn as well, leaks will also appear around the handle and the outer cover. Because you will have to dismantle the tap to replace either the washer or the seals, it is usually worth doing both jobs at the same time. If fitting new ones fails to cure the drips, the washer seating itself is probably worn. This is a common problem with older taps, and the cure is to regrind the tap seat.

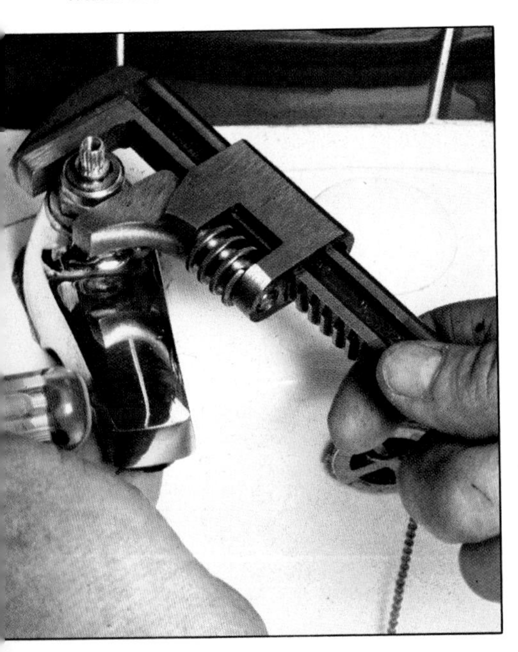

Replacing a washer

To replace the washer on a conventional type of tap, start by turning off the water supply to the tap. Turn the tap on fully to drain away any water left in the pipe. Plug the basin, sink or bath to prevent any of the tap components slipping down the plug-hole.

The assembly which holds the tap washer and the spindle is known as the head. On older taps, it is covered by an outer shield which screws into the tap body. Newer taps have a combined shield and handle which must be removed as one unit.

To remove a conventional shield, make sure that the tap is turned fully on. Loosen the shield with a spanner or a wrench and unscrew it.

Modern shields/handles are either simply a push-fit on to the spindle or else are secured in place by a screw through the top.

If it stays fast, dig out the plastic cover in the top to expose the securing screw.

Left: A dripping tap can be extremely annoying for all concerned. But it can be easily corrected with the minimum of skill and expense

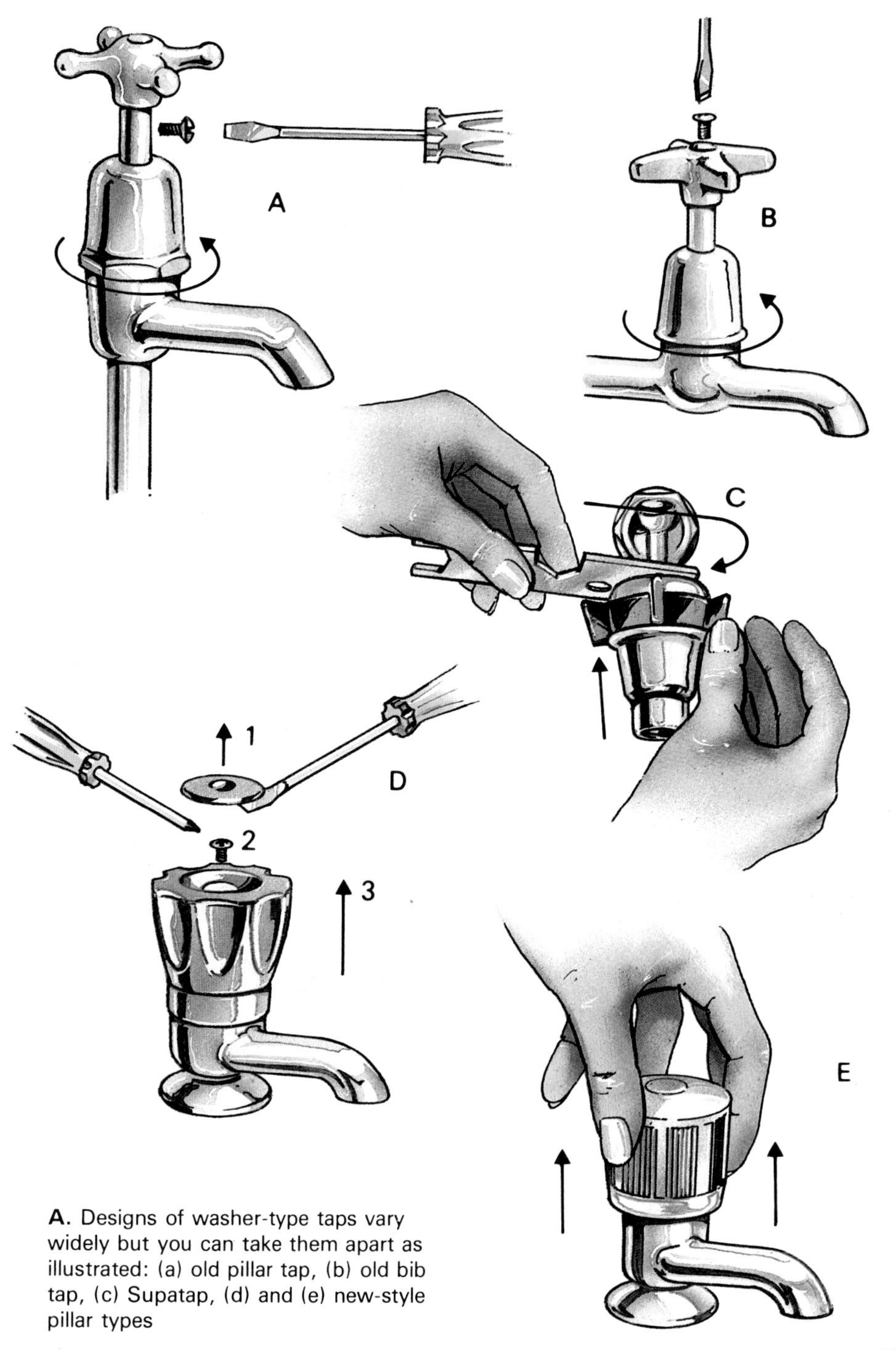

A. Designs of washer-type taps vary widely but you can take them apart as illustrated: (a) old pillar tap, (b) old bib tap, (c) Supatap, (d) and (e) new-style pillar types

1 On this type of tap, remove the cover to expose the securing screw. Completely undo this and pull the loosened handle upwards to expose the spindle. When you undo the locking nut, try to wedge the body of the tap against the nearest firm support to avoid putting any undue strain on the pipe

2 Unscrew the head assembly so that you can get at the washer. Check the seating in the tap body for corrosion while the tap is dismantled. On some types of tap, the washer is held to its jumper by a small securing nut on the base of the head—you will first need to carefully undo this with a pair of pliers

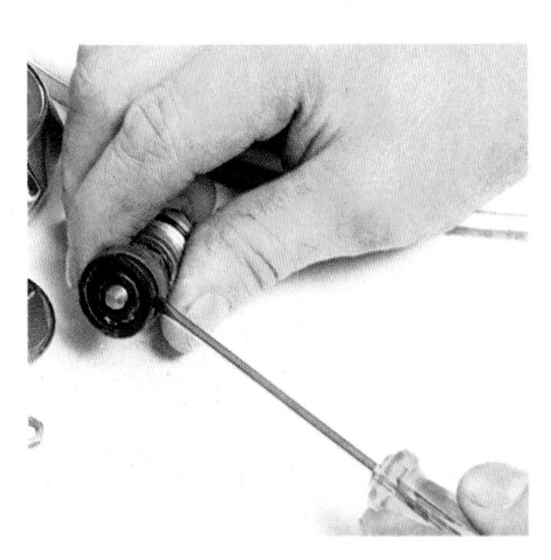

3 You can then manage to dig out the old washer and replace it with a new one. For a temporary repair you can actually reverse the old washer. To replace the spindle O-ring seals, you should dig out the circlip holding the spindle to the tap head. Take care not to damage the circlip

4 Once the circlip is loosened, you can slide the spindle out. You can then see the various O-rings used on this particular design of tap. If the seals are very worn, prise them off carefully with a pin. Slide on new ones and make sure these are properly seated before you start to reassemble the tap

With this removed, the handle can be pulled off (fig. 1).

The next stage is to remove the head. Locate the hexagon nut at the bottom of the assembly and loosen it, again using the wrench or spanner. Unscrew the head from the body of the tap and remove it. At the base, you can see the washer (or what remains of it) seated in its *jumper.*

On older taps the head assembly will be made of brass and the washer will be held in the jumper by a small nut. Loosen this with pliers, remove the old pieces of washer and put on the new one, maker's name against the jumper.

On newer taps, the entire head is made of nylon and the washer and jumper are combined in one replaceable unit which slots into the bottom of the assembly. To replace the washer, you simply pull out the old jumper and push in the new one.

Once you have fitted the new washer, you can re-assemble the tap and turn the water supply back on. If the new washer is seated correctly, there will be no drips from the nozzle and you should be able to turn the tap on and off with little effort.

Supataps

When replacing a washer in a Supatap, there is no need to turn off the water supply—this is done automatically by the check-valve inside the tap. To gain access to the washer, hold the handle in one hand while you loosen the gland nut above it with the other. Holding the gland nut and turning in an anticlockwise direction, unscrew the handle from the tap. As you do this, there will be a slight rush of water which will stop as soon as the handle is removed and the check-valve drops down.

Protruding from the dismantled handle, you will see the tip of the flow straightener. Push or knock this out on to a table and identify the push-in washer/jumper assembly at one end. Pull off the old washer/jumper and replace it with a new one. Before you re-assemble the tap it is a good idea to clean the flow straightener with a nail brush.

5 To replace a Supatap washer, start by loosening the locknut above the nozzle assembly. There is no actual need to turn off the water supply. The flow straightener can then be knocked out using light taps from a hammer. The washer and its jumper are situated at the other end of the tap

6 With the Supatap type of design, the washer is combined with the jumper and it needs to be carefully prised away from the flow straightener and then thrown away. A new washer—which must be exactly the same size to fit properly—can then be firmly and securely slotted into its place

Leaking spindles

If the leak is coming from around the spindle of the tap rather than the nozzle there are two possible causes. Either the O-ring seal around the spindle has worn out or else the gland nut which holds it is in need of adjustment.

To service the spindle, you have to remove the tap handle. On newer types of tap, this may have been done already in order to replace the washer, but on older cross-head taps the handle will still be in place.

The cross-head will be held on either by a grub screw in the side or by a screw through the top, possibly obscured by a plastic cover. Having undone the screw, you should be able to pull off the handle.

Once you have done this, mark the position of the gland nut at the top of the tap head against the head itself with a screwdriver. Next loosen the nut and unscrew it completely. Check the condition of the O-ring or packing around the seating below and, where necessary, replace it.

If the seal around the spindle appears to be in good condition, the leak is probably due to the gland nut above working loose. Replace the nut and tighten it gently so that it just passes the mark that you made against the head. Temporarily replace the handle and check that the tap can be easily turned. If it is too tight, slacken the gland nut. But if, with the water supply turned on, the tap instead continues to leak, then the gland nut will require further tightening to solve the problem.

Leaking swivel nozzles

Mixer taps with swivelling spouts are often prone to leaks around the base of the spout itself, caused by the seals in the base wearing out. Providing you are working on the spout alone, it will not be necessary to turn off the water. Start by loosening the shroud around the base, which will either screw on or else be secured by a small grub screw at the back.

Around the spout, inside the base, you will find a large circlip. Pinch this together with pliers and remove it, then pull out the spout.

Dig the worn seals out of the exposed base and discard them. Fit the new ones around the spout.

7 To cure a leaking nozzle, undo the shroud at the base—either by unscrewing or by releasing a screw. Pinch together the large circlip at the base. Use pliers for this but wrap cloth all around the nozzle so that you do not scratch the chrome surface

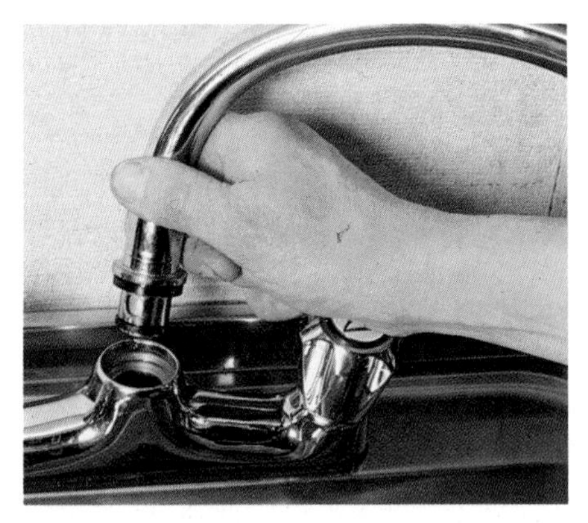

8 Then pull the spout from its seat and then dig out the worn seal in the exposed base. Place the replacement seal on the spout before refitting this. Replace the circlip and then firmly screw the shroud back on. Test the tap and check for leaks

Airlocks and water hammer

Rattling pipework, irregular and spluttering water flow from the taps and—occasionally—split pipes and joints are symptoms of two of the most common domestic plumbing faults: water hammer and airlocks.

Neither problem is serious if corrected quickly, and the work is not too difficult if you possess some plumbing skills. But if problems are ignored for any length of time, they are likely to worsen—and they can wreak havoc with other parts of the house if a pipe bursts or a joint starts to break up.

Note: In the UK, you must inform your water authority of your plans at least seven days before work starts. As well as giving practical advice, they will warn you against any possible infringement of their regulations.

Water hammer

This is a term used to describe any noise emitted by your pipework or water tanks. Identification is easy—you will notice the pipes rattling and vibrating as water flows through them, or else you will hear a succession of bangs and rattles whenever you turn a tap on or off.

The primary cause of water hammer is the water pressure of the mains supply. In areas where this is high, turning a tap on or off suddenly can produce a rapid build-up of hydraulic pressure in the water pipes—especially when the rate of flow through the pipes is quite high. The pipes then expand and contract under the increased pressure and the resulting vibration causes a shuddering noise that is amplified by pipes, tanks and other metalwork units.

The problem is made worse by insecure pipework which rattles against its supports, by faulty taps, or by a ball valve in a cold water storage tank that bounces on the ripples in the water (see below).

Curing water hammer

If your plumbing suffers from water hammer, do not immediately assume the worst: go about curing the problem in a logical manner, starting with slight adjustments to the mains water pressure.

Find the main stop valve—usually fitted under the sink in the kitchen—and adjust the setting so that the flow of water is slightly reduced. The cold water tap in the sink is usually supplied direct from the mains so turn this on and use it to check the flow rate. Very often a slight adjustment will cure the problem completely.

If this does not work, the pipework itself could be faulty. Check all the affected pipe runs for loose fittings and unsupported pipes. You may need to replace old bracket fittings with new plastic ones, but you could also fit soft rubber cushions between the pipes and the brackets to stop them vibrating.

Horizontal pipes need supporting every 1800mm or so along their length, though polyethylene or PVC pipes may need more frequent support—say, every 500mm or so. Vertical runs need less support as they tend not to sag, but you should make sure that they are secure and cannot vibrate.

In an indirect system, make sure the rising main is securely fixed to rafters and joists in the roof space—and not solely to the cistern. The pipe moves slightly as water passes through it, and if it is connected only to the cistern it may produce a low rumbling noise, especially if you have a galvanized cistern.

If this does not do the trick turn off the supply and remove the final 1m of copper piping. Replace this with a polyethylene or PVC pipe of the same internal diameter and connect it to the copper pipework and cistern using compression joint adaptors.

Taps

Leaking taps can often cause water hammer in the rising main or the distribution pipes from the storage cistern. More often than not the fault can be traced to a faulty gland in the tap body. The gland is a type of seal situated between the spindle and the washer which normally prevents water from leaking up the sides of the spindle. If the gland becomes worn or needs adjustment, water may leak through it when the tap is turned on and—more importantly—the spindle spins on and off very easily. When this happens, the sudden cessation of water flow through the tap can cause an abrupt expansion in the pipework and consequently some water hammer.

The first thing to try is tightening the gland nut. Put the sink plug in position to prevent your losing screws or nuts, and do not bother to turn off the water supply. Remove the tap handle and cover to expose the gland nut, then use an adjustable spanner to turn the nut slightly clockwise—but no more than half a turn. Replace the tap handle, then try to turn the tap on and off; re-adjust the gland nut if necessary until the tap can be turned without undue effort, but does not leak. Then reassemble the tap, applying petroleum jelly to the screw threads to protect them.

If readjustment of the gland is unsuccessful, you will have to repack it completely. Turn off the water supply and turn on the tap to empty the pipe before dismantling it. Remove all the nuts and washers above the gland nut and unscrew this to expose the packing around the spindle. Pick out all the

1 One cause of water hammer is broken clamps and fittings in the pipework. Check along all your pipes to look for these faults throughout the house. Where clamps and brackets have managed to spring loose, either replace them or refit them making sure that they hold the pipe tightly and securely in place

3 Any length of water piping which goes along horizontally for quite a distance will need some strong form of support at regular intervals. In the picture a notched length of timber, secured to the floor, has been used to support the rising main pipe which is situated in the roof space

2 Check that long unsupported pipe runs do not come into contact with any other fittings such as shelves, picture rails and ceiling joists. Support loose pipework with clamps or, alternatively, by squeezing small blocks of rubber between them and the fittings they are continually knocking against

4 Sometimes water hammer can be easily cured by just reducing the water pressure going through the water system. Go to the main stop valve, often under the sink in the kitchen, and turn it down slightly. This could well be enough to slow down the water flow and stop the irritating hammer

packing with a sharp instrument but take care not to scratch or damage the internal seating surfaces. Repack the gland using knitting wool steeped in petroleum jelly, packing it evenly round the spindle. Alternatively you can use an O ring seal bought from an ironmonger or plumbers' merchant. When you reassemble the tap, adjust the gland nut as described above before fitting the tap cover.

Air chambers

Even with the mains pressure turned down, water hammer can still occur in almost any pipe connected direct to the mains. What is needed is some way to cushion the pressure shock wave created whenever a tap or ball valve is turned on and off.

The solution is to fit an *air chamber* on the offending pipe—a sealed tube containing air which evens out the changes in pressure. With the indirect type of system which is commonest in the UK, you may need an air chamber at the highest point of the rising main.

Air chambers can be bought ready-made, or you can make your own from a length of pipe—preferably larger in diameter than the pipe you are connecting it to. Fitting one usually requires nothing more than turning off the water supply, cutting the pipe at the appropriate place, and inserting a plumbing fitting (see figs 6 to 10). Then turn on the main supply: inflowing water will trap air in the chamber automatically.

Storage tanks

Water flowing into a cold water storage cistern (or tank) can cause ripples on the surface of the water already in the tank. This sets the ball float bouncing, rhythmically opening and closing the valve—and causing water hammer.

The easiest solution to this problem is to buy a purpose-made stabilizer to fit on to the arm of the float. The stabilizer is a plastic or metal disc attached to a short, adjustable arm which clips on to the float arm. The disc is adjusted so that it is sus-

5 A leaking tap gland is another potential cause of water hammer and can be easily identified. Remove the tap cover to check this out. Tightening the gland nut slightly may cure both the water hammer and the leak. If it does not, make sure that you replace the washer and repack the gland

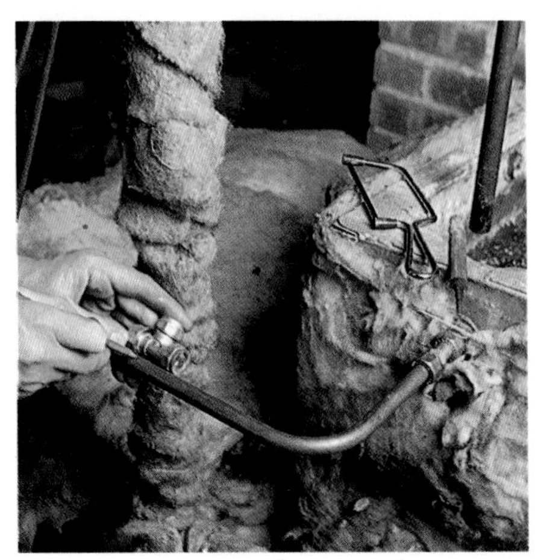

6 An air chamber need be nothing more than a length of sealed pipe inserted, with a T-piece, into the rising main near to the water tank. Turn off the water at the mains and depress the ball valve so that you completely empty the pipework. Then cut through the rising main with a small hacksaw

9 Cut a length of copper pipe about 500mm long to fit into the third nozzle of the T-piece and so complete the assembly of the air chamber. Then seal the open end of the pipe with a brass top end, having first used plenty of proprietary sealing compound to make sure that the pipe is absolutely watertight

10 The next and final stage of work is to firmly secure the pipe to the T-piece section and then turn on the water supply at the mains again. This then actually traps air throughout the pipe. This final action completes all the preparation work that is necessary in creating an air chamber

7 Remove the cut end of the rising main from the cold water tank so that you can cut out the length of pipe required for the T-piece connection. Before using any compression or soldered joints, clean the cut edges of the pipe with a file to ensure that you get a really close, watertight fit

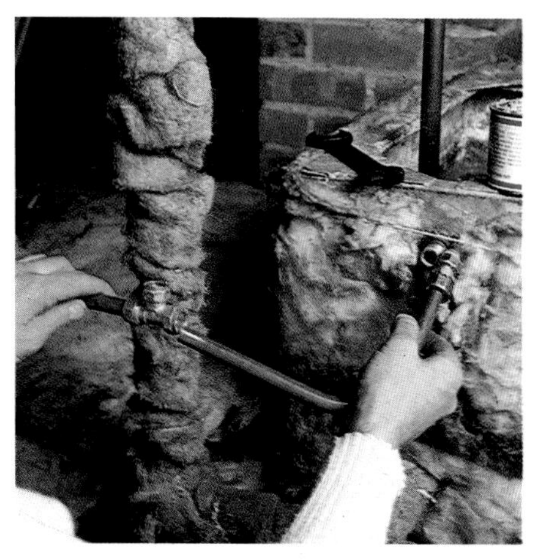

8 Fit the T-piece to the end of the rising main, using a proprietary sealing compound to ensure that the compression joints remain completely watertight. Firmly tighten the joint on the cold water tank and make sure that the T-piece is fixed at the correct angle before you actually secure this as well

11 However, you will still need to replace any lagging for the pipes that you may have removed in order to fit the air chamber. You will also need to carefully lag the new air chamber. Make sure that all the pipes are covered securely. The operation is then completely finished and the system ready to be used

12 Use a spirit level to check that all horizontal pipe runs slope down slightly from the water tank, so allowing air bubbles to rise. Air-cocks should actually be fitted in the same way as air chambers or stop valves. They can be opened with a small key to allow trapped air to escape

pended a few centimetres below the surface of the water and acts as a damper, preventing the float from bobbing quickly up and down.

If the ball is a metal one, you could, instead, solder a flat disc of copper to the underside, taking care not to puncture it. The disc should be about 100mm in diameter to be effective. As an alternative, temporary, measure you could hang a light colander below the actual ball assembly.

If none of these methods are effective, fit an equilibrium ball valve in place of the existing one. This is fitted in exactly the same way and is designed so that the water pressure on both sides of the piston valve is equal. The bouncing is thus damped out, although the ball is free to move up and down with the level of the water in the tank.

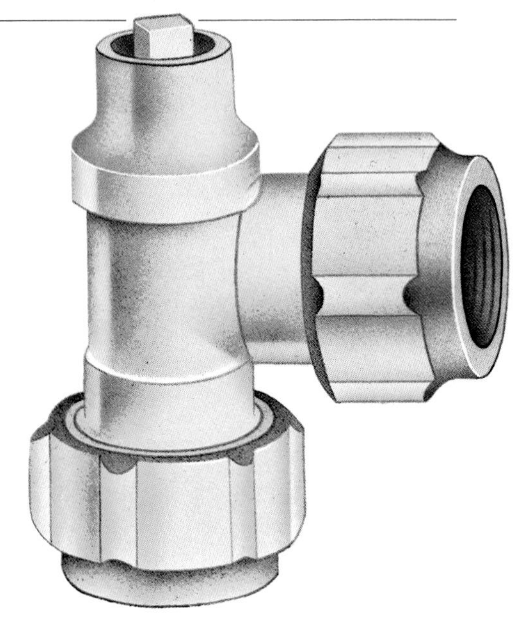

A. A typical example of an air-cock (**above**) and an equilibrium ball valve and air chamber which is found in a normal type of cistern (**right**)

Pipework

One further cause of water hammer is faulty pipework. This can affect the water flow in two ways: a long, straight pipe run allows the rate of water flow to build up to the point where turning off a tap abruptly can cause a very sharp build up in pressure in the pipe. The second problem arises when hard water deposits in a pipe constrict the flow at some point. When this happens the speed of the water increases as it passes through the constriction, and falls again as it reaches a wider part of the pipe. This causes pressure changes along the pipe with the inevitable vibration and noise.

The cure for the first problem is to reduce the rate of flow slightly by re-routing the pipe so that it has a few bends in it which slow the water down. But when you are doing this, be careful not to create an inverted U-bend in the pipe which could encourage airlocks.

If hard water is the problem, you must drain the entire system and flush it with de-scaling agent. To discourage future scale build-up, you could suspend scale-inhibiting crystals in the cold storage tank or consider fitting a water-softening device.

Airlocks

An airlock is exactly what its name implies—a body of air trapped in a pipe between two volumes of water. When this happens the flow of water along that pipe becomes sporadic and irregular. In extreme cases the flow may be cut off altogether.

If you must drain the water system to allow yourself to work on it, take great care when you come to refill it. A common mistake is to try to fill the system too fast. If you have a direct water system where all the cold taps are supplied directly from the rising main turn down the main stop valve slightly so that the fast-flowing water does not trap air.

In the case of a more conventional indirect water system—where all the taps and appliances except the kitchen cold tap are supplied from the cold water tank—partially tie up the ball valve in the tank or turn down the stop valve on the pipe supplying it so that the tank fills slowly.

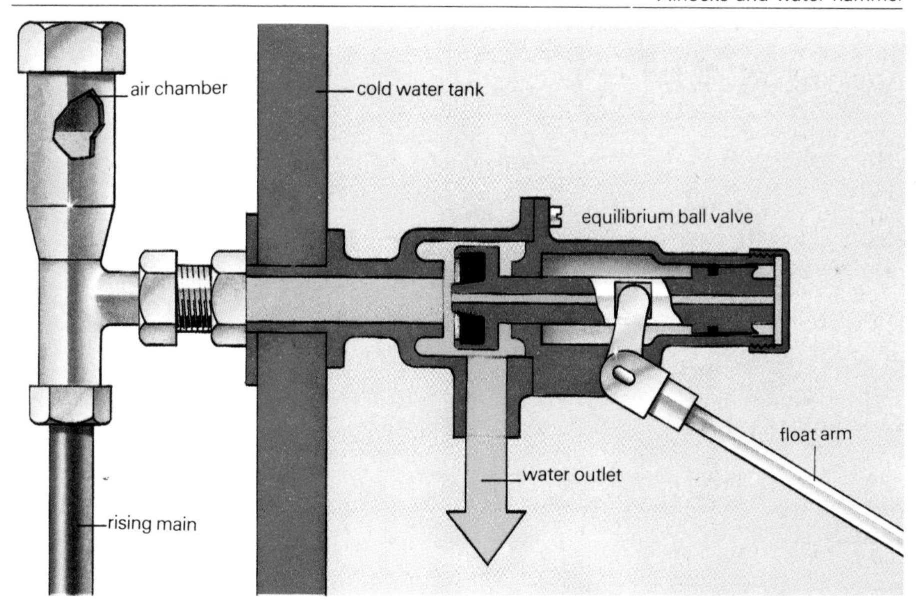

If after all this you still have an airlock in one of the pipes, you may be able to remove it using water pressure. Connect a length of hose between the kitchen cold tap (or any tap supplied directly from the main) and the tap on the end of the affected pipe. Secure the hose at each end with hose clips and turn both taps on for a couple of minutes. The pressure from the mains tap should blow the bubble out of the affected pipe and back up to either the water tank (if it is a cold water pipe) or the hot water cylinder vent pipe.

Another cure for persistent airlocks is to fit an air-cock at the highest point of the affected pipe. This is fitted in the same way as an ordinary stop valve.

Persistent airlocks indicate design faults and should be investigated carefully. The most common of these is the incorrect choice of pipe diameters for the various parts of the system. Pipe diameters must be closely matched to the appliances they supply and some appliances—such as baths and hot water cylinders—need a greater supply rate than others. The size of the pipe as well as the head of water determines the rate at which water is supplied. Consequently small-bore pipes should never supply larger bore pipes and fittings because the smaller pipe would not be able to supply enough water to the larger one and air would enter to fill the spaces.

The exception to this rule is the rising main supply to the cold water tank: the diameter of the overflow from the tank should be greater than that of the main so that, in an emergency, water flows out of the tank faster than it is supplied.

One further cause of persistent airlocking is that so-called 'horizontal' pipe runs are indeed horizontal. 'Horizontal' pipes should, in fact, slope away slightly from the storage cistern or hot water cylinder so that air bubbles in the pipe get a chance to rise through the system while the water is stationary, and can eventually escape through the vent pipe.

If this is the problem with your plumbing you will have to drain the system and realign the pipes to allow the air to escape. Similar measures must be taken if you have very convoluted pipe runs where pockets of air can be formed. At the very worst, you may have to reroute the pipe run completely.

Cold water cisterns

In the indirect cold water systems widely used in the UK, most of the household water is distributed through a cold water storage tank or *cistern*. The main exceptions to this rule are taps for a garden water supply and a direct junction from the rising main to supply fresh drinking water, usually at the kitchen sink.

There are a number of advantages with this system. Firstly, it evens out the water demand loading for the water supply authority. In this way water is stored at off-peak times, such as overnight, and is then ready for instant use at times of maximum demand—such as between seven and nine in the morning.

Constant pressure is vital for both domestic hot water and central heating systems; and the lower-than-mains pressure helps to reduce stress in piping, as well as reducing the noise caused by the water flow.

Some modern cisterns combine hot and cold water storage in one but the majority of houses are still supplied from a single, large water cistern, usually

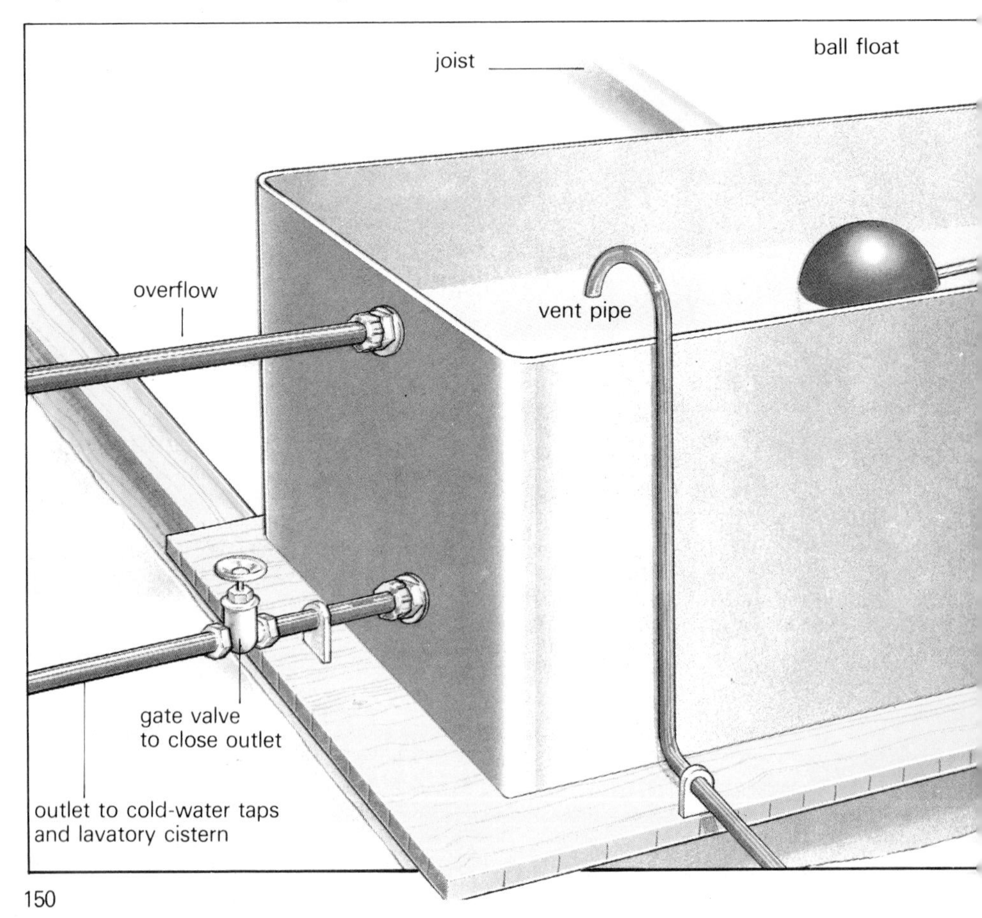

located somewhere in the roof space. Additionally, where an indirect system of hot water supply or central heating is installed, there is a smaller cistern to act as an expansion chamber and water supplier to the primary or sealed circuit.

In the case of a typical indirect water heating system, the heat exchanger coil within the water cylinder is supplied from this smaller expansion tank, while the water that is actually heated and used comes from the general cold water storage cistern (fig. 13). On no account should an expansion tank be fed from a cold storage cistern; it should have its own supply direct from the rising main.

A. The main features of a normal cold water tank, with two outlets for cold water, an overflow pipe, a rising main, and a vent pipe which extends right from the hot water cylinder

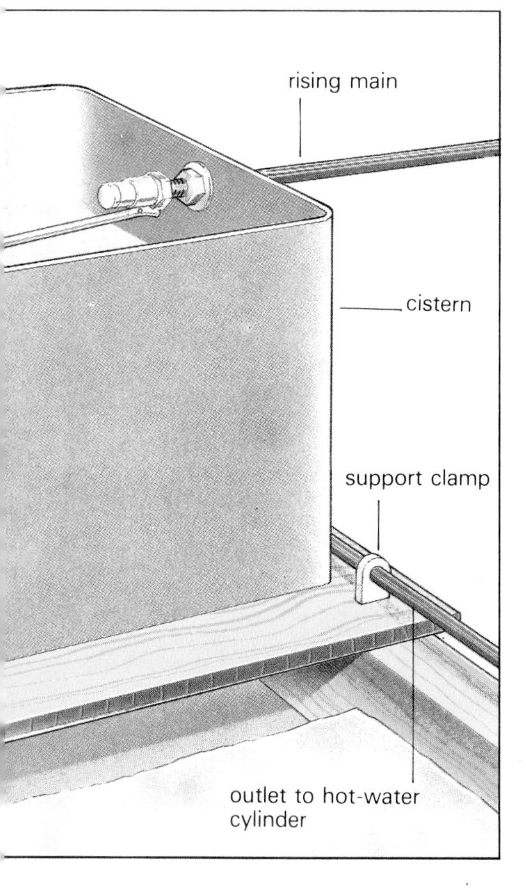

Your cisterns will house ball valves at the inputs from the rising main to keep the water inside at a constant level.

Usually there are two main outlets. One supplies cold water for the bathroom and is later branched to run to both taps and the WC cistern. This pipe should be 22mm in diameter at the cistern. The other outlet runs directly to the hot water cylinder. This pipe should also be at least 22mm in diameter but preferably it should be 28mm.

In modern installations both these pipes will be copper, and they should be fitted with gate valves so that either part of the system can be drained independently for repair. It is also a good idea to fit a stop valve to the inlet pipe from the rising main so that the whole sorted water system can be shut off for maintenance while still leaving a kitchen water supply.

Although electrically heated showers can be plumbed directly to the rising main as and where local regulations permit, mixer showers must take their cold water directly from the storage cistern. The reason for this is that a shower needs constant water pressure, otherwise there is a real danger of scalding when water is drawn somewhere else in the house. It is also essential to maintain equal pressure between hot and cold supplies. This is possible if both are pressurized by the same storage cistern, even though they may have independent supply pipes.

Shower outlets generally need a minimum head of water between the shower rose and the storage cistern of about 1m though this can be reduced to 900mm where the pipe run is very short and mainly straight.

Another vital piece of cistern pipework is the overflow pipe. This is fitted to the cistern approximately 25mm above the normal full water level and vents directly to the outside to prevent it from overflowing if the ball valve fails.

If your house water heating system

incorporates a hot water cylinder, either direct or indirect, the outlet of the vent pipe which rises up from the top of this will hang over the water storage cistern. Its purpose is to allow for the expansion of heated water, and to discharge any overflow caused by excessively high pressure in the hot water system (fig. 3).

A standard cistern filled with water weighs over 200kg and for this reason most cisterns are centrally installed in roof spaces.

Traditionally, cisterns were made from galvanized steel. These are heavy, subject to corrosion and are difficult to manoeuvre into the roof space. Consequently, they are increasingly being replaced by circular polyethylene cisterns which are light, corrosion free, and flexible enough to be squeezed through narrow trap-doors in the roof.

1 In this installation the storage cistern is placed above the hot water cylinder, which helps to insulate it and prevent the pipes from freezing

Cistern maintenance

All cisterns need to be dust and vermin proof (but not airtight) and insulated from winter frost. Whenever you take over a house you should make cistern inspection an early priority.

If the cistern is full of debris, it must be drained and cleaned. Make sure that all boilers and immersion heaters are switched off before you attempt this.

In most cases, draining is simply a matter of closing the stop valve on the cistern inlet pipe and then opening the cold taps around the house until the cistern reaches its maximum drain level —you will have to bale out the last few millimetres by hand. But in some older houses there will be no handy stop valve and you will either have to locate the rising main stopcock and turn off mains supply from here or tie the ball valve closed.

Once you have cleaned away all the debris in a galvanized cistern, search carefully for signs of corrosion. You can minimize future corrosion by suspending a 'sacrificial' anode of magnesium—available from plumbers' merchants—in the water. This should be connected to the tank rim by a short length of copper wire or sheet. The magnesium will slowly dissolve away leaving the cistern walls relatively unscathed.

Non-toxic bituminous compounds manufactured specially for this purpose can be painted on new metal cisterns to protect them from corrosion.

Old metal cisterns can have their lives prolonged by this same treatment, but all traces of corrosion must be removed first. You can do this by vigorously attacking the surface with a wire brush and then rubbing down with wet and dry paper.

As you remove corroded layers, it is possible that small holes and cracks in the steel will be exposed. These can be effectively filled with epoxy resin adhesive or a glass fibre repair kit.

There may be borderline cases where you can temporarily patch holes using glass fibre filler and perforated metal sheet. And some clean holes can be repaired in the short term by drilling through the damage, then inserting a bolt

2 This galvanized steel water cistern has a corroded and dirty interior, consequently it is long overdue for replacement. Insulation around the tank is also a problem; polystyrene is an excellent insulator. It can easily be cut to fit around the pipes going to and from the cold water cistern

3 This is a properly insulated system with the cold water cistern, the expansion tank, and all the pipework properly protected. If the insulation is at all neglected to any of these areas, there could well be serious freezing problems during a very cold spell of weather during the winter months

4 To prevent the pipes from shaking and to protect the joints, you should firmly fix them to the roof joists with screw clips or suitable brackets. If you do not take these precautions you might well suffer from water hammer noises in the pipe system

5 Plastic cisterns must be laid on a flat but strong surface to prevent them collapsing under their own weight when filled up. Also, to ensure an adequate head of water for showers, the cistern should be raised even higher in the loft on a strong timber plinth

6 With the new cistern in place, carefully mark the positions of the various pipes leading to it at convenient points on the outside wall. Then you should make the necessary holes for the pipe connections using a power drill which is fitted with a suitably sized hole cutter attachment

7 A plastic screw connector is all that is required to secure the overflow pipe, but make sure that this is tightened up properly. If, for some reason, you cannot get a hole cutter to match the fittings exactly, enlarge the holes carefully with a file and clean up the raw and ragged edges

10 The outlets should be situated far enough above the bottom of the cistern to prevent any debris from getting into the pipes. Fit the outlet stop valves with compression joints and seal them with jointing compound. The arrow on the tap shows the flow direction

11 With all the fittings in place you can see how much easier it is to have them all on the same side of the cistern. If you decide to use soldered joints, remember the fire risk with plastics: do not solder immediately beside the cistern without adequate protection

8 One of the most important points to note with connecting pipework is to have a good seal on the fittings. Thoroughly coat the flanges on the interior sides of the outlet pipe connectors with proprietary mastic to ensure that you get a really good seal when you connect everything up

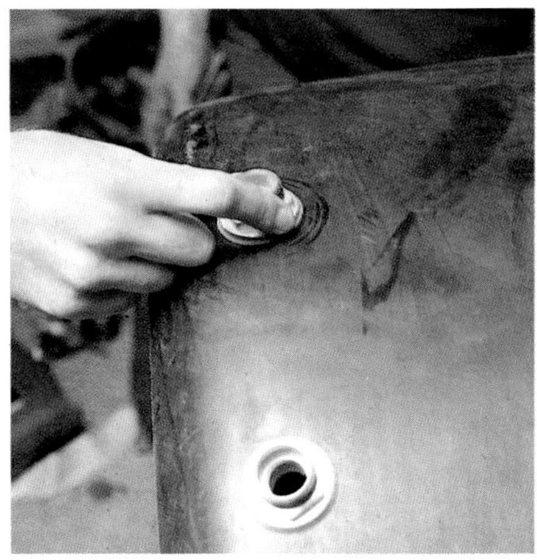

9 The next stage of work is to use compression joints to secure the outlet pipes to their actual fittings. You will need to make sure that the nuts are really screwed up tightly or you might well find, in the future, that the joints will leak and possibly cause some damage around the tank

12 The overflow pipe from the cistern should feed directly through to the outside. To save going to all the trouble of making up the necessary joints, you can just feed it straight through a small hole that you have drilled in the wooden plinth platform

13 The plumbing installation is now finally complete with only the necessary lagging and insulation to the cistern, overflow tank and piping to be fitted. Stop valves fitted on every outlet now make isolating the system much easier than ever before

with washers either side of the cistern wall. When tightened up this will provide a moderately watertight seal.

Once the repairs are made good, you must protect the cistern from further corrosion. Use at least two coats of the bituminous sealer, making sure that it is applied right up to the joints where outlet pipes leave the cistern. Leave the sealer to dry out thoroughly before refilling by opening the stop valve on the rising main.

If your cistern does not have a suitable cover, you should make or buy one.

Finally, check that the cistern and all its associated pipework are thoroughly lagged to prevent freezing. While it is rare for a cistern itself to freeze up, the ball valve nozzle—which stands out of water—is particularly vulnerable. If it should freeze, you can free it by wrapping a partially filled hot water bottle around the body of the valve for a few minutes.

For total winter protection, insulate the whole cistern—except the underside—with glass fibre lagging, loosefill chips contained within a hardboard frame, or specially designed fire-retardant polystyrene or strawboard lagging units.

At the same time, lag all other pipework in the roof space. Take care when you do this not to block the hot water vent pipe outlet which discharges into the cistern.

Ball valves

Your cistern might be fitted with any one of a number of ball valves, but the older types, where the float moves a washered piston inside a barrel, are more likely to be troublesome.

If you do have trouble with an old valve, cut off the water supply to it, then remove the float and arm by taking out the pin on which they pivot. If the valve is a 'Croydon' pattern, discharging downwards, the washered plug will simply fall out. But if the valve is a 'Portsmouth' pattern, discharging horizontally, you will need to unscrew the end retaining cap and then push the plug out through its hole.

If a plug is sticking because of scale build-up, you can cure it simply by cleaning the plug with abrasive paper and then smearing it with petroleum jelly. To replace the washer, hold the body of the plug firmly in a vice and unscrew the retaining cap with pliers. If the retaining cap is stuck fast, you may have to pick out the old washer and force in a new one. Make sure the new washer lies flat in its seating.

If neither of these two repairs remedies the valve malfunction, it is probably time to fit a brand new valve.

Replacing an old cistern

Cut off the water supply to the old cistern and then completely drain it by running off water through the cold taps and baling out. Next, disconnect all the old pipe fittings and carefully lift out the old

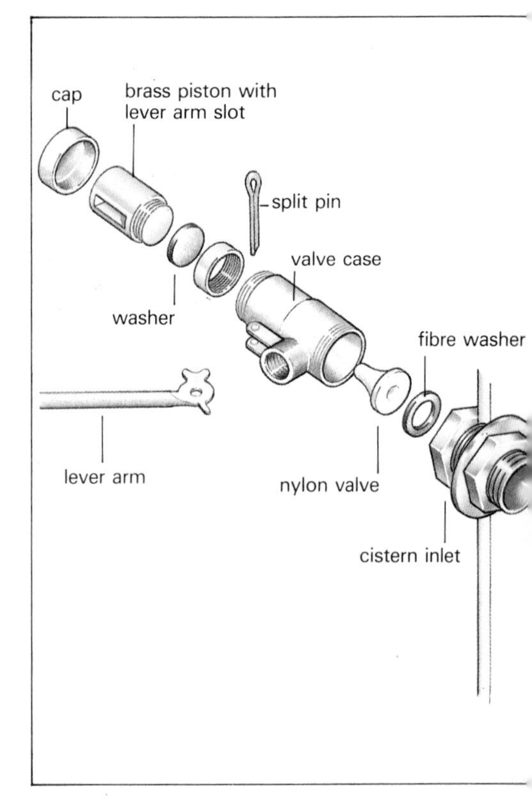

cistern system.

At all the removal stages lay down boards to distribute the weight of the cistern evenly over the joists and never step between them.

If your replacement cistern is exactly the same size as the old one, there will be little extra work involved in rerouting the pipework. Because of this, rectangular plastic cisterns reinforced with glass fibre are often more suitable for replacement work.

Although your old galvanized cistern may simply have rested across the joists, the new plastic one must stand on a flat base of 25mm board. Adequately support this with timber or it will buckle as soon as you fill it up.

It is far easier to cut the tapping holes in the new cistern before you manoeuvre it up into the roof space.

But if the trap door is too small to accommodate the old cistern, you may find that only the drum shape polyethylene cisterns are sufficiently flexible to be squeezed into the roof space. In this case you must site the new cistern before rerouting existing pipework and marking the tapping holes.

Tapping holes in plastic can be cut either by heating up a suitable piece of copper pipe and burning the hole through, or by using a hole saw drill attachment.

The ball valve is fitted about 25mm down from the top edge of the cistern and most cisterns are reinforced at this point to bear the additional weight of the valve and its piping. Push the threaded tail through the appropriate hole and secure it on both sides with its locking nuts. Then connect the rising main to the valve using a compression joint which includes a special valve connector. If you do not have a stopcock fitted at this point, take the opportunity to fit one.

Special compression joint tank connectors, secured with locknuts, are attached to the cistern at each of the other tappings. Compression-joint the remaining pipework to these, rerouting or extending pipes where necessary.

Finally connect up the overflow pipe and ensure that the hot water vent pipe can discharge properly. Test the cistern in operation and secure any pipes subject to vibration with clips screwed to the joists before insulating the entire installation.

B. Exploded views of the Portsmouth (left) and Croydon (right) ball float valves, widely used today in the UK

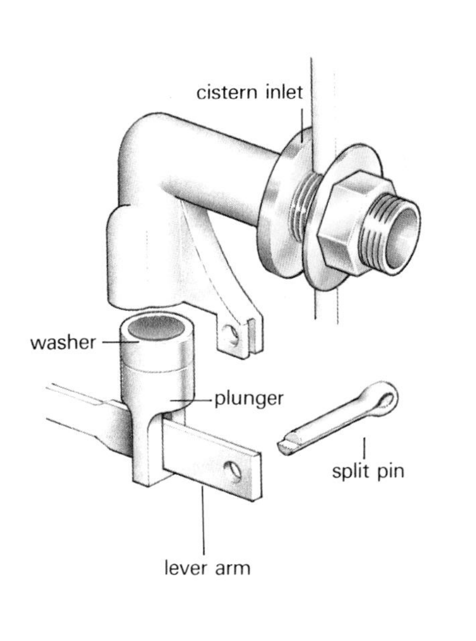

Insulation

When you have completed the installation it is essential to ensure that the tank and surrounding pipes are correctly insulated. All of the pipes, including the overflow and hot water vent pipe should be covered with thick lagging or pipe insulation.

Also make sure that the sides of the tank are insulated. Do not insulate the underside of the tank. Instead, lift the insulation from between the joists below so that warm air can rise and prevent the water in the tank from freezing.

Renewing your guttering

However well they are maintained, old metal gutters and downpipes may eventually begin to show signs of decay. If the decay is far advanced, it is well worth considering replacing the system with PVC guttering.

PVC rainwater systems have several advantages over the various metal types. They do not corrode, nor do they require painting for protection—though they can be painted to suit colour schemes. Because PVC guttering is light, sections of it are easier to handle than their metal counterparts—an important consideration when you are working on a ladder. Being cheaper than cast-iron, PVC has virtually replaced it for home building and renovation in Britain.

Planning the new assembly

Sections of PVC guttering can be joined together in a variety of different ways. But with all types of half-round guttering, you fix the system to the exterior of the house in more or less the same way. The gutter sections are clipped into brackets screwed to the fascia boards beneath the eaves of the roof. The downpipes have wrap-around pipe clips which are screwed directly to the walls. Some other systems require no brackets for the gutters because they are screwed directly to the fascias.

Before you take down the existing guttering, measure it carefully to give you the lengths for the new gutters and pipes (fig. 1). Count and measure the stop-ends, outlets, shoes, swan necks and internal and external angles to work out the number and size of each part you will require.

When you are calculating the number of support brackets and pipe clips needed, bear in mind that the existing system may not have been fitted with an adequate number. Gutter support brackets should be spaced no further than 1m apart, and pipe clips a maximum of 2m apart.

Removing cast or galvanized iron guttering

When you have bought all the replacement PVC components, you can start to dismantle the existing system. If your house adjoins another property, start at the joint nearest the dividing line between the two houses. If not, start at any convenient point along the run.

Remove the bolt holding the first joint together, using a junior hacksaw if necessary. Repeat the process for the joint at the other end of the length and then remove the section (fig. 3). When removing a long piece of guttering, take care not to let its weight catch you off balance while you are on the ladder.

When you have removed a section and taken it to the ground, unscrew the supporting brackets from the fascia board.

If you are dealing with Ogee-section guttering, either unscrew the fixing screws holding the lengths to the fascia board, or, if they are corroded, cut through them with a junior hacksaw.

Some cast-iron systems are supported by brackets which are screwed to the roof rafters. To gain access to the fixing screws on such brackets, you may have to remove the slate or tile immediately above it with a slate ripper.

When you come to dismantle a downpipe, start by removing the outlet section

Above: When you come to fix the downpipe of a PVC gutter system, firmly secure a plumbline with a nail or drawing pin to the fascia board immediately behind the outlet. This gives you a good guideline for positioning the pipe clips down the wall and fixing the pipe so that it runs vertically

at the top and, if fitted, the swan neck. You should be able to dislodge these by hand by pulling upwards, but if not, use a hammer to knock them from place (fig. 5). Remove the downpipe brackets by levering out the pipe nails with a claw hammer. Where necessary, hold an off-cut of timber against the wall so that you get more leverage.

Assembling the new system

Before you erect the new guttering, check that the fascia boards are in a sound condition.

1 Before you take down all the existing guttering, measure it carefully to give you the lengths for the new, substitute gutters and downpipes

2 The bolts holding the old gutter together may be badly corroded. In this case saw right through them using a junior hacksaw

5 You should be able to remove the swan neck of a downpipe by hand but if it is not possible, knock it out gently with a hammer

6 Before you start to assemble the new guttering, use a spirit level to check that all the fascia boards you are using are exactly horizontal

Scrape off any paint that has formed in ridges around the old guttering, then wash down the fascia and when dry apply primer to any bare wood. When this has dried, key the surface by rubbing it over with a medium grade of glass-paper. Paint the boards with two undercoats and one top coat then leave them to dry out before erecting the new guttering.

Boards in particularly bad condition may have to be replaced altogether.

3 Lift the freed guttering out of its brackets and take it to the ground making sure that the heavy weight does not catch you off balance

4 If the fixing screws of a fascia bracket are too corroded to unscrew, then use a claw hammer to lever it completely away from the board

7 To assemble the system, begin by screwing the supporting fascia brackets firmly into place alongside the existing fascia board

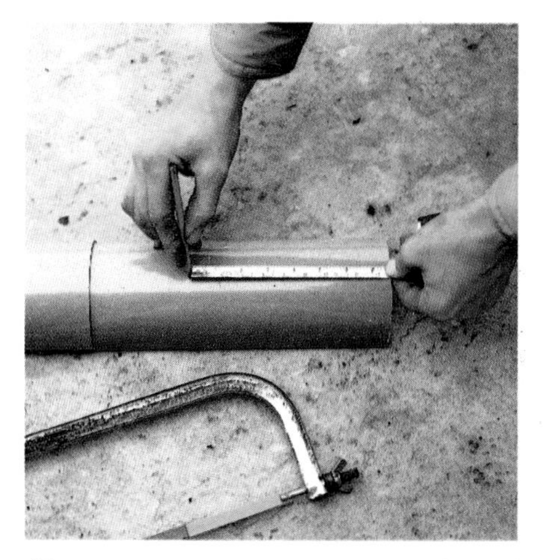

8 When you are cutting a new piece of gutter to length, make a pencil mark on the underside of the section at the correct distance from the end

To assemble the system, begin by fixing the supporting brackets. Place one bracket at the top end of a run to correspond with the old one, and one at the bottom end in a similar position (fig. 7). Attach a length of string between the two brackets and make sure that it is taut. Check the string with a spirit level to make sure that it slopes towards the outlet position—the correct slope need be as little as 25mm in a 15m run—then use it as a guide for positioning the interven-

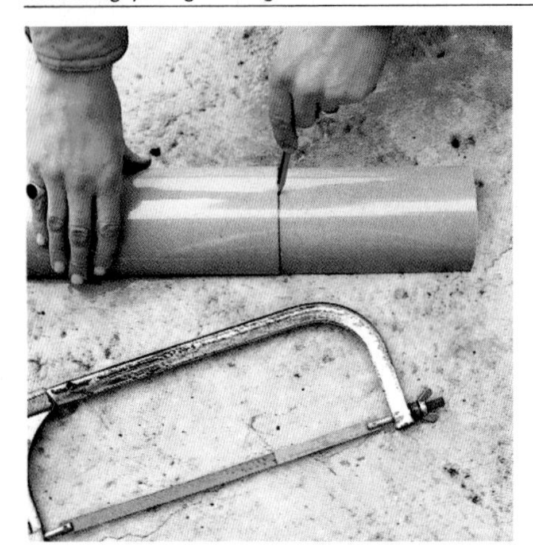

9 Fit a spare gutter section over the piece which is to be cut. Align its edge with the pencil mark and firmly draw the cutting line

10 Hold the length of guttering in place and cut through the line with a hacksaw. Then smooth down the cut edges with a medium file

13 When cutting a piece of downpipe to length, wrap a paper template around the pipe to make sure the cut edges are square

14 Mark and drill the pipe clip screw holes. In masonry walls, plug the holes with wall plugs, place a clip around the pipe, then screw it into place

ing brackets. It may be that you can fix all the new brackets in the positions of the old ones. But check constantly that both the spacings and the fall are correct.

When you come to an internal or external angle at the corners, hold the appropriate part in place and mark the appropriate bracket positions: these vary according to the brand of system that you are installing.

When you have marked all the bracket positions, drill holes for the mounting screws into the fascia boards and screw each bracket home. With all the brackets

11 To join PVC guttering to an existing cast-iron system, clean the end of the iron piece, then apply some sealing compound to the area

12 Fix the special adaptor fitting into the end of the iron gutter and neatly clean off the underside with the point of a screwdriver

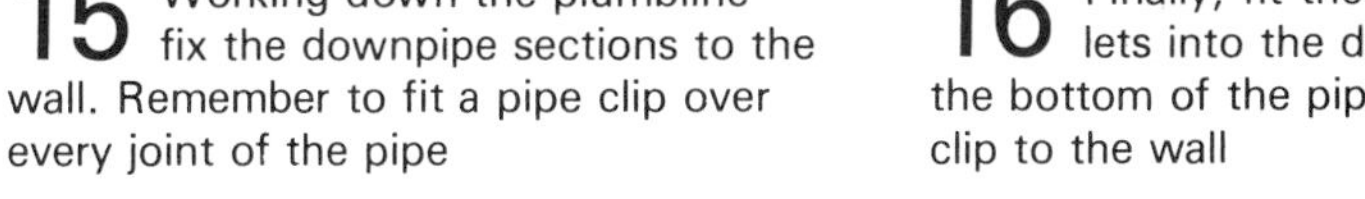

15 Working down the plumbline fix the downpipe sections to the wall. Remember to fit a pipe clip over every joint of the pipe

16 Finally, fit the shoe piece that lets into the drain or soakaway at the bottom of the pipe and attach the last clip to the wall

in place, you can start to position the guttering lengths within them.

Cutting and fitting

When you are cutting new gutter lengths, it is important to make sure that the cut ends are square. You can do this by fitting a spare section over the piece to be cut and using it as a template to draw the cutting line (fig. 9). Once you have sawn through a section, smooth the cut edges with a medium file.

Start fitting the guttering at the top end of a run. Clip the lengths into position in the brackets and join sections together.

Because PVC tends to expand and contract, even with quite small temperature variations, some systems make allowance for movement at each joint. In this case, the union clips holding sections together have marks on either side with which the ends of adjoining gutter sections are aligned. The resulting gap between sections allows for maximum expansion and contraction without weakening the new seal.

If you are faced with the problem of connecting the new guttering to a neighbour's iron system, special adaptor fittings are available for joining the two materials. Dry out and clean the end of the iron section, using a wire brush to remove any traces of rust. Apply sealing compound to the area then press the adaptor into place (fig. 12).

Fitting a downpipe

Unlike cast-iron systems, the swan necks for PVC guttering are not manufactured in one piece. Instead they are made up of an offset socket, an offset spigot and an offcut of pipe. The length of pipe determines the angle of the bend, thus giving you more flexibility in positioning the downpipe than you would have with cast-iron or galvanized metal.

To erect the downpipe, fix a plumbline with a nail or drawing pin to the fascia board behind the outlet. You can then use the string as a guideline down which to mark the pipe clip screw positions.

Place one of the clips around the bottom of the offset spigot, hold it temporarily in place on the wall, and mark its screw holes. Next, measure and cut the length of pipe to fit between the socket and spigot. To make sure that the cut end of the pipe is square, mark the length to be cut, then wrap a paper template around the pipe at the mark (fig. 13). Bore the holes for the pipe clip screws into the wall (fig. 14), plug the holes with wall plugs, then fit the swan neck in position.

Fit the downpipe down the wall, joining the sections according to the manufacturer's instructions, and fix a pipe clip at each joint to support the pipe. Finally, fit the shoe piece that lets into the drain or soakaway at the bottom of the pipe and attach the last clip (fig. 16).

Once the whole assembly has been fitted and joined, test the system by emptying a bucket of water into the gutter at the highest point of each run to check that there are no leaks.

Left: Make use of your rainwater by diverting it from a section of guttering into a storage barrel. These are readily available from garden centres

ELECTRICS AND LIGHTING

How electricity works

Electricity in the home is something which we all take for granted—and would be lost without. Yet electricity is also highly dangerous if it is not treated with the respect it deserves. For the do-it-yourself enthusiast, this means having a sound knowledge of the way in which domestic installations work before tackling any electrical job with confidence.

Electricity and the law

In the UK, regulations covering wiring are compiled by the Institute of Electrical Engineers. Anyone may do his own wiring, but the IEE regulations must be complied with. These require that all electrical installations be tested on completion by the relevant electricity supply board.

Electrical measures

An electric current consists of a flow of minute particles called electrons. This flow can be likened to the flow of water from a tap connected by a pipe to a tank.

For water to flow when the tap is opened, the tank must be at a higher level than the tap. And the greater the height of the tank, the higher the pressure of the water that comes out of the tap. So water at high pressure has a greater rate of flow, or current, than water at low pressure.

The *voltage* in an electrical circuit corresponds with the *pressure* of the water in the pipe. The *rate* of flow of an electric current is measured in *amperes* and is equivalent to the flow of water along the pipe—that is, how much comes out at any given time.

Electrical power is measured in *watts*. This term applies to the electrical equipment itself and is a measurement of the rate at which it uses electricity. An average electric light bulb uses only about 100 watts, whereas a powerful electric heater might use 3,000 watts

Below: Electricity enters the house through an armoured service cable connected to the company fuse. From here, power flows through to the meter

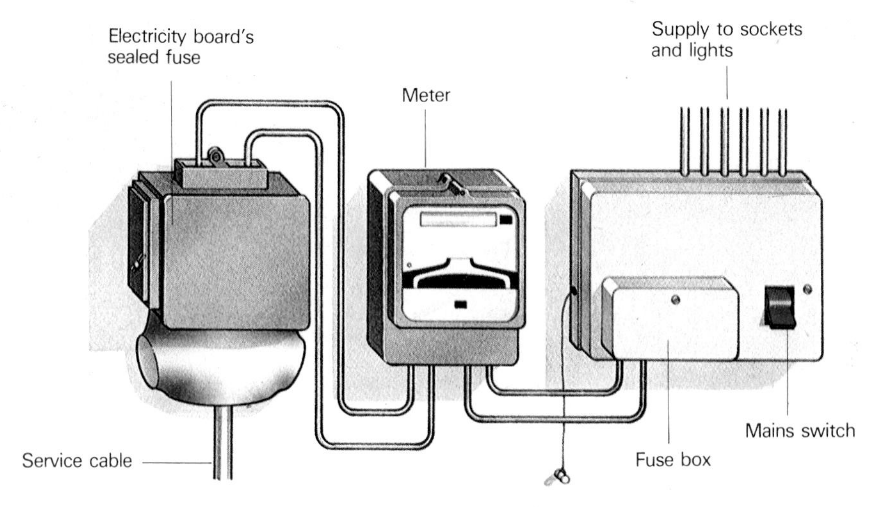

A: Power runs to an electrical appliance via the live wire and actually returns via the neutral wire. To be a double safeguard against electric shocks, the switch to the appliance is always placed on the 'live' side. The earth wire carries power to earth in an emergency

B: For a wall switch, the live current must be diverted down the wall and back again. Usually a standard two-wire cable is used, with wires of—confusingly—different colours. But both of these wires are in fact 'live' connections. A separate earth wire is connected to the rose

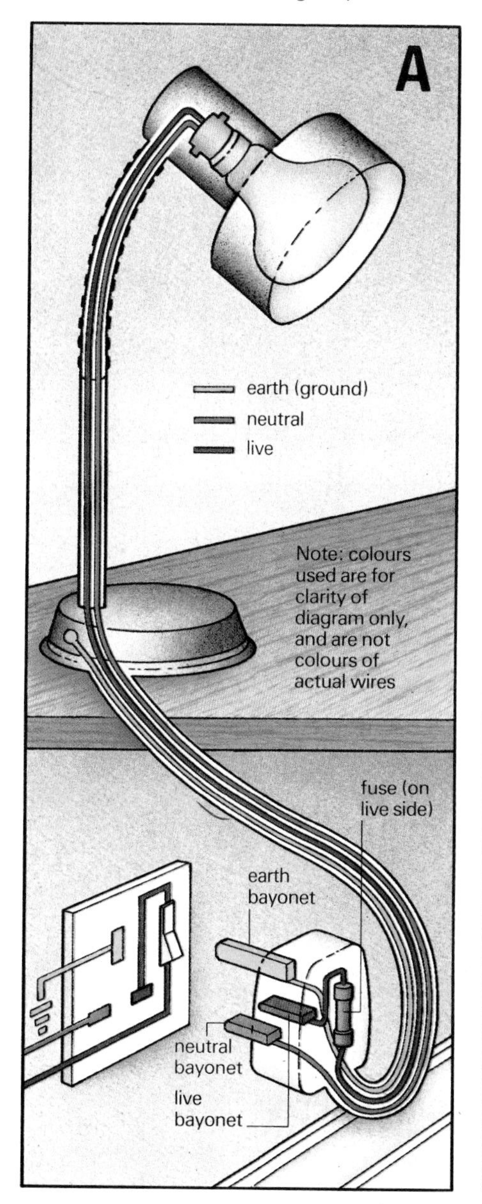

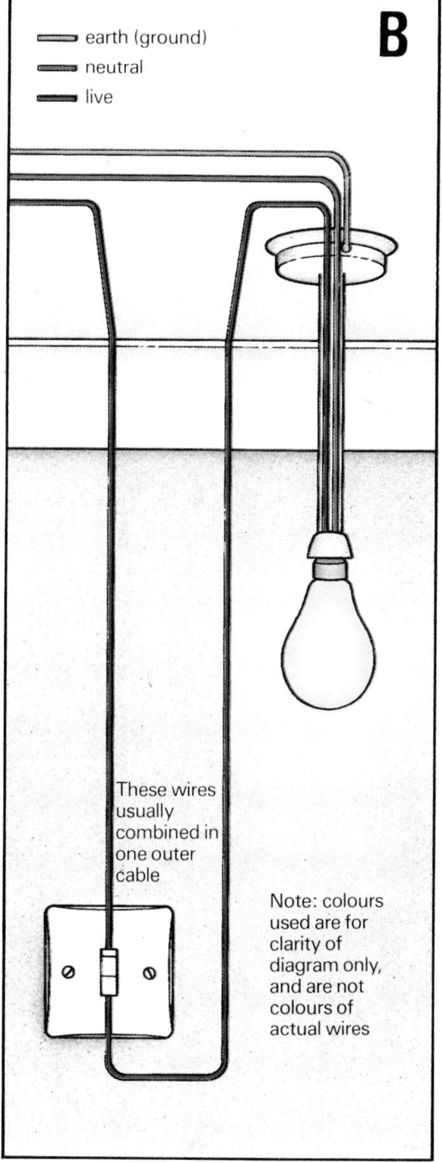

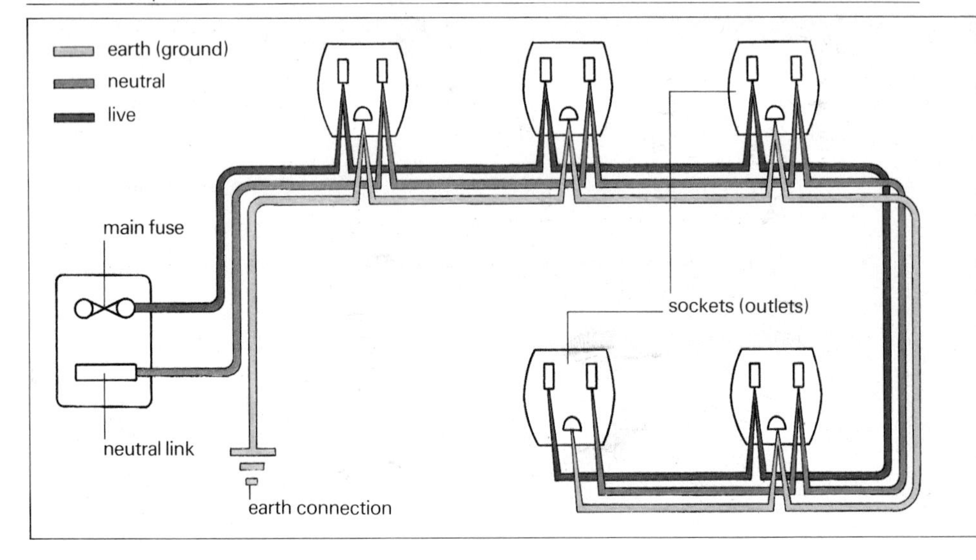

(3 kilowatts). The relationship between amps, volts and watts is expressed in the formula:

$$\frac{\text{Watts}}{\text{Volts}} = \text{Amps}$$

This formula is useful for determining both the correct size of cable to use for an appliance and, in British systems, the correct size of cartridge fuse inserted in its plug.

Domestic installations

The comparison between the flow of water in a pipe and an electric current in a wire is not exact: electricity requires a closed loop—a circuit—in order to work.

Electricity comes into the home from a local transformer through an armoured service cable or via overhead wires. The service cable is connected to a fuse unit—called the company fuse—which is sealed by the electricity board or company. From here, power flows along the live supply wire and through the meter to the consumer unit—a combined fuse box and main switch, one particular type of which is shown on page 2. The live supply wire is usually encased in two separate sheaths. The electricity then flows through your lights and appliances before returning to the local transformer along the neutral wire. A third wire, the earth, connects the appliance casing to the main fuse box casing and then to the ground. Unless a fault develops in the system, it carries no current.

Loop circuit

C: A typical loop electrical circuit, with each light or power outlet 'looped off' from the one before it. In circuits throughout Britain, the live wire is red, the neutral black, and the earth is bare copper covered with a green/yellow striped PVC sleeve whenever it is exposed. Loop circuits are not very common in Britain—the radial or ring main system is far more usual. Most loop circuits are, in fact, radial circuits which have been extended to create more socket outlets. The ground wire is bare copper, sometimes terminating in a green plastic-covered 'jumper'

Loop circuits

In the US and Canada—and most other

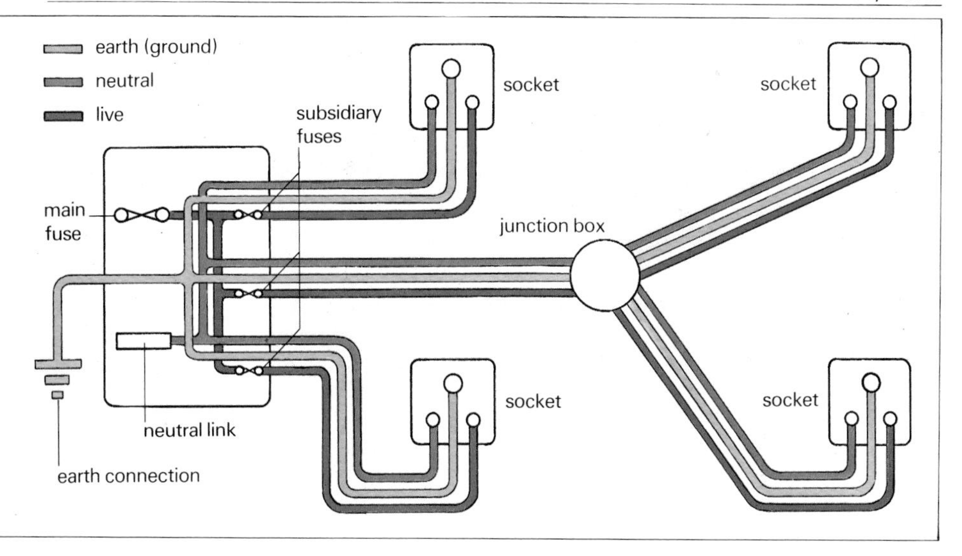

Radial circuit

D: A radial circuit of the type used in all British installations before 1947. The wire colours are exactly the same—red (live), black (neutral) and green/yellow (earth) as in newer wiring, but the sockets have no fuses at all, being protected instead by the fuses at the main switchboard. When re-wiring, the metal conduit from the old system is often useful as a means of feeding new wires through the wall plaster. But the ends of this metal conduit often have to be cut off so they cannot possibly touch any of the wires in either the new sockets or in the switches

parts of the world—power and lighting outlets are served by a system called *loop* wiring (fig. C). In this system the live, neutral and earth wires run outwards from the main switch to the first light (or power socket). From there they are 'looped off' to the second light; from the second light to the third; and so on. The number of lights and/or power outlets on each circuit is limited by local ordinances, so that every house needs a number of circuits. In some such systems, an individual circuit will supply both lighting and power outlets. In others, the lighting circuits and those that supply wall sockets (for appliances and so on) are separate installations.

In the UK, lighting circuits are still of the loop type. And up until 1947, power circuits were also of a similar type called *radial* wiring, in which each socket was served by a live, neutral and earth cable direct from the main fuse board. These older British systems are fitted with three varieties of round pin sockets rated at 15 amps, 5 amps and 2 amps. The configuration of the pins is the same in all three cases but reduces in size with current rating.

In all loop and radial systems, because the plugs that fit the sockets have no fuse of their own to help protect appliances, the circuit fuses in the fuse box must be kept to as low an amp rating as possible in order to give both the cable and the appliance a reasonable degree of protection from overload.

Ring-main system

In Britain, houses wired since 1947 use, for power socket circuits only, a different

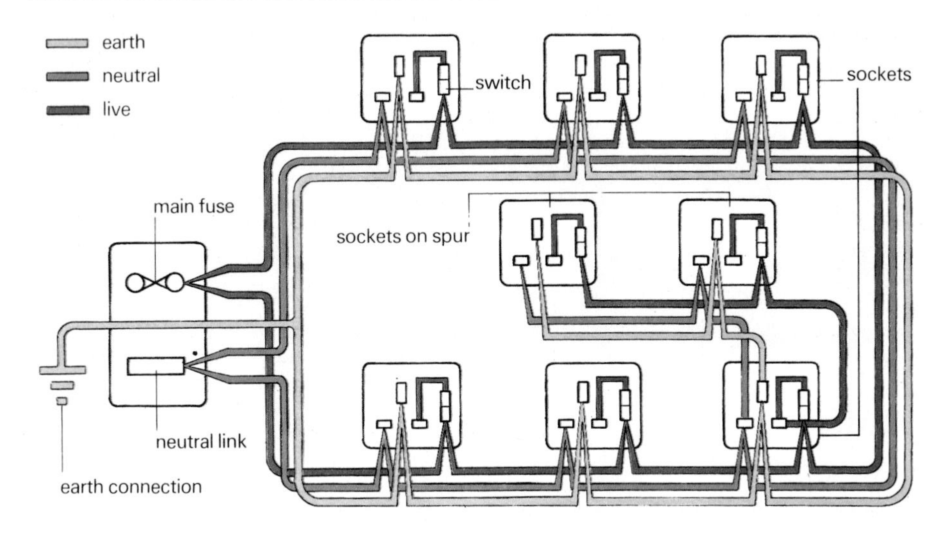

wiring system known as the *ring main* circuit (fig. E). In this system, the live, neutral and earth wires run in a complete circle from the main switch to each socket in turn, and then back to the consumer unit. There is generally one ring for each floor of a house, with 'spurs' reaching out from it to supply isolated sockets and appliances.

Plugs and socket outlets in ring-main circuits are of the 13 amp rectangular pin type. These are much safer than the old round-pin types because the sockets have shutters inside which automatically close when a plug is withdrawn. Furthermore, ring main plugs, unlike other types, carry their own cartridge fuses. This means that should an individual appliance become faulty, only the fuse in its own plug—and not the main fuse for the whole circuit—will 'blow' and break the circuit.

Earthing

Should a live wire come into contact with the metal casing of an appliance, anyone who touches the appliance is liable to receive a severe electric shock. For this reason, domestic appliances—apart from ones that are double insulated—have an earth wire connected to their outer casings and led indirectly to ground.

This is so that, if a live wire makes contact with the casing, the electricity will follow the path of least resistance to the ground. That is, it will flow through the earth wire instead of the person's body. At the same time, a live wire coming into contact with earthed metalwork will result in a large current flow that will blow the fuse.

Ring main

E: The ring main is a circuit exclusive to British houses. Each wire (the red 'live' for example) goes from the consumer unit to each socket in turn, and then back to the consumer unit, where the 'inward' and 'outward' ends are wired in together into the same terminal in the appropriate fuseholder. Each ring main is protected by its own fuse in the consumer unit. In addition, each appliance that it serves has a fuse in the plug, lessening the chance of actually blowing the main fuse and breaking the circuit. For this reason, the ring main is the safest and most widely used of all wiring systems

The electricity flows from the live wire in this way because it is trying to reach the neutral—which is connected to earth back at the electricity board transformer. This system has been found to be the safest way of disposing of unwanted current.

Fuses

A fuse is a deliberately weak link in the wiring, thinner than the wires on either side. If an overload occurs, the fuse wire melts and cuts off the current before the heat from the overloaded circuit can damage any equipment or actually cause a fire.

Fuses should always be of the nearest available size above the amperage of the appliance or circuit that they protect. Most electrical appliances have their wattage marked on a small plate fixed to the back or base of the unit. So, for an appliance connected to a ring main, you can use the formula above to find the amp rating and hence the correct fuse that should be inserted in the electrical appliance's plug.

For example, say an electric fire has a rating of 3 kilowatts and the voltage of the mains is 240 volts. The current taken by the fire is found by dividing the watts —3,000—by the volts—240—which gives a result of 12.5 amps. Therefore, the fire should be protected with a 13 amp fuse, which is the nearest higher size of fuse available.

In Britain, it is recommended practice to use 3 amp cartridge fuses, colour coded red, for all appliances rated up to 720 watts, and 13 amp fuses, colour coded brown, for all the other appliances up to a maximum electrical rating of 3 kilowatts.

Most plugs come fitted with 13 amp fuses, the largest available size. But some appliances can be damaged by a current of less than 13 amps. So it pays to use the formula and check that the plugs on appliances are fitted with the correct size of fuse.

F. Types of fuse holder available.
1: Bridge wire fuse holder. 2: Cartridge fuse holder. 3: In a protected wire fuse holder, the wire run all the way through a tube. 4: The wire in this type of holder runs right across an asbestos mat.

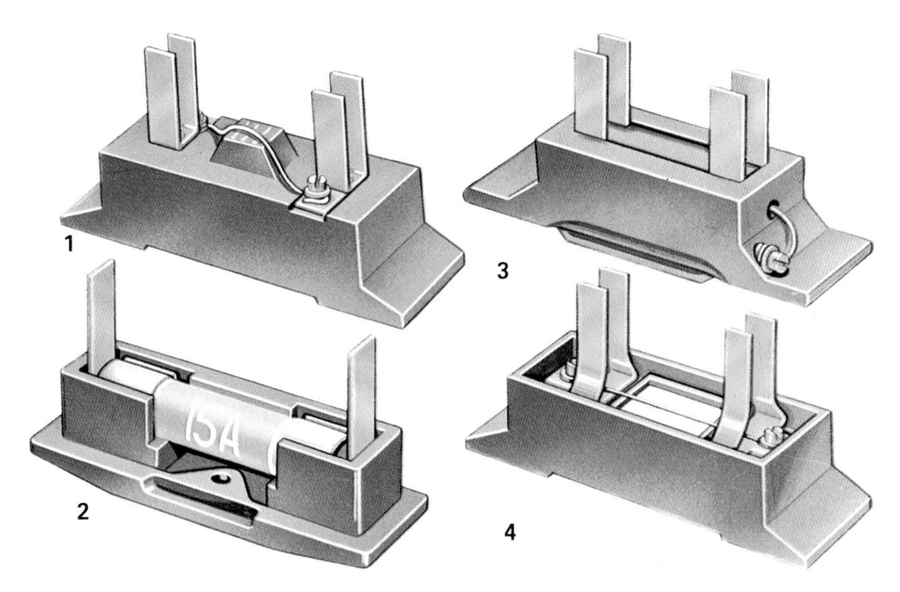

Mend a fuse

There are three main types of circuit fuse: wire fuses, cartridge fuses and circuit breakers. It is important to know which type you have and to keep a supply of spare fuse wire or cartridges. Circuit breakers need no spares as they are switches which shut off if the circuit is overloaded; you will need, however, to rectify the fault.

Most fuse boxes are covered by a plate which either clips on or screws into place. **Always turn off the mains switch before removing the plate or touching any fuse.**

With the plate removed you will see a row of fuse carriers. Some are colour coded on the back: white for 5 amp lighting circuits, blue for 15 amp heating circuits and red for 30 amp power socket circuits.

Take out the first fuse—the holders simply pull out and clip back into place—then replace the cover and turn the mains switch back on.

Check each circuit until you find the one that has stopped working.

When a fuse blows, the first thing to do is to discover the cause and rectify it. If you suspect that the failure is due to a faulty appliance, unplug it and do not use it again until it has been mended.

To mend a wire fuse, loosen the screws and discard the broken wire. Cut a new length of wire of the correct amperage rating. Wrap the ends of the wire around the screws in a clockwise direction so that when you retighten the screws the wire is not dislodged. Finally, replace the holder and fuse box cover and switch the power back on.

Wire a plug

G. Secure the flex in the cord grip by tightening its fixing screws. Strip the insulation from the end of the three wires, baring only enough wire to wrap safely around each terminal. Twist the strands and form a loop. Remove the plug cover by unscrewing the large screw between the pins to reveal the three terminals. The terminal at the top connects to the green and yellow earth wire. The brown live wire connects via the fuse to the live pin on the right and the blue neutral wire to the neutral terminal on the left. Some older appliances are coloured: green, for earth, red for live and black for neutral. Loosen the cord grip screws at the base of the plug. Remove the wire sheathing about 60mm and put under the grip and tighten the clamps. Cut the three wires and remove insulation. Twist the wires into strands, fix round each terminal and tighten the nut. Ensure that the right fuse is in place and then tighten the screw on the cover. Then test the plug to see if it is working correctly

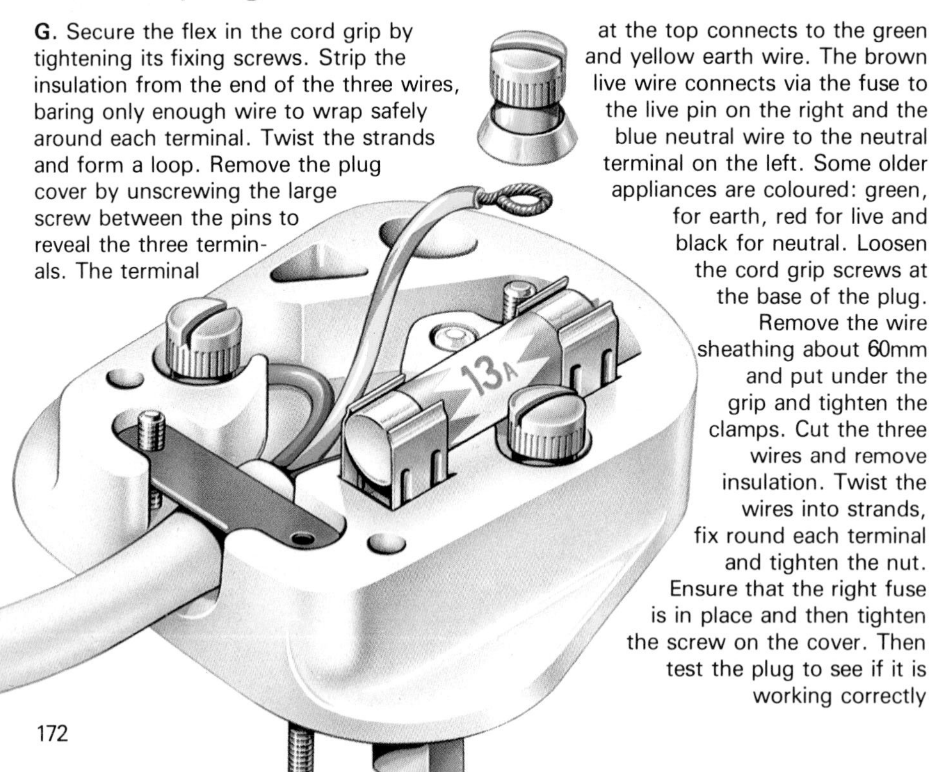

Understanding the wiring

The bulk of the work in any electrical project is actually installing all the wiring. In Britain you can do your own wiring, provided the work is always carefully inspected by the supply authority in your district.

Electrical wiring in the home is made up of *fixed* wiring and *flexible* wiring. Fixed wiring, housed within the 'fabric' of the home, carries electrical current from the consumer unit (main fuse box) to fixed outlets such as sockets and lights. Flexible wiring provides the final link from a socket to an electrical appliance, or from a ceiling rose to a lampholder.

Electrical cable

Fixed wiring consists of *cable*. This is made up of individual wires, or *conductors*, which carry the current, and *insulation* to prevent the current from leaking. In new wiring, the live and neutral conductors are usually insulated separately in colour-coded plastic sheaths then laid together with a bare earth wire in a common, outer sheath.

In some older installations, each conductor runs separately within its own inner, colour-coded and outer sheaths. In others the live and neutral conductors are housed in the same outer sheath but the earth insulation runs separately.

In **Britain**, the colour coding for cables is: red for live, black for neutral, and green/yellow striped for earth where this is insulated.

Modern cable is insulated with PVC which has an indefinite life and is impervious to damp and most common chemicals. Older installations may have been wired with rubber-insulated cable. This has a life of only about 30 years, after which it may begin to break up and become a potential danger. If your wiring is of this type, do not attempt to extend it, but replace it with the PVC type.

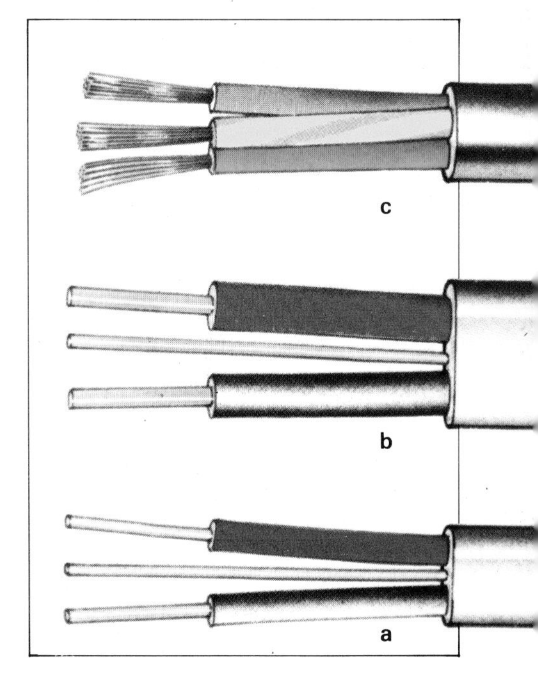

A. Some types of flex and cable that are in common usage at the present time in the UK. **(a)** Twin and earth cable used for the low amperage lighting circuits. Red is live, black is usually neutral, but might be live if connected to a light switch. **(b)** The same sort of cable but larger and used particularly for ring mains which take higher amperage. **(c)** Flex—commonly used for connecting plugs on appliances. The colour coding is different

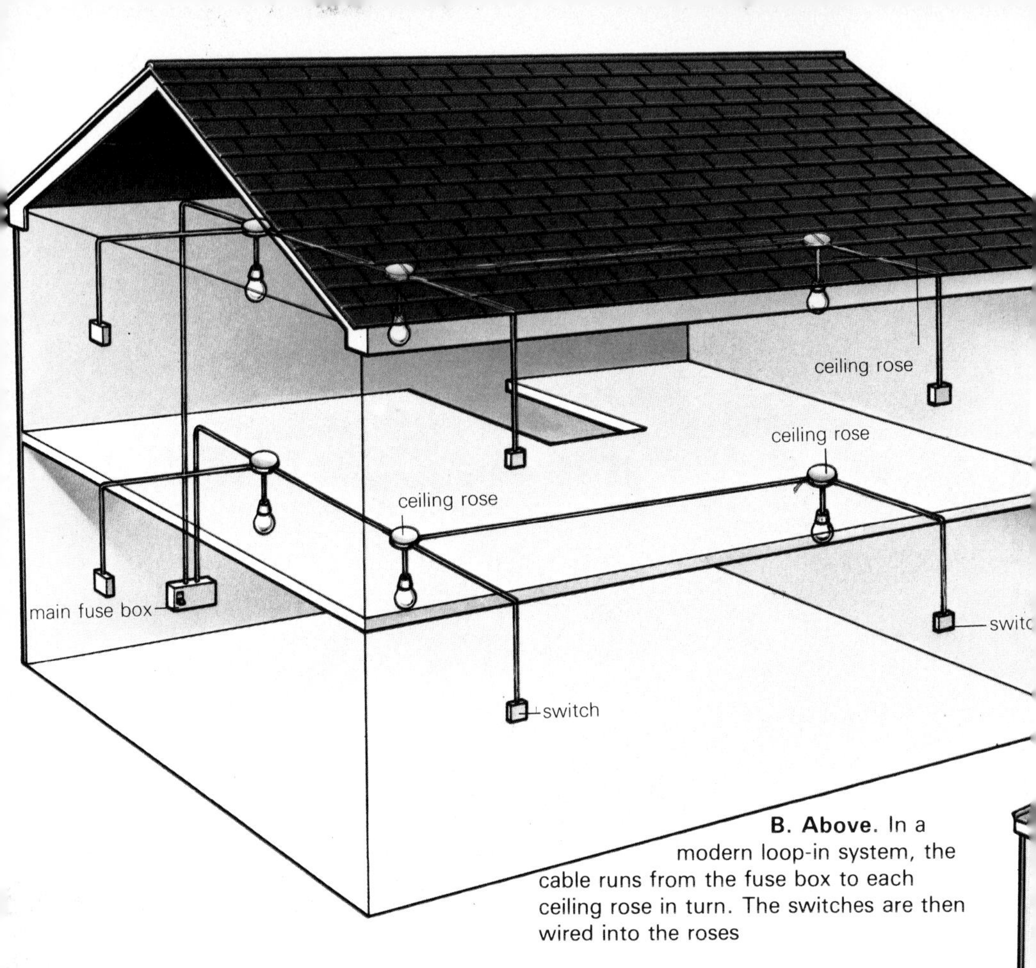

B. Above. In a modern loop-in system, the cable runs from the fuse box to each ceiling rose in turn. The switches are then wired into the roses

Fixed wiring runs around the home hidden beneath floorboards and buried in walls. When recessed in solid plaster, the cable is protected by a length of plastic or metal tube called a *conduit*. Beneath floorboards, the cable can run freely along the sides of, or through holes bored in, the floor joists.

When laid beneath floorboards, the cable should really be quite slack, but well supported—either by lying on the ceiling of the floor below, or by being carefully secured in place with strong cable clips.

Electrical flex

The conductors in flexible wiring, or *flex*, are made up of a number of thin wires. This enables them to stand up to repeated twisting and coiling, as occurs when the flex is wrapped around an unused appliance. But though flex is strong along its length, it should never be strained at the ends. Never pull a plug out of a socket by the flex or you may strain the terminals and pull the wires loose, making the plug and flex potentially very dangerous.

In **Britain**, the conductors in three-core flex are colour coded brown for live, blue for neutral, green and yellow for earth. Older appliances, of which there may still be several in existence, may have flex with the same colour coding as

Right: In a junction-box lighting circuit, each ceiling rose and switch is wired to a junction box above the ceiling

cable: red (live), black (neutral) and green (earth).

The two-core flex for double-insulated appliances requiring no earth is not always colour coded. The conductors in a table lamp flex, for example, are often insulated in transparent plastic because on non-earthed appliances, it does not matter which conductor is actually connected to which terminal.

There are various thicknesses of flex conductor—appliances of high wattage ratings requiring thicker conductors than the ones which have a lower rating.

If you need to lengthen a flex for any reason, make sure that the new length is of the same type as the existing flex and use a factory-made connector of the correct amp rating to connect the two. Remember never to use insulating tape to join the conductors together.

Lighting circuits

Older houses often have *junction-box* lighting circuits. In this system, the cable runs from the fuse box to junction boxes above the ceiling. Separate cables then run from the junction boxes to ceiling roses and light switches. You should not add a light to a junction-box circuit without first seeking expert electrical advice.

In the modern *loop-in* system the wiring is continuous, running from the fuse box to each ceiling rose in turn. The switches are wired directly to the roses. A light controlled by its own switch can be added to a loop-in system by wiring an extension from the circuit cable running into an existing ceiling rose.

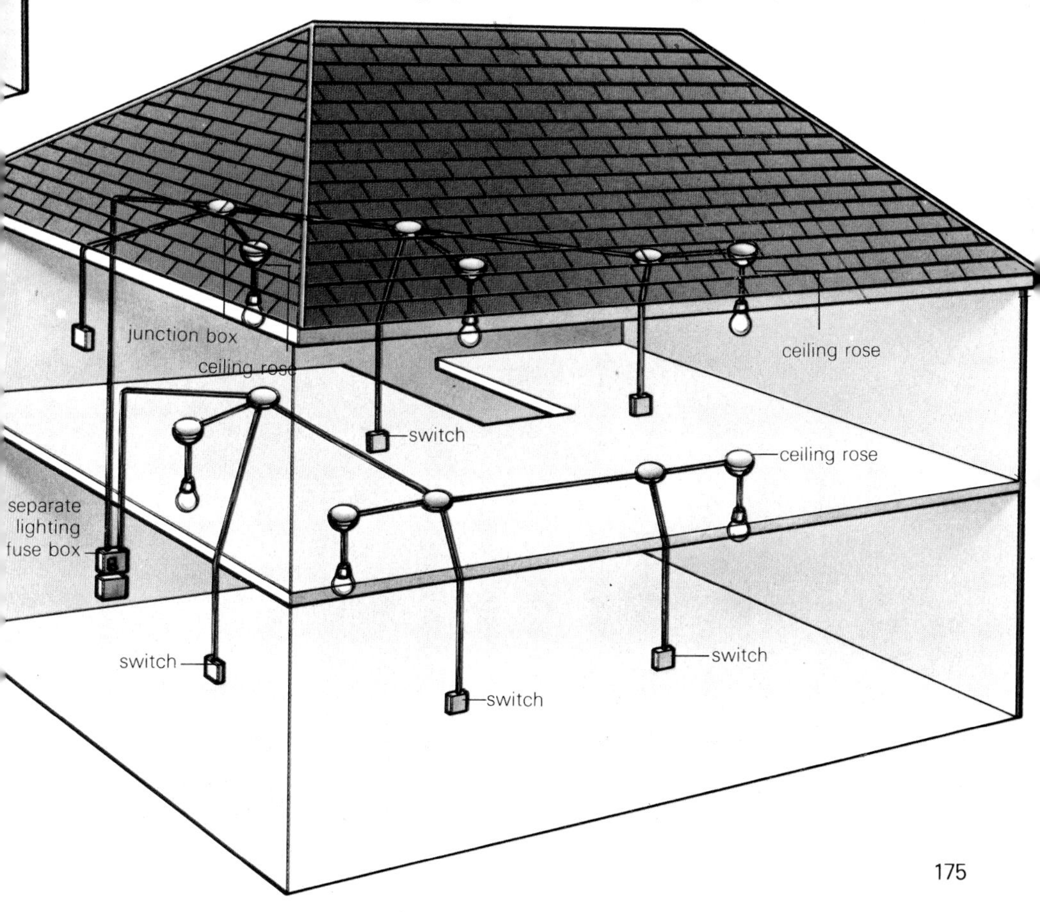

An extra light in the ceiling

Installing an extra light connected to an existing one, and controlled by the same switch, is a straightforward project.

The main items you need are a lampholder and a new ceiling rose. For connecting these two, buy $1mm^2$ flex. If the lampholder you plan to use is brass, it will have to be earthed, so buy three-core flex. Otherwise buy two-core. For connecting the new ceiling rose to the old one, buy $1mm^2$ twin-with-earth cable, allowing about 0.5m extra. Also buy a short length of 2mm green/yellow PVC sleeving to insulate each earth wire.

Decide where you want the light and drill a hole in the ceiling.

From the floor above, locate the hole and the existing ceiling rose. Enlarge the hole with a 13mm bit.

To mount the new ceiling rose base, a piece of 150mm × 25mm timber is fitted between the joists over the hole. Measure the distance between one of the joists and the hole and transfer the measurement to the piece of board. Drill a 13mm hole in the board, fit it over the hole in the ceiling and attach it with angle brackets to the joists on either side. You can now fix the rose base to the ceiling below.

Go back into the ceiling and run a length of cable from the existing light's ceiling rose to the new rose. If the cable route is parallel with the joists the cable can lie unclipped between them. If it runs at right angles to joists which are carrying floorboards, however, you will have to drill holes through the joists. Drill these at least 50mm from the tops of the joists to prevent damage from nails.

Next, prepare the cable for connection. First slit it for about 50mm from the end by sliding the blade of a handyman's knife between the live wire and the bare earth wire. With the sheathing removed for about 50mm (fig. 2), strip about 6mm of insulation from each wire.

Left: An extra light can be readily fitted to a ceiling to bring a gloomy, dull corner of a room to life

Wiring the new ceiling rose

Return to the floor below and prepare both ends of the flex that will run from the ceiling rose to the lampholder. Remove about 75mm of sheathing from the end to be connected to the ceiling rose and 50mm from the end for the lampholder. Sleeve the bare earth wire of the new cable (fig. 2) and connect the cable and the flex to the ceiling rose. It does not matter which of the ceiling rose terminals you use as long as you group the wires correctly in the same terminal block—the two lives (red cable and brown flex) together; the two neutrals (black cable and blue flex) together; and both earth wires together if your flex has them.

Tighten all the terminal screws and hook the flex wires over the two anchor pieces in the base of the ceiling rose. Slip the ceiling rose cover up over the flex and screw it onto the base. Then connect the lampholder to the other end of the flex, again hooking the wires over the anchor pieces and again checking the terminals.

Wiring-in the extension

Before wiring-in the extension, you need to isolate the electric circuit you plan to work on. To do this, turn on the light to which the extension is to be made, and keep pulling fuses out of the consumer unit until the light goes off. (Turn off the power at the main switch as you withdraw or replace each fuse.) Once you have found and removed the fuse for the circuit you want to work on you can turn the main switch on again. This allows you, if you need light during the wiring process, to plug a standard lamp into a wall socket.

Since both lights are to be operated by the same switch, they are connected to the same terminals in the lighting circuit.

So the first thing to do is to identify the terminals to which the **flex** of the existing light pendant is connected. These are the terminals to which the live and neutral wires of the new cable must also be connected.

If the existing pendant flex has coloured conductor wires, wire the red live wire of the new cable to the same terminal as the brown flex wire of the old light pendant. Similarly, wire the black neutral wire of the new cable to the same terminal as the blue flex wire.

If the existing flex is not colour-coded, you cannot tell which side is the live. Your new cable must then be connected to the same terminals as the **old flex**, and not to any other terminal.

In either case, you may find you have to push one old wire and one new one into the same terminal hole.

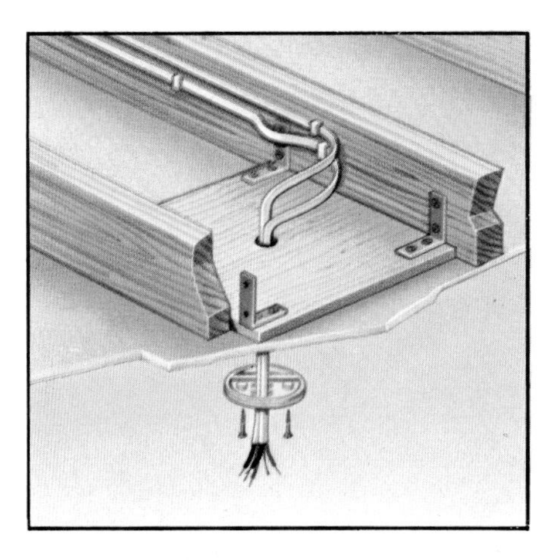

1 Drill a hole in a board and fit it. The cables go into the hole and the rose

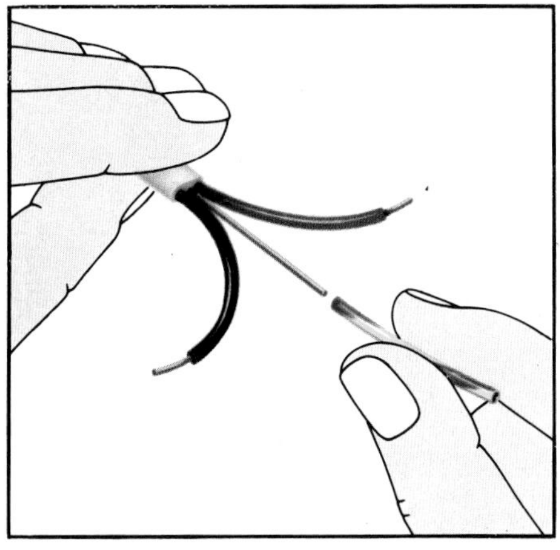

2 Before connecting a cable, sleeve the earth wire with PVC sleeving

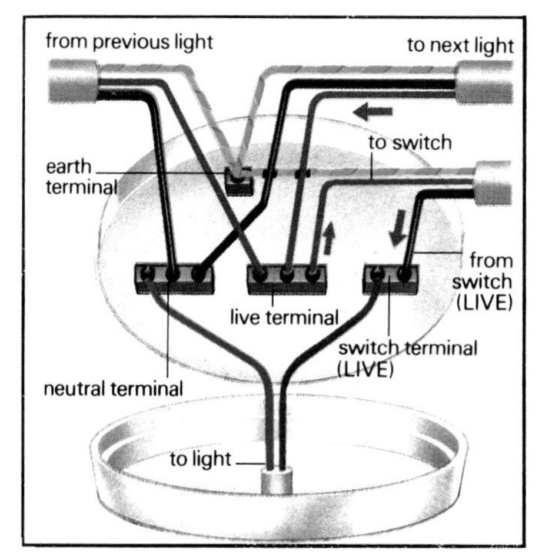

3 In a modern rose, identify the groups of terminals

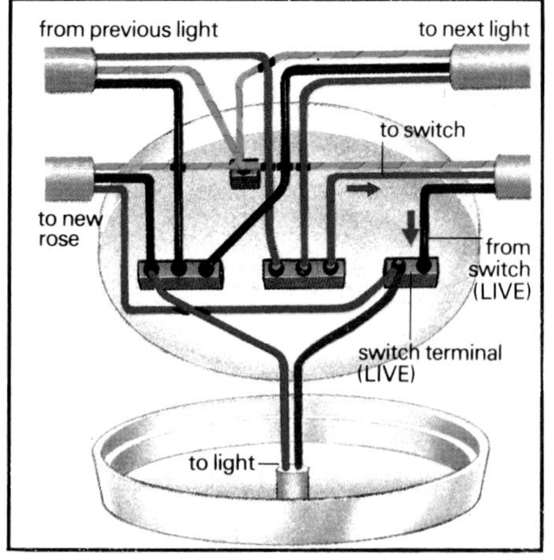

4 Connect the cable for the new rose to the terminals

Persistent fuse blowing

A circuit fuse is relatively simple to mend, but when a fuse continues to blow each time you replace it, either the circuit is overloaded—in which case you should switch off some appliances—or there is a serious fault somewhere along it which must be located and rectified before the circuit will function again. On no account must you replace the blown fuse with a length of wire or any other bridge, such as a nail. To do so would be tantamount to lighting a fire.

Note: Never work on a circuit until you are certain that it is not live.

Having a thorough understanding of the theory of fuses and the faults which cause them to blow will help you to maintain the electrical circuits around the home. And even if you do not intend to carry out the repair work yourself, being able to locate the area of a fault will help to save on the cost of repair.

Why fuses blow

A fuse is a deliberately weak link included in the wiring of a circuit. If a surge of current occurs in the circuit, caused by a wiring fault of some kind or by overloading, the thin fuse wire is melted by the resulting extra heat generated by the current surge.

Fuses often blow because two wires in the circuit are in contact with one another. If the live and the neutral wires make contact, this is called a short circuit; when the live wire touches the earth it is called a line/earth fault or a short to earth. Or the live wire may be in contact with earthed metalwork —such as the mounting box of a flush-mounted light switch—to which the earthing core is always attached via a screw-type earth terminal.

Although a fuse is a 'weak' link in the wiring, it requires quite a large amount of current before it blows. For example, a cartridge fuse requires a current of one and a half times its current rating before it melts, and a wire fuse may take a current of twice its rating.

But when a short circuit occurs, the resulting current surge is enormous. This is also the case with a line/earth fault—if the earthing is in good condition. If the earthing is faulty, there may be insufficient current to blow the fuse, in which case the fault will remain undetected and a potential fire hazard—the earth return will heat up due to the high resistance it meets.

A fault in an electrical appliance is unlikely to keep blowing the circuit fuse, if the circuit is protected by a cartridge

1 This type of protected wire fuse holder has a window to let you see if the wire is broken. Cut a length of wire of the same amperage and fix it in place

2 In the case of a blowing fuse in a lighting circuit, replace the fuse then test each light. Start at the lampholder

3 Check that the wires in the rose are intact and that there is no contact between the earth and a live terminal

fuse in the appliance's plug as in UK 13 amp ring main circuits. But a circuit fuse may blow if the circuit is heavily overloaded—drawing far too much current.

Miniature circuit breakers

All the faults and checks described below apply equally whether your consumer unit is fitted with wire or cartridge fuses, or with the modern miniature circuit breakers. A miniature circuit breaker (MCB) is a single-pole switch which is automatically cut off when excessive current caused by a fault flows right through the circuit.

The principal differences between MCBs and normal fuses are that they require less current to shut them off than is needed to blow a fuse of the same current rating, and they operate more quickly. When a fault in the circuit persists, the circuit breaker trips immediately an attempt is made to switch it on.

Cable faults

If a circuit fuse continues to blow each time it is replaced, a possible cause is that two wires are in contact with each other somewhere along the cable of the particular circuit in question.

If the wiring in your home is old, persistent fuse blowing may just be an indication that the wiring needs replacing altogether.

Trying to locate a specific fault on a relatively recent cable is a tedious job which is best left to an expert using special test equipment.

Cables are often damaged in the course of alterations to a home, so begin by checking the wiring around the site of any recent work.

Also check any recently installed wiring: you may have disturbed the old when running additional cable to new lights or socket outlets, or you may have failed to make proper connections to the new wiring.

Lighting circuits

If the main fuse of a lighting circuit keeps blowing, turn off all the light switches fed by that circuit, shut off the electricity supply at the mains then replace the fuse.

Turn on the mainswitch, then switch on each light switch in turn. When the fuse blows, you will have found the part of the circuit in which the fault lies. Now you must track it down.

4 If necessary, try to inspect the underfloor boxes for clues such as a smoky discoloration or melted insulation

5 A typical source of trouble is an unsheathed earth wire meeting a live terminal behind the switch plate

The first thing to check is the flexible wiring which connects the lampholder to the ceiling rose. This may be worn or damaged, particularly if it is of the obsolete, twisted twin type. Once more, turn off the electricity supply and remove the relevant fuse holder. At the light, unscrew the lampholder to check the condition of the flex and make sure that the cores are securely connected to the terminals. If necessary, renew the faulty flex.

Now check the wiring in the ceiling rose by unscrewing the cover from the base which is fixed to the ceiling. A common problem here is that the earth wires are left unsheathed and make contact with one of the live terminals in the rose. If you find that this is the case, disconnect the wires from the earthing terminal, slip lengths of green and yellow PVC sleeving over them—leaving about 6mm of bare wire protruding—and reconnect them.

Where a bare earth wire is not the problem, check the condition of the remaining wires. If the insulation of these is all intact and they are connected tightly to the correct terminals, replace the rose cover and turn your attention to the light switch itself.

Remove the cover plate of the switch and check the wiring. The most likely fault is, again, that the earth wire is bare and in contact with the live terminal. But it may be that the fixing screws of the cover plate have penetrated the insulation of one of the wires and that, with a flush-mounted switch, a section of live wire is in contact with the earthed metal box.

If it is the live return wire that is damaged in this way, the fuse will blow only when the switch is turned on; but if it is the live feed wire which is damaged, the fuse will blow whether it is on or off. The latter fault is easily recognized by the burnt insulation and smoke marks around the damaged area.

Where the area of damage is slight, you can make do by firmly wrapping some insulating tape around the bare section then laying the wires carefully back into the box so that the screws will not interfere with them. But if the damage is particularly bad—such as where a wire has almost been severed—the length of cable must be replaced.

If, after examining the lampholder, ceiling rose, switch and any accessible

6 The best way to insulate the bare insulation wire is to disconnect it then slip on a suitable length of green and yellow PVC sleeving

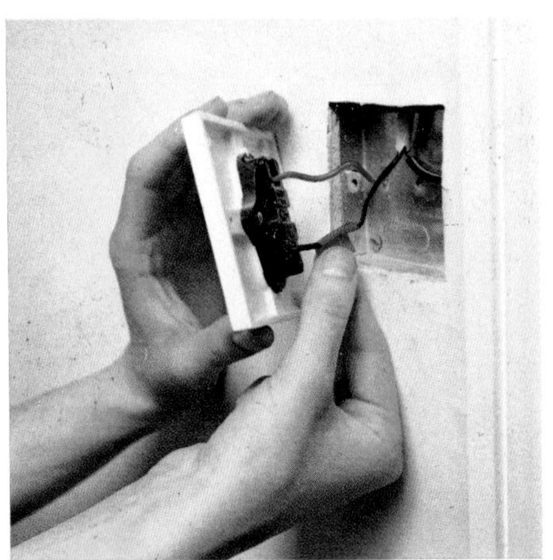

7 In the case of slight damage to the neutral or live wires, bind the affected portion tightly with insulating tape and then refit the switch

cable you are still unable to find the fault, call in expert help.

Power circuits

When the circuit fuse of a ring main circuit continues to blow, the fault is unlikely to be in one of the portable appliances plugged into the circuit: when these are faulty, the cartridge fuse in the plug will blow leaving the circuit fuse intact. However, before you start work on locating the fault, unplug all appliances and check that the fuse in each plug is of the correct amp rating.

On a ring main, the next step is to check the 30 amp main fuse. Very occasionally, when the circuit is already loaded to near its capacity, a fault on a small appliance may cause it to blow.

Other than an overload or a damaged circuit cable, the most likely fault in a ring main circuit is in the mounting box behind one of the socket outlets. Turn off the electricity supply at the mains and examine each socket in turn.

Unscrew the cover plate of the first socket and examine the wiring attached to the terminals on the back: the likely faults are similar to those that are found in lighting switches.

Earth wires are often left uninsulated and therefore can easily make contact with the live terminal. This is particularly likely on a socket outlet as the earthing core is connected to a terminal on the back of the socket plate, rather than to one on the box, and can therefore be bent into a dangerous position. Cover with lengths of green and yellow PVC sleeving, then check the insulation of the live and neutral wires. These sometimes perish, if the terminals are not tightened properly or where a cheap—or faulty—plug or adaptor has been used in the socket and has overheated. Alternatively, the insulation may have been pierced by the socket's fixing screws. Deal with this problem as described above and, if necessary, use shorter screws to fix the socket plate into place.

When you have checked the first socket, replace the cover plate and move on to the next. Even if you think you have found and rectified the fault, it is worthwhile checking the remaining socket outlets.

If you do not find anything wrong with any of the sockets, the fault probably lies

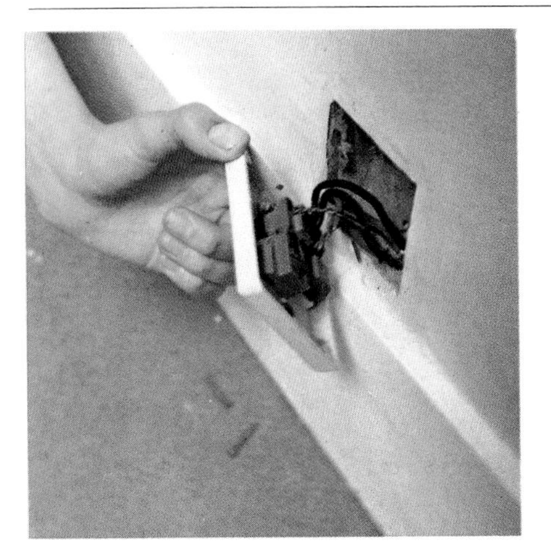

8 In the case of a ring main circuit, it is necessary to check each socket in turn. A common fault is a bare earth wire touching a live wire

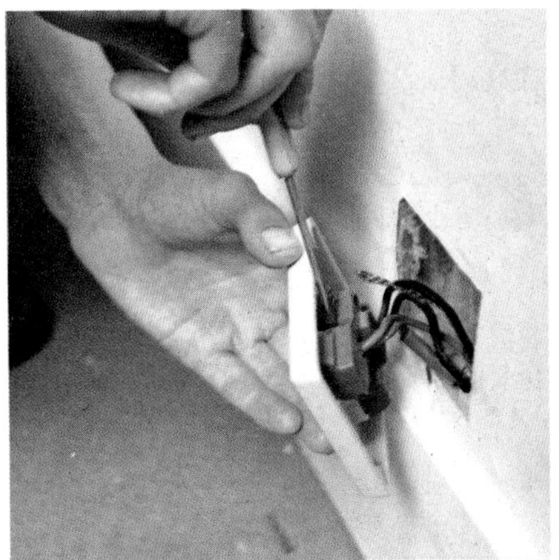

9 Undo the bare earth wire and refit the live wire to the live terminal. Then sheath the earth wire with PVC sleeving and reconnect to the socket

somewhere along the cable of the circuit, so it is best to call in expert assistance, such as a qualified electrician.

Cooker circuits

Because of the large amount of electricity it consumes, a free-standing electric cooker is always connected on a separate circuit protected by its own fuse in the main fuse box. The appliance is connected to its circuit by a special cooker control unit, which contains a switch and sometimes includes a separately controlled socket outlet. Neither the cooker nor its control unit contain a fuse, so a persistently blowing circuit fuse usually indicates a fault in either the control unit or in the appliance itself.

To find out whether the fault is in the unit or in the cooker itself, turn off the control switch, replace the circuit fuse with the relevant size of fuse wire or cartridge and turn on the power. If the fuse immediately blows again, the fault lies in the control unit or in the cable from the fuse board; with the power turned off, remove the unit's faceplate and inspect the wiring for damage as decribed above. If the fuse only blows when the cooker control switch is in the 'on' position, the fault is in the cooker itself and you should call in expert assistance to locate the fault.

Immersion heaters

An immersion heater is usually supplied directly from its own circuit fuse with no other fuse intervening. When this circuit fuse blows, the fault is most likely to be in the immersion heater itself and therefore requires expert attention.

Other circuits

Tracing faults on other sorts of circuit follows much the same methods as described above. First switch off at the mains, then unplug or disconnect all appliances and switch off lights on the faulty circuit. Switch on the mains, and carefully re-connect all appliances and switch on lights one by one until you find what causes the fuse to blow. Then check out the appliance or relevant part of the circuit, following the details above.

Whatever repairs you make to the fusebox, sockets or wiring, be sure to turn off the electricity supply at the mains switch before starting work.

How to install sockets

Today, the average home is equipped with a far greater number of electrical appliances than was the case a few years ago. And if many of these appliances are in use at the same time, there may not be enough sockets.

Socket outlets

In the UK, the sockets that have three rectangular holes to accept the pins of 13 amp plugs are used on ring main circuits and on some partially modernized radial circuits. Socket outlets with round holes for 2 amp, 5 amp and 15 amp plugs are used only on radial circuits and usually indicate that the circuit is over 30 years old.

Modern socket outlets can be flush- or surface-mounted. The flush type is screwed onto a metal box which houses the cables and is recessed into the wall. For surface mounting, the same sort of socket is used, but this time screwed to a plastic box which is fixed to the wall surface.

Socket cover plates and, in the case of surface-mounted sockets, the box as well, are usually made of white plastic. But for installations in places like garages where outlets have to be more durable, sockets with metal cover plates and boxes are available.

In the UK, regulations require the live and neutral holes of 13 amp sockets to be fitted with protective shutters to prevent people (children especially) from poking metal objects inside with possibly fatal results. Most sockets also have a built-in switch to minimize the danger of touching live parts when you insert or remove a plug. Some switched sockets include a neon indicator light to show when the socket is on. Switches are usually single-pole, cutting off the supply in the live wire only. This is usually sufficient: to totally isolate an appliance, remove the plug.

In a bathroom, where the presence of water increases the risk of electric shocks, the only sockets that can be installed are those specially designed for electric razors.

Plug adaptors

In rooms where there are too few sockets to go round, or where appliances are too far from free sockets, plug adaptors—sometimes called socket adaptors—are often used to plug two or three appliances into the same socket.

A two-way adaptor with a fuse of the correct size is satisfactory for temporarily connecting low wattage appliances, such as table lamps or the hi-fi. But it is not advisable to use an adaptor for long periods or to plug in a high wattage appliance, such as a bar heater. By far the best approach is to add extra sockets.

Adding socket outlets

If a room has an inadequate number of socket outlets and you have a ring main circuit, you can add extra ones without too much difficulty.

A ring circuit can have an unlimited number of socket outlets and, ideally, each room should have at least four—more in a kitchen. The circuit should serve a floor area of not more than $100m^2$, which is more than the area of an average two-storey house. So, if you decide to install extra sockets, there is no limit to the number you can add as long

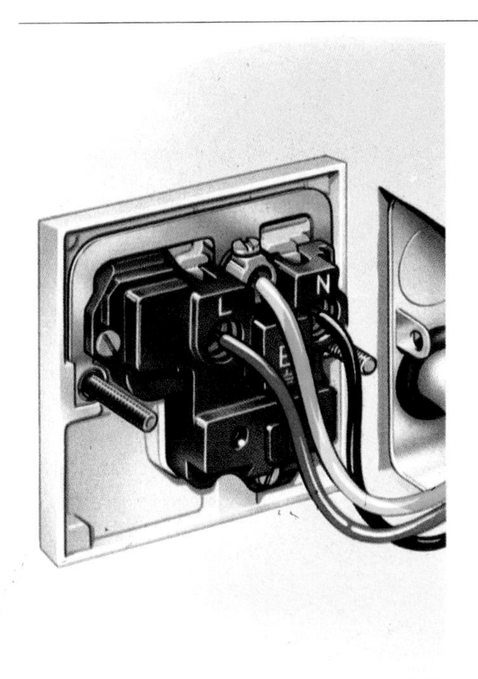

A. Wiring up a single socket. Strip about 20mm insulation from the cores and then connect to the terminals

as they do not extend the circuit beyond the 100m^2 maximum.

Sockets are almost always mounted on a wall and should be positioned at a minimum height of 150mm above the floor level, or the working surface in a kitchen.

Though new sockets can be installed directly from the ring, it is often easier to wire it on a *spur*—an extension taken from the back of an existing socket.

Each existing socket outlet, or double outlet, can supply only *one* extra outlet—one single or one double socket.

Single into twin socket

An even easier method of adding sockets is by converting single socket outlets into double ones. Where single sockets have been installed, the number of outlets in a room can be doubled, though none will be in new positions.

If you are working in an area of good natural light, turn off the electricity supply at the mains. If not, isolate the supply by removing the relevant circuit fuse and leave the lighting circuits functioning.

You must now find out whether or not your chosen socket is suitable for conversion. If it is on the main circuit, the socket can be converted without any problems. But if it is on a spur, no more outlets can be added to the spur.

To check the position of the socket in the circuit, unscrew the cover plate, ease it from the wall and examine the wiring. Two sets of wires connected to the plate suggests that the socket is probably not a spur. To make quite sure, examine the wiring in the nearest sockets on either side. If either of these has one set,or three sets of wires, the socket is on a spur and should not be converted. If the selected socket has three sets of wires, it is supplying a spur already and so cannot be used.

When you have satisfied yourself that the socket outlet is suitable, undo the terminal screws holding the cable cores into the plate and gently remove the cores inside. If the live, neutral and earth cores are twisted together, untwist them and then undo the mounting screws holding the metal box into its recess. Prise the box from the recess with a screwdriver or an old chisel.

To house the new, twin socket box, the recess must be extended. Mark the position on the wall and cut out the plaster and brickwork to the depth of the new box with a hammer and bolster. Knock out the punched holes in the box to accept the cables, feed these through, and position and screw the box into place using wall plugs. Twist the wires together again and wire up the twin cover plate as shown in fig. E. Screw the plate on to the box, switch on the power and test the socket.

The above procedure also applies to fitting a surface-mounted twin socket, though in this case no recess is needed—the box simply screws on to the wall.

A spur from the ring main

Running a spur from an existing socket means that you can place the new socket almost anywhere you like.

To wire the spur, you need a sufficient length of $2.5mm^2$ cable 'twin with earth' to stretch from the existing socket to the site of the new one. You also need oval PVC conduit with securing clips and about 1m of green and yellow PVC sleeving. Choose as your source for the spur a socket as close to the proposed site as possible.

Before starting work, isolate the supply. Unscrew the cover of a possible socket and carefully compare the wiring. If a spur has already been taken from it or the socket itself is on a spur, it is not suitable. Unscrew a suitable socket and remove and untwist the wires. Prise the box away from its recess and knock out the relevant punched holes.

Hold the new box in position on the wall and draw around it to mark out its recess. Using a straight edge as a guide, draw two parallel lines—25mm apart—between the new position and the existing recess, for the cable chase. Next cut the new recess and the chase with a hammer and bolster. The chase should be about 6mm deeper than the thickness of the conduit.

Knock out one of the punched holes in the new box and install it in its recess. Refit the box of the other socket as well, then cut the conduit to length so that it will protrude about 10mm into each box when installed in the chase. Fit the conduit, secure it and make good the plaster.

Wait until the plaster is dry then push the cable through the condúit so that about 200mm of cable protrude into each box, then remove the outer sheathing back to the edge of the box at both ends. Strip about 20mm of insulation from the live and neutral cores and sleeve the earth wires with lengths of green and yellow PVC sleeving, leaving about 20mm of bare wire protruding. Wire up the new socket cover plate as shown in

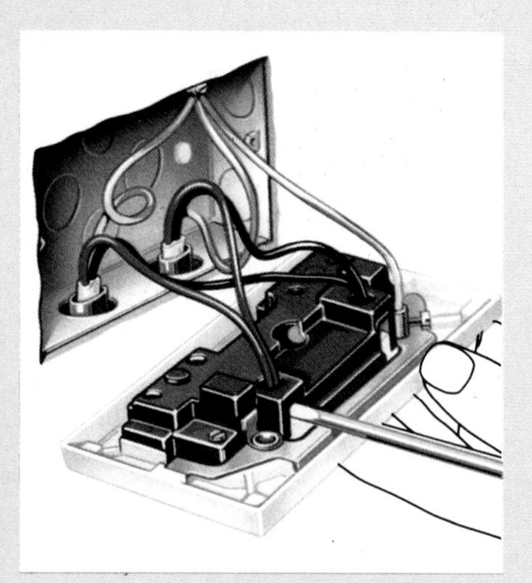

B. Unscrew the cover of an existing socket to check that it is suitable for connecting to a spur

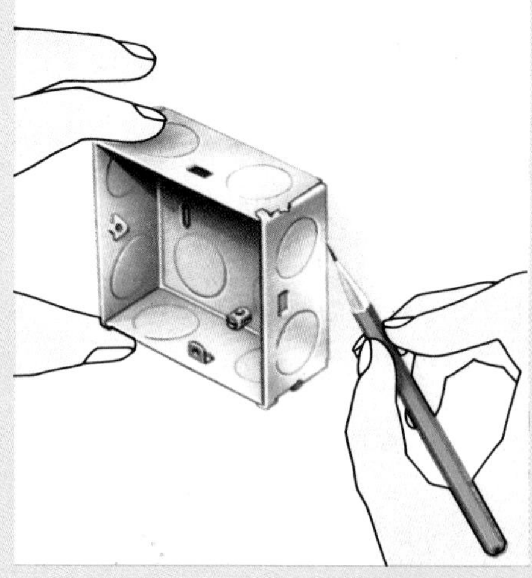

C. Mark the position for the new spur socket, then cut the recess for the box and the cable chase

fig. A and screw the plate in place.

Returning to the other box, connect the three red wires together and the three black wires together. Sleeve the earth wires if necessary, then twist together as shown in fig. F. Wire the plate up, carefully as shown in fig. F. Then screw it back on to the wall. Finally, switch back on at the main fusebox and plug an appliance into the new socket to check that it works correctly. Recheck wiring if necessary.

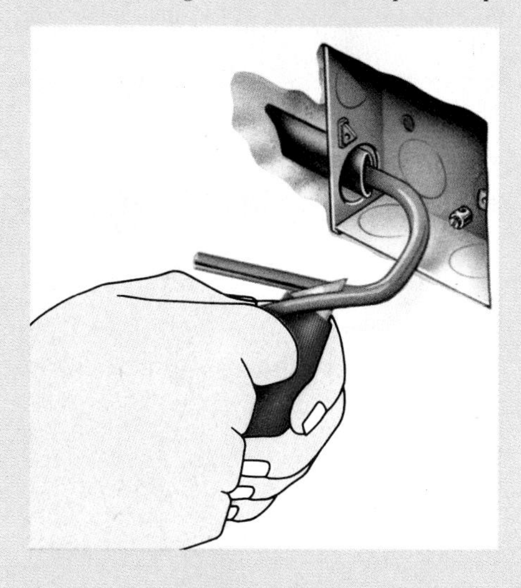

D. Push a cable through the conduit from the original box. Then remove the outer sheathing

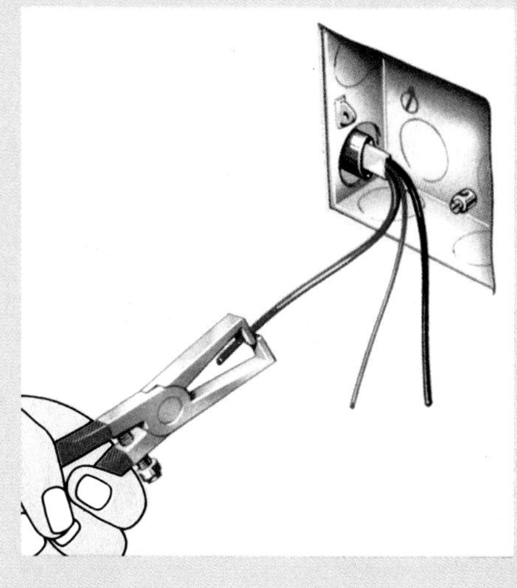

E. With the sheathing removed back to the edge of the box, bare the ends of the wires with wire strippers

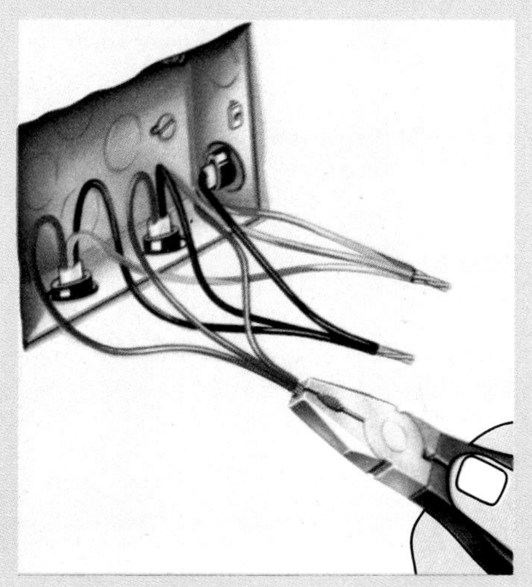

F. With older cables, using separate strands, twist the ends of each group of wires firmly together

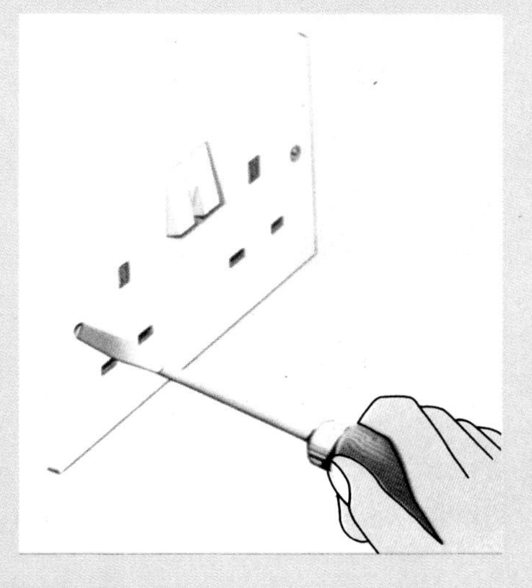

G. Wire up the cover plate and screw it back into place on its mounting box. Then test the new socket

Light switches

Having light available at the flick of a switch is something we have all come to take for granted. But there is more to domestic switching circuitry than the simple on/off device. Innovations like two-way switching and dimmer switches make lighting more flexible.

Lighting switches

Switches work by interrupting the flow of electricity through wires connecting the mains supply to the light itself. Most switches are *single-pole*—they make or break the supply passing through only one wire. It is important that this is the live wire of a circuit so that the light is isolated from the live supply when the switch is off. In no circumstances should a single-pole switch be inserted into the neutral pole; if it were, the light fitting would be live even when the switch was in the off position.

The type of switch usually installed in UK homes is an all-insulated unit with rocker action. This has a plastic or metal cover plate which is usually part of the switchgear. For surface mounting, the switch can be screwed to a plastic box which is fixed to the wall surface; for flush mounting, it can be screwed to a recessed metal box.

Pull-cord switches are used in bathrooms and kitchens where it is particularly important that people with wet hands cannot directly touch electrical fittings.

Note: Always remember *never* work on a circuit until you are certain that it is not live.

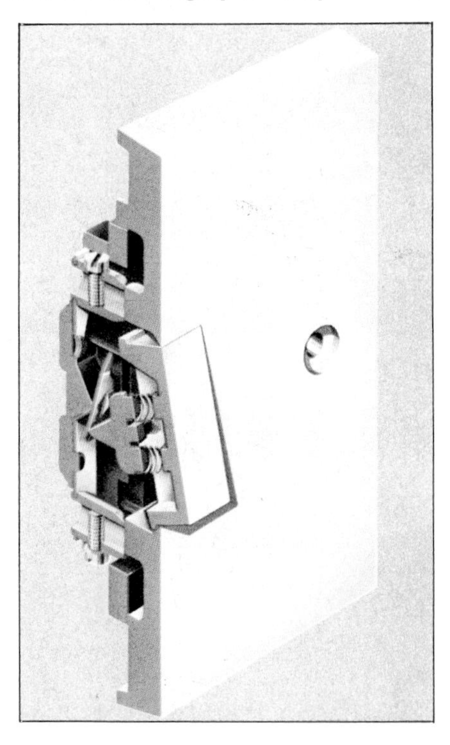

A. A cross-section through a rocker switch. This is the switch most commonly used in British houses. It is an all-insulated unit with a rocker action

Two-way switching

It is often convenient to be able to switch on a light at either of two locations. Ordinary switches cannot do this independently of each other—you can always switch the light off at either switch, but you cannot always switch it on. If you want to switch at two places independently, then you need two-way switches.

An ordinary one-way switch has two terminals, one for the live feed and one for the live return, but a two-way switch needs three terminals, marked in the UK, *common*, *L1* and *L2*. In the basic two-way switching circuit, the switch drop is linked to the L1 and L2 terminals of the first switch, and its three terminals are then linked to the corresponding three terminals of the second two-way switch using three-core and earth cable.

Dimmer switches

As an alternative to a simple on/off switch, a dimmer switch greatly increases finger-tip control.

A dimmer switch is an electronic device, the main components of which are a semi-conductor called a *triac* and a printed circuit. Modern dimmer switches also contain a 2 amp fuse to protect the triac from the surge in current when a light bulb blows.

By rotating the knob of the dimmer, you can reduce the intensity of the light from the full, normal strength to any lower level: an effect which is achieved by blocking out part of the incoming current.

There are various types of dimmer switch on the market, the simplest and cheapest of which have a rotary dial which switches the light on and also controls the brightness. But this means that each time you switch on, you have to reset the desired level of illumination. Another type gets round the problem by having a normal rocker on/off switch alongside a rotary dimming wheel and a third type has a single knob with push/on, push/off switching action.

A more recent development in dimmer switches is the 'touch' dimmer. This has no moving parts, but is fitted instead with two separate touch pads. A quick tap of the finger on the upper pad turns the light on and a continued gentle touch raises the level of brightness. Touching the lower pad decreases the light intensity, and a quick tap turns the light off.

When choosing dimmer switches, bear in mind that fluorescent lights require a special type and that changes must be made to the light circuitry.

Multiple switches

If you want to control more than one light independently, then you will need, obviously, more than one switch. Although you can of course always have separate switches mounted in their own boxes, it is neater and easier if the switch mechanisms are close together, sharing a mounting box.

In the UK, this is usually done by using multi-gang switches. Up to three separately-controlled switch mechanisms can be mounted together on a plate that covers the same area as a standard, single-gang switch. Four- and six-gang switches are also available. All these multi-gang switches are of the two-way type, but of course any two-way switch can be used on a simple one-way circuit. Use the common and L1 terminals.

Damaged switches

To replace a damaged switch, turn off the electricity supply at the mains, remove the switchplate from its box and disconnect the wires attached to the terminals.

If the damaged switch is a two-way switch, note which wire goes to which terminal and be sure to replace it with a switch of a similar type. If more than one wire is connected to any one terminal, keep these joined together and treat them as one wire. Wire up the replacement switch in the same manner as the old one and screw the cover plate into place.

If you have a cord-operated switch that is sluggish in action, turn off the power, remove the cover and squirt aerosol lubricant into the mechanism. When a cord snaps or is pulled out of its socket, it is better to buy and fit a replacement cord.

If a dimmer switch fails, isolate the supply, remove the switchplate and check that the wiring is correct and intact. If it is, the problem is probably due to a current overload having damaged the triac or some other component. In this case, the dimmer will have to be returned to the manufacturer.

One-way to two-way switching

Almost any one-way switched light can be converted simply and economically to a more convenient two-way system. For this you require two two-way switches:

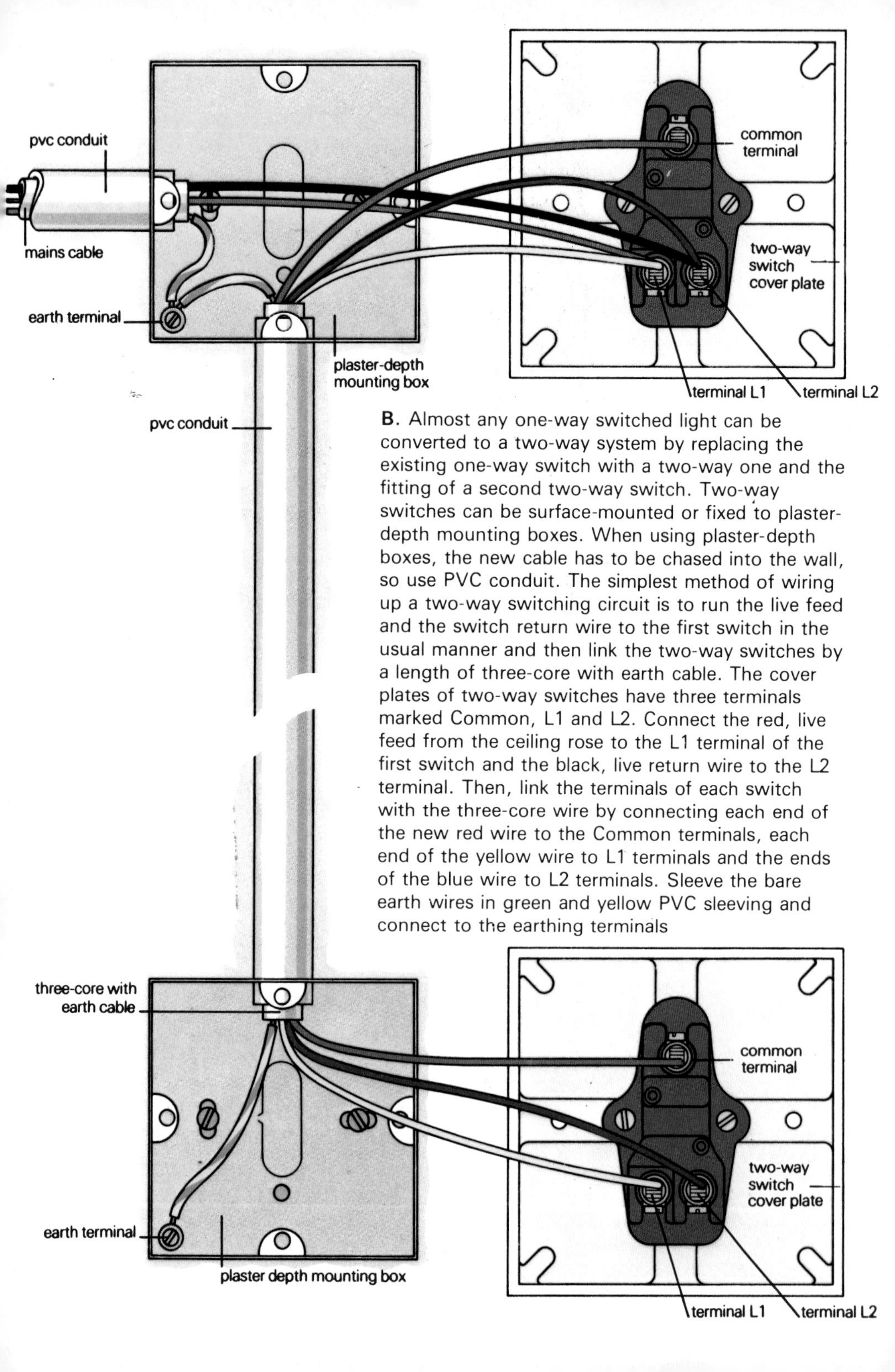

B. Almost any one-way switched light can be converted to a two-way system by replacing the existing one-way switch with a two-way one and the fitting of a second two-way switch. Two-way switches can be surface-mounted or fixed to plaster-depth mounting boxes. When using plaster-depth boxes, the new cable has to be chased into the wall, so use PVC conduit. The simplest method of wiring up a two-way switching circuit is to run the live feed and the switch return wire to the first switch in the usual manner and then link the two-way switches by a length of three-core with earth cable. The cover plates of two-way switches have three terminals marked Common, L1 and L2. Connect the red, live feed from the ceiling rose to the L1 terminal of the first switch and the black, live return wire to the L2 terminal. Then, link the terminals of each switch with the three-core wire by connecting each end of the new red wire to the Common terminals, each end of the yellow wire to L1 terminals and the ends of the blue wire to L2 terminals. Sleeve the bare earth wires in green and yellow PVC sleeving and connect to the earthing terminals

one to be fitted in place of the existing one-way switch and the other for fitting in your chosen new position.

Before you buy the new switches, turn off the electricity supply at the mains and remove the switchplate on the existing switch. If it has three terminals on the back marked as described above, it is a two-way switch wired for one-way operation and you need buy only one new two-way switch.

For mounting the wall switches you will need a mounting box—two, if you are replacing the existing switch with one of a different pattern. The boxes can be either flush- or surface-mounted.

Although switches can be wired in practice as shown in fig. A, this method is rarely used, and is particularly inconvenient when modifying existing wiring. The usual method makes use of special cable—1.0mm^2 three-core and earth cable. There are three insulated cores coloured red, yellow and blue, plus a bare earth wire. Buy enough to run from the existing switch position all the way to your additional switch.

You also need a length of green and yellow PVC sleeving for sheathing the ends of the bare earth wires and some red insulating tape to stick around the yellow and blue wires so that they are easily identified as live.

If you are installing two-way switching in a room with two doors, it is usual to place the switches near the doors so that you can chase the plaster out for the cable to run up the side of the architrave. If, on the other hand, you intend to run the new cable over the surface of the wall, the architrave can be used to secure the clipping. Better still use a box section conduit with a snap-on lid section: this can be stuck to the wall with contact adhesive. Box section conduit is not only safer than bare surface wiring but also looks a lot neater.

Wiring a two-way switch

Begin by turning off the electricity supply at the mains, then remove the cover plate of the existing switch and unscrew the wires attached to the terminals. Next, prepare any cable chases and any recesses for boxes. If boxes are to be flush mounted, knock out one of the punched holes in the back for the cable and fit the box.

Where necessary, install your PVC conduit then run the new cable from the existing switch position to the new position, clipping it to the wall surface or feeding it through the conduit as necessary. Then make good any damaged plaster at this stage.

Remove about 150mm of outer sheathing from each end of the cable, leaving 12mm protruding into each box, then strip about 10mm of insulation from the end of each wire and double the ends over. Bind a short piece of red insulating tape around each yellow and blue wire, about 20mm from the end, and slip a length of green and yellow PVC sleeving over both bare earth wires and the earth wire of the original cable, if not already sleeved. If there is no red tape around the existing black insulating wire, put a piece on at this stage.

Now wire up the two switches as follows:

- At the original switch position, connect the earth wires to the box earth terminal
- Connect the original red wire and the new blue wire to the terminal marked L1
- Connect the existing black wire and the new yellow wire to the terminal marked L2
- Connect the new red wire to the 'Common' terminal
- At the new position, connect the red wire to the 'Common' terminal
- Connect the blue wire to the terminal marked L1
- Connect the yellow wire to the terminal marked L2
- Connect the earth wire to the box earth terminal.

Lay the wires neatly in the boxes and fix the switchplates in place with the screws provided. After you have turned on the power at the mains, the new switching arrangement can be tested.

Fitting a dimmer switch

To replace a one-way switch with a standard dimmer, begin as always by turning off the power supply; then remove the cover plate of the existing switch and disconnect the two wires on the back. Try the dimmer switch plate in the wall box and arrange the wires so that they will not be trapped.

As the black wire carries the current back from the switch, and is therefore also live, it is best to clearly mark it as live with a piece of red insulating tape.

Now check that the wires fit properly into the terminal holes on the back of the dimmer switch plate. Some dimmers have terminals with holes that are much shallower than those of a normal switch. If this is the case, trim each wire to make sure that no bare wire is left protruding from the terminals (fig. 4).

Having made sure that the new dimmer fits neatly into the box, connect the two wires as for a normal switch, following the instructions, or diagram.

If the switchplate of the dimmer is metal, it will have an earth terminal on the back. Make sure that this is connected to the box earth terminal by a short length of green and yellow PVC insulated wire (fig. 3).

Now fit the switch into place, making sure that no wires are trapped, and screw in the fixing screws. Switch the dial off if necessary. Turn the power on again and your new dimmer is ready.

If you want to replace a two-way switch with a dimmer, make sure that the type you choose for the job has three terminals on the back. Dimmers that incorporate a rocker switch alongside the dial or a push switch are the most suitable.

Touch dimmers and time lag dimmers will replace both one-way and two-way rocker switches. Make the connections according to the manufacturer's instructions.

1 To replace a one-way switch with a standard type of dimmer, first turn off the electricity supply at the mains and then unscrew the switch cover plate. With the cover of the existing switch completely removed from the mounting box, carefully unscrew the terminal screws so that you can easily free all the attached wires

2 If you discover when you have managed to free the wires that the earth wire, which is connected up to the box terminal, is bare, loosen the terminal screw so that you can free the wire. You should then firmly sleeve it in a short length of green and yellow PVC sheathing for insulation purposes and to give the wire better protection

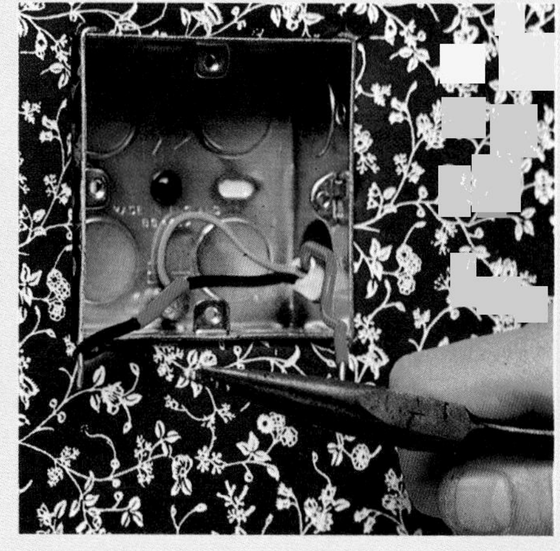

3 Make sure when you sleeve the earth wire that about 6mm of bare wire is left protruding at the end. As the black wire in a switch is also live, it is best to highlight this fact, for any necessary future work, by carefully wrapping a piece of red insulating tape around it as marker for future reference

4 If the terminal holes in the new dimmer are less deep than those existing in the switch, trim the wiring so that no bare end is left protruding. When you have trimmed both wires to length, connect up the switch following the detailed wiring instructions which will be given by the manufacturer

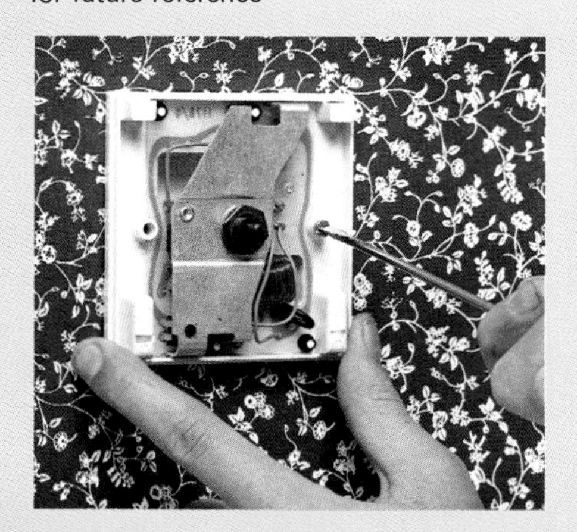

5 Next, having connected up all the wiring on the switch you should use the mounting screws provided to actually fix the switch plate to the mounting box already on the wall. The last piece of work to do on this project is then to screw or clip the fixing cover, which houses the rotary dimmer switch control into position

6 Now you should make sure that the control knob is fixed in the 'off' position. Then turn the electricity supply back on at the mains and rotate the switch back and forth to test out the performance of your new dimmer. You will then begin to appreciate the attractive and special effects achieved by dimmed or subdued lighting

Time switches

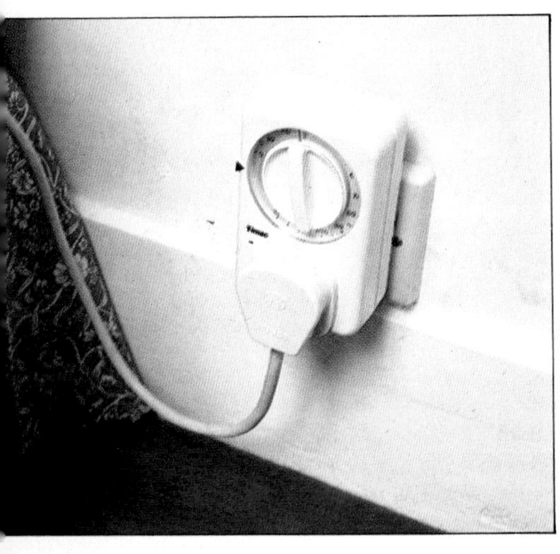

Above, top: A variable time delay switch can be used to control small appliances such as electric blankets. **Above, bottom:** A time switch featuring a photo-electric cell is an easily fitted deterrent against burglars

With fuel costs spiralling all the time, anything that enables you to control your electricity consumption is worth considering. Electric time switches offer a way of doing just that—particularly for heating and ventilating appliances.

A time switch can be fitted to almost any appliance and will automatically switch it on and off at preset times.

Types of time switch

A time switch is quite simply a rotary switch—usually single pole—driven by a small electric clock. The switch has a dial which generally makes one revolution every 24 hours, although some models make one every week.

The dials are usually calibrated at

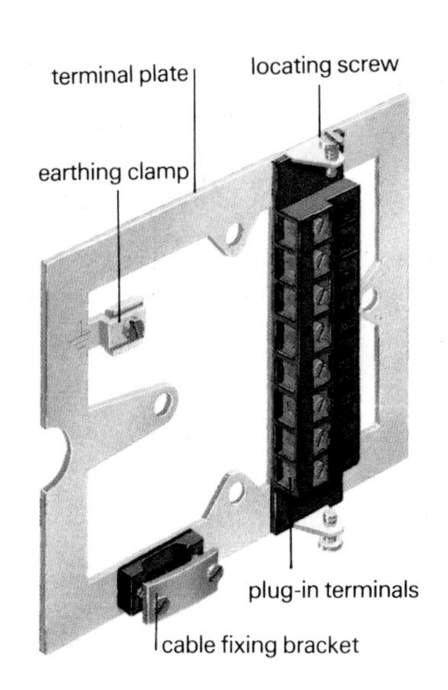

intervals of 15 minutes so that the control periods can be selected with reasonable accuracy. Most units have two sets of tripping cams on the clock which provide two control periods every 24 hours, while some provide for several control periods but with a minimum interval between ON and OFF of about half an hour.

Some models of time switch contain a reserve battery to keep the clock going if the mains power supply is interrupted.

Once set for a programme of ON and OFF switching, a time switch continues with the programme until it is changed. However, most have a manual override switch allowing you to switch the appliance on and off at your own convenience.

Although time switches are usually wired to a circuit, several models plug into an ordinary socket or mains outlet. These models have their own socket into which, in turn, appliances can be plugged and, like other time switches, include a manual override.

Plug-in time switches have a maximum rating of about 3000 watts, while units that are plumbed into the mains have a variety of higher ratings. The usual rating is high enough to cover most requirements.

Applications

A time switch can be used to control almost any appliance, but on no account should it ever be used to control a radiant electric fire: surprise switching could scorch an unsuspecting child or burn furniture and fittings, causing a fire hazard.

One circuit where a time switch is par-

A. Below: One type of time switch has separate supplies for switch and appliance, allowing the appliance to be isolated without actually stopping the clock

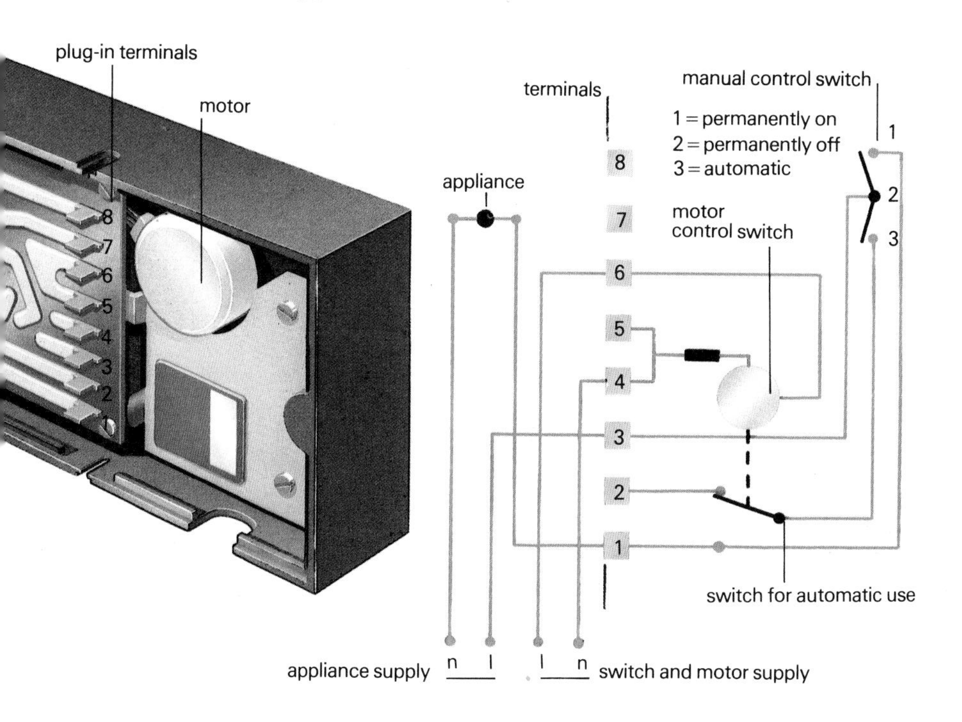

ticularly useful for energy-saving is the one supplying an immersion heater for electric hot water heating. You can programme the timer to switch on the heater about an hour before hot water is required (three hours for a bath) in the morning and evening.

Another useful place for a time switch is in the circuit supplying fixed electric heaters used as background heating (even when these have built-in thermostats). Among the heaters most suited to time switch control are tubular heaters, skirting heaters, and the oil-filled type of electric radiators.

The timer will usually be wired in the circuit supplying power to the heaters. So ensure no other appliances are fitted in the same circuit 'downstream' of the timer—otherwise these will be switched on and off in time with the heaters.

Controlling storage heaters

If you wish to take advantage of the cheap off-peak rates offered by the local electricity boards in the UK, a storage heater controlled by a time switch is a sound investment. You can set the controls so that it draws electricity at the cheapest rate, and then emits heat throughout the day while it is switched off.

Although the electricity boards install storage heaters with their own circuit and consumer unit, you can install and run a single storage heater from a 13 amp socket using a plug-in time switch to turn it on and off. If you wish to install more than two heaters, however, it is best to supply each of them from a spur on the ring main with its own, wired-in time switch.

Burglar deterrent switching

Lights left burning all night are just as likely to arouse the attentions of a would-be intruder as a house left in perpetual darkness. Time switches controlling table lamps in the bedrooms, kitchen and living room make excellent deterrents for this very reason, though the timers need resetting every few weeks to follow lighting-up times reasonably closely. Set the timers so that different rooms are lit up at different times up to about midnight.

Installing a time switch

The first stage in installing a wired-in time switch is to find a suitable location for it. However, when doing so there are a few things you should bear in mind.

A time switch does not need to be next to the appliance—it can be placed in any convenient and accessible position: next to the consumer unit (fuse box), alongside the meter, in a cupboard. But if the appliance has a manual control switch, it is best to install the time switch between this and the consumer unit so that you can turn off the appliance manually without stopping (and having to re-set) the timer.

Another factor to consider is the layout of the wiring. If you are installing a new appliance, and are extending an existing circuit, then the time switch will need to be somewhere in this new run—look for a discreet but fairly accessible location.

Fitting a time switch in an existing circuit is often a simple matter of breaking into the circuit and connecting up the unit as described below. Where you have to run a new circuit to the appliance, installation details will depend on whether the new circuit forms an extension to a lighting circuit, a spur off a ring main, or a separate circuit. Make sure you use a timer of a sufficient current rating for the circuit you are connecting into, and that you use the right size cable.

Note: Make sure you never work on a circuit until you are certain that it is not live.

Like a light switch, the time switch itself must be partially dismantled before it can be fitted and wired; most time switches have a screw-on cover which must be removed to allow access to the terminals inside it. Remove this carefully, taking care not to damage the clock mechanism, and locate the holes in the casing for the cables, and the screw terminals for connecting the wires.

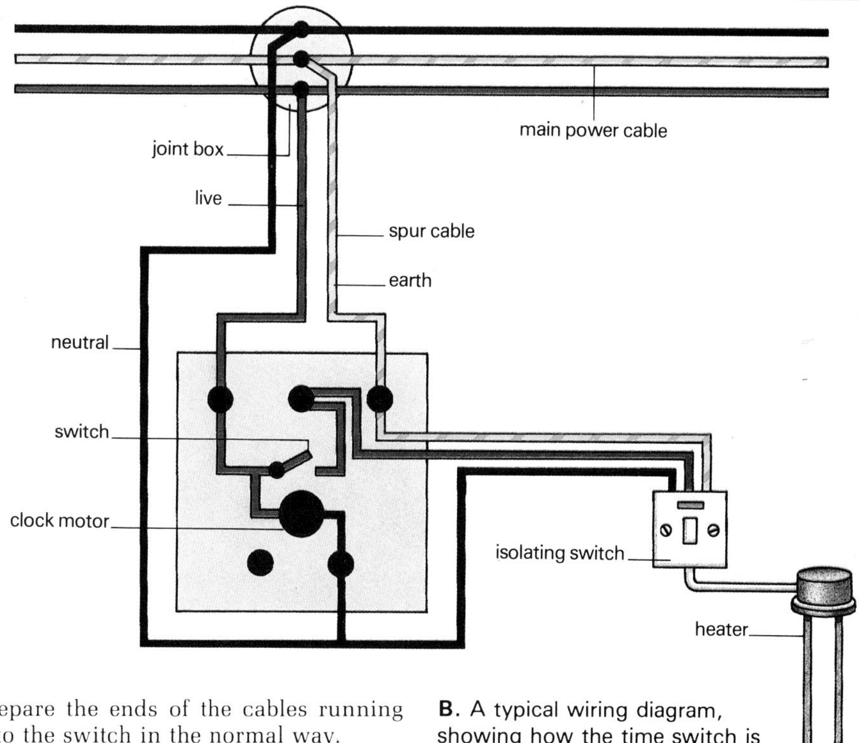

B. A typical wiring diagram, showing how the time switch is fitted on a spur cable so that its operation does not affect other appliances in the home

Prepare the ends of the cables running into the switch in the normal way.

The next step is to fix the unit to a wall, using screws and wall plugs, or to a convenient shelf near the consumer unit. Having done so, start connecting the wires from the supply and the appliance. The live wire from the supply is connected to one side of the clock/switch mechanism, the live wire to the appliance is connected to the other. The neutral wires may have a common terminal, as may the earth wires, so be sure to consult the manufacturer's wiring diagram and find out which is which (fig. A).

Sheath the bare earth cables before fitting them, then fit the remaining wires, tighten up the screw terminals, and replace the top cover. Set the timer to the switching periods you require, set the clock to the correct time, and switch on the supply.

Thermostatic control

Thermostats serve a similar purpose to time switches: they provide automatic control of your heating system, switching heaters on and off as they are required and maintaining a constant temperature so that no energy is wasted raising the temperature of a room to an unnecessarily high level.

Some heaters have a built-in thermostat that can be set to any temperature you require, but the majority do not. For these you can buy a unit similar to a plug-in time switch, which plugs into a socket outlet and into which the heater itself is plugged.

To achieve accurate control you should make sure that the unit is plugged into a socket well out of the way of draughts. But as with time switches, radiant electric fires should never be used with thermostats due to the risk of fire.

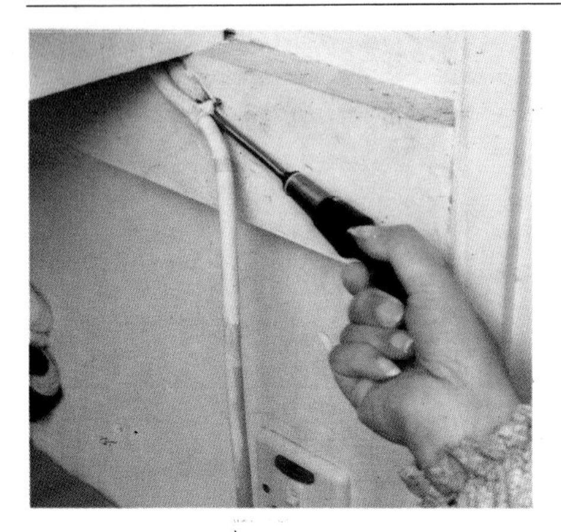

1 To install a time switch in an immersion heater circuit, you should first isolate the circuit and then remove the cable clips securing the cable. Next, take the fixing plate off the time switch, and using a loop of the cable, find a suitable location for it, as close as possible to the isolating switch

2 When you have found a suitable location, mark the screw hole positions. Drill the screw holes through the pencil marks. Use wall plugs if fixing the switch to plaster. Otherwise use wood screws of the correct size, secure the fixing plate of the time switch to the wall. Make sure that it is the right way up

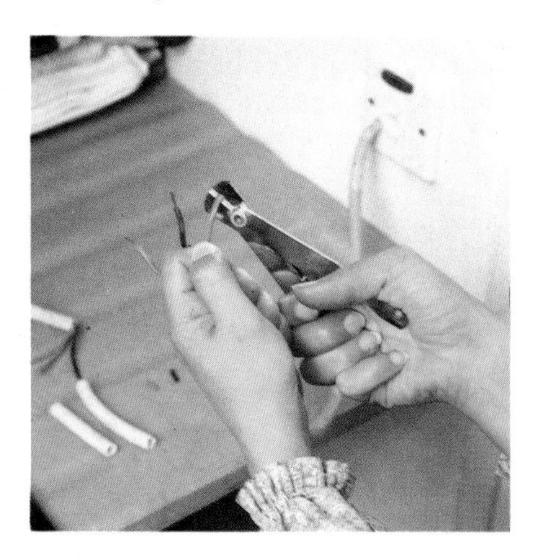

3 Lay the loop of cable carefully over the fixing plate and, allowing 50mm for connections on each side, cut it in line with the middle of the plate. Then strip back the cable sheathing for about 50mm, and then you should strip the insulation on the wires inside down to a depth of about 10mm

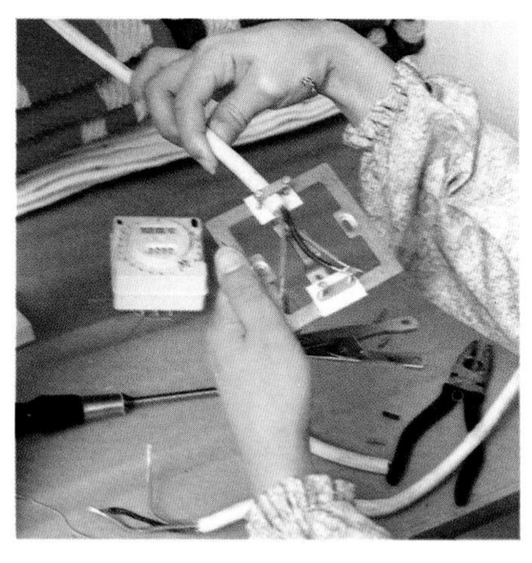

4 Now feed the unsheathed wires into the metal backing plate and then fix the cables using the cord grips, which are provided on each side of the plate. The earth wires on this switch have a common connection terminal. In this case twist the bared ends firmly together with the help of a pair of pliers

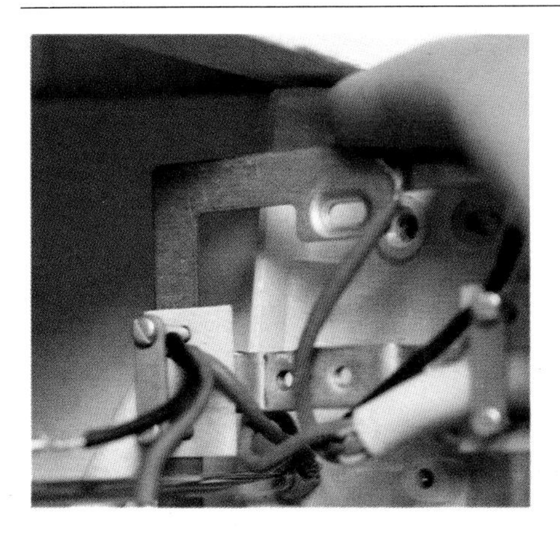

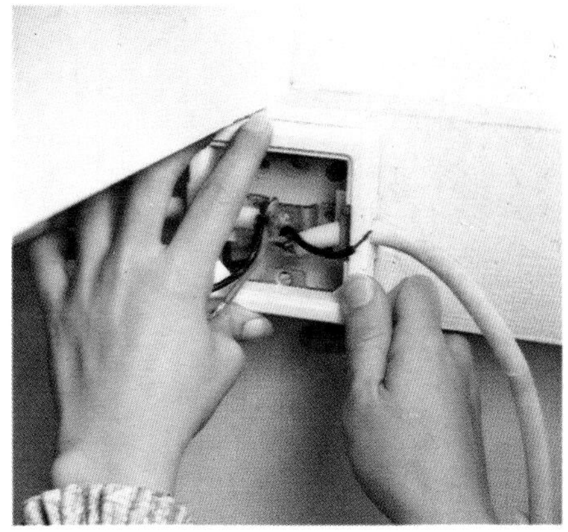

5 When you have done this, fit the earth wires into the earth terminal on the fixing plate and then tighten up the terminal screw firmly. Now using the screws, which have been supplied in the kit, fit the backing plate to the fixing plate—first making sure that it is being fitted the right way round

6 When the backing plate is fixed firmly in place, turn your attention to the next task which should be completed. The piece to be fitted next is the adaptor for the clock and the switch mechanism. This should simply be pushed firmly and securely into the correct place and just left there

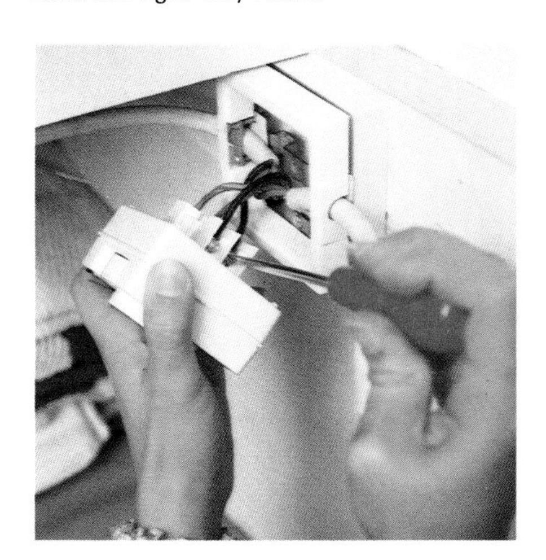

7 Look out the manufacturer's wiring diagram for the timer and make sure you follow all the instructions carefully. Then connect up the live and neutral wires to their terminals on the back of the switch. Do not forget the neutral wires may have the same terminal as may the earth wires, so check the instructions first

8 Having made sure you have sheathed the earth wires, you now need to tighten up the single screw which holds the switch mechanism in place. Then set the clock to the correct time and set the tripping pins to the switching periods you require. Then you can begin to test the timer to see that it works correctly

Channelling electric cables

Few things are more unsightly and potentially dangerous than electric cables running across ceilings and down walls. Your first consideration when wiring sockets, switches or light fittings should always be to hide such cables safely and unobtrusively.

When a house is wired during its construction, cables are usually hidden from view in various ways—in chases or channels cut in masonry walls; behind the wall covering of timber-framed walls; hidden under the floor or above ceiling level.

New cables can be hidden in much the same way—by cutting chases in masonry walls; dropping them through the hollow centre to be found in most timber-framed walls; or by lifting floorboards and threading cables along or through joists.

An alternative, which can save a lot of redecoration, is to run the cables along the surface of walls or ceilings—but neatly hidden in plastic box-shaped channels called trunking.

Planning wall cables

Cables channelled into walls are usually connected to wall switches or wall-mounted lights, but they are sometimes also used to carry power to socket outlets or to individual appliances such as cookers.

During the construction of new houses, wall-run cables are fitted into plastic conduits prior to being channelled into the wall. This keeps the cable in position during construction and offers some means of protection once the walls have been plastered.

But when you are channelling through walls that are already plastered you can use plastic conduit, plastic cover strip, or—even safer—galvanized steel cover strip.

Once a channel has been cut to the required depth, the cable is fed into it and then covered with protective capping. The work is completed by plastering the channel level with the existing wall surface.

When planning cables to run along walls, make sure that they are placed according to accepted practice so that anyone drilling into the wall at a later date can avoid them.

Channelling wall cables

Before cutting out channels to accommodate the cables, carefully mark their proposed positions on the wall. Hold a long straightedge against the surface and draw two parallel lines across the wall, slightly more than the width of your conduit or capping apart.

Once the whole run has been completely marked out to your satisfaction, including the position of power points and switches, reposition the straightedge against the lines and run the blade of a handyman's knife along it. Try to cut through wall-coverings—if there are any—and into the top layer of plaster (fig. 1).

Once the channel has been cut along both sides, peel away any wall coverings from the centre until the plaster below is fully exposed. Then use a sharp bolster to cut first down the centre line, then the outside edges, of the channel until you have removed all the plaster.

The channel should be at least 20mm deep, and to achieve this you may have to cut into the brick or block work. Use an 18mm cold chisel, and be sure to wear

1 When channelling cable through walls, mark all the proposed positions. Then place a straightedge along the marked out lines and run a handyman's knife along them to cut through the wallcovering. Peel and scrape away the paper until the plaster below it is fully exposed and ready to cut away

2 With a sharp bolster cut first down the centre and then down each outside edge of the proposed channel. Continue to do this until you reach the brick or blockwork behind it. Since the channel needs to be at least 20mm deep you may need to use an 18mm cold chisel and hammer to cut into the masonry

3 First screw the back of the protective channelling firmly into place using plugs drilled and fixed into the wall behind the recess. Then thread the cable into place making sure that it is all straight, does not have any kinks, and that it fits neatly into the backing part of the channelling

4 Snap the front of the channelling on the backing to cover the cable and help protect it from damage. Secure the whole channel by spacing galvanized nails along both sides. Finally you should plaster the channel so that it is level with the existing wall. Use a straightedge to clear away any loose material

5 Before channelling cable under floorboard level, mark its route in straight lines across the floorboards with a piece of chalk. Then raise all the marked-out floorboards using a bolster. Once the joists are fully exposed, mark the position of the intended run midway between the two adjacent floorboards

6 Use a spade or flatbit attachment to drill the necessary holes. Make them all slightly larger than the cable—but they should be no wider than 25mm. If space between the joists is very cramped make more room for the drill by cutting the drill bit in half with a medium-toothed hacksaw

7 Another alternative to the awkward problem of drilling holes in the joists is that you can actually fit a right-angle adaptor to the power drill. This particular attachment is very useful as it allows you to insert the drill and to work in comfort from a point above each of the joists you need to drill into

8 Unkink the length of electrical cable and thread it through each drilled hole in turn. Take care that it does not become at all damaged or twisted in the process. When you replace each floorboard again, keep the nails well away from the chalked cable line you have previously marked on the floor surface.

safety glasses or goggles to protect your eyes from flying chips of masonry. Always angle the chisel in towards the centre, to avoid accidental damage to the rest of the wall.

Once all the channelling is complete, cut out chases for light switches and power points in the same way. Check the depth of each chase carefully to ensure that the relevant fitting can be mounted flush with the wall, then knock out the cable entry blanks nearest the channel feeding it and fix the fitting securely in position.

If you are using plastic conduit to protect the cable, fix it in the channel at this stage, using galvanized nails. Then thread the cable into position in the conduit and connect it to the fittings, but not to a power souce.

Then plaster over the top of the conduit using the same techniques employed to plaster a small hole. Make sure that the plaster is pushed hard into the channel, then place the straightedge across and move it up and down in a sawing motion to remove excess material and leave a smooth, flat finish.

Clear loose plaster from around the live terminals at each fitting, then leave the wall to dry for at least three to four hours before connecting the circuit to the mains and switching the power back on.

Underfloor cables

Much of the cable used in house wiring is run in the space under a suspended ground floor or between the ceiling of a downstairs room and the floor of the room above. Here the cable is relatively safe, requires the minimum of fixings to hold it in place, and is protected from damage by the timbers around it. Where the cable has to pass across joists, you should feed it through holes drilled in them. These holes must be at least 50mm below floorboard level, and must noi extend below the centre lines of the joists.

Plan where you want the cable to run, marking the floorboards with chalk if necessary. Try as much as possible to

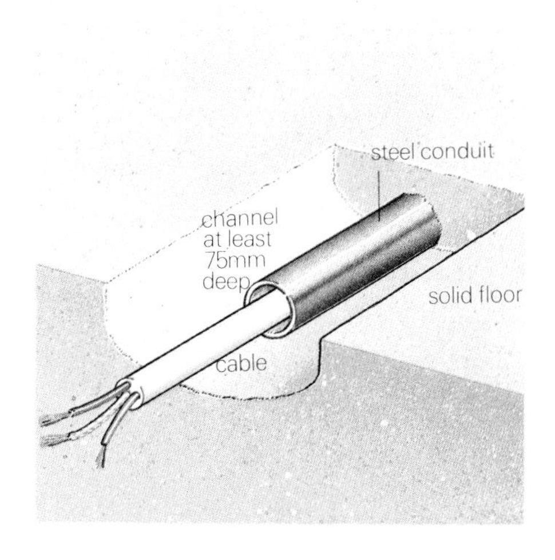

A. Above: Through a solid floor cut a 75mm deep channel using either a cold chisel or otherwise a power chasing tool

keep these marks in straight lines running across the joists so that you have to lift as few floorboards as possible (fig. 5).

With the cable route clearly planned, raise all of the marked floorboards and expose the joists below. In many cases the joists may already have been drilled to accommodate cables and if you notice a line of holes running near where you have lifted floorboards, use these to accommodate your own length of cable. But if no such holes exist, you will have to drill fresh ones.

Mark the positions of the holes on the joists so that they lie midway between the two adjacent floorboards.

Use either a flooring brace or a power drill, fitted with a 90° adaptor and a flat bit, to make the holes. If you do not have these tools, there should be enough space between the joists to insert a power drill fitted with a spade or flatbit cut in half. Always make the holes slightly larger than the cable so that you can feed it through without difficulty.

When you replace the floorboards, make sure that you keep the nails well away from the chalked cable line marked on the surface.

Cables in the roof space

PVC sheathed cables run in the roof space to supply lights and switches in the rooms below. But unless the loft is converted into an extra room there is no need to drill holes in the ceiling joists to accommodate them. They can be run across the joists, fixed at intervals with cable clips, or alongside joists and rested on the ceiling.

However, where the roof is insulated with expanded polystyrene granules, protect the cable with plastic conduit fixed along the top of the joists. If the plasticizer contained in the PVC cable sheathing comes into contact with the granules, it eventually damages the cable itself, leading eventually to dangerous, bare wires in the roof space.

Skirting boards and architraves

If you have a room where the floor is solid, or is decorated with tiles or some other permanent floor covering, an alternative to cutting chases in the wall is to hide the cable behind skirting boards and architraves. Although this involves removing these features, the final result is neat and comparatively safe if it is done well.

Prise the skirting board and architrave away from the wall and then make sure that there is enough space to accommodate the cable once these have been replaced. If necessary, use a bolster or cold chisel to cut a shallow channel in the wall behind.

Then position the cable, pushing it deep into the recess behind the skirting board and into the gap between the architrave and the door frame. Then replace the skirting board and architrave,

B. Below: A plastic conduit system provides you with all the straight sections, angled adaptors and boxes for covering up any ugly exposed wiring

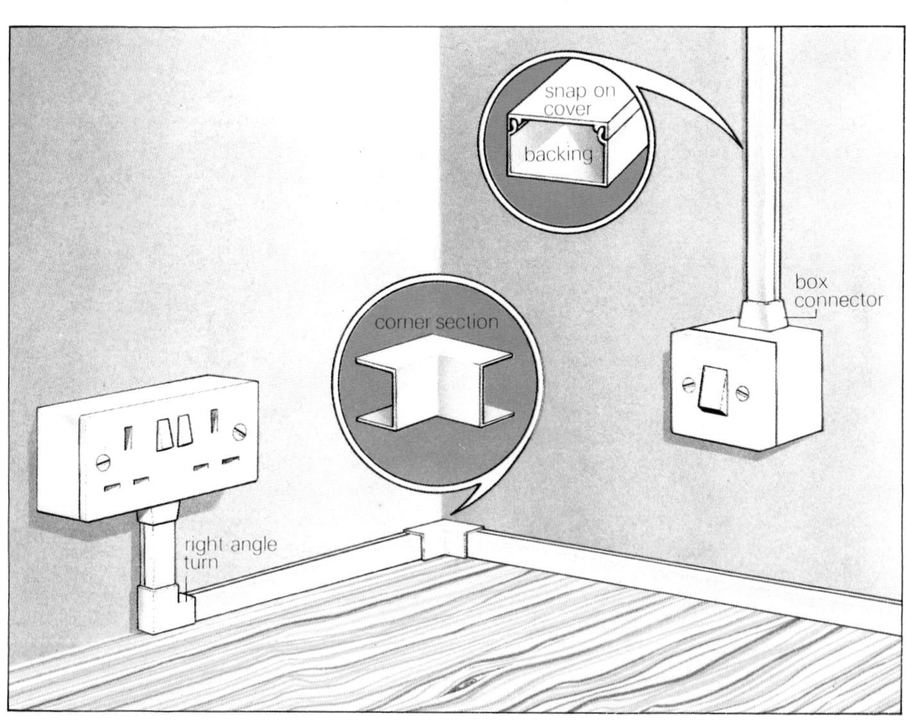

making absolutely sure that none of the fixing nails are positioned near the cable run.

If the floor is of bare concrete, it may be more practical over short distances to channel straight through it. And although you can cut such a channel with a hammer and bolster, it is a great deal less work to hire a power chasing tool for the job.

Cables running through concrete must always be encased in steel conduit—available from electrical stores and builders' merchants—and the channels themselves must be at least 75mm deep. This may breach the floor's damp-proof membrane. To ensure its continuity, brush two coats of bitumen-based damp-proofing liquid into the chase.

After you have fed the cable through the conduit and laid the latter in position, make good the channelling with a mortar mix of one part cement to three of sharp sand with a little PVA bonding agent added.

Using plastic trunking

Plastic trunking provides a means of safely channelling electric cable without either cutting into walls or lifting floor-boards. The box-shaped channel runs across ceilings and can be used to accommodate any type of two or three core cable for lights, switches or power points.

The trunking is designed in two parts, the back being easy to fix in place while the front snaps off to allow the cable to be inserted. The system includes boxes for switches, socket outlets and fused connection units, and these, too, are fixed directly to the surface of the wall. Trunking can be screwed in place, or stuck with impact adhesive.

Fix the baseplates of switches and so on first, then fix the back part of the conduit. Lay the cable in place, make the electrical connections and snap on the covers. Finally, connect up the cable to the mains.

You may have some problem linking power from an existing socket to the new one. If the existing socket is directly below the new outlet, simply drop a length of cable down the cavity to where you want it. If the existing socket is some distance away, it is best to drop the cable down the cavity and then lead it behind the skirting board.

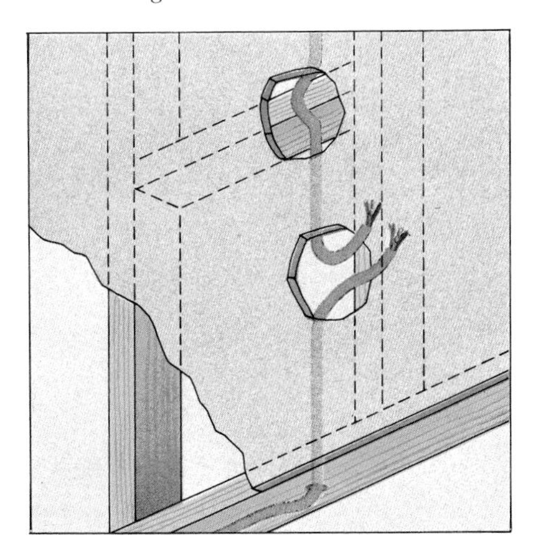

C. Above: Cables can usually be hidden in timber-framed walls, though you may have to use some ingenuity to cope with the framing members

Timber-framed walls

With timber-framed walls, it is usually easy to drop cables down the hollow between the wall coverings on either side of the framing, fishing it out through a hole in the covering at the site of any switches or power points. At the top or bottom of the wall, you can either drill holes in the horizontal timber plates as you would with flooring joists. Or—especially where the wall is of lath and plaster—cut a small chase at these points and lead the cable round the plates. You will have to do something similar if you are unfortunate enough to encounter horizontal noggins along the site of the cable drop, or if you have to run the cable horizontally at any point (though in this case it is probably easier to replan so that horizontal runs are in the floor or across the ceiling).

Install a 30 amp supply

Most homes in the UK are equipped with one or other of the two main types of 30 amp electrical circuit. Modern houses have a 30 amp ring circuit—a multi-outlet circuit supplying numerous 13 amp sockets and fixed appliances via fused outlets. Some older houses have a 30 amp multi-outlet radial circuit which supplies a limited number of 13 amp socket outlets and/or fixed appliances via fused outlets. In all cases, the outlets have a maximum capacity of 13 amps.

But some appliances, notably electric cookers and electric shower units, require their own separate 30 amp or 45 amp circuit (called a *radial final sub-circuit*) because of their high power rating.

Note that you should not confuse a 30 amp radial circuit with the older, 15 amp, 5 amp and 2 amp (round pin) radial circuits installed until about 1947. If you have one of these, your house is due for complete rewiring.

Electric cooker circuit

Essentially, electric cooker circuits consist of a cable running from a circuit fuseway in the consumer unit to a control switch, and then on to the cooker itself.

The current rating of the fuse, or MCB (miniature circuit breaker), and of the cable in the circuit is determined by the current demand of the cooker. The majority of domestic electric cookers have a loading of between 10,000 watts and 13,000 watts. On the 240 volts electricity supply standard in the UK, the maximum possible current demand of a 10,000 watt cooker is 42 amps, and of a 13,000 watt cooker, 54 amps.

However, because of the oven thermostat and variable controls of the boiling rings, there will never be more than a momentary maximum demand. UK regulations provide a simple formula for assessing the current demand of a domestic cooker, in which the first 10 amps are rated at 100 percent, and the remaining current at 30 percent. A socket connected to the control unit is rated at 5 amps.

This means that a socket and a 10,000 watt cooker drawing a theoretical 42 amps have an assessed demand of 25 amps. And a 13,000 watt cooker with a theoretical 54 amp demand, plus socket, is assessed as 28 amps. Consequently, most cookers fall well within a current rating of 30 amps. Only very large ones and those with double ovens require a 45 amp circuit.

Consumer unit to control switch

Hopefully your existing consumer unit will have a spare fuseway from which to run the cable.

However, where there is no spare fuseway—and usually where you have a large cooker requiring a 45 amp circuit—you must install a separate mains switch and fuse unit, called a switchfuse unit.

The cable

The only difference between a 45 amp and a 30 amp circuit is the size of the cable. If your calculations have shown you that a 30 amp fuse is adequate for your cooker, then you need cable with a current rating of at least 30 amps—6mm^2 twin and earth PVC sheathed will usually do. With a 45 amp fuse, 10mm^2 cable is needed.

The cable should obviously take the shortest possible route from the switchfuse unit to the cooker control unit. Where there are no solid floors it is an easy task to run the cable straight down from the switchfuse unit, under the floorboards, to emerge once again immediately below the planned position of the control unit.

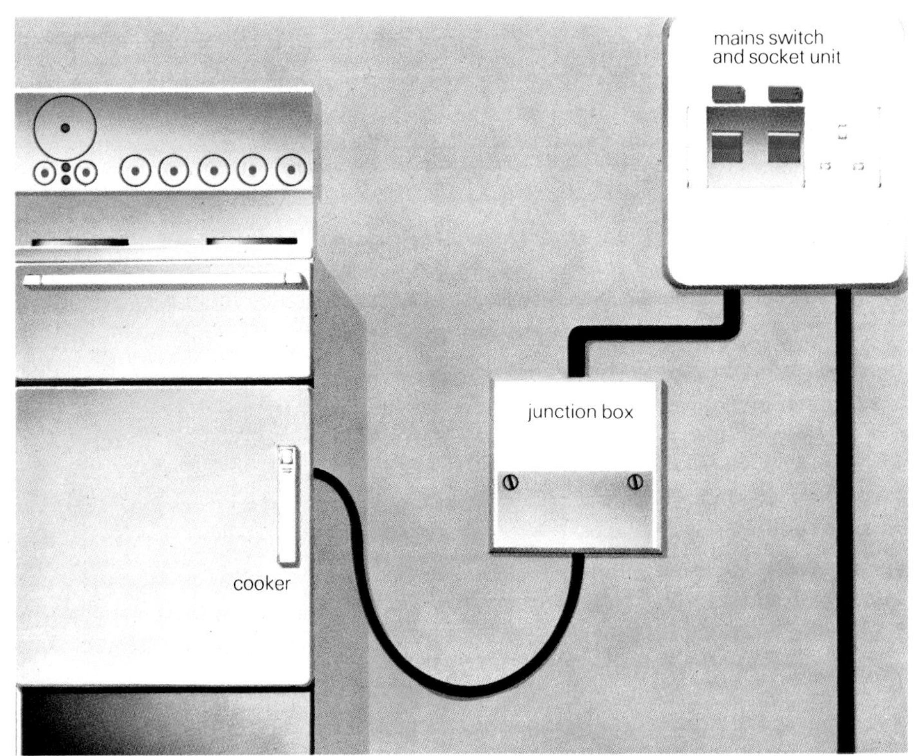

A. Above: The 45 amp double-pole main switch and 13 amp switched socket is used in the circuit to the electric cooker to isolate the supply. The control unit is fixed at about 1.5m above floor level

However, should you need to run a cable across the direction of the joists, these must be drilled—not notched—at least 50mm below the top edge of the joist.

But, where, as in many kitchens, there is a solid floor, it is advisable to take the cable up from the switchfuse unit, into the ceiling void, across and between the joists, and then down the kitchen wall to the control switch.

Positioning the control unit

The control unit is normally fixed at about 1.5m above floor level, and to one side of the cooker. UK regulations require that the switch should not be more than 2m from the cooker, to allow for rapid access in emergencies.

Control units come in various styles, either surface or flush mounting, with or without neon 'power' indicators, and with or without a kettle socket outlet. The current rating is usually 45 amps. If it is necessary to fix the switch above the cooker, one without a socket is recommended to avoid the risk of a flex trailing across a hot ring.

Control unit to cooker

To allow a free-standing cooker to be moved for cleaning or servicing, you must run the last section of cable in the form of a trailing loop. The first few feet can either be fixed to or buried in the wall immediately below and behind the unit.

If you opt for burial, you must install an outlet box. You can either use a through box, simply anchoring the uncut cable with a clamp, or a terminal box, which would make it possible to remove the cooker altogether.

Split-level cookers

In the UK, wiring regulations regard the separate hob and oven sections of a split-level cooker as a single unit. They should therefore be on one circuit—providing that both sections are sited within 2m of the control unit itself.

Following these rules, you can install the two sections up to 4m apart as long as the control unit is midway between them. And if one of the sections is installed more than 2m away from the control unit, it can share the circuit but needs a second control switch. In all cases, you must ensure that the cable fitted on the cooker side of the control unit is exactly the same size as the circuit cable.

Electric shower unit circuit

An electric shower unit is an instantaneous electric water heater in which the water is heated as it flows over the element unit. To provide adequate hot water the element has a loading of 6000 watts or in some cases 7000 watts, with respective current demands of 26 and 29 amps.

To install a shower unit you will therefore need a 30 amp fuseway, a length of $6mm^2$ twin and earth PVC sheathed cable, a double pole isolating switch, and a length of sheathed flexible cord or cable to connect the shower unit to the isolating switch. In some cases a flex, or *cord*, outlet unit is required for the final connection to the shower unit.

Running the cable

On an electric shower installation, use a twin and earth PVC sheathed cable with

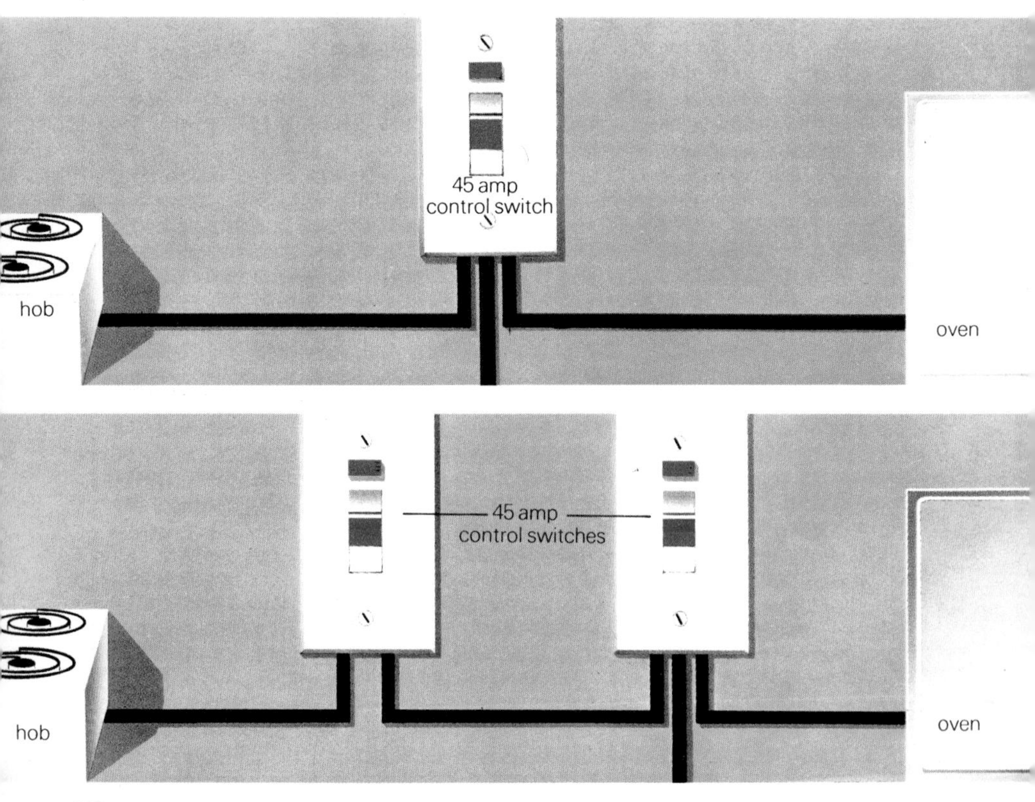

a current rating of not less than 30 amps to match the circuit fuse or MCB in the consumer unit. The circuit cable running from the 30 amp fuseway to the 30 amp double-pole isolating switch should run in the same way as that for a cooker.

It is dangerous to have an electric switch or socket within reach of wet hands, so you must install either a cord-operated ceiling switch in the bathroom or a wall-mounted switch outside (fig. C).

A special 30 amp double pole switch with neon indicator is available for cord operation and is mounted on a standard, square-moulded plastic box. To install this unit, first remove the knockout blank in the base for the two cables; one is the circuit cable, the other is the shower unit connecting cable. Pierce a hole in the ceiling for the two cables, connect them to the switch, then fix the unit to a timber joist using wood screws.

B. Use a 45 amp control switch without a socket if you prefer. If both sections of a split level are within 2m of the control unit, you can just use a single switch. **Above left**: A simple way of wiring a split level cooker circuit. **Below left**: Where the two sections are more than 4m apart it becomes necessary to use two cooker control units. **Right**: An alternative method of connecting up the oven and hob sections by linking them together in series—both the sections are controlled from the same switch in this method

Some shower units are supplied with a three-core circular sheathed flex. Do not remove this; instead, run both it and the cable from the isolating switch into a cord outlet unit mounted on a square-moulded plastic box and fixed near the shower unit.

In rooms other than the bathroom mount a 30 amp double-pole switch outside the showering cubicle, in a position where it cannot be reached by anyone using the shower.

Connecting up the switch

The 30 amp cord-operated ceiling switch is a double-pole switch and therefore has two pairs of terminals. Each respective pair is marked L for live and N for neutral. One pair takes the cable from the consumer unit, and these are marked SUPPLY or MAINS. The other terminals are for the cable to the shower unit, and are marked LOAD.

Connection at the consumer unit

With all the other wiring completed, your final task is to connect the cooker or shower circuit to the mains, either at a spare fuseway in the consumer unit or—if that is not possible—to a separate switchfuse unit.

To connect to a fuseway, turn off the mainswitch and remove the consumer unit cover. On some models you must first remove the fuse carriers or MCBs.

Cut the new circuit cable, allowing about 300mm for the inside of the unit.

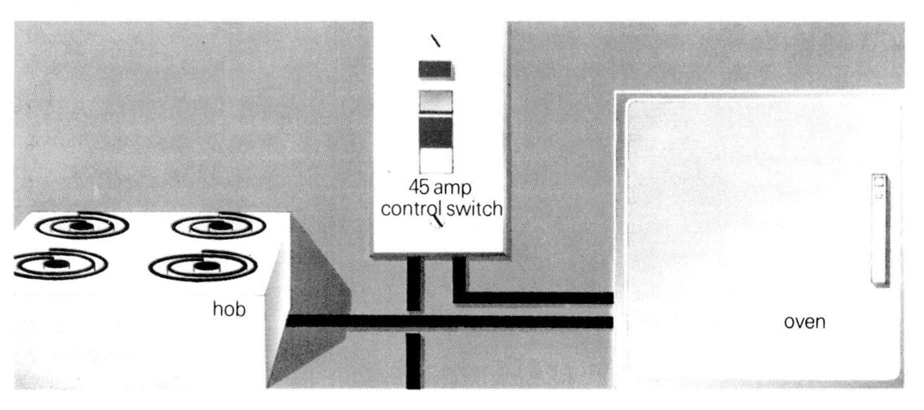

Trim about 250mm of outer sheathing from the cable, strip about 9mm of insulation from the live and neutral wires, then sheath all but 9mm of the bare earth wire with green and yellow PVC sleeving.

Next, knock out a blank from the consumer unit case and thread in the three wires until there is about 50mm of sheathing within the unit. Connect the red wire to the terminal of the spare fuseway, and the black wire to the neutral terminal block—which will already have some neutral wires connected to it in any case. Connect the sleeved earth wire to the common earth terminal block. Carefully replace the fuse carriers or MCBs, if you have had to remove these. Then put back the cover.

Finally, fit the new 30 amp fuse unit (or MCB), and if the fuse is rewirable, check that it contains a 30 amp fuse wire. Replace the cover of the consumer unit, turn on the mainswitch and you are ready to test the new installation. If any appliances refuse to work recheck the wiring very carefully.

Connecting a fuse unit

Where there is no spare fuseway on an existing 30 amp consumer unit, or the circuit requires a 45 amp installation, you must install a switch-fuse unit.

In the UK, you cannot make the final connection to the meter yourself, but must contact the Electricity Board to do it for you. At the same time, they can check over the rest of your installation to ensure that it is safe.

A switchfuse unit is a one-way consumer unit consisting of a double-pole mainswitch and a single-pole fuseway fitted with either a fuse or an MCB (an MCB is best, and a cartridge fuse next

C. Below: In this type of shower installation, the double-pole cord operated switch is actually fitted to the bathroom ceiling. You should then run the supply cable through the ceiling and connect up the shower through a standard cord outlet unit

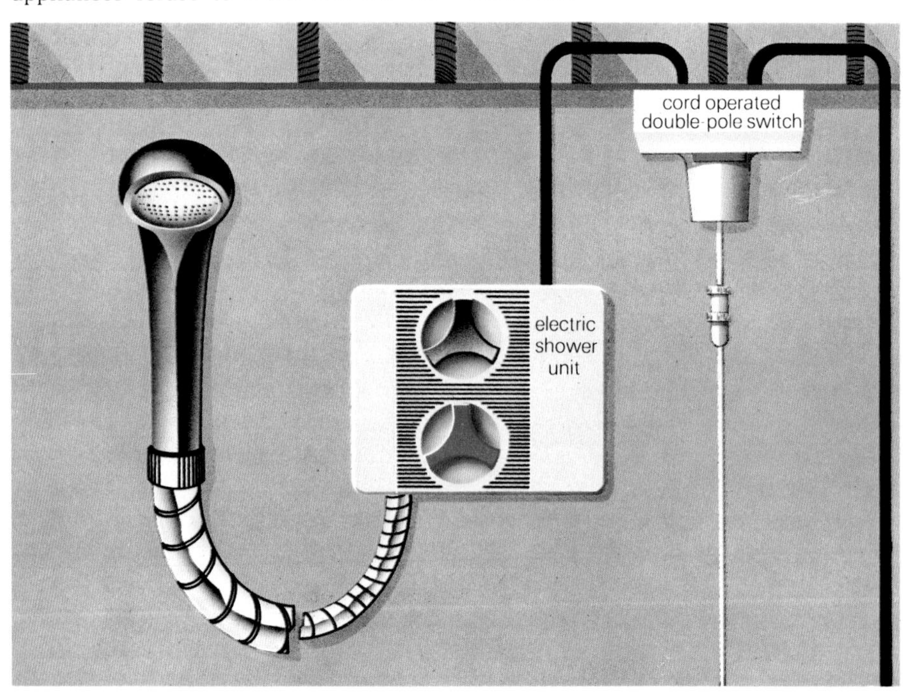

best). Both two-way and three-way consumer units are available, and you should consider installing these if future electrical extensions are anticipated.

Fit the unit to the wall adjacent to the existing consumer unit. Then connect three single-core, double insulated PVC sheathed cables—one with red, one with black, and one with green and yellow insulation—to the appropriate L (live), N (neutral) and earth mains terminals. The cables should be cut to about 1m in length, and then left for the Electricity Board to connect up. The Board stipulates the cable size—usually 16mm^2—which is determined by the current rating of the Board's service fuse.

To prepare the end of the circuit cable first cut it to the correct length, allowing a short amount for the inside of the switchfuse unit. Trim about 300mm of outer sheathing from the cable, strip about 9mm of insulation from the live and neutral wires, then sheath all but 9mm of the bare earth wire with green and yellow PVC sleeving.

Connect the wires to the appropriate fuseway terminals, insert the fuse unit if necessary then notify the Electricity Board that the circuit needs connecting to the mains.

Earthing the fusebox

When the board makes the connections they may want to check the earthing of the installation. For safety's sake it's as well to check this yourself. The earth wire usually runs from the outside of the box to a nearby water pipe, gas pipe or some other metal object which runs to earth. Check the connections carefully, making sure that the earth wire is correctly bared and that the connections are tight and secure.

D. Sometimes it is necessary to install a switchfuse unit adjacent to the consumer unit from which to take the mains supply. Electricity Boards often insist that a 60 amp double-pole terminal block (below) is fitted adjacent to the meter—the Board has to connect it up by law

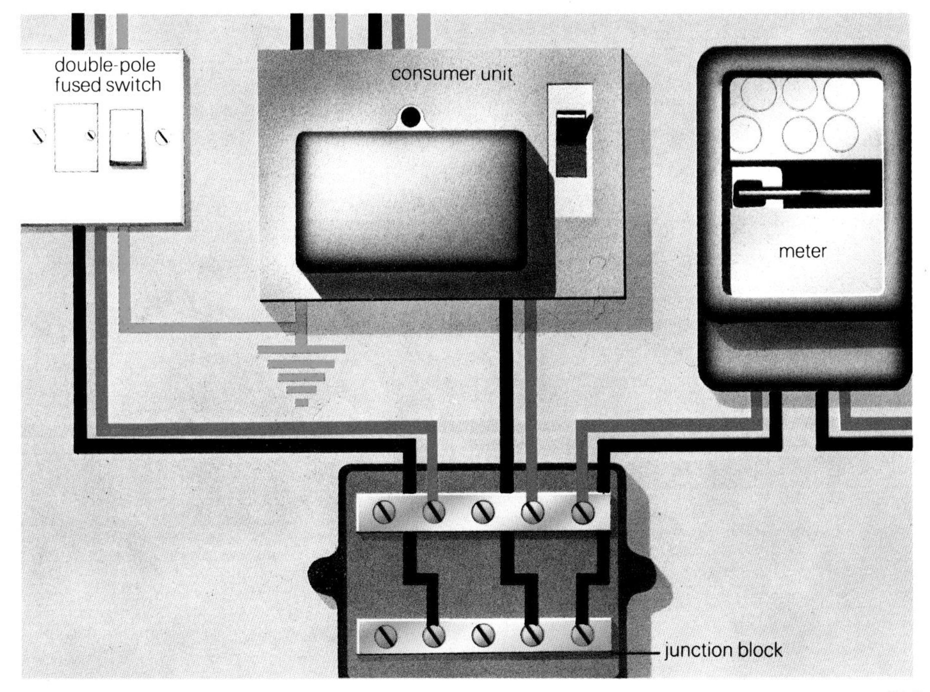

Doorbell systems

Choosing a bell that is both efficient and yet attractive to look at is not an easy proposition. First you must decide whether you want to install a manual model or one powered by either batteries or mains electricity.

Manual bells: These are ideal if you do not want to be bothered with wiring or replacing batteries, but they are less sophisticated in appearance and often give a poor sound.

Manual bells are of two types. The most common—and strictly the only variety that is truly manual—consists of a metal bell, gong or plate which is struck once the doorbell is operated. Other manual bells have a wind-up clockwork mechanism and these usually give a ringing signal.

Battery-operated bells: These depend for their power on two or four small batteries stored inside the chime unit and save you having to check whether or not the mechanism is correctly wound.

Electric bells: Doorbells powered by mains electricity are by far the most popular since they have so many advantages over the more simple manual or battery-powered models. Unlike manual models (where the chime has to be mounted directly behind the push button) electric bell chimes can be fixed in almost any unobtrusive spot, providing they can be heard anywhere in the home. Indeed a single push button can operate more than one chime unit—providing this is wired correctly. Alternatively, you can connect more than one door push to a single unit, with two different signals so that you can tell whether someone is at a back or side door.

If you want something a little more unusual, you can install an electronic chime which plays one of a variety of tunes once the push button is depressed. These tunes can either be pre-selected by the householder or chosen at random by the unit.

Transformers

All electric doorbells work on a very low voltage—usually between 3 and 12 volts—so you could not possibly connect them directly to the mains supply. Instead you must incorporate a transformer into the system, situated somewhere between the mains supply and the chime unit. Most manufacturers of doorbells will be able to supply you with a transformer suitable for this purpose.

Door pushes

Once you have chosen which type of bell or chime unit you want to install you should turn your attention to the choice of button push. Care is needed here

Below and right: A whole range of different and unusual chime units is available so there is plenty of choice—both of the housings and signals

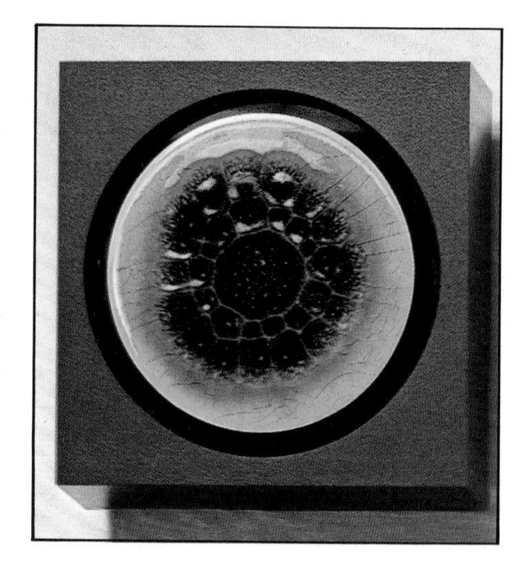

because the push must match the chime you have bought and also look attractive.

Door pushes come in a variety of sizes and widths, so choose one that fits neatly into place. They can be mounted either on the door itself or on the frame, but non-manual models are often better on the latter, because of the difficulties that might otherwise be caused by trailing wires as the door opens and closes.

Fitting a manual or battery bell

Manual or battery-operated bell systems are easily fitted. All you need to do is to determine the position of the bell push, drill a hole in the door frame to accommodate it and then fit the push and chime unit into place.

Once you have finally decided on a suitable position for the bell, mark the spot carefully. To accommodate most manual or battery models you will need to drill a fairly large diameter hole all the way through the door or the adjoining frame. To avoid splitting the timber, fit a suitably sized twist or auger bit into a hand brace and drill through the wood slowly (fig. 1).

Try the bell for size before fitting it permanently in place.

The whole mechanism can then be screwed into position. Some models are held by screws driven through from the front of the door while others are screwed from both sides. Once this is done, fit the chime unit into place—if necessary checking first that the batteries (if battery operated) are correctly seated. Finally, check that the bell is operating correctly. It should require little maintenance other than battery renewal, but it is a good idea to oil all the moving parts occasionally.

Installing electric bells

Electric bells are not particularly difficult to install. The key to success lies in checking carefully where each component part goes and in tackling the work systematically.

Before you buy an electric bell decide first which type you want to install. You can then decide roughly where each of the component parts are to be mounted and from this calculate how much wire you will need to complete the job successfully. You should also decide at this stage whether you want to wire up just the front door or any back or side doors as well.

Mounting the chime: Once you have purchased your bell kit the first task is to position the chime unit. You should already have decided roughly where you want it—usually in the kitchen or the hall. But bear in mind that it should be heard both inside the house and also by the person pressing the button, otherwise the visitor will go on ringing the bell—something which might create mutual annoyance. Alternatively, you may want to fix up two chime units—perhaps one on each floor—so that if anyone comes to the door, the bell can be heard more easily.

In general the most suitable position for mounting chime units is about 2m above ground level. At this height they produce the best sound and can usually be hidden away fairly unobtrusively. However, if you are installing an electronic chime, you may want to mount it slightly lower for easy adjustment.

Mounting the push: The techniques required to install an electric bell push are

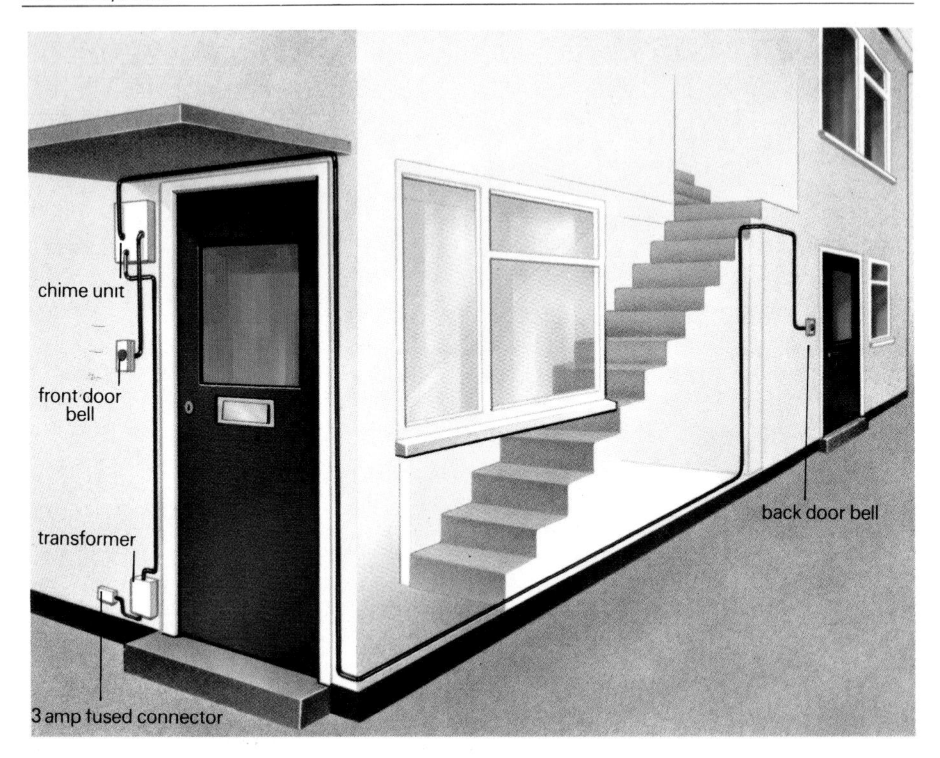

A. Above: An electric bell system employing a two-tone chime, which is then connected up to both the front and the back doorbell pushes

the same as those used to fix a manual model except that the hole you need to drill to accommodate the push is generally smaller.

Once the push and the chime are in position you can wire one to another. The push should be connected to the output terminals on the chime and the wire fixed neatly around the room with cable clips.

Wiring the chime unit: If your chime unit is not powered by batteries it needs to be connected to the mains electric supply via a transformer.

First, fix the transformer securely to the wall. It can be mounted next to the chime or in some other less obtrusive position between the chime and the power source. Once it has been secured firmly in position, wire the output terminals of the transformer to the relevant terminals on the chime according to the maker's instructions.

The next stage is to connect the input side of the transformer. One solution would be to plug the transformer into a nearby socket outlet, using a length of mains flex (not bell wire). But this could tie up a valuable outlet.

A better solution is to treat the transformer as a fixed appliance and connect it permanently into the house wiring.

In the UK, the transformer could be wired into a ring main via a fused connection unit fitted with a 3 amp fuse.

Alternatively, because of the low current needed to operate a chime, it is also possible to connect it into a lighting circuit. And as the transformer is likely to be mounted near the ceiling this may be easier and neater than trying to connect it to a power circuit. Connect the transformer to a suitable outlet as if it

1 To fit a bell push, start by drilling a hole through the door frame using either a hand-held brace or alternatively an electric drill with a large diameter bit. Then carefully thread the wire through from the back. Try to ensure that the cable has no kinks in it and that the plastic sheathing remains intact

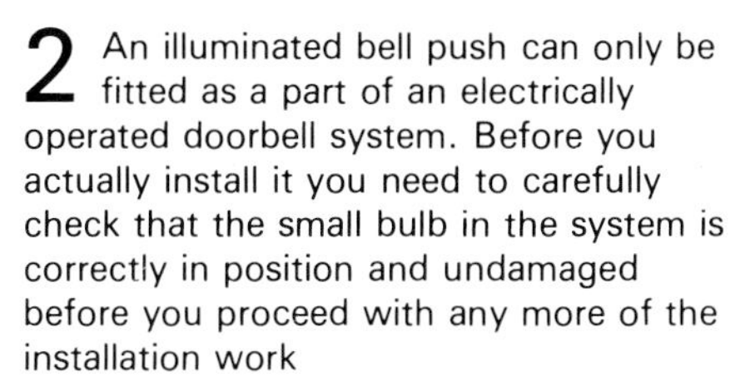

2 An illuminated bell push can only be fitted as a part of an electrically operated doorbell system. Before you actually install it you need to carefully check that the small bulb in the system is correctly in position and undamaged before you proceed with any more of the installation work

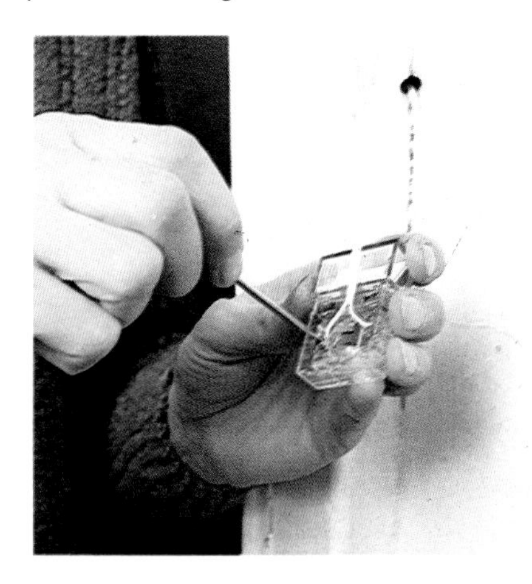

3 Bare the ends of both wires and attach one to each of the two retaining screws, which are located just inside the bell push housing. Then you should turn the bell push system over and screw it firmly and securely to the door frame. If the push has a see-through section for a name card to be fitted to it, this can then be inserted

4 Lead the wire back inside the hall, pinning it neatly, every so often, to the top of the skirting board or running it in conduit, until you reach the chime unit. If you are also installing a back doorbell push, fix this in position at this stage and then run the wires to the chime unit, keeping them out of sight as much as it is possible

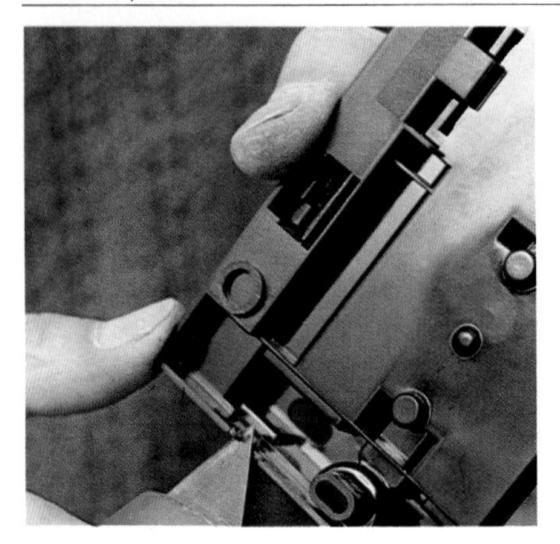

5 Before you fix up the chime unit, use a sharp handyman's knife to clear each of the wire entry points, which are located on the back of the unit. Then secure the unit firmly to the wall using the necessary wall plugs. To ensure that the sound carries it should be positioned about 2m above ground level

6 Having secured the chime unit in place, the next task is to fix the transformer firmly into position. This can be located in a suitable spot anywhere between the chime unit and the spur connection to the electricity mains. Then you should connect up the back of a 3 amp fused unit to the wall

7 Connect the wires from both the front and back doorbell pushes to the output side of the chime unit according to all the manufacturer's instructions. Then link up the input side of the chime unit with the transformer, taking care to choose the two terminals that give the correct voltage needed for this particular type of bell unit

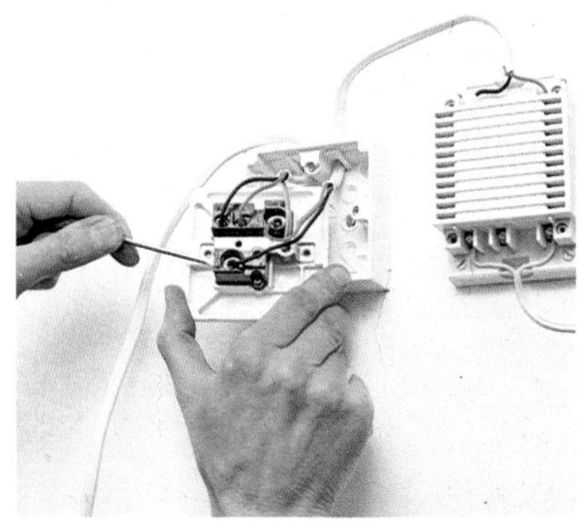

8 The wiring is completed by connecting the transformer input to the fused connection unit and then linking this to the mains. You can then replace the fronts of each box and check that all the wiring is pinned neatly to the wall out of sight. Finally check that you have the right fuse in the connection unit, turn on the power and test the system

were an extra light—though of course you will not need to provide it with a switch as you want the connection to be permanently live.

Complex wiring schemes

Most people will probably be content to have a single bell push mounted on the front door. But if visitors often call at more than one entrance you can easily fit up a second bell push on a side or back door, wired to a central unit.

If you want to do this you should buy a chime unit which has a dual tone. This gives a different sound from each of the different pushes—even though both pushes are wired to the same chime. In this way you can tell whether someone is at the front door or the back door.

B. Below: Doorbell systems incorporating telephones are easily installed and give a greater degree of security than the traditional bell unit

The only problem you may have is in connecting the wires to the transformer. Most transformers are capable of being wired to more than one bell push, but you should seek advice from the manufacturer before you attempt to do this.

Door security devices

Increasingly a number of sophisticated devices are being used to complement or even take the place of traditional doorbells. The most popular of these—available in kit form for the do-it-yourselfer—consists of a speaker system linked from the front door to a telephone situated inside the house. The system gives the householder a greater degree of security than the traditional push bell and its very presence can often deter burglars and house thiefs.

The door security system is connected up in a very similar way to the electric bell system (see above) with a small speaker unit in place of the push button.

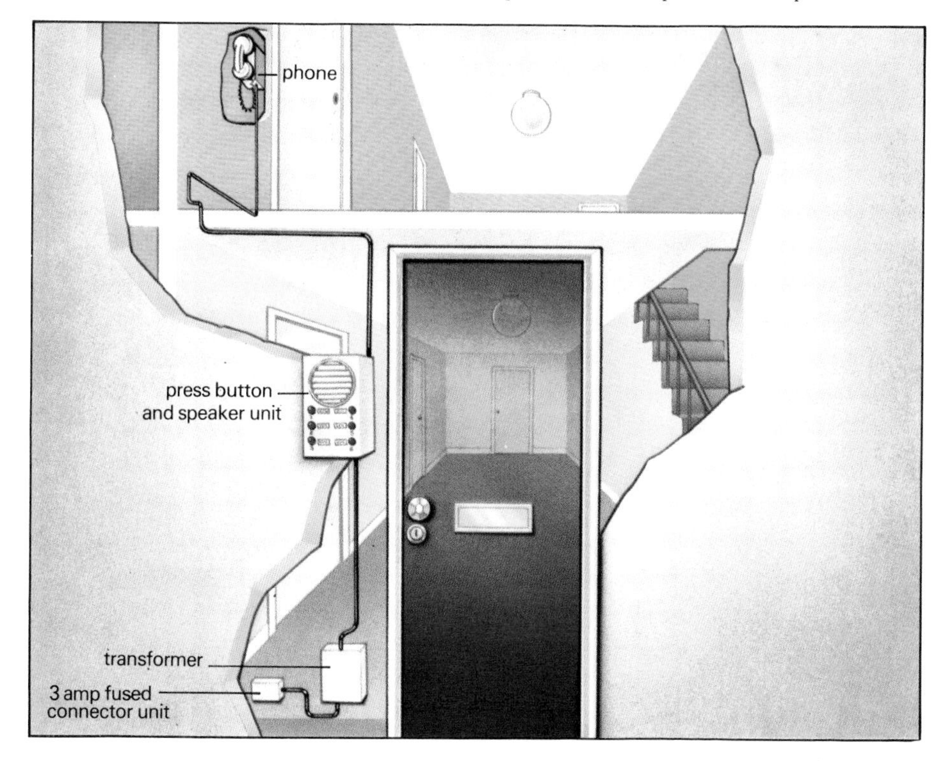

Installing a burglar alarm

Burglary is one of the most worrying types of crime to both householders and flat dwellers alike. Not only are possessions vulnerable: senseless vandalism and personal attack have become increasingly common.

Burglar alarms help to make your home secure in a number of ways: they warn you of an intruder if you are asleep at night; they alert your neighbours if a burglar strikes while you are away; their presence helps deter would-be thieves; and the sound of the alarm should frighten a burglar out of your home

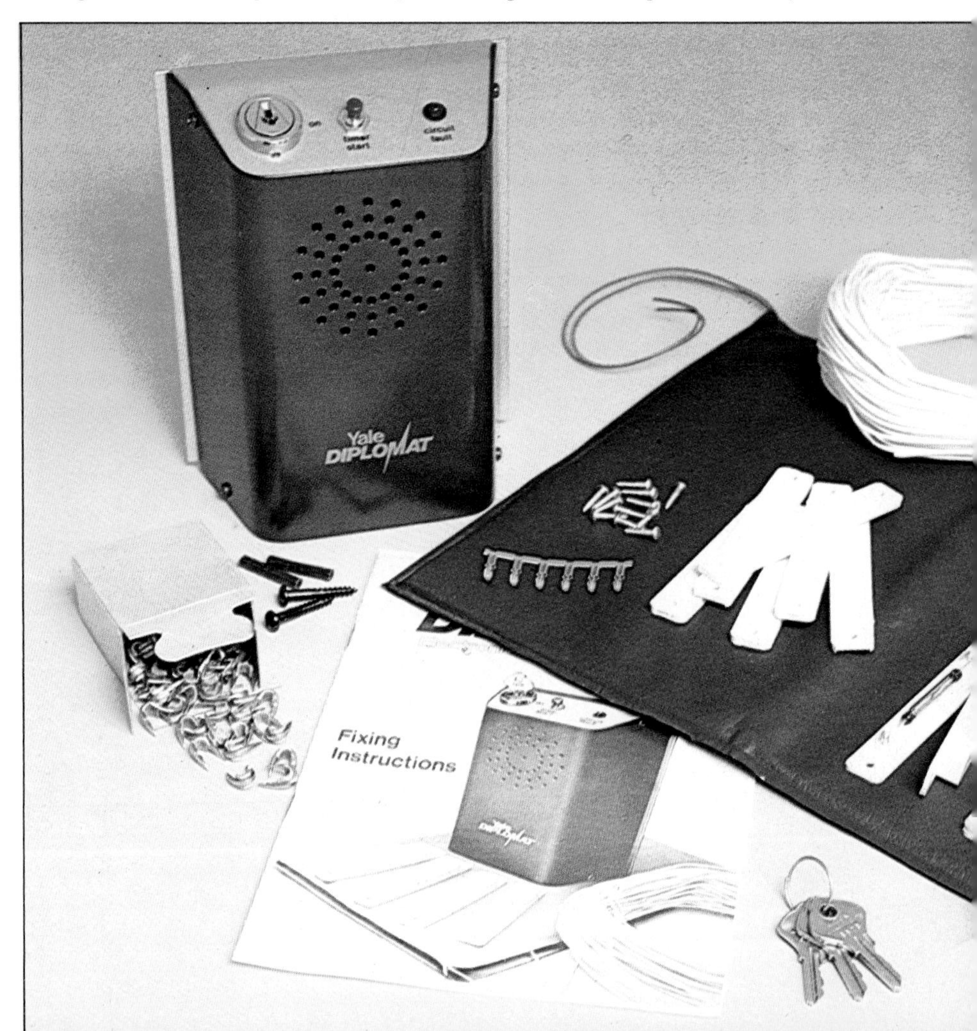

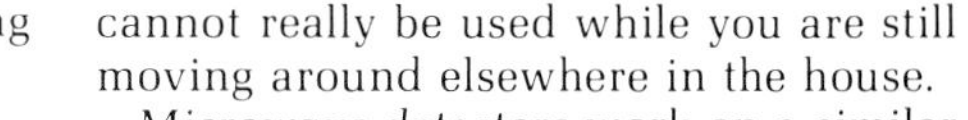

before he has a chance to take anything or do any damage to your property.

Types of burglar alarm

There are several types of alarm available, some of which you can fit yourself. *Ultrasonic detectors* are alarms that employ frequency sound pulses generated by a tiny speaker. The pulses are bounced off room surfaces and are constantly monitored by a microphone, usually housed in the same unit. Any change in the sound pattern triggers the alarm.

The disadvantages of this system are that they may be triggered by such things as traffic noise or blustery wind, and they cannot really be used while you are still moving around elsewhere in the house.

Microwave detectors work on a similar principle to ultrasonic detectors, except that they use radio waves. This kind of alarm is simple to fit, is easily disguised, and very effective. It is less prone to false alarms than the ultrasonic system, but, again, is of little use when the house is occupied.

The basis of electronic loop systems is an unbroken wiring circuit, along which is strung a number of different sensors, all fixed at strategic points. There is nothing to stop you moving about the house once the system is activated.

Open circuits are completed when one of the sensors is activated. As soon as current flows, the control box triggers a bell or siren. The bell circuit is electrically latched so that it cannot be switched off except by a master key.

Closed circuit systems are kept alert by a trickle of electric current. When a sensor is activated the circuit is broken and this triggers the alarm in the same way as an open circuit.

Alarm systems of this type are available for do-it-yourself fittings. Electronic loop systems can be powered by mains or battery, or a combination of the two to guard against mains failure.

A projected beam of invisible light aligned between an emitter and a sensor forms the system used by *infra-red detectors*. If the infra-red beam is broken, the alarm is triggered. To increase their effectiveness, beams can be laced over an area using a series of reflectors. Such systems are complex to install, and are best left to a professional security firm.

Types of sensor

Sensors are the detection devices fitted along a loop circuit to doors and windows and other possible break-in

Left: Several different types of burglar alarm kits are available for the do-it-yourselfer. They can be mains or battery operated but a combination of both is the ideal system

entry points. When a door is opened or a window smashed the circuit is disrupted and the alarm is activated.

There are several types of sensor on the market:

A *microswitch sensor* is a tiny electrical switch activated by a plunger arrangement. The plunger is held down by a closed door or window to complete a closed circuit. If that door or window is opened, the plunger is released, breaking the circuit and triggering the alarm.

A *magnetic reed contact* is a very simple sensor which is featured in very many alarm packages in one form or another. Current is passed through two fine magnetic reeds, sealed in a glass tube. The tube is fitted in a case, in line with the loop circuit, to the frame of a door (or certain types of windows). A

A. Microwave and ultrasonic detectors should be positioned to scan entry points

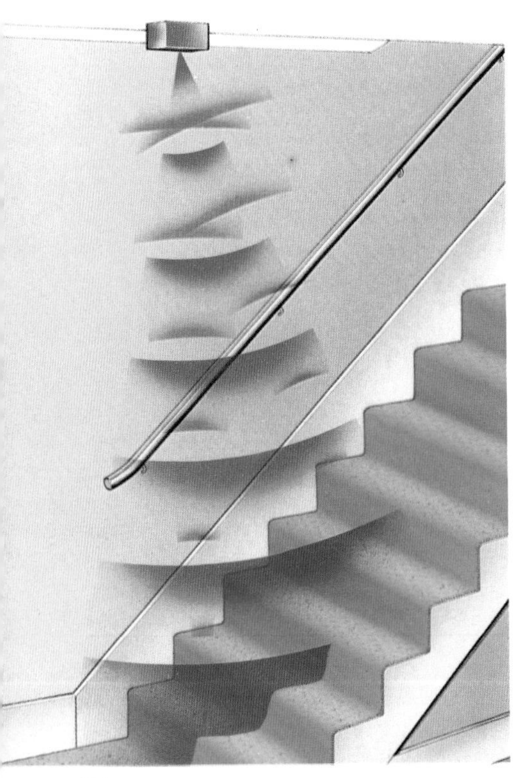

similar case containing a magnet is fitted adjacent to the reed tube, on or in the door itself. The two cases are fitted parallel to each other at the opening edge of the door, usually less than 3–5mm apart. It is particularly important that the two halves of this sensor are correctly aligned.

While the door remains closed, the magnet holds the two concealed reeds together to complete a closed circuit. If the door is then opened by more than the release distance the reeds spring apart and activate the alarm. Concealment is important, as an experienced burglar will certainly be able to use a magnet to keep the reeds together as the door is opened.

Metallic foil detectors are available in self-adhesive rolls for attachment to window glass. Current flows down the foil in a closed circuit and if the window is broken, this is disrupted and the alarm sounds.

Metallic foil detectors have the advantage of advertising to the would-be intruder that your home is protected. They should be fitted to the inside of the glass, close to any window catches.

Vibration contacts are taking over from metallic foil as window sensors because they look neater, are easier to install, and are a better safeguard for modern, large-area widows. They are closed circuit devices contained in self-adhesive cases which can be mounted at suitable points on the glass itself. Heavy vibration breaks the circuit and the alarm sounds.

Most installations also include one or more *pressure mats*. These are open-circuit devices, wired up to a separate pair of contacts in the control box (fig. 7). An intruder stepping on the mat completes the circuit and activates the alarm.

Pressure mats must be installed against a firm floor, under both carpet and underfelt.

Panic buttons (or personal attack buttons) are open circuit devices linked to their own separate terminals in the control box and, usually, they can be kept constantly activated during the day. If you are attacked by an intruder, you

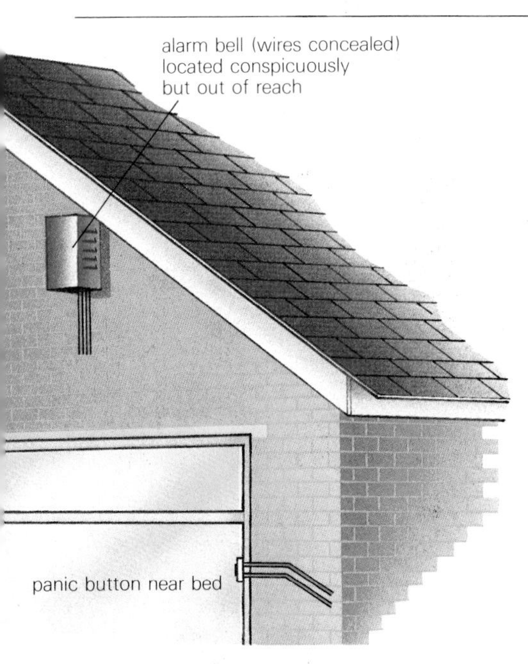

B. It is sometimes advisable to fit an exterior alarm at the back of the house where it is least noticeable. Panic buttons can be sited by your bed.

press the button to activate the alarm.

Loop alarm kits

Most alarm kits come complete with a range of different sensors; they also contain wiring and instructions for linking them to the *control box*. This contains a number of terminals for connection of open circuits, closed circuits, panic buttons and—sometimes—smoke detectors.

Into the control box comes electric power to maintain the closed circuits in the alert mode and to power the alarm bell itself.

Some systems rely entirely on battery power. They use very small currents to maintain the circuits, but the batteries drain rapidly once the alarm is sounded.

The disadvantage of a mains-powered system is that it is affected by power cuts. Also, the power and alarm bell cables must both be well concealed to prevent tampering, as the easiest way to immobilize this kind of an alarm system is to disconnect either of these.

The best alarm kits use a combination of mains and battery power so that if the mains fails or is tampered with, the system switches automatically to battery power.

All alarm systems have some kind of keyed *master control switch* which enables you to set the alarm and turn it off. There is usually a time delay to give you a few seconds to enter or leave the house or get away from the alarm-sensitive areas.

Some systems merely have a key switch on the control box. Others can incorporate remote switches and these may be elsewhere in the house, often by the front door.

Alarm systems usually make use of small bells that produce a very loud sound. Once the bell is activated it can only be turned off by the master switch key.

The purpose of interior bells is to frighten the intruder out of your house, so locate these in an inaccessible spot such as at the top of the stair well. Exterior bells, which come in weather-proof cases, are intended to alert neighbours and passers-by. They should be installed high, out of reach, with the wiring to them passing directly through the wall to prevent tampering.

Planning and fitting the system

When you plan your alarm system, concentrate the alarm sensors at vulnerable points such as windows and doors, and around any inside region where the burglar is likely to go—such as the hallway. Start by thoroughly surveying your ground floor and draw up a plan, noting the vulnerable areas likely. Mark out a circuit line for the closed circuit sensors which links them up in the most economical way.

All doors to the outside should be included in the closed loop, especially those with any areas of glass such as sliding patio doors. The latter can be fitted

1 Plan a convenient location for the alarm control box and mark the position of fixing holes for this. Then screw the box firmly into place

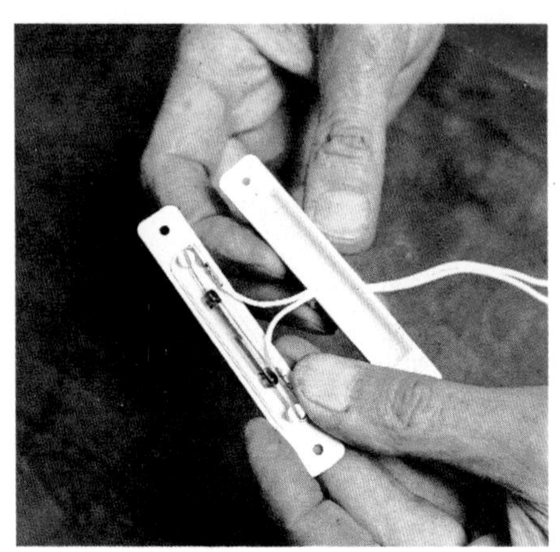

2 If necessary, wire up the magnetic reed contacts using wire provided with the kit. Check that the magnetic action is in satisfactory working order

5 For a cylindrical reed sensor, drill a hole in the frame. Then wire up the reed contact and put it carefully in the hole. Feed the wire into the back

6 Fit the magnet section neatly into a hole drilled in the door edge. Then connect up the reed contact to the closed circuit loop

with a magnetic reed sensor that is shielded from the metal.

Fit sensors to some interior doors as well.

All ground-floor windows are vulnerable, but pay special attention to large bay windows, and windows concealed from general view at the back of the house and down alleyways. Fit either metallic tape sensors or vibration sensors.

Fit pressure mats at strategic points, such as at the bottom of the stairs or in front of valuable objects. Small pressure

3 The reed section of the sensor is located on the door frame. In some types of kit, this is set into the woodwork to remain completely out of view

4 Shut the door and butt the magnet section against the reed section and screw into place. Then pin the wires to the corner and behind the door frame

7 Another commonly used sensor is a pressure mat, which is best located near a likely entry point or passageway or close to valuables

8 All connecting wires should be completely concealed from view to discourage tampering—but this is not an essential requirement for closed circuits

mats can be fitted up the stairs.

Locate the control box in a position that is out of sight, but not so far from the door that you cannot leave the house having just activated the system. The control box is fixed to the wall, or a mounting panel, using plugs and screws.

Where wiring must cross a door, run it under the carpet, over the door frame or through a flexible door cable, which most kits offer as an accessory. Power and alarm bell connections should be concealed at ground level: if possible run the wiring beneath floorboarding.

Installing fluorescent lighting

Fluorescent lights with their characteristic, glare-free light are today very much a part of the home lighting scene. And placed with care, they can create effects well beyond the capabilities of ordinary light bulbs.

Their light output, measured in lumens per watt, varies according to the colour of the light, but for general lighting it is more than three times that of an incandescent bulb. For example, the light output of a 40 watt fluorescent tube is about the same as that of two 100 watt bulbs.

The main disadvantage of fluorescent lighting is that it produces a shadowless light which can destroy the attractive character of a room. Although the hard shadows produced by some tungsten lights can be objectionable and dangerous in the vicinity of stairways, a living room without shadows can be unbearable.

Choice of colour

Fluorescent tubes are available in either 'warm' or 'cool' colours, and whereas the cool colours—such as the 'natural' commonly found in offices—may be acceptable in the domestic garage or workshop, you are likely to need a much warmer colour in a living area.

For example, the Philips Softone 32, or a de-luxe warm white tube has good colour rendering and a warm colour similar to that of tungsten lighting. These features make it and similar lamps particularly suitable for decorative lighting above curtains, pictures and cupboards.

Circular lamps are found only in the warm white series, but because they are normally enclosed by a decorative diffuser of either plain or tinted glass, lamp colour itself is not critical.

Types of tube

The standard straight fluorescent tubes are made in a number of lengths and wattages, ranging from 125 watt down to 15 watt and 2400mm down to 450mm, though 40 watt tubes, either 1200mm or 600mm long, are common.

Miniature tubes are also available. These are from about 525mm long down to as little as 150mm and are rated at only a few watts. They are typically used in shaving mirrors, cooker hoods and inspection lamps.

Circular fluorescent tubes are made in a number of sizes—from 60 and 40 watt, both 400mm diameter, down to tubes of about half that size.

Installing a fluorescent fitting

The typical domestic fluorescent fitting consists of a metal batten or casing, which contains the ballast gear, switch-starter (where appropriate) and associated components including a capacitor, internal wiring and a terminal block. Two bi-pin lampholders project from the underside of the batten to support the tube.

Note: Remember never to work on a circuit until you are certain power is switched off at the mains and it is not live.

Start by removing the cover of the batten to gain access to the cable entry holes, the screw fixing holes and the terminal block. Decide where you want to position the fitting, then hold it against the fixing surface and use a bradawl to

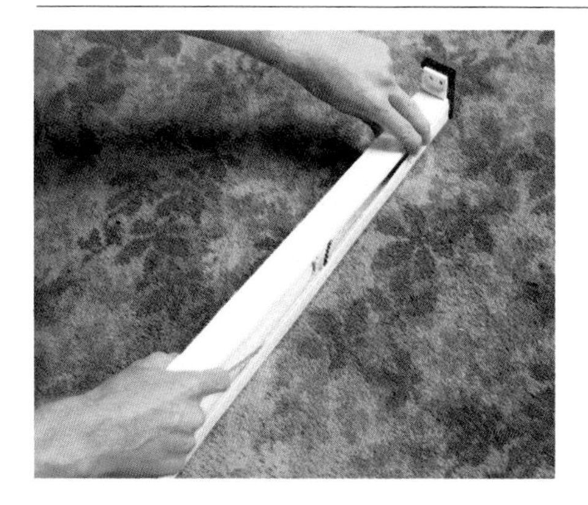

1 To wire up a standard fluorescent light, start by removing the diffuser (if there is one) then unclip the cover from the body of the fitting

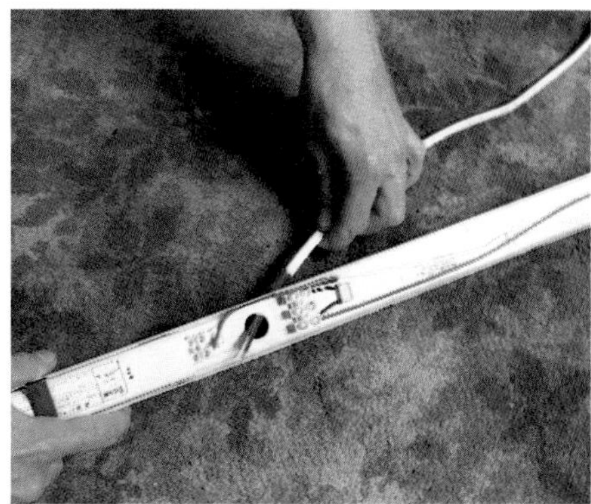

2 Feed in the appropriate length of 1.5mm^2 twin and earth PVC cable through the large hole that is punched in the back of the fitting

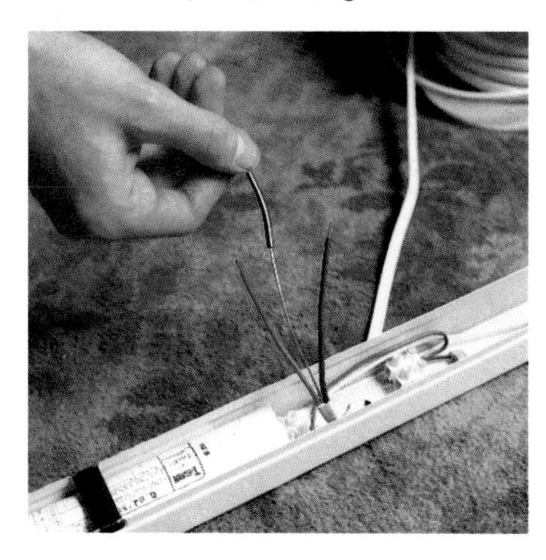

3 Before you go any further, make sure that the bare earth wire is covered with a suitable length of green and yellow PVC sleeving insulation

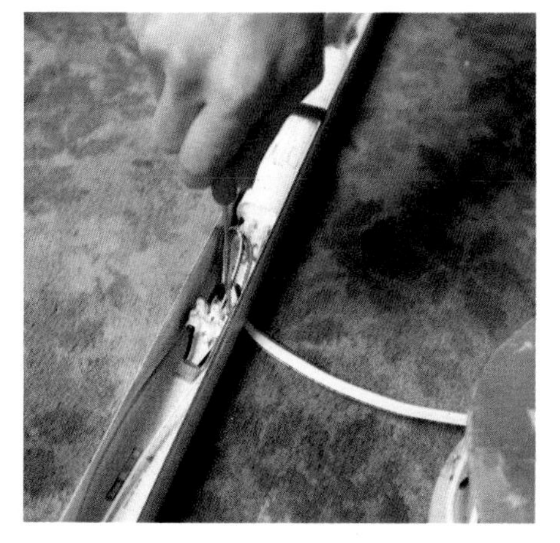

4 Next connect up the wires in the cable to their appropriate terminals inside the fitting—red to L, black to N, and green and yellow to Earth

mark the screw holes. Bear in mind that where you are replacing an existing fitting you may have to allow for the position of the cables already there.

In the case of a ceiling mounting, once you have marked the holes check where they fall in relation to the joists. If one or more holes are between joists, you may have to drill additional holes in the base of the fitting or fit a piece of timber between the joists in the relevant place. But in many cases, slightly adjusting the fitting position saves either task.

Before handling the existing wiring, remember to turn off the electricity and to remove the appropriate fuse or fuses. Once you have arranged the cable run to the fitting (see below), feed this through the entry hole then secure the fitting to the ceiling using No. 8 woodscrews.

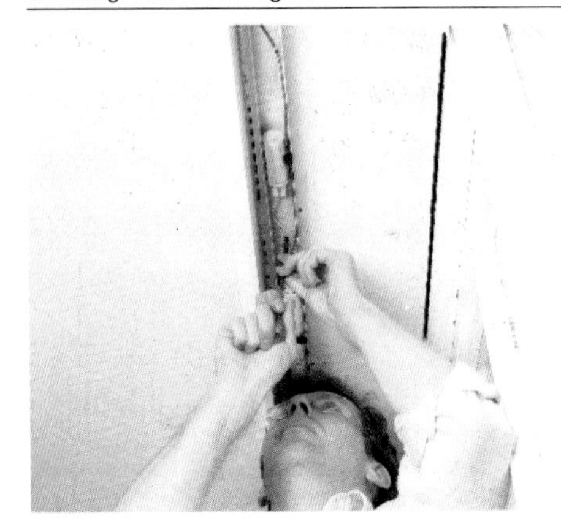

5 Use the fitting as a template for marking the fixing positions. Check that these are really secure before you finally screw the fitting in place

6 If you cannot actually get to the ceiling void, run the cable down a door or window frame and then take the supply from a fused spur

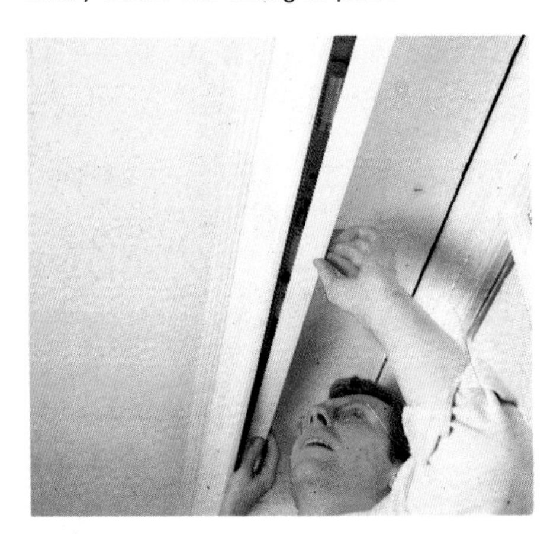

7 Make sure that the connections in the fitting have not dislodged themselves during installation, then you can put the cover back in position

8 Finally, fit the tube itself. Check that it is securely held in the bi-pin lampholders at either end before you attempt to switch on

Wiring up

If you are replacing an existing light fitting, it is possible in most cases to use the cable from this for the new installation. Having prepared the ends of the cable as necessary, simply connect the wires to the terminal block on the fitting.

The one exception is where your fluorescent light is of the *switchless* type and your lighting circuit of the older, non-earthed variety. In this case you must run a length of 1.5mm^2 single-core PVC insulated non-sheathed cable from the earth terminal in the consumer unit to that of the fitting.

Where the new fitting is to replace two or more lights on the same circuits, the wires to these must be disconnected and drawn back to a junction box situated

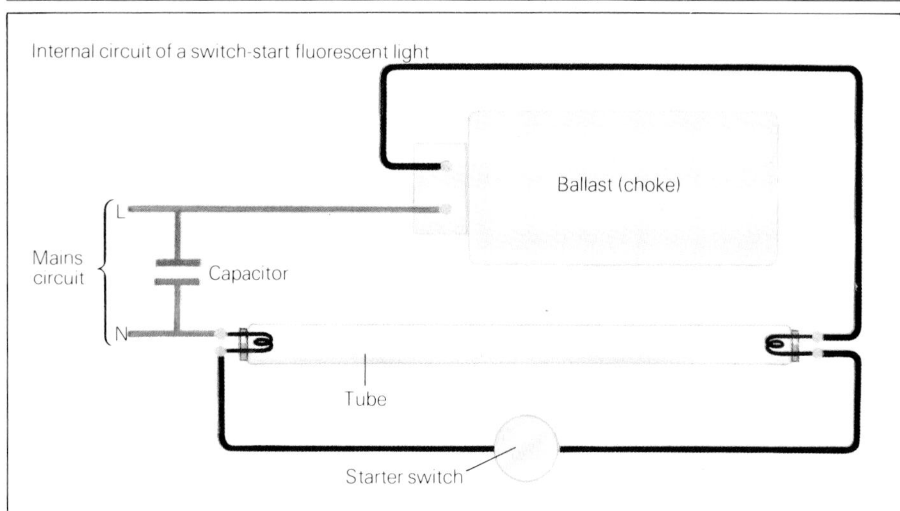

A. Top: The circuit of a switch-start fluorescent light contains several parts but has no need of an independent earth connection. **B. Bottom**: The simpler switchless circuit. In both types, the colours of the wires marked black vary according to makes and you must trace them back to source if difficult to identify

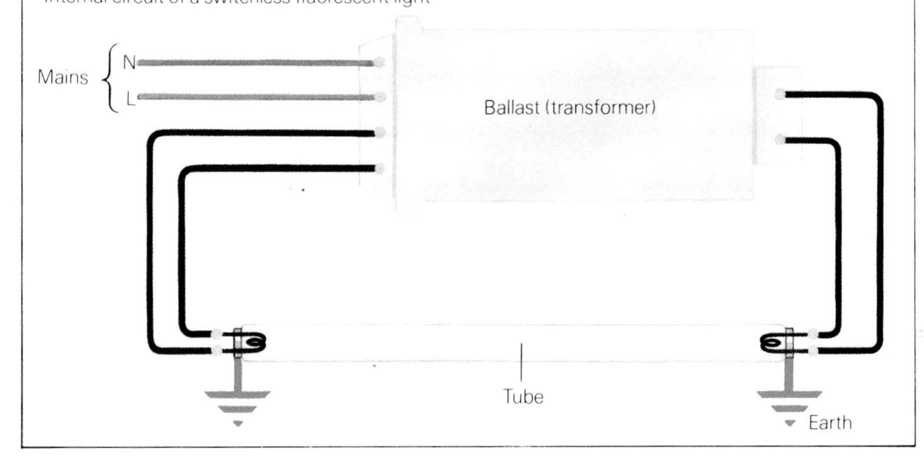

in the ceiling void.

Entirely new installations can be wired either from the lighting circuit or from a 5 amp fused spur taken off the ring main. Where access to the ceiling void is easy, the former is usually the obvious choice. Identify and break into the three-way junction box and light switch, then run a new length of cable to the fitting.

But where the new installation is to be at a lower level—such as underneath fitted cupboards above a worksurface—it is often easier to take a switched fused spur from the ring main, fit this adjacent to the installation and then connect it to the batten or holder.

Other fittings

Circular fluorescent fittings are even simpler to fix than the strip type. Simply secure the metal backplate to the fixing surface and connect the wires to the cable connector, then install the lamp and fit the diffuser.

Shaving lights, bulkhead fittings and other miniature tube lighting fittings are fixed and connected in the same way as ordinary light fittings.

For pelmet lighting use the thin, batten type of fitting with reflector tubes to produce maximum downward light. Though the fittings are installed in the normal way, positioning is important if the right effect is to be achieved. The lights must be no less than 150mm in front of the curtains, two or more tubes must be overlapped to prevent dark patches, and the end of the tube (or tubes) must extend a good 50mm beyond the curtain width.

Dimmer switching

It is not possible to use an ordinary dimmer switch to control a fluorescent light. Where a fluorescent fitting replaces a tungsten filament light controlled by a dimmer switch, it is simpler to replace the dimmer with an ordinary type of switch.

How fluorescent lights work

The most important component in a fluorescent light is the glass tube. This is coated on the inside with a fluorescent powder, and contains mercury vapour and a small amount of argon gas to assist starting. At each end of the tube is an electrode with a small heating element—similar to the filament of an ordinary light bulb—which is coated with an electron-emitting substance.

When an electric current is applied to the heated electrodes, electrons flow along the inside of the tube. These bombard the glass, causing the powder to fluoresce and so produce the characteristic light.

Once it has been started, a fluorescent tube needs nowhere near as much current as an ordinary bulb. Consequently, it requires a controlling device called a *ballast* to limit the flow of current. The ballast and its associated components are usually contained in the fluorescent fitting.

There are two methods of starting, or 'striking', the flow of electrons in the tube. The first, termed the *switch-start*, uses a starter switch—a canister similar in appearance to the flasher unit of a motor car or 35mm film canister—which is installed in the side of the fitting. The other is known as the *switchless* or 'quick start' because there is no delay between switching on the light and the tube striking in the familiar 'flashing manner'.

When a switch-start fluorescent light is switched on, current flows through the ballast unit—which contains a choke—on to the starter and then through the electrode heaters. After a short interval, the switch starter contacts open and produce a surge of high voltage from the choke which is discharged between the heated electrodes to start the continuous flow of electrons and keep the tube alight. The job of the switch is then finished, though the choke remains in circuit to control the current flow.

When a switchless fluorescent light is switched on, current flows through a transformer, which has a low voltage tapping to the electrodes, causing them to emit electrons. The high voltage surge which starts the flow of electrons is provided by a special earthed tube, which has a metal strip running from one end to the other and is earthed to the circuit through the lamp caps.

When installing a switchless fluorescent fitting or replacing a tube, you must therefore make sure that the tube is of the switchless type; although a switchless tube will operate in a switch-start fitting, the opposite does not apply.

A fluorescent tube has an average life of 7000 hours compared with 1000 hours for a standard electric light bulb. For average use this represents over ten years of life.

When a fluorescent tube fails it does not fail completely like a tungsten bulb. Instead it behaves in a characteristic manner usually flashing on and off or dimming before the light finally fails.

Concealed lighting

Use fluorescent lights to give an effective treatment to high, narrow or badly lit corridors.

Many older houses with high ceilings have corridors that are very tall and narrow and difficult to light. Fitting a suspended ceiling reduces the height and alters the proportion of the corridor.

This design includes circular fluorescent lights for a spread of even, bright light. They are concealed behind a pierced grid, which gives an interesting surface and patterns the light. It is based on commercially available, pre-formed chipboard ceiling panels, but you can use softwood slats as an alternative. The pre-formed panels are 600mm square, so you will have to fit your design to this size and add intermediate supports for ceilings with a larger span.

Fit bearer battens to the wall and add a soffit on which to support the lights. The latter are simple 300mm diameter tubes with a remote choke. Paint the soffit matt black then clip the tubes in place and wire them up.

The ceiling panels are held to the battens by sliding clip fittings designed for the purpose.

Spot and track lighting

The traditional method of lighting a room—a single central bulb hanging from the ceiling—leaves a lot to be desired. True, the light levels in the room may be enough for most purposes, but a single bulb makes for a very stark lighting scheme with little atmosphere.

There are many ways of creating this elusive atmosphere using carefully planned lighting systems, but one of the most effective is to use spotlights.

Spotlights—whether mounted like an ordinary ceiling or wall light, or on lengths of track—can be used for two main purposes: *task lighting*, where they serve to illuminate a desk or working surface; and *mood lighting*, where they play on and subtly highlight pictures, ornaments and plants.

Choosing spotlights

Once you have decided how a room is to be used and decorated you must decide how to light it. At first glance the choice of available light fittings is bewildering, but your first priority is to choose the type of spotlight bulb (more correctly called the *lamp*) that will give you the type of illumination you want.

There are four basic types of spotlight lamp in general use: the general lamp service (GLS); the internally silvered lamp (ISL); the crown-silvered lamp (CS); and the parabolic aluminized reflector (PAR) lamp. They all give roughly the same amount of light for a given wattage, but because they concentrate and diffuse the light in different ways, each produces a different intensity of light at any particular distance.

GLS lamps: This is an ordinary light bulb and must therefore be mounted in a reflective light fitting. The beam of light emitted is broad and diffused, but up to 2m away from the subject a 60 watt lamp is sufficient for reading.

ISL lamps: Probably the most common spotlamp of all, the back of the lamp is silvered so that nearly all the light output is in a strongly directional beam with a 35° spread. Used in the same way as the GLS lamp and at the same wattage the ISL gives a higher levei of illumination.

CS lamps: These are silvered at the front so that the light is reflected back to a parabolic reflector in the fitting. The resulting forward-facing beam has a concentrated spread of about 15°, which gives a very intense level of light around the subject. This beam is seen to best effect when mounted on a high (4m) ceiling and used to illuminate a table.

PAR lamps: These have a parabolic reflector and are available with coloured lenses. They can be bought as spotlights with a narrow beam or floodlights with a wide beam and because they are totally sealed they can be used out of doors.

Lamp caps: All four types of lamp are available with one of three caps (the part that goes into the fitting) namely, bayonet, single centre contact, and Edison screw. Like ordinary lamps, the smaller sizes have smaller caps.

Types of light fitting

Once you have decided which type of lamp is best suited to each lighting position, you can choose a light fitting that will take it.

CS lamps, for example, need a parabolic reflector—and this obviously restricts your choice of fittings somewhat. GLS lamps also need a reflector of some sort, though unless you need a fairly concentrated beam of light the shape of the reflector is not so important. With ISL and PAR lamps no reflector is necessary to control the spread and shape of the light beam, so the choice of fitting open to you is potentially vast.

Controlling glare: Glare can be an irritating problem when reading or working. CS lamps with their narrow beams do not create much sideways glare, but others almost certainly will. The answer in this case is to use a recessed fitting.

Left: Spotlights and track lighting look far more complicated to install than they actually are. For a modest outlay and a little work you can greatly alter (and often improve) the lighting and atmosphere in any of the rooms in your home

1 When you decide you want to install a recessed spotlight, start by selecting a suitable site for it, then use a cardboard template and pencil to mark its position clearly on the selected ceiling. Then drill a hole carefully through the ceiling inside the circle and cut carefully around the circumference of the marked-out hole with a padsaw

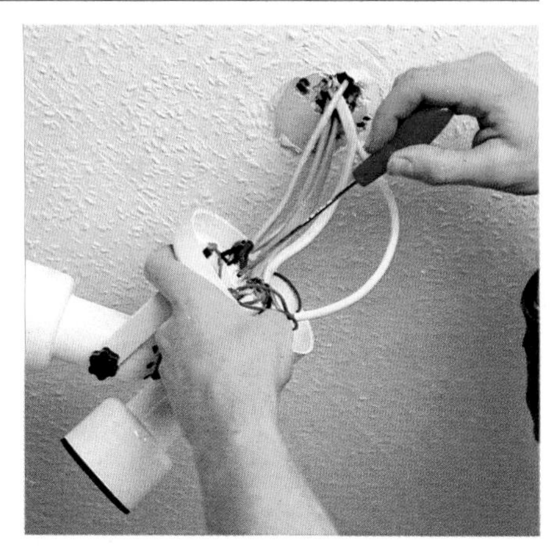

2 When you have cut out the hole in the ceiling and taken care not to damage any of the surrounding plaster work, you can draw a power supply from a nearby loop-in ceiling rose. This can be very easily done by connecting heat-resistant cable to the existing ceiling rose and then running it along to the position of the new lamp

5 An important point which should always be carefully noted when you decide to fit a recessed spotlight into the ceiling is to make sure you get the correct match of lamp and fitting. The particular fitting detailed does not feature a reflector unit, so the only lamps that will be really suitable for it are the ISL or PAR type of lighting units

6 If you decide you want to power a section of track light from a loop-in ceiling rose, replace the two-core flex running to the lampholder with a length of three-core flex. Next you should strip off the sheathing and insulation from the flex and connect it up to the track's electrical adaptor—this is also known as the 'live end'

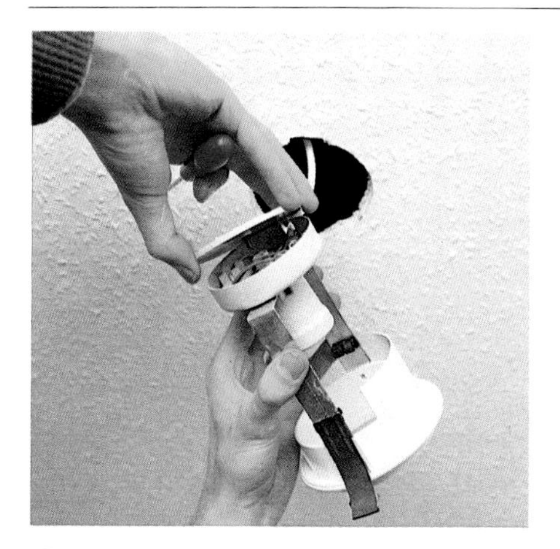

3 Connect up the heat-resistant cable to the recessed fitting at its other end. In this particular case no thermal insulation was necessary to protect the roof space area. You can then fit the protective cover safely over the terminals, but make sure that the cable sheathing does not finish short of this box so as to expose the cores

4 This unit has adjustable steel brackets that rest on the ceiling and support its weight. Set them correctly and then slip the fitting into the hole. To prevent any disturbance from glare many recessed spotlights have a black ribbed drum on the inside. Slip this in place inside the fitting before you actually install the selected lamp

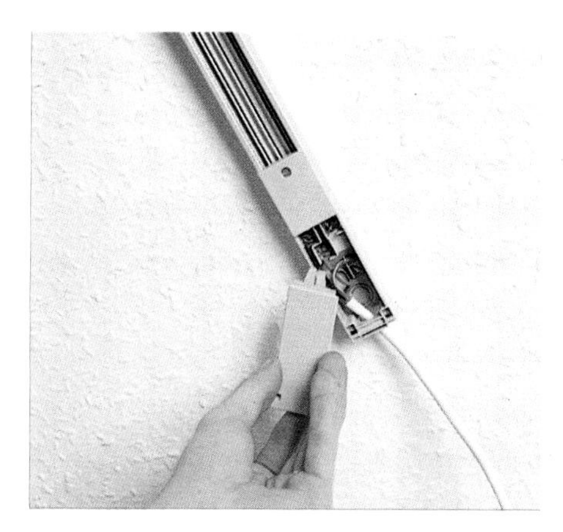

7 Screw the light track to the ceiling using woodscrews and cavity plugs, plug in the electrical adaptor, and then snap the conducting strip firmly into place. The next stage is to clip the top cover into position on the electrical adaptor, making sure the flex insulation terminates well inside the actual unit and that it does not overlap

8 You can buy an adaptor which replaces the ceiling rose of a joint box system. The unit is screwed to the ceiling and the live end is wired up in the normal way. Fix the track to the ceiling next to the adaptor, plug in the live end adaptor, and then screw the top cover in place to neatly conceal the hole and all the flex

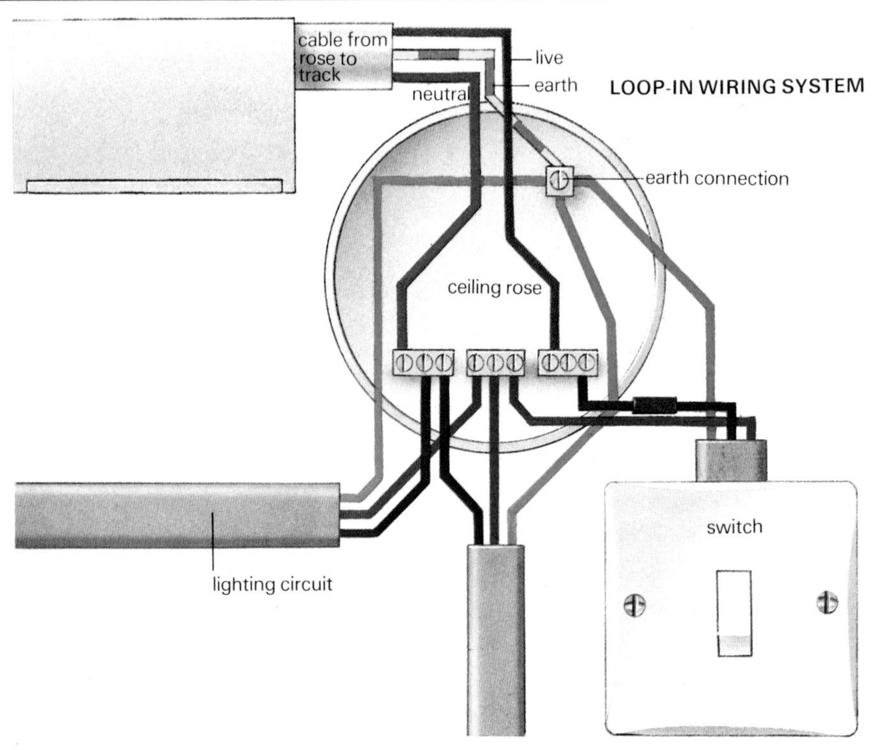

Types of mounting

Light fittings are often mounted on adjustable brackets so that the light beam can be pointed in any direction. Many fittings can be mounted directly on walls or ceilings, and most can also be bought with special adaptors for mounting on tracks.

Light fittings are available for recessing into a ceiling. Most are fixed so that the bulb points straight down—a *downlighter*—and drum-type fittings are the most popular. Other fittings have baffles which push the light out more horizontally than vertically. These are known as *wallwashers* because they are often used to illuminate a picture below them or part of the wall.

Track lighting

One disadvantage of having permanently mounted spotlights is that you cannot alter the character of the lighting system in a room without a great deal of trouble.

For this reason, track lighting with its built-in flexibility has become extremely popular. A light track is a length of metal or plastic incorporating continuous live, neutral and earth conductors which cannot be touched accidentally. This is screwed to the wall or ceiling and spotlights are then mounted on it using special adaptors. The lights can be slid along the track, mounted or dismounted easily, and all the lights on one track operate from the same power supply.

Track generally comes in lengths of about 1m; some makes can be cut shorter, while all makes clip together to form longer lengths or different shapes. The electricity supply is connected to an adaptor which clips into one end. Some light fitting adaptors have built-in switches so that you can switch lights on and off individually, but unless you use adaptors with pull-cord switches this may present problems.

The most important thing to remember

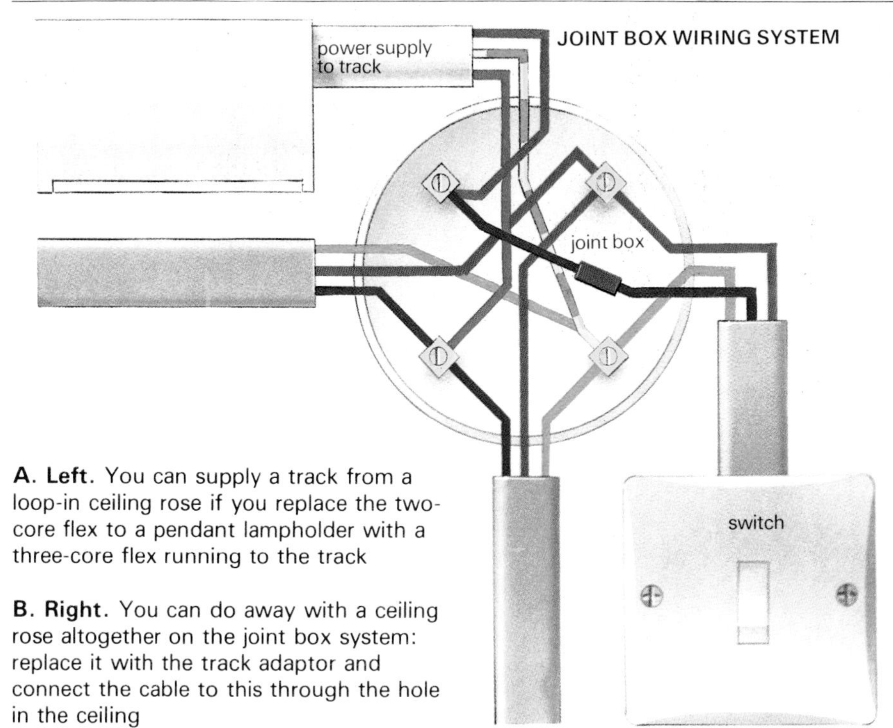

A. Left. You can supply a track from a loop-in ceiling rose if you replace the two-core flex to a pendant lampholder with a three-core flex running to the track

B. Right. You can do away with a ceiling rose altogether on the joint box system: replace it with the track adaptor and connect the cable to this through the hole in the ceiling

about track is that it is not always possible to mix and match it with light fittings and adaptors; if you are considering buying a track lighting system, make sure you can get light fittings.

Installation

The installation details that follow refer mainly to UK wiring practice. Wherever you live, never take chances with electricity: *switch off* at the mains and check the current is dead before starting work.

Spotlight fittings are installed in much the same way as other light fittings, but there are two special factors to take into account.

First, there is a limit to the number of lights you can have on a circuit. In the UK, most lighting circuits are 5 amp, and the practical limit is 12 lamps—which can soon be reached if you plan to add several spotlights to an existing circuit. There are two main ways round this problem. You can install an extra lighting circuit—if you have a spare fuseway on the consumer unit (fuseboard)—or you can fit an additional consumer unit. Or you can connect some lights to a ring main circuit. You can take a spur off the ring main at any convenient point, and wire it using 2.5mm^2 cable to a fused connection unit fitted with a 13 amp fuse. From this, you can run a circuit using 1.5mm^2 cable for up to 24 lamps, incorporating switches and so on as for any lighting circuit.

Of course, if you have room on an existing circuit, you can wire spotlights in a number of ways. If you are replacing an existing fitting, or adding a light to be run off the same switch, simply wire to the existing ceiling rose. For a separate light with its own switch, you can either run the new circuit from a loop-in rose if there is one conveniently placed or from a new joint box fitted into the existing lighting circuit. Many fittings have only

Above: Several kinds of spotlights can be used to create bright or subdued effects

three wiring terminals inside: if you want to wire such a fitting on the loop-in system, you will have to add an additional terminal block to the fitting for the switch wire.

The second problem is that old lighting circuits have no earth wire. For spotlights that need earthing, you will have to run an earth wire from the fitting back to the consumer unit.

Many fittings have no backing plate on the mounting piece: the UK wiring regulations require such a plate. One solution is to fix the mounting piece over a circular conduit junction box.

Installing track lighting

In general, track lighting installation is the same as for other fittings: the track is screwed to the wall or ceiling and the lights are then plugged into it.

You can draw the power supply for the track in many of the ways described above. But the electrical adaptor pieces are usually rather small and do not allow room for you to add a loop-in terminal, so you may need to use the joint-box method of wiring.

Recessed fittings

Most manufacturers offer light fittings that can be recessed into the ceiling to be used as downlighters and wall-washers. There are two basic types: one is dropped through a hole in the ceiling from above and is supported by brackets which rest on the ceiling; the other is offered up from below and has a bezel which is screwed to the ceiling using woodscrews and plugs.

Before buying and fitting recessed light fittings there are a few points to consider: first of all make sure that there is sufficient space above ceiling level for the fitting; secondly check that there are no restrictions on how close to a ceiling joist you can mount the fitting; and thirdly ensure that there is no way that the fitting could overheat and become potentially dangerous.

The last point is very important, as spotlights operate at very high temperatures. Follow any fitting instructions closely, if necessary lining the nearest joists and laths and the undersides of the floorboards above with asbestos mat to protect them from the heat. If you are mounting the fittings into a ceiling with a loft or roof space above it, keep any thermal insulation well away from the fitting or it will overheat very quickly. The best solution is to make a heat-resistant housing for the fitting, over which you can re-lay the insulation.

You may be required to use heat-resistant flex within 1m of the fitting. In this case, run the flex from the fitting and connect it to the power cable and the switch using a suitable joint-box wiring system.

Free-standing lamps

The passing of the oil lamp should be mourned. It represented a highly civilized form of domestic lighting for two obvious reasons—it could be easily moved to where light was needed and you could adjust brightness. An additional bonus was the colour temperature of the oil light, which was 'warm', because it was primarily at the red end of the colour spectrum.

Contrast this to the stark and clinical cold/blue light produced by a ceiling-mounted fluorescent tube, and you can soon appreciate the advantages of localized, warm lighting.

Table or standard lamps have superseded oil lamps and these generally use hot filaments, which also give off light towards the red end of the spectrum. They are movable, as far as the lamp flex will allow, and, by selecting a suitable wattage bulb, can be adjusted for brightness.

In addition to being used to provide localized light—for reading, needlework or even background illumination for TV viewing—standard and table lamps can also, if carefully located, be used to give dramatic effects. Dark corners or alcoves can be illuminated with relatively high-intensity localized light. This provides a natural contrast with main room lighting, helping to counter shadows and also contrasting the 'flatness' which is created by a predominantly overhead lighting system.

Below: This decorative brass table lamp with an unusual glass shade really complements the highly ornate side table

Above: A free-standing lamp with an adjustable neck and high-intensity spotlight is perfect for a modern setting.
Left: This pretty lamp adds a colourful touch to the simple wall display

Equally, table lamps can be used to concentrate light on ornaments, plants and so on, without recourse to the colder light often produced by wall-mounted spotlights or fittings with internally silvered lamp bulbs. Free-standing standard lamps are designed to throw light either upwards or downwards, depending on the shade. Some shades are semi-translucent, which allows some light to go through sideways and gives a softer effect.

With traditional table or standard lamps you can restrict the spread of light by choosing the right type of lampshade. Dense, drum shades will spill light up and down while only a little escapes through the shade's fabric. And dense shades also prevent glare at eye level, even though they illuminate effectively the table upon which the lamp is placed. For TV viewing this arrangement is ideal. There is little reflected light from the screen to cause distraction, yet the room is not in complete darkness, and is less likely to cause any possible eye strain.

Another way of altering the intensity of a lamp is to move its shade around, experimenting to see which way the shadows fall to achieve the best effect.

The only practical restriction on where you can position either table or standard lamps is the location of a suitable power point. Simply using long flex is no answer, especially if it stretches over a walkway.

A sensible approach is to first plan thoroughly where you intend to position lamps and then to introduce power

Below: This old-fashioned type of oil lamp has been cleverly converted to use electric power to provide a pretty and decorative light source

points as close as possible to these locations. It is a good idea for you to add these fittings before, say, you decorate a room.

In some cases in the UK, table and standard lamps can be incorporated into the lighting circuit using approved plugs, sockets and fittings. This leaves the 13 amp ring main circuit free for components which operate at higher wattages.

There is a huge choice of lamps and shades available today. With table or standard spotlights, the units are integral and must therefore complement your interior decoration as a complete assembly. But with more traditional lamps the style can be altered quite substantially by the choice of shades, both in terms of colour and fabric. Shades can be covered to match the wallpaper or curtain fabric so that they become part of a well-planned and co-ordinated scheme.

Oil, Victorian and art deco lamps are now very popular and there are good reproductions available to give you a considerable choice of colour and different styles. Search around junk shops and antique shops to see if you can find lamps of this type which are suitable.

Remember that free-standing lamps can be relatively inexpensive devices for changing the entire appearance of a room. Whether you need them for practical puposes or simply to achieve a mood, they can be invaluable for highlighting or disguising special features.

Below: A decorative fringed shade on a standard lamp gives ideal light for reading by and adds character to the room

Lighting outdoors

Well-designed exterior lighting can turn your patio or garden into a night-time wonderland. On warm summer evenings, garden lights enable you to extend your living space outside. And even in colder climates, when there is frost or snow in the air, exterior lighting adds a sparkling new dimension to the view from your windows.

But exterior lights serve more than just a decorative purpose. You can use them to light up a porch and front door; or to illuminate drives and pathways so that visitors can see the way in.

Choosing exterior lights

The variety of exterior lights and lamps almost equals that of interior lighting. Long gone are the days when you could buy only rather crude floodlights which made the garden resemble a football pitch. Modern exterior lights range in function from spotlamps to hanging lanterns, and in style from old-fashioned brass to ultra-modern bulbous glass.

Wall-mounted lamps which cast a soft, diffused light are suitable for lighting a porch, a patio or even a gate in a garden wall. Many shops sell beautiful old brass lanterns converted for this purpose, and replicas are just as easily available. Cast-iron, cottage-style lamps have a similar function and, with frosted glass windows, lend a Dickensian glow to the porch. More suited to modern-style houses are the cylindrical, circular and oval designs with frosted or clouded glass.

Floodlights and spotlamps, casting a swathe of light through the darkness, can pick out anything from trees to the whole front or rear elevation of the house. You can buy them hooded to restrict the light path, or fully exposed to cast a broader beam.

Mounted in the ground they can be

Below: Add drama and mystery to your garden by using spotlights to highlight statues or attractive ornamental features such as dark garden pools or perhaps rockeries

pointed in any direction, in trees they appear as a secret source of light and on a sweeping driveway they can illuminate the house as though it were day.

For lighting paths and driveways—and for any part of the garden, patio or terrace which would benefit from general illumination—there are many kinds of pole-mounted downlighters which cast a diffused light over a fairly wide area. The styles vary from miniature street lights to elegant bowl-shaped lamps perched on tall poles.

Wiring up

Any exterior light fitting, unless it is sheltered in a porch, must be fully sealed and insulated because it will always be exposed to the elements—even if it is not always switched on. Porch lights and lamps mounted on exterior walls can generally be connected directly into the interior lighting circuit. But with lights fitted some distance from the house, this is not always possible.

Installing an exterior lighting circuit is a job that requires great care—the results must remain safe even after years of exposure to the weather. If you have any doubts about your skills, let a professional do the job.

Use only fittings—lights, sockets, bulbs and so on—that are designed for outdoor use. Unless your lighting circuit is very simple, wire it to a separate fuse on the fuseboard—the circuit should have its own isolating switch as well. In the UK, you could wire a lighting circuit via a fused switched connection unit, fitted to a spur on the ring main. Use suitable

Below: Spotlights are invaluable for garden lighting. They help create a romantic, gentle atmosphere

cable—in the UK, mineral insulated or armoured PVC sheathed, buried at least 450mm below ground, or ordinary PVC cable protected by heavy-gauge conduit and buried at the same depth.

It is sensible to have the circuit checked by a professional before connecting it (or having it connected for you) to the mains.

Positioning lights

Choosing what to illuminate and where to place the lights is almost as critical as selecting the lights themselves. At all times bear in mind that once you have positioned a light outside and buried the cable, it can be a lengthy job repositioning it. Always experiment with different locations before you make any final decisions—the extra effort will be well worthwhile.

If you simply want to illuminate a drive or pathway, the kind of lights you choose and where you position them will depend mostly on the surroundings. If you have trees lining a sweeping drive or even a narrow path, the lights should be positioned to offer a clear line to the house.

A long drive is often adequately served by just one pole-mounted downlighter near the entrance and another closer to the house. Casting a glow over a wide area, these lamps will create a welcoming atmosphere without being excessively obtrusive.

Remember that a powerful single lamp close to the house can also serve to illuminate the house itself, so here you might consider a spot or floodlamp more effective. Positioned behind a shrub or rockery and pointing upwards to the house, the secret source of light can have a most entrancing and mysterious effect.

Many families now enjoy barbecue parties on warm evenings and some kind of lighting is essential to make the most of the occasion. In a well-appointed patio, there may be separate eating and cooking areas which would best be served by individual lighting of different types.

Above: Why not give your visitors a double welcome and clearly spotlight your house number on an outside wall as well as on the front door

Powerful spotlamps pointing up towards the house would undoubtedly create too much glare: softer, glowing lamps which cast a more diffused, softer illumination over a wider area would be a better choice. Position one close to the barbecue as this is where you will need the most light.

If there are surrounding walls, they might be the ideal places on which to mount the lights.

It can be very disconcerting to be confronted by a black gloom just a few feet beyond the patio, so consider adding one or more lights some distance away in the garden. A single lantern in a tree will probably not be enough, particularly in a large area, so experiment carefully with other lights until you achieve a satisfactory compromise for both patio and garden.

Drawing the eye to one or more points of interest in the garden not only relieves the gloom lying beyond the house, it also enables you to make fuller use of the garden when you are entertaining. Just as lighting a driveway introduces a welcoming atmosphere at the front, so lights in the back garden make it a friendlier place.

The shape and texture of many natural

Above: Bring your patio to life at night with a brilliant display of outdoor lighting, using spotlights to pick out features, or diffusers for a gentle background glow. However, it is essential to use only special waterproof lights

features in the garden take on quite a different aspect when illuminated at night. A lamp mounted in the trees creates moving patterns of shadows in the slightest breeze, while spotlamps pick out the delicate tracery of the leaves. Patches of rocks and bricks, shrubs and flowers are all enhanced by illumination: try lighting them from spotlamps hidden away in a tree or bush.

Even from inside the house, especially during the colder months of winter when the trees sparkle with frost or are covered by fingers of snow, the garden itself can become a picture in a window frame.

Illuminated from below by spotlamps, a pergola can be transformed into a night-time roof of greenery; because of the effects of shadows, any foliage thickens and becomes glossy—the very shape and proportion of the garden is often altered beyond recognition at night.

But of all the features in a garden that are transformed by exterior lighting, the most spectacular are pools of water. A fountain or even a pond will sparkle when lit from above by spotlamps. Plants and ornaments in water become more distinctive, goldfish shimmer and the contrast with surrounding shadows is striking.

Lighting the house

The house itself can benefit from some illumination and again spotlamps work best at picking out the most attractive and decorative features.

Lamps mounted on the walls are not generally very effective in this respect because they tend to cast shadows that distort the exterior features.

It is better to position a pair of spotlamps centrally, some distance from the front of the house, so that they can be angled to either side. This ensures that the entire front elevation is evenly illuminated.

Alternatively, individual spotlamps can be placed at the sides pointing inwards. In both cases, the lights should be positioned at ground level pointing upwards. Take care not to buy excessively powerful lamps (unless you have a very large house) since even the low-powered variety create some glare.

CENTRAL HEATING AND INSULATION

Planning central heating

Installing central heating is a major home improvement project with real benefits—improved comfort, cheaper fuel bills (often) and an increase in the value of your home being the most significant. But the benefits come only if the system is properly installed, which means taking painstaking care over all aspects of its design and the way you assemble the components. And, as you are only likely to tackle the job once, you must be sure of getting the job done right first time.

Often the first problem facing the do-it-yourself installer is which system to choose. And with so many different fuels and ways of transmitting heat around, it is easy to be put off before you start. But as it is not possible here to give a detailed comparison of the many different systems, this section will cover installing only one—gas-fired, low-temperature hot water, small-bore pipework, using conventional radiators. This system is relatively easy to install and includes a hot water storage cylinder.

However, most of the information applies equally to small-bore systems using other fuels, boilers or heat emitters. Many of the details on planning and design would also be of use if you wanted to install the warm-air type of central heating system.

By far the most complicated—and difficult—part of the job is designing a system that suits your own home and requirements. This section will therefore

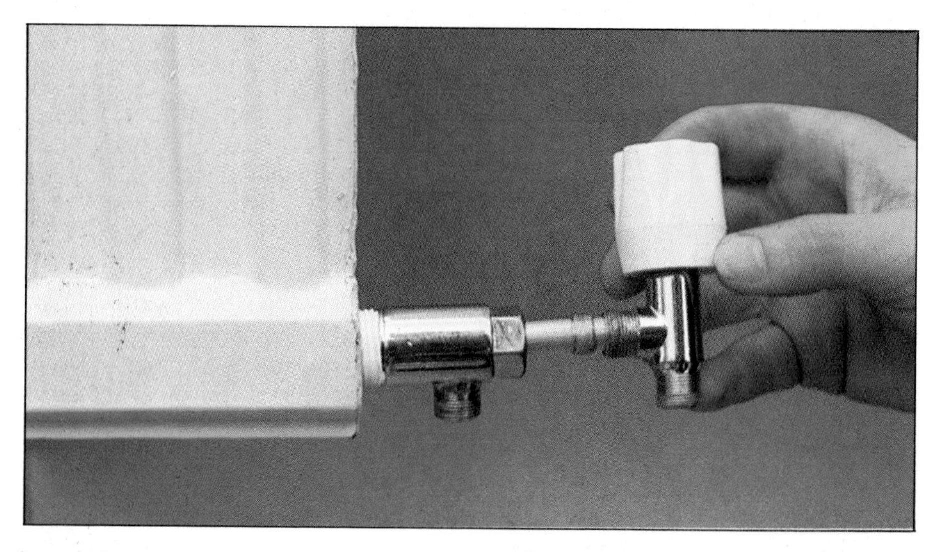

Above: Control valves must always be fitted to radiators as they enable you to have room by room control of the actual temperature

concentrate on this aspect and present it in the greatest detail. Providing you get the design right and work out properly what you need, the business of installation is quite straightforward and well within the scope of the DIY enthusiast who already has a fair amount of plumbing skill.

'Wet' central heating systems

Originally, hot water heating systems using radiators made use of gravity to help circulate the water. But as this imposed severe limits on design and called for very large-bore, expensive pipework, it has generally been abandoned in favour of the pumped system, which is still in common use. Here, an electric pump promotes the flow of heated water from the boiler to the radiators, the pressure being more than enough to keep it flowing in a continuous closed circuit.

The temperature of the water in the system has an important part to play in its design. In a system open to atmospheric pressure, water hotter than 95°C (203°F) has a tendency to turn to steam and so become potentially dangerous. But if the system is sealed and under pressure, the water temperature can safely be increased to around 120°C (248°F). This in turn allows smaller bore pipework and smaller radiators to be used without any noticeable loss in efficiency and can also increase the flexibility of the design.

The drawbacks to *pressurized*, or *medium-temperature hot water* systems are that they demand a much higher standard of design knowledge and workmanship than *unpressurized*, or *low-temperature hot water* systems. Although they are often the best choice for bungalows and flats where height is restricted, in most two-storey homes the savings made on smaller radiators and pipes is offset by the cost of the extra control gear and valves that are needed.

Radiator pipe layouts: The way in which the pipes connecting the radiators run to and from the boiler also has a marked effect on the running of a hot water system and here, too, advances in design have been made over the years.

In the *one pipe* system (fig. B) the advantages of a simple pipe layout are outweighed by the fact that cooler water leaving radiator 1 mixes with hot water entering radiator 2 and so on—progressively lowering the overall temperature of the water as it moves around the system. Though the problems can be eliminated by—amongst other things—carefully sizing the radiators to match these temperature differences, it is generally far easier to opt for the more complicated *two pipe* system (fig. C) as used in the featured installation.

Here water flows to each radiator at near boiler temperature, all of it under pump pressure, so making for a more evenly balanced distribution. It is by far the most practical system for an average-sized home, but where a large number of radiators are needed, balancing becomes difficult and it is usually rejected in favour of the *three pipe* type of system (fig. D).

This is a modified version of the two pipe system, but is so designed that the sums of the lengths of the flow and return pipes to each radiator are equal—a characteristic which makes balancing appreciably easier in larger homes but which can also impose more limitations on the design.

As well as being classified by type, radiator pipe layouts are also known by the way in which they are actually installed in the home.

In the *downfeed* or *drop* (fig. E), the main flow is taken to a high level—such as the roof space—and then dropped to feed radiators at a lower level. Such a layout is well suited to homes which have a roof space, but which also have solid floors where conventional pipe laying would be difficult and time consuming.

The opposite of this—suited to homes with no roof space—is the *upfeed* or *riser*. Here, the main flow is at the lowest possible level and rises to feed radiators above.

Most common of all in domestic installations is the *ladder* or *tree*, where the main flow rises up the building and feeds branches at each floor level. In a two pipe system (as featured) these *main branches* are divided into *sub-circuits*. These in turn divide into the *branch circuits* which supply each individual radiator.

Similar to the ladder is the *manifold*, the system most commonly employed with micro-bore tubing (see below). Here the main flow rises up the building and the main branches at each level run to centrally placed manifolds. From these, smaller branch circuits radiate outwards to each radiator in turn.

Pipe sizes: As described above, the advent of pumped hot water systems led to much smaller diameter pipework—15mm and 22mm—being used, hence the term small-bore system. But as these pumps became more efficient and capable of handling greater pressures, so it became possible to reduce the pipe size still further—to 6, 8, 10 and 12mm outside diameter.

These very thin pipes, which look like—and bend almost as easily as—thick cable, are known as micro-bore tubes. Although they are easier to install, current opinion associates them with a multitude of maintenance problems. They also tend to limit possibilities in the design of a system.

Superficially, micro-bore is easier to work with and requires less jointing than small-bore. The pipes are often easier to run and conceal and, since there is less water in any one section of pipe for less time, heat loss through the pipework is often reduced.

However, micro-bore systems installed by the inexperienced hand are more likely to give trouble—foreign matter left in the pipes can easily cause a blockage and slight design defects can lead to draining-down problems later. About the only situation where micro-bore really does come into its own is when the structure of a home makes it almost impossible to conceal pipework, in which case it is less obtrusive. Good examples of this

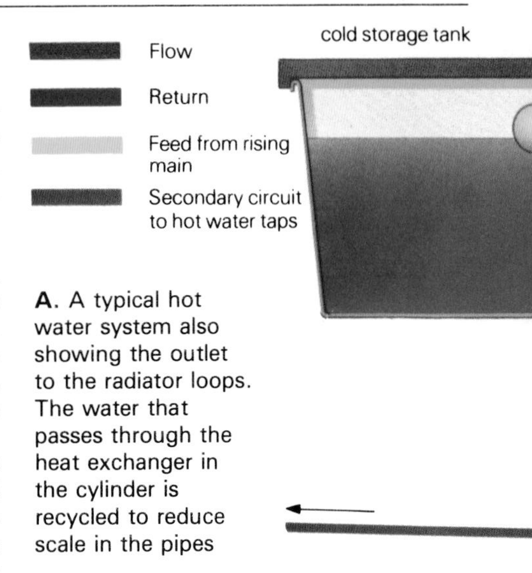

A. A typical hot water system also showing the outlet to the radiator loops. The water that passes through the heat exchanger in the cylinder is recycled to reduce scale in the pipes

are homes with solid floors on two or more storeys.

If you think that micro-bore might be of more use to you, many of the details of the featured small-bore installation will still be relevant, but you should seek the advice of a qualified heating engineer and also consider having the system installed professionally.

Components of a system

By now you should have a good idea of the principle of a two pipe, small-bore low temperature heating system and some clues as to how the radiator pipe layout will fit into your home. The next stage is to familiarize yourself with the workings of the system as a whole—the boiler, pump, expansion tank, hot water cylinder—so that you can get a clear idea in your own mind what the installation entails.

Figure A shows a typical two pipe system supplying radiators and a hot water cylinder. Heat is generated by the boiler and transmitted to the water. This is then transmitted by the pump via the flow pipe to the radiator circuit, the hot water cylinder circuit or both—some systems have *motorized valves* to share

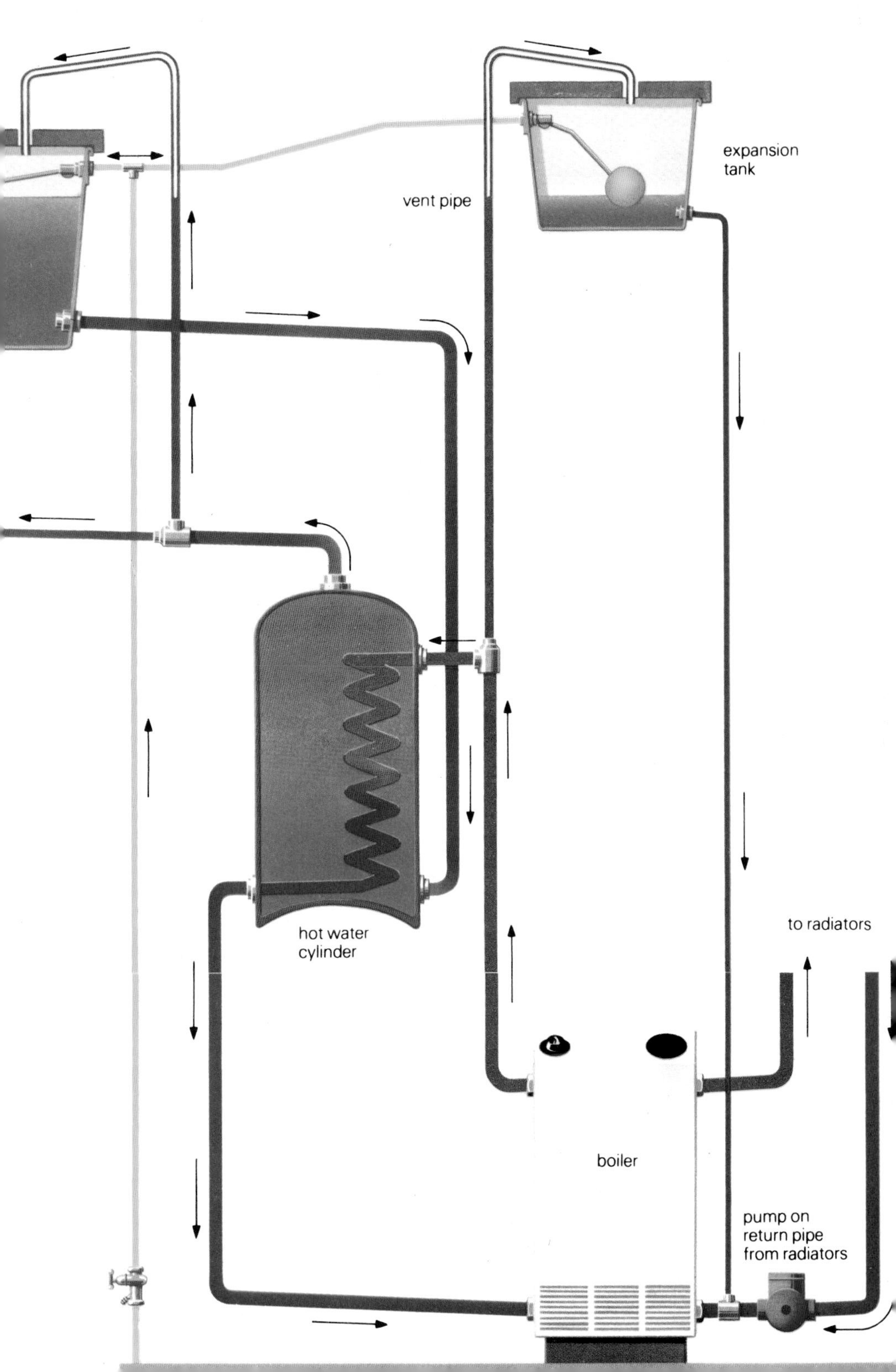
expansion tank
vent pipe
hot water cylinder
to radiators
boiler
pump on return pipe from radiators

the water flow between all the different circuits.

Having released its heat at the radiators or in the cylinder to heat up cold water for the hot taps, the water in the system then returns to the boiler via the return pipe to be reheated for another cycle.

Expansion of the volume of the water due to its being heated is accommodated

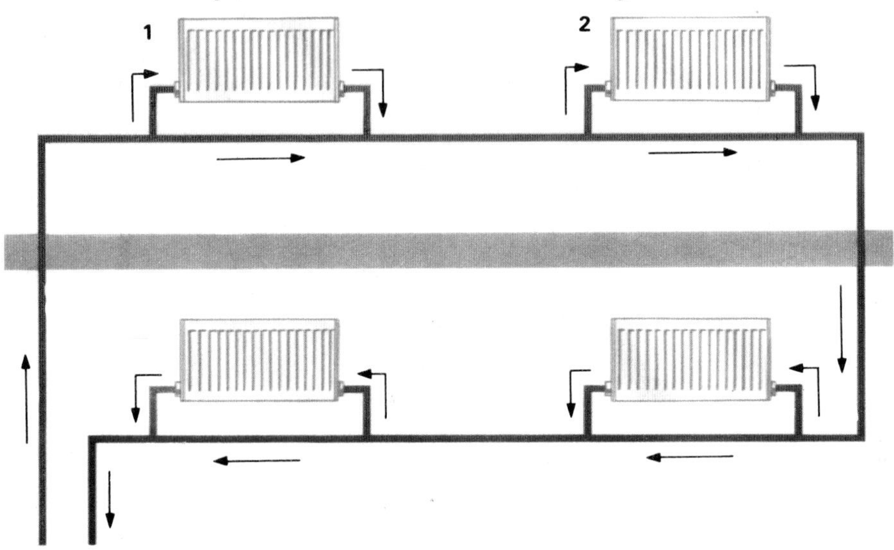

B. Above: The one pipe system. Although the pipework layout is very simple, the system itself is inefficient and the radiators need careful sizing. **C. Below:** The two pipe system is a better system and is far more efficient in distributing heat throughout the house and the sizing of the required radiators is very simple

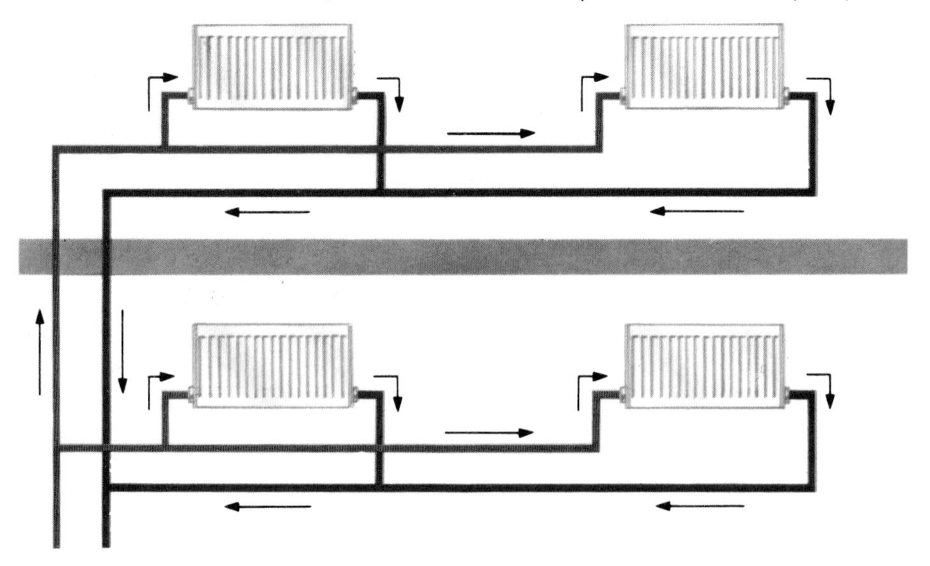

in the feed and expansion tank and in the feed and expansion pipe which connects this with the boiler. The tank, which is fed from the cold storage tank, also serves to 'top up' the system if there are slight losses through evaporation.

To accommodate expanding air—and for safety's sake in the event of overheating—an open vent pipe must be run from the boiler to discharge over the expansion tank. Some boilers (combination boilers) act like multipoints—providing instantaneous hot water when a tap is turned on. Otherwise, they heat the radiator circuit only. They dispense with the need for the hot cylinder and the motorized valve altogether.

Buying the components

Getting together the components which go to make up a hot water central heating system is a job that must be done in stages, as the design falls into place. However, it is as well to make contact with a reputable supplier right from the start and if possible to get catalogues showing the choice in radiators, boilers and control systems. It is also a great help to have some idea of the costs you will be letting yourself in for at this early development stage.

In the UK, plumbing and heating stores which specialize in advising and supplying do-it-yourselfers are by far the best source of new parts. But if you have to go to a trade supplier or wholesaler, bear in mind that he will expect you to know exactly what you are talking about and may not have either the time or the knowledge to give specific advice.

Finally, but most important, many heating suppliers and outfitters now offer a special DIY service—they will design a system to suit your house and present you with detailed plans of the job and the components to use. This leaves you with the relatively simple task of installing the components they supply.

Installation procedure

First decide whether to plan the design yourself but get experts to install it, or whether to get experts to design the system so that you can install it yourself. For DIY installation, make sure you have

D. Below: Where a large number of radiators is required the heating system will be better balanced if a three pipe type of system is used

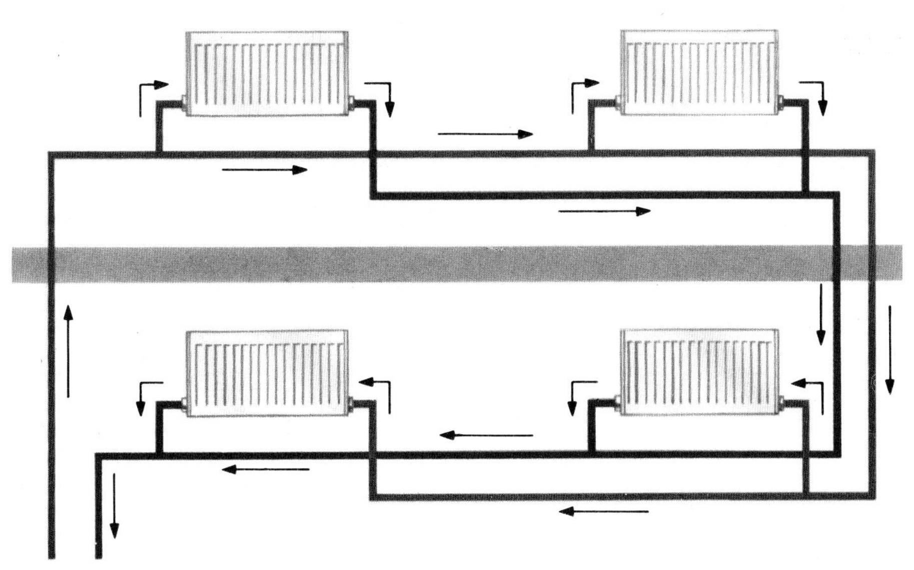

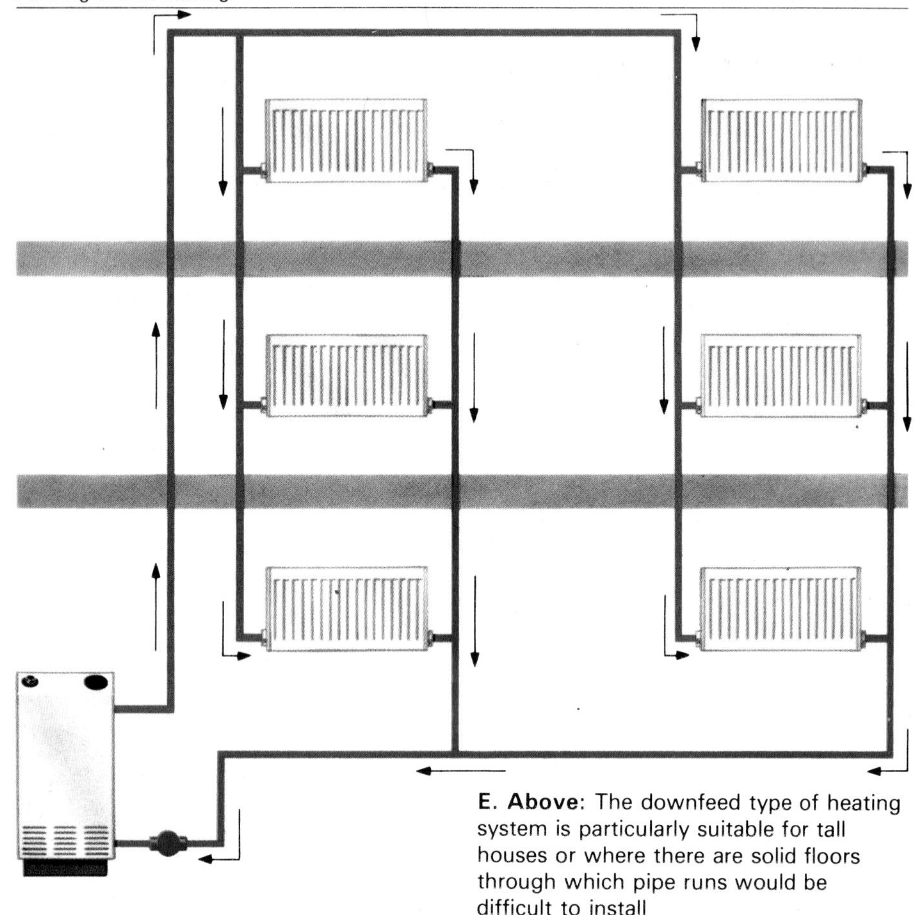

E. Above: The downfeed type of heating system is particularly suitable for tall houses or where there are solid floors through which pipe runs would be difficult to install

the necessary knowledge and skills for the plumbing work involved.

The work sequence for installing the featured system is based on working out what you need as accurately as possible, designing a system around this and then assembling the components for installation. Though there are short cuts to be taken, especially at the design stage, there is no point in doing so if you want your system to be truly efficient and to save you money. Briefly, the sequence runs as follows:

- Work out the total heat loss through ventilation and the house structure for each room in the house.
- Use these figures to determine the size and position of each radiator.
- Decide on your hot water requirements, then use the information gathered so far to gauge boiler size and position.
- With the design coming together, determine the pipe and pump sizes and the actual pipe layout.
- Work out a suitable flue arrangement for the boiler.
- Finalize design of the hot water system.
- Choose the control system best suited to your needs.
- Install, commission and test the system.

Maintaining central heating

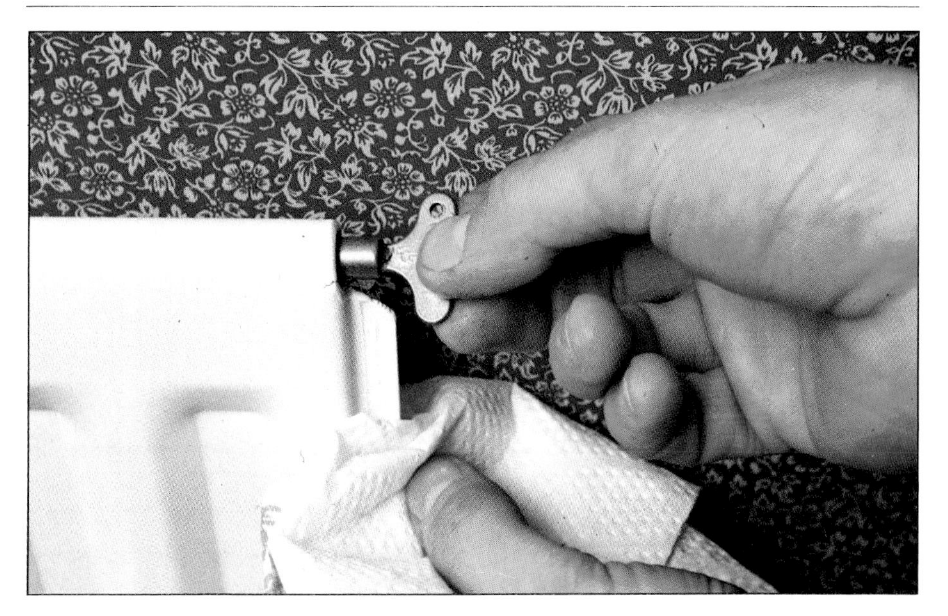

When a central heating system ceases to function properly, it becomes an expensive liability. But it does not always take an expert to repair it. Many common faults can be cured just as easily by the householder.

The most complicated part of the average domestic central heating system is the boiler. This may require specialist knowledge and tools to put it right should it fail—but failures in boilers which are regularly serviced are rare. More prone to trouble are circulation pumps, thermostats and radiators which have only a limited life.

Wet central heating systems

In order to identify a particular fault in a central heating system, it is worth having some idea of how the system works.

Above: All the radiators in a central heating system should be bled of air about once or twice a year. If there is a substantial air lock in a radiator, it will not get very hot and will not function as well as it should

In most modern systems, hot water flows from the boiler to the radiators and hot water cylinder, releases its heat and returns to be reheated. The flow is created artificially by an electric circulation pump which is normally mounted adjacent to the boiler. The pump is controlled by a time clock and, in most cases, by a room thermostat as well.

At pre-selected times, the mechanism in the clock switches on the pump. The pump then sends hot water to the radiators, heating the house.

Maintenance of the system

Although all central heating systems should be serviced at least once a year by qualified engineers, you can keep the system running reliably by correct use and regular maintenance.

It is not advisable to switch off heating at night during cold weather. A small amount of heat—to ensure that the temperature throughout the house never falls below 10°C (50°F)—cuts the time needed to reach full operating temperature and may, in the long run, save fuel.

The boiler should never be run at too low a thermostat setting. The boiler thermostat in a conventional small-bore system should be set at up to 82°C (180°F) in winter. In summer, when the system is required for hot water only, it should be kept at not less than 54°C (130°F).

If the system is oil-fired, the oil tank should be examined annually. Any noticeable external rust should be completely removed with a wire brush and glasspaper and then painted over with black bitumen paint.

To clean the oil filter on an oil tank, turn off the stop cock and remove the filter bowl. Clean the element with paraffin, dry it and refit. At the same time check the oil line from the tank to the boiler for leaks, tightening joints where necessary.

When a solid fuel boiler is not in use it should be left clean. Remove sooty deposits from the combustion chamber and flue and leave the damper and boiler doors open to allow a current of air to pass through. Have the flue cleaned at least once a year.

Overheating

Overheating is one of the most common faults found in wet central heating systems. In all cases of overheating, if the fault cannot be rectified at once, the supply of gas or oil to the boiler should be cut off as a precaution. If you can run the circulation pump with the boiler off, keep it circulating water so that the heat is dissipated through the radiators. With a solid fuel boiler, rake the fire into the ashpan and remove it.

To check a room thermostat, turn it down to its lowest setting and then back up again. A click should be heard as the switch inside turns the pump on. If there is no click, the unit is damaged and will have to be replaced.

If the whole system is overheating seriously, the radiator pipes may make prolonged knocking or hissing noises and there will be excessive temperature in the boiler delivery pipe. One possible reason for this is failure of the circulation pump.

To find out whether the pump is working, hold one end of a screwdriver against the casing with the other end to your ear and listen for the hum of the rotor inside (fig. 2): if there is no noise, this is probably stuck. On pumps with a screw-on glass inspection cover, the rotor can be freed quite easily. Turn the pump off, unscrew the cover and insert a screwdriver into one of the slots in the rotor. If the rotor does not spin freely, it should be possible to free it by levering gently with the screwdriver (fig. 3).

On pumps that have all-metal casings, the water supply must be cut off before opening the cover. In most cases, there are stop valves on each side for this purpose, but where no such valves are fitted, the system will have to be drained before carrying out any work on the pump.

If the pump is heard to be working but water is evidently not circulating, there is probably an air lock. At the top of the pump you will find a vent valve—operated either by a key or a screwdriver—from which the pump can be bled (fig. 4).

To do this, turn the pump off and leave it for a few hours to allow the water in the system to settle. Then open the valve to bleed the air off. A hiss of air will be followed by a trickle of water: when the trickle becomes constant, close the value.

If the fault is not in the pump, the boiler thermostat may have failed. The thermostat, a small box with a dial on the top, is located behind the boiler casing. Remove the casing and check that the electrical connections on the thermostat are sound. Check also that the sender bulb on the end of the copper capillary from the thermostat to the boiler has not fallen out of its socket (fig. 5). If so reposition it and replace the securing clip.

Note the setting on the boiler thermostat dial and turn it down low. After a few minutes turn it back towards its maximum setting and listen for a click. If there is no click, it may mean that the thermostat has jammed and you should call in a qualified engineer to check it.

Central heating too cool

If all the radiators are cool and the boiler is working correctly, the fault probably lies with one of the thermostats, the time

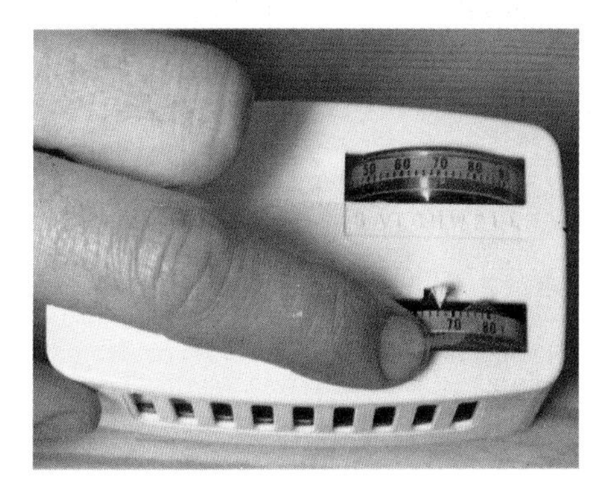

1 To check that both a room thermostat and a boiler thermostat are working properly, you will need to turn them down to their lowest setting and then turn them up again. If you do not hear a click they are jammed

2 To check a circulation pump, hold a screwdriver against the casing with the handle to your ear. On pumps with metal casings, you may have to drain the system and take out the unit before removing the casing

3 When you open up the pump you might find the rotor has seized. If so, you might be able to free it by inserting a screwdriver into one of the slots and then levering it gently up and down

4 To free an air lock in the pump you should unscrew the vent valve, which is located at the top of the pump. When water begins to trickle out steadily, close up the valve again

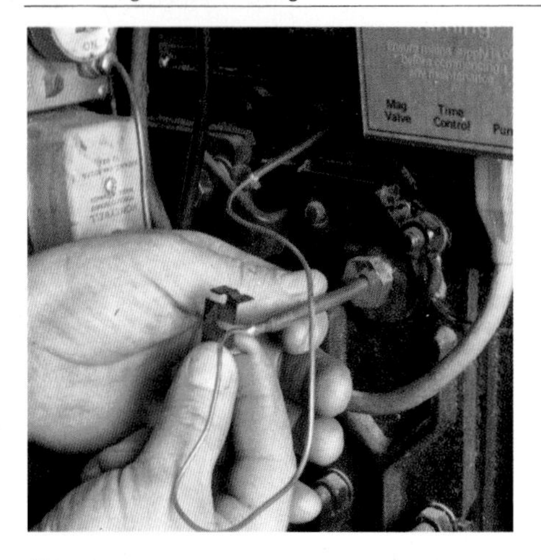

5 Another problem which might be encountered with the boiler system is that the sender bulb on the end of the copper capillary might have somehow come out of its place. If this is the case, it is quite easy to just reposition it and replace its securing clip to keep it firmly in position again

6 Another part of the heating system which should be checked now and then is the expansion water tank. The water level should never be more than about 150mm away from the actual valve outlet. If, when you check the tank, the water is below this level you must top it up straightaway

7 Before completely draining a central heating system, turn off the electricity supply to the time clock and also to the immersion heater if there is one fitted. You should then shut off the water supply to the boiler, by closing the stop valve tap on the pipe which leads in to the expansion tank

8 When the system has had time to cool down, attach one end of a garden hose to the nozzle of the main drain cock which is situated on the boiler. Then run the other end of the hose to an outside drain. Open up the drain cock by carefully turning the nut beneath it with an adjustable wrench

9 Pipes often creak running through the floor joists. Cushion them with felt or carpet to stop the noise. If a pipe rubs against wood, pack it with suitable padding. Metal pipe brackets should be bent back and pieces of felt inserted if they are noisy

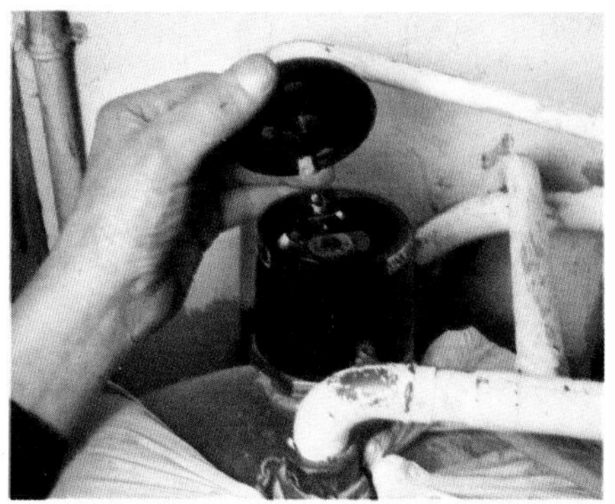

10 To adjust the thermostat of an immersion heater, unscrew and remove the element cover on the top or side of the cylinder. Now you can locate the temperature dial. Turn the dial by hand or with a screwdriver to the desired temperature setting

clock or the circulation pump. Carry out checks outlined above under 'Overheating', paying special attention to the position of a room thermostat if fitted.

To work efficiently, the thermostat should be mounted on an internal wall at least 1.5m above the floor and away from draughts, radiators and direct sunlight.

Draining the system

Before doing any major repairs or modifications to your central heating, you will have to drain, or partially drain, the system. Start by turning the boiler off and leaving the system for a few hours to cool down. Turn off the electricity supply to the time clock and the immersion heater.

Shut off the water supply to the boiler by closing the stop valve on the pipe into the expansion tank (fig. 7). If no stop valve is fitted, lash the ball valve in the expansion tank to a piece of wood laid across the tank.

When the system has cooled, return to the boiler and identify the main drain cock. This is usually at the front end of the boiler near the pump where it is always built into the lowest pipe. Alternatively, it may be found on a ground-floor radiator. Attach one end of a garden hose to the nozzle and run the other to an outside drain. Open the drain cock by turning the nut beneath with a spanner or adjustable wrench and allow as much water as you require to drain away.

Refilling the system

Before refilling, close the main drain cock securely. Open the valve on the pipe leading to the expansion tank, or untie the ball valve, to admit fresh water into the system. Regulate the position of the valve so that the tank fills slowly—keeping the risk of air locks to a minimum. Also check the drain cock for leaks.

Noise

Noise is another common problem with wet central heating systems. Creaking under the floorboards and around radiators is caused by pipes—which expand and contract according to the temperature of the water—rubbing against the floor joists on which they rest. Creaking can also occur where a pipe rises through the floorboards to feed a specific radiator.

If the noise persists, take up the floorboards around the suspect area. Eventually you will find a point where one or two pipes cross a joist and are notched into the woodwork. If the notch is so small that it causes the pipes to rub against each other, enlarge it to give a better clearance.

Use a trimmed piece of rubber pipe lagging, felt or carpet to cushion the pipes firmly (fig. 9).

Where a pipe rises through a gap in a floorboard, either enlarge the gap by filing it away or pack the space around the pipe with padding.

Creaking behind radiators is usually caused by the hooks on the back of the panels rubbing against their corresponding wall brackets. For serious cases, on smaller radiators, special nylon brackets can be fitted in place of the normal pressed steel type. A simpler solution is to place pieces of felt or butyl between each hook and bracket.

Immersion heaters

In many systems, hot water for sinks and baths is heated by a thermostatically controlled immersion heater in addition to the boiler-fed heat exchanger. The thermostat is pre-set to turn the heating element off when the water reaches the selected temperature. If the water is unbearably hot, the thermostat may simply need adjusting.

The thermostat control is found at the top or on the side of the hot water cylinder. To adjust it, turn off the electricity supply to the heater then unscrew the element cover where you will find a small dial marked centigrade, Fahrenheit, or both. By hand, or with a screwdriver, turn the regulator screw to the desired temperature—normally 60°C (140°F) in hard water areas or 80°C (180°F) in those with especially soft water.

If the water heats up slowly, or the hot tap cools too quickly, check that the cylinder is sufficiently lagged and that the lagging is in good condition. If it is, try adjusting the thermostat. When water fails to heat up at all, either the thermostat control or the heating element are defective and will have to be replaced.

Radiator controls

Most radiators are fitted with two valves —a *handwheel* and a *lockshield* valve. The handwheel allows radiators to be shut down individually or the temperature of a radiator to be reduced by restricting the flow of water. The lockshield valve is set when the system is installed, to give a balanced flow of water through the radiator.

In some cases, thermostatic radiator valves are fitted in place of handwheels. A radiator thermostat can be pre-set to maintain any desired temperature and is controlled by temperature-sensitive bellows. As the water temperature falls, the bellows contract to allow more hot water into the radiator. Radiator thermostats are usually only suitable for use in a two pipe system.

Bleeding a radiator

When air accidentally enters a wet central heating system, it can find its way to a radiator and prevent this from functioning efficiently. All radiators should be bled of air once or twice a year to clear the small amounts that inevitably get into the system. But if a radiator becomes cold whilst others are functioning normally, the cause is probably a substantial air lock and the radiator should be bled immediately. The top of a radiator remaining cold while the bottom is scalding also suggests an air lock.

On most radiators a square-ended hollow key—obtainable from ironmongers—is needed to open the air vent valve at the top. To prevent air being sucked into the system, turn down the room thermostat and switch off the time clock so that the pump stops working.

Place a towel underneath the radiator to catch any drips, then open the valve by turning the key anticlockwise until a hiss of escaping air is heard. As soon as water begins to flow freely, quickly re-tighten the valve nut.

Central heating control systems

The cost of heating your house is rising all the time as fuel becomes more and more expensive. Reducing central heating bills not only means cutting down heat loss from the house by such measures as loft insulation, but also using your heating system in the most economical and efficient way possible.

Automatic control of the central heating system helps you to do this by regulating the amount of heat emitted by heaters throughout the house at different times of the day and night. If this results in less wasted heat than simple manual control would do, then you can make savings on your fuel bills.

Automatic controls are not as complex to understand as many would believe, and the installation of control valves and thermostats to a 'wet' control heating system is not difficult and within the capability of the do-it-yourself plumber.

Automatic control

The basic principle of a comprehensive control system is that the house is divided into areas that receive no more or less heat at any time of the day or night than is absolutely necessary.

In a typical system the heating would be switched off while the house is empty during the day and would be set automatically to give a lower temperature during the night. Thermostats and valves ensure that all the rooms are at a constant—but not unnecessarily high—temperature, with the living room slightly warmer than the bedrooms or the hall.

A programmer (see below) ensures that the heating and hot water systems switch themselves on only in the morning and evening.

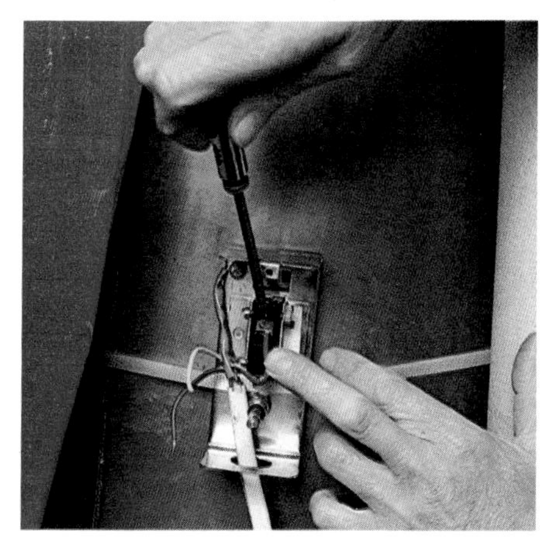

1 Install a cylinder thermostat a short way up from the base of the cylinder and wire it to the relevant control valve

2 To install a 3-way motorized valve, choose a site on the main flow pipe from the boiler to the heating circuits

Obviously it is best to consider the benefits of automatic control before you install the central heating, but an existing system can be adapted—often very easily—to most types of control.

If you intend fitting automatic controls to an existing system, there are a number of factors to consider. Small-bore and microbore systems are easily adaptable, and the type of fuel your boiler uses is largely immaterial. The boiler must be of recent design, however, and must contain a thermostat. This is because certain systems use the boiler thermostat to control the temperature of the water supplied to the system.

Automatic controls are effective with both pumped and gravity primary systems but the hot water cylinder must be of the indirect type. If yours is not, you can buy a conversion kit incorporating a heat exchanger which replaces the original immersion heater. This in turn is plumbed into the boiler.

Controls explained

The principal controls for a central heating and domestic hot water system are: room thermostats; programmers; thermostatic radiator valves (TRVs); cylinder thermostats; motorized and electrically actuated valves—both diverting and zone valves; and the boiler thermostat which comes fitted into the boiler when you buy it.

Boiler thermostat: This prevents the boiler overheating and is usually handset with a maximum temperature of 85°C (185°F). It does not, itself, operate as a comfort control.

Room thermostat: This switches the circulation pump, boiler and motorized valves on and off to maintain a steady temperature in the house. Some models incorporate a setback facility which reduces the temperature of the house during the night.

A room thermostat should be screwed to the wall and wired up in the same way as a light switch. Position it about 1–1.5m above floor level in the living room, bedrooms or hall. Make sure it is well away from sunlight and electric fires and that it is not fixed to an outside wall.

Frost thermostat: Fitted to override all other controls and switches when the system is switched off for an extended period during the winter, this switches the heating on temporarily to prevent the system from actually freezing during a hard frost.

Outside thermostat: You can fit a thermostat outside the house where it senses temperature changes before the room thermostat, thus cutting out the delay before the heating comes on and preventing excessive temperature variations inside the house.

Cylinder thermostat: This is used to control the temperature of the domestic hot water supply inside the cylinder. It is strapped or stuck to the outside of the cylinder below the lagging, about one-third of the way up from the base. A setting of about 60°C (140°F) is satisfactory for most domestic installations. The thermostat is wired up to operate the pump, boiler or motorized valves, depending on the system you use.

A cylinder thermostat can also be fitted to a direct cylinder to control an immersion heater.

Time switches: These can be used to switch the pump and the boiler fuel system on and off at times already preset.

Control valves

These are devices that are plumbed into hot and cold water pipes in the heating system. They open and close to control the flow of water, and can also divert the flow from one pipe to another, or simply vary the rate of flow in a pipe. There are various types available, and these may be controlled remotely by thermostats, by the temperature of the water in the pipe or by time switches or the surrounding air temperature.

A number of control valves are operated by electric motors or actuators. Non-electrical control valves are operated by the expansion and contraction of a liquid in a capillary tube, or by the

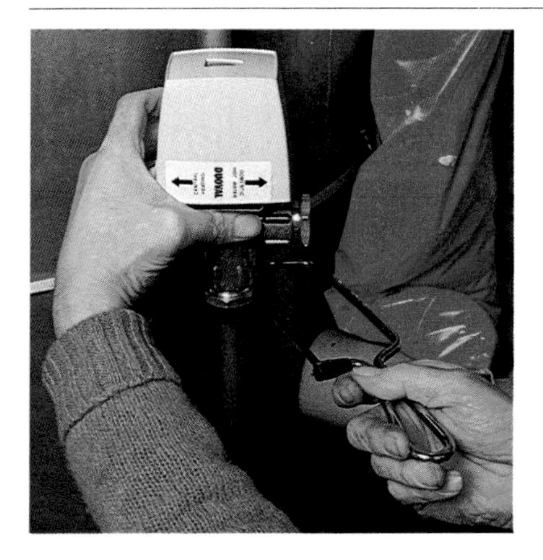

3 Thoroughly drain the system then sever the flow pipe with a fine-toothed hacksaw, using the valve as a guide. Then remove any surplus pipework

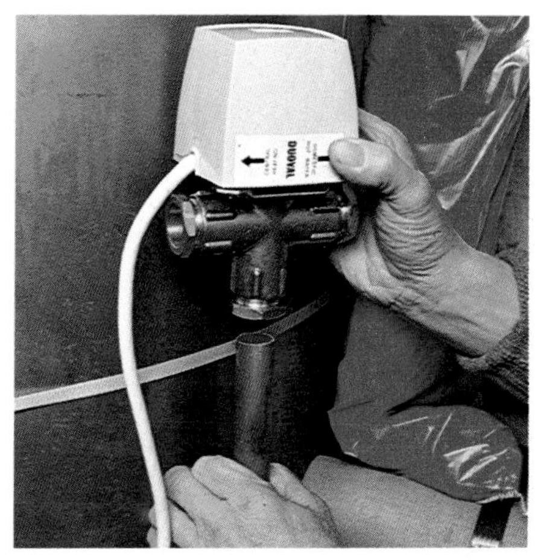

4 Fit the inlet port of the valve to the boiler end of the severed flow pipe, making sure you tighten the compression joint on the valve body

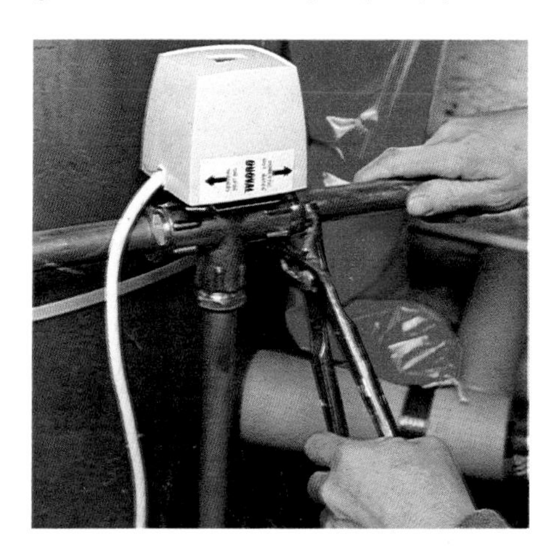

5 Then run separate flow pipes from the hot water and heating circuits and fit them to the valve outlet ports. Refill the system and test for leaks

6 Finally replace the cylinder and pipe lagging, make sure that the cylinder thermostat is not covered up, then adjust this to the required temperature setting

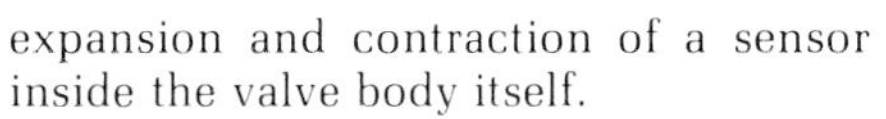

expansion and contraction of a sensor inside the valve body itself.

Motorized valves: There is a wide variety of models available, each differing according to its function—which may be diverting or mixing. All types are manufactured for different pipe sizes.

Motorized valves have either two or three ports, the latter having an inlet and two outlets which allow pumped hot water to be diverted from the heating to the hot water circuit and vice versa. A midway position on the valve allows the hot water to be shared equally between

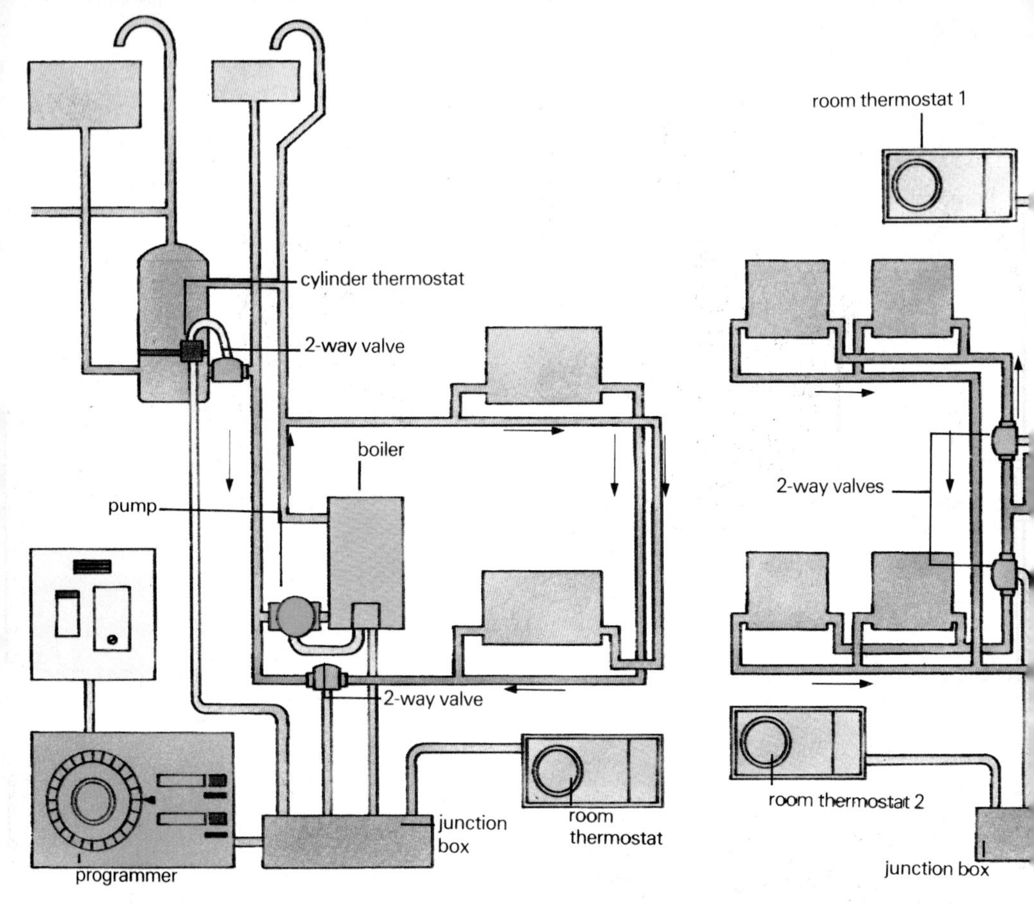

A. Above: Here the heating circuit and pumped hot water circuit are given individual control by fitting two 2-way motorized valves which are then themselves operated by room and cylinder thermostats respectively. **B. Above middle:** In the 'zoned' system, the upstairs and downstairs radiator circuits each have a 2-way valve and a separate room thermostat for individual control.

the two systems. When the thermostats in both systems indicate that the required temperatures have been reached, the valve closes completely.

The electric motor operating the valve is bolted to the valve body. This motor has a protective plastic cover and is connected to the electrical circuit controlled by the programmer, time switch or thermostat controls.

Spring return valves: These are similar to motorized valves and cover an equally wide range of types. In this case, however, the actuator operates the valve as a simple two-position switch in which the motor opens the valve, and a spring closes it when the motor is switched off. The actuator itself is fitted to the valve body and wired up after the valve has been plumbed in.

Non-electrical valves: The most common of these are thermostatic radiator valves (TRVs). These are fitted to a radiator in place of the hand-operated type and automatically maintain the temperature in a room by regulating the amount of hot water supplied to the radiator. They have a temperature range of between 10–20°C (50–68°F) and many have an anti-frost facility, enabling the

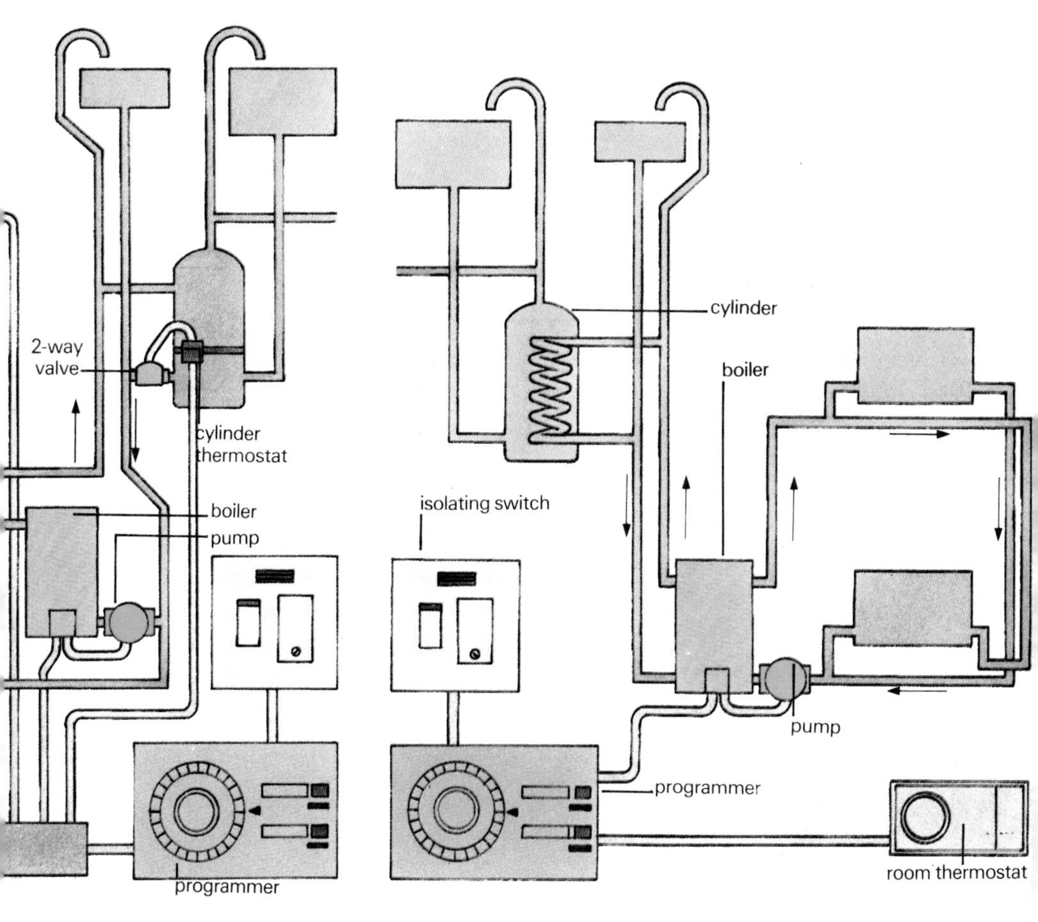

A third 2-way valve (with a thermostat actually on the cylinder) controls the circulation of all the hot water. **C. Above right:** Simple controls for a system with a gravity hot water circuit. The programmer determines the times when the heating is on, the room thermostat activates the pump to provide heating up to a suitable temperature which has already been pre-set at these times

valve to be set at a few degrees above freezing to protect the system.

The valve head contains a sensor which expands with the rise in room air temperature to close the valve and stop the flow of hot water through the radiator. If the radiator is in an awkward position or is covered by heavy curtains at night, a TRV with a remote sensor can be fitted. The sensor—which is fitted to the wall nearby—is connected to the valve body by a capillary tube and this operates the valve remotely. Detailed installation instructions for TRVs are usually provided by the manufacturers.

HWS control valves: HWS is an abbreviation for Hot Water Systems, and HWS valves are non-electrical units fitted into the primary circuit of a hot water supply system. Their purpose is to reduce the risk of scalding when the boiler is run at space heating temperatures—usually by stopping the flow of water to the heat exchanger in the hot water cylinder once this has reached a certain temperature. There are different models for both pumped and gravity hot water supplies, but the basic design is similar to that of a TRV.

The sensor is fitted under the cylinder

lagging and operates the valve through the expansion of liquid in a capillary tube running to the valve body.

A different type has no remote sensor, but is fitted instead to the primary return from the cylinder to the boiler, where it senses the return temperature of the water. This temperature is directly related to that of the water in the cylinder, and at a predetermined temperature the valve shuts off the flow in the primary circuit.

Programmers

A programmer basically provides time, rather than temperature, control. Models vary in complexity: the simplest and cheapest is manually operated and contains two rocker switches—one for heating, the other for hot water. This allows one to be switched on without the other, or both to be on or off at once. The time switch allows you to select the control periods.

More complex versions control the entire system. The various thermostats are wired to the valves, pump and boiler through the programmer. If either the hot water system or the heating system are in an 'On' period then the thermostats will switch them on or off as required to keep the system at the chosen temperature. During an 'Off' period the thermostats will not operate at all.

In addition, the programmer controls the pump, valves and boiler so that they cannot be switched on during an 'Off' period unless it is by the use of a manual override switch.

The most modern units are electronically controlled with a digital display. This shows the time of day and—when required—the type of programme for each system and its current state. These also allow the heating in two parts of the house to be controlled separately.

Most programmers come complete with fitting instructions and a wiring diagram, but despite the fact that all are wall-mounted units, not every one is compatible with package heating control systems offered by rival manufacturers.

Choosing your control system

Your choice of control system depends on the service you require and on the type of system you already have or that you intend to install. There are a number of choices open to you, and the most popular are shown in figs A to C.

Wiring

Most systems come with a junction box which should be supplied from the mains through a 13 amp switched and fused connection unit. The unit can be on a spur from the ring main and the supply cable should be three-core flexible PVC sheathed. The separate components wired through this junction box such as the valves, thermostats and programmer, each have colour-coded wires and their own wiring diagrams—which you should follow exactly. Pay close attention to safety considerations when doing the wiring.

Installation

Fitting the thermostats and programmer presents no real problems. Depending on the type and the position you have selected for them they can be flush-mounted like light switches on the wall, with the wiring chased into the plaster and run under the floorboards, or surface-mounted with the wiring running down the wall in plastic conduit.

All controls have a base plate, which must be unscrewed from the cover plate and fixed and wired first. The cover plate can then be screwed in position.

To fit motorized valves, you must first turn off the water supply to the system and drain and flush it to remove any grit or sludge that could block the valves at a later date. Next cut out the required portion of pipe—according to the type of valve you are using—and prepare the cut ends for connection. If you are installing a 3-way valve, you will have to reroute the pipe supplying part of the system so that it comes to the third port in the valve. Do not forget to seal off the other part of this pipe when you have actually done so.

Choosing a solid fuel fire

An open fire or stove burning solid fuel is an attractive way of heating a room. For this reason more and more fireplaces that were sealed up when central heating was installed are being opened up and restored to use. And even those modern houses where no chimney and fireplace exist can have these features added so that the benefits of a fire can be enjoyed.

This section of the book deals mainly with the advantages and disadvantages of solid fuel heating and describes the type of open fire or stove you can install. It does not give you full details about installing a solid fuel appliance—either by unblocking an existing opening or building a new chimney, fireplace and flue, but will help you choose the right solid fuel system for you.

Choosing a fire

It is easy to get carried away by the appeal of a solid fuel fire without stopping to consider whether it is the most suitable and effective form of heating for you. Start by looking at the main alternatives—which may be electric or gas fires or some form of central heating system.

The cost of running the appliance will

A. Below and Left: This is the most common type of solid fuel appliance. The fire burns in an open grate

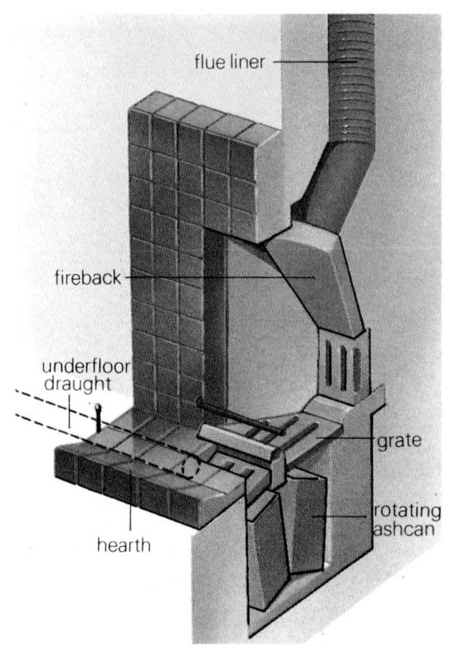

B. Left and Above: The underfloor draught fire has its own ducted air supply which comes from below. **C. Below:** Some different types of room heaters—like this unusual and attractive slimline model—are actually gravity-fed with fuel

obviously be of prime concern. All manufacturers of fires are obliged to give their heat output—usually measured in kilowatts. Try to find alternative appliances with the same kilowatt output. You can then do a direct comparison between the two—taking into account the price of installing each fire and a rough estimate of how much each will cost to run.

Another point to take into consideration if you are thinking about buying a stove or open fire is the availability of fuel. The wood or coal you buy must be easy to get hold of and you must have an available space to store it. Remember that if you live in a smokeless zone you will have to burn a smokeless fuel. This is more expensive than other fuels but burns more effectively.

Convenience too must be taken into account. A solid fuel appliance takes a long time to light and can never give instant heat like a gas or electric fire. It needs constant attention and refuelling to keep it alight. So if you are going to be out of the house for long periods of time you should buy a solid fuel fire or stove

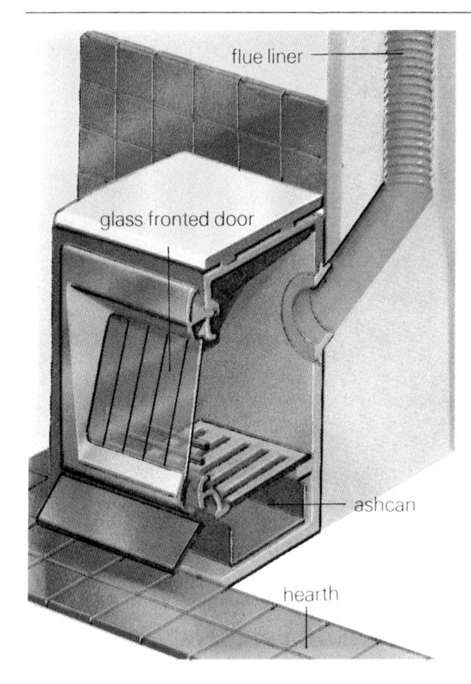

D. Left and Above: A hole-in-the-wall fire is set right into the chimney breast situated above floor level. **E. Below:** Box-shaped room heaters are very common and popular and can either be completely free standing or inset into the wall

which can be stoked up and kept going.

Many solid fuel appliances can be used with a back boiler, which provides hot water for domestic use and can also be used to feed a number of radiators in a central heating system. If you fit a back boiler remember to connect it up before lighting the fire.

Solid fuel appliances

If you have considered all the alternatives and decide that a solid fuel appliance is right for you, next choose the exact model you want to install. Five main types are available:

Inset open fire: The commonest type of fire—the inset—burns in a square- or oblong-shaped opening made from bricks. The opening is lined with a shell-shaped fireback, individual firebricks or some type of render (fig. A).

The fuel itself burns in a grate. The most common type of grate has a front plate fitted with vents which control the rate of burning by regulating the airflow (fig. A). Alternatively, some fires have a basket grate supported at each end by either firedogs or andirons. Although this often looks more attractive than the vented grate it is a less efficient way of burning solid fuel since the air entering the grate cannot easily be controlled.

The efficiency of some fires—especially the basket grate variety—can be raised by fitting a metal fireback or a front canopy. The metal fireback is fixed behind the fire basket and radiates much of the heat that might otherwise be lost. The front canopy—fitted above the fireplace opening—increases the draught of the fire and stops it smoking.

Underfloor draught fires: Any solid fuel fire depends on a good supply of air to help it burn. If the air is merely drawn from the room itself—as it is with inset fires—it can cause cold draughts and impair the fire's efficiency. A better method is to give the fire its own ducted air supply from beneath floor level which is then heated and passed into the room.

If you want an underfloor draught fire check carefully that your floor and walls are suitable. Normally the grate is at, or slightly below, hearth level and the waste falls into a deep ashpit below the fire (fig. B). Ash can be removed without disturbing the fire—either by providing rotating ashcans, which are pulled out of a hole in front of the fire, or by building an access door into an outside wall directly behind the fireplace.

Air is led to the fire through fireproof pipes. With a solid floor two pipes must be buried at right-angles to one another leading to outside walls. The air pipes meet in a balancing chamber—designed to stop through draughts—situated just below the front of the fire. From here a short duct takes the air to the fire via the air inlet connection.

Suspended floors pose less problems if they are well ventilated underneath by airbricks in the outside wall. Two short lengths of pipe can be led from the air inlet connection to the underfloor air space. Before you install such a system check that the airbricks are in position back and front and that there is an uninterrupted flow of air under the floor.

Hole-in-the-wall fires: Some fires—known as hole in the wall—are set into the chimney breast above floor level. Apart from their height, these are normal open fires with or without an underfloor air supply (fig. D).

Room heaters: These are enclosed fires which can be free-standing—with their own separate flue—or fitted into a fireplace opening. They have front doors which can be opened for refuelling, but only on a few models can the doors be left open (figs C and E).

The fact that the fire is completely enclosed allows the fuel to be burned economically and efficiently. Not only does the box itself radiate heat but the amount of draught entering the heater can be controlled very finely to adjust the rate of burning. And, like many inset fires, room heaters can be fitted with back boilers which heat water ready for domestic use and for a central heating system.

Some models are designed to burn only specific fuels—like coal—while others can be used with a range of different fuels. So before you install one of these heaters check carefully which fuel it uses. You can then find out whether this fuel is readily available and—in a smokeless zone—if it complies with

F. Below: A free-standing open fire that has a prefabricated flue is both striking and very original

Sizing chart for open fires

The chart below gives guidance in the selection of an open fire of a suitable size to heat a particular room effectively. It is difficult to ensure even distribution of heat through rooms over 100m^3 and expert advice needs to be sought. Climatic conditions may alter these figures.

Type and size of appliance	Size
Open fires:	
—inset 350mm	not suitable for main living areas
—inset 400mm	max. room size 50m^3
—inset 450mm	max. room size 57m^3
—convector 400mm	max. room size 64m^3
—convector 450mm	max. room size 71m^3
Open fires with back boilers:	
—inset 400mm	max. room size 42m^3
—inset 450mm	max. room size 50m^3
—with adjustable throat	+7m^3 to room size

the regulations that are in existence.

If you have an existing fireplace, the heater can either be fitted into the existing opening or sit on the hearth in front of it. Which one of these you decide to do depends on the size of the opening compared to the heater as well as how you want the fireplace to look.

If you decide to stand the heater in front of the fireplace opening it must sit on a hearth projecting some way in front of it. If your present hearth does not meet the specific requirements set out in the installation instructions you will have to extend it or, if no hearth exists, build a new one.

Remember, too, that if the heater stands in front of the opening it must be linked to the flue with a special connector so that smoke and combustible gases can be carried away safely. Most manufacturers provide connectors which fit all the room heaters that they make and give advice on correct installation.

Free-standing room heaters can be situated almost anywhere but must be fitted with a prefabricated, insulated chimney and gather. Most manufacturers provide full and detailed instructions on how these should be used, including advice on roof fixings and suitable chimneys. Although these fires are more difficult to install than many other types, the insulated chimney means that overall efficiency should be a little higher.

Free-standing open fires: Many free-standing fires, instead of being completely enclosed, sit on an open grate. The smoke is carried away by a chimney with a wide gather situated directly above the grate (fig. F).

If you decide to install one of these fires it must be in an area with few draughts. Also, the grate must be surrounded by a suitable hearth to prevent any risk of accidental fire. The manufacturers will be able to advise you on a suitable site for such a fire and give advice on installation and the type of flue necessary.

Solid fuels

Apart from wood the main type of solid fuel is coal or one of its by-products. It is important that the correct type and size of fuel is selected for each appliance to ensure satisfactory performance. And of course it is essential to use only smokeless fuels in smoke control areas.

Housecoal: This is available in a number of carefully graded qualities and sizes. It ignites very easily and burns with a bright flame.

Above: A solid-fuel fire can blend in with the different styles of many rooms, but it always adds a really cosy warmth and natural glow

Welsh dry steam coal: This is a naturally smokeless fuel which can be used in both closed appliances and underfloor draught open fires. Available in a range of sizes it burns slowly with a high heat. It is available as large or small nuts and is particularly popular for boilers.

Anthracite: A popular smokeless fuel which is dense and burns slowly. It is normally sold in a range of six sizes—French nuts are the largest, followed by stove nuts, stovesse, peas, beans and grains.

Coalite: This is a manufactured smokeless fuel. It is lightweight and burns with a good, steady flame. Coalite is intended for open fires, while coalite nuts are much more suitable for room heaters and boilers.

Homefire: This is an octagonal-shaped smokeless fuel which is easy to light and burns for long periods with a bright warm flame.

Rexco: This is a manufactured smokeless fuel produced in four sizes—multipurpose for all appliances, nuts and superbrite for room heaters and boilers, and Rexco Royal for open fires.

Sunbrite: A lot denser than other manufactured fuels, this needs to be used in closed appliances or on open fires with underfloor draughts.

Keeping the house warm

About three-quarters of all heating in an uninsulated house is lost to the atmosphere, much of it through the roof. Insulating your roof space is a cheap way of counteracting this loss and will noticeably cut your heating bills. Insulation also helps keep the house cool in summer.

Regardless of the exact type of material used by the house builder, there is nearly always room for improvement. And because of fast-rising fuel costs, in the long run you will save money whatever the actual cost and quantity of your insulation.

Note: Remember also that you can apply to your local authority for an insulation grant, but this must be done before you start work.

Insulating materials

The cheapest and simplest way of insulating the roof space is to place insulating material between, or over, the ceiling joists. Various types of natural and man-made material are available, either in rolled blankets or in granulated form. But as there is little to choose between them in terms of effectiveness you should base your choice on the cost and selection of what is available locally.

Mineral-fibre or glassfibre matting and blanket comes in roll form, cut to fit the average space between floor joists. On its own, this is normally adequate for insulating a roof; awkward nooks and crannies can be filled with off-cuts from the rolls once the main insulation is laid.

However, in older houses, where the ceiling joists are likely to be more narrowly spaced than is usual today, laying a standard-width roll material is a wasteful business—every bit has to be turned up at the edges. In this case, loose-fill insulation is much easier.

Loose-fill comes in bags, either in granule form or as pieces of loose fibre. Among the materials used are polystyrene, vermiculite—an expandable mica—and mineral wool.

Besides being handy where the space between floor joists is narrow, loose-fill insulates inaccessible corners more effectively than offcuts of rolled material.

Whichever type of material is chosen and however this is laid, depth of insulation is the crucial factor. About 100mm is considered a satisfactory compromise between cost and effectiveness. Roll materials are available in thicknesses of about 75mm or 80mm for topping up existing insulation, and of about 100mm for dealing with a loft that has no insulation.

Calculating quantities

Inspecting the loft gives you a chance to estimate both the quantity of material required and the extent of work involved. To help you move around, and to avoid accidentally damaging the ceiling below, place stout planks across the floor joists.

If you are considering adding to existing insulation, think in terms of bringing it up to the 100mm depth of loose-fill or blanket insulation recommended for uninsulated roofs.

In Britain, a typical roll of blanket material of 100mm depth measures about 6.25m in length. 'Topping up' rolls, with depths of about 75mm or 80mm, are slightly longer at about 8m—and usually more expensive. The easiest way of working out your needs is to add together

1 Take blanket insulation right up to the wall-plate at the eaves, and firmly tuck in the edges at the joists if the blanket is too wide

2 Where possible, tuck the insulation under any obstructions. Note the use of a stout plank as a movable working platform across the joists

3 Blanket material can be easily cut to shape with large scissors or a handyman's knife. Offcuts can be used for pipe lagging and elsewhere

4 Loose-fill material is a quick and effective way of dealing with awkward spots such as around the chimney stack and wiring boards

5 Level off the loose-fill right to the top of the joists. If these are very deep, use a 'T'-shaped board cut to give the required depth of material

6 Allow plenty of overlap when covering the loft door—this really does prevent draughts—but do not insulate beneath the water tank

Reducing heat loss

Below: The points 1–6 are jobs that should be undertaken by a specialist, points 7–12 are jobs that can be done by yourself.
1. With an unused fireplace have the chimney stopped and vented. 2. Some types of insulation need to be carefully fitted to prevent damage. 3. Cavity wall insulation is effective but expensive. 4. Insulation can be fitted over a false ceiling —useful when there is no access to the roof space. 5. Sealed-unit double-glazing is best fitted by a professional. 6. Floor cavity insulation ideally needs to be fitted at time of building. 7. Some blanket insulation can be tacked to rafters and covered by board. 8. Insulation between the joists and lagging of tank and pipes is easily done. 9. An inexpensive job is to insulate doors and windows. 10. A bigger job is to panel insulate the inside of a cavity wall. 11. Secondary sash double-glazing is easily fitted. 12. Thicker carpets help reduce heat loss

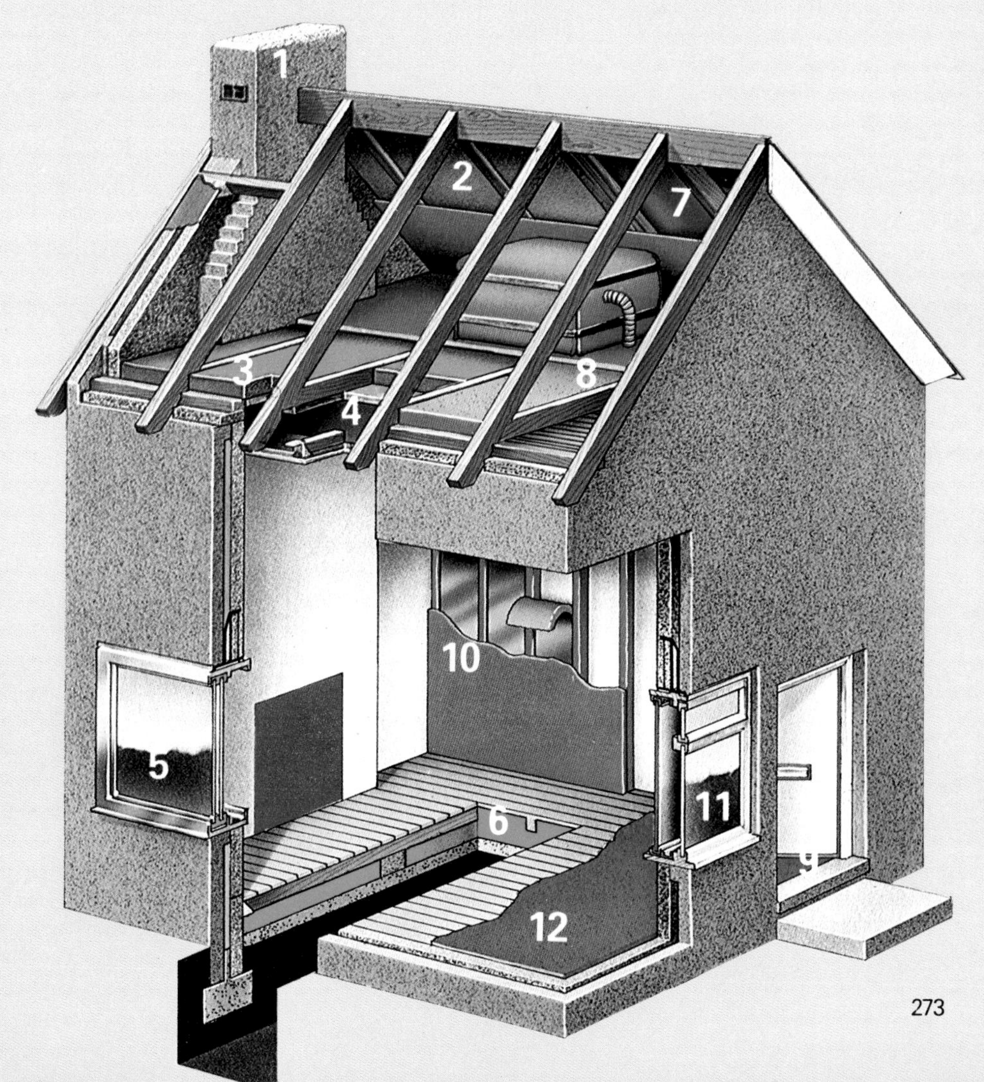

the total length of the strips of ceiling to be covered, and divide this by the length of the roll material you are using to do the job.

Add to this number of rolls a generous surplus to take care of trimming and overlap. Remember to allow for the turn-up at the eaves (see below), and add extra to wrap around the water tank and its piping, and to cover the trapdoor.

If you are using loose-fill material, your requirements are best based on the manufacturer's own tables and recommendations—on the assumption you will be adding insulation up to the depth of 100mm.

While you are in the loft, inspect the areas below the flashings which exclude water at the junction of the roof and other surfaces, such as around the chimney.

On no account should you proceed with insulation if there is any evidence of roof leakage or wet rot, as loft insulation can aggravate both these problems considerably.

At the same time, take a look at the electrics. Wiring perishes in time—especially the older cloth-covered rubber-insulated type—and in any case may not take kindly to repeated knocks while you are laying the insulating material.

Planning the work

When laying blanket insulation, it is infuriating to find that every roll ends short of the mark or repeatedly needs cutting at, say, a particularly large roof member—leaving an almost useless offcut.

The most convenient place for rolls to end is away from the eaves—it is difficult enough having to stretch into these inaccessible areas just to push the insulation home. You should therefore plan on working away from the eaves wherever possible. Any offcuts can be used up later to insulate a more accessible strip in the middle of the loft area.

Laying materials

When you come to lay your insulation, simply follow the set pattern of joists across the roof. Loose-fill material can be levelled to the correct depth using a template made from thick card or wood offcut. Shape this to fit the space between joists (fig. 5). Like roll materials, loose-fill should be laid working inwards from the eaves. Level the filling smoothly towards a clear space in the middle of the loft where addition and removal of the filling will present far less of a problem.

Roll material can be cut with large scissors or slashed with a handyman's knife, but wear protective gloves and clothes at all times. Awkward shapes are more conveniently torn from a supply length. Be generous in the cutting length so that you can tuck in the surplus at the end. Where two lengths join, either tightly butt the two ends or leave the excess to overlap by about 100mm. Offcuts can be used to fill small gaps between lengths.

Around the edges of the loft, strong draughts can be prevented by arranging for the roll ends to be turned up between the rafters—allow extra material for this if necessary. But in most cases you need insulate only as far as the wall-plate—the barrier between the joists and eaves (fig. 1).

The loft area is finished off by insulating the access trap or door with spare lengths of rolled insulation, glued, tied or tacked in place. Allow the material to overspill when the trap or door is closed.

Partial loft conversions

Boarding over the joists after you have insulated the loft will reduce heat loss still further. But if you may want to carry out a full-scale loft conversion later, do not lay a permanent floor; your ceiling joists (probably only 100mm × 50mm, in UK houses) will have to be strengthened for a permanent habitable room. Instead, lay a temporary chipboard floor, screwing down the chipboard so you can lift and re-lay it later.

If the loft already has a floor, lift about one board in five and force loose-fill material between the joists.

Insulating the loft

Above: The illustration shows the various ways of insulating (left) an unused loft and (right) another in the process of being converted into a living space—the basic form of insulation is the same but is used differently.

Blanket insulation such as batts is inexpensive and need only be taken up to the joist end (1). Roll the blanket inwards from the eaves (2). Also use to line and draughtproof the loft door (3) and insulate between the rafters (4). A double thickness is particularly good for a noisy floor (5), but no insulation should be laid beneath a water tank (6). Loose-fill 'rock wool' is better insulating a 'bitty' ceiling (7); increase the depth for further insulation (8). It is also good for a water-tank box, but a softboard box (9) will be needed around the tank.

Remember to also lag pipework using insulation offcuts or polystyrene tubing (10). A draughty roof can have a special lined blanket between the rafters (11)—attached to the tile battens (12). Completely cover the rafters with insulating softboard (13)

In a conversion for a living area, box in insulation behind a false wall (14) to keep the sound down. Chipboard, fitted with screws, is ideal for the floor (15). Also think about fitting a sealed-unit double-glazed window (16) for further good and effective insulation

Draughtproofing

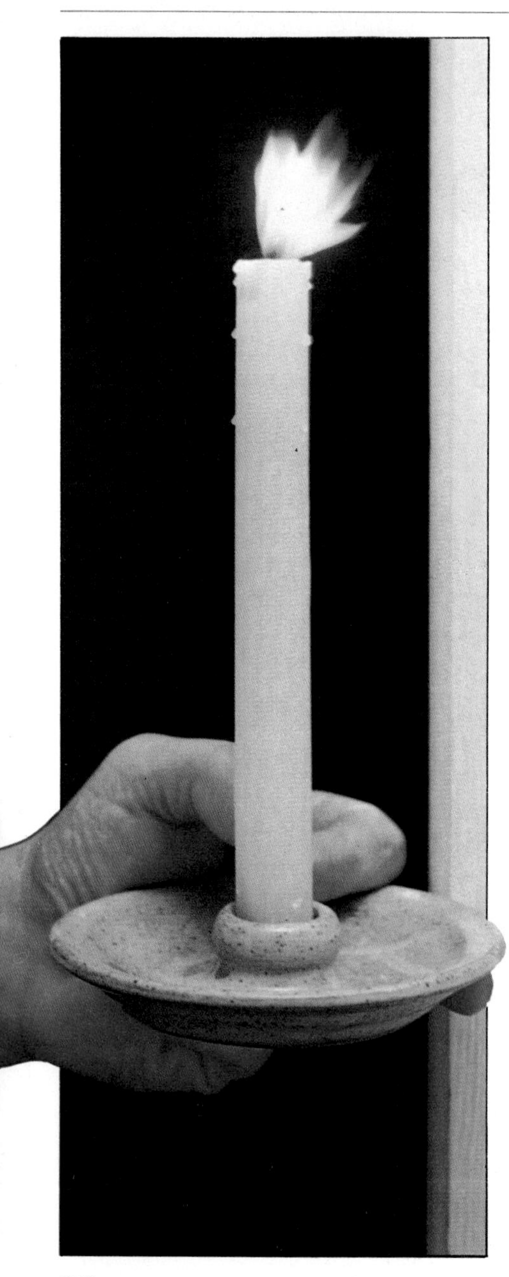

Heat losses caused by draughts are effectively, easily and cheaply eliminated with efficient draughtproofing. Of all the forms of home insulation, draughtproofing brings with it the most quickly noticed improvement in personal comfort—and immediate savings in fuel costs.

The causes of draughts

Draughts are mostly the result of air pressure differences within a house, but they will also occur wherever there is a large gap to the outside, or between a cold and a heated room such as hall and sitting room.

Convection currents are the main cause of air pressure changes, however slight, and the effect can extend from a single room to a whole house. In a single room a large expanse of cold single-glazed window often gives rise to cold down-draughts, even if the whole room is sealed off as a unit. More usually, this cold window down-draught combines with seepage around doors and cracks to make living conditions very uncomfortable.

Locating draughts

If there is any doubt about their whereabouts, the job of locating draughts is best done on a cold and windy day. Use a bare candle flame (away from curtains and other inflammable fittings) to detect the slightest movement of air. If you have one, a smoking taper will give better visual indication and is safer.

Hold the candle flame or taper close to suspect areas around windows and door

A. A flickering flame indicates the presence of a draught and an unnecessary loss of heat which is easily and cheaply remedied. Use a candle for draught detection only where it is safe to do so

frames, watching carefully to see which way the smoke is drawn. Also, check through-wall fittings and pipework where filling looks to be in need of repair.

If possible, seal each area as you proceed. Work from room to room, taking in the hall and other connecting areas as you go.

When draughtproofing each room do not forget to allow enough ventilation for any fuel-burning appliance that may be in use there. Even if a ventilator grille is provided, this may be positioned badly in relation to the appliance. Consider repositioning the grille closer to the appliance to reduce cold draughts across a room. A ventilator grille can be let into suspended flooring or into a nearby external wall.

Building and safety regulations insist on suitable arrangements for ventilation of fuel-burning appliances and this point must be considered in any project that involves extensive draughtproofing.

Sealing doors and windows

Sealing doors and windows accounts for most of the draughtproofing that is likely to be needed. Though in each case the job can be simple and inexpensive, better-looking fittings are available at greater cost.

At the cheapest end of the scale of proprietary draught-excluding products is strip-plastics sponge, attached to a self-adhesive backing and cut to length off a supply reel. With the backing peeled off, the sponge strip can be stuck in place on the cleaned contact surface between a door or window and its frame (fig. C).

Strip-plastics sponge is an effective draughtproofer—providing it is used around the whole frame. However, it does tend to get dirty and tattered, and may disintegrate if exposed to damp and sunshine for any length of time. The wipe-clean surfaced type should last longer but is more expensive.

Perhaps as cheap—and certainly more effective when used in old, warped or rustic frames—is one of the new generation of mastic-like sealants such as silicone rubber. Squeezed from a tube in a continuous, even length along the contact area between window and frame (fig. D), it acts as a rot-proof barrier against moisture and draughts.

Rigid strips of polypropylene, vinyl, phosphor-bronze or aluminium can be used in place of foam strip. Though no

B. A badly hung or warped door may need extensive repair work or, in some cases, total replacement

C. Strip material—here ribbed rubber—is easily fitted and an inexpensive and useful draughtproofing aid

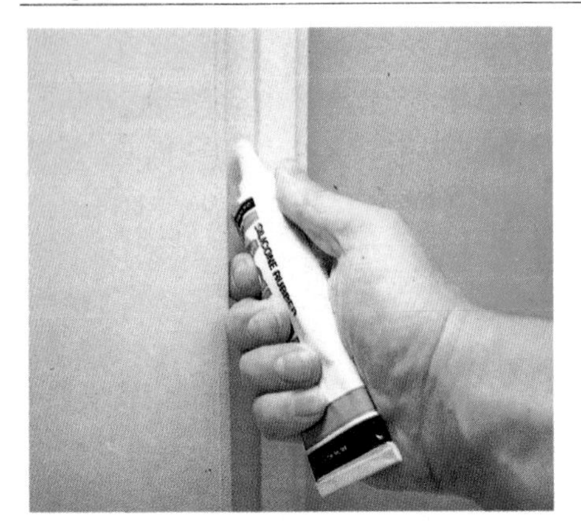

D. Sealant can be easily squeezed into the most inaccessible parts of a door or window frame to firmly seal it

E. Take a close look at the underside of window sills, and use filler to make good any gaps you might find

F. Gaps between wood sidings and window frames can be sealed with mastic applied from a gun

G. Draughtproofing the rear of a letterbox using a brushpile screen which is then screwed in

more efficient, these sprung, hinge-like strips do last indefinitely and are a better proposition on doorways to the outside.

Cut to length and tacked in place round the door or window rebate the strips are easily fitted. As the door or window is closed the two halves of the 'hinge' close together—one side fixed to the door frame, the other sprung against the door.

Secondary-sash double-glazing also acts as a fairly efficient draughtproofing aid for windows but ought to be used in conjunction with excluding strip and anti-condensation crystals to prevent build-up between them.

Mastic can again be used for making good small gaps between a door or window frame and the accompanying brickwork where the filler mortar has crumbled. But purpose-made cellulose or vinyl-based filler is cheaper and usually easier to apply.

Take a particularly close look at the underside of window sills—especially

H. Draught-excluding strip is easily attached to the door base although plastics types do not last long

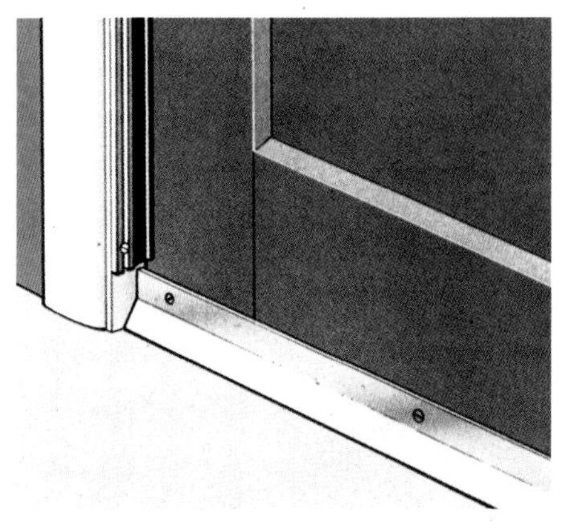

I. A rubber seal set into a metal frame acts as a heavy-duty draught-excluder that is ideal for outer doors

J. A combination of threshold seal and door-mounted weather shield is the best option for heavy-duty applications

K. Brushpile strip is easily fitted to the base of a door and is ideal for areas where floors are uneven

large ones such as those found in some types of bay window—and check for draughty gaps there. Use cement or filler to seal these (fig. E).

Even the finest of cracks can still let in a powerful draught if the conditions are right. In this case, an inconspicuous fillet of wood filler may be all that is required.

Timber-clad houses

One source of draughts in timber-clad houses is the inevitable gaps between the weatherboard, clapboard or shingles sections, and between these material and door and window frames. These gaps should be filled with an appropriate mastic (caulking compound)—these days, often silicone. Clean out the old caulking, and wipe the area with a rag soaked in white spirit, turpentine or other solvent. Caulking is available in disposable cartridges, and is forced into the gap using a cartridge gun (fig. F). Make sure the bead of caulking adheres to both sides of the joint. Modern screw-head cartridges do not need an application gun.

Door strips

There are many types of draught excluder for the gaps under a door.

Strips of inexpensive rubber or plastic draught-excluder about 30mm wide can be screwed or tacked to the lower edge of the door on one or both sides (fig. H). But these tend to wear quickly, especially if positioned too low and hard against the floor covering. Position each strip so that the edge just indents, or is bent by, the floor covering against which it rests.

A better long-term proposition is a metal door sill and door seal arrangement (fig. I) fixed to the outside of the door. A weatherproofing shield can be fitted instead of this to protect a sill fixed to the floor (fig. J).

Better for inside the house—and well suited to sliding doors—is the brushpile type of strip, the bristles of which compress to form a very effective seal (fig. K). This can be used in conjunction with full carpeting in most instances, but is particularly suited to polished wood or tiled floors.

Another solution is to use a 'rise and fall' excluder, particularly where a hard object—such as a door mat—has to be crossed. In this case, adjustable strip with an angled striking face is kept in place by a hollow moulding attached to the base of the door. In the closed-door position, the strip self-levels (if it can be arranged, against the mat or carpet being used). As the door is opened the strip is forced upwards as its angled face strikes the floor covering.

At the other extreme, a substantial gap of more than 20mm ought to be built up to reduce the eventual gap between the fitting and the base of the door. Threshold strips provide a partial answer, but you may find that these have to be fitted over thin battens to fill the extra space. Battening used on its own and covered by carpeting can also act as an excellent seal and this inexpensive idea is well worth considering. Use padding in the form of offcuts of carpet to build up either side of the batten before laying the main carpet over.

Dealing with other draughts

Bare floorboards may look great, but they can also be a source of strong draughts which you cannot afford to neglect. The tongued-and-grooved types are designed to get round the problem, but even so, some joins—especially those near the skirting—may need attention. The worst offender is the old, square-edge boarding. Here, even fitted carpet is not always successful at excluding draughts.

The best solution is to fill the gaps between the boards, either with one of the proprietary mastic-like compounds described above or with papier mâché.

When using filler, smooth it into each joint with a piece of electrical flex. If you decide on papier mâché, use a wood stain to match it to the colour of the floorboards.

If the gaps below skirting boards are the problem use fillets of mastic, filler paste or cement as necessary. This gap is a common source of draughts and can usually be eliminated by wall-to-wall carpeting or by tacking quadrant beading into the corner.

If suspended flooring is being installed or repaired, or if you have crawl space under the house, you can prevent quite heavy heat losses by insulating between the joists. There are two kinds. Paper-faced glassfibre batts, commonest in Britain, have flanged edges for easy stapling to the joists.

Make sure the loft trap or attic door is treated in the same way as others using the same methods of draughtproofing. If the loft area has been properly insulated, overlapping material at the edges of the door normally provides a good seal.

Then there's the letterbox. Here, you can fasten a piece of rubber or old carpet to the inside of the flap. But for a better-looking job, fit a stronger spring and line the slit with foam strip, or exchange the old flap for the new type with brush inserts.

Double-glazing

Above: Fitting most forms of simple double-glazing requires no more than a screwdriver, drill and some cutting implements. Here, the side track of a Polycell fixed window kit is being firmly screwed into place in line with the top and bottom tracks

Glass is not a very good material for keeping in heat—for a given area, you will lose more heat through the windows of your house than through the walls or roof. The way to reduce heat losses via windows, and so cut your heating bills, is to double-glaze them—instead of having a single pane of glass, the windows have two parallel panes separated by a trapped layer of air; it is mainly this air gap that gives a double-glazed window its increased insulation value.

The benefits of double-glazing

The most obvious reason for double-glazing is to reduce fuel bills. In the UK, however, the amount of fuel saved is not likely to make anything but the very simplest and cheapest form of double-glazing system worthwhile.

Double-glazing does have other benefits, though. Particularly with large windows it reduces the cooling down-draught effect that can make a room feel chilly even when heated properly, and can severely restrict the area of the room that is comfortable to sit in. It reduces condensation and, if the right system is chosen, can dramatically improve sound insulation. It is also worthwhile working out the cost-benefit of double-glazing if you are installing a new central heating system: with double-glazing, you will need a smaller heating system, so you can offset some of the costs against the savings here.

There is a huge variety of double-glazing systems available.

Simple systems are at the cheapest end of the scale, and the cheapest of these are based on plastic sheeting, which comes in many thicknesses, ranging from that used for food-wrapping to acrylic sheet such as Perspex. In between there are numerous other plastics forms, including the popular middle-of-the-road choice for double-glazing on a budget: acetate sheets, available in various thicknesses.

The disadvantages of thin plastics film, such as food wrap, is that even when fitted well it tends to look terrible. Polythene sheeting is little better, as it tends to whiten and become more brittle when exposed to sunshine. Acetate sheet, which keeps its clarity well, is a better choice. Another choice is a thin plastic film that is stuck to the frame with double-sided clear tape and which stretches taut under blown hot air.

It is possible to incorporate thicker plastics sheeting within a frame arrangement constructed from wood battening or plastic channelling, perhaps using components from a double-glazing kit. The frame can clip into place for easy removal when cleaning is required.

For thicker plastics sheet or, even, another sheet of glass, you can make a more substantial frame. But this or any other frame must be capable of taking the extra weight of the glazing material and be easily removed in the case of fire.

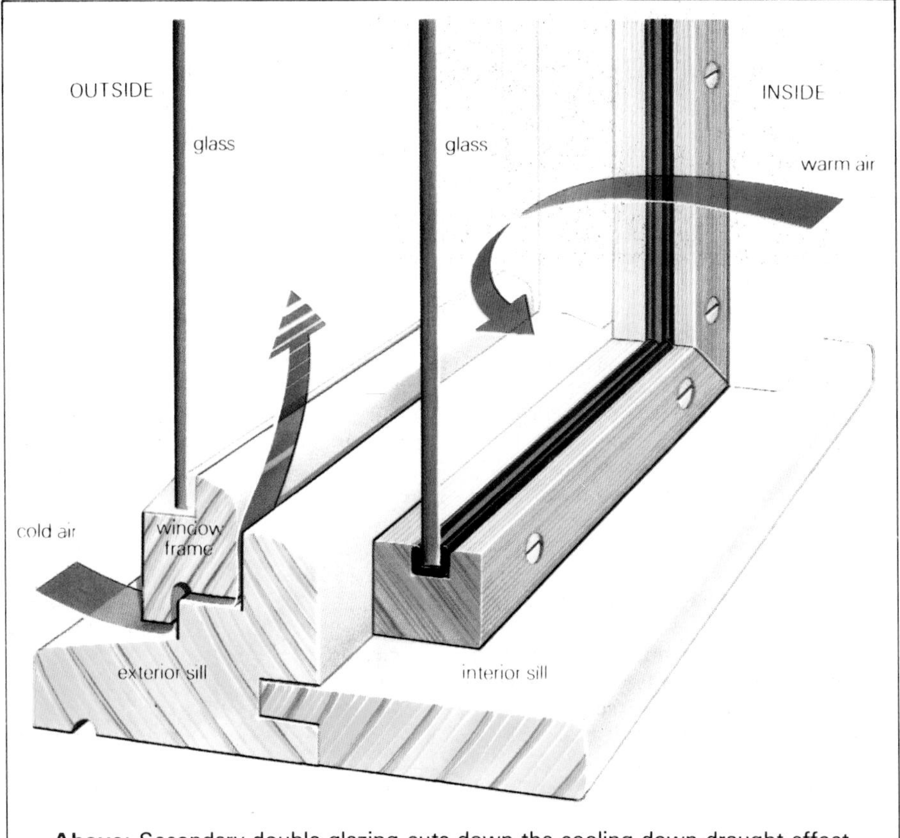

Above: Secondary double-glazing cuts down the cooling down-draught effect of large areas of glass and also eliminates frame draughts

If you choose to use glass, 4mm float is normally sufficient, but your glass supplier will be able to advise on glass thickness if you are in any doubt.

Secondary-sash glazing describes several methods of providing a more permanent form of double-glazing. With these, the second sheet of glass is supported against the frame by clips, hinges, or in channels which permit either vertical or horizontal sliding for opening and closing. Some of these frames can be supplied ready-glazed and complete with all fittings, including the seals so important to these designs. Alternatively, you may prefer to construct your own secondary-sash arrangement using components from some of the many kits available. The best forms of secondary-sash double-glazing permit access for cleaning of inner window surfaces, and enable you to open the window for ventilation in dry weather if required.

Extruded aluminium frames are most commonly used for secondary-sash systems, particularly those that are supplied ready-glazed.

Coupled glazing is an even more 'permanent' variation where, in effect, two window frames are employed in place of one. This arrangement is particularly suitable for windows with a narrow sill that cannot take a sliding secondary sash or other form of glazing frame. Both windows open and close as one, but the additional one is hinged and clipped to enable easy separation for cleaning.

Storm windows, although also mounted on the outside, are not often coupled to the original window, but are rigidly fixed to the frame.

Sealed units (sometimes called insulating glass) consist of two layers of glass, with an air gap between, sealed together in the factory. You install the complete unit in the window frame opening in place of the existing single sheet of glass. These are covered in the next chapter.

Width of air space

The heat insulation property of double-glazing varies with the width of the enclosed air space. The optimum space depends very much on the temperature difference between the inside and outside surfaces, but is usually taken as 20mm in temperate zones when heating is up to normal standards. For easier fitting, this gap is reduced to 12mm in factory-sealed insulating glass and the difference in heat loss can be considered negligible. A gap of less than 12mm leads to progressively greater heat losses.

The heat loss, or *thermal transmittance*, of a single pane of glass under average conditions of use and exposure is taken to be 5.6 watts per square metre of glass, for each degree centigrade temperature difference between the inner and outer surfaces. This is expressed as $5.6W/m^2$ °C. A 20mm air gap between two sheets of glass almost halves the heat loss to $2.9W/m^2$ °C. Insulating glass (factory-sealed double-glazed units) yields figures of 3.0 and $3.4W/m^2$ °C for air gaps of 12mm and 6mm respectively.

Sound insulation

Sound insulation is often one of the most important considerations when planning a double-glazing scheme, particularly if your home suffers greatly from the noise of a busy road or nearby airport.

Any double-glazing reduces noise on account of the trapped airspace between panes and as this gap increases, so sound insulation improves. However, the gap needs to be at least 100mm—and preferably 150mm with 4mm glass—for the best combination of sound and thermal insulation. While a bigger gap of up to about 400mm improves sound insulation, thermal insulation is greatly reduced because of the convection currents that then have space to form between the two panes of glass.

Whatever type of double-glazing you use, fitting it to allow a gap of 100mm or more is often difficult on most types of domestic window. So, if thermal insulation is important, you may have to make modifications.

Factory-made sealed units usually have

1 The Polycell kit for fixed secondary glazing and the few tools required for cutting and fixing. Glass of the right size is an extra item to buy. Measure off the required length of the deeper top track to fit across the width of the soffit or lintel. Use a try square to mark the necessary cutting lines

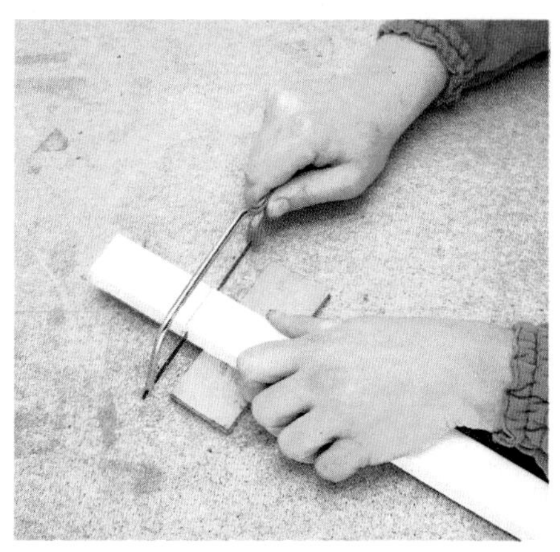

2 Use a small hacksaw or fine-bladed saw to carefully cut the track to length. Unless the window frame is truly square, individually measure off and cut the remaining tracks to length. Then position the top track to leave as wide an air gap as necessary before marking screw positions with a bradawl

an air spacing of between 5mm and 12mm and the sound insulation properties these may have are due only to the weight of glass involved. However, if used as a secondary unit this insulating glass can be positioned to provide the necessary gap, in which case further benefits are provided by the additional trapped layer of this multiple glazing set-up.

Where the gap width permits, you can achieve additional sound insulation by using acoustic tiles to line the soffit, reveal and sill of the window. Bear in mind that this insulation should not impede drainage arrangements which may have to be provided.

Condensation problems

A frequent problem with single-glazed windows is condensation, which can reach severe proportions if the atmosphere indoors is very humid. Over a period of time this ruins fixtures and fittings and may even cause wood framework to rot, replacement of which must be the first priority in any double-glazing project.

Although double-glazing does not always eliminate condensation, it goes a long way towards curbing the problem—especially if fitted properly.

Drilling a series of holes, at an angle downwards through the window frame, enables the air gap to 'breathe'—but no more—and so prevents a build-up of too much moisture. Or, you can place *silica gel*, a moisture absorber, in the air gap on shallow trays made of up-ended channelling. The silica gel has to be removed and dried from time to time.

Insulating glass normally has a filling of inert gas sealed within the unit. Condensation between the panes should not be a problem and there is usually some form of replacement guarantee to this effect, providing the seal remains intact.

Condensation is likely to occur if there is a poor seal between a secondary-sash and the supporting frame, a very real problem with some of the cheaper DIY double-glazing kits as adequate precau-

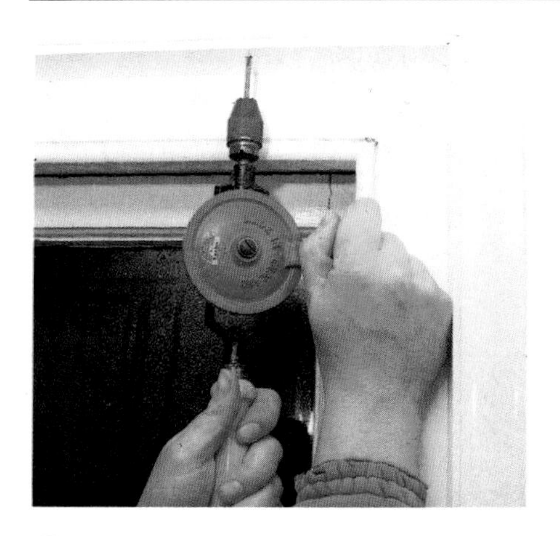

3 Drill pilot holes in the top frame or soffit. Use a masonry bit on your drill if you are screwing into plaster, brick or concrete. Then screw the top track into place, plugging screw holes with rawl plugs if fixing plaster and brick or concrete. Firmly drive the screws home into the necessary position

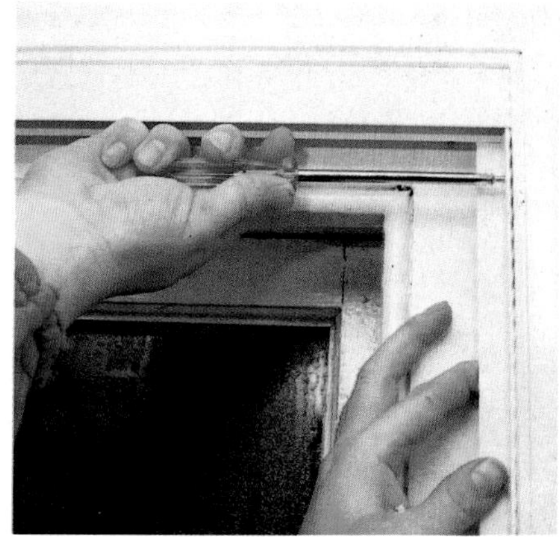

4 With the top and bottom tracks completely aligned with each other and set squarely in the window reveals, position and fix the side tracks into place. Use a wood offcut to tap and, if necessary, force edging strip fully into place on the glass edges. Then slip the glazed frame into the window tracks

tions cannot normally be taken. Always provide a generous and effective seal if you can, but make sure you install your glazing on a cold, dry day as the moisture content of the air is at its lowest then. Even with removable double-glazing arrangements such as secondary-sash systems, it may be worth adding a temporary or permanent 'bedding seal', particularly for opening windows.

Curing draughts

Draughts are an unwanted feature of every house, and many originate from badly fitting windows or doors. Most problems of this nature are easily put right and must not be allowed to go unchecked when double-glazing is installed as many of the benefits may then be lost. Draughtproofing between an air gap and the inner glazing sheet is especially important if condensation is to be minimized or eliminated.

If a frame, window or door is in a particularly bad state of repair, it may be easier and cheaper in the long run to consider fitting a double-glazed replacement from the outset.

Where to glaze

In most cases, double-glazing is an improvement job which is undertaken in stages as both weather and funds permit. Deciding quite where to start can be a problem, so base your choice on those rooms which you use a lot, those kept at the highest temperatures, and those which have the largest area of glazing.

The living room, sitting room and kitchen are obvious starting points and as these are likely to account for much of the ground-floor glazing, it is a good idea to choose one, matched system for all of them. Double-glazing upstairs is a luxury by comparison, but should be considered in your long-term plans. Temperatures here are usually kept lower, and even if heating is turned off at night, this hardly matters when you are snugly asleep.

Take care to match the likely strength of a glazing kit with the area of glass that it has to support.

Fitting simple double-glazing

Most forms of double-glazing in kit form are easily installed by the home improver. Of these, the various forms manufactured from aluminium section tend to be more durable and better looking than their plastics counterparts, which often cost as much.

With all forms, particular care should be taken to ensure clean, square cuts as errors here can greatly mar the finished appearance. Take care to avoid scuffing aluminium, which readily shows this ill-treatment.

Always buy height and width kits which are oversized to allow for any possible error in calculations.

The Cosyframe kit which is featured in the step-by-step pictures consists of the aluminium glazing frame, some glazing strip and sealing strip and it also features all the necessary corner components

5 Measure off the required height and width of frame needed for the window; carefully matching the opposite sides to ensure you have absolute squareness. Then use a fine-toothed hacksaw for making a clean, square cut. Remove any uneven burrs, which might have occurred with the cut, with a file as these could impede assembly of the kit

8 Protect the aluminium with an offcut of wood when tapping frame fully home. The frame must be particularly tight fitting for the necessary safety. Use a wood offcut, if need be, to remove an incorrectly positioned frame. Thoroughly lubricate the glazing seal with soap and water before repeating

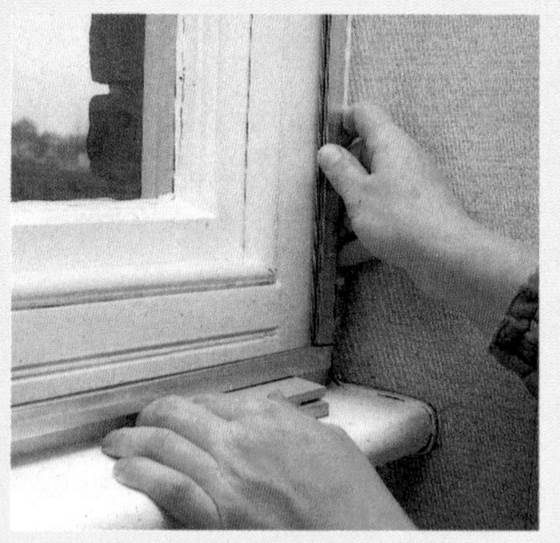

9 Again using the soap and water, lubricate the sealing strip as it is inserted within the frame. A blunt screwdriver or knife is useful here. Then once the frame corner screws have been tightened, position the glazed frame in the window. Use wood offcuts again to help position the frame

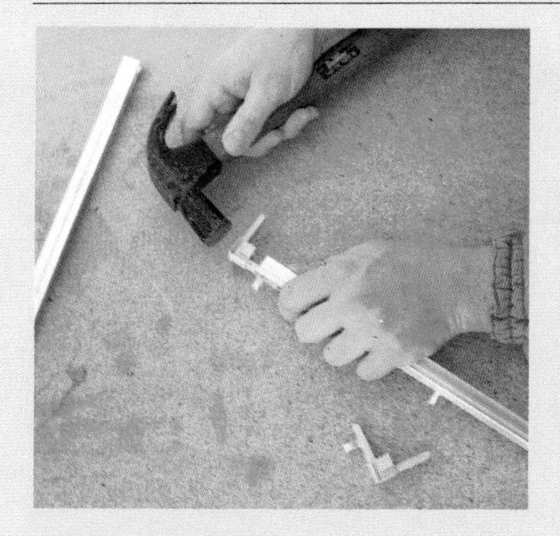

6 Firmly tap home the corner pieces with a hammer so that they are securely in place—with this particular type of kit, self-tapping screws are located but they do not need to be tightened up at this stage. Then slip some glazing strip along the edges of the glass sheet, cutting to length only when any stretching has actually contracted

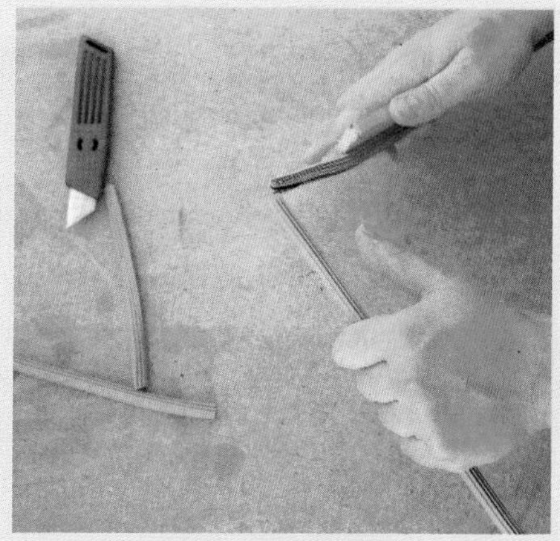

7 Use a spare block of offcut wood to push the glazing strip firmly into the right place, making the final trimmings of length as you find it necessary. Then thoroughly lubricate all the glazing strip with plenty of soap and water and slip into the required position the first of the four parts of the actual aluminium frame

10 Use a bradawl tool to make and drill pilot holes for fixing all the frame hinges. On high windows you will need to provide additional sets of hinges. When the hinges have all been screwed into position, carefully check that the frame opens and closes properly along its supporting length

11 The final stage in fitting this simple Cosyframe double-glazing kit is to position neatly the turn-catches as close to the top and bottom of the opening side of the frame as is at all possible. These should, however, be very tight fitting or they will just not operate in the correct way needed

Further double-glazing projects

Even the simplest forms of double-glazing can be effective at keeping heat in, and possibly at keeping noise out. But many of these simple types are not very attractive, nor are they very durable.

A short step from some of the simple double-glazing kits is the installation of home-made, permanently glazed secondary windows which can have a much more attractive appearance.

Secondary frames may fit either inside the existing window, or outside it as a coupled window, or a storm window. The frames may be fixed in place—the best solution for a good, tight seal—or sliding or hinged—to give easy access for cleaning and ventilation.

The greatest problem with secondary systems and coupled windows is preventing draughts and condensation. It is essential that your double-glazing system fits the window properly to keep maintenance problems to a minimum. Envisaging problems of this sort, you may prefer to buy a factory-made secondary glazing unit and install this yourself.

Secondary glazing

If you decide to stick to a secondary glazing system and choose to employ a more rugged and permanent method than that provided by many of the simple kits, a fixed secondary frame is often the answer.

But although a fixed secondary glazing system is attractive from the point of view of long life, installation is often an involved process. You must take particular care to prevent condensation forming after assembly, and to make provision for cleaning and ventilation.

'Breathing holes' of 2–3mm diameter are drilled in the frame to dissipate moisture drawn through the woodwork surrounding the air gap without directly admitting outside damp.

Fitting becomes more difficult if the frame has a shallow sill, or if a frame is being fitted against an existing metal-framed window which has no woodwork. In this case, a sub-frame of 30mm × 30mm timber can be fitted to the window reveal, leaving a sufficient gap for clearance of existing protruding handles and other immovable fixtures. But fitted properly, the frame should be suitable for all forms of double-glazing, including the simpler types.

Secondary glazing of this type differs only slightly from that for a coupled window and fitting problems are much the same.

Factory-made units

The first major step up from simple systems is the fitting of factory-made ready-glazed secondary systems. Some firms can provide these units for you to fit yourself, whereas others may insist on an all-in professional service.

In most systems, an extruded aluminium frame is attached to existing window framework with a mastic or other suitable sealant used to make good small irregularities and to prevent draughts at the frame edge—a potential cause of condensation.

A brick window opening is rarely truly square, and to offset this fact the better-quality units usually employ a sub-frame. This is fitted first, either to the bare brickwork at the window reveal or to the existing window frame, if this is in good condition. The new frame is then

attached to the sub-frame, the fixing screws concealed beneath moulding.

The sub-frame should be made of hardwood to eliminate long-term problems such as warping and splitting. And if the frame is attached to brickwork, it is essential that fitting and construction are of a high standard.

A similar procedure is employed for the installation of complete replacement windows and patio doors. A variation is the use of an additional aluminium sub-frame, which must be carefully fitted to avoid reducing the glazing's insulating

Above: Insulating glass is quickly and easily installed—ideal for the person wanting to install quality double-glazing

properties and—over the long term—to prevent a build-up of trapped water.

Insulating glass

This is one name given to double-glazing that consists of two panes of glass sealed together in the factory with a gap between them—*sealed units* is another name. The gap between the units is filled with dehumidified air or an inert gas to prevent condensation. The units are fitted as replacements for existing single panes, but the window frames must be able to support the additional weight. If the rebate in the frame is not deep enough to take a standard unit, a stepped type can be used.

But you can obtain greater benefits by combining these insulating glass sheets within secondary glazing arrangements, so that triple or multiple glazing results.

Used in place of single glazing, insulating glass should—under identical conditions—show a noticeable reduction in the amount of condensation on the inner surface. Claims can seem exaggerated if the influencing factors—relative humidity, surface temperature differences and ventilation—alter.

The sealing methods used for insulating glass—and also for secondary glazing units—are also worth comparing. Choose systems and methods which employ a tight-fitting, but supple, 'soft' seal, as this reduces movement and vibration of the glass. Opening windows and doors, and large-area sheets exposed to strong winds are particularly susceptible to trouble of this kind.

Consider using professional help to install a particularly large area of insulating glass (or, indeed, standard glass) as experienced handling and fitting is required to avoid damaging the seal.

Comfort, safety and security

Draughtproofing and double-glazing can literally seal up a home, so providing adequate ventilation is particularly important. It comes down to striking a happy balance between heating and ventilation from the point of view of comfort, otherwise a build-up of internal humidity will result in severe condensation problems—perhaps far worse than you experienced before double-glazing.

You must provide adequate ventilation for fuel-burning appliances, even if this means going to the lengths of installing a ventilator grille near the appliance once the double-glazing (and draughtproofing) has been installed.

The reduction in heat losses brought about by double-glazing often encourages greater use of windows and patio doors—both as a replacement for existing walling and windows, and as part of the design of structural extensions. The resulting increased area of glazing poses safety and security problems which cannot be ignored—even in terms of the single window, where one large area of glass is likely to be used in place of several small ones in individual frames.

Windows near doorways or stairs are particular danger areas. In these and similar instances, the risks of injury can be reduced if you employ safety or tempered glass in place of float or decorative glass. Safety glass goes through an annealing process which increases its resistance to smashing. And if it does break, the glass fractures into small, comparatively safe pieces rather than splinters.

All forms of glass should be handled with care, using heavy-duty gloves at all times—even on sheets with ground edges. Sharp edges can damage the plastics seals of many of the systems you can glaze yourself. Ask your glass supplier to remove these, or do the job yourself with a carborundum block.

For safety in the event of a fire, ensure that one or more easily accessible windows on each floor can be unlocked and opened quickly.

Large areas of glass or a window with two sheets of glass instead of one is unlikely to deter an intruder intent on forcing an entry—and quite possibly the reverse will apply. Opening windows should incorporate—or be provided with

—locking handles or catches. Recessed locks and safety bolts (fitting into adjacent panels) should feature on all patio doors.

Maintenance

The more expensive your initial installation, the less likely the need for maintenance and running repairs. The seals of insulating glass should be inspected for wear every few years, but faults here are likely to show up in the form of condensation. Carry out these and other checks before wet and cold weather sets in.

Cleaning away dust and condensation is likely to be the most frequent maintenance job on most forms of secondary glazing—particularly the cheaper units —but many systems allow for this to be done quickly and efficiently.

1 You can install insulating glass instead of single glass when reglazing. Remove old putty then carefully check the fit of the insulating glass

2 Line the bead with back putty, keeping to an even depth of about 5mm. Then push the glass into the frame and fix with glazing pins

3 Apply nodules of exterior-grade putty and smooth this down evenly using the curved part of a putty knife

4 Insulating glass should only be used in windows with strong frames and deep rebates to support the extra weight

Double-glazed patio door

Professionally installed double-glazing is a major home-improvement expense. A typical job is replacing old French doors with a custom-built unit having sliding doors. A patio door conversion of this nature may require the removal of the low walling on each side of the threshold. This type of structural work is usually carried out by the firm installing the system.

The picture sequence shows the installation of a Therm-A-Stor patio door.

Sealed units of up to 32mm thickness can be accommodated by this design, permitting an air gap of 20mm, which is considered the optimum by this manufacturer.

Safety and security are important aspects to consider. With this design—capable of withstanding gale-force winds—a hook-type lock is employed

1 The first stage of installing a double-glazed patio door is the complete removal of the existing old door and window frame and all the short-wall brickwork at the sides. The wooden sub-frame is custom built by the manufacturers to fit the required aperture. This is normally made on the spot for the greatest possible accuracy

4 The 'fast' frame is then carefully inserted within the main frame. The weight of glass is substantial and the design of the frame has to consider this aspect. Edge stripping and draught excluders are then added to the 'fixed' and 'moving' frames and also to the main frame itself to insulate the door

5 The moving frame runs back and forth on small nylon or stainless-steel rollers which have to be adjusted before the installation of the frame. The sliding door is then fitted in place. Then all the final fittings—handles, the lock and side trims—are added to the basic door structure

2 The sub-frame is then carefully checked for accurate fit and screwed firmly into place. A bedding seal of suitable proprietary mastic helps prevent any possible frame draughts. The aluminium frame is then put together at the same time as the sub-frame is constructed to ensure that you get the necessary perfectly matched fit

3 On this particular type of double-glazed patio door installation, the aluminium main frame has to be firmly secured to the hardwood sub-frame with several fixing screws. The realistic number of fixings that will need to be attached to the frame depends on the actual height and width of the door you are having fitted

6 The inner and outer walls are then made good. Any extensive repairs to the actual frame surrounds have to be made earlier. Gaps and cracks can then be filled using a suitable general-purpose mastic. Efficient draughtproofing of the whole frame is also considered a really essential job

7 The final stage of installing the frame is varnishing the hardwood frame both indoors and out. A polyurethane type of varnish is best for this purpose. The complete patio door installation should look very good and be capable of putting up with considerable wear and tear in all kinds of weather

Soundproofing

Noisy neighbourhoods, and very noisy houses, are an increasingly common cause for complaint in urban areas; even if you have the most considerate neighbours, intrusive noise is often intolerably high. Fortunately, there are a number of steps you can take to insulate your home effectively and efficiently against noises from within and without.

The nature and types of noise

Sound is produced by the creation of variable waves in the substances through which it passes. These waves can pass through gases, liquids or solid materials and the sound you hear is determined by their nature; that is, by their frequency and intensity. When the frequency is fast, we hear high-pitched noises; when it is slow we hear low-pitched noises. Most people can detect a wide range of frequencies—between 62 and 16,000 cycles per second—though this faculty will vary from person to person.

A. Above: When planning soundproofing you have to identify the different noise sources: airborne—from cars and planes—and impact—from noises like footsteps

Noise level (or volume) is measured in *decibels* (dB). Decibels are points on a logarithmic scale which record the volume of noise produced in different situations. The higher the decibel reading, the louder the noise. But because the scale is logarithmic, doubling the volume of noise does not double the decibel reading—it only increases the decibels by about three.

Consequently, the difference between 60 decibels and 90 decibels is quite enormous; an appropriate comparison would be between the noise from a television in a living room (60dB), and heavy urban traffic at a distance of 5m (90dB).

The degree to which a noise is annoying is dependent on a variety of factors. In certain circumstances, the ticking of the watch on your wrist (approximately 30dB) will be annoying, while in others the background noise of a television may not be.

Most importantly, you have to consider the source of the noise and this means understanding how the noise is reaching you. In this respect, it is important to bear in mind that sound travels into your home in two ways: through the air, when it is called 'airborne noise'; and through solid objects, when it becomes known as 'impact noise'. Bangs, thumps, footsteps and vibrations cause impact noise, but this in turn can create reverberations which produce airborne noise. Impact noises travel far faster and further in solid, dense objects, while, ironically, such objects are particularly effective in cutting out the passage of airborne noise.

Airborne noise

Airborne noises are the most common invasion of your privacy and your moments of relaxation, but luckily they are also the easiest to deal with. They can range from aircraft and traffic noise, to the hi-fi system of the people in the house opposite, to the noise of children playing.

Airborne noises from the outside will enter buildings through the weakest links; windows, doors and ventilators providing the easiest access. Consequently, the sound level close to the window will be mainly determined by the insulation value of the glazing. However, the average noise level in the room —which is what is important to the occupants—will be determined by the wall and window in combination. In this respect, the net insulation value of the room is always closer to that of the window than of the wall and so in general, the larger the window, the lower the insulation value.

Because of its high density, even thin glass gives insulation ranging from 23dB for 3mm glass, up to 34dB for 25mm glass. But ill-fitting frames reduce these insulation values enormously. Firstly, then, check all the seals on casement windows.

On casement windows, overpainting of the edges will damage the effect of the seal because the paint builds up and prevents the frame from closing properly. If this is the case, scrape or burn off the excess paint before priming and painting both closing edges. When the paint has dried, fit one of the many types of seals that are currently available.

Seals that have been developed to save heat are useful in this respect because you can make them serve a dual purpose. Wherever possible, use compression seals, rather than brush seals, because they are more effective. Before doing so, however, make sure that the casement is capable of exerting the necessary compressing force: often only metal frames are sturdy enough to seal a compression joint.

Despite the density of glass, and the use of seals, the insulation value of a window is likely to be low unless it is double-glazed. However, while two thin sheets of glass, separated by a gap of less than 50mm, may be an efficient heat insulator, such an arrangement may let in more noise than a heavy single pane of glass. This is because if both panes are of an equal thickness, they tend to produce a 'coincidence loss' for noises of a particular frequency. This will be heard as a 'hiss' on the inside. Therefore, where the width of the air gap is limited to less than 100mm for practical reasons, use different weights of glass. With a gap of 50–80mm, and panes of different thicknesses, double-glazing gives an improvement of some 3–4dB over double-glazing that uses the same weight of glass.

For sound insulation of greater efficiency, use a much wider gap between panes than you would for insulation against heat-loss—if possible as much as 200mm—and stick strips of absorbent lining in the reveals between the panes. Carpet strips, mineral-fibre board, or strips of foam plastic are sufficient to reduce noise escaping into the reveals or around the frames.

You can improve the sound insulation of existing windows by installing secondary glazing behind them. Give the existing windows good seals first, particularly at the edges of opening casements. This may improve the insulation by as much as 10dB immediately. Use sliding panes as the secondary glazing, placing the frame at least 150mm behind the existing pane of glass.

Using heavy, lined curtains could improve the sound insulation still further, though give some thought to the loss of ventilation which this might entail.

Improving door insulation

Like windows, doors break the insulation qualities of solid brick walls, which are normally quite efficient. And because few doors are well sealed, the insulation value of a wall can be as much as halved by the sound entering via the gaps around them. Your first concern is to make sure that the doors fit as well as possible. Where a door is warped or the frame is out of alignment, make this good.

Fitting seals around the edges of the doors can improve their insulation value by as much as 5dB immediately. The best seals, but also the most expensive, are the magnetic type used on refrigerators. Fit them into the rebate on the door frame to protect them and to form an unobtrusive and effective seal.

The threshold is the most difficult part of the door to seal and here you should use the type of threshold seal which has a raised bar containing a rounded, resilient strip. Make quite sure that the bar is accurately aligned with the bottom of the door and that it is in contact with the complete length of the bottom rail. This will make the door more difficult to open and close, but will greatly improve the sound and heat insulation.

Wall insulation

Many party walls are only of a single brick thickness, and often a partition wall within a house is constructed only of timber and plasterboard. Because the weight of such walls is relatively light any airborne sounds can quite easily pass through.

There are two things you can do to improve the insulation of such walls. The first is the most obvious method, but often the least practical: simply increase the weight of the wall itself by adding an extra leaf of brickwork. The increased solidity prevents the passage of significant amounts of airborne noise, but the feasibility of such a step depends on the layout of your house and on whether it is possible to support the extra weight; certainly you should never build such a wall without adequate foundations. And although this method reduces the transmission of airborne noise, it will not reduce impact noise at all. You will still clearly hear banging or vibration of any sort from the other side.

An alternative method for reducing airborne noise transmission, and which also reduces impact noise, involves constructing a false wall which conceals an insulating glass wool blanket. Along the ceiling, about 100mm from the noisy party wall, nail a 100mm timber lath parallel to the line of the wall. Hang a 75mm glass wool blanket from the lath by sandwiching the blanket between the timber and a strip of hardboard screwed or pinned along the length of the timber. Make sure that the blanket hangs from the ceiling to the floor, without resting on the floor itself or touching the wall; this slight air gap all round is most important. On the inside of the room, erect a stud partition frame and clad the frame with plasterboard, hardboard or a lightweight surface material. When this has been done, finish the wall as you would do for any normal partition wall.

Use a similar method for insulating internal stud partition walls, and improve the insulative qualities of the wall surface still further by adding polystyrene sheets behind the sheet panels. Stagger the joints of the layers to avoid undue settlement and cracking. In both these cases, the system works because of the interaction of air space and sound absorbers.

B. To insulate a suspended floor, raise the floorboards and then lay 'silver' 'pugging' sand between the joists. Then refit the boards over a glassfibre blanket

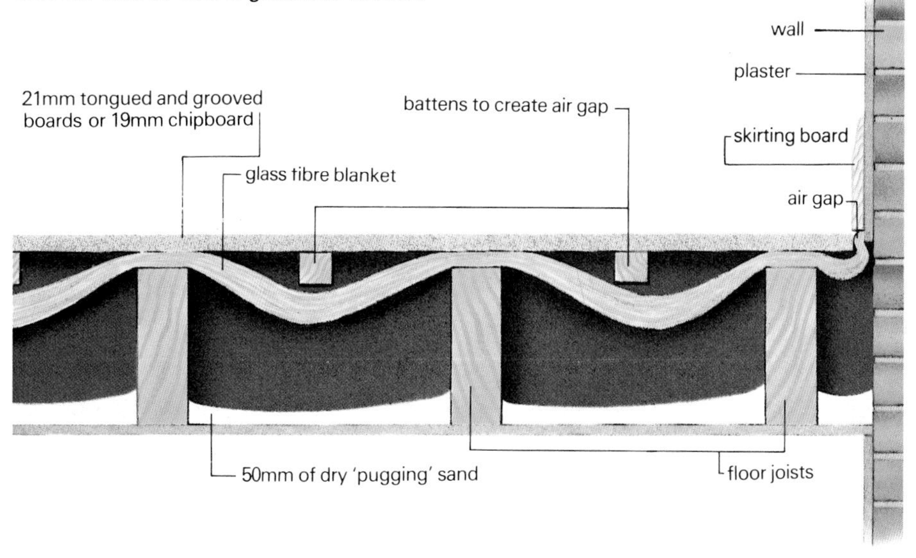

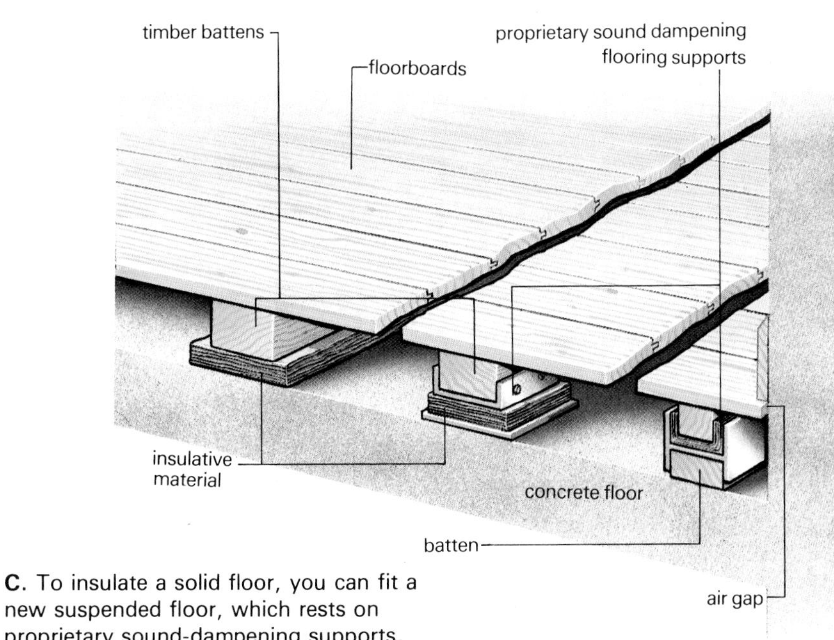

C. To insulate a solid floor, you can fit a new suspended floor, which rests on proprietary sound-dampening supports. Three common types are detailed

D. Loadbearing glass blocks make good sound insulators because of their thickness; but merely fitting thicker standard window glass would produce some noticeable benefit

Noises from above and below

Noises from the room or flat above may be of both the impact and airborne type, but you will be unable to reduce their level simply by fitting acoustic tiles to the ceiling. Acoustic tiles are sound-absorbent; that is, they will only absorb the sounds created within the room itself. Likewise, soft furnishings, heavy curtains and thick carpets will absorb—rather than reflect—noise.

Suspended floors

Noise travels easily through normal suspended floors into the room below. Most annoying is the intrusion of impact noise from footsteps, furniture and machines in the rooms above. Where the noises are not excessive, but are nevertheless annoying one measure is to lay a 50mm layer of the fine, dry sand ('silver sand') underneath the floorboards of the room above.

To do this, you must first make sure that the ceiling lining is capable of bearing the weight of the sand or *pugging*, as it is known and, if necessary, strengthen it by nailing the lining more firmly to the floor joists from below. To lay the pugging, you do of course have to remove all of the upstairs floorboards to gain full access. Afterwards, spread the sand evenly between the joists, including the narrow gaps at the edges. Pugging alone can improve the insulation properties of the floor by as much as 10dB—a significant amount.

With the floorboards removed and the pugging laid, you can now take the opportunity to restrict the passage of further airborne noise. Level the floor joists and remove any remaining nails. Then lay a resilient quilt of glassfibre wool or mineral wool loosely over the top of the joists and overlapping up the edges of the adjacent walls. Select the first floorboards or sections of chipboard flooring and, on the undersides, mark the mid-points between the floor joists. At these mid-points, nail or screw timber battens which will hold the quilt away from the flooring to provide an air gap. This is shown in fig. B.

At the same time, the battens will allow you to cramp the floorboards together, because the object is to create a floating floor separate from the main structure. Therefore, do not nail the floorboards to the joists; any connection between the floor and the room below will enable impact noise to travel downwards.

Instead, cramp the floorboards together and fix them to the battens. Fix three or four boards together at a time. In this way the floor will be separate from the floor joists and 'float' on the resilient quilt. At the wall ends of the boards, draw the quilt up against the walls' surface where it will be covered by the skirting boards. Fix these directly to the walls once the floor is laid, but leave a gap between the floor and the skirting boards to avoid creating a sound bridge into the room below (fig. B). Such a method can improve the insulation of a normal suspended floor from about 35dB to as much as 50dB, so virtually eliminating impact noise.

Solid floors

Most complaints about noise concern the transmission of sound from the room or flat above. This is especially the case in large blocks of flats, though if these were constructed properly, complaints need not arise. The problem is caused almost entirely by impact noise, which is transmitted easily through the solid floors, and is flanked by noise travelling through the concrete and into the adjacent walls. Virtually no airborne noise is involved.

A thick carpet, with two or three layers of thick foam underlay, will improve the sound insulation greatly; but the best solution is to construct a floating floor, free from the structure through which the sound travels. This is much the same as the method for suspended floors.

Again, it is essential that no solid connections exist between the floor surface and the building structure. Construct the floating floor by spreading a layer of expanded polystyrene, glass wool or mineral wool over the floor and constructing a timber raft above it. Remove the skirting boards first, then lay the blanket over the entire floor area. Lay 75mm × 50mm timber battens on top of the quilt at 50mm centres, but do not secure them to the floor.

Nail or screw 21mm tongued-and-grooved floorboards or 19mm chipboard to the battens. Take particular care at the wall edges; here, you should leave a gap between the floor and the walls so that any noises are not passed into the wall. Make sure that the skirting boards are separate from the floor so that they do not act as a sound bridge. Fix them directly to the wall leaving a slight, even gap between the floor and the skirtings.

An alternative method is to apply sound-damping flooring supports to the floor itself, so that the battens can be fixed to them. Such supports are available in a variety of designs, some of which rest on the floor and some which need to be embedded into the floor itself (fig. C). For the latter type, mark out the positions for the supports, then drill holes in the floor to accommodate the lugs. Fill the holes with mortar and push the lugs home. The battens then rest inside the support brackets (fig. C).

Planning air conditioning

Nearly everyone has experienced air conditioning in theatres, shops, office buildings and hotel rooms, but very rarely in a UK home.

It is generally thought that air conditioners are essentially air coolers. However, many models also function as space heaters, and can be used during cold weather at about half the cost of an equivalent electrical heating appliance. At the same time, the air conditioning machine filters the air to remove dust and odours, and also condenses excess moisture. Central heating fan convectors may be used in the same way.

How air conditioners work

Air conditioners are cyclical: first, a fan extracts stale air through a return grille. The extracted air is then passed through a filter, which removes dust, pollen and other particles. The filtered air next passes over a refrigerated coil, which reduces its temperature to a preselected, thermostatically maintained level and at the same time reduces excess moisture. Finally, the extracted heat is dissipated outside by a fan, and clean, cooled air returned to the interior under pressure from another fan. The conditioned air forces the stale air out of the interior, so continuing the cycle.

Room heating is achieved by switching the refrigerating unit so that it functions

A. Bottom: This type of split air conditioning room system can easily serve one or two rooms. Its noisy compressor is situated on the outside of the house so the operation inside the house is quieter

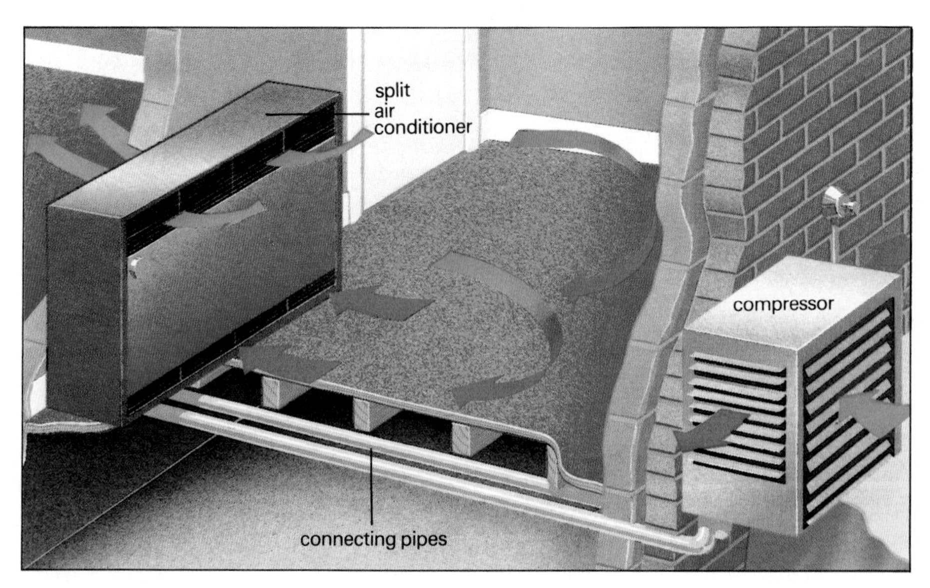

in reverse mode—taking exterior heat inside; in cold climates a heating element is also included. And, if you do not want either cooling or heating, you may use the air conditioner to circulate filtered air throughout the room.

The choice of systems

There are basically two main types of air conditioning system: the *ducted* system; and the *room* system. The systems can be further divided into 'split' types and 'package' types.

The ducted system allows several or all of the rooms in a house to be treated simultaneously. As the term implies, the conditioned air is carried from the coil fan unit—usually located in the roof space—through ducts or tubes, to air supply grilles mounted in the ceilings. Alternatively the ducts may run under the floors to flush-mounted grilles in the flooring.

The ducted system is usually a 'split' type of air conditioner. The split unit has a separate coil fan and compressor, which means that while the former, air handling, unit is located inside the house, the noisy condensing unit may be outside.

Ducted systems are expensive and difficult to install, and should only be considered at house construction stage.

The split type of air conditioner is also available in units designed to condition one room only. The interior air handling unit is available in ceiling- and floor-mounted versions.

Generally, a split air conditioner should back on to an external wall, but there are several dual-head (or 'two-way blow') versions that are promoted as being suitable for location on any internal wall of the house and capable of conditioning two adjacent rooms at the same time (fig. A). Like all split systems, the refrigeration unit with its noisy compressor is relegated to a convenient position outside the house. Normally, however, the condenser may not be sited more than 10m from the coil fan unit.

The most popular room air conditioner is the package type, so called because it houses both the air handling unit and

B. Below: The package-type room air conditioner is a unit that is completely self-contained and it is one that can be easily installed in quite a short space of time

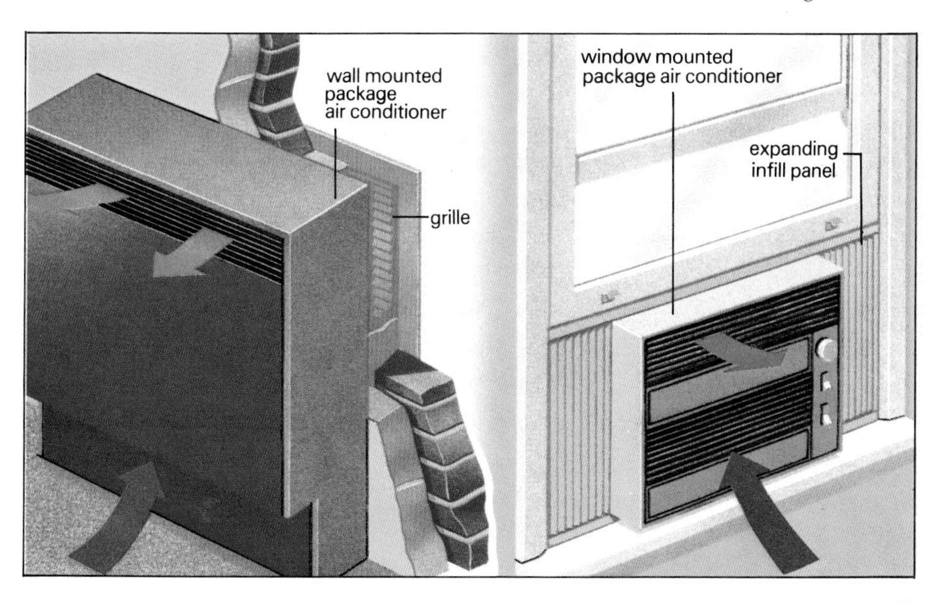

compressor condenser unit in one compact box.

These units are especially designed for installation in a properly prepared opening in an external wall, or for mounting in a window (fig. B). They range from basic 0.5hp versions to luxury 2hp models. The former, usually capable of cooling only, can cope well with the average bedroom, or small room. The latter, usually a reverse-cycle type, will cool or heat comfortably a much larger room.

A major problem with all package system air conditioners is excessive noise. It is one to which manufacturers have devoted a considerable amount of research, incorporating in their products various sound-damping devices.

Siting the unit

Unlike the split type of floor-mounted console, which can sometimes be located on an internal wall, a package unit must always be positioned so that it extends through an external wall. This is because it is essential to have an unobstructed flow of air to the condenser air grilles at the rear of the cabinet outside, and an equally unrestricted flow to the evaporator air grilles at the front inside the room (fig. B). For the same reason the package unit must not be sited in a corner where the flow to the side grilles might easily be impeded by the adjacent wall.

Where cooling is the prime consideration it is best to place the unit where it will be shaded from strong sunshine; this is important because for every unit of coolness the machine blows into the room, it blows an equivalent amount of heat to the outside; and, if the condenser outlet is facing the fierce afternoon sun, the hot air is less easily dissipated and the conditioner's efficiency is thus impaired considerably.

The size of unit

Perhaps the first thing that you must consider when choosing an air conditioner is whether you need a simple cooling unit only or a more sophisticated model which features a reverse-cycle facility to provide heating as well.

Having decided which type of unit is most appropriate for your needs you

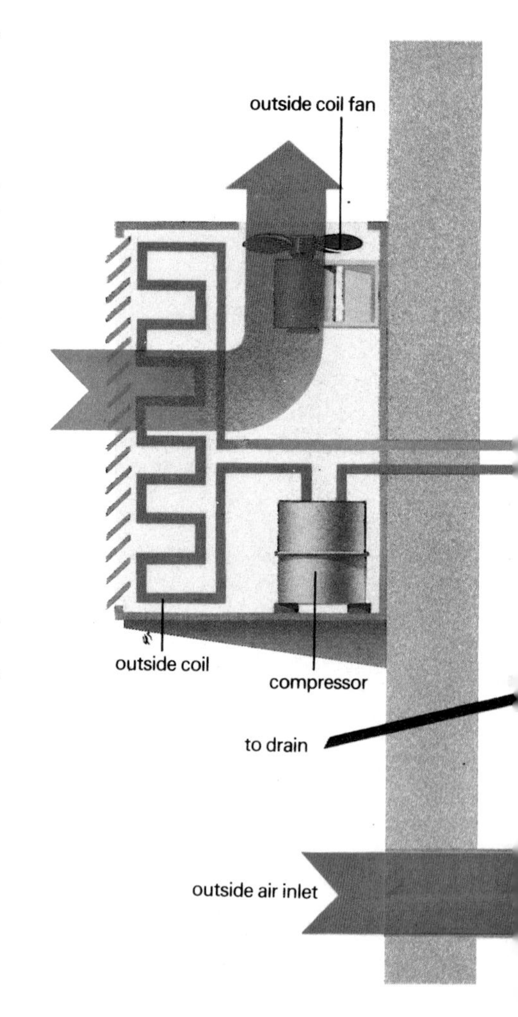

C. Right: An air conditioner does not merely cool and recirculate the air. Air drawn from the room is first passed through a filter to remove any accumulated dust and pollen, then through a heat exchange coil, which can either refrigerate and dehumidify the air or, in the case of reverse cycle models, heat it

must then work out which size will be the most economic. There are two factors generally used in the trade for assessing the correct sized unit: the effective 'capacity' of the unit, and the 'heat load' of the room.

The manufacturer's literature may quote 'capacity' in two ways: the capacity, or output in watts, of the compressor itself; and, a lower figure, the cooling capacity of the conditioner as a whole. The lower figure is the important one because it gives an indication of the actual effect you can expect the machine to achieve in your room, subject to the heat load.

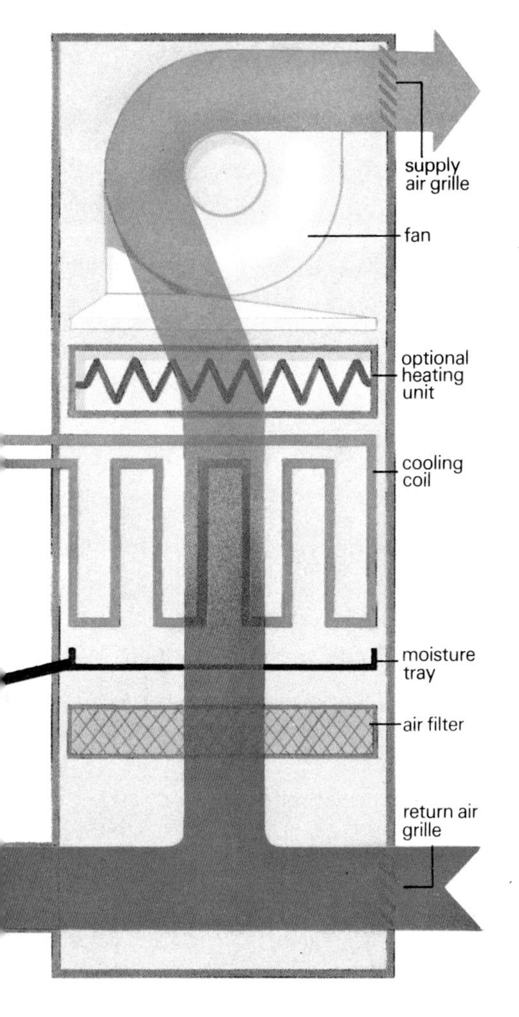

If you are given only one capacity figure, it is more than likely to be the one representing the compressor output which is measured under 'bench' conditions.

The effective capacity is important for several reasons. If you buy a unit with too small a capacity for the area to be served, you are bound to be disappointed with its performance and, because it has to work too hard, the machine will eventually break down. If you buy a unit with much too large a capacity for the area to be served, you will be spending more than you need both in initial outlay and in running costs. Furthermore, the machine is likely to wear out faster than it should because, operating automatically to maintain the room temperature you select through the thermostat, it will have to keep adjusting its output. Make sure that the unit you buy is exactly the right capacity.

Note that wiring-up is often easier with small units. For example, in the UK, units with an input rating of up to 3000 watts can be plugged into an existing power point (though it would be better to wire the unit on its own circuit). With larger units, a separate circuit must be provided.

The heat load that a room carries represents the amount of opposition the machine will have to overcome in order to maintain the temperature level you demand when you set the thermostat. This depends on a number of factors, including the materials from which the house is constructed, the insulation in the walls and roof and the number and size of windows in the room (including the direction in which they face).

Calculating heat load is an involved process best left to the manufacturers or to your dealer. But to enable them to make the calculations accurately, it is best to draw up a scale plan of the room and mark on it all of the house's constructional details; this will then make their job much easier.

Installing air conditioning

Once you have decided that you want an air conditioner, and have chosen the model most appropriate to your requirements, the next stage is installation. As mentioned in the previous chapter, the *ducted system* calls for extensive installation, which, in most cases, is not a practical possibility unless carried out when the house is first built. This part of the book is therefore concerned only with the planning and the installation of the *package-type room system* air conditioner in a window opening.

The easiest installation to make is the 'sill mounting' in a sash window. But when ease of installation is not the most important consideration, you can construct a framework that holds the conditioner unit centrally in the window opening. And using the same 'framing' technique you can mount an air conditioner in non-opening hopper, casement and horizontally sliding windows.

First considerations

Installing an air conditioner in a window is not a difficult task. The main considerations are to ensure that the unit is securely fixed in position and that the spaces around the machine are sealed adequately.

Bear in mind that you must take care to ensure that the complete unit can be removed for servicing and that, when this is done, the window can be made secure against the weather and possible intruders.

The kit should comprise a weather sealing strip, two safety brackets for fixing the lower sash of a double hung window at the required height, and the necessary screws.

On-sill installation

Raise the lower sash and lightly mark the centre of the bottom rail. Remove the front panel of the air conditioner and the air filter, then manoeuvre the unit into the window opening. Rest the steel channel welded to the base of the cabinet on the space normally occupied by the sash bottom rail when the window is closed. To centre the unit in the window opening, align the centre screw hole in the mounting frame with the centre line on the rail. Allow for proper drainage of condensation moisture by making the unit tilt slightly rearward.

Now slide the expanding slide panels out against the window stops. Lower the sash and check that the bottom rail is tight against the top of the cabinet. Also check that the side panels fit squarely against the window stops. Then lock the unit in place by screwing the expanding panels to the bottom of the lower sash rail, and the mounting frame to the window frame.

Fit the safety brackets to the top of the lower sash top rail and to the pocket pieces on both sides. These will prevent the window from being raised, which could allow the unit to fall out. Fit window bolts through both sash stiles to prevent intruders opening the top sash.

Because the window will be permanently open, it is essential that the gap between the upper and lower sash is sealed properly. To do this first cut two lengths of 30mm wide by 3mm thick rubber strip to the width of the window. Then secure the strips to the bottom rail of the top sash.

To waterproof the outside joint between the top of the air conditioner housing and the lower sash rail, you can apply a bed of mastic to the joint angle then screw a strip of aluminium angle to the lower sash rail.

Replace the air filter and the front panel, and plug the mains cord into a power point or connect it to its own electrical circuit (depending on its rating). Then, following the manufacturer's instructions, test the unit.

Larger models: In the case of larger units a sill-mounted installation is slightly more complicated because of the need to accommodate the conditioner's greater weight and bulk.

Although aesthetically you may prefer to centre the unit in the window aperture, greater stability is afforded by positioning it against one side of the window frame.

It is normal when fitting a large air conditioner to remove the mechanism from the metal cabinet, install the cabinet first, then refit the mechanism. In most models a slide-out chassis facilitates this operation.

When you unpack the unit from its case, remove any bolts or screws that have been inserted at the factory to prevent movement and damage during transportation.

Start the installation by raising the lower sash as far as it will go, then measure up from the sill the height of the housing plus a fraction (no more than 2mm) for clearance, and mark the side frame at the appropriate point. Afterwards lower the sash so that the underside of the bottom rail just comes to this point. Drill pilot holes through the stiles

Below: Use this chart only as a very rough guide to the size of conditioner units in the UK

Conditioner sizes

Room Size	Ceiling Insulated				Ceiling Not Insulated			
	Windows facing west		Windows not facing west		Windows facing west		Windows not facing west	
Square metres	Large windows	Small windows	Large windows	Small windows	Large windows	Small windows	Large windows	Small windows
9	1300W	1050W	1050W	810W	1440W	1170W	1170W	900W
12	1730W	1400W	1400W	1080W	1920W	1560W	1560W	1200W
15	2160W	1760W	1760W	1350W	2400W	1950W	1950W	1500W
18	2590W	2110W	2110W	1620W	2880W	2340W	2340W	1800W
21	3020W	2460W	2460W	1890W	3360W	2730W	2730W	2100W
24	3460W	2810W	2810W	2160W	3840W	3120W	3120W	2400W
27	3890W	3160W	3160W	2430W	4320W	3510W	3510W	2700W
30	4320W	3510W	3510W	2700W	4800W	3900W	3900W	3000W
33	4750W	3860W	3860W	2970W	5280W	4290W	4290W	3300W
36	5180W	4210W	4210W	3240W		4680W	4680W	3600W
39		4560W	4560W	3510W		5070W	5070W	3900W

1 Every installation presents its own particular problems—metal casement windows need to be removed. Open the windows and undo the securing screws around the rebate of the frame—jar them if necessary

2 Use a bolster and hammer to prise the frame away from its housing. Then once the frame has been loosened, carefully lower away the complete assembly making sure you have the help of an assistant

5 Place the metal housing on the support platform and screw it securely to the timber. Cut a piece of 50mm × 50mm timber battening to the window width, house it around the frame and secure it firmly with screws

6 Using the same timber, cut two indentical uprights and then secure them to the horizontal batten and sill with dowelled joints. Then pin a suitable architrave to the front and sides of the battening

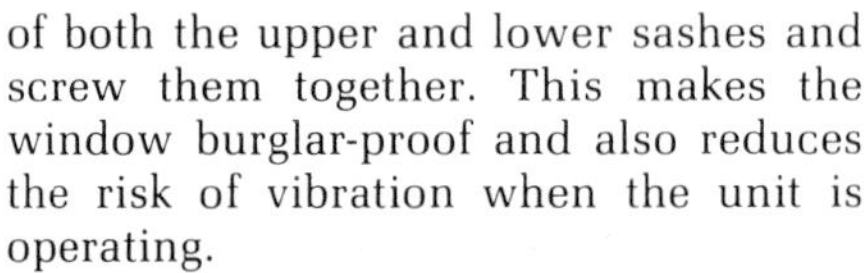

of both the upper and lower sashes and screw them together. This makes the window burglar-proof and also reduces the risk of vibration when the unit is operating.

You must complete the frame for the unit housing by securing an upright between the sill and the lower sash rail. Use 50mm × 50mm softwood, and cut it 5mm longer than the distance between the sill and the sash.

Measure from the relevant window

3 To fix the unit on the sill, cut timber battens, drill and plug the brickwork below and screw the battens down. Secure the battens to the outer sill and firmly screw a timber platform right across the sills

4 Screw metal angle brackets to both sides of the platform and secure them to the wall. Larger package units have an easy-sliding chassis feature. Remove the fascia then slowly slide out the mechanism

7 Mitre the joints of the battening to achieve a neat corner. To finish, seal the metal housing to the frame with mastic, prime the frame and then glaze the window and paint the frame in the desired colour

frame the width of the housing plus a small allowance for clearance, and mark this on the sill and sash rail. Then mark off an additional 50mm to allow for the width of the upright.

You must make a housing for the upright in the lower sash rail. To do this, first mark the depth, then make three or four saw cuts inside the limit of the housing up to the depth mark. Remove the waste with a firmer chisel, then clean up the housing with glasspaper wrapped around a block. Put the upright in place, and skew-nail it to the sash rail and sill.

Now lift the conditioner housing into place, taking care to position it so that all the air grilles are unobstructed, and that it has a slight rearward tilt. Fix it firmly to the sash rail, the window frame and the new upright with the screws supplied.

To provide additional support, you can fix galvanized steel or aluminium angle brackets to the rear underside of the housing and the wall below the window sill.

The next job is to provide an infill panel to screen the space left between the upright and the window frame. The simplest way of doing this is to fix a sheet of waterproofed plywood or metal into the space, then paint this to match the interior and exterior decoration. But, provided the area is not too small—for example, less than 150mm wide—you can achieve a more pleasing effect by glazing the space with glass panels cut to size. Pin fillets of quadrant moulding around the 'frame', lay putty around the fillets, put the glass in position, and fix this in place with putty. Paint the putty when it has set.

All that remains is to weatherproof the joint between the air conditioner housing and the window frame as described above. Similarly, seal the gap between the now permanently open windows.

Finally, get an assistant to help you lift the mechanism and slide it into the housing. Follow the manufacturer's instructions for replacing the front panel and other procedures for putting the unit into operation.

Framed installation

Although the on-sill installation described above is usually satisfactory, some manufacturers recommend that the lower edge of the unit is positioned about 1.5m above the floor. This provides an optimum air circulation pattern, and prevents any discomfort caused by strong draughts of air directed below shoulder height.

In this case you must construct a sturdy framework of 50mm × 50mm softwood inside the window opening, consisting of two uprights and two cross bars. The system can be adapted for use in practically any type of wooden-framed window, including casement and horizontally sliding windows, the upper sash of a double-hung window, and fixed (non-opening) sashes. In every case you must house the frame into the window frame, and glue and screw or skew-nail it in place.

The dimensions of the frame obviously depend on the dimensions of the conditioner housing and in many cases the metal housing may be slightly out of square. Do, therefore, measure the housing width top and bottom, and on both sides. If there are discrepancies, make the frame accordingly to ensure a snug fit all round.

On a plain framework, it is wise to

Cutting the glass

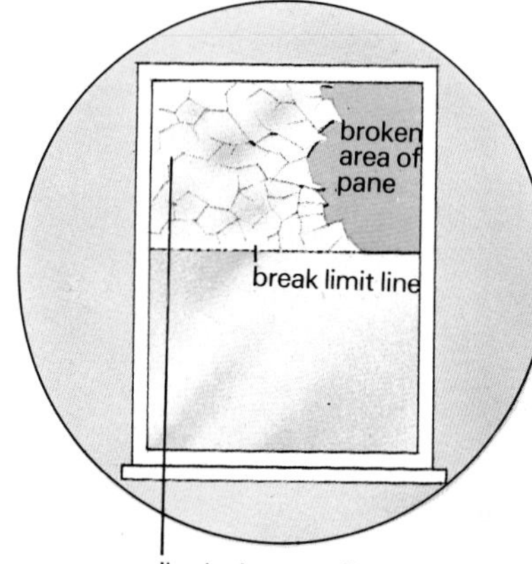

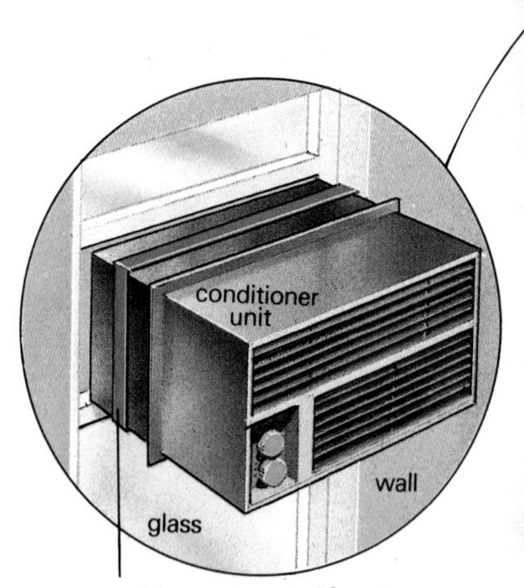

A. Below: Installing a package air conditioner through any part of a non-opening window necessarily involves you in some reglazing work

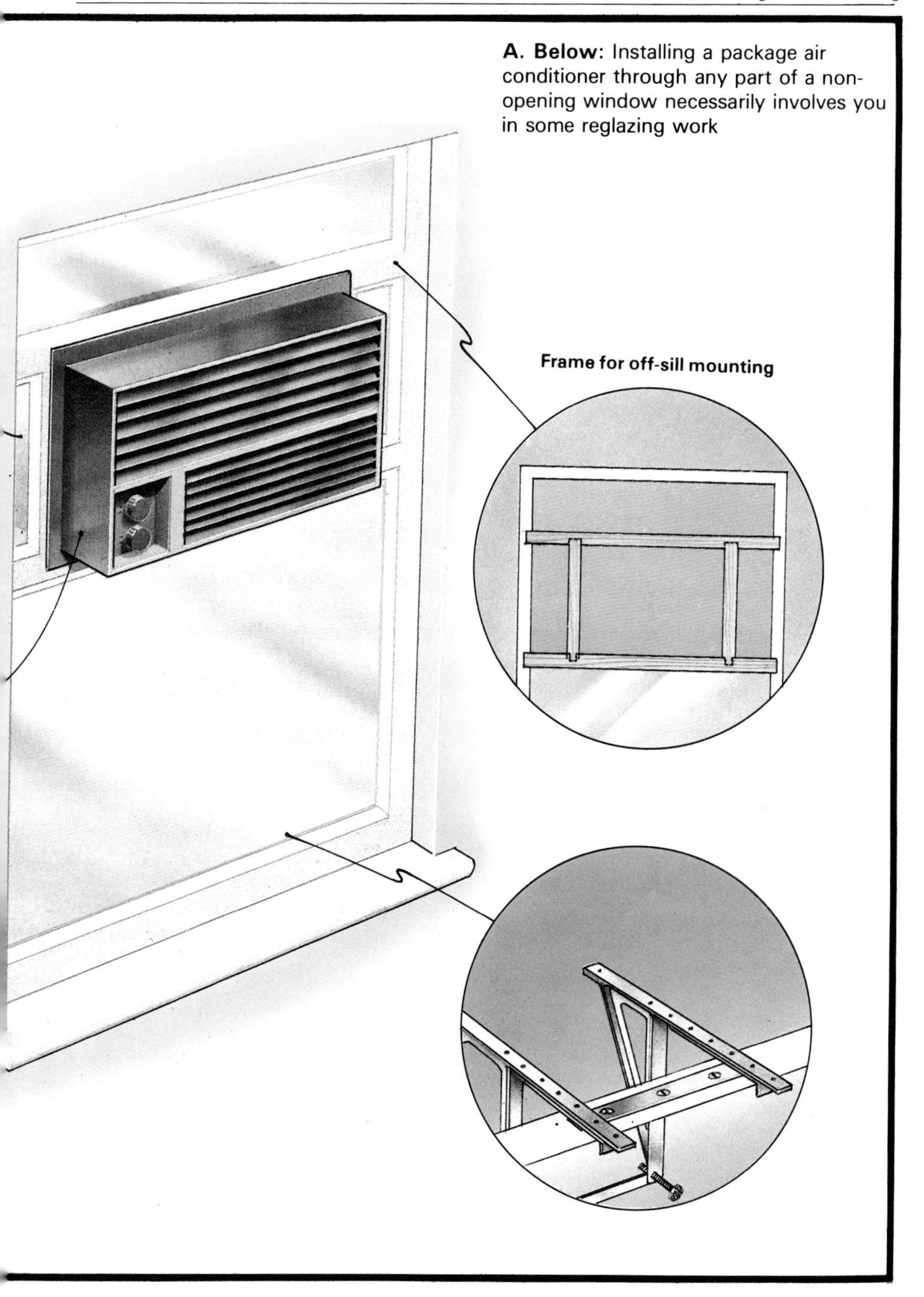

allow a 2mm clearance on each dimension. However, you may wish to surround the conditioner housing completely with an anti-vibration pad of sponge rubber, 50mm wide and 6mm thick. In this case be sure to allow for two thicknesses of the rubber strip on the internal height and width of the frame. In the absence of a rubber strip, fill any space between the housing and frame with mastic once the conditioner is in place.

When you have cut the timber to size, cut housings for the uprights in the cross members then glue and screw the frame together. Cut corresponding housings in the existing window frame and glue and screw or skew-nail the new frame in place.

Other installations

The installation of an air conditioner above sill height in a non-opening window is a challenging project calling for a fair amount of skill in inserting the supporting framework, because it entails removing some of the glass. In this case you can either remove the whole pane, and cut out the infill panels from it, or cut out a panel of glass from the pane and build the framework into the window aperture.

To start with draw a line in felt-tip pen across the glass at the height of the lower edge of the conditioner, less about 50mm, to allow for the thickness of the lower cross bar. Then measure up from this line the height of the conditioner housing, plus the combined thickness of the upper and lower cross bars.

From now onwards wear protective goggles and gloves to avoid injury from broken glass. Score along the marked lines on the inside of the glass using a glass cutter and a metal straightedge. Then, with the cutter, tap gently along the lines.

Next score and tap a third line roughly midway between the original two, and make a series of diagonal score marks in criss-cross fashion over the whole area. Arrange a blanket on the inside of the window to catch the fragments of broken glass, and proceed to tap out the scored portion from the outside. Finally, use a pair of pliers to pick out any remaining pieces and nibble away the rough edges.

Cut housings for the new frame in the existing window frame and install the upper and lower cross bars in place. Skew-nail all the joints. Then fix the two uprights, the required distance apart, between the cross bars, using simple skew-nailed butt joints. Punch all the nail heads below the surface and fill the remaining holes. Where applicable, glue the sponge strip all around the inside of the frame. You can now insert the conditioner housing, without the mechanism, positioning it with proper attention to the air grilles as described above. Secure it to the frame through the top and sides with the screws provided.

If additional external support is necessary, you can mount a piece of timber or angle across the window—below the housing so that the brackets can be fixed to this at the required 45° angle.

Glaze all the remaining spaces, utilizing the glass removed. Sandwich the panes between putty-lined mouldings, pinned to the window frame and the new framework. Finally, paint the frame, then replace the conditioner mechanism in its housing and firmly screw the fascia back on.

Other window types

Constructing a suitable support frame along the lines described above is the key to installing an air conditioner in other types of window, though each project demands minor variations in treatment. For example, in the case of hopper and casement windows, it is better to remove the sash completely to make way for the new unit. For a horizontally sliding window, you must provide a locking device to hold the movable sash in the required position. In this case, the verticals of the framework will extend the full height of the opening and one of them can act as a stop for the sliding sash (which will be fixed to it).

Ventilation in the kitchen

Lingering cooking smells and an excessive amount of steam condensation create an unpleasant and unhealthy environment in the kitchen. Fitted ventilation gets round the problem, and still allows you to keep the room warm and comfortable.

The higher the room temperature, the

Below: Extractor fan mounted at the top of a non-opening window pane.

larger the potential moisture content (humidity) of the air and the greater the likelihood of condensation forming. This can ruin paint and wallpaper—and, given time, plasterwork—in the same way as damp. In the kitchen, condensation can cause unsightly mould growths, while moisture-borne particles of grease act as a breeding ground for germs.

Raising the room temperature increases the moisture-carrying capacity of the air but is not in itself a successful way of preventing condensation. For this to be achieved the moisture-laden air must be carried out of the house altogether—the job of a ventilator or extractor fan.

Calculating your requirements

The cheapest form of kitchen ventilation is a self-actuating, window-mounted plastic ventilator. But although these are comparatively easy to fit, they cannot normally cope with the demands of a kitchen and some form of mechanical ventilation should be used instead.

If a combination of moisture and cooking fumes is the problem, the choice of kitchen ventilator is normally between a wall- and a window-mounted extractor fan.

Extractor fans blow stale inside air to the outside. Unless draughtproofing is completely efficient—a most unlikely possibility—this air is replaced by seepage into the kitchen from elsewhere. Between ten and twenty 'air changes' an hour are considered necessary for a kitchen. The lower figure applies when the room temperature is high and the cooking times are short, the higher figure when the kitchen is particularly cold or hot and steam and fumes are obviously troublesome—such as when cooking for several people.

One air change is equivalent to the volume of a room, so to help select the right extractor fan calculate your kitchen's volume (length × height × width, in metres) and multiply this by between ten and twenty, as outlined, to find the hourly capacity required. Divide this figure by sixty if a fan's capacity is quoted in minutes. Always err on the side of a more powerful machine if in doubt.

If draughtproofing is efficient, an extractor may reduce the air pressure in the kitchen to a point where the efficiency of the fan is impaired. The problem can be made even worse by having a fuel burner in the room. To get round it, you must fit an air inlet, preferably as far from the extractor fan as possible.

If cooking fumes alone need to be removed, an extractor hood mounted above the stove may provide adequate ventilation. This can be either of the recirculating type—where steam-borne grease and smoke are filtered out before air is returned—or an extractor type—where partly filtered air is ducted to the outside. The latter type is considered more efficient, though installation procedures are more involved.

Heat, too, is expelled by extractor fans, but this should not be much of a problem at cooking times. Recirculating cooker hoods require frequent cleaning and replacement of their filters to keep them fully efficient. Some models can be converted into extractors by fitting an optional blanking plate and duct.

Heater ventilation

If your heating system uses a fuel-burning appliance, an adequate fresh air supply to this is essential —for both good combustion and the removal of toxic waste gases.

Unless your appliance incorporates a 'balanced flue', which lets in as much air as it expels fumes, effective draughtproofing of a room could starve the appliance of air and cause fumes to be drawn down the flue.

Central heating appliances are often located within the kitchen area in British homes, and this is another consideration in any kitchen ventilation project. An air vent on a door, or airbrick on an outside wall close to the burner, is a simple solution which should not impede other arrangements.

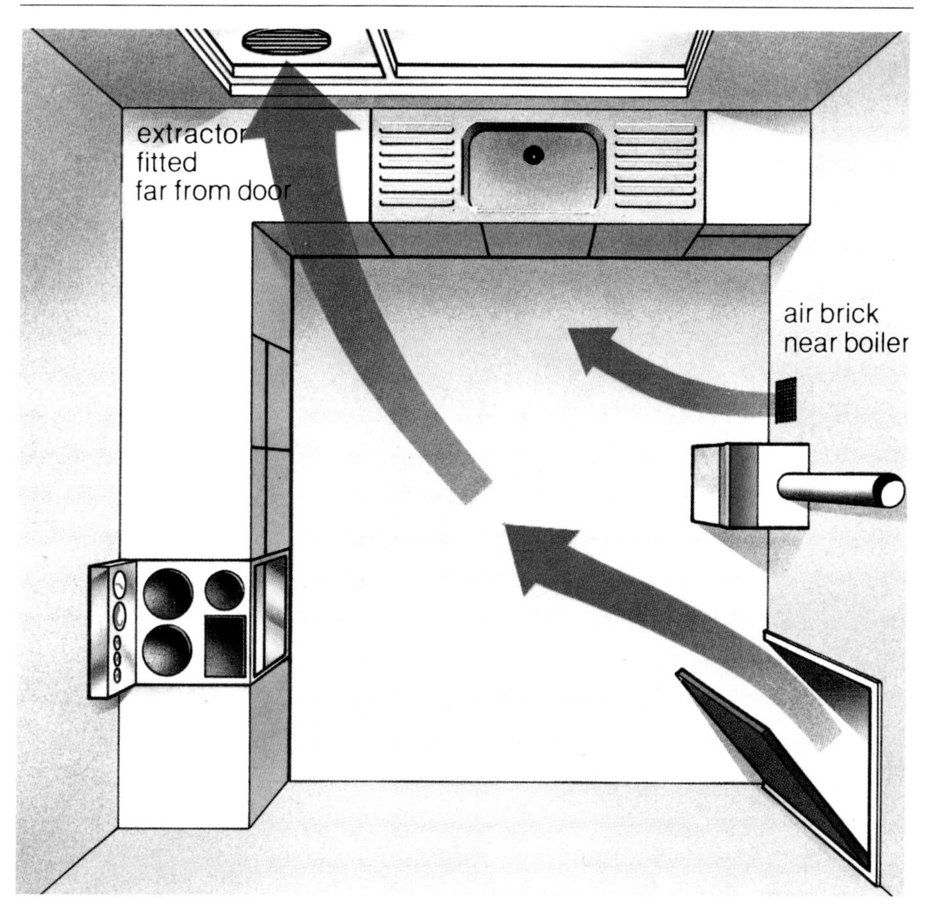

Above: Position the extractor unit as far as possible away from air inlets such as the door and ventilators

Another method is to fit a ventilator plate in floorboarding close to the appliance, though this is possible only if you have a suspended floor. The grille should be placed as close to the burner as possible to prevent the occurrence of floor-level draughts.

At its extreme, an adequate air supply to a burner can be provided by a wall or underfloor duct which is linked to the outside.

Ventilation for other appliances

Another appliance that may need ducting to the outside is a clothes drier. A wall- or window-mounted extractor fan can be used as an alternative but is usually less effective at preventing condensation build-up.

The procedure for fitting a duct is the same as for a stove hood, though the specific instructions supplied by the appliance manufacturer should be followed.

In the case of a clothes-drier duct, avoid sharp bends and fine-meshed grilles, which may collect minute, moisture-borne fibre particles. These need cleaning from time to time in any case, so leave some access to the duct ends and make sure the outside grille can be removed for cleaning.

Fitting an extractor fan

You can mount an extractor fan in a convenient external wall or window. Either way, it should be located as close to the ceiling as possible, near the sink and stove but not right above these unless the window or wall here is really high up.

Window mounting requires that a hole be cut in the glass. Although not a difficult task (see opposite) accidental breakage is all too easy. Using a replacement pane with a hole cut in it by the glazier makes fan installation much easier.

1 When the hole has been cut out, fit the flange and gasket assembly of the unit in place. The components screw together with this particular unit

2 A fused spur needs to be wired to a junction box situated close to the fan. Conceal the wire using plastics duct back to the junction box

3 After you have completed the wiring, fit the face-plate by snapping it firmly into place on the lugs which are provided on the box

4 Pull-cord switches hanging from the extractor fan allow you to operate the fan easily and conveniently, and also with complete safety

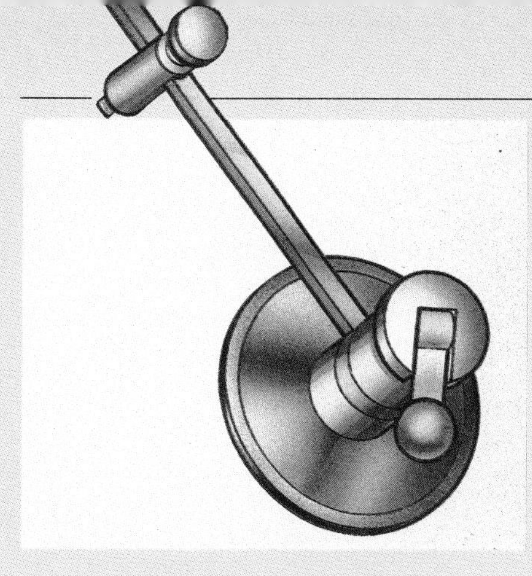

1 Adjust the circle scribe and the clamp

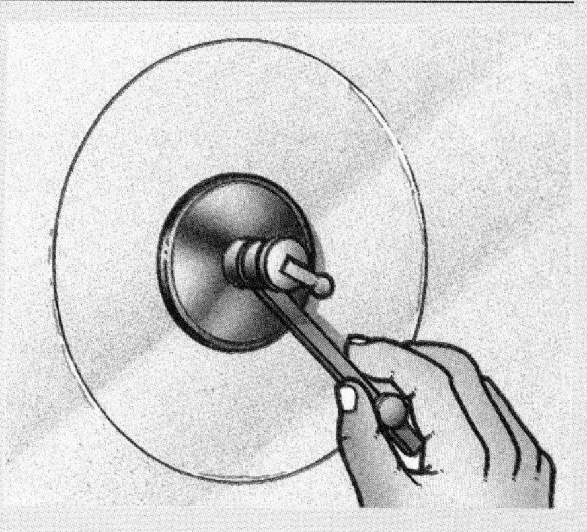

2 Scribe outer and then inner circle after oiling cutter and work area

3 Score criss-cross lines over area of inner circle

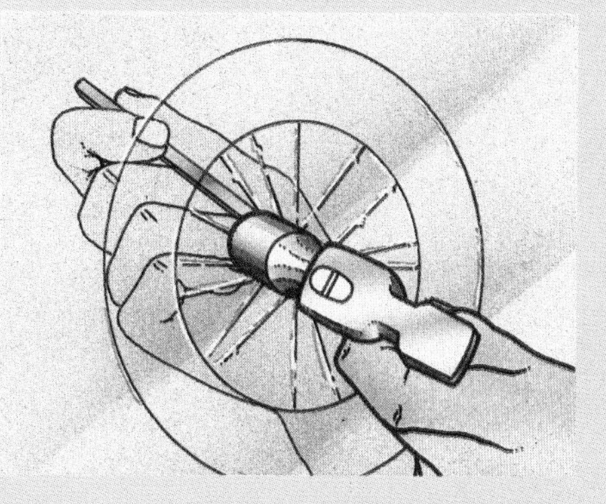

4 Tap scoring and then knock out the circle

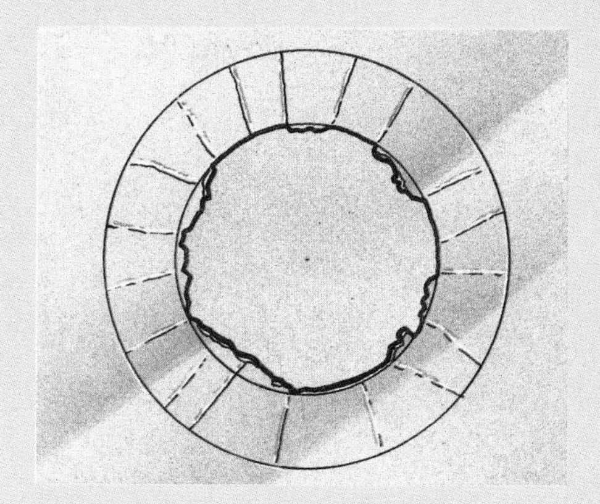

5 Score to outer circle then tap and knock out

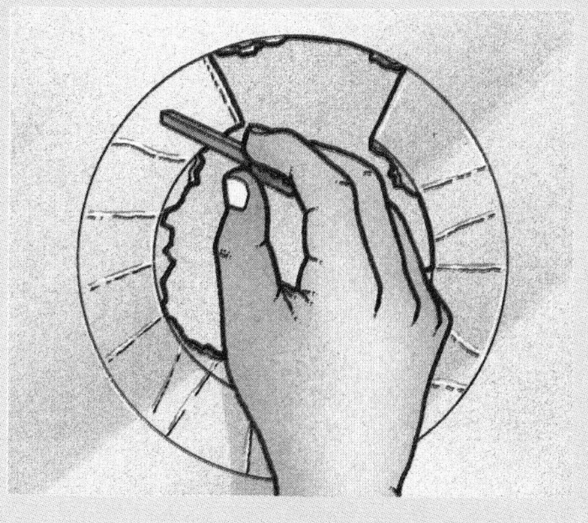

6 Nibble away any remaining bits gently, using a pair of pliers

Fitting an extractor hood

A cooker hood is placed directly above the hob, and is not normally used in conjunction with stoves having an eye-level grill assembly. The hood should be sited squarely over the cooking area and no less than 600mm above it. Most cooker hoods hook or slip on to brackets fixed to the wall, enabling them to be removed easily for maintenance of the filter and for good general cleaning which is always necessary.

If the hood is to be used as an extractor with ducting to the outside, consider relocating the stove if this will make the work easier and shorten the path for the duct. Hoods can be ducted directly to the outside, but, if the stove is to remain in the most convenient spot, a length of flexible duct piping is usually required (see figs 1 to 10). This can be concealed by a dummy section fitted cupboard, or by purpose-made boxing-in. Flexible pipe duct can be used for an extractor fan which cannot be located on an outside wall, but remember you should always keep the length of the ducting short.

Fitting a cooker hood above a stove or mounted hob unit presents very few difficulties. If the hood is of the type that simply filters and recirculates the air, little work is required. An extraction hood is much more efficient in clearing cooking fumes. However, additional work is required in providing a duct to an outside wall, making a hole in the wall and concealing the flexible hose that connects the hood to the outside. Taken individually, none of these jobs is particularly complicated, but a full day should be allowed to completely finish the project.

Making a hole in the wall is a straightforward but major part of the operation and quite a bit of time should be allowed to do the work. Line the hole to prevent draughts and heat loss. Slope the hole downwards to the outside slightly if this is possible. A purpose-made ducting kit (which may or may not be supplied with the extractor hood) should be fitted very carefully according to all the manufacturer's detailed instructions on installation.

If possible, re-plan your kitchen so that ducting can be reduced to a minimum by placing the stove nearer to an outside wall.

1 Expose the brickwork at the point where the duct is required. Carefully drill or chisel the hole right through to the outside of the wall

2 Widen the hole in the wall from the outside to a width slightly greater than the duct fitting. Then insert the liner and make good around the gap

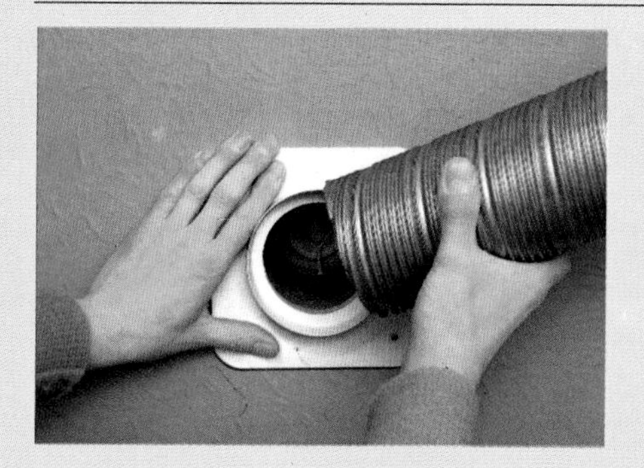

3 Attach the flexible duct hose to the fixed inner duct plate. The hose is then carefully directed to the cooker hood as tidily as is possible

4 Fix a cover on the outside if one is not included in the kit. This one simply nails into place after it has been neatly fitted to the duct liner

5 The cooker hood itself should be positioned about 600mm above the cooker hob. A template is usually provided to give the fixing location

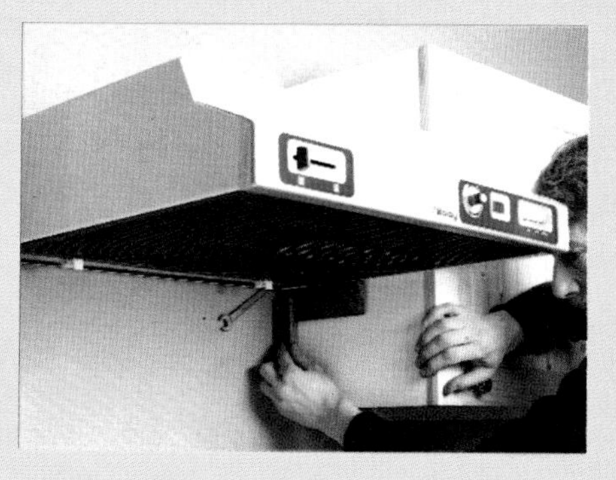

6 For efficient operation—and the final look—the hood should be levelled off. Fine adjustments are made by using the nut and screw arrangement

7 To fit the duct to the hood attach the supplied hose plate to the rear of the cooker hood unit, following the manufacturer's specific instructions

8 The duct will have to pass through any surrounding built-in cupboards. Prepare and drill the necessary holes through these as they are required

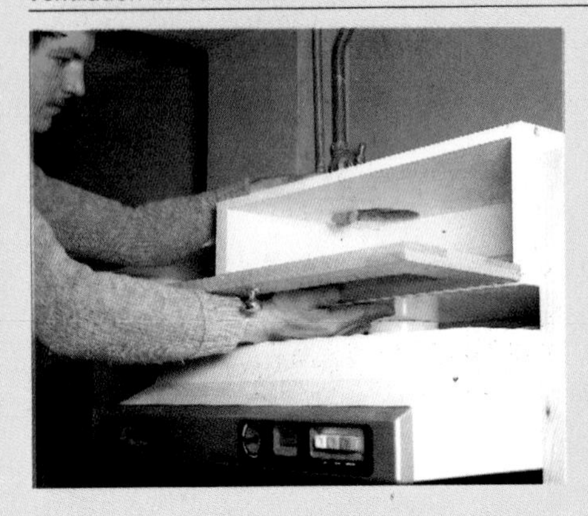

9 When the duct hole has been completed—a power jig saw is the best tool here—mount the cupboard in the required position above the hood

10 Prior to fitting the last section of cupboard or boxing, connect the flexible hose to the hood and smoke test to see if there are any leaks in the hose

Ventilation in the bathroom

Traditionally the smallest room in the house, a WC can quickly become unpleasant to those who have to use it afterwards unless special care is taken to provide adequate ventilation. An opening window is an effective solution but is sometimes uncomfortable, especially in cold weather when there is the additional problem of household draughts and resulting heat loss.

A power extractor fan, operated either by the light switch or independently, is a simple solution and a provision considered essential—by law in the UK—for WCs that do not have windows.

A slightly different problem exists when it comes to bathroom ventilation. Here, the high moisture content of the air produced by running a bath or shower quickly condenses to form water droplets

Below: A ceiling-mounted fan is an unobtrusive and effective method of relieving the condensation problems of a bathroom which is badly ventilated

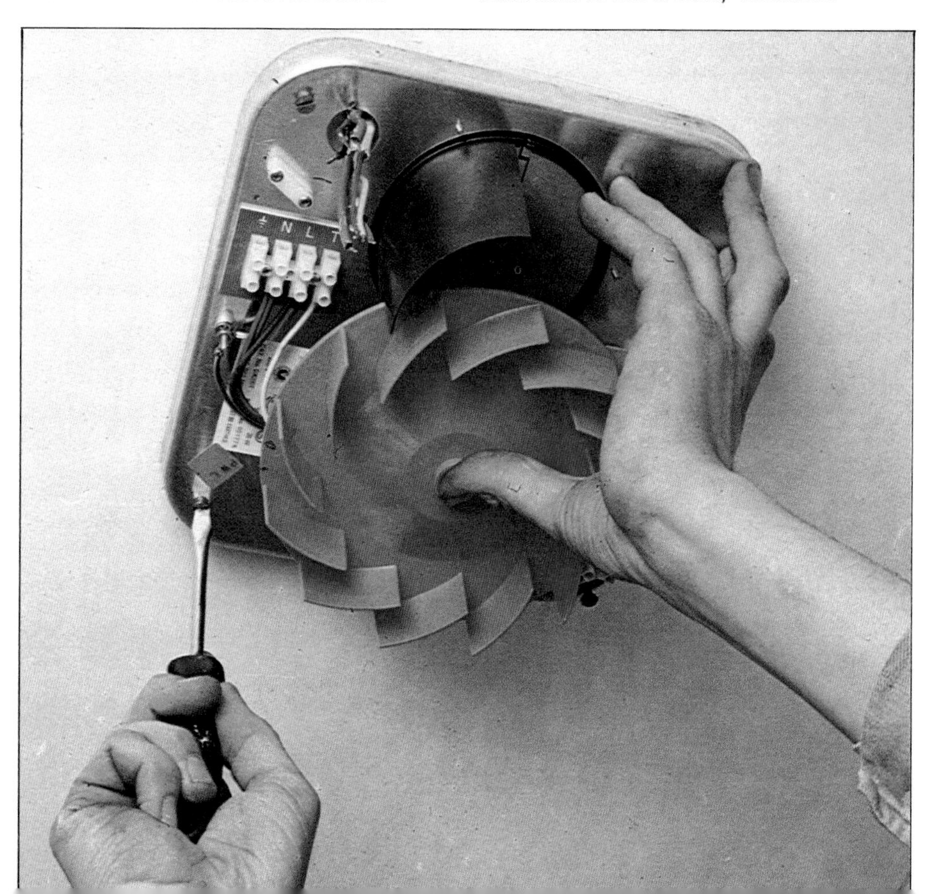

and puddles which are not readily removed simply by opening a window for a few minutes. The problem is aggravated by the fact that the room is likely to be used only for a short time, thus discouraging opening of the window both during and after bath time.

An efficient extractor fan is the only convenient solution, and its cost can be weighed against the improved atmosphere of the bathroom when it is being used, and the reduced risk of damage to fixtures and fittings resulting from the lower levels of condensation that then form.

Siting the fan

The best place to put an extractor fan is on the wall opposite the main doorway for the room, as high up as you can and above any source of moisture. Replacement air then has to travel across the room, ensuring that ventilation is complete.

You can mount the fan in a non-opening section of window, either by cutting a hole in the glass (see last chapter), or by replacing the whole pane with a suitable sheet of wood and fitting it within this.

The wall position which best meets the ventilation requirements is high up, next to the window, where there is often an air-brick or ventilator grille. This can be removed and the ventilator fan installed in its place.

Moisture is the main problem in bathroom ventilation and it must be discharged where it will do no harm. This requirement means that, if an outer wall is not available for mounting the fan, special care has to be taken in ducting the fan to the outside.

Fitting a wall-mounted fan

The best place to locate a wall-mounted fan is on an outer wall as this means that no additional ducting is required for the outlet. In most cases, a hole of 100mm diameter would be required for this. In addition an access hole (for a 20mm conduit) needs to be provided for a through-wall electrical connection. Alternatively a chase has to be made so a wire can be run from a suitable source out of the room.

Take great care to avoid concealed pipework and wiring. Taps and switches in the same vertical plane could indicate trouble, so locate the fan just to one side if you can.

With a masonry wall, carefully chip away covering plasterwork and old wallpaper using cold chisel or small bolster so that you expose brickwork beneath. Try to locate the corner of a mortar joint as the plaster is gradually removed and use this as the 'weak spot' for making the outlet hole.

Carefully nibble or drill away the mortar and adjacent brickwork corners, then split the first whole brick with a hammer and bolster. Continue in this way until the hole is just larger than that required for the outlet hole and connecting duct.

If you are dealing with a cavity wall, you also have to breach the outer leaf—a job that is better done from the outside. But first drill through pilot holes from the inside to avoid making any mistake in the position. Arrange to drill these through mortar joints so that afterwards you can remove whole bricks.

The covering of a timber-framed wall is usually easy to cut away with a jig saw or similar. Avoid positioning the fan over vertical studs. Find studs by tapping or drilling small trial holes.

When assembling the fan components, use a length of sleeving to line any cavity and prevent moisture-laden air from discharging into it. The sleeve should slope slightly to the outside, which can usually be arranged during final fixing of the fan.

Follow the manufacturer's assembly instructions to install the fan unit itself. Much of the making good will probably have to be done beforehand, which means shaping the surrounding brickwork, repositioning cut bricks, and finally using heavy-duty filler or a suitable mastic to entirely eliminate through-wall draughts.

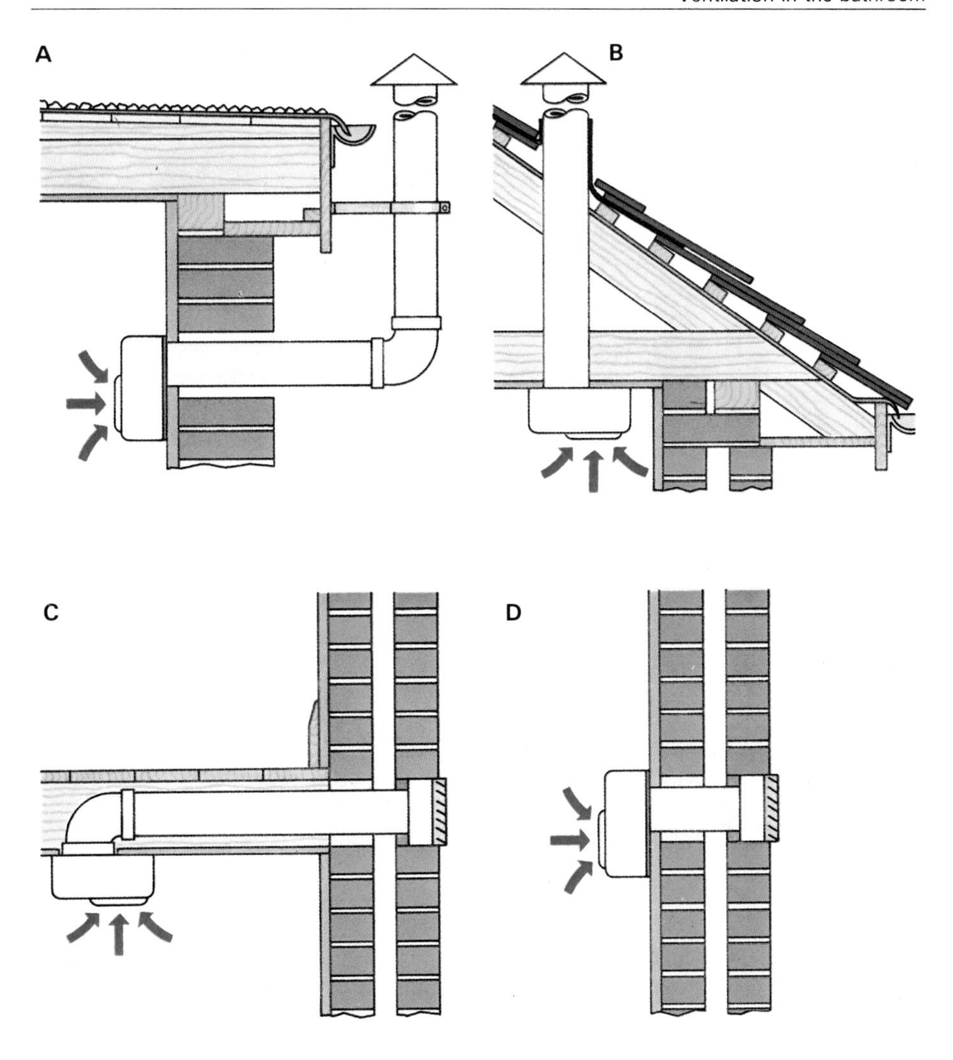

Above: Various methods of ducting an extractor fan to the outside. Which method you use depends principally on the location of the fan. Although rigid pipework is shown, flexible ducting may prove easier to install, especially through walling and partitions. Fix a protective grille or cowl to the exposed pipe end

Inner walls usually present much less of a problem, but additional work may be involved in providing suitable ducting to the outside, where again a hole must be made. For health reasons and personal comfort a WC ventilator must not be vented to another room—it must vent to the outside wall.

Panel mounting

If a wall fixing is required, it is sometimes more convenient to use some method of panel fixing—especially if a purpose-built boxed-off duct has to be

1 Position the fan slightly away from the wall and mark the screw holes and duct and conduit holes. Then drill a pilot hole in the waste area of the duct aperture and check the position

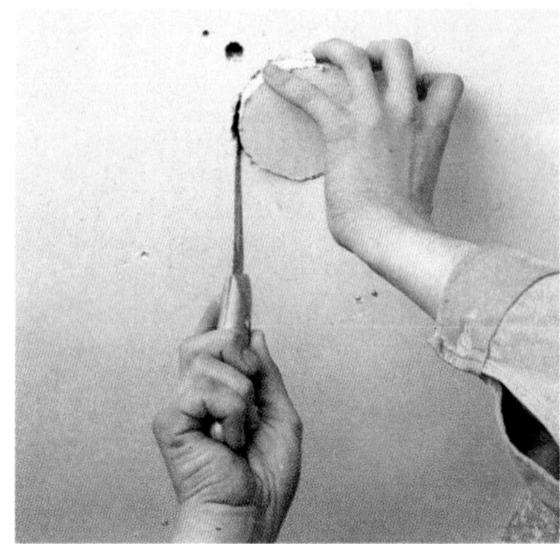

2 Then cut out the duct aperture using a padsaw. Make good any plaster then pull the power and lighting cables through. These connect to the mains and lighting switch as specified by the maker

5 Screw on the fan cover and then do a test run on all the connections. Some models may have a separate timer, which will need adjusting to get it right

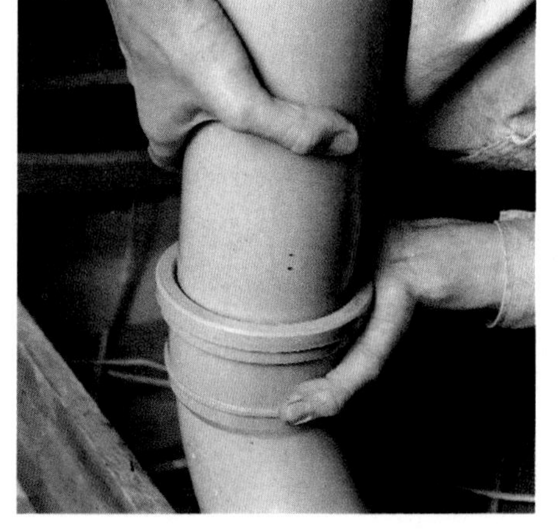

6 Push-fit PVC pipework has been employed for the ducting. Ready-made bends are used for ease of fitting and the pipe run is kept short

constructed with the room design in mind. A similar approach could be used if you are installing a ceiling-mounted fan.

A panel-mounted fan can also be installed where additional work may prove difficult. So instead of bricking up a small and useless WC 'high window', you could use inner and outer panels of suitably treated exterior-grade plywood to seal up the window after you have removed the glass. The wood then could be cut accurately to size to accept the extractor fan.

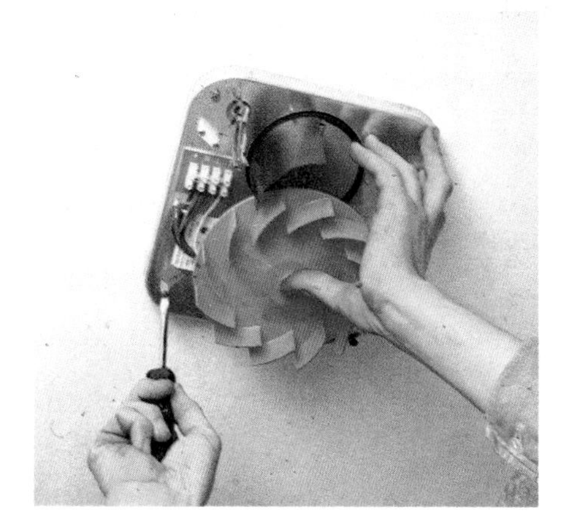

3 Fix the fan to the ceiling using the cavity wall type of fittings. When you are installing a heavy fan unit you may find it will be necessary to have additional support from above

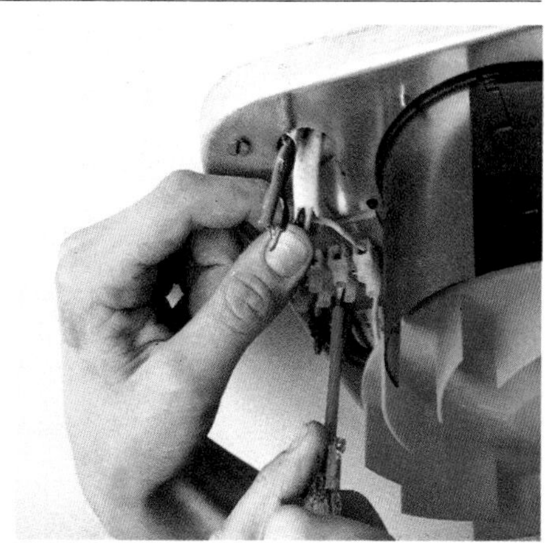

4 The next job is to connect the electrical parts. These are not normally difficult to do but you must ensure that the instructions of the manufacturer are followed very carefully

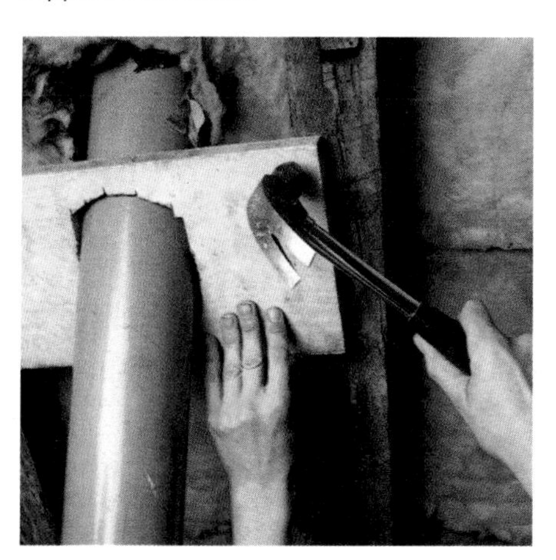

7 Secure the upright that goes through the roof with a brace nailed to the rafters, vital if the outside is exposed at all to strong winds

8 Then fit some form of cowl as protection to the exposed pipe end. Use mastic and apron flashing to completely waterproof the roof joint area

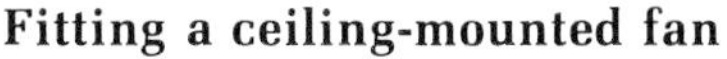

Fitting a ceiling-mounted fan

The best place to put a ceiling-mounted fan is right above the bath or shower enclosure, as most of the problem moisture is likely to originate from these. The fan must be located between the joists and requires a hole in the ceiling of up to 300mm diameter, the exact measurement varying between models and makes.

The first stage is to make a pilot hole through the ceiling. Go into the roof space first to check the area for pipes, wiring and obstructions around where the hole is to be made. Use support walling and lamp wiring roses to get your bearings.

Drill the pilot hole from the bathroom side. Check its position from above, if necessary drilling another hole from below until the true centre of the fitting aperture is obtained.

When you have an accurate centre, mark the cutting line for the aperture. This is likely to be a circle, so rig up a simple compass affair using two pencils and a length of string to produce this. Alternatively, use a suitable template such as a large-diameter biscuit tin lid or similar.

The hole must be cut very carefully, both to avoid cracking and damaging the plaster beyond it and to minimize the amount of making good required after the fan is fitted.

To be absolutely safe, drill further pilot holes along the circumference, then gently chip away the plaster or use a padsaw or power jig saw to remove it. Offer up the fan fixing to check it for fitting. You may also need to nail battens between the joists above to support the weight of the unit—fit them so that you can screw the flange to them.

From here onwards follow the specific installation instructions that apply to your fan. If you have been careful, you are likely to find that the fixing flange and the bodywork of the fan are sufficient to conceal small irregularities in the hole, so that making good becomes unnecessary except to strengthen the fixing. Use general-purpose filler for making good unsightly cracks and dents which remain exposed. If you plan to decorate the ceiling, do this before fixing the fan base permanently.

Providing ducts

Ducting has to be used when the fan is mounted on an internal wall and needs to be discharged to the outside, and also when steam and condensation occur. Moisture-laden air must not be discharged into the roof space or eaves as damp damage may occur over a period of time. If the ducting cannot go through a wall, but must pass through the roof, a roof cover must be fitted at the outlet.

For the small-sized WC ventilator shown, standard 102mm plastics ducting is used. This can be led along the inside of a deep stud-partition wall, beneath floorboards and between joists, or along purpose-built boxing to an outside wall where it ends in a special grille. Similar forms of ducting are used for ceiling-mounted extractor fans when moisture-laden air has to be led to the outside. You can use rigid PVC pipework components in place of flexible ducting, but additional bracing will probably be required to hold the pipework firmly in place.

Where possible, use flexible ducting hose instead of rigid uPVC type.

Moisture content is much less of a problem with WC ventilation, so the ducting can be terminated high up in unused roof space, or in the eaves.

Electrical connections

It is important to follow manufacturer's specific instructions when you come to make the electrical connections, particularly where a fan is being used in damp conditions such as a bathroom or separate shower. The details given here are suitable for UK electrical systems.

The WC fan installed in figs 1 to 8 is connected to the supply via a suitable on/off double-pole isolating switch using 0.5mm three-core cable. Protection is provided by a 3 amp fuse if a 13 amp plug is used for the connection, or a 5 amp fuse if wiring is carried from the distribution board. Alternatively, install it on a fused spur. Then ensure that the fan is earthed properly.

This fan has a timer and remains activated for up to twenty minutes after the light is switched off if connected in this way.

In the UK, the ceiling-mounted bathroom fan must be wired to the supply in such a way that plug and socket are outside the bathroom itself. Either run a fused spur to the ceiling—perhaps via adjacent walling—or use existing supply wiring in the roof space.

HOME IMPROVEMENTS AND EXTENSIONS

A basic DIY kit

A good selection of tools is a pleasure to own and an investment for the future. Anyone who takes pride in doing a good job will enjoy working with the best tools and in the majority of cases these will never need replacing as long as they are properly treated and maintained.

Holding and supporting

One of the most useful and important tools in carpentry is a workbench. Having somewhere to do your joinery without having to clear the kitchen table makes life much easier, and if you have a proper bench you can store your tools in it tidily and conveniently.

A solid and secure vice—either built-in, or of the clamp-on type—is indispensable for securing timber and other items on which you are working, and G-cramps will help to secure longer lengths of work in addition to their normal duties.

Measuring tools

Accuracy in measuring and cutting is reflected in the quality of your finished work so you should always buy the best and most robust measuring instruments available in your price range.

Buy a good quality—and preferably a long—spirit level for checking levels and verticals. If you can afford it choose one with an adjustable glass which you can use for checking angles as well. A less accurate, but nonetheless useful, tool is a simple plumb bob and line which can be used for checking verticals on a larger scale. A steel rule is also an essential item.

A woodworkers' try square is essential for checking right-angles as well as the accuracy of planed timber edges—look for one with a sprung steel blade and a stock protected by a thin brass strip. You will also need a combination square for marking angles and mitres: this has a stock which slides along a calibrated steel blade that is used as a depth gauge. A marking gauge is essential for scribing marked-up joints and for multiple marking-up on a large job.

Cutting tools

Accurate cutting is an essential requirement of almost every DIY job so a variety of reliable cutting tools is essential. Two saws—a panel saw which should be about 550mm long and a tenon saw which should be about 250mm to 300mm long—are enough, though separate rip and cross-cut saws are better than a general-purpose panel saw.

Carpenters' chisels are almost indispensable, but they must be looked after properly if they are to give the best results. A selection of three or four bevel-edged chisels is the best choice for a basic tool kit—6mm, 12mm, 25mm and 37mm blades are the most widely used. Whether your chisels have wooden or plastic handles you should never use anything except rawhide, plastic or wooden mallets to hit them with.

Bench planes are available in a wide variety of types and sizes, but an excellent basic choice is a unit about 250mm in length and about 50mm in width. A handyman's knife is a useful item with its interchangeable and replaceable blades.

Abrasives

Files and rasps for shaping and smoothing metals and timber are a necessary part of any tool kit, but because they are fairly expensive you should buy them only when you need them. From the wide variety of shapes and styles available a half-round file is probably the best choice as it can be used for both flat work and concave work such as smoothing the insides of holes.

1 Cramps are vital in most types of carpentry work. G-cramps are useful in securing longer pieces of timber in addition to their normal purpose. Sash cramps are good for long pieces of timber but are expensive. Less expensive, and equally good, are cramp heads pictured in the illustration

2 Accuracy in measurement in any type of do-it-yourself is essential if you are going to achieve the perfect finish. Therefore buy the best try and combination squares and marking and sliding bevel gauges. Also don't forget the importance of having a long, good quality spirit level and the useful bob and line

3 If you find you need to do a great deal of joinery work, a mortise gauge saves a lot of time. It is a necessary item for accurately marking out mortise and tenon joints. A sharp, handymans' knife with changeable blades is also very useful. It is particularly good for marking cutting lines

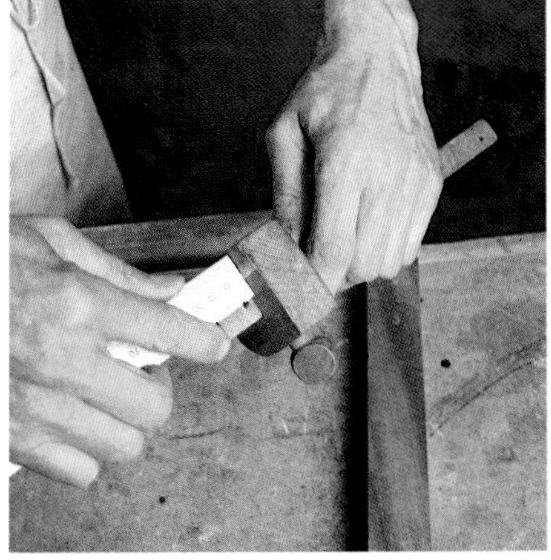

4 One of the most important items you can buy for your tool kit is a good quality steel rule. They come in lengths from 150mm to 1m and apart from being ideal for the usual measuring tasks, they can also be used as straightedges and cutting guides. A folding boxwood rule for general joinery work is also handy

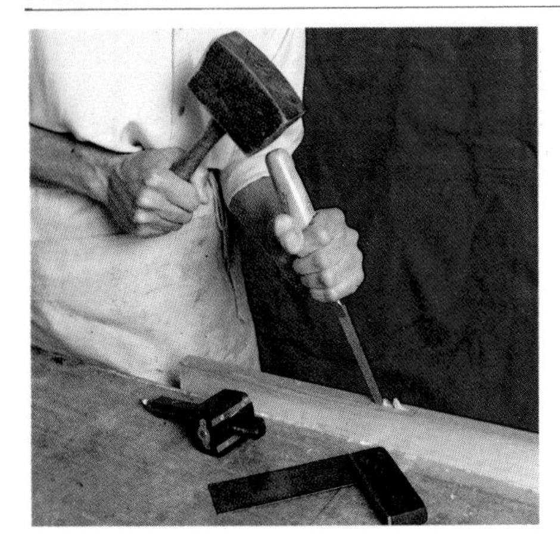

5 Chisels are indispensable tools for joinery work and need to be carefully looked after. To have a selection of about three or four bevel-edged chisels is the ideal number. Always use rawhide, plastic or wooden mallets to hit your chisels or you may seriously damage the handles over a period of time

6 Planes are again very useful items for the do-it-yourselfer. Bench planes are the best ones to handle the rougher planing work, but block planes complement these very well. They can be used for those finer, more meticulous, aspects of cabinet work, such as bevelling or trimming or just to plane end grain

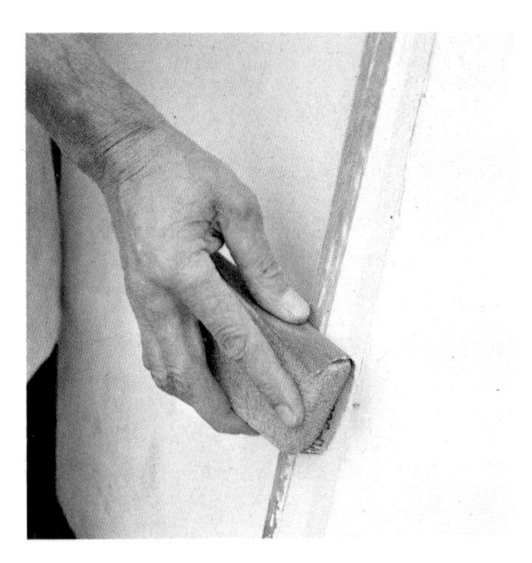

7 Sanding requires a firm touch and you must at all times use the correct grade of paper for the relevant task. Glasspaper is best for most timber finishing while wet and dry paper is better suited to metal and glass fibre work. Harder masonry or painted surfaces may call for something harder, like silicon carbide

8 A power drill is one of the most useful assets of your tool kit as it is so versatile both inside and outside the house. Buy the best drill you can afford. Multi-speed units which have a full range of accessories and a hammer action for drilling through masonry are a particularly good choice

9 A comprehensive screwdriver kit, which includes some cross-head screwdrivers and both long and stubby flathead examples, does not cost a great deal of money and can be used almost anywhere. The kit is essential to all those fiddly everyday tasks. Use a good file to keep the screwdrivers true

10 If you embark on a major home improvements project, you will need some specialized tools to work with. A 2kg club hammer and steel bolster are the first items needed for breaking up masonry and stripping old plaster. They can also prove extremely good for prising up nailed-down old floorboards

11 Pliers are other tools which always come in handy—self-locking pliers, such as a Mole wrench, are particularly good when dealing with nuts, bolts and compression joints in pipework. A comprehensive set of spanners is also very good to have as is a tin of penetrating or possibly lubricating oil

12 Tools which are used for cutting obviously require the most frequent attention—chisels and planes particularly need regular sharpening. To ensure a good cutting edge, a honing guide and an oilstone are worthwhile investments. Saws and drill bits should be taken to an expert to sharpen

A good selection of abrasive paper together with a rubber or timber sanding block is essential both for finishing timber and for preparing surfaces for painting and papering.

Drilling

The most useful and versatile drilling tool that you can buy is of course a power drill. It is worth spending a little extra on a unit made by one of the more reputable manufacturers for which a full range of accessories is available. You can buy these as the need arises, but it is worth buying a multi-speed drill at the outset so that you can use all accessories properly on both metal and masonry.

Despite this, a hand-operated wheel brace is essential for times when there is no power or where an electric drill would be too powerful.

Another essential item for use especially with metal is a countersink or rose bit—these are available for both hand drills and ratchet braces.

To mark the hole before drilling use a bradawl for timber, and a centre punch for metal.

Hammers and screwdrivers

The choice of tools under this heading is vast, and you can spend a great deal of money buying tools that you rarely, if ever, use. For general work you can get by with three hammers: a claw hammer of around 680g is a good all-purpose tool, while a 225g cross-pein hammer is best for driving in panel pins and small nails. An engineers' or ball-pein hammer is the best for metalwork and for driving masonry nails.

For joinery work and chiselling you will need a carpenters' or joiners' mallet.

Other tools

As well as the tools mentioned above, you will find some others extremely useful. Chief among these is a pair of pliers: the most common types are the bull-nosed variety, but needle-nosed pliers are also extremely handy for electrical work.

Build a mitre jig

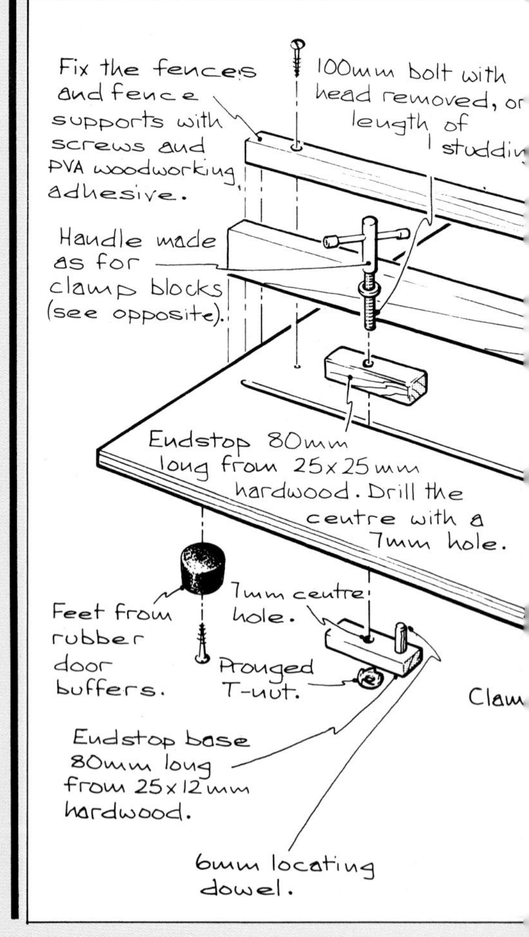

This mitring jig is good for all kinds of projects, but is ideal for picture frames using frame mouldings.

It has two fences so that the parts are aligned squarely, and two sets of saw guides for square and angled cuts. There are two clamps to hold the workpiece in position and an adjustable end stop for gauging the length of the sections.

It is not very complicated, except for the clamps, but the accuracy of assembly will determine the accuracy of the jig.

Start by cutting out the baseboard and marking two square lines on it for the fences. Mark the cutting lines at the right angles to this. Then cut the slot for the end stop. Glue and screw the fences in—make sure you get them dead square, otherwise the jig will be inaccurate.

Make up the saw guides from dowel and tubing. Drill the baseboard and press them into position. Do not fix so they can be replaced. Make sure they are set on the cutting lines.

Make up two clamps from hardwood blocks. The clamping mechanism is made from nuts and bolts and tubing. Drill the blocks for fixing screws. When using, adjust the clamps to lock timber, butt it against the end stop and cut between the saw guides making sure that you do not cut into the wood of the jig itself.

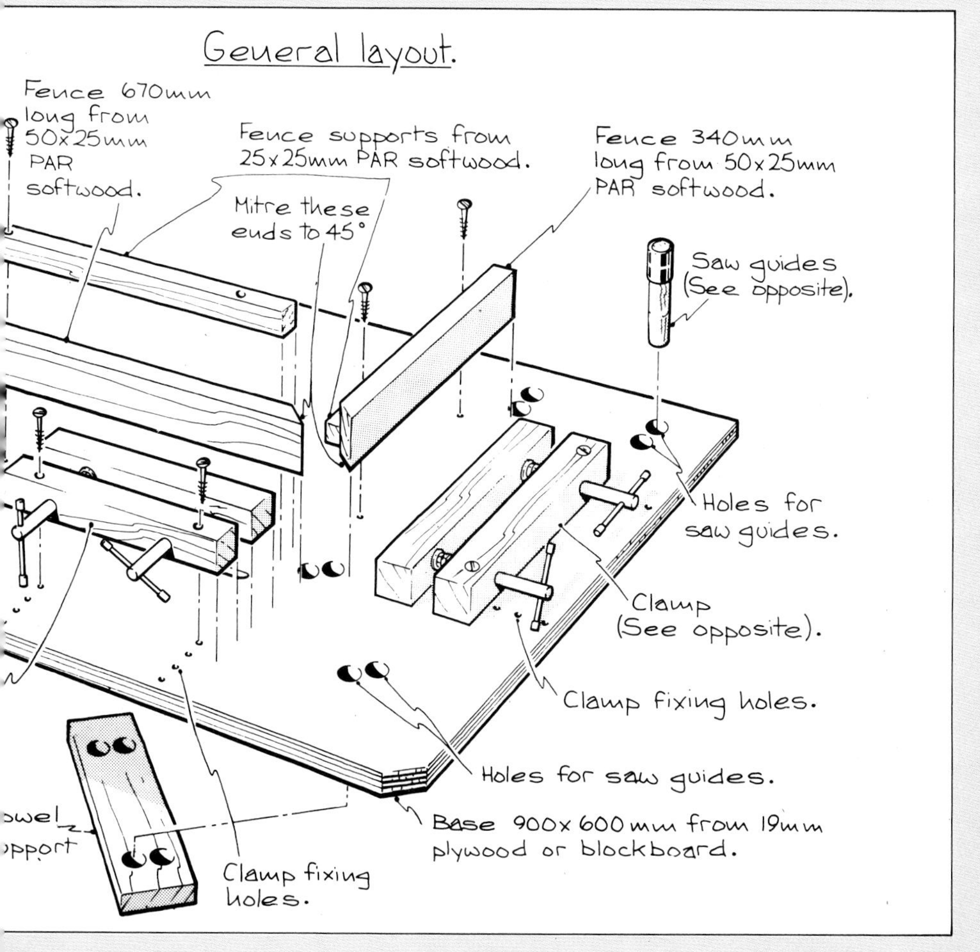

Using a chisel

Knowing how to use a chisel correctly is one of the most important aspects of carpentry. And once you have mastered the skills and techniques involved, a whole new range of do-it-yourself projects becomes possible.

Types of chisel

The chisel is the basic wood-shaping tool and is used for paring, cutting joints and chopping out areas of wood for hinges and other fittings.

Bevel-edged chisels have tapered edges which allow the chisel to get easily into tight corners. They are ideal for cutting dovetails and shallow housings, such as hinge recesses, and for vertical paring.

Firmer chisels have strong blades of rectangular cross-section which make them stronger than bevel-edged chisels and thus more suitable for heavy work such as fencing, frame construction and notching out for pipes running over joists.

Mortise chisels are the strongest chisels of all and are designed to withstand both

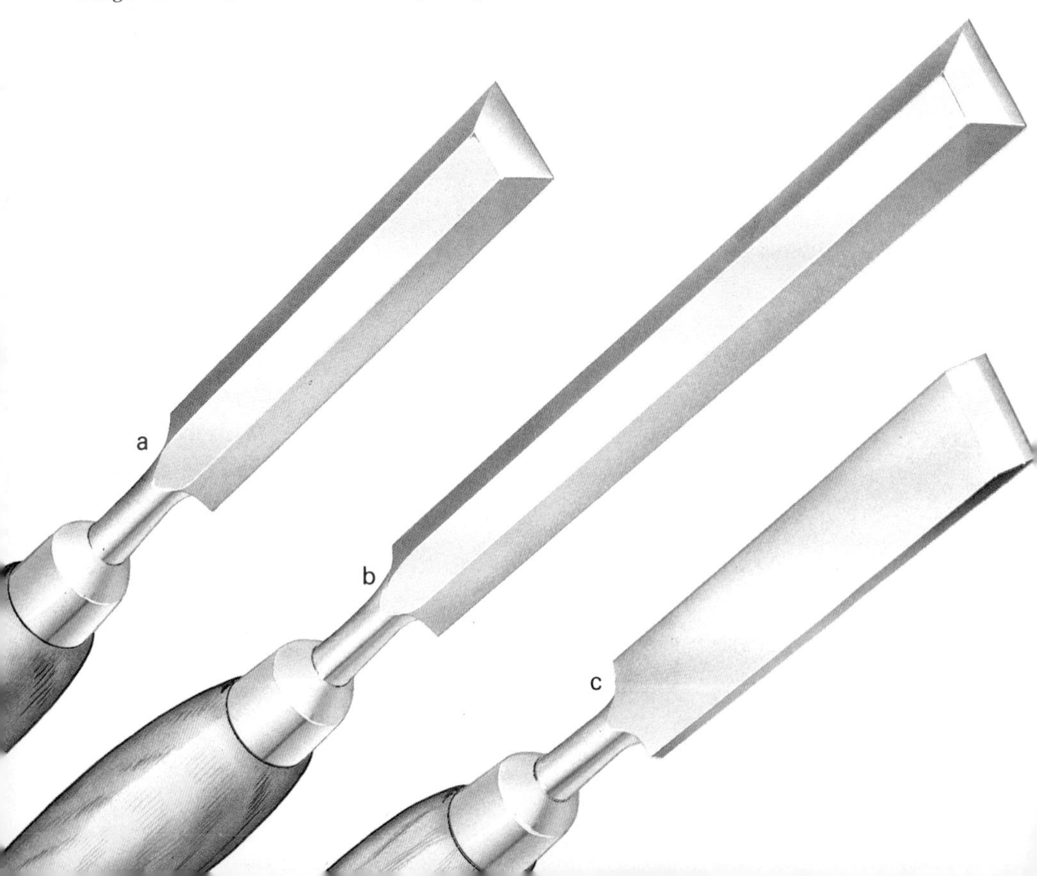

A. Three types of chisel. (a) Bevel-edged chisel has a blade with tapered sides, to get right into the corners. (b) Paring chisel has a long bevelled or rectangular blade. (c) Firmer chisel, with its strong rectangular blade, is used for heavy work

continual striking with a mallet and the levering action required when cutting the mortises for mortise-and-tenon joints.

Paring chisels have long blades of either firmer or bevel-edged type. The long blade is so designed for reaching into awkward corners and for paring out long housings, such as those used in bookcases.

Buying chisels

Bevel-edged and firmer chisels are available in a wide range of widths from 1mm to 38mm. Initially, a set of 6mm, 12mm and 25mm chisels should be adequate for most requirements. Mortise chisels do not come in such a range of sizes and it is unlikely that anything other than 6mm, 8mm and 12mm mortises will ever be required. Buy paring chisels only when the need for a particular one arises.

Chisel safety

Chisels are often supplied with plastic guards which fit over the end of the blade. If the chisels you choose do not come supplied with guards, it is well worth buying a set.

Horizontal paring

Horizontal paring is a technique used when constructing joints—such as housing joints for supporting the ends of shelves and halving joints used in framework.

When making such a joint, define the area of the slot by marking out width lines on top of the wood, and width and depth lines on both sides. Make a saw cut slightly to the waste side of each width line and cut down to the depth line.

Hold the wood securely in the vice so that it will not move as you work and make sure that it is horizontal (fig. 1). Hold the chisel in both hands, safely behind the cutting edge, with the elbow resting comfortably on the bench. This gives extra control over the chisel's movement.

Start by chiselling out the waste adjacent to the sawn lines, making angled cuts to half way across the wood (fig. 2). Push the chisel firmly, holding it at a slight angle, keeping your arm horizontal and level with the work. When the cuts are half way across the joint, reverse the wood in the vice and complete the angled cuts from the other side (fig. 3).

Now turn the chisel over so that the bevel is facing downwards and remove the bulk of the remaining waste by slapping the handle of the chisel with the palm of your hand (fig. 4). Because the bevel side is facing down, the chisel blade works its way up to the surface and no levering action is needed to clear the waste. Again chisel only half way across the joint, then turn the wood around and work from the other side with the bevel side of the chisel facing upwards once more (fig. 5).

When most of the waste has been removed, work the chisel across the joint, keeping it absolutely flat across the bottom, to shave off the last fibres of wood (fig. 6). Finally, hold the chisel vertically in one hand and work the blade into the corners to clean them out and sever any remaining fibres (fig. 7).

Vertical paring

Vertical paring is necessary when you wish to round off a corner or to make a curve in a piece of wood.

Hold the wood on a bench hook, to protect the surface of the work bench, and support the other end, if necessary, with a timber offcut of the same height as the hook (fig. 8). Hold the chisel upright in both hands with the thumb of the upper hand over the top of the handle to give control and downward force.

Mark the required curve on the wood and cut off the corner, to an angle of about 45°, with a tenon saw. Holding the chisel as described, pare off the corners left by the saw cut. Keep paring off the corners, taking off thin slivers of wood not more than 1mm thick (fig. 9). If you take off thicker cuts than this, the extra effort involved may cause you to lose control of the chisel.

1 For horizontal paring, hold the wood firmly and securely in the vice so that it does not move as you chisel. Rest your elbow comfortably on the bench

2 Hold the chisel with both hands, keeping them behind the cutting edge and paıe angled cuts which are adjacent to the sawn guidelines

5 Turn the wood in the vice once again, and remove the remainder of the waste from the other side. The bevel edge should then be facing up once more

6 When most of the waste has been cleared out, work the chisel across the joint with its blade flat against the wood to remove the fine shavings

9 Remove slivers of wood, gripping the blade tightly between your fingers. Hold your thumb over the handle to provide more downward force

10 When cutting a mortise, cramp the wood and carefully protect it with a timber offcut. The tail of the cramp should then be beneath the work

3 When the angled cuts are half way across the wood, turn it around in the vice and then finish the cuts from the other side

4 Turn the chisel over so that its bevel-edged side is facing down and quickly slap the handle with the palm of your hand to remove the waste

7 To sever any remaining fibres in the corners, work the blade carefully into each corner with the chisel held strongly in one hand

8 For vertical paring, place the wood on a bench hook and support the end with a timber offcut. Keep your head bent closely over the work

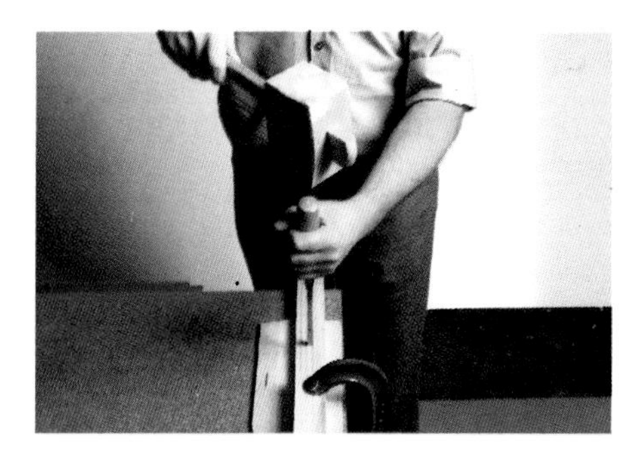

11 Keep your body right behind, and completely in line with, the work and drive the chisel firmly into the wood with a wooden mallet

12 For paring out long housings, use a paring chisel. The long blade can be worked flat over a long distance to achieve an even finish

13 To sharpen the blade of a chisel, hold it at an angle of about 30° on to an oilstone. Rub the blade slowly in a figure of eight motion

14 When a wire edge begins to form, turn the blade over. Rub the other side over the oilstone keeping the blade flat upon the surface

Work as closely in to the curve line as possible, then finish off by smoothing with a file.

Cutting a mortise

A mortise is a rectangular slot cut into a piece of wood into which a tongue—called a tenon—from another piece of wood is fixed. The mortise and tenon make a strong joint which is used to form T-shapes in frames. The mortise should always be made with a mortise chisel.

To mark out a mortise accurately you need a mortise gauge. Using a chisel of the exact width of the planned mortise, set the gauge to the chisel blade and mark out the width lines on the wood. With a try square as a guide, draw the two setting-out lines which determine the length of the mortise.

When cutting a mortise, the wood should be held securely on a solid part of the bench rather than cramped in the vice: as the chisel is struck with a mallet, it would dislodge the wood from a vice. Use a G-cramp to hold the wood in position and protect the top with a timber offcut (fig. 10). Make sure that the tail of the cramp is beneath the work or injury may result. Drive the chisel into the wood with a mallet.

Start by driving the chisel into the mortise to dislodge a deep wedge of waste. Use three separate strokes of the chisel to remove the wedge, making it equal on both sides. Keep your body behind, and in line with, the work (fig. 11). Work, with a series of small chops, from the centre towards one of the setting-out lines keeping the chisel in the same vertical plane at all times. Stop at the line, turn the chisel round and approach the other setting-out line with a further series of chops.

Clear out the waste and dislodge another wedge in the centre to the depth of the finished mortise. A band of tape wrapped around the chisel blade to the required depth makes a good depth indicator. Chop up to both setting-out lines, again to the required depth.

Sharpening chisels

No matter how correct your technique or how expensive your chisels, you cannot produce good work with a blunt chisel. You should always check that cutting edges are sharp before use and hone them if necessary.

Sharpen a chisel on an oilstone. Apply a light oil liberally to the surface to prevent metal filings clogging the stone. Hold the chisel with one hand gripping the handle, the other steadying the blade.

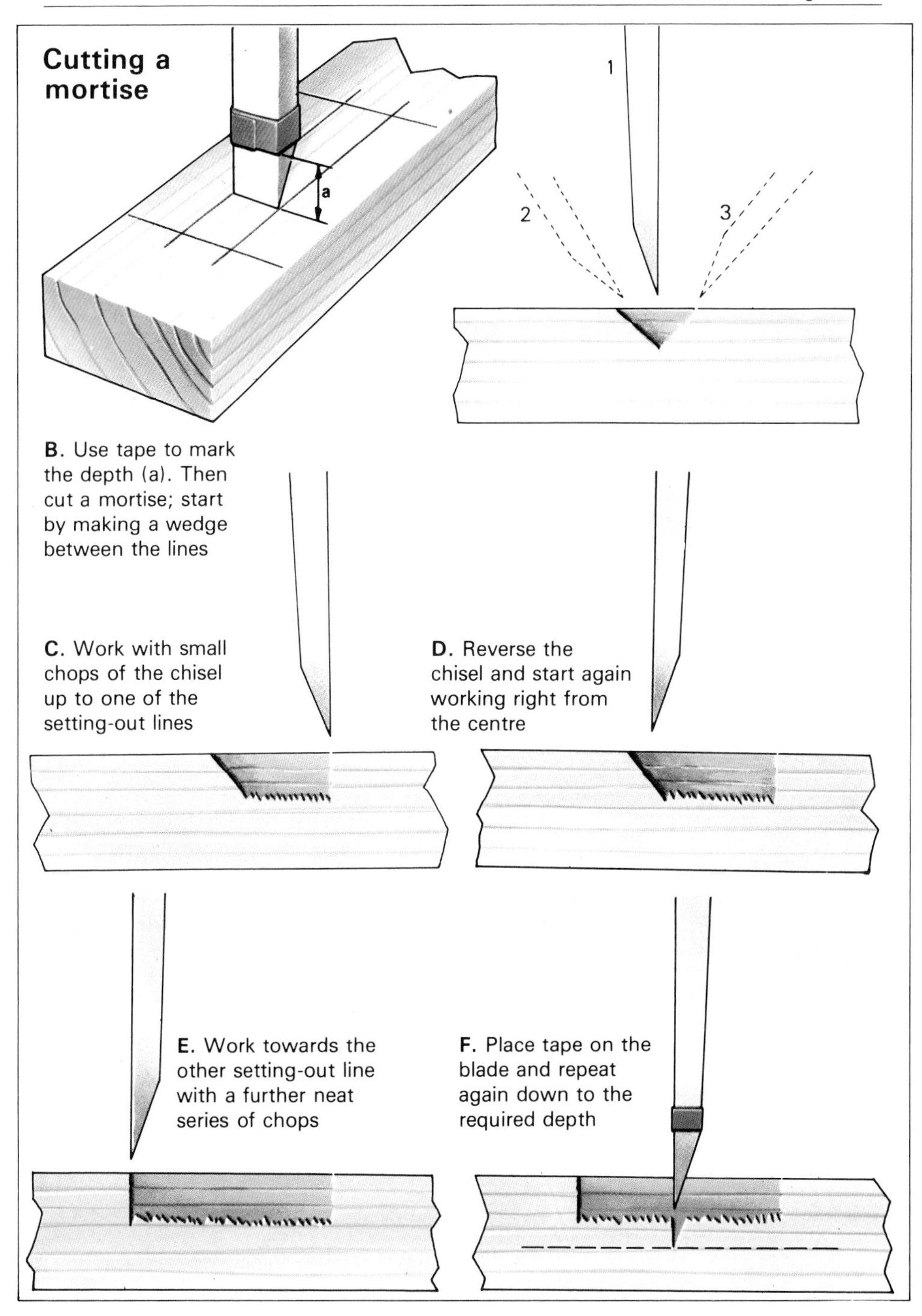
Cutting a mortise
a
1
2
3
B. Use tape to mark the depth (a). Then cut a mortise; start by making a wedge between the lines
C. Work with small chops of the chisel up to one of the setting-out lines
D. Reverse the chisel and start again working right from the centre
E. Work towards the other setting-out line with a further neat series of chops
F. Place tape on the blade and repeat again down to the required depth

Fixing wood to wood

Nails and screws are the two most important fastening devices used in carpentry, but how well they do their job depends almost entirely on how correctly they are used.

Tools

The two hammers used most frequently in carpentry are the claw hammer and the cross-pein, or 'Warrington'. The first is useful for levering out old nails and lifting floorboards while the second is more suited to finer nailing work.

If you are starting a tool kit, opt for a 450g claw hammer and a 280g Warrington. Later, you can add a 100g 'pin' Warrington for light, accurate nailing and pinning.

For burying nails below the surface of the wood, you need a set of nail punches. These come in quite a variety of sizes—to suit different sizes of nail—and help to avoid bruising the wood with the hammer head.

Some kind of drill is essential for screwing work. A power drill is the obvious choice because of its versatility, but where there are no power points or access is limited, a wheel brace (hand drill) will serve well.

To drill larger holes by hand, you need a swing brace and a set of special bits—not a priority for the beginner's basic tool kit.

Good quality screwdrivers are essential to any tool kit and cabinet screwdrivers, with blades of about 300mm, are the most useful. Two of them—one with an 8mm tip and one with a 6.5mm tip—should cover you for most jobs. To deal with crosshead, Philips or Posidriv screws, you need screwdrivers with the appropriate tips.

Using a hammer

Using a hammer properly requires a little bit of practice. Take a firm grip right at the end of the handle and form your arm into a right-angle, looking straight down on the work as you do so. Start the nail by tapping it lightly, keeping your wrist controlled but flexible and letting the

Above: Start short nails with a cross-pein hammer. Tap gently with the wedge end until they stand firm, then drive in firmly with the hammer face

Above: Very small nails and pins should be held with a pair of pliers. Use the cross-pein hammer to hit the nail with fairly gentle taps

hammer head do the work.

On well-finished work, remember not to drive nails right in—leave a bit protruding for the hammer and nail punch to finish off.

Start light nails or tacks with the cross-pein by tapping gently with the wedge end of the hammer head. Drive them home with the hammer face using a number of fairly gentle taps rather than

Commonly used nails

Round wire
For rough carpentry work: large ugly head ensures a firm grip. Liable to split wood

Oval wire
Commonly used in carpentry. Oval cross section makes it unlikely to split wood if the long axis follows the grain

Lost head
General carpentry nail. Head can be punched below the surface and the hole filled

Panel pin
Small nail for securing light pieces of wood; usually used in conjunction with glue

Clout nail
Large headed for fixing roofing felt, sash cords, wire fencing to wood. Galvanized for outdoor work

Flooring brad
Used to hold down floorboards. Good holding power and unlikely to split wood

Glazing brad
Headless: used to hold glass to picture frames and lino to floorboards. Will not grip if driven too far in

Masonry nail
Hardened steel nail for fixing wood to soft brick, breeze block and concrete

Hardboard pin
Special head shape countersinks itself in hardboard and can be filled over

Upholstery nail
Decorative head used to cover tacks in upholstery work

trying to knock them in with one blow, which will probably bend the nail.

Nailing techniques

For accurate, well-finished work, nails alone do not normally make a strong joint. However, if the nails are angled in opposition to each other, a reasonable joint can be made. When used in conjunction with one of the modern woodworking adhesives, a very strong joint can be achieved. Seldom are nails driven straight—a stronger joint can be made if they go in at an angle or *skew*.

Removing nails

The claw hammer is used to remove partially driven nails. To avoid damaging the surface of the wood, place a small offcut under the hammer head before you start levering. Extract nails with a number of pulls rather than trying to do the job in one.

Use pincers to remove small nails and pins which are difficult to grip with the claw hammer.

Drilling screw holes

All screws must have pilot holes made before they can be driven home. For screws into softwood smaller than No. 6 gauge, make these with a bradawl. Drive it into the wood with its chisel point across the grain, to avoid splitting.

Screws into hardwood and screws into softwood larger than No. 6 gauge need

Nailing tips

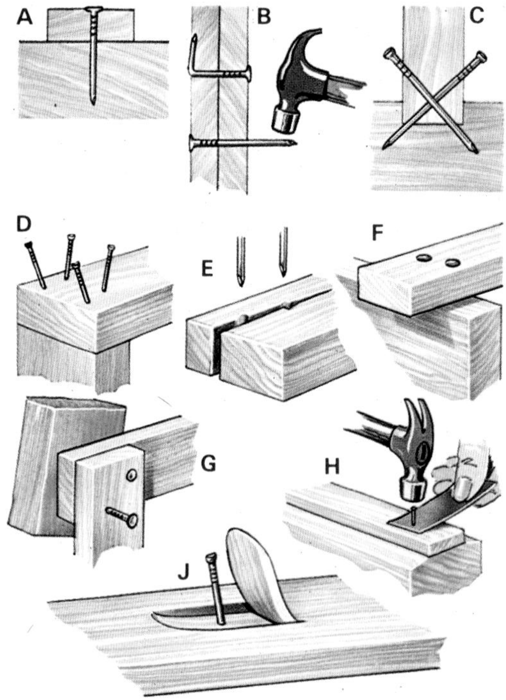

A. Use nails about 3 times as long as the workpiece. Always nail smaller to larger. **B.** On rough work, clench-nailed joints are much stronger. **C.** Skew-nailing is one of the best ways of securing a housing joint. **D.** When nailing into end grain, drive in nails at opposing angles. **E.** Driving more than one nail along the same grain line risks splitting the wood. **F.** Nail small battens overlength to avoid splitting the end. Afterwards, saw or plane off the excess. **G.** Avoid 'bouncing' by placing a block under the workpiece. **H.** Small nails can be positioned with the aid of a cardboard holder.
J. Secret nailing. Prise up a sliver of timber with a chisel. Glue down after nailing

two pilot holes. One is for the thread—the pilot hole—and one for the shank—the shank hole.

For all except the largest pilot holes, use twist drill bits. Those for pilot holes should be the same size as the screw core to which the threads are attached. Those for the shanks should match them.

Screws: types and uses

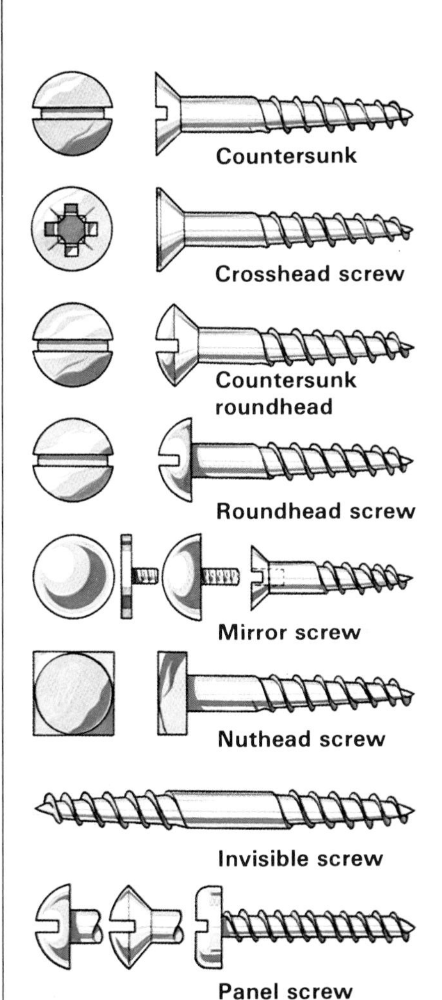

Used for general woodwork. The head sinks in flush with, or slightly below, the wood surface

Used for general woodwork, but needs a special screwdriver which does not slip from the head

Used for fixing door-handle plates and other decorative fittings with countersunk holes. The head is designed to be seen

Used for fixing hardware fittings without countersunk holes. The head protrudes from the work

Used for fixing mirrors and bathroom fittings. The chromed cap threads into the screw head to hide the screw. Do not overtighten

Used for fixing heavy constructions together and heavy equipment to timbers. Tighten with a spanner

Used for invisible joining of two pieces of timber

Used for fixing thin sheets of metal and plastic. Cuts its own thread as it is screwed in. Various types of head are available

Used for securing chipboard and its derivatives. Various types of head are available

When drilling pilot holes, mark the required depth on the drill bit with a piece of masking tape. This will tell you when to stop and cannot damage the workpiece should you overdrill.

As with nailing, where two pieces of wood are to be fixed together, screw the smaller to the larger. Drill the shank hole right through the smaller piece so it is pulled down tight as the screw is driven home. If the shank hole goes only part of the way through you will find it very hard to pull the top piece of wood down tight and may risk breaking or damaging the screw. Brute force should never be used—it indicates that either the thread hole or the shank hole is too small.

Countersinking

Countersinking is normally the easiest way of recessing screw heads flush with, or below, the surface of the wood. The recess is made with a countersink bit after the pilot has been drilled, to the same depth as the countersunk screw head. Take particular care if you are countersinking with a power drill or the recess may accidentally become too large.

Drilling techniques

Using the correct drilling technique makes all the difference to the quality of the finished work. Whether your drill is power or hand operated, you should always hold it at right-angles to the work surface so that the pilot hole is straight. If you find this difficult, rest a try square upright near the bit and use it as a guide.

With bit drills, operate the drill in bursts and lift it frequently to allow debris to escape. To give yourself as much control as possible, always hold the drill with both hands and never press too hard—you are bound to overdrill.

Keep the chuck key taped to the cable, so it is handy whenever you want to change bits.

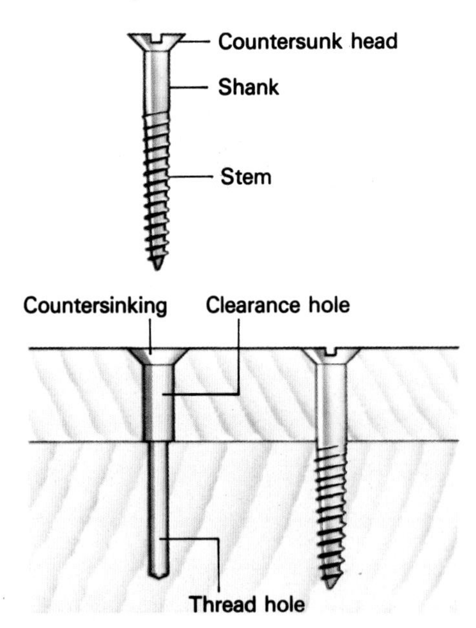

A. Drill two pilot holes for each screw—the top one to accept the shank in a 'push fit', the bottom one should be about two sizes smaller

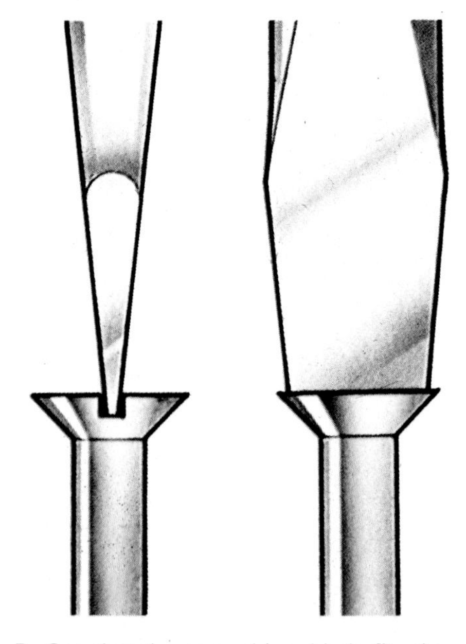

B. See that the screwdriver blade fits the screw head exactly and that the tip is kept ground square. If not, you run the risk of 'chewing up' the screw

Using a hand-operated wheel brace requires slightly more effort, but gives more control than a power drill. When drilling vertically, grip the handle with your thumb on top. Turn the wheel steadily to avoid knocking the drill out of line.

To drill horizontally, grip the handle with your thumb towards the wheel. Alternatively, where a side handle is fitted, grasp this in one hand while you turn the wheel steadily with the other.

Driving screws

Always make sure that the tip of your screwdriver is in good condition and that it fits exactly into the slot in the screw head. A blade which is too narrow or rounded damages the slot, while too wide a blade damages the wood.

When using a pump-action screwdriver, hold it firmly in both hands—one on the handle, the other on the knurled collar just above the bit—and make sure that you are not off-balance. Any loss of control could cause the blade to slip out of its screw slot and damage your wood.

To make screwdriving easier, the screws can be lubricated with wax or candle grease before driving. Brass screws are quite soft, and to prevent damage when screwing into hardwood, the resistance can be lowered by driving in a steel screw first.

Below: When you have acquired some of the basic carpentry skills you could easily progress to doing something more ambitious, like making this attractive bunk bed for children

The art of planing

Above: A fairly long plane should be used for long pieces of wood so that the plane levels out the timber rather than following any profile it might have. The plane should be held comfortably with the body weight positioned over the top of it to give all the pressure that is needed to make the cut

A plane's job is to slice off unwanted portions of wood, reducing the wood to the exact size required and leaving it smooth and flat.

Bench planes

These are made up of the same parts and have the same adjusting and sharpening procedures. They come in four lengths. The jointer plane is the longest, measuring approximately 550mm, the fore plane is about 450mm, the jack plane is 350–375mm and the smooth plane 200–250mm.

The plane blade has two angles forming the cutting edge—the ground angle of 25° and the honed angle of 30°. The plane's ground angle is already formed on a new plane and will need only occasional renewing on a grinding stone, but the honed angle has to be sharpened before you can use the plane.

Taking apart and sharpening

Referring to the diagram detailed, remove the lever cap by releasing the cam and sliding the cap upwards until it will lift off. Remove the plane blade and the cap iron. Place them on a flat surface and undo the cap iron screw. Slide the blade forward, twist it through 90° and remove from the cap iron.

If you have a honing guide for sharpening the blade, set this up according to the manufacturer's instructions. Alternatively, use an oilstone box with a medium stone.

Use enough oil to keep the surface of the stone moist. Hold the plane iron so the blade is at 90° to the stone with the bevel side of the blade down on the stone. Tilt the iron until you feel the bevel flat on the stone—this will be about a 25° angle. Tilt through another 5° to get a 30° angle. Then rub the blade evenly up and down the stone, maintaining the angle.

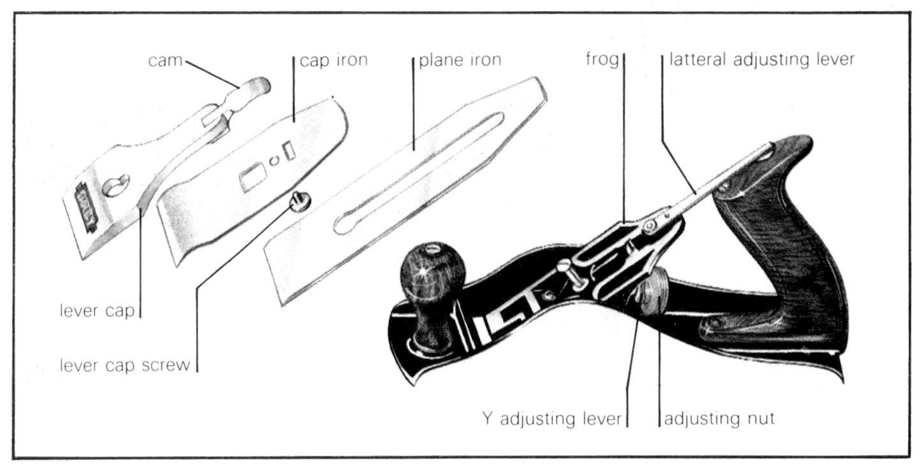

Above: A new plane is easily taken apart for sharpening the blade

Continue doing this until you feel a burr or wire (a roughness) on the flat side of the blade. When you feel it burred evenly all the way across, turn the blade over and place it flat on the stone. Holding it flat with both hands, move it up and down at a slight angle until the burr has been removed from the edge.

Repeat on a fine stone and then, if you want a very sharp edge, do the same again on a leather strop impregnated with motor car valve grinding paste to provide a good abrasive.

Re-assembling

To put the plane together again, hold the cap iron screw side up and place the blade at right-angles to it over the screw. Slide the blade so that the screw goes three-quarters of the way up the slot, then twist it back through 90° and slide it back until only 1.5mm of blade projects beyond the cap iron.

Finger-tighten the screw and readjust the blade to a clearance of 0.5–0.7mm. Hold the blade flat on a bench and tighten the screw. Place the blade back on the plane—taking care not to damage the sharpened edge—so that it lies flat on the frog. Then replace the lever cap. Look along the bottom of the plane from the front at eye level and move the lateral adjusting lever to the right or left, if the blade is not level. It must be exactly level to give an even cut.

Block planes

These are very like the bench planes but they are smaller. They are made up of similar parts but there are fewer of them. They have to be taken apart and the blade sharpened in exactly the same way as the bench plane.

The standard type has the same cutting angle as a bench plane. Others have a cutting edge of 20° and 12°, which make it easier to use on small items. They can be used one-handed quite easily.

Block planes are particularly suitable for using on small pieces of timber, for working on the end grain of timber and for trimming plastic laminates.

Preparation

Put the wood on a solid, level surface so that it will not move while you are planing. Have the end of the wood against a stop.

If you are supporting the workpiece in a vice, make sure that it is sandwiched between two offcuts to prevent the jaws from bruising the wood.

The frog part is adjustable, which means that the mouth of the plane can be altered according to the type of material

1 Always remember to make sure before you even contemplate a planing job that your plane is very sharp. Otherwise it will badly tear the surface of the wood, probably making it unusable. Moisten the stone with oil. Tilt the iron to a 30° angle and then rub the blade evenly up and down the stone maintaining that particular angle

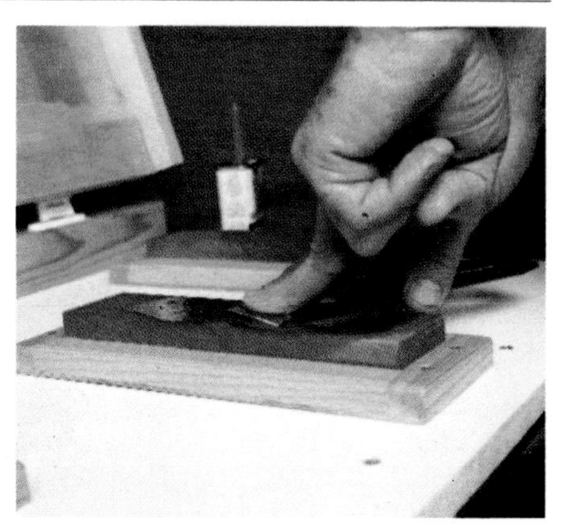

2 Keep rubbing the blade evenly up and down until you feel what is known as a burr or wire—basically a roughness—on the flat side of the blade. When you can feel it has got an even roughness, turn the blade over, putting it flat on the stone. Then holding it flat move it up and down at a slight angle to remove the burr from the edge

5 Then hold the blade completely flat on a bench or workmate and firmly tighten up the screw with a large screwdriver. Place the blade very carefully back on the plane—making sure that you do not damage the sharpened edge—so that it lies completely flat on the frog section. Then you can safely replace the lever cap

6 Then look along the bottom of the plane from the front angle, and at eye level, and move the lateral adjusting lever to either the right or left so that the blade is level and protrudes less than 0.5mm. This adjustment is particularly critical as the blade must be completely level to give the necessary even cut when you are using the plane

3 If you want a very sharp edge on your plane, rub it at a slight angle on an oiled leather strop to provide a good abrasive. Put the plane back together again by holding the cap iron, screw side up, and place the blade at a 90° angle to the screw. Slide the blade so the screw moves further up the slot and then twist it back through 90°

4 Slide the screw further back until only about 1.5mm of blade is still visible projecting beyond the cap iron. The next thing to do is finger tighten the screw and to accurately readjust the blade to a clearance of 0.5–0.7mm. You can probably judge with your eye, but if not, measure the clearance just to be on the safe side

7 Now the plane is sharpened and ready to use. Put the wood on a solid, level surface or have it fixed in a vice between wood offcuts so that the jaws do not damage your piece of wood. Hold the plane with both hands and with your body balanced over the top, push the plane over the wood, keeping the cuts shallow but very even

8 When you are planing long square edges, you will need to apply more pressure on the front knob of the plane at the beginning of each stroke. So use your fingers to support the plane and help keep it in a square position. At the end of the stroke, apply pressure to the back of the plane. Always make the stroke along the whole length of wood

you are planing. For rough planing and soft timbers, the blade should be set with half to three-quarters of the mouth open. For fine finishing of hard woods and for planing end grain, the frog should be adjusted to give a very fine mouth opening of about 1.5mm.

Method

Hold the plane firmly but comfortably with both hands and with your body balanced over the top of the plane. Push the plane forward over the wood keeping the cuts shallow and even. Never plane against the grain of the wood or the blade will catch on the ends of the fibres.

If you are planing correctly you should be producing ribbon-like shavings of equal width and thickness.

When planing long edges apply more pressure on the front knob of the plane at the beginning of the stroke, even out the pressure in the middle of the stroke and at the end of the stroke apply more pressure at the back of the plane. Make the stroke the whole length of the wood each time.

As you plane, make *sure* by frequent checking with the try square that the edge you are working on is at right angles to the other surfaces. And use the edge of the try square, or a steel rule, to see that the edge is straight.

End grain

If you are planing end grain, cut the wood 6mm longer than it needs to be. Put the piece of wood upright in a bench vice, with a waste piece of wood behind. Plane across both pieces of wood—that way any splitting will occur on the waste wood rather than the wood you want to use.

Alternatively, you can bevel all the four corners and then plane from one end towards the middle. Turn the wood around and plane from the other end towards the middle. Remove the piece left in the middle very carefully. Even when using a method such as this, take great care to avoid putting undue pressure on the plane.

9 If you are planing correctly you should be producing long ribbon-like shavings of equal thickness and width. Do not spoil the rhythm of planing by stopping in mid-stroke. When you are planing across a wide width of wood, twist the plane so that it is at an angle to help reduce the natural resistance of the wood

10 To plane end grain, put the wood securely in a vice with an offcut fitted neatly behind it and then plane smoothly across both pieces. Another method is to bevel all four corners of the wood and then plane evenly from one end to the middle. Turn over the wood and repeat the process

Repairing window sills

Above: Obvious signs of rot, if left unattended, can cheapen the appearance of your entire property

The purpose of a window sill is to protect the wall underneath the window from rain. Although this may not seem necessary—after all, the rest of the wall is not protected in this way—rainwater striking the glass panes forms a concentrated, downward-running cascade which could penetrate a masonry wall or even start rot in wooden siding.

Some typical sills are illustrated. They project well beyond the frame of the window itself so that rainwater is directed well clear of the supporting wall.

Unless rainwater runs off quickly, wooden sills may rot and stone or cement sills crack through frost action.

A drip groove on the underside of the sill is a small but important feature. Whatever the angle of slope on the top surface, some rain inevitably creeps around the front face of the sill; accumulated drips then work along the bottom edge and onwards to the wall—where they can attack the joint with the sill. The drip groove prevents this by halting the water's progress, causing it to form into larger droplets that then fall harmlessly to the ground.

Some sills are formed in one piece with the rest of the window frame. Others are installed separately and if any joint between the two is left unprotected or badly sealed, you can almost certainly expect trouble later on.

Dealing with design faults

If you want to avoid recurring problems, it is important to correct any design faults during the course of routine maintenance or repair work.

Start by checking the drip groove. Appearance can be deceptive: there may be a drip groove, but well hidden under layers of paint. Probe around to see if you can find one and, if you do, scrape the recess completely clear then prime and paint it, taking care not to repeat the fault.

Where there is no groove, you might be able to rout or chisel one. But a stop of some form is a much easier solution which should work just as well. You can make the stop from a length of quadrant (or even square) beading and fix it to the underside of the sill with impact adhesive, about 35mm back from the front edge.

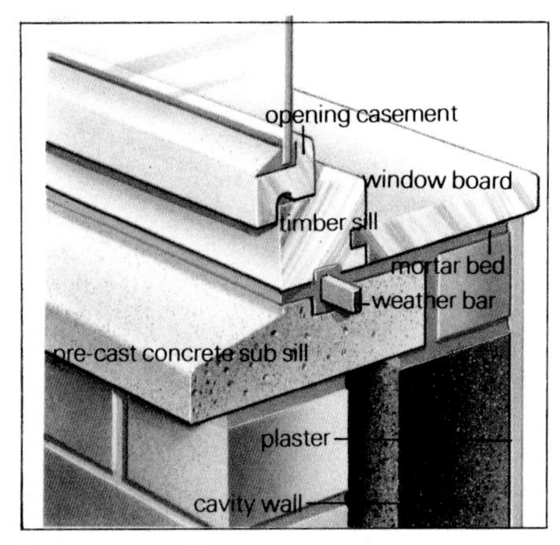

Composite sill

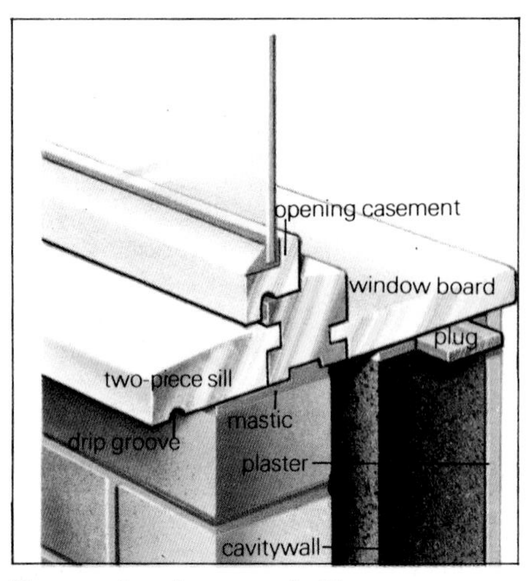

Tongued-and-grooved sill

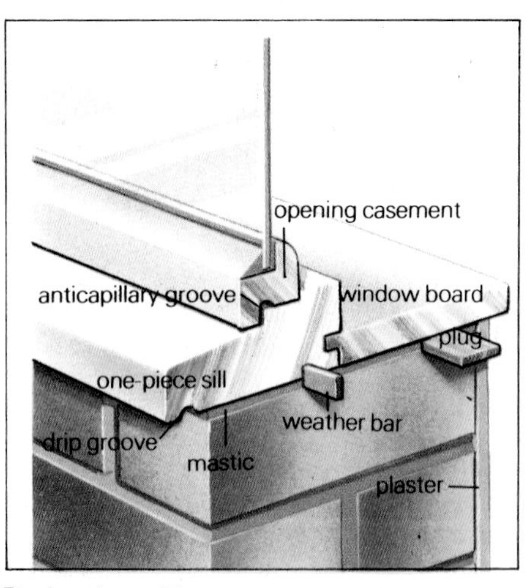

Projecting sill

Prod a wood sill with a pointed blade or bradawl to check for wet rot, and look for fine cracks and flaking on stone or concrete sills—typical signs of an inadequate slope.

A wooden sill is easily corrected by planing it to a suitable slope, though you can do this only if the timber is sound and deep enough.

A stone sill can be repaired and sloped by forming a mortar fillet on top.

Paint the surface with PVA adhesive so that the new mortar mix of one part cement to three of sand adheres properly. Run over this with an offcut of timber to give the slope you want, then remove the former and shape a rounded front edge.

Rotten window sills

If you have caught the rot in good time you may need to do nothing more than burn off all the paint on the sill, scrape the surface back to sound timber, and flood the area with wood preservative before repainting.

But if the damage is at all extensive, it is sensible to cut out the affected part and replace it. Some joinery stockists sell ready-shaped sills and if you can find one which has the same profile as your sill (or nearly so), it can be used for patching gaps. Otherwise you have to trim a piece of suitable timber to the correct shape.

Most modern wooden sills are made of softwood—usually redwood—which is perfectly suitable providing it has been properly treated with pressure-impregnated preservative.

Hardwood is a better material for sills because of its resistance to decay, but there are problems. Susceptibility to surface 'checking' may make traditional materials difficult to paint, while some hardwoods such as Ramin have poor resistance to decay.

Replacing a sill

If the sill is formed in one piece with the window frame, you must cut it free at a suitable point in order to replace the whole sill. If possible, arrange the cut so that the joint with the new sill will be covered by the next window frame member up. Otherwise simply cut off a generous width of sill, well beyond the depth of rot.

Clean up the cut face of the remaining part of the sill by chiselling and planing until it is smooth and flat. Treat the face generously with preservative (fig. 4).

The new sill is bonded firmly to this surface. Although galvanized screws driven in at angles from below through the two pieces might do in some cases, a better solution is to make dowel joints between the two.

Whatever main method of fixing you choose the two surfaces must also be glued together, using a urea or resorcinol formaldehyde adhesive. When the wood is well bonded, rake out all the gaps between the new sill and the wall or the old sill and flood them with preservative. Finally, pack the gaps with a suitable waterproof mastic.

To repair just a small section of sill, cut out the affected part with a saw and chisel then use this as a template to cut the patching timber to size. Thoroughly treat the new wood with preservative, then glue it in place with a urea or resorcinol formaldehyde adhesive. Finally, screw the patch to the existing sill using galvanized screws countersunk well below the surface. Cover the heads with filler.

Painting

Prevention is much better than cure, so making sure that your window sills are properly painted is essential.

The old paint will probably have to be removed completely if it is in poor condition and in this case burning off is better than using stripper because it keeps the wood dry. Sand the surface smooth afterwards and treat any knots with knotting compound to seal them. Rub a fine wood filler into the surface to seal the grain—do not forget the ends of the sill. Finally paint with primer, undercoat and two top coats, making sure that no bare timber is left overnight.

1 Use a pointed tool and knife to investigate the extent of the rot in the window sill. You should expect trouble at exposed joins in old sills. Then, carefully mark an angled cut line on each side and well clear of the rot, and use a tenon saw to completely remove the rotten section

2 Chisel well into the sound wood to the rear, levelling the wood as you proceed, so that the replacement pieces will fit easily into the gap. Then from direct measurements, cut the necessary replacement sill sections. Carve or rout a drip groove to join the one already in existence

5 Another task before fixing this sill section is to apply a suitable adhesive—urea resorcinol formaldehyde adhesive is best—to all the contact areas on the sill and the new piece of wood. The adhesive used should always be a waterproof type

6 Now carefully place the wood section into position and immediately drill holes with a power drill for the secondary fixing. Do not forget to countersink the holes so they will not be visible. Then firmly fix the plated screws in with a screwdriver

3 Where the sill rot has spread to nearby framework, a replacement section must be fitted. Build this up from any suitable pieces of timber you might have around. It is sometimes easier to shape wood in situ. Use countersunk fixing screws, and then plane the wood to reduce it to the correct size

4 Before you permanently fix the first sill piece in position, one of the things you must make sure you do is to apply liberal quantities of a good wood preservative with a paintbrush to all the points of contact. Make sure you work the preservative well into all the cracks and crevices

7 Check the remaining pieces of wood that need to be fitted for accuracy of measurement and then coat these and the contact positions with the waterproof glue. Then screw into position as the previous section and make good any gaps with a well-known make of filler

8 The last thing to complete the repair is to plane all the new sill pieces so that they blend in completely with the existing section of sill. Then carefully sand down the new wood and filled sections ready for the necessary priming and subsequent painting

Door repairs

There is nothing more annoying than a door which is difficult to open and close. And although the trouble can usually be put right quite easily, neglecting such a door may cause more extensive damage which is costly and difficult to repair at a later date.

Choosing hinges

Plastic, nylon, or—better still—pressed steel hinges are suitable for light internal doors, but if you are fitting hinges to a heavy, outside door, use the strong type made of cast steel.

Above: This small kitchen is made even more cramped by a door which opens inwards. By rehanging the door to open outwards more space is immediately created

By finding out the thickness, weight and height of your door, you can estimate what size of hinge you require. For example, a lightweight door, 32mm thick, would need a 75mm × 25mm hinge, whereas a heavier door, 45mm thick, might require a 100mm × 38mm hinge. To find the size of a hinge, first measure its length and then the width of one of its leaves to the middle of the knuckle where it swivels.

Most doors are fitted with butt hinges and you can buy either the fixed or the rising variety. The rising butt hinge allows the door to rise as it is opened but shut down closely on to a carpet or threshold as it closes. This means that though the door does not scrape against floor coverings, it will stop draughts.

Marking and fitting

Before you fit the hinge decide which side you want the door to open. Panelled doors can be hinged on either edge but most modern flush doors can only be fitted with hinges on one edge.

Once you have decided which edge of the door is to be hinged, arrange it so that it is resting on the opposite edge. Support the door by wedging it into a corner, cramping it to the leg of a table, or by holding it in a vice.

The best positions for the hinges are 215mm from the top of the door and 225mm from the bottom, but make sure that this does not leave them over any joints or the door may be weakened.

Use a marking knife and try square to mark the hinge positions on the door edge, starting from the knuckle edge where the hinge will swivel. Mark across all but 6mm of the edge then continue on to the face of the door, marking the thickness of one hinge leaf (fig. 1).

Next, open one of the hinges and lay it in position on the door edge to check that the lines you have drawn are accurate. Hold the hinge in position and use a marking knife to mark each end (fig. 2). Then neatly scribe the width and depth of a hinge leaf on to the door edge and frame (fig. 3).

Cutting out

The hinge recesses are now ready to be cut out. Use a bevel-edged chisel and start by chopping downwards across the grain in a series of cuts 5–6mm apart. Leave a thin uncut border of about 2–3mm around the three edges. Now hold the chisel flat, bevel side up and pare away the chipped-up timber. Finally, keep the flat side of the chisel parallel to the door edge and clean out the rest of the recess (fig. 4).

The hinge should now press firmly into place flush with the surrounding timber.

Fixing hinges

Once the hinge is comfortably in position, carefully mark the screw holes with a sharp pencil then remove the hinge and remark the screw centres with a centre punch. Try to mark these a little off centre—towards inside of the recess—so that once the screws are inserted, the hinge will be pulled snugly into position.

Drill pilot holes to the depth of the screws and then clearance holes deep enough for the screw shanks. For heavy butt hinges use No. 7 or No. 8 × 38mm screws. Insert the screws so that they finish level with, or slightly below, the hinge plate (fig. 5).

Fitting the door

Position the door in its frame by supporting the base with wooden wedges made from offcuts (fig. 6).

With all types of hinge, make an allowance at the base of the door for any proposed floor covering and adjust the gap as necessary by altering the positions of the wedges. Then scribe around the hinges with a marking knife to mark their positions on the door frame.

With the door removed from the frame, mark out the hinge recesses—their length, width and depth—accurately with a marking knife and adjustable try square. Use the same technique to cut the recesses as you used for those on the door.

Replace the door and position it exactly using the wooden wedges, then

1 Before fixing new hinges, stand the door on its edge and support it securely with a vice firmly clamped to either the top or bottom. Accurately position the hinges 215mm from the top of the door and 225mm from the base. Remember to keep the hinges well clear of any joints on the door

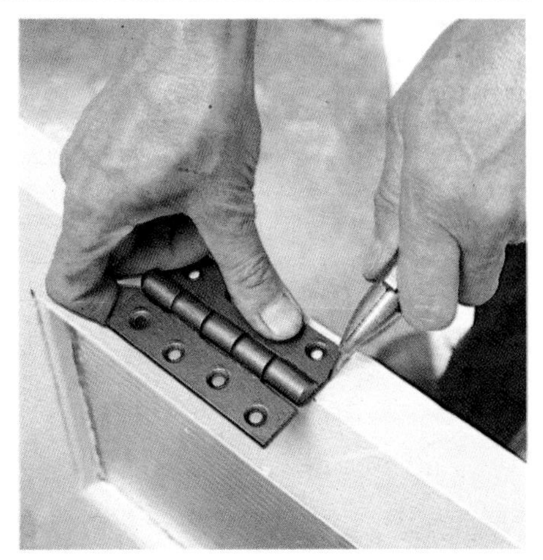

2 You should then use a sharp marking knife and a try square to indicate the position of the hinges on the door edge, starting from the knuckle edge where the hinge will actually swivel. Make marks across all but 6mm of the edge and then carry these marks right on to the face of the door

5 Mark the screw holes slightly off centre towards the inside of the recesses. This allows the hinge to bed securely once it is fixed. Drill the pilot and clearance holes and then insert the screws, with a big screwdriver, so that they are slightly below the level of the hinge plates

6 Actually positioning the door into the frame is not that easy a task. So to make it easier for yourself, fit wooden wedges, made from any spare offcuts, under the base of the door. This then gives you the flexibility you need to lift or lower the door and adjust it to exactly fit the frame as is required

3 Then set a marking gauge to the width of a hinge leaf and scribe this on the door edge between the two other lines previously marked. Then reset your marking gauge to the depth of one hinge leaf and mark this on to the face of the door frame right in between the two knife cuts

4 Use a bevel-edged chisel to cut out the hinge recesses. Make a number of cuts about 5–6mm apart so that you leave an uncut border around the edge. Cut out the chipped-out timber in the hinge recesses with a chisel—held bevel side up—until the recess has become completely clean and smooth

7 Broken or damaged joints can be strengthened by first drilling out the old wedges to a depth of 75mm using a 15mm twist power drill. The holes can than be filled with 15mm thick dowels which have been glued. These should be chamfered at one end and have longitudinal cuts

8 When removing a planted door stop, first use a blunt, wide chisel and a mallet to actually prise the stop away from the door frame. The next stage is to insert the claws of a hammer well into the gap. The door stop can then be slowly worked loose and away from the nails holding it to the frame

9 When rehanging a door which was hinged on the other side, pin pieces of wood block to fill all the gaps and then plane the door smooth

10 If the door is rehinged to swing in a different direction, a new door stop must be added to the door frame so that the door will close properly

tap the hinge leaves into place in the waiting recesses. Finally, mark and pre-drill each screw hole then insert one screw in each hinge so that you can check that the door opens and closes properly.

Sticking doors

If a door sticks and you can find nothing wrong with the hinges, it may be that part of the door frame has swollen. Where the swelling is slight and there is plenty of clearance between door and frame, investigate the possibility of bringing the swollen part away from the frame by either packing or deepening one of the hinge recesses.

Where the swelling is more severe, you have no choice but to plane off the excess and redecorate the door. The planing can be done with the door in situ providing you first wedge the base, to take the weight off the hinges.

Older doors and those particularly exposed to damp may warp or become loose at the joints, causing them to fit badly in their frames. In the case of slight warping, one answer is to make a small adjustment to one of the hinge positions so that you take up the twist. Do this on the frame—not on the door.

However, a more satisfactory solution is to remove the door so that you can cramp and strengthen the frame. Take off all the door furniture—the hinges, knob, lock, key escutcheon—place it flat on a workbench, then cramp the frame square using a sash cramp with a long bar.

Where gaps appear in the joints, scrape out any dust, accumulated grime and old glue with a chisel or knife. Then bring the joints together by cramping across the frame in two or more places. Use softwood offcuts to protect the door from being bruised by the cramps.

Next, drill out the old wedges holding the tenons at each frame joint to a depth of 75mm; use a 15mm twist drill bit. Make up some 85mm lengths of 15mm dowel with longitudinal cuts in them to allow for compressing (fig. 7) and chamfers at one end to give a snug fit.

Liberally smear each piece of dowel with external grade waterproof wood-working adhesive then drive them home into the drill holes with a mallet. Check that the cramps are still holding the frame square by measuring across the diagonals—which should be equal—and leave the adhesive to set. When it is dry, cut off the excess dowel with a tenon saw and finish the edges in the normal way.

Changing direction

It is often useful to change the direction in which a door swings—to make more space in a small room for example—or to hang it from the opposite side of the frame.

Making a door open in the opposite direction involves removing and resiting the door stop, altering the hinge rebates and possibly changing the door furniture. You may or may not have to change the hinges, depending on what type you have. Ordinary butt hinges can simply be used the other way up.

Removing a planted stop: Remove the door from the frame and clear the space around you. Then use a blunt, wide chisel and mallet to cut into the joint between stop and frame and lever the stop away. The stop is bound to be securely fixed and you may have to use considerable force. The job becomes easier when you can insert the claws of a claw hammer and ease the stop away, working upwards from the base of the door (fig. 8).

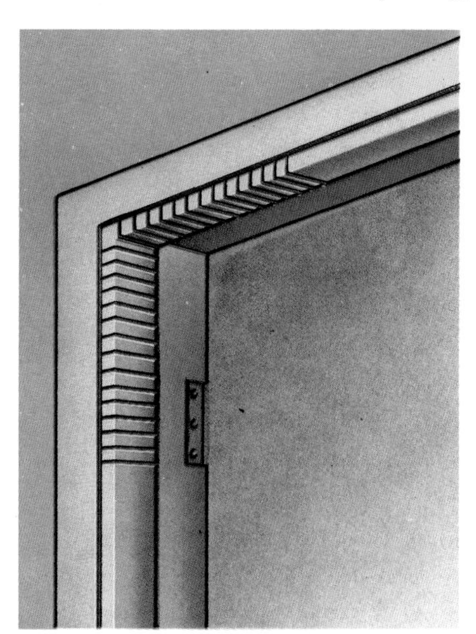

Once the door stop has given way, remove any old glue or chipped wood with a chisel, plane and glasspaper.

Removing a rebated stop: Start by measuring by how much the stop protrudes then mark this amount down and around the outside face of the frame with a marking gauge.

Next, take a tenon saw and make a series of cuts 12–18mm apart in the top corners of the door frame. Remove the waste between these with a wide chisel as you would that in a halving joint. This done, you can insert a rip saw or power saw and cut downwards through the remainder of the door stop. Afterwards, plane the cut timber flush with the rest of the frame and use a chisel to clean up the corners.

Rehanging

When you come to rehang the door, the hinge recesses may well have to be moved. Do this by chiselling them across to the other side of the frame. Then make up wood blocks to fill the now unused parts of the recesses and pin and glue these in place (fig. 9).

Refit the door stops—or make up new planted ones in the case of rebated stops—in accordance with the new door position. Make sure that the stops are firmly pinned and glued (fig. 10).

If the door lock or latch is handed, you must exchange it for a new one and fit it according to the manufacturer's instructions. Alter the position of the striker plate and make good the old recess as you did the hinge recesses. Finally, rehang the door as described above; start by fitting the hinges.

A. Left: If you want to remove a planted stop, first make a series of cuts 12–18mm apart around the corners of the stop on each side of the door. Chop away the waste wood with a mallet and chisel. Then insert a rip saw or power saw and cut away the stop across the top and down both sides of the door

Basic plastering repairs

Above: Plaster is applied to a wall with a laying-on trowel. When you are spreading plaster, keep the trowel's top edge tilted towards you

Plaster can be applied to solid surfaces, such as bare brick, cement rendered brick, building blocks or concrete, and to surfaces to which a key for the plaster—such as metal lathing or wooden slats—is attached. On most solid surfaces two coats of plaster, known as the floating coat or undercoat and the setting or finishing coat, are applied. When lathing is fixed to the surface, an additional first rendering coat is necessary called a pricking up coat.

Plasters

The main constituent of ready-mixed plasters is gypsum, calcium sulphate, which has been partly or wholly dried in a kiln. The extent to which the gypsum has been dried, and the addition of further constituents during manufacture, determine the type and grade of the plaster.

Lightweight, pre-mixed gypsum plasters are the most commonly used nowadays, by both professionals and amateurs. They come in several types, each used for a specific purpose.

Browning is a floating coat (undercoat) plaster used on semi-porous surfaces such as bricks, clinker blocks (breeze blocks) and concrete blocks.

Bonding is a floating coat plaster used on less porous surfaces such as poured concrete, where getting good adhesion is difficult.

Finish plaster is used for the thin surface coat that is applied over the undercoat.

Special plasters are also available for stopping and skimming plasterboard.

If in doubt on which undercoat plaster to use, ask the advice of your builders' merchant.

Always store plaster in a dry place. If any water comes into contact with plaster before it is used, the properties of the plaster will be altered. You should use plaster as soon as possible after buying, as the retarder—the constituent which governs the setting time—grows less effective with time. Plaster is usually date stamped on the bag and, whenever possible, you should use the plaster within six weeks of the date.

Tools for plastering

Most of the tools you need for plastering can be made yourself. They include:

Spot board: This can be a piece of exterior-grade ply about $1m^2$ and is used for holding the mixed plaster. A couple of coats of exterior-grade polyurethane wood lacquer will help to preserve the wood. The board should be placed on a stand—a wooden crate or sturdy stool will do—at a convenient height from the floor. The board should overhang the stand slightly so that the hawk can be held under the edge when transferring the plaster on to it.

Hawk: A board about 300mm × 300mm for carrying plaster from the spot board to the work area and for holding the plaster as you work. Professionals use aluminium hawks with moulded-on handles, but you can get by quite comfortably with a home-made one. Cut your square from an offcut of timber or plywood and screw on a handle about 200mm long cut from 50mm × 50mm timber with the edges rounded off.

Laying-on trowel: Used for applying and spreading the plaster. It has a rectangular steel blade about 280mm × 120mm attached to a wooden handle. Some trowels have curved handles which are easier to grip. A trowel of good quality is important as it is hard to obtain a smooth finish with a worn or inferior blade.

Gauging trowel: Available in a variety of sizes and used for repairing areas too small to be worked with the laying-on trowel. Also useful for mixing plaster.

Below: Tools for plastering include (**A**) home-made scratcher, (**B**) laying-on trowel, (**C**) gauging trowel, (**D**) hawk, and (**E**) skimming float

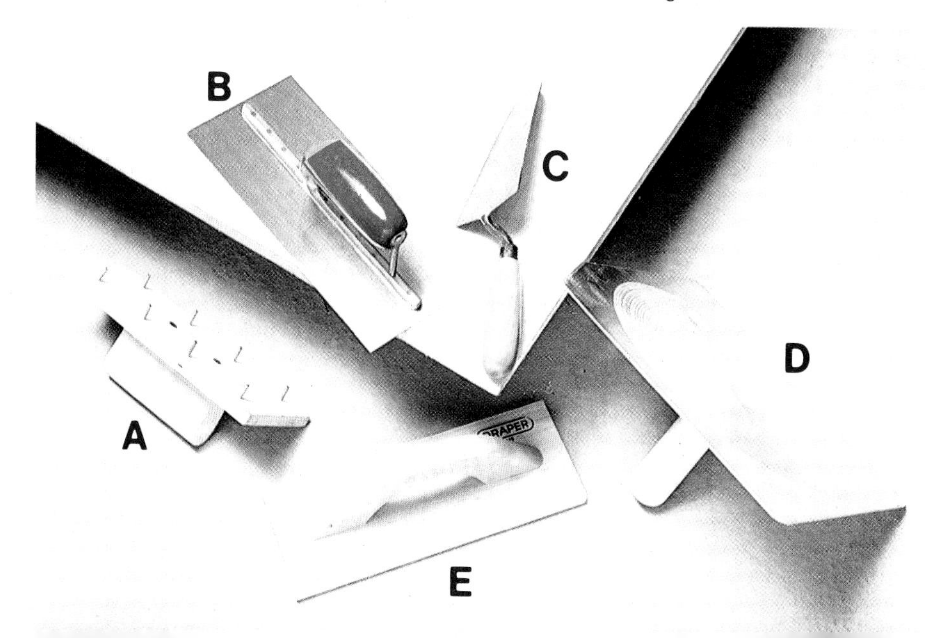

1 Before you begin to plaster a large patch on the wall, use a good hammer and a bolster to cut straight lines round the area. This will help to make the subsequent plastering that much easier to apply and level

2 Scrape some of the mixed plaster from the spot board on to the hawk with the laying-on trowel. Then make sure you carefully trim off any excess plaster. Hold the trowel at an angle over the hawk and take up a small amount of plaster

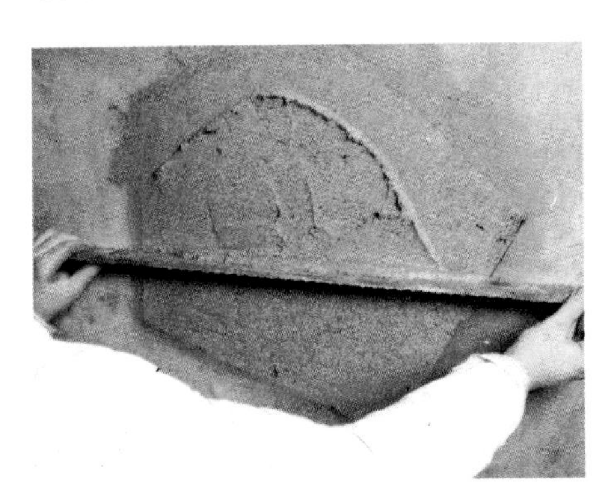

5 Now take a straight-edged length of wood that is a little longer than the patch and draw it upwards in even strokes so that you make sure the plaster is completely flush with all the edges of the patch

6 Next, again use the laying-on trowel to finally trim any excess amounts of plaster. These may have accumulated around the edges of the patch and possibly on to the surrounding area of the main wall

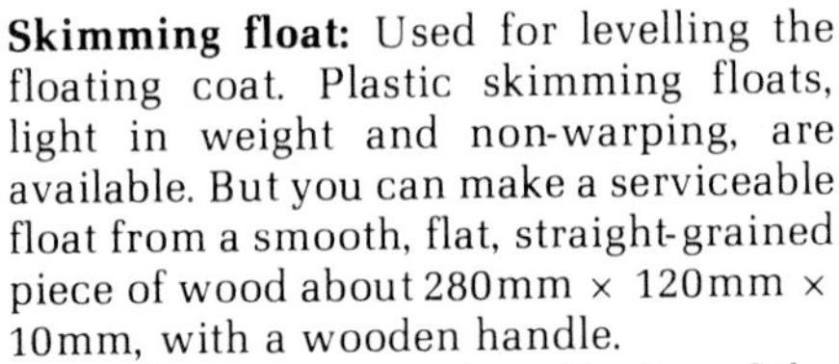

Skimming float: Used for levelling the floating coat. Plastic skimming floats, light in weight and non-warping, are available. But you can make a serviceable float from a smooth, flat, straight-grained piece of wood about 280mm × 120mm × 10mm, with a wooden handle.
Scratcher: To ensure the adhesion of the next coat of plaster, the surface of an undercoat is scratched over. A suitable scratcher can be made by driving a few nails into a piece of wood and then cutting off their heads with a pair of pincers or pliers.

In addition, you will need two buckets —one for mixing the plaster in and one for holding water—a distemper brush and straight-edged rules of various lengths depending on the size and nature of the job. Also required, for chipping off

3 The next step is to hold the trowel against the wall surface, keeping its upper edge tilted backwards at an angle of about 30°. Then smoothly draw it upwards, spreading the plaster evenly over the patch

4 Keep applying further amounts of plaster from the trowel until the patch is completely filled in. The new plaster should then be smooth and level with the surface of the old surrounding plasterwork

7 To make room for the necessary, final coat of plaster, you will need to go over the surface of the undercoat again with the skimming float. This will help to really flatten the plaster and cut it back

8 Using the straightedge again, draw it across the patch once more to check that the undercoat surface is level all over and that it is actually slightly lower than the old plaster on the wall which surrounds it

old plaster, are a hammer and a bolster.

Preparing the surface

Before you start, clear the room of furnishings as much as possible, as the plaster dust will fly everywhere and can scratch polished surfaces. Cover what you cannot remove with old dust sheets. Have ready a suitable receptacle to receive the old plaster.

If the wall behind the plaster is of new brickwork it will need only brushing down and damping with clean water before you start to apply the new plaster.

Concrete wall surfaces require special preparation as their smoothness provides a poor 'key' for plaster and their density gives low suction. Before you plaster, paint the concrete with a PVA adhesive such as Unibond, applied neat.

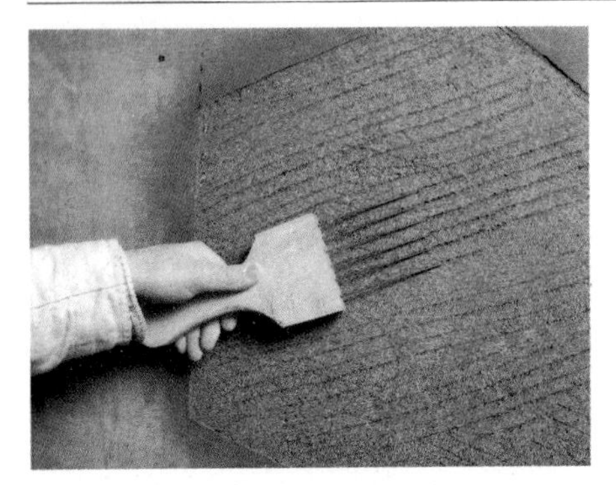

9 Run the scratcher lightly across the undercoat surface to form thick and noticeable ridges. This helps to key the surface of the patch, ensuring that the coat of finishing plaster does adhere properly. Then mix up the necessary finishing plaster and apply it smoothly and accurately to the patch using the laying-on trowel. Use firm pressure all the time and make quick, upward movements with the trowel

10 As the finishing plaster begins to set, dampen it slightly with the distemper brush. However, take great care not to use too much water at this point or it will become too messy. Wet the laying-on trowel and smooth it over the surface in slow, circular movements. Finish off with light, upward strokes and you will begin to see how well the new plaster does blend in with the old surface of the wall

Mixing the floating coat

When mixing plaster of any type use only water that is fit for drinking. Any impurities in water may be detrimental to the properties of plaster.

Pre-mixed lightweight undercoat for plastering small areas should be mixed a third of a bucket at a time. This is sufficient to cover a patch of about 300mm × 300mm to a depth of about 10mm. If the area to be plastered is larger than this, it is better to mix further amounts later. Pour water into the bucket first, then add the plaster. If the plaster is put in first, it clogs when the water is added and sticks to the bottom of the bucket. Add the plaster, while stirring the mixture with a stick, until a stiff but workable mix is obtained.

Whenever you have finished mixing any plaster, pour it on to the spot board. Then clean the bucket out immediately, or any remaining traces of plaster will set and then be extremely difficult to chip off. Traces of old plaster in the bucket will also speed up the setting time.

Applying the floating coat

Mix the floating coat plaster and place it on the spot board. Hold the hawk beneath the overhang of the spot board—if you are right-handed hold the hawk in your left hand and vice versa. Use the laying-on trowel to scrape some plaster on to the hawk them trim away any excess (fig. 2). Tilt the hawk and 'snatch up' a small amount of plaster on to the trowel. Keep the trowel horizontal until the edge connects with the wall, then tilt the outer edge upwards until it is at an angle of about 30° to the wall (fig. 3).

Begin in the centre of the patch and work upwards, exerting slight pressure. Keep the laying-on trowel at an angle, with its upper edge clear of the wall, so that plaster is fed to the wall all the time (fig. 4).

If the patch is 10mm deep or less, fill it until the new plaster is level with the old surrounding plaster. If the patch is more than 10mm deep, do not attempt to fill it in with one coat as this results in the plaster shrinking back from the edges and cracking. Instead, fill the area to half its depth, then use the scratcher to key the plaster with criss-cross lines. Apply a second layer of plaster when the first layer is dry.

Now, take a straight-edged rule a little longer than the patch and, working from the bottom upwards, draw the rule from side to side over the plaster to make it flush with the edges (fig. 5). Fill in any hollows with more plaster and draw the rule over the surface again.

To make room for the finishing coat, the plaster in the floating coat must now be cut back to a depth of 2mm lower than the surrounding plaster. First, flatten and cut back the floating coat with the skimming float (fig. 7). Next, run the scratcher over the surface of the floating coat to provide a key for the finishing coat (fig. 9). Then, go over the plaster with the skimming float again to flatten the burrs left by the scratcher. The scratch marks should remain but their edges should not protrude too far.

Below: If a patch of plaster has to extend round a corner, nail a thin piece of batten to one side of the corner and plaster up to it

Clean the surrounding wall area to remove any adhering plaster and leave the floating coat to set. Ready-mixed plasters take between 1½ and 3 hours to set.

Before mixing your finishing coat, clean all tools and the spot board.

Mixing the finishing coat

Lightweight finishing plasters are applied thinly so they can always be mixed in a bucket. Pour water into the bucket until it is about a quarter full. Slowly pour in the plaster until it appears above the water and stir with a stick. Once the plaster has settled, add more and keep stirring until the paste reaches the consistency of thick cream. Then pour it on to the spot board.

Applying the finishing coat

Lightweight finishing coat plaster dries very quickly. So until you are experienced, mix and apply only enough to cover a small area at a time. Scrape some plaster from the spot board to the hawk and lift a small amount with the laying-on trowel. Use firm pressure to apply the plaster, using upward strokes as much as possible.

When the finishing coat is level with the existing plaster at the edges, draw the straightedge over it until it is flush, filling in any hollows. As the plaster begins to set, dampen it with the distemper brush to keep it workable while you trowel it smooth. Do not use too much water as this can kill the gypsum plaster in the surface and cause crazing. Wet the laying-on trowel and, keeping it as nearly flat as possible, run it over the surface in circular movements, finishing off with light upward strokes (fig. 10). If you do not achieve a smooth, flat surface at the first attempt, try again.

Patching corners

If a patch extends around an external corner, nail a batten with a smooth, straight edge to one side of the corner so that its edge is level with the existing plaster on the other side.

Designing shelf systems

Installing shelving is perhaps the easiest way to provide a home with storage and display space. And wood, which is both attractive and easy to work with, is usually the first choice as a shelving material.

When you are planning your shelving requirements, your judgement must be based on looks, function and location. For example, there is no point in using expensive materials and elaborate supports for shelves in a workshop. Nor

can you plan for a set of shelves to carry heavy books or a TV set unless you know that the wall they are to go on is capable of taking the weight.

Types of shelving

Considering what types of shelving are available is a good way to start planning. There are three main types of shelf system, which for convenience we shall call types A, B and C. Various designs are available within each type to suit all situations. They are available in a range of materials and will fit in with practically all decorative schemes and tastes.

Type A uses softwood battens to support solid wood or manufactured board shelves. Though it is only suitable for three-sided locations—such as an alcove—it is the strongest design providing the span of the shelves is not too long.

Type B standard and bracket shelving consists of vertical, slotted standards which hold brackets for the shelves themselves. Proprietary systems which use this design come with or without the shelving, but are made to suit a variety of different loadings. So if you opt for this system, make absolutely sure that the brackets and standards are strong enough to match your needs (fig. A).

Though some of the proprietary shelves comes with book-ends—and if you make your own shelves you can make the ends too—this type of design can look insubstantial on an open wall unless used solely for display; in most cases it is better suited to a corner, alcove or workshop.

Left: This is a self-contained type of shelf unit which is very flexible. The unit can either be made free standing or can easily be fixed to the wall. It is the ideal design to use for temporary shelving or where no obvious location for the shelving is immediately apparent. Timber standards can be used to support the shelves if the alcove walls seem to be very uneven. Otherwise one of the many different types of upright supports can be used

Location

The simplest way to build sturdy shelves is to make use of the existing house walls as supports, so look at any corner or alcove where space might go to waste.

Apart from this, the type and state of the walls are your most important considerations. With timber-framed walls, it is far better to fix through into the studs themselves, rather than to rely just on the covering, which can take only the lightest of loads.

Where the walls are very uneven or slope noticeably—as in some alcoves—simple batten supports may be impractical, obliging you to opt for type B or C shelving. So always bear in mind such restrictions before you decide on a particular design.

And in some cases, the location may also influence your choice of shelf material.

Function

Having decided on a shelf design and a location, the final form your shelves take depends a great deal on what they are to carry. In consulting the shelf loadings panel which classifies loads as light, medium and heavy, bear in mind the following points:

- Many of the materials listed are too strong to justify their expense when constructing shelves which will take only a light load.
- The span between supports is in some cases determined not by the load but by the length of unsupported material you can use without this sagging under its own weight.
- Laminated or veneered boards may be used for heavy loads with very short spans, but they are not recommended, nor is timber less than 16mm thick overall.
- Plywood and softwood have similar strengths but plywood is less likely to sag or warp.
- Shelves which are built to support heavy loads are best constructed using a solid batten system.

Estimating the width of shelves requires less judgement than the span. Where light and medium loads are concerned, all you have to do is measure the objects you wish to put on them. Remember, though, that it is false economy to buy materials that are wider than you really need; for instance, kitchen jars or spices may need only about 100mm, and paperback books around 150mm–175mm. Also bear in mind that narrower shelves require less elaborate supports than wider ones.

Only where heavy loads are to be carried does width become a critical factor. Here, the longer the length of the brackets or distance between supports, the more downward force is exerted on their fixings. Shelves wider than 300mm are definitely not recommended for heavy loads unless they are supported on three sides by a suitable batten or housing arrangement to provide even support.

Of course, there is no reason why all your shelves should be of the same width. Standard and bracket systems are available with different sizes of brackets, though you must arrange the shelves carefully or they will look out of place; graduate them evenly.

Shelving supports

Though your choice of shelving supports may already have been settled by the type of system, you may just as easily be faced with a bewildering list of alternatives. In this case, you need to consider carefully the relationship between the location, the weight and the look of the shelves.

Simplest of all supports—whether for an alcove, corner or free-standing unit—are fixed battens of metal or wood. The shelves themselves can be either secured or simply rested on the battens; and if you attach lips to the front of the shelves, these will strengthen them and help hide the battens from view.

Slightly more sophisticated are the

Safe shelf loadings

	LIGHT	MEDIUM	HEAVY
LOAD	load less than 0.75kg per 100mm length	load 0.75–3kg per 100mm length	load over 3kg per 100mm length
OBJECTS	spices, ornaments, paperback books	stereo equipment, larger books, foodstuffs	L.P. records, TV sets, heavy books, crockery
MATERIALS	glass: for very light objects man-made boards solid wood 12mm thick plywood from 9mm	thicker boards (possibly reinforced)* solid wood 15mm thick and above or plywood	strong or man-made boards at least 15mm thick (possibly reinforced)* softwood and hardwood 15mm thick and above
SPAN BETWEEN SUPPORTS	up to 610mm for rigid shelves up to 760mm for boards	up to 760mm for thicker wood or plywood—less for boards	maximum of 560mm for man-made boards 15mm thick 710mm for softwood 19mm thick and above 760mm for hardwood 19mm thick and above

*Boards can be reinforced by fixing battens to the underside.

various forms of bracket support, least attractive being the L-shaped steel supports commonly employed in garages and workshops. Where these are used for shelves mounted on a single wall, the entire arrangement can be made more sturdy by fixing battens to the wall and then securing the brackets to these. And in greenhouses and potting sheds, an alternative is to use heavy wooden brackets.

Wire clip arrangements actually hold the shelf from above and have the added virtue of acting as book-ends. And finally, the wide range of standard and clip-in bracket systems can all be used to support unenclosed shelving.

Enclosed shelf supports: Where your shelves are to be enclosed—either by an alcove, timber side sections or both—your choice of support is greater. In the case of a free-standing unit with its own uprights, the most difficult—but also the neatest—method is to cut housing slots in the uprights and slide the shelves into these. More sophisticated still is to use stopped housing joints so that no joins are visible at the front of the unit.

Simpler by far—but nevertheless easy to get wrong—is to screw the shelves to the uprights. Here, you are faced with the problem of screwing into end grain, which is not advisable unless you take additional precautions, such as a filler plug.

With hardwood shelves, drill pilot

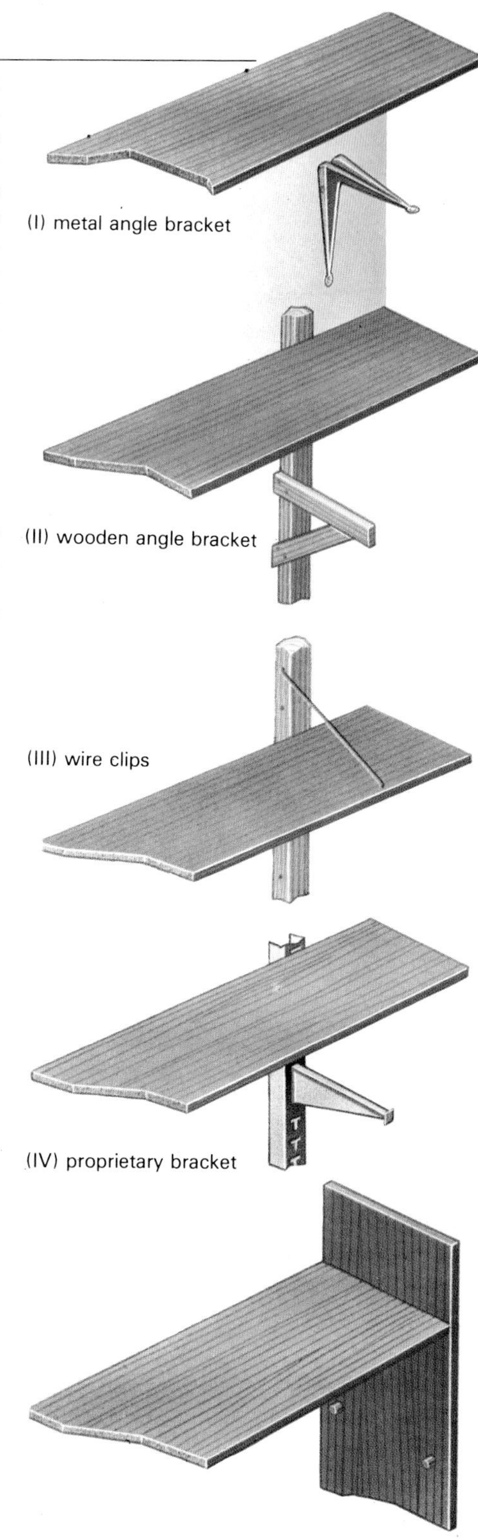

A. Right: This type of shelving consists of brackets to hold the shelves, usually supported by an upright. Shelf supports are also detailed.

holes in the end grain slightly smaller than the threaded portion of the screws and dip the latter in PVA woodworking adhesive before you fix them. In the case of softwood or manufactured board, plug the pilot holes in the end grain with fibre plugs dipped in PVA adhesive. Make the holes themselves slightly on the generous side—both in width and depth—to avoid splitting the wood when the plugs expand.

In both cases, using double-threaded 'Twinfast' screws will make for a much more secure fixing.

Among the many ready-made enclosed shelf supports, the simplest consist of plastic or metal studs (fig. A(v)). These can be screwed directly to solid timber and plywood, or into ready-made hole liners where a soft material such as chipboard is being used. Because the shelves simply rest on the supports, they are best suited to lighter loadings.

Similar, but more substantial, are the many varieties of knock-down fitting more usually employed to joint box frame constructions.

Many self-assembly furniture kits make use of the disguised wire clip as a shelf support. For this, you need timber uprights with holes for the clips and grooved shelf ends—making softwood or hardwood the most obvious choices of shelf material.

Of the more sophisticated proprietary enclosed supports, one of the best uses two metal side brackets attached to the upright-mounted, clip-in brackets on which the shelves rest. This is both strong and attractive providing you cut small pieces out of the shelves themselves so that they fit snugly around the square U-shaped uprights. A similar system has the main support housed flush, vertically into the uprights.

Where you simply wish to use the side walls of an alcove as uprights, fittings are available which screw to the undersides of the shelves and are then jacked outwards against the walls. The pressure of the fittings against the walls holds the shelves in place and is secure enough to support medium loads safely. Because they are not permanent, the shelves can be adjusted at any time and they do not have to be cut exactly to fit.

Hanging shelf supports: Though you can buy ready-made, metal-framed hanging

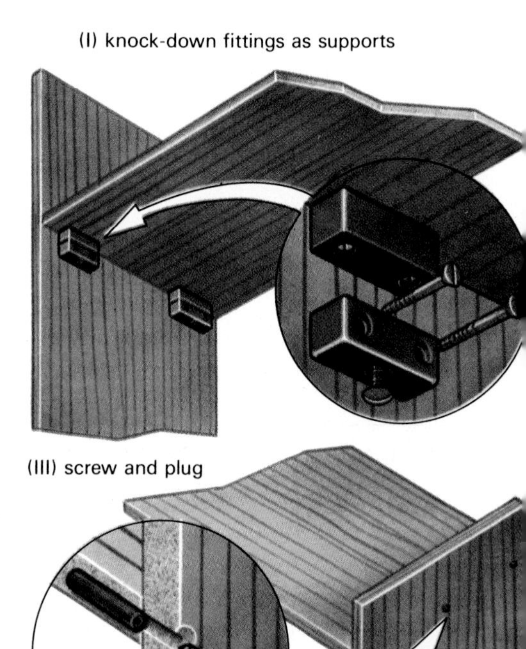

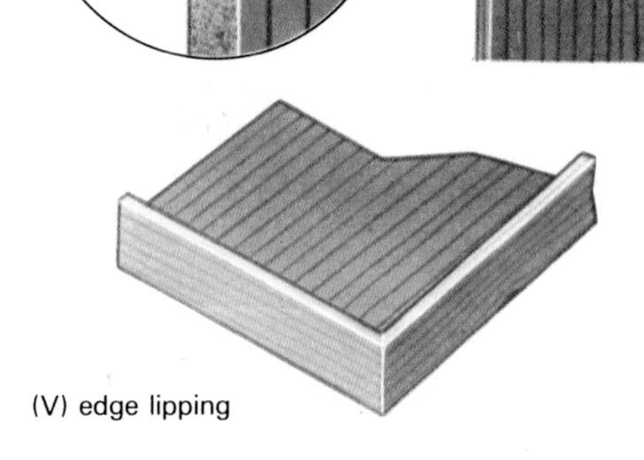

B. Right: KD fittings and screwed joints can be used on free-standing units. Shelves can be hung from a metal frame or knotted cord. Bare shelves may be lipped if necessary

shelf supports, a knotted cord arrangement can often work just as well (fig. B(v)). Use a pre-stretched or non-stretch synthetic fibre cord available from yacht chandlers and figure-of-eight knots—fiddly to adjust but non-slip once they are in position.

Fixing shelves to walls

Often, the greatest difficulty with wall-mounted shelves is that the walls themselves are rarely true or evenly surfaced. This makes it absolutely essential to fix upright standards, battens or other supports in conjunction with a plumbline or spirit level. If you work carefully, even the most uneven wall can be tackled successfully.

In the case of standards, temporarily pin the first one in approximately the right position then hold a plumbline next to it to show the true vertical and mark the other fixing holes in pencil. Use the same procedure on the other standards, having first run a straightedge and spirit level between them to check the horizontal. Then drill and fix the battens into place using wallplugs and screws.

Fix vertical battens and timber uprights in the same way, having first predrilled their fixing holes.

When you are considering how many standards—or how much battening—to use, never be tempted to economize. Standards, though sold singly, are normally used in pairs, but fit more if the shelves are to receive heavy loads. In the alcoves, remember that a back batten in addition to two side battens will lend extra strength to the shelves themselves as well as giving more support.

As you fix uprights in place, check again with the spirit level or straightedge to ensure that these are vertical and not distorted by the surface of the wall. If necessary, use fillets of timber, cardboard or hardboard to pack out depressions or make good the unevenness.

(II) ladder supports

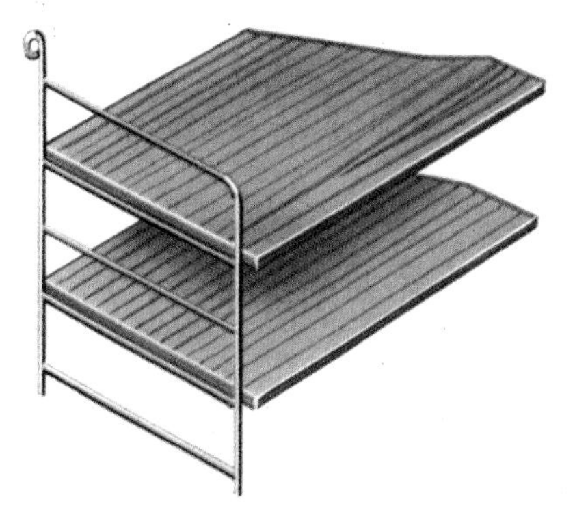

(IV) knotted rope

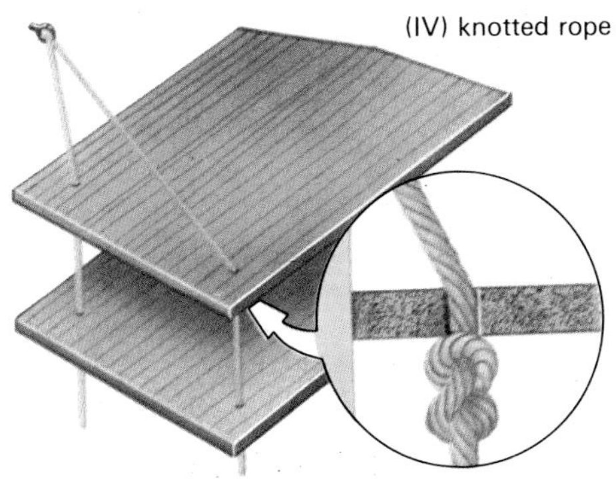

(VI) simple bookend

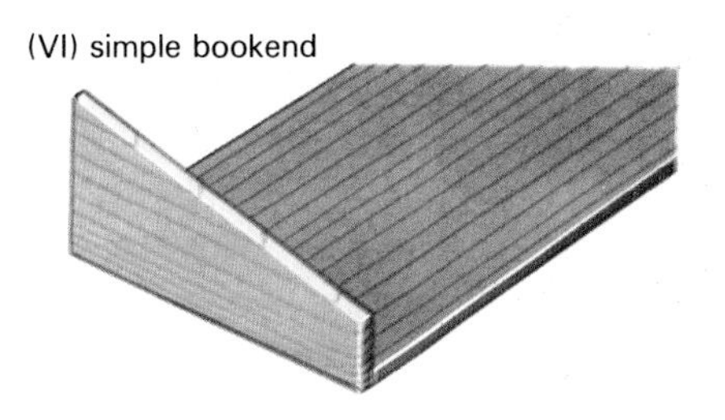

Fixing shelves in alcoves

One of the most space-effective spots to fix shelves is in an alcove—one either side of a chimney breast, for example. This is a space that usually goes to waste but can serve as an ideal place for storage and for showing off ornaments.

When you come to cut the shelves for an alcove, measure and mark out each one individually. Though gaps between the shelves and the back wall are unlikely to show once the former are filled, unsightly gaps at the sides can be avoided by measuring for length at both the front and back of the alcove.

Simple ornament shelves

Storing and displaying a collection of small ornaments and mementoes can be a real problem. Small objects often look lost on standard-size shelves, and the shelves themselves take up more space than is necessary for showing small items.

This simple shelf unit solves these problems by creating what is really almost a flat pictorial display within a frame.

You can make it really cheaply from softwood battening, stained or painted to your taste. Or, for a richer look, use hardwood such as utile which is readily obtained in the sizes needed.

Make up the main frame from 25mm square stock, using glued and screwed joints. Chipboard screws give a better fixing into end grain. The only joint needed here is the central dross halving joint, which is easy to cut if you use a tenon saw and chisel.

Divide the frame into whatever divisions to suit your collection. The dividing frames again use cross halving joints and have butt joints at their ends which are secured tightly with the use of pins and glue.

When the frame is complete, sand the entire surface smooth, and finish it as you prefer. Fit suitable brackets to the top frame and screw these to the wall to support the frame.

Boxing-in

In ideal circumstances, all pipework in the house should be run out of sight—beneath the floorboards or else hidden behind walls or fitted furniture. But often, when a new central heating system has been fitted, or when new water pipes have been added, these and perhaps gas pipes as well are left exposed. This is especially likely where there are solid floors, or where vertical runs cannot be hidden inside fitted furniture such as cupboards and wardrobes.

Preliminary considerations

If you do have some exposed pipework to deal with, it is unlikely that you will be able to re-route it without going to considerable trouble and expense. The ideal solution would be to incorporate it in fitted furniture of some kind—perhaps by building a fitted wardrobe or cupboard around it. In some cases, however, sheer lack of space will make this impossible and boxing-in is the only solution.

In most cases—especially if the pipes run in a straight line, close to the wall—boxing-in is a cheap and simple operation. But even if the pipework is rather more awkward, a simple panelled timber framework will usually do the job quite adequately. All that you have to do is tailor the boxwork to your particular circumstances, though this means giving a great deal of preliminary thought to the design of the boxwork, and to the materials and finishes that you select.

Planning the work

You are unlikely to run into any insurmountable technical problems with boxing-in; the actual work involved is fairly simple. But it is the amount of time that you spend planning the work that will make the difference between an ordinary job and a significant improvement to your home.

Start by assessing the scale of the work. If you are dealing with a single pipe, then a simple solid boxwork construction will suffice—but you must still consider whether or not you have to provide access to valves or stop taps.

One possible solution if you are covering a low, horizontal pipe is to cover the boxwork with the same material as the flooring—either by extending the carpet, or by covering it with tiles.

Further planning is necessary if you have to build a larger structure—one that covers more than one pipe, or which conceals a meter or other plumbing units. For anything other than fairly small-bore pipes running close to a wall, a framed structure will be necessary.

A typical example would be an older bathroom in which the walls are festooned with pipes that you would like to conceal. Instead of boxing-in just the pipes, it might be possible to make a bigger boxing unit that would also provide cupboard space beneath an inset basin.

Solid boxwork

In many cases, where you have a single run of pipework, this will be the most convenient technique of boxing-in. The material that you choose for the construction should be solid enough to be jointed—examples are 12mm solid timber, plywood and chipboard. A simple butt joint is usually sufficient, with the top piece resting on the side piece for strength.

As an example of the technique, if you wish to box-in a low, horizontal pipe running along a wall, start by carefully measuring the total length of the boxwork required. The height of the boxwork will obviously depend upon the height of the pipe, and the width upon the diameter of the pipe combined with the distance from the wall along which it runs. But take care if you are dealing with hot-water pipes; in this case you should allow more room and insulate the pipes first—to avoid wasting heat, and to prevent the boxwork from shrinking and splitting, particularly if you are using solid timber.

Secure the boxwork with screws to a length of 12mm square batten that is itself screwed to the wall; in most cases, this will be sufficient support, but if you wish to make the fitting more secure, you can screw a similar batten to the floor as well—making sure that you do not drill or screw into pipes or wires running beneath the floorboards.

Drill screw holes in the boxing and battens, and countersink the holes so that the screw heads will sit flush with the surface. Finish by assembling the boxing, remembering to fit the top piece above the side piece so that the finished unit has sufficient structural strength.

Three-sided enclosures: To box-in exposed pipes, start by fitting battens to the wall on each side of the pipe and then screw projecting timbers to each of them; the timbers should project from the wall a few millimetres more than the pipe (although more space should be left for hot pipes—see above). Fit a third panel between the two timbers to conceal the pipe, securing it as detailed above.

Below: The simplest form of boxwork is solid boxwork concealing a pipe run in a corner. The materials and techniques used are very straightforward

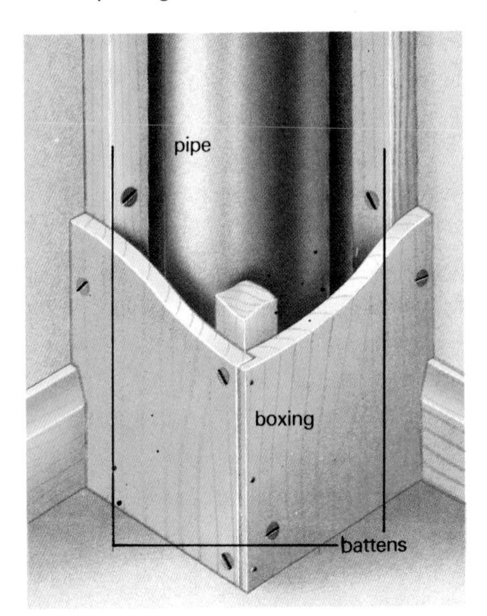

Framework boxing

You should use this method when covering meter units, sinks and pipes that run more than a few millimetres away from the wall, and also when extra strength is required—either when the boxwork is to double as a shelf, or when it is possible that children will climb up on to the structure.

In most cases you should make the frame from 25mm square softwood, but if any heavy weights have to be supported on the finished structure, use sturdier timber such as 50mm × 25mm softwood. The members at the back of the frame are screwed directly to the wall, so there is no need to screw separate battens to the wall first.

Building the frame

The actual building of the frame is not difficult—the corners are butt-joined and secured with screws, oval nails or corrugated fasteners—so no great carpentry skills are required. However, as mentioned above, you have to take care to ensure that the positioning of the rails and side members is such that you have adequate access to the plumbing.

First, measure the overall dimensions of the area to be covered, and then make an accurate plan and cutting list.

You can build the framework over tiles or linoleum, but carpets will probably have to be cut back. When marking up the position, make quite certain that you have allowed adequate clearance all round the pipework to be covered, particularly if any hot pipes are involved.

Start the construction by fixing the back batten to the wall. You may have to make this in sections, fitted between obstructions, but in either case you

1 When boxing-in, measure up and compile a cutting list. Then fit the back batten first. Use a spirit level to make sure it is straight

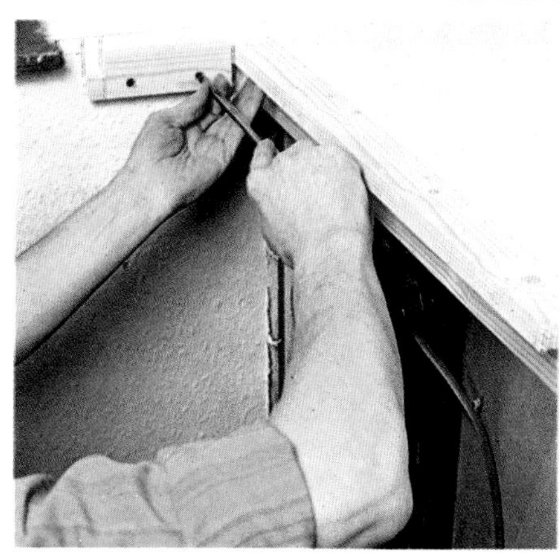

2 When you have to build a frame in a corner, fit the upper end support next— then you should add the two end supports and the bottom batten

3 Make sure you check the depth of the unit by offering up the toe board and then carefully marking the position of the floor noggin on the floor

4 Firmly nail or screw down the floor noggin using the toe board as a guide. Solid floors must first be drilled and plugged to take woodscrews

should use a spirit level to ensure that the battening is level and correctly aligned.

Next make up the front frame. This consists of a member running parallel with the back batten, joined by a series of uprights. If the floor is uneven, you may need to scribe the bottom batten to fit, so do this first. Then cut the top batten to fit and try it in position level with the bottom and the back battens. Wedge or pin the top batten temporarily in place and then check the clearance between it and the bottom batten; if the floor is uneven, the clearance may vary.

To complete the front frame, you will need vertical supports; the spacing between these will depend on the cladding material and the weight to be supported, but around 600mm is a good average. Make sure that none of the intended positions will make access to stop valves difficult, and remember that any panelling joints must coincide with the positions of the battening. Mark the support positions on the battens and check the clearance at these points to ascertain the length needed for each support batten.

Remove the battens and cut the supports to length. Make up the complete front frame using butt joints held with PVA woodworking adhesive and dowels, screws, nails or corrugated fasteners. When complete, fix the front frame in place and mark in the positions for the top supports. As with the vertical supports, their position will be governed by the weight to be supported and the access that will be required. Check the lengths of the supports needed and cut them to size. You can join them to the front frame using any of the methods described above, and at the back using dowels, corrugated fasteners or skew nails. Alternatively, you can remove the back batten entirely and nail or screw the supports from behind. Fix the completed frame to the walls.

If you want to panel your bath, build a framework as described above and fit it beneath the rim; the framework should be screwed to the floor and walls and then panelled as described below. In this case, however, you must provide access to the waste trap, either by means of a removable panel, or by designing the panelling so that it may be lifted off as a whole.

Similarly, you can box-in a sink, WC cistern or other units to include cupboards and shelves so that they become useful pieces of fitted furniture in their own right.

Fitting the panelling

Thin plywood and hardboard both make ideal panelling materials, but although hardboard is a very cheap material, it may be more difficult to finish satisfactorily. To avoid any problems with warping, you should condition the wood in the same room in which it is to be used.

Plywood is stronger and has the advantage that it can be sanded and lacquered to give an attractive, natural finish. 4mm plywood will be adequate for most purposes, but where heavy weights are to be supported, use a thicker material or add extra framing. In bathrooms, use resin-bonded marine ply.

Cut the panels slightly oversize and plane or sand the protruding edges once they have been fitted to the frame. Where panelling has to fit against a wall, this will not be possible, and you must scribe the board to fit accurately.

Fix the panelling to the framework with hardboard pins or small panel pins, set at close intervals. Before hammering make sure that the relevant section of the frame is braced against something solid. Each pin should be buried slightly with a nail punch and then covered over with a dab of wood filler which can then be sanded smooth with glasspaper.

Where you will need to remove panels in order to gain access to the pipework or stop valves, fix the panels with screws and cup washers; the latter help to spread the load of the screws on the thin panelling material as well as improving the overall appearance.

Providing access

If you are boxing-in a meter that has to be inspected regularly, then obviously a door hatch will have to be included in the boxing structure. The simplest method of making one is to cut the opening out of the front of the panelling using a jig saw. Do this before the panel is pinned to the frame, then simply fit hinges and a catch and handle.

If your completed boxwork structure is to take the form of a cupboard, do not forget that proprietary louvred or parallel doors are available in standard sizes, and these can make your boxwork look far more attractive.

5 Offer up the top front frame member and mark up any necessary joints to be made between the end supports and vertical frame members

6 Next, nail the toe board to the vertical support, then hold the support firmly in position while you nail it tightly to the floor noggin

7 Nail the top front frame member in position and offer up the top panel to check whether the corners of the room are completely square and true

8 Fix the top panel to the front and rear upper battens by screwing them from underneath, then fit the side panels to the vertical supports

Finishing boxwork

The main consideration when finishing boxwork is how to lessen the visual impact of what is essentially an intrusion on a smooth wall.

You can simply paint the boxwork, perhaps in the same color as the surroundings; if it is a fairly small construction, this will not draw too much attention to it. You may, however, have difficulty obtaining a really good paint finish on materials such as chipboard. If necessary, sand and fill the panel with a one-part fine filler paste. Alternatively, on a wallpapered wall it may be possible to hide the boxwork with matching paper.

Making window frames

Mass-produced joinery units have revolutionized the window frame business. Almost every new house built today makes use of off-the-shelf windows.

But nowadays, as the woodwork of the properties of a generation or more ago begins to fall into disrepair, the carpenter is back in demand.

To begin with it is most important to produce a rough working drawing. You will also need a list of the materials required, but this necessarily follows from the drawings.

Making a sash window

A double-hung sash window consists of a pair of pulley stiles, a head and a sill. The boxes at each side, inside which the sash weights are suspended, are formed with linings.

Making up the frame

The methods of making the joints in a sash window frame vary. The stiles are usually housed into the head and sill, while both stiles and head may be tongued to mate with grooves in the linings. The sill and head are cut wider than the frame, the protruding parts being called *horns*. The upper pair are cut off when the assembly is complete, but those on the sill are set into the brickwork at each side of the window opening when the frame is installed. The sashes themselves are of wedged mortise and tenon construction—the stiles mortised and the rails tenoned into them.

Left: A well-made sliding sash window provides excellent noise and heat insulation and, if looked after, should last for several lifetimes

First cut the head and sill to the required length—approximately 150mm wider than the actual window opening. Set them side by side on the workbench, and mark them up together with the positions of the housings for the stiles.

Next, cut the two pulley stiles to length. These must be the overall height of the frame, less the thickness of the head and sill, plus the depths of the housings into which they fit. Lay the two stiles side by side, and mark with dotted lines the areas that will fit into the housings. Then mark the four pulley positions on the stiles, and also the outline of the pocket pieces.

The slots for the pulleys are usually positioned 75mm to 100mm down from the tops of the stiles; use the actual pulleys that you will be fitting to mark out the slots.

Carefully cut out the slots with a mallet and chisel, after first drilling out the bulk of the waste wood. You can then screw the pulleys into place.

The pocket pieces can be positioned at one edge of the stile, as shown in fig. 8, or cut out from the centre.

To cut them, first drill a hole through the centre groove of the stile at one end of the pocket piece position, thread in a coping saw blade, and use the saw to cut down the groove to the other end of the piece. Now use a fine-toothed tenon saw to make the three subsequent cuts, and then chisel away the pocket piece.

Next you must cut the housings in the head and sill. Cut the housing in the head right across the width, but stop the cut in the sill.

Assembling the frame: Place the sill face up on the workbench, then glue, wedge and skew nail the stiles into place. Next glue and nail the head on to the top of the stiles, driving the nails down through the head into the ends of the stiles. Afterwards lay the frame flat on the bench, check for squareness by measuring the diagonals, then cramp it up while the adhesive sets.

Making the sashes: Making up the sashes is a little more complicated. Remember that the mortises are cut in the vertical members and the tenons on the horizontal ones. Cut the various stiles and vertical glazing bars in pairs and lay them alongside one another ready for marking out. Similarly cut the top, bottom and meeting rails, plus the appropriate number of cross glazing bars and line them all up as shown.

Now the various mortise and tenon joints can be made. Glazing bars can be joined together either with mortise and tenon joints or halving joints.

Cut the long dimensions of all the mortises slightly wider than those of their corresponding tenons so that wedges can then be driven into each joint during assembly.

The actual assembly of the sash proceeds as follows. First you must assemble the centre section of the cross bar and two vertical bars. Then cramp the bottom (or top) rail in a bench vice and drop the tenons on the H-shaped bar assembly into the mortises in the rail and place the meeting rail in position. Next, fit the outer sections of the cross bar into the mortises in the centre of the stiles, and join this assembly to the main assembly in the vice.

It is advisable to perform this operation 'dry', when you are satisfied with the fit and size of the assembly, lay it flat on the bench, cramp it up and test it for squareness. Then smother small hardwood wedges with adhesive and tap them into the overwide mortises.

Meanwhile, lay the frame flat on the bench with the outside face uppermost, so that the outside linings can be pinned in place to the edge of the head and the stiles. These are wider than the inside linings and provide a 'bead' against which the top sash bears. Next, add squaring strips to hold the frame square during installation. Then turn the frame over and pin the inside linings into place. Finally, add plywood strips to each side to enclose the weight compartments.

Installing the frame: With the sashes and frames completed, you can now install the new frame in the opening. Start by removing the old frame.

1 Make an accurate, full-sized drawing of the frame and sashes, with clear details of each joint, using the actual proprietary mouldings as guides

2 Use a sliding bevel to mark out the sloping side of the wedged mortise after you have clearly marked out the width of the mortise

5 The top rail is joined to the vertical glazing bar with a mortise and tenon joint. Also join the cross glazing bars with a mortise and tenon joint

6 The bottom sash stiles are joined to the bottom rail with a haunched mortise and tenon; the sashes' meeting rails are jointed to the stiles

The construction of a sash frame means that any fixings to masonry walls are usually made through the head and sill of the frame; if made through the pulley stiles they would interfere with the movement of the weights and would also tend to pull the frame out of square. Try to duplicate the type, size and number of fixings found on the old window. In the case of newer windows the fixings will be ordinary galvanized woodscrews.

Drill holes for the fixings in the frame while it is still on the bench, then counterbore each hole to a depth of about

3 Having cut the pulley stiles to size, place the cord pulleys in their correct positions and firmly scribe round them prior to cutting

4 Insert the pulley stiles into the wedged housing and hammer wedges into each housing. Then place head over the pulley stiles and nail securely

7 Assemble the construction to make sure it fits and glue and cramp the completed sashes. Pin a batten across the corners. Glue and insert the wedges

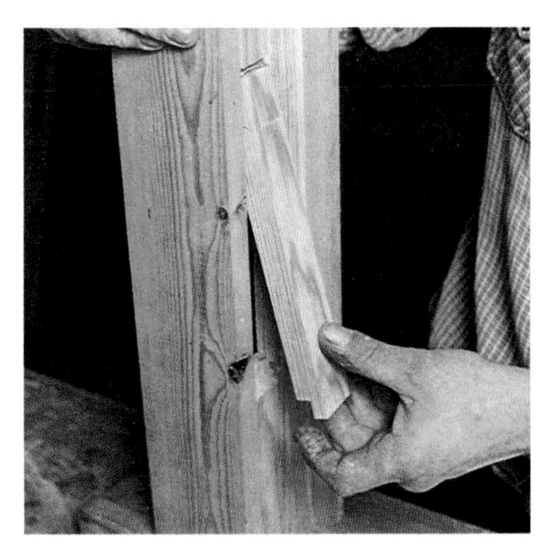

8 Pin the pocket pieces, your only access to the weights and cords, in place and then screw the pulleys into the pulley stiles using the brass screws

10mm so that the screw heads will be hidden later. Afterwards offer the frame up to the opening, and use rough timber wedges to hold it in place while you mark through the fixing holes to the masonry behind with a long nail.

Now remove the frame, switch to a masonry bit, and drill holes at the marked points on the wall to take the wall plugs or expansion anchors. Having inserted the plugs, mark their positions with chalked lines then reposition the frame.

Make one final check for squareness,

9 Install the parting slip in the weight box with its tip through the head and secure it firmly in place with a small wooden wedge

10 Hold the top sash in the frame and put some parting bead into its rebate to mark where it meets the meeting rail. Then trim the meeting rail

wedging the frame as necessary, then screw it securely to the wall. Fill the bolt or screw heads with wooden plugs or filler, make good the outside of the opening with mortar, and pipe a bead of non-hardening mastic all round the frame to seal the small gap between it and the masonry.

With the frame installed, the sashes are ready to be fitted into place. If you are using the sash weights from the old window make sure that the lighter pair are fitted to the bottom sash and the heavier pair to the top one. Next, glaze the window.

Making a casement window

Casement windows are a great deal easier to construct than sliding sash windows. Mortises are cut in the horizontal members of the window frame—head and sill—and tenons are cut on the vertical members—jambs and mullions. For the casement sashes, however, the order is reversed; the stiles and bars are mortised, while the horizontal members—rails and cross bars—are tenoned into them.

The first stage in constructing a casement window is the same as for a sash window. Cut the head and sill to the required lengths, and set these out side by side for marking out. Similarly, cut the jambs and set them out in the same way. As before, cut the head and sill wider than the actual window opening to create horns; those at the head can be cut off when the frame is installed.

Next, cut the various mortises and tenons. And, where mullions or a transom are involved, extra joints—for example, mortises in the jambs to take the tenoned ends of the transoms—will have to be cut. Note also that as with the glazing bars on a sash, the transom is usually cut into sections prior to assembly, while the mullion or mullions run unbroken from the head of the window to the sill.

Assembling the frame

With all the components cut and the joints prepared, assemble them in a dry run on the bench. The basic principle is the same as for the sash frames. First set the sill on the bench, glue the jambs into position, and finally add the head. In a frame with a mullion or mullions but no

11 Tie the top sash to the head and spring the parting beads into the pulley stiles' rebates. Pin sash cords to the bottom sash and put in frame rear

12 Pin the loose staff beads around the frame with 30mm ovals, mitring them to produce a neat joint. Finally, glaze and decorate the window.

transom, you must add the mullions at the same time as the jambs. Similarly, where a transom is involved, you must assemble the jambs, mullion(s) and transom flat on the bench, then offer up this complete sub-assembly to the mortises in the sill, and finish by adding the head as with the sash window.

With the frame assembly complete, lay it flat on the bench, cramp it up and check it for squareness. Secure the mortises with small hardwood wedges smeared with adhesive. Then, once this has set, trim the wedges flush with the frame.

Cut and mark up the components for the casements as before. But remember that, in this case, you must cut tenons on all the horizontal members and mortises on all the vertical ones. Where glazing bars are involved, the assembly follows exactly the same sequence as for the top and bottom sashes of a sash window. On a simple casement or top light which will hold only one pane of glass, you must assemble the four components in the same order as the casement frame. The joints are then similarly glued and wedged after the frame has been finally fitted together and you have checked for square.

Installation: When the casement joints are set, clean them up all round and test the fit of the assembly within the frame. There should be a 3mm clearance all round.

Finally, hang the casements in place in the frame using galvanized hinges. Then add the rest of the ironmongery attached to the window. Screw all of the catches, handles, stays and locks into place and check that they are operating correctly.

The installation of the new frame is a relatively straightforward matter. As with the sash window frame, the horns are left on the sill, to be set into the brickwork at either side of the window opening. In this case, however, the frame is usually fixed within the opening by bolts or screws driven through the frame sides, rather than through the head and sill. To finish off, make good, weather-proof with non-setting mastic, add the interior window sill and glaze the window. Once the window is firmly in place make sure that it closes correctly and that the catches and handles all work perfectly.

Converting attics and lofts

With the high cost of housing nowadays, most people can no longer afford the luxury of a rambling attic filled with discarded bits and pieces that just 'might come in useful one day'. Space under the roof can generally be put to more practical uses.

Most homes with a sloping roof, unless it is of very shallow pitch, have an area which can be utilized in some way. For example, a restricted space or one in which people cannot stand up can still be converted into a well-designed storage unit. Larger areas offer more scope for perhaps a small study or TV viewing room, a bedroom, bathroom or a playroom. Very extensive attics might even be turned into guest suites or bedsitters.

If your attic is so small that its scope

for development is restricted just to storage space, you will still need to plan it carefully. First of all think about what you want to store there and the possible methods of doing so—shelves, cupboards, nets slung from the top of the roof or even a combination of these. Consider, too, how often you will need access to the stored items. For example, if you want to save money and bulk-buy things like canned foods, detergents and toilet rolls, you need to get at them fairly frequently. But if the area is simply to be a home for more seasonal items like garden furniture, skis or Christmas nick-nacks, quick and easy access is not so important.

Try to use easily available space. If the roof slopes down to the floor, use that side for storing awkwardly shaped objects and put shelves on the straight walls. Avoid putting too much weight on any one joist, however, as they are not designed to carry heavy loads individually.

It is a good idea to cover the joists with some form of solid flooring to avoid the risk of accidentally stepping off a joist and through the plaster ceiling of the room below. There is no need to go to the expense of laying a proper floor—sheets of chipboard which are laid side by side across the joists will be sufficient, and will also stop you damaging or dirtying any insulation there is between the joists.

If your attic is entered via a trap door you will need a ladder to reach it. An outdoor ladder brought inside when required will do if you use the attic only occasionally, but for regular use it is better to fit a folding loft ladder which is stored inside the trap door and can easily be pulled down.

The light switch is best sited on the floor below to avoid you having to stumble about in the dark looking for the switch or trap door. A multi-directional spotlamp or series of spots on a track will enable you to see what is stored all over the area.

Be sure to check that the whole area is watertight. Look at the roof to see if there are chinks of sky visible and replace any damaged tiles or fit waterproofing inside. Nail heavy-duty polythene sheets to the rafters, taking care to overlap them in such a way that they neither let rain through nor trap it. Or, for a more durable solution, put up foil-backed plasterboard which also acts as good insulation and can be painted inside to improve the appearance of the area. Choose light, bright coloured paint.

Opening up a room

It is often very difficult when crawling

Left: A very large roof space which has been given a very cosy atmosphere. Note how the original roof timbers have been cleverly blended into the design

about in a dark, confined attic to imagine how it could be opened up to provide a real room. To a large extent, what you can do depends on the planning and building laws which exist in your country or area. Since these regulations can affect markedly what you are ultimately allowed to end up with in the way of a loft conversion, it makes sense to

Below: Quite a unique way of making use of roof space is to convert it into a small kitchen. This is by no means as impossible as it might first seem. A lot of thought, however, should be given to the amount of light and headroom available and to installing all the necessary services, particularly electricity and running water, before you start the conversion work

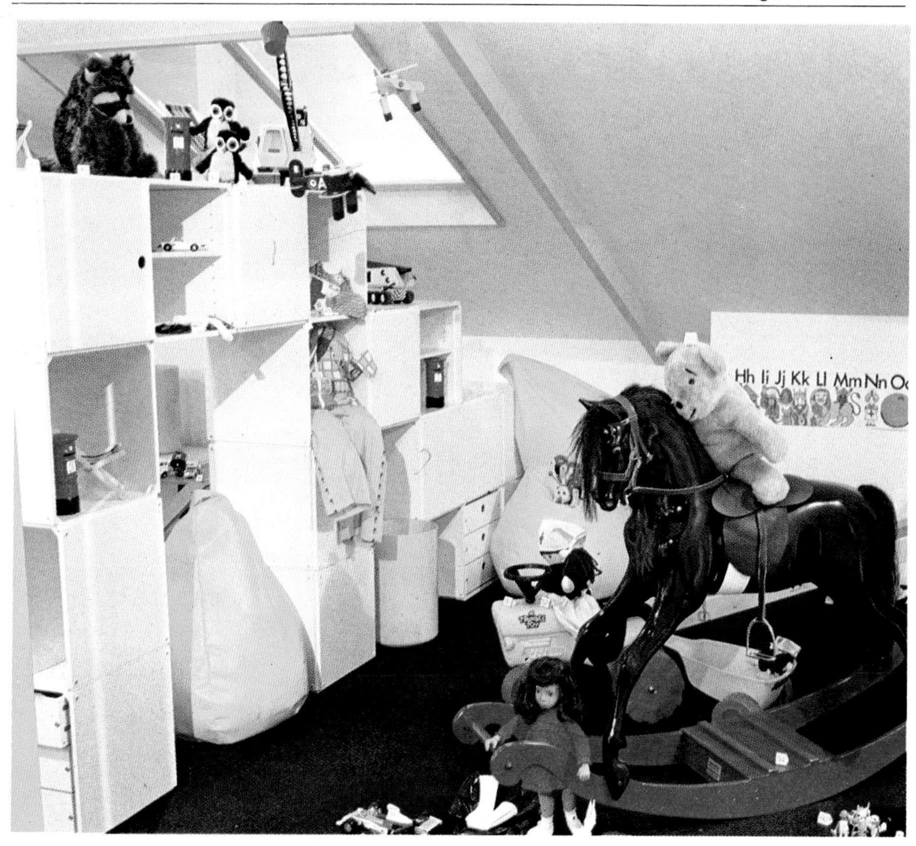

Above: Totally different, a small roof space with a simple roof light transformed into a child's playroom. Storage follows the roof slope to save space

check out your initial ideas with your local authority before getting too involved with the details.

Fire-proofing is vital since you are opening up a whole new area and some authorities may insist that not only is the new structure properly fire-proofed but that you fit self-closing hinges to every door in the house and also cover all the upstairs floors with hardboard.

While it is possible to do some alterations yourself, a major conversion generally requires professional advice and it is a good idea to consult an architect or specialist conversion firm before starting anything. They will draw up plans of the area and show you what can be done. Be clear when studying the plans about such things as usable floor area and the amount of natural light the room will get, and make adjustments as necessary. You are likely to end up with an irregularly shaped room, perhaps with one or even two sloping walls, but these are part of an attic room's charm and can be used to good decorative advantage.

While increasing the size of a house also increases its value (both rateable and saleable) it is important to make sure the extension harmonizes with the rest of the house. Try to choose window frames which match those you have already; and if you are building up the wall, use bricks or wall cladding which match those in the rest of the structure. Inside your home, complete harmony is not so essential. After all, if you are opening up a whole new floor it means you can adopt for it a whole new style.

If the attic is already reached by stairs there will be no problem with access. But if you have previously used a ladder and trap door you will need to install a staircase. And here you will need to check with your local authority for any regulations regarding type and size of staircase.

In an older house it may be possible to fit an original or specially made spiral staircase which does not look out of place and has the advantage of blocking out very little light. But even this will take up more space then you imagine and you must make sure there is a fair-sized landing to site it on. Otherwise you can opt for a conventional closed-tread set of stairs and look for banisters to match in a secondhand or reproduction furniture retailers.

Windows are important in an attic conversion and can turn a previously dark hole into a habitable room. On the front of the house, try to match the size and scale of existing windows. But at the back—providing they are not totally alien to the design of the other windows—you might consider installing large panes to let in as much light as possible and also maximize the extent of any view you have gained.

If money is not a main consideration

Below: A teenager's room converted from an average-sized roof space. The effectiveness of the finished room belies its simplicity and low cost

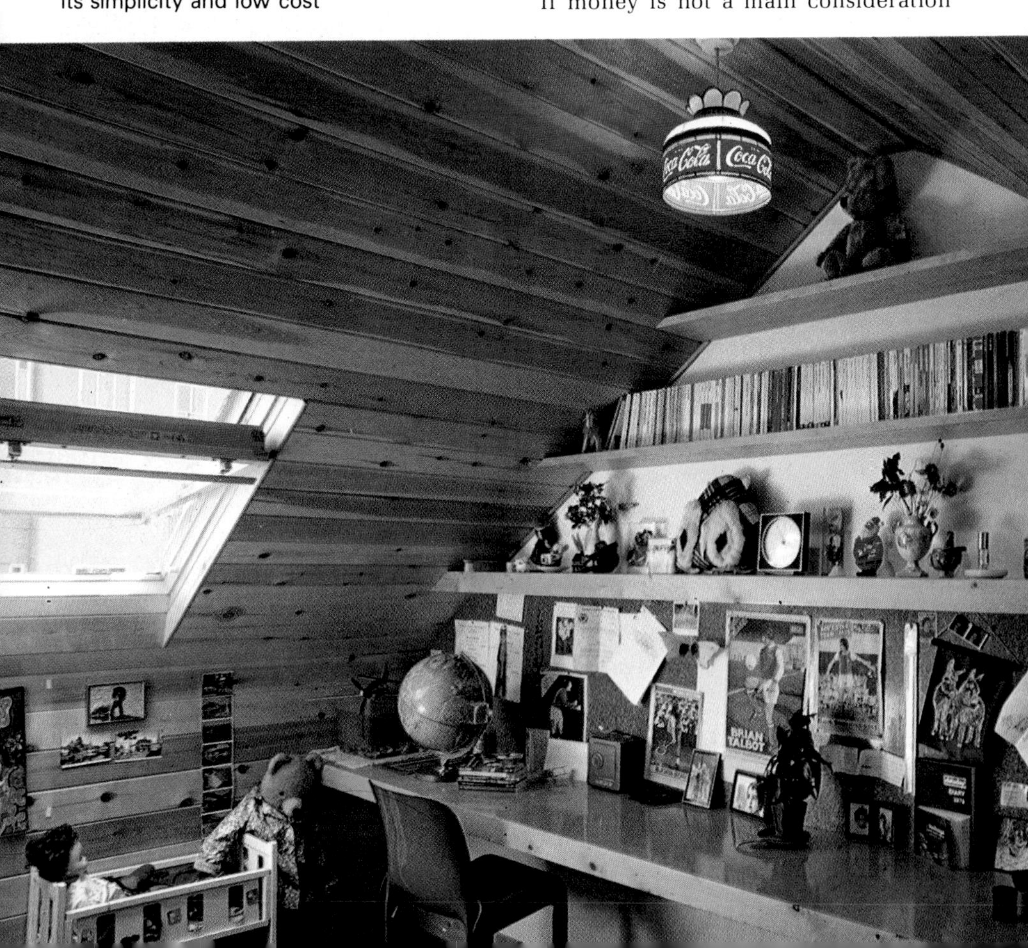

and if space allows, a most attractive conversion can be made by fitting an inverted dormer window which is set back into the roof—instead of sticking out—with a small area outside. While this diminishes the space available inside the room, it does provide a small balcony for sunbathing in the summer or just giving a more attractive view. An inverted dormer would be especially good for a bedsitter or a teenager's room, especially if it overlooks the garden or some other attractive view. But if you do intend to install an inverted dormer, make sure that it is surrounded by a well-constructed wall or fence, particularly if young children are going to use the room. The balcony of an inverted dormer also makes an ideal spot for showing off plants and flowers.

Colour and design

Before choosing the decorative scheme for your new area, see how the light falls in the room at different times of day, and see how it can best be used in terms of shape. This gives you a better idea of how much light or shade is needed, how much pattern the room can take and which features need highlighting by paint or paper.

If the room has unusual angles and slopes, avoid large patterns—as well as being difficult to match when hanging, these detract from the charm of the shape and tend to overwhelm the room. Go instead for small prints or plain colours, perhaps picking out features such as beams or small areas in natural or contrasting shades.

If you prefer to retain an authentic attic feel, you might consider installing wood panelling in the form of tongued-and-grooved boarding. Hang the boards horizontally to increase the apparent size of the room, or vertically to increase its height.

For a warm, intimate feel—in a study or bedroom for instance—choose warm, dark shades of paint or wall-covering. But for rooms used in the daytime go for light colours and minimum pattern.

Where walls are uneven in texture, use a disguising covering such as hessian, anaglypta (painted in the colour of your choice) or flock. For a lighter feel use lining paper with emulsion paint on top.

Flooring should meet the needs of the room. Thick carpeting will minimize the amount of noise transmitted to the rest of the house, but sheet vinyl or cork—which are easily cleaned—are better choices if the floor is likely to become messy.

Window dressing is often a problem in an attic. Small dormers can look cluttered with thickly gathered curtains and are best fitted with a blind. Larger dormers look good with floor-length curtains, although to let in maximum light these may need to be secured with ties during the day.

Sloping windows are common in many attics and are difficult to fit with either curtains or blinds. The simplest solution here is to fix a piece of battening or a curtain pole across the bottom of the window, mounted on small blocks so that you can hang the curtains behind it. Choose a pole to match the one the curtains are hung from for an unusual and attractive effect. Bear in mind that you will need to allow extra length on the curtains for there to be enough weight for them to stay in this position.

A blind will stay in the drawn position if it is fixed firmly to a hook at the bottom of the window; on wider windows, however, you may need a hook and cord on each side.

A more expensive solution is to have a roller blind fitted between double-glazed panels though this must be more or less a permanent choice in terms of colour and pattern and is only supplied by a few specialists.

If the room is to be used mainly in the evenings—perhaps as a study, library or TV viewing room—you do not need to ensure that it is brilliantly lit. Go rather for subtle lighting effects with directional lighting placed where you need it. Spot-lamps can look too harsh in this situation so choose low-level lighting in the form of lamps or wall lights.

Installing a dormer window

Above: A carefully planned dormer should look attractive from outside as well as providing enough light for your converted loft or attic

A loft conversion is a convenient way of adding space on to a house, but in most cases it is necessary to install one or more dormer windows in order to gain sufficient headroom and window light in the roof space.

Installing a dormer is, however, a large-scale undertaking, and you should not begin any work until you are sure that the finished job will be a sturdy and attractive addition to your house.

Building regulations

In all cases, you will have to apply for approval under the building regulations (local building code) for your dormer window—and, of course, for any associated work for the loft conversion itself.

You will certainly have to draw up detailed plans for submission to the building inspector. A qualified surveyor or architect can do this for you—and will, of course, know all the ins and outs of the regulations as they may affect you. But, as long as you can check through the regulations yourself, there is no reason why you should not do this work yourself.

The building inspector will be concerned to make sure that the structure you propose for the dormer window is itself structurally sound and weathertight, and that it does not make the roof any less structurally stable. You may find there is a requirement to make sure that it is suitably fire resistant.

If the dormer has opening windows or ventilators, these must not be situated too close to either a chimney (unless it now cannot be used) or the top of a soil or vent pipe. In the UK, the top of a chimney must be at least 1m vertically and 2.3m horizontally from the window. The top of a soil pipe should be at least 0.9m above the window if it is less than 3m horizontally from it.

Most regulations require habitable rooms to have adequate ventilation—either natural or mechanical. In the UK, the minimum area of openable window for ventilation should be five per cent of the room's floor area.

In England and Wales (except for Inner London) rooms are not strictly required to have windows (though if they do, there are complicated regulations to ensure that the space in front of them is not obstructed). But most other regulations require windows with a total glass area of between five and ten per cent of the room area.

Planning permission

In Scotland, loft conversions always require planning permission. In the rest of the UK, the loft conversion itself is not likely to require planning permission unless your house is 'listed'. Any dormer window, though, will require planning permission:

- If the dormers, together with any other extensions to the house, increase the size of the original house by more than 70 cubic metres or fifteen per cent of the size of the original house. The limit is 50 cubic metres or ten per cent for terraced houses (including end-terrace), and all house in Conservation Areas, National Parks or Areas of Outstanding Natural Beauty.
- If the dormer is higher than the ridge of the existing roof.
- If the dormer projects beyond the front of the house.

Dormer types

Before you draw up detailed building plans, you must decide which of the two main dormer types you want to install. Your decision will depend not only on the amount of extra space you want to create but on how you want the window to look once the work is completed.

Bay dormers: These are, in effect, room extensions which project to an outside wall of the house (fig. A). The bay adds maximum possible amount of space to the original loft without the need for total rebuilding and guarantees that the whole structure can be easily and safely supported on the wall below. They can be regarded by some planning authorities as constituting a fire risk and must be carefully sited to avoid this; you should check with your building inspector on the exact fire regulations which apply in your local area or county.

Roof dormers: These are lightweight structures situated partway up the roof slope (fig. B). They are sometimes built in rows, often stretching along nearly the whole length of the roof.

Roof dormers can enhance the appearance of a house if planned correctly.

However, roof dormers also have some disadvantages which should not be overlooked. Perhaps the most important is that, compared to the bay dormer, the amount of extra space they create is minimal.

A third type—the inverted dormer—is not really a dormer at all but a construction in which an area is cut away from the roof instead of being added to it. Inverted dormers are rarely used, since they add no extra space to the loft but they can be useful where an existing chimney or some other permanent structure cannot easily be removed.

If you need to create a large amount of extra space and light, think about installing a 'through' dormer—two dormers in line with one another, one on each side of the house. This also has the advantage of providing a box-shaped loft room rather than one with sloping walls.

Dormers can have flat or pitched roofs depending on the design.

Preparatory work

Once your plans have been approved by the local building inspector you can start work.

Most of the equipment you need for the work—including scaffolding and ladders—can usually be hired locally. You should also buy or hire a large tarpaulin or a number of rolls of strong polythene sheeting which can be used to cover the open roof at night in case of rain.

Dormer construction

Described in outline, dormer construction is not particularly difficult or complicated.

Figure C shows a typical dormer construction giving details of the types and sizes of materials used. The front of the dormer consists of a light 100mm × 50mm timber frame enclosing the windows.

Jointed to the front of this frame are two beams which run across the whole width of the roof. They are fixed to each set of rafters with 260mm × 12mm coach bolts. Additional support is provided by two lengths of 100mm × 100mm timber positioned where the beam crosses the existing roof. To give added stability, each support rests on a 300mm length of 100mm × 50mm timber placed on top of an existing floor joist.

A large roof beam is fitted where the dormer meets the main house roof; calculate its dimensions carefully. Add 10mm to the width of the beam and 25mm to its depth for every 300mm of the span. A beam spanning 2.4m, for instance, will need to be 200mm deep × 80mm wide. In many cases these dimensions can be made up by nailing two pieces of timber together to make a single, larger beam.

The dimensions of the lintel which stretches across the front of the frame above the window should be calculated in a similar fashion. For each 300mm of the span you should add 10mm to the thickness and 25mm to the depth of the lintel. If the span is 2.3m or more make the lintel at least 150mm thick.

The carcase is completed down both sides and across the top with lengths of 100mm × 50mm timber. These can be connected to the rest of the roofing timbers with joist hangers.

If you want to build a dormer with a small pitched roof construct it as shown in fig. C. The rafters spaced at 400mm intervals are made from lengths of 100mm × 50mm timber, with a ridge

A. Above: The Bay dormer is the most common type of window. It allows the maximum amount of space to be used within the roof or loft area

B. Above: Roof (Standard) dormers are lightweight structures sited partway up a roof slope. They look neat but add less extra space than many other types

board measuring 175mm × 13mm. The roof can be covered in felt, although tiles or slates may be more decorative.

Opening the roof

Before you cut away any of the roofing material, erect temporary supports to take the weight of the roof during construction, otherwise there would be a very real danger of collapse. For this you need two adjustable steel props and two 150mm × 50mm planks of wood slightly longer than the dormer width. Erect these as shown in fig. 1 under either the collar ties or a suitable purlin. Try to position the props to either side of the proposed dormer so they are well clear of the main building work.

With the props in position you can begin to open up the roof. You may find it easier to do this from outside but you can, if you wish, clear the entire opening from inside the roof space. Try to remove a few more tiles or slates than is absolutely necessary to give you enough space to erect the frame.

Once all the rafters are exposed, cut through each one in turn and remove it from the area.

Building the frame

Start by inserting the large roof beam positioned across the bottom of the cut-away rafters where the dormer meets the main roof. Make a neat birdsmouth joint between the cut rafter ends and the trimmer and then, to ensure that the trimmer is firmly seated, make a mitred halving joint in each end and nail it to the two adjoining rafters.

Next erect the front frame. This consists of two vertical struts making up the side frames of the window and two cross members—one resting on the wall and the second forming the window sill. In particularly wide dormers, the two cross members can be strengthened by a number of vertical struts running between them (fig. C). The struts can be skew-nailed to the rest of the frame.

The front frame should be secured by simple halving joints or by skew-nailing one piece of timber to another; this will provide a robust structure which will not be seen once the window is complete.

Then fix the two roof beams in place. Use a mortise and tenon joint to secure the front of each beam to the top of the front frame (fig. C). You can then support the rest of the beam with a stout prop and attach it to the rafters with two 260mm × 12mm coach bolts (fig. C).

Next fit the lintel across the front of the frame. It can either be screwed to the top of the vertical uprights or securely fixed with a mortise and tenon joint. The rest of the frame can then be completed by filling the gaps along each side and across the roof with 100mm × 50mm studs spaced at roughly 300mm intervals. These are usually skew-nailed into place, although the ends of the roofing timbers often rest on joint hangers. If your design includes a pitched roof, this should now be added.

Small roof dormers are constructed along the same principles.

Cladding the outside

The exterior cheeks and gable end of the dormer can be covered in either tongued-and-grooved boarding or clad in the existing roofing material (or a mixture of both). Which you use depends on taste and the requirements of the local building regulations, but a slate or tile covered dormer often looks a lot neater and can help the dormer to blend in with the remainder of the roof.

Use 19mm chipboard to form a base for the cladding; nail it in position and then add a covering of roofing felt or waterproof paper to protect the timber. The slates or tiles themselves are hung on lengths of 19mm square battening running in closely spaced horizontal lines across the cheeks and gable end of the dormer. The exact spacings you require will obviously vary according to the size of tiles or slates you are using, but as a rough guide try to position them a half-tile or slate length apart; in this way you will achieve a good watertight overlap. Make sure the battens are well

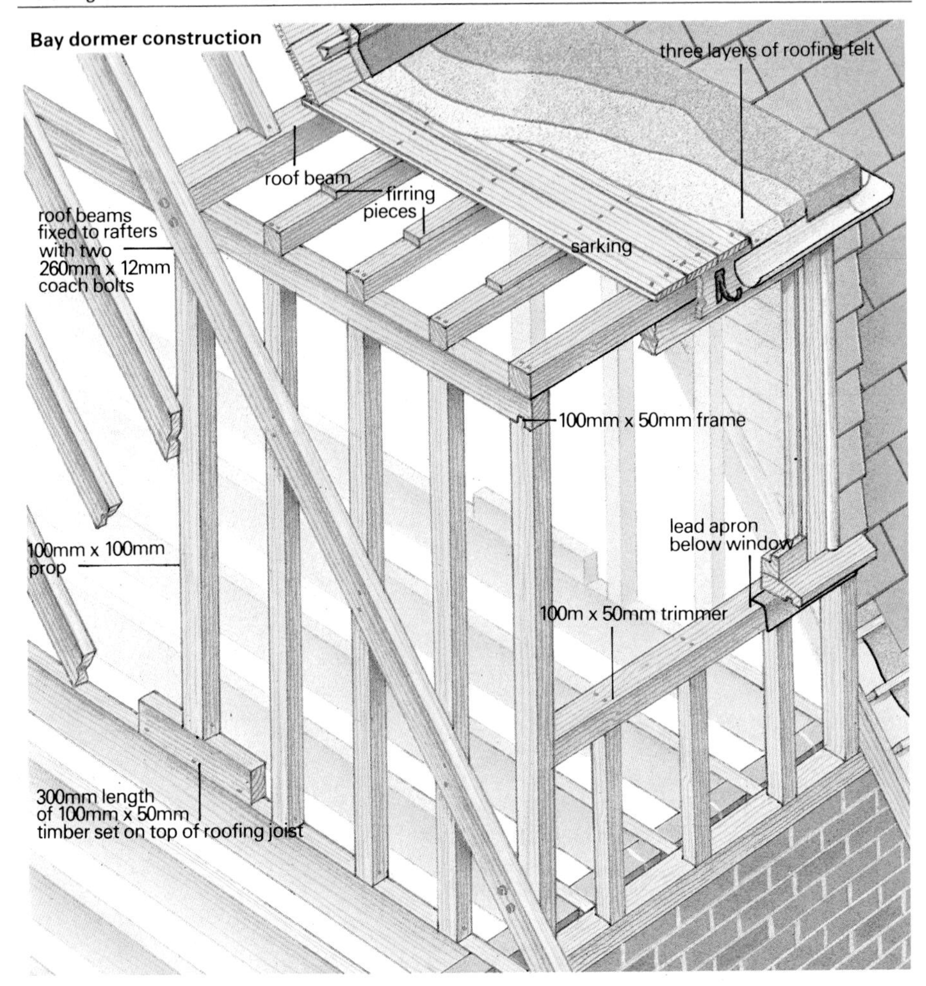

coated with preservative and fix them with galvanized nails.

Before you nail the cladding in position, fill in the gaps around the outside of the dormer with fresh roofing material. Complete the tiling beneath the window first, starting at the eaves and working up to the bottom of the window. You may find that fresh tiling battens have to be fixed in position so that you can complete the job effectively.

Fit a lead, zinc, or semi-rigid bituminous asbestos apron over the bottom of the dormer. This should stretch from the base of the window frame, run over the top of the lower horizontal trimmer, and lap the top course of tiles (fig. 8). Extend the apron to cover at least one full tile on either side of the dormer, then dress it to follow the contour of the roof covering.

Replace the missing tiles down both sides and across the top of the dormer next. The roof on each side of the window is made watertight by nailing short sections of flashing—called soakers —to the edge of the frame, and alternating these with either slates or tiles.

The cladding can then be fixed in position. Start from the bottom and work

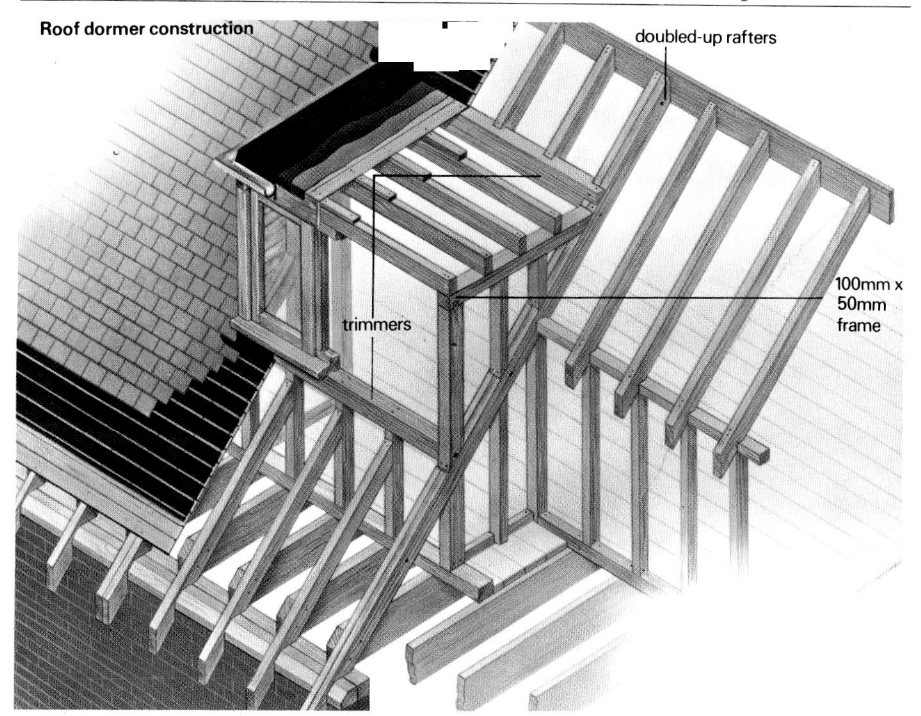

C. Left: Bay dormers can be built with either a flat or sloping roof.

D. Above: Doubled-up rafters and trimmers make the roof dormer very strong

upwards. The tiles or slates can be nailed either one above the other or so that their joints are staggered; use whichever method matches the existing roof. Try to ensure that each tile or slate is securely fixed and that the cladding is trimmed to fit neatly along both outside edges.

Roofing

Once the cheeks and gable end of the dormer are covered and fully waterproofed you can tackle the roof.

In the case of a flat roof, fix 19mm water-resistant chipboard laid at a slight slope on firring pieces, then 3-layer roofing felt on a layer of building paper. Ensure that the junction of the flat roof and vertical side cheek cladding is weathered by a flashing. If you decide on a pitched roof, lay sarking felt with 150mm laps, 40mm × 25mm softwood battens treated with preservative at centres to suit the tiles. Nail the tiles to the battens and finish off at the ridge with half-round tiles bedded in mortar to match the roof tile colour.

Finishing off

All that remains is to fit a window frame and finish off the inside of the dormer. The window frame can be purchased ready-made in either wood or aluminium. It may be well worth installing double-glazing or fitting a sealed glazing unit while you are at it.

Lay a 100mm thick layer of insulation around the inside of the frame and between the rafters, then clad the interior with sheets of foil-backed plasterboard. Once the joints between the plasterboard have been covered with a thin skim of plaster, you can paint the dormer and redecorate the roof space.

1 Before you actually begin the task of installing your new dormer window and begin to cut away any of the existing roofing material, erect two adjustable steel props—otherwise known as acrows. These are necessary supports and should be carefully placed in position under either the collar ties or a purlin

2 With your supports firmly in position, you can now begin the process of stripping the roof. Remove all the felt, battens and tiles in the designated area for the dormer. Each of the rafters, as they become exposed, should be sawn through near the top and then carefully removed

5 Now you will have to make the decision about the type of roof structure you want to use for your dormer. There are two choices—it can either have a flat or a small pitched roof. Joist hangers can be used to support the cross members if you decide on using the flat roof type of building construction used on most dormers

6 The side timbers situated along the dormer cheeks can be nailed to an adjacent rafter or continued to the floor depending on your particular style of window design. The roof of the dormer—whether flat or pitch—should then be completed using the standard methods of roofing construction, normally water-resistant chipboard covered with felt

3 Doing this sort of roofing project you really need to work very steadily and accurately. Try to open a neat hole in the roof—slightly wider than the space needed for the dormer frame—to give yourself more than enough space in which to handle all the work easily and comfortably

4 To actually build the main frame of your dormer window you will need to buy 100mm × 55mm sections of timber available from your local timber merchants. Employ simple halving joints or skew-nail one member to another to really provide a robust and safe building structure

7 A lead, zinc or bituminous flashing strip can now be fixed to the top part of the frame. You should also fit an apron to the underside section. The window frame can then be fitted in either at this stage or when the dormer has been completely finished off. You should screw or nail the window securely to the actual dormer frame

8 Now your new dormer window is almost completed. The last stage of building to finish the construction is to dress the apron—whether it be lead, zinc or bituminous—carefully over the lower tiles of the adjacent section of the roof of the house. It should be lapped for at least 100mm to ensure complete water-tightness at this important junction

Greenhouses and conservatories

A conservatory is one of the most delightful ways of adding more space to your home. You can add a space for casual dining to the exterior of the house. Access is through the living room, but, to make the serving of food convenient, the window has been turned into an open hatch giving a very pleasant view from either side.

Hanging plants and the light-coloured cane furnishings add to the bright, cheery atmosphere. In a conservatory it is best to choose light colours to keep the room from becoming dreary on rainy days. Select furniture that can easily be moved from outdoors to indoors. A slate floor (or you could use tiles instead) gives an outdoor feeling to the room and is very resistant to water. Other types of flooring may be spoiled when watering plants.

Right: A casual, airy dining area can be created by attaching a room to the back of the house. **Below:** A neat greenhouse, which can be filled with plants, can be built as a small extension to your kitchen window

The serious plant lover may find in time that the addition of a greenhouse in the back garden is the best place for putting a growing collection of house plants. You can grow tender, flowering potted plants that include pelargoniums and fuchsias give a splash of colour to the garden throughout many months of the year. In the summer you can place them outdoors or bring them inside the house for special occasions.

Perhaps the smallest practical greenhouse is one that is built as an extension to your kitchen window. An array of colourful flowering plants, especially in the winter months, gives you something pleasant to focus on when you are doing the washing up. A small kitchen greenhouse is the ideal spot for growing herbs that will not only add a decorative touch to the kitchen but will provide a convenient means for getting the right ingredients to cook good food.

Exterior walls at right-angles are an ideal area to add a conservatory to your house. A patio can be converted into a conservatory, but still retain the feeling of being outdoors.

The warmth created by sunshine, however, means that the patio can be enjoyed for a longer time of the year. It means also that outside walls in the home receive extra insulation especially when, as in the picture, there are several French windows which would otherwise be a source of draughts.

Wrought iron supports are a lovely decorative touch—they were widely used in Victorian times, which is when conservatories became common.

Left: You can easily convert your patio into a bright conservatory with some simple building work

Below: To give a different look to your garden you can construct an attractive gazebo greenhouse

Above: To prevent your plants from being scorched in the conservatory, a roller blind on the roof can be the ideal answer

Beautiful arched and stained glass windows can give a conservatory a very special quality, and it can be greatly enhanced by rows of plants that extend the width of the wall.

Your plants need not take up precious room space in the conservatory. The addition of shelving may be all that is needed for grouping your plants.

In a conservatory with glazed ceiling panels, protection is often required during periods of the day when there is strong sunlight—otherwise plants could scorch and the room would become unbearably hot. A roller blind is a very good idea as it will diffuse light coming into the room; bamboo blinds also keep out some sunlight. For a really good screening your best bet is an inexpensive blind of pinoleum—very fine wood strips woven with cotton.

Whether you are thinking of attaching a conservatory to your house or building a greenhouse in your garden, you need not limit yourself to the usual traditional designs. You could in fact construct a very charming greenhouse in the style of a Victorian gazebo. A number of prefabricated greenhouses exist, which when installed in your garden, will not only be functional but add to its overall appearance. The gazebo-type of greenhouse can also provide a pretty and tranquil place for sitting and relaxing.

But the important thing to consider when choosing a particular design of greenhouse—or conservatory for that matter—is that it fits in with its surroundings. Natural wood and a geometric shape can complement the straight lines of paving stones and flower beds. But formality can be well balanced by a more informal layout of items like the rockery and by the choice of flowering shrubs and other plants.

Below: A large greenhouse filled with flowering plants throughout the year can really add colour to your garden

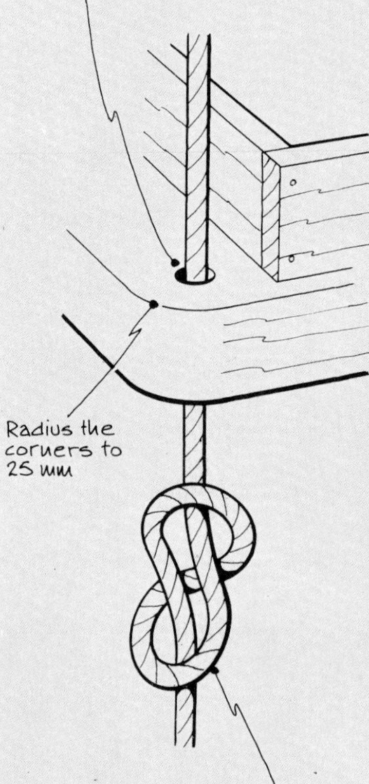

Left: The hanging rack can hold many plants on three levels to dress up windows or hide awkward corners

Hanging rack for plants

Display your plants in this simple hanging rack. You can hang it across a window where the plants will get plenty of light or fit it into a corner.

Make each tray from softwood boards. You can buy plastic flower trays to take your plant pots and stop drips. Use these to give you the size of the trays. Finish the timber with lacquer.

Fix the trays on four ropes tied to hooks on the ceiling, and tie off under the trays at equal heights.

MASONRY AND BRICKWORK

Which concrete?

Although concrete and mortar are two of the most basic building materials, they often give rise to a great deal of confusion. Deciding on which mix to use and what materials you need is frequently the hardest part of a masonry project.

Concrete

Concrete is a mixture of water and two dry ingredients: a matrix or binder, usually Portland cement, and aggregate.

Aggregate is a term about which there is often confusion. Generally, it describes anything from fine sand, through shingle and river gravel, to small pebbles. But when builders speak of concrete 'mixes', they sometimes take the sand separately and call the gravel component 'large aggregate'. Hence a typical concrete mix would be 1:2:3, meaning one part cement to two parts sand to three parts gravel.

The size of the particles of gravel goes a long way towards determining the exact nature of a particular concrete mix. For example, one commonly used type of aggregate contains particles up to about 18mm or so in size, and this may be described as '18mm aggregate', or simply 'coarse aggregate'. This sort of aggregate, when mixed with cement and sharp sand, should give a concrete which is suitable for most DIY jobs.

But it is far more convenient for the DIY enthusiast to buy the sand and gravel ready mixed, when it becomes known as '18mm all-in ballast' or 'combined aggregate'.

All-in ballast may be available in bags, but if more than $0.25m^3$ is required, it is much cheaper to buy it in loose bulk form. When mixed in the proportions of 1 (cement) to 6 (ballast), it gives the ideal general-purpose concrete mix for the DIY enthusiast (see table 1).

In the finer mixes of concrete used for some rendering and screeding jobs the large aggregate is replaced by 9–10mm gravel mixed with sand, or by sharp sand used on its own. At this stage, they are better referred to as mortar mixes.

Water content

The water content of concrete is a critical factor, but one for which there are unfortunately no hard and fast rules

Table 1 — General-purpose concrete mixes

	Portland cement	Sharp sand	Coarse aggregate	Combined aggregate	Applications
MIX A	1 :	2½ :	4		Foundations, drives and floor slabs, fence post setting, any small job which requires a 75mm thickness of concrete or over
	1 :			5–6	
MIX B	1 :	2 :	3		Stronger than Mix A. For paths, pools, steps and jobs calling for a concrete thickness of less than 75mm
	1 :			3.75	

1 Mix the dry ingredients together thoroughly using a suitable spade. Fold the mix over as you add from the edge to the middle

2 Form a crater in the dry pile and add most of the water. Until you have acquired some experience of mixing, add this slowly in stages

3 Mix the material to an even consistency and colour, again folding edge mix into the centre so that all of the dry mix is used up

4 Use a sprinkling water can to add water—very gradually—until the consistency and workability of the mixture seems completely right

5 If a boot leaves a lasting impression in the mix—without making it ooze or crumble—the mix has reached just the correct consistency

6 Test the workability of mortar for doing blockwork by seeing if it sticks firmly to a metal float when this is held upside down

Table 2— Mortar mixes

Applications	Portland cement	Non-hydraulic lime	Builders' sand	Sharp sand	Plasticizer	Remarks
External walls and outer leaves of cavity walls above DPC	1	1	5–6		×	
	1		5–6		√	
	1	2	8–9		×	for calcium/silicate bricks—summer use only
	1		7–8		√	
External walls below DPC	1	½	4–4.5		×	
External free-standing walls	1		3–4		√	
Internal walls, inner leaf of cavity walls	1	1	5–6		×	winter or summer use
	1		5–6		√	
	1	2	8–9		×	summer use only
	1		7–8		√	
Copings & sills, also retaining wall and engineering bricks	1	0.25		3	×	
	1	0.5		3–4	√	calcium/silicate bricks
	1	0.5		4–4.5	×	
Parapets and domestic chimneys (rendered)	1	1	5–6		×	
	1		5–6		√	
	1	2	8–9		×	calcium/silicate bricks
	1		7–8		√	summer use only
Parapets and domestic chimneys (not rendered)	1	0.25	3		×	winter use only,
	1	1	5–6		×	not calcium bricks
	1		5–6		√	
Joints for paving	1		3–4		√	use fine sand
Bedding for paving	1			3	×	large and small slabs
	1			3–4	×	to take light traffic
		1		8	×	large slabs pedestrian
	1			10	×	traffic only

for the DIY person. Aggregate is usually damp when you buy it, so it is impossible to generalize.

The most useful rule of thumb is to add only as much water as you need to bind the dry ingredients together.

Concrete additives

Although most concrete mixtures contain only cement, water and aggregates, it is sometimes necessary to include additives or admixtures to give the mix special qualities. For example, ready-mixed cement may contain an air-entrained admixture.

Concrete can be coloured by using a special type of aggregate or cement—only your supplier can advise on this—by adding pigment, or by painting the finished concrete.

Applications		Portland cement	Non-hydraulic lime	Builders' sand	Sharp sand	Plasticizer	Remarks
Pointing for brickwork		1		2		×	engineering bricks
		1	2	8		×	other bricks
		1		4		√	
Floor screeds		1			3	×	waterproofer/hardener may be added
Insulating floor screed		1				×	6 parts vermiculite (50kg cement + 2 × 110 litre bags vermiculite) lay 36–50mm thick
Topping screed for vermiculite substrate		1			4	×	
Repairing flaunchings		1	1		6	×	
round chimney pots		1			3	×	
Rendering, internal	first coat	2		3	3	√	change plasticizer for waterproofer/hardener to prevent damp
	subsequent coats	2		6	6	√	
Internal walls	all coats	2		6	6	√	
		1	2	4.5	4.5	×	
Rendering, external	first coat	2		3	3	×	plus waterproofer/ hardener
	subsequent coats	2		4.5	4.5	√	
Hard brick		1	2	4.5	4.5	×	

NB If colouring is added, a different mix may be required; follow colour manufacturer's instructions exactly.
Where alternative proportions of sand are given they refer to the grade of sand used. Use lower limit if sand is either coarse or fine, higher if sand is evenly graded.

Calculating quantities

When you are concreting, it is vital to have an adequate supply of materials with you: there is nothing more annoying than having to stop half-way through a job in order to buy more.

Begin by finding out the volume of mixed concrete you need. This is simply done by multiplying the area to be concreted by the depth of concrete

Above: This comprehensive table gives you the typical mortar mixes needed for the many different applications inside and outside the home. The figures which are detailed refer to the necessary proportions of each different ingredient used. A tick in the plasticizer column indicates that it is perfectly all right to use this particular type of additive. Pay attention to the remarks at the end of each entry

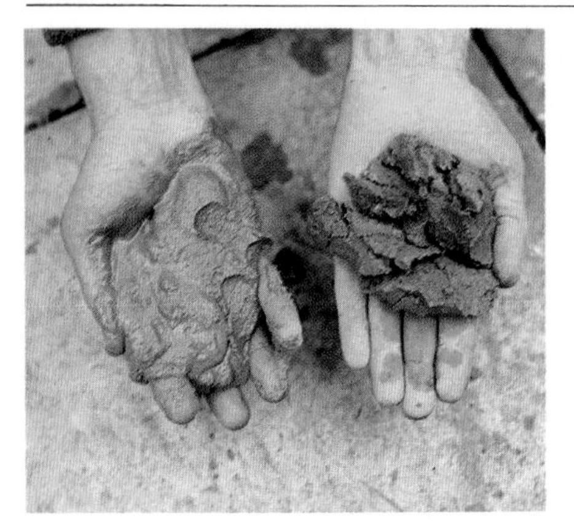

7 The 'squeeze test' for checking the consistency of concrete—the mix on the left is too wet, that on the right is just too dry

required and adding on about 10 percent for wastage. For example, on a drive 6m × 3m, the area is $18m^2$. If it is to be covered to a depth of 100mm you get $1.8m^3$ ($18m^2 \times 0.1m$). Adding on 10 percent for wastage gives you a final requirement of about $2m^3$.

If the area is irregularly shaped, draw a scale plan of it on graph paper. Find out the area of one square, multiply this by the number of whole squares then make an estimate of the area covered by the part-squares.

Buying concrete

Mixing concrete by hand is an extremely laborious business and for all but small quantities, is not worth the effort. This may leave you with three options: to hire a small concrete mixer, to order the concrete ready mixed or to employ a specialist company to mix the concrete for you.

Ordering concrete ready mixed saves you a lot of effort on really large jobs but most firms charge proportionately more for small amounts.

For amounts between say $1m^3$ and $7m^3$ the choice is between hiring a mixer and getting a firm to mix the concrete for you on-site. The latter is preferable if there is a firm offering this service in your area and if you have enough room for their lorry.

Though mixers can be hired quite cheaply from plant hire shops, using this method involves you in buying and arranging transport for your own supply of materials.

Storing cement

Cement deteriorates if it is stored for any length of time, so buy it in batches as required. Whether you store it indoors or outdoors, it is important to keep the cement dry and off the ground.

Remember that if you have a considerable quantity of concrete to lay, it may be worth buying, rather than hiring, a mixer. Apart from saving money, this means that you can carry out the work over a longer period than if you were hiring the machine and needed to take it back to the shop in a hurry.

Mortar

Mortar differs from concrete in that it contains none of the heavier forms of aggregate such as ballast. It is simply a mixture of cement and sand.

Older forms of mortar used lime, instead of cement, to bind the sand together. This produced a flexible mortar which could take up quite large settling movements without cracking, but which had little resistance to the weather.

Cement-based mortar is much more robust. The addition of a small amount of lime or plasticizer to some mixes (see table 2) improves their flexibility and makes them easier to work with.

Where lime is specified in the mix (see table 2), you may have a choice between hydraulic and non-hydraulic lime. The majority of bricklaying jobs call for the latter, which is dry or slaked and needs plenty of air around it if it is to set properly.

Mix mortar in the same way you would concrete: the dry ingredients first, then the water. Like concrete, the water content of mortar is always the most critical factor.

Shuttering concrete

All timbering used to contain concrete temporarily is known by the universal terms *shuttering* or *formwork*. The only exception is the term *centring* which is used to describe the temporary support for brick, stone or artificial stone in an arch over openings.

Materials

Although it is not necessary to use first-class timber for formwork, you must nevertheless be careful if you are buying some specially for the purpose, because the wood may behave adversely under the varying conditions of shuttering.

The best new timber to use is a partly seasoned softwood such as spruce or pine, but deal in also suitable.

There is a plywood made specifically for formwork use, which, although it contains inferior quality pine (it may be knotty), is resin bonded and will not distort when in contact with wet concrete.

The support timbers—props, braces and bearers—can be purchased new as sawn timber which is cheaper, but all timber must be planed smooth or *wrought*.

Always treat the insides of the formwork with mould oil, soft soap or whitewash to make it easier to remove once the concrete has set.

Paths and bases

The simplest formwork is that used to form the edges of paths and patios and unless these are to be left exposed, you can use any odd pieces of timber. The boards should, however, never be less than 100mm.

Start by setting out the position of the path or patio with pegs and twine. Place the boards in position and carefully allow for a slight fall to prevent water from flooding the finished concrete. Then drive waste wood stakes into the ground at intervals along the outside edges of the boards.

It is important to realize that wet

1 Use rough lengths of softwood—offcuts are particularly ideal. The timber must be about the same width as the required depth of the concrete

2 When you nail wood pieces as battens to the formwork, always blunt the nails first. Mark and then nail the correct position of the battens

3 When pouring concrete on to the ground you must dig away the top-soil until you reach the subsoil, then lay the formwork carefully in position

4 In order to check that the assembly is square on the ground, measure both of the diagonals and adjust the formwork if at all necessary

5 Next, check the level. In the absence of a sufficiently long spirit level, use a long parallel-sided piece of timber as a suitable substitute

6 When the formwork is complete you must apply a coat of releasing agent to its inner surface. Used motor oil is an economic and efficient solution

7 When you cast concrete on to soil you may need to lay a hardcore base. Keep it away from the sides to produce a smooth outer casing

8 Mix up the concrete, pour it into the formwork, dig it well into the base hardcore, then tamp it down and make good any visible holes

concrete exerts considerable pressure on formwork and that the stakes should never be spaced at more than 24 times the thickness of the board or the latter will buckle. For example, a 25mm board should have stakes not more than 600mm apart, and a 12.5mm board must have stakes not more than 300mm apart.

In order to make removal easier, you should not use nails on formwork unless it is absolutely essential. Temporarily support the boards against the stakes by sandwiching them between bricks or large stones, removing them as you pour the concrete into the formwork.

Where the ground is rough or stony and the pegs cannot be driven in accurately, place them as near as possible, but behind, the correct position. Afterwards align the boards properly, then fill the space between the stakes and the boards with thin packing pieces.

If a base is to be laid on ground where the levels vary, a different method of support for the formwork will be necessary. One side can be supported by stakes as described above or, if possible, be braced against one side of the excavation. But the other side must be braced either against an existing structure or supplementary pegs driven into the ground a short distance from the position of the formwork.

Whenever the base is to be finished above the level of the surrounding ground it is good practice to set the brickwork or blockwork back about 50mm or 75mm from the edge of the base.

Steps

Formwork for single steps needs no further explanation: because a step is simply a miniature base.

But in the case of multiple steps, accurate and properly constructed formwork is necessary. One of the most convenient ways of making the sides of the formwork is to use boards of the same width as the rise of the steps.

Each subsequent step down must be a tread width longer. The riser boards are the same width and are simply straight boards cut to the same length as the finished width of the steps. Bevel the bottom edges of the riser boards (fig. A) to allow the poured concrete to extend right to the junction of each tread and riser.

This is the most economical way of making the sides of the formwork because you can use offcut lengths of board, but it does leave ridges on the concrete along the lines of the joints between the boards. To get rid of these, remove the formwork while the concrete is still 'green' and rub over them with a brick or some other abrasive material. But if a good quality finish is essential, the side formwork should either be lined or made from the 19mm resin bonded plywood made specifically for formwork.

There are several methods of supporting step formwork in position but the best is to drive pegs around the base formwork to retain it and then tension each riser with twisted wire (fig. A). To do this, drill the sides of the formwork and feed double lengths of wire through the holes so that each riser has a double wire across its outside face, about one third its width from the top edge and 25mm from the face as shown in fig. A.

Afterwards, place short pieces of wood, metal bars or nails between the centres of the wires and twist them until sufficient tension is produced to hold the sides of the formwork tight to the ends of the riser boards. When the concrete has been poured and set, you can cut the wires and allow the formwork to drop away.

Another method of supporting the formwork is to nail wooden cleats to the structure against which the steps are being built.

Manhole and cesspit surrounds

Although most manholes are small enough to accommodate an iron cover and frame built directly on top of the brickwork, occasionally the need arises to cast a concrete surround which will close up the gap.

The formwork for this is essentially the

same as that for standard bases. Nail the outside boards to the joints in the manhole brickwork, and support them with struts braced against the sides of the surrounding excavation. In order to stiffen the sides of the formwork and prevent it from buckling when the concrete is poured, you can nail additional braces across each corner.

Unless the slab is excessively large it is easier to support the *soffit* (the underside of the concrete) with a sheet of stout asbestos cement or similar material—but not wood—and leave it in place after the concrete has set.

Place the soffit on top of the brickwork, allowing it to overlap approximately 100mm beyond the inside faces of the manhole. Next, using a series of drill holes and a padsaw cut a hole in the middle of the sheet to provide future access through the manhole cover. Make this smaller all round than the final inspection hole by the thickness of your formwork boards, so providing a projection on which to support those boards that form the sides of the opening.

Make the inside frame of the box from 100mm or 150mm wide board, according to the thickness of the concrete required for the slab. Finally, screw battens around the tops of the outside boards to form a rebate in which to recess the metal frame and cover after the slab has set.

Lintels

Concrete lintels can be bought ready made or cast on the ground, which means that the formwork is relatively easy to construct. But situations sometimes arise where it is either difficult or impossible—for reasons of weight or access—to raise a pre-cast lintel into position. In such a case you must cast the lintel in situ.

Although constructing the formwork for an in situ casting is straightforward, you need to know what weight of concrete the boards will carry without deflection and also how well they will resist sideways buckling. The table shows the maximum span of board that may be used for different weights of concrete.

The method of construction is similar

Safe sizes for formwork

Depth of slab in mm	Safe span for 19mm board	Safe span for 25mm board	Safe span for 31mm board	Safe span for 38mm board	Safe span for 50mm board
76	566mm	716mm	865mm	1016mm	1268mm
100	535mm	685mm	838mm	970mm	1220mm
127	532mm	683mm	812mm	939mm	1200mm
152	510mm	660mm	793mm	926mm	1169mm

Note:. 1. Small intermediate bearers will double the span permissible

2. Multi-ply resin-bonded sheeting is stronger than narrow boards of the same thickness, and the permissible span may be increased if it is used in large sheets and supported at all joints

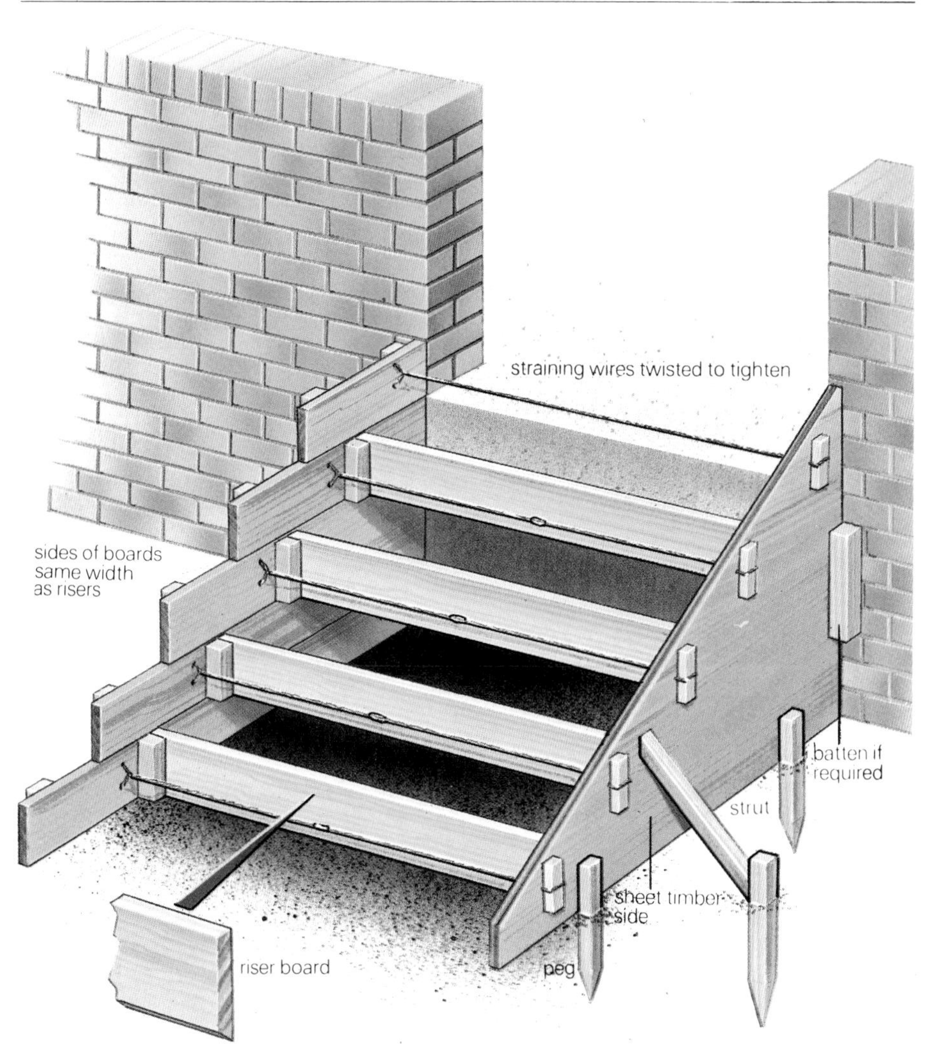

A. Above: Formwork for a staircase. If you use separate boards you can remove the inevitable ridges in the concrete by rubbing a brick over it

whether the lintel is to span a solid or a cavity wall. But in the latter case the lintel is usually of the 'boot' type; the depth of concrete on the outside wall being 150mm and on the inside wall 228mm. This ensures that any moisture within the cavity is directed towards the outer leaf, rather than towards the inner, where it could cause penetrating damp which would be very destructive.

The ideal material to use for the formwork is 19mm resin-bonded plywood. The soffit board should be wider than the wall to allow the side boards to rest on it —screw on 25mm × 50mm battens to support them.

The soffit itself is held in position by a cross bearer, which is in turn supported by one or two timber props at each end

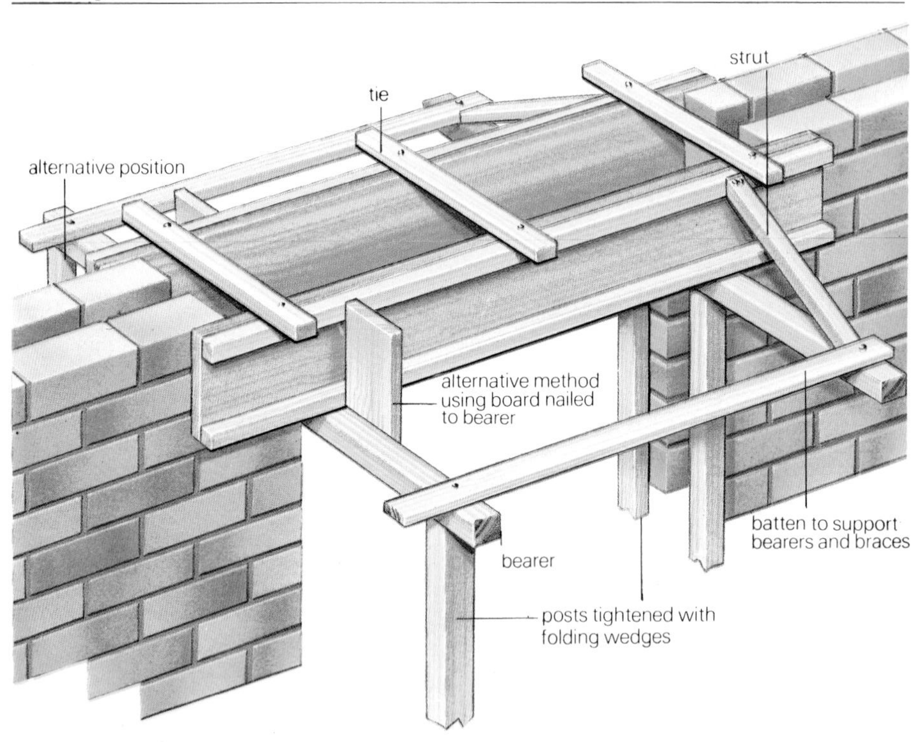

depending on the width of the wall. Adjust the props to correct the level using pairs of folding wedges. The wedges also make it easier to remove the formwork from the cured concrete. Nail one or more battens across the tops of the side boards to stop them spreading or closing. Allow the battens to project past the outer edges of the sides to avoid the possibility of the struts pushing upwards.

The method described above is perfectly adequate for most applications, but if your local building inspector requires you to form a superior lintel, you must stop the brick or blockwork at the soffit level until the lintel is cast. This allows the end formwork to be fixed and removed after setting.

The end pieces should be a stepped shape. Secure them in position by placing them upright against the insides of battens screwed to the side boards. Then lay a small piece of slate or similar material to seal the cavity between the end of the soffit board and the ends of the lintel. This will remain as part of the lintel when the formwork is removed and should overlap the surrounding brickwork by 50mm to add strength.

B. Above: The formwork for a lintel. You must check with current design building regulations as to whether any metal reinforcing rods are necessary

Nail a 25mm × 50mm batten across the top of the formwork. Give this a bevelled edge to provide an edge and a guide for trowelling off the slope between the two levels of the lintel.

It is not easy to fix battens across the top of a lintel this shape, so the boards must be held together with wire in the same way as the formwork for multiple steps; the wires are left in the concrete after it has set and the formwork has been removed from around the outside.

Laying raft foundations

Raft foundations are the large slabs of concrete on which rest garden sheds, greenhouses and outhouses. Their function is to spread the load of the structure above, together with its contents, over a wide area.

Laying a stretch of concrete—for a patio, path or driveway—is a good introduction to the concreting techniques used in making rafts.

Planning the project

Make a scale drawing of your proposed project before you start work. If you are planning a patio, path or driveway it will be much easier to run this right up to one wall of the house. Multiplying the final area of the project by the required thickness of concrete gives you a guide to how much concrete you need. For a drive, aim for a minimum thickness of about 100mm concrete over 100mm well-tamped hardcore. This can be reduced to 75mm concrete for paths and small patios or a minimum 50mm concrete over 75mm well-tamped hardcore.

Ordering the concrete

For work of this kind use a mix of one part cement to 2½ parts sand to four parts aggregate or gravel, plus enough water to bind the ingredients together. If your estimates call for more than $1m^3$ of concrete, consider having it delivered ready mixed by a local concrete firm.

If you are mixing the concrete yourself, the volume of concrete you will get will be roughly equal to the volume of the aggregate (only).

Setting out

You will find it helpful to choose a site which is more or less level: ground which is heavily sloping calls for more involved concreting techniques.

If you are working from an existing house wall, take this as your base setting-out line and take other measurements from it. If not, drive in two wooden pegs and stretch a length of mason's line or twine between them. Ensure that the pegs are well outside either side of the work area.

Your second setting-out line will run at

Left: The final section of a large raft foundation is filled and tamped after the concrete in the adjacent bays has been laid and has set

right-angles to the baseline and mark one side of the project. Having measured and marked where the line will cross the baseline (or wall), set it up with pegs and line. Use a builder's square to ensure that the angle between the two lines is exactly 90 degrees.

The third line—marking another side of the project—should run parallel to the baseline. Measure out from both sides to the baseline to ensure that this is so then set up the pegs and line.

The fourth line—marking the final side of the project—runs parallel with the second. Measure and set it out in the same way as the others.

Preparing the site

Start by removing all obstructions and traces of vegetation—such as weeds and roots—from within the boundaries of the site.

To get the site level, you need a straight piece of timber 2-3m long and a supply of wooden pegs, about half as long again as your proposed depth of concrete.

Decide where you want the final level of the concrete to be—normally against a lawn or base of the house—then drive one of the pegs into the ground on the edge of the site. The top of the peg will mark the final level of the concrete and is known as the datum. Ensure that the finished level of the concrete is a minimum of 150mm below any adjacent damp proof course—also that the concrete slopes away from the house in about a 1:60 fall to deal with surface water.

Use the straight piece of timber and a spirit level to check the height of the peg against the point you are taking your level from.

The site can now be excavated to the required depth, working away from the datum peg. As you progress, more pegs must be driven in to help you keep an eye on both the level and depth of the site.

Once the whole site is pegged out in this way, you can measure down the pegs to the required depth of concrete and level off the ground at this point. Keep

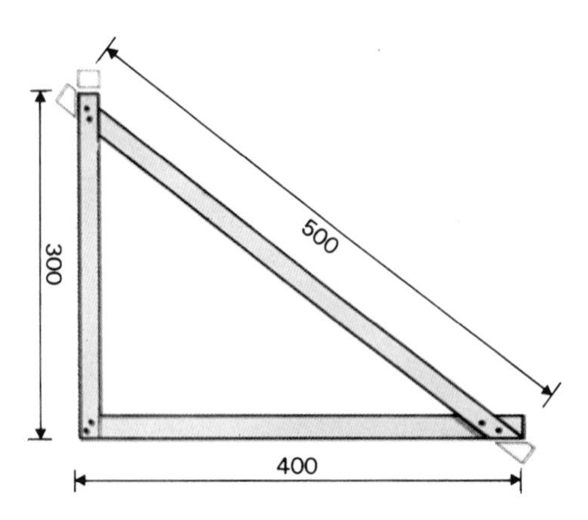

A. Use a builder's square, made from wood offcuts, to check that the setting-out lines are perfectly square

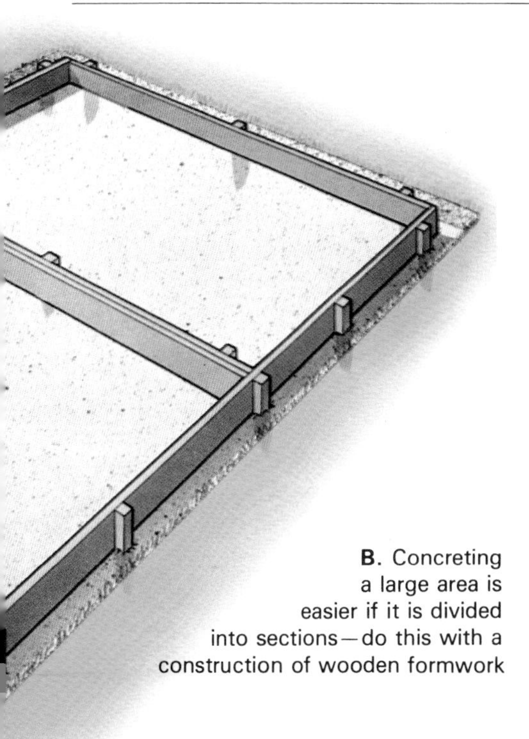

B. Concreting a large area is easier if it is divided into sections—do this with a construction of wooden formwork

the edges of the site sharp, and in line with the setting-out lines.

Foundations such as driveways which are going to bear the weight of a car need to be strengthened. This is done with wire mesh of about 3mm diameter which can be cut to size with bolt cutters (fig. 1).

At this stage, any obstructions on the site, such as drains, should be boxed off to prevent them being concreted over (fig. 1).

Lay the mesh down on lengths of timber—which are level with your setting-out lines—prior to concreting. Nail another length of timber on top of the first to hold the mesh in place while concreting the various sections (fig. 2). These lengths of timber act as the sectioning formwork necessary for concreting large areas. They should be removed after the adjacent section has been concreted.

Constructing the formwork

The purpose of formwork (fig. B) is to stop the wet concrete from spilling haphazardly over the boundaries of the site. It can also be used to split large sites into smaller areas, which can then be concreted in stages.

Make the formwork from lengths of timber, as wide as the depth of your concrete and about 25mm thick.

To hold the timber in place, drive in more wooden pegs against the outside faces (fig. 3) then nail all the pieces together.

If a large area is to be concreted or if the concrete is to run up to an existing wall, more formwork must be used to divide the site into sections of about $2m^2$.

Where a path is being laid along a wall, the site should be divided into 'bays' (fig. B). Alternate bays can be filled, levelled and left to harden.

Construct the sectioning formwork in the same way as that for the boundaries of the site.

When all the formwork is in place (fig. 4), use the straightedge and spirit level to check that the top edges of the boards are level with the tops of your marker pegs (fig. 5).

Concreting

The actual job of concreting will be much easier if you have an assistant to help you.

Shovel in the concrete by hand and level it off roughly 15mm above the height of the formwork (fig. 6). When you have filled a section, the concrete must be tamped.

The tool for doing this is called a tamping beam. You can make one from a length of 100mm × 50mm timber with wood offcut handles at either end. The tamping beam should be at least 150mm longer than the concreted section (fig. 7).

With the aid of an assistant, run the beam over the freshly concreted section in a sawing, chopping motion. The weight of the beam should be enough to tamp the concrete down to the height of the formwork.

1 If necessary, the wire mesh for loadbearing foundations can be cut to size. Before concreting, box in obstructions such as drains

2 Lay the wire mesh on lengths of timber which have been checked for level and then another length on top to hold the mesh firmly in place

5 Use a straightedge and a spirit level to check that the top edges of the boards are completely level with the top of the marker pegs

6 Shovel the concrete into the first bay and level it off to about 15mm above the actual formwork. It can then be tamped down level

9 When one section is finished, remove the sectioning formwork between the first and the next. Then concrete this section as before

10 After the concrete of these alternate sections has set, remove all the formwork and then fill in the last intervening bay

3 Drive in wooden pegs against either side of the formwork and then nail all the pieces together to make a really secure construction

4 All the formwork is in place—including the sectioning timber—ready for the first bay to be filled with the already prepared concrete

7 Use a heavy length of timber as a tamping beam. To be effective, the beam must be at least 150mm longer than the width of the bay

8 With the help of an assistant run the beam over the freshly concreted section in a chopping motion to give a rippled effect

11 A steel edging trowel should be used to smooth off the edges of the concrete to give the foundation a good, smooth finish

12 Freshly laid concrete needs at least a week to dry out—longer in damp weather—and heavy loads should be kept off it for at least ten days

If the tamping shows up any low spots, fill them immediately and re-tamp. When you are happy with the surface, two passes of the beam should be sufficient to complete the tamping process.

The final surface

This can be left as it is—rippled—roughened or smoothed. For a rough surface, brush over the concrete with a stiff broom. To smooth the surface skim it over with a piece of timber or (better) a plasterer's wooden float.

Concreting subsequent sections

If you must complete the concreting in one go, you will need to provide expansion joints so that the concrete does not crack as it dries out. To do this, make up your sectioning formwork in the usual way. With the first section poured, place a thin (say, 9mm) board against the next length of sectioning formwork and check it for level. When you have poured the second section, carefully remove the formwork, but leave the thinner board permanently in place. Repeat this procedure for subsequent sections.

If you are concreting in 'bays' fill in alternate sections with the sectioning formwork left in place. After the concrete has hardened (see below), remove the formwork and fill in the intervening sections (fig. 10).

Use a steel edging trowel to flatten down the edges of the concrete for a really neat finish (fig. 11).

Drying

The freshly laid concrete (fig. 12) should be given at least a week to 'cure'—longer if the weather is especially cold or damp. Heavy loads should be kept off it for seven to ten days.

In warm weather, the concrete must be prevented from drying too quickly. Do this by covering the whole site with dampened sacking or a similar material. Every day, sprinkle the covering with water to keep it moist, but try to avoid splashing water on the concrete itself.

Below: One way of mastering the skills of raft foundations is to make a path or a section of crazy paving with pavement slab oddments

Basic bricklaying

Although there is no need to collect a full set of bricklayer's tools just to build a simple project, a few are essential and will stand you in good stead later on.
Bricklaying trowel: absolutely vital for spreading the mortar.
Spirit level: another essential tool; make sure that you buy the 1m bricklayer's level.
Ball of twine: for setting out your project.
Shovel: for handling and mixing the mortar.
Bucket: for carrying materials.
Brick hammer and bolster: for cutting bricks.
Measuring tape: for checking, as the work proceeds.

Materials

Always buy a few more bricks than you need: some may get damaged in transit and others are certain to be spoilt when cutting them.

As well as bricks, you need the materials which go to make up mortar—soft sand and cement—plus a square of blockboard or similar material, to carry the finished mix.

Setting out

It is essential to make sure that the main wall in any project runs in a straight line and remains level throughout—you can do this by constructing a marker line, to indicate the edge of the proposed wall. First, tie a length of twine, at least 1m longer than your proposed wall, around a brick. Place the brick on-site at one end of the line of the wall: put two others on top to weight it, then stretch the twine out in the direction of the wall. Finally, tie the twine to another brick, weight it and pull the line taut. The main wall of your project can start anywhere along it.

When you come to mark your first course—each layer of bricks is called a 'course'—your marker bricks will be laid to one side of the line, as close to it as possible without actually touching.

Mixing the mortar

You can mix the mortar on any clean, hard surface near the site. Start by thoroughly mixing four shovelfuls of sand with a shovelful of cement. Turn the mixture over with the shovel until it is thoroughly mixed.

Next, mix up some clean, soapy water, using washing-up liquid. The soap acts as a plasticizer, binding the mortar and keeping it malleable when you come to trowel it. Form a crater in the mortar mix, then add a little of the water.

Finally, transfer the fresh mortar to your spotboard ready for use.

Simple bonding

In order to create a rigid structure and to spread the load on any one point, bricks are laid so that they overlap one another or are *bonded*. The simplest and most common bond is the *half-bond, stretcher bond* or *running bond*. With this arrangement, the bricks in any one course overlap those above and below by half a brick's length.

Gauging

How successful a brick structure is depends a great deal on the continuity of its size or *gauge*. This not only applies to the bricks themselves, but also to the mortar joints between them. The ideal width of a joint is 10mm. Although you may not be able to achieve this on your first course, great care should be taken on subsequent courses to get as close to this as possible.

Cutting bricks

In order to achieve a proper bonding pattern, you will inevitably be faced with the task of cutting bricks. Bricklayers simply judge by eye the length they need, then whack the brick with the laying trowel until it severs. To begin with, though, it is easier to mark the length required in pencil, allowing 10mm for the mortar joint. Then, using the hammer and bolster, tap the brick firmly on its top, both edges and bottom at the point where you want the break to be. A final, hard whack across the top will sever it.

Arrange the mortar into a neat pile on one side of the spotboard. If you are right-handed, the left-hand edge of your trowel as seen from above will be a straight edge. Use this to cut a section of mortar from the pile (fig. 2), keeping the blade of the trowel angled slightly towards you.

Roll the mortar down the spotboard towards you, smoothing it to form a sausage shape with tapering ends. This section of mortar is known as a *pear*. To pick it up, slide the straight edge of the trowel under it and then up again in a sweeping movement. Practise doing this

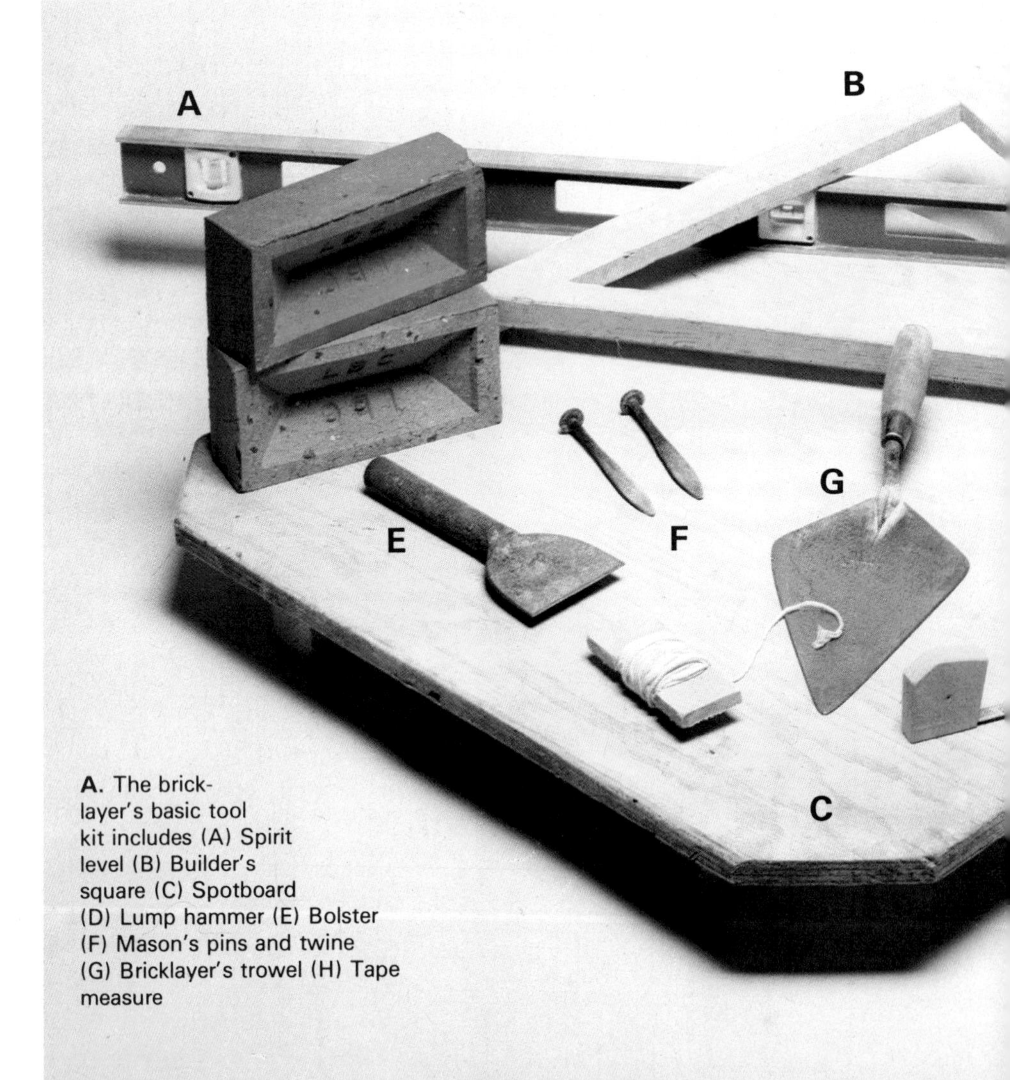

A. The bricklayer's basic tool kit includes (A) Spirit level (B) Builder's square (C) Spotboard (D) Lump hammer (E) Bolster (F) Mason's pins and twine (G) Bricklayer's trowel (H) Tape measure

until you can pick up the whole of the pear in one sweep.

Marking your first course

Start by arranging the bricks which go to make up your main wall 'dry'—without mortar—along the setting-out line (fig. 3). Adjust them until there is a gap of about 10mm between each one.

The first job is to lay a series of marker bricks to which all the others can be aligned and levelled. Take up the brick at one end, and in its place lay down a pear of mortar. Flick it off the side of the trowel to start with, then flatten it out to the area of a brick. Before you lay the brick on top, trowel a depression in the middle of the mortar to help it spread flat.

Use the spirit level to check the brick for level in both directions, making small adjustments with gentle taps of the trowel handle (fig. 4). Stretch the level out along the dry run of bricks so that one end remains on the brick you have just laid. Now lay the brick at the far end of the level. Check it for level as before. Then stretch your spirit level back to the first laid brick and check that the two bricks are level with each other.

Follow this by checking them both for line, with your level pressed against the side faces. When you are satisfied that they are in the right position, lay a third marker brick, 'one level's length' from the second.

Continue laying marker bricks until you reach the end of the dry run. You should end up with a series of laid, squared, level, marker bricks at intervals along the first course. Make a final check to ensure that they are all level and in line with one another, then remove the intervening bricks.

Laying the first course

Start by stretching your setting-out line tautly along the edge of the marker bricks (fig. 5). Use the line as a guide for the positions of the intervening bricks. The procedure for laying them is as follows:

- lay down a pear of mortar
- flatten and indent it
- take up your brick, gripping it as shown
- draw off another piece of mortar, about the size of a cocktail sausage
- scrape it hard against one heel edge of the brick
- do the same for the other heel edge
- lay the brick in position, against the adjoining one
- check it with the spirit level for level and see that its top edge aligns with your setting-out line

1 To set out a simple project, like a barbecue, stretch a length of twine taut between stacks of bricks and then use it as a guideline. If you have a lot of bricks to cut use a wooden template as a guide. Cut a brick neatly using a bolster and a hammer. Tap all round and then give a final tap to sever it

2 To trowel a pear of mortar, separate a trowel-size section from the heap, roll it down the spotboard in a series of chopping movements. Practise until you can do this smoothly and quickly. Then pick up the rounded pear by sliding the trowel sideways under the mortar and up again in one movement

5 With all the markers laid, weigh down your line to touch them; use this to align the remaining bricks. Scrape hard as you 'butter' the end of an adjoining brick or the mortar will crumble

6 There is no need to check further bricks for level—tap them in line with the marker brick. Gauge small corners by holding the spirit level next to the end brick as a straightedge

• scrape off the excess mortar and return it to the spotboard

Turning a corner

On large projects, bricklayers use a builder's square (fig. A) to help them judge corners correctly. For small projects a spirit level will suffice. Having laid your corner brick, butt the level up against the heel of the end brick and then tap the corner brick into line (fig. 6).

Laying subsequent courses

Subsequent courses of brickwork are laid in much the same way. Before each course, re-position your setting-out line

3 To start the first course, line up the base bricks in a dry run to see if they fit. Then, taking the brick at one end as a marker, flick some mortar into the exact position you intend to lay it. Before you lay the marker brick on top, flatten out the mortar slightly and make a small depression so that it will spread

4 With the brick firmly in place, use your spirit level to check that it is true. Make any necessary small adjustments with gentle taps of the trowel handle. Lay your second marker brick at the other end of the spirit level. Once it is completely level, match it up to the level of the first brick

7 As you now proceed to the second course, make sure that the mortar you are laying completely fills in and covers each cross-joint that has been made on the first course

8 With a brick laid firmly on top, the bed mortar for the second course of bricks should be (when measured) about 10mm deep. This then shows what is known as the stretcher bond

one course higher than before. As you lay down a pear, make sure you cover the cross joint between the bricks below (fig. 7). If a bit of mortar slips down, simply replace it with more.

Finishing the joints

Finishing the joints, half an hour after they are set, will improve the overall appearance of the project and protect the mortar from erosion.

For small projects, a *round tooled* finish is the most suitable. You can do this by scraping a piece of 12mm rubber hose along the half-dry joints and then brushing away the excess mortar.

Make yourself a barbecue

To actually start to build the barbecue you will need about 300 standard size bricks, two bags of cement and 30kg of sand, which you can easily get from your local builders' merchant.

The seats shown are each made from three boards about 1585mm × 75mm × 50mm. They should be battened under either end and then carefully sanded and varnished.

For the fireplate, you should use mild steel plate, about 450mm × 450mm × 6mm, with a piece of angle iron bolted to the front edge. You will need to make the grille above from steel lattice of the same size. Remember you must allow a gap of 20mm all round between these and the surrounding area of brickwork.

You will also need to build supports into the bedding mortar to hold the plates firmly in place. These can be constructed from 25mm flat iron or 6mm mild steel dowel which has been already cut into 100mm lengths. You will need to use four of these supports per plate

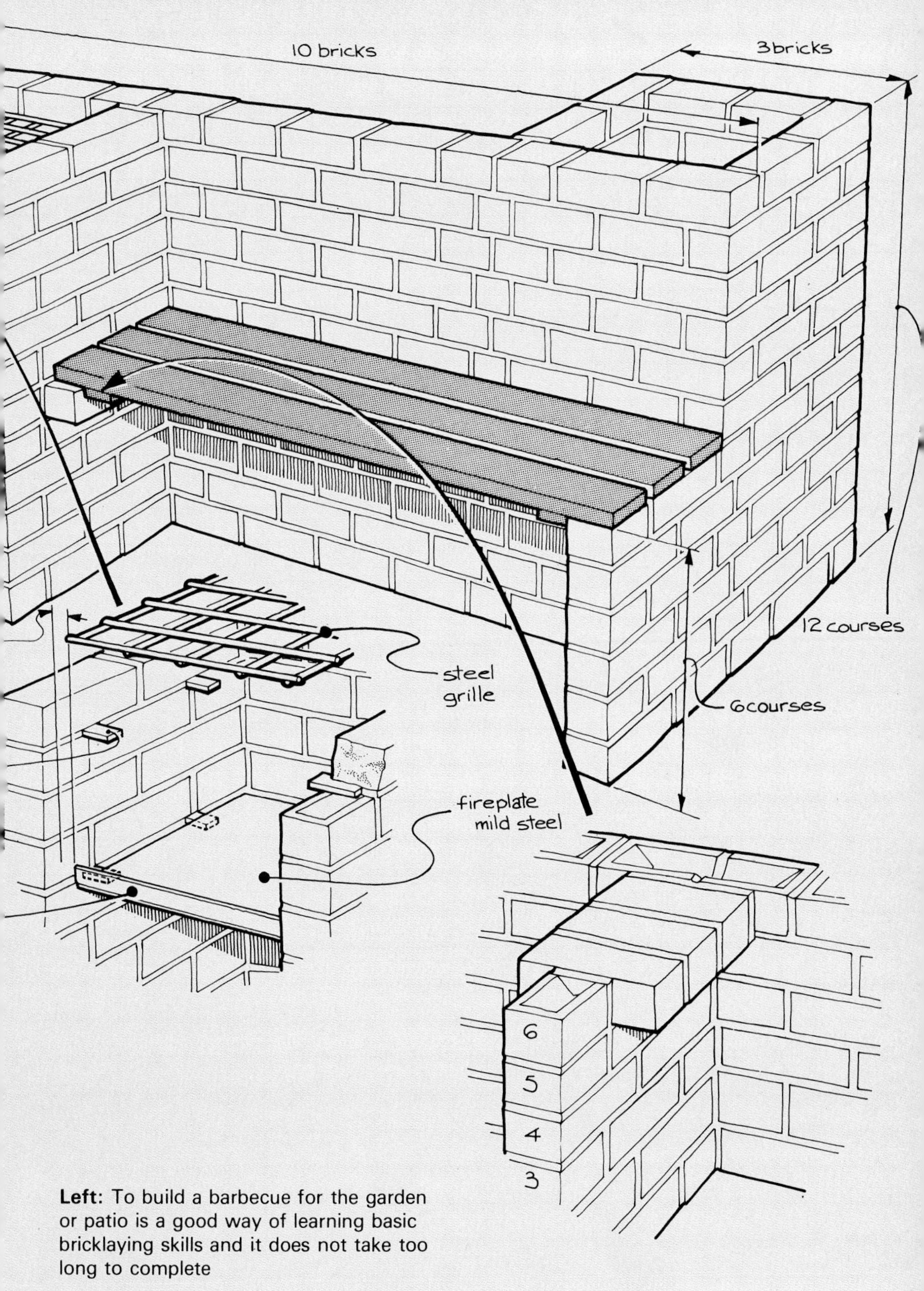

Left: To build a barbecue for the garden or patio is a good way of learning basic bricklaying skills and it does not take too long to complete

Lay a brick path

The porous nature of some ordinary bricks—especially internal soft types—makes them unsuitable for paving work. Coming into direct contact with the ground, with no damp proof course to protect them, they quickly become saturated and start to crumble. For this reason you must use either engineering bricks or purpose-made paving bricks.

Paving bricks vary in size from 215mm × 65mm × 33mm to 215mm × 215mm × 35mm and come in a variety of colours, allowing them to be laid in different combinations like quarry tiles.

Remove the old mortar on the bricks with any sharp-edged instrument or trowel. Clean a good number before you start work. You can use the old mortar as hardcore for the foundations.

Brick patterns

Brick paths, drives and patios can be laid in a variety of patterns—basket-weave, herring bone, running or half bond, transverse bond (fig. A). Norfolk bond and Flemish bond look particularly good.

The running bond is easy and quick to lay, being exactly the same as the stretcher bond used for walls, and the bricks can go either across the path or lengthways. The transverse bond is thought to be stronger because it runs across the direction of traffic.

You can make the patterns even more attractive by varying the colours of the bricks.

For a more varied appearance you can lay a ragged brick edging (fig. A), though this uses more bricks than the simpler bonding methods. For wide areas—such as a patio or drive—it is a good idea to start by paving one or two longitudinal courses each side to act as a gutter and border.

With transverse bonds, you should always start and end the alternate courses with a half brick—it is easier and saves on cutting bricks to awkward sizes.

Preparing the site

Before starting to lay any foundations drive in pegs at each corner of the proposed path. Stretch twine taut between them, check this for level, then adjust the height of the pegs where necessary so that you have a level guide for the foundations.

Left: A brick path can be laid in a normal way or in different patterns and colours to create attractive and unusual effects

Where a path is to curve, fix one peg to the middle of the site and attach a length of twine as long as you want the furthest part of the curve to extend (fig. B). Stretch this taut to another peg, level it, then move the second peg around as you dig out the foundations. Shorten the twine, and repeat for the inside edge of the path.

If the ground is soft, you must lay down a layer of rubble or stones, compact it with a roller then cover it with sand.

Where soft patches occur in otherwise firm ground, fill them with rubble, tramp it well down and roll it level. In extremely wet conditions, or where the site is below ground level, it is a good idea also to install a 25mm wide subsoil drain in a bed of clinker beneath the hardcore. If possible, the drain should have a slight gradient and discharge into a ditch or soakaway. However, it is a good idea to consult your local building inspector at the planning stage.

Ideally, all paths should have a gradient of 25mm in one metre. To obtain this, check that the marking-out pegs are level then adjust their heights so that the twine between them slopes away from the house. As you use the twine as a guide for digging the foundations, the gradient will eventually be transferred automatically to the bricks themselves.

A paved patio which butts up to the house must be at least 150mm below the level of the damp proof course so that rainwater cannot splash up to the wall above it.

A gradient of 25mm every three metres is sufficient for a level patio, but a site which slopes dramatically away from the house also needs a soakaway at the far end—a shallow, gravel-filled trench will do the job.

When the patio site slopes heavily towards the house, bring the adjoining edge up to ground level with hardcore and insert a vertical DPC against the wall of the house. When you lay the concrete, form a gutter in it with PVC guttering which slopes out to a soakaway.

A. Below and overleaf: Among the various patterns you can lay are (A) single herring-bone bond (B) raking bond (C) diagonal basket weave (D) double herringbone bond (E) basket weave bond and (F) a mix of half bond and Flemish bond. You should bear in mind that the more complicated patterns will require some cutting of the bricks which is both difficult and extremely wasteful of material, not to mention the actual expense

Large, flat areas often look as if they are concave—turning up at the edges. To avoid this, introduce a slight camber of, say, 25mm every three and a half metres by gradually lowering the marking-out lines from the middle of the site outwards.

Bedding material

The site for paths and patios needs to be excavated to about 100–150mm, depending on which bricks you use. Though bricks can be laid directly on to a well-tamped bed of clay or gravel, the path is best protected against subsidence by laying a sub-foundation of concrete. Make the concrete bed from one part cement to six parts all-in ballast and with just enough water to make the mix workable.

Lay the concrete to a depth of between 50mm and 75mm and hold it in place with formwork. The surface need only be roughly levelled at this stage, as the mortar in which the bricks are laid will help to take up any irregularity. Hardcore is not really necessary for paths and patios, but is for loadbearing driveways or sites where the subsoil is very bad. At least 100mm should be laid—plus a layer of small chippings or stone dust and sand as the final layer.

Laying bricks on sand

Where the ground is naturally hard, brick paths can be laid loose on a bed of sand—although you may have to excavate to a depth of 180mm before you reach sufficiently firm and level subsoil. In this case level off as much as possible, roll out the area, then spread a layer of sand over the site. Lay down the bricks in the desired pattern, spacing them about 15mm apart and removing or adding sand as necessary to level them.

When you have laid all the bricks, spread sand over the surface and brush it well into the cracks. Then, to hold the bricks together, make up a concrete joint filler from one part cement to one of sand. Mix this with just enough water to allow it to run freely, then spread it over the path so that it fills the joints.

Laying bricks on mortar

Before you start to lay the bricks, prepare two lengths of board, about 2m long × 125mm wide and prop these at the side of the path as the bricks are being laid. Move the boards along as you work and lay a straightedge, with a spirit level on top, across them to act as a gauge to keep the surface level.

Use a guideline stretched taut along the length of the site to indicate their correct

height; place this to the right if you are right-handed and vice versa.

Start at the lowest point of the project and lay the bricks in the usual way. Position the bricks about 5mm proud of the line to allow for slight movement when you are tapping them into place.

Press the bricks into the mortar bed and tap them gently into position with a lump hammer handle until the straight-edge passes cleanly over them.

Brick borders

Adding a border to a brick path or patio serves two purposes—it makes the work look more attractive and helps to hold the bricks together.

Always use new, purpose-made bricks —soil piled up against them will make them more vulnerable to decay.

Brick steps

All the bricks suitable for paths can be equally suitable for steps, although you must be careful to choose a type which does not become slippery when wet and therefore dangerous.

Before deciding how many steps to make, determine the height and horizontal width of the slope or incline by banging in a post—at least as high as the ground you are measuring—at the foot of the slope. Use another piece of wood to run from this to the level gound at the top of the slope.

When you have checked that the horizontal piece is level, measure exactly the height at which the posts meet. Measure the horizontal distance between them as well, then divide the proposed number of steps into this measurement to give you the width of the treads.

Before finally deciding on the number of steps, consider your proposed number in relation to the gradient of the slope: if it is steep, the riser should not be too high and the tread should be as wide as possible—at least 300mm.

Normally, it is possible to divide the height equally into steps with risers of about 100mm. But if this leaves too narrow a tread, reduce the height of the risers slightly.

The next stage is to roughly cut out the shape and number of steps and dig a trench to form the footing of the first riser. Continue this trench around the sides of the steps in preparation for the side walls.

Next, excavate the steps to allow for a riser equivalent to the depth of two courses of the bricks you are using plus a 50mm mortar bed and two 15mm mortar joints. Check for level all the time.

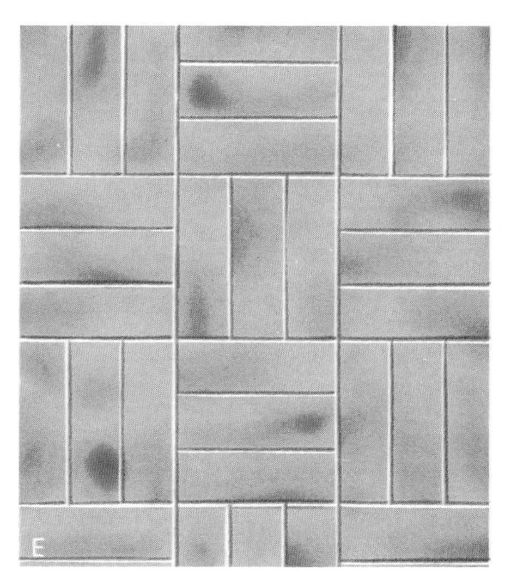

1 If you are laying the path on firm ground you should first fill in any holes and take away bumps then roll it out smooth with a heavy roller

2 Mark out the path with twine stretched between pegs. Adjust the twine with the help of a spirit level to obtain the right kind of slope

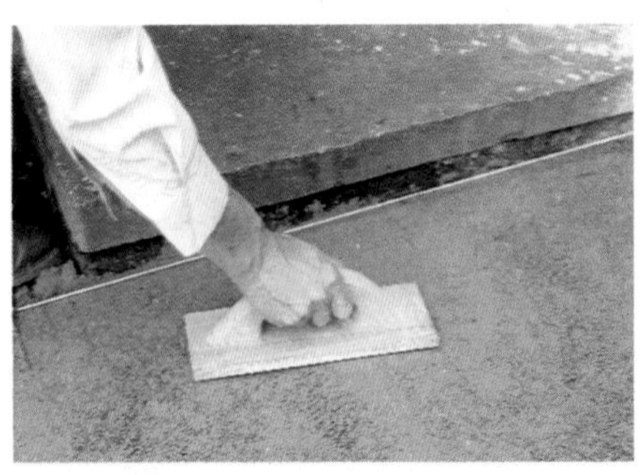

3 To make a sand foundation spread the sand over the site and then carefully smooth it down so that the level is about 50mm deep all over

4 Now lay the bricks down in the desired pattern, spacing them about 15mm apart and removing or adding sand to make them level

5 Protecting the bricks with a spare piece of wood, tap them with a heavy club hammer to make sure the surface is as level as possible

6 Spread some sand over the path and brush it well into the cracks, leaving a trough of about 30mm deep between all the bricks then fill with concrete

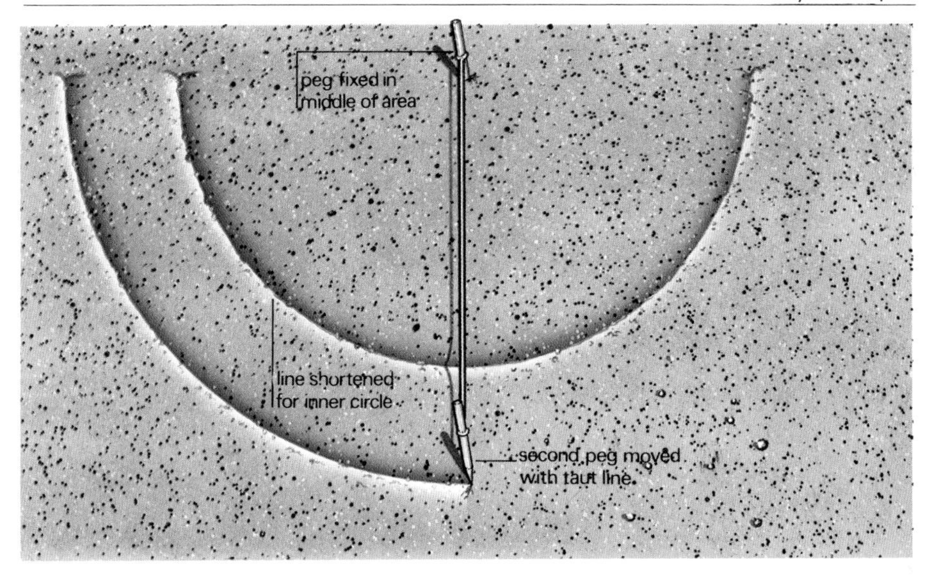

When you are satisfied that the steps have been correctly cut and are level, fill in the trench with a 1:5 mix of cement and all-in ballast. When this is set—and it will probably take at least a day—the first riser and tread can be laid. For this, you need a mortar mix of 1:3 cement and builder's sand. Lay the first course of bricks for the riser in a stretcher bond on a 50mm bed of mortar and lay the next course on a 15mm bed.

For laying the front course of the tread, single bull-nose bricks are satisfactory, although for comfort and safety the nosing should be of a small radius. If you use conventionally shaped bricks, adjust the level of the mortar to allow for a drainage gradient to stop water gathering.

Lay the front course flush with the second course of the riser and complete the tread in the normal stretcher bond. Carry on this way until all the steps are complete, but check each course for level before moving on to the next.

To prevent subsidence of the soil from the steps and to give them a more attractive appearance, you should now build a side wall. Check that the ground is level before you begin, then build the wall in a stretcher bond using the same bricks for uniformity. Mark out and build the quoin in the usual way, cutting the bricks so that the edging is flush. The top of the wall should finish as shown in fig. A with the topmost course extended along the path above the steps and butted up to it to form a border.

B. To mark out a curved path, scratch the lines with this make-shift compass. Then simply shorten the line to mark the necessary inner edge

Below: The finished path—clean off any excess concrete with sand

Basic blockbuilding

Concrete building blocks are a particularly versatile type of building material. They are lighter, cheaper and often easier to work with than bricks.

Types of concrete block

Pre-cast concrete blocks come in all shapes and sizes. The term building block properly refers to the rectangular units used for building solid walls. These in turn are classified as either common or facing blocks.

Pierced blocks are the open, decorative kind used for garden screen walls like the

project detailed. As they are non-loadbearing and always laid unbonded (not overlapping), pierced block walls must be supported by piers or pilasters.

Special, hollow blocks are available for building piers, though bricks can be used instead. Thin, dense blocks known as copings or cappings are used to line the top of such walls.

Building blocks

Concrete building blocks come in a variety of materials, depending upon what material is available locally, and what structural and/or insulating properties are desired.

Dense aggregate blocks: Made from heavy aggregates such as granite, limestone and gravel, these heavyweight blocks can be used both below damp-proof course level and for wall structures. They are difficult to handle, hard to cut or chisel and can be laid only two or three courses at a time, since the mortar must be allowed to dry out at this stage.

Lightweight aggregate blocks: Made from a huge variety of materials, including clinker aggregate, pumice aggregate, pottery dust, clinker or fuel ash. They come in both solid and hollow forms and in both loadbearing and non-loadbearing grades. Some are unsuitable for garden walls, and (in Britain) all must be rendered externally if they are used in house construction, to comply with the Building Regulations.

Aerated blocks (for example, Celcon, Thermalite, Lignacite): Formed of similar materials to lightweight aggregate blocks but by a different process, these are much lighter blocks and have better insulating qualities. These are the blocks that are much used in Britain for the internal skins of cavity walls, since two skins of brickwork no longer comply with the insulation requirements of the Building Regulations.

Mortar mixes

As with brickwork, the mortar used to bond blocks should never be stronger than the blocks themselves. Because the strengths of blocks vary manufacturers

A. Common types of building block which are normally used: (1) Aerated building blocks, used in Britain in cavity walls and sometimes for solid exterior walls (2) Two types of screen wall patterned blocks (3) Dense aggregate blocks (4) Pilaster block for the end of a garden wall (5) Hollow lightweight block (6) Decorative facing block

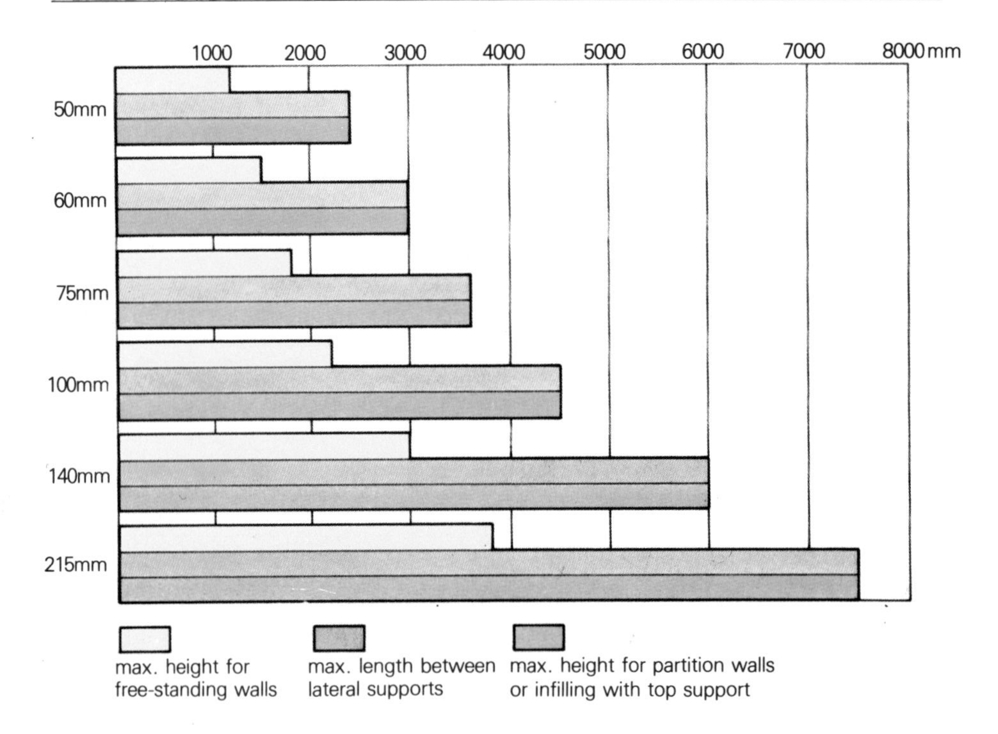

B. When building with blocks it is important not to exceed the maximum dimensions specified for each size

normally give very specific instructions on the correct mortar mix.

As a rough guide, loadbearing blocks take a mix of around one part Portland cement to six of sand while the lighter, non-loadbearing type require a one to eight mix.

Foundations

Where the foundations for lightweight, loadbearing and non-loadbearing blocks are concerned, there are no special factors to consider. Simple footings or rafts can be constructed in the same way as for brickwork. The only constructional difference occurs in the foundation for a screen wall. Here, steel reinforcing bars for the piers must be set in the wet concrete.

The foundations for heavyweight blocks may need to be 1.2m below ground level—your local building inspector can advise you on this point. The building inspector should, in any case, be consulted if you are planning a loadbearing block wall.

Piers

If it is necessary for a block wall to continue beyond the maximum permissible free-standing height and length (fig. B), some form of support must be used. This can either be a parallel wall which forms a lateral bracing or a pier.

Piers can be made in brick or from more blocks and should be twice the thickness of the wall. In both cases, the pier must be incorporated into the structure of the wall with wall ties.

Use either standard, galvanized wall ties or strips of expandable wall tie, set into the mortar joints on each course.

Pilasters made from hollow concrete blocks are a very special kind of pier,

1 When you have carefully pressed the reinforcing bars into the wet concrete—making sure that they fall right in the middle of the pilaster block—check with the spirit level that the foundations are completely level before you proceed any further

2 Once the concrete in the foundations has firmly set, a bed of mortar can then be laid down around the base of the reinforcing bar. Lay down enough of the mortar so that you form a good, solid even base for the first block you lay of the proposed pier

3 Slide the first pilaster block over the reinforcing bar, making sure that the slot for the pierced block is facing the right way. When it is safely in position, tamp it down with a piece of wood and check, again with the spirit level, that it is completely level

4 When you have accurately established that the pilaster block is level, its hollow inside can be filled up with concrete. Make sure that the concrete is tightly packed in around the bar so that more than sufficient support is given to it

5 Check that the first block is still level, and then lay down an even 10mm mortar joint on the top. Slide the second block into position and press it down on to its mortar bed. Check again that it is level and fill as fully described previously

6 Having built up the pilasters to the desired height, they should then be left to set and the top of the bar cut off as considered appropriate. Then set the first screen block in position on a 10mm mortar bed and carefully check it for level. Adjust as necessary

7 When this block is level, stretch a piece of twine between the two ends of the wall and use this as your guideline to position the intervening screen blocks. You must check that each block is completely level as you lay it carefully down in position

8 Always build up at least four courses of a pier before you start to build the intervening wall. When the wall is completed it can then be topped with coping blocks, both as protection from the damp and for a neater, more attractive-looking finish

particularly suited to supporting screen walls.

Constructing a pilaster

The strength of a pilaster is derived from a hook-ended steel reinforcing bar which runs through the hollow blocks into the foundations below.

Having dug your footing and filled it with wet concrete, decide on how many pilasters are needed. Then, mark at the side of the footing exactly where the first block of each pilaster will go—bearing in mind that an exact number of pierced blocks must run between them.

Use the marks as guides to positioning the reinforcing bars—which must fall roughly in the middle of the pilaster blocks—and press the bars into the concrete (fig. 1).

When the concrete in the footing has gone 'off', lay down a bed of mortar around the first reinforcing bar and slide on the first pilaster block (fig. 2). Make sure that the slot for the pierced blocks is facing the right way for the construction.

Next, fill the hollow in the block with concrete, tamp it down with a piece of wood and check the block for line and level (figs 3 to 5).

The pilaster can now be built up to the desired height as follows:

- Lay down a 10mm mortar joint around the block already in position
- Slide a further block on top
- Fill the hollow with concrete and tamp firmly
- Check for line and level
- Repeat for the next block

When you have built up the pilasters to the desired height, leave them to set. When hard, any protruding reinforcement can be sawn off and the pilasters finished with coping blocks for neatness.

Building screens

Pierced blocks for screen walls are always laid unbonded, to preserve their pattern. The slots in the pilaster blocks are sufficient to bond the screen to the pilasters but intervening vertical joints must be strengthened with strips of expandable metal wall tie. The strips are laid across the vertical joints between the blocks on every course and must be well bedded in to the mortar. To make sure of this, lay down a thin bed of mortar, position the tie and then cover it over with more mortar, up to a 10mm thickness.

When filling in a screen of blocks between pilasters, start laying according to the arrangement shown in fig. 6. With a length of twine stretched between ends, you will then have a guide to positioning the intervening blocks. Check each block, as you lay it, for line and level (fig. 7).

Like the pilaster blocks, screen blocks can be topped with coping blocks for a neater finish.

Conventional blockbuilding

Building a wall with blocks calls for much the same techniques as building with bricks.

Normally, only the half-lap (running) bond—where one block overlaps those above and below by half its length—is used. This involves some cutting.

For lightweight aggregate blocks, the cutting technique is to mark off the block then chip around it with a club hammer and bolster until it splits of its own accord. This is much easier on solid—rather than hollow—blocks, though pre-cut half blocks are sometimes available.

Heavyweight blocks can be cut in the same way, though more force is required. Aerated blocks can be sawn, using either a masonry saw or general-purpose saw.

When planning the first course of a blockwork structure, you can keep cutting to a minimum by laying out the blocks in a 'dry run' and then adjusting the width of the vertical joints between them.

Unlike brick walls, long concrete walls need to have some expansion joints about every 6m or so along their length. These must run the full height of the wall. The usual method is to build a strip of bituminized building paper into the vertical joint, then fill in the rest of the joint with mortar.

Build a garden screen wall

A screen wall constructed in pierced blocks is a useful and attractive way to divide up a large garden or break up an uninteresting view. You can construct quite large walls with no special reinforcement, or you can make them as small or low as you like. The blocks are not intended for loadbearing structures, but you can use them to support a lightweight roof such as a softwood frame covered in translucent acrylic sheeting, which makes them suitable for covered patios or car ports. This project is for a simple free-standing garden divider, but it could easily be adapted to use in this way by adding a simple light roof framework.

It uses standard pierced screen wall blocks with matching pilaster blocks and coping stones. Use whatever sizes are commonly available in your area. In the design shown, exactly 48 blocks are used between the piers, the edges of which are recessed to take the screen blocks. Special blocks are available for corners and ends of the wall to give a neat finish.

The way to build this project is detailed in the photographs on the previous pages. You start by laying and levelling the foundations. This is the most important part, as it governs the overall stability and evenness of the finished wall.

Plastering a brick wall

A professional plasterer can achieve a smooth, flawless finish in a relatively short time and with seemingly little effort. But the skill needed to do this takes years to master, and to achieve the same result the less experienced plasterer needs to spend some time in mastering the basics before starting important work.

Preparing the base

Plaster can be applied to any solid surface such as bare brick, cement rendering or building blocks and to surfaces which are relatively smooth—such as concrete and metal—providing they are adequately prepared. As well as checking that these materials are sound and dry it is often necessary to roughen them to provide a key for the plaster coating.

Brick and building blocks: These usually provide an excellent base for plastering since their rough exterior surfaces allow the plaster to adhere well. However, many of these materials become badly damaged over time and efforts should be made to patch up cracks and to replace broken bricks before plastering.

Blown plaster: When dealing with walls that have already been plastered previously, it is essential to carry out extensive investigations to check whether sections of the plaster have 'blown' or separated from the wall beneath. Plastering on top of these would be a waste of time since the new plaster would increase the weight on the wall and result in pieces breaking away and unsightly holes appearing.

To test for blown plaster tap the wall at intervals with the handle of a hammer—a hollow sound indicates the material is loose. Hack away all the affected plaster using a hammer and wide bolster until you get back to a sound base.

When carrying out these repairs it is worth considering why the plaster has worked its way loose. Sometimes it is a case of poor adhesion if the wall was inadequately prepared when the work was first done. But blown plaster is more usually a sign of penetrating damp and if you suspect that this is the case a cure must be found and the wall sealed before you start plastering.

A. This corner shaping tool is one of the specialist items you must hire or buy for the best possible finish

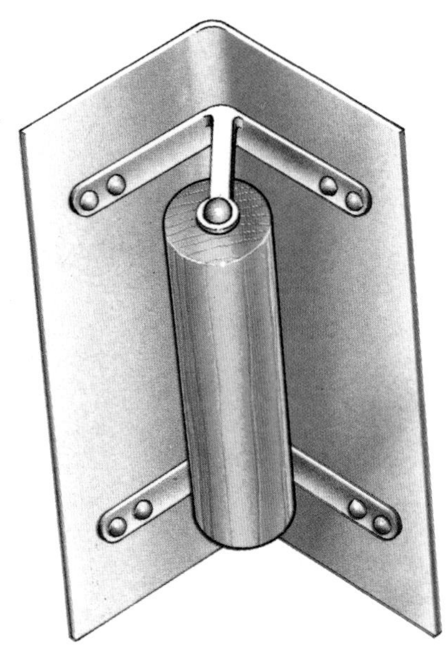

Plasterwork: Some surfaces such as plaster are usually too smooth to provide a good key for replastering and must be roughened in some way to aid adhesion.

To do this, mark a grid of criss-cross lines on the material carefully using a heavy hammer and wide bolster. Wear safety glasses when doing this to protect your eyes from flying masonry. The lines should be about 50mm apart and need not do more than break the surface to be effective.

To increase adhesion even further use a PVA bonding adhesive on the surface before plastering.

Tools for plastering

For any plastering job, even a small one, it is essential to have good quality equipment. For larger jobs you will need:

Setting-out boards: A number of battens of wood 12mm square and the length of the wall to be plastered are necessary for setting out the wall prior to the floating coat. These are placed at about one metre intervals along the wall and at each end of it. They should be cut exactly 12mm wide since this corresponds to the depth of the first coat of plaster.

A length of board about 100mm wide and the height of the wall is also needed when plastering corners.

Straightedge: For levelling out areas of plaster, a straightedge about 1.5 metres in length is used.

Plumbline and spirit level: To align the setting-out boards accurately prior to plastering it is essential to have an accurate spirit level and efficient plumbline.

Mixing bucket: To avoid unnecessary mess when preparing the plaster it is useful to have a large plastic bucket for mixing. For cleaning tools and wetting down walls it is also useful to have a second bucket full of clean water.

Wetting brush: To help the plaster to adhere, the surfaces need to be wetted down and a wide paint or distemper brush makes this task easier.

Shaping trowels: Once the finishing coat

B. How to use a scaffold square to plaster into awkward corners such as window reveals. The edging board fixing nails or screws will have to be spotted when the reveal plaster has dried and the board is removed

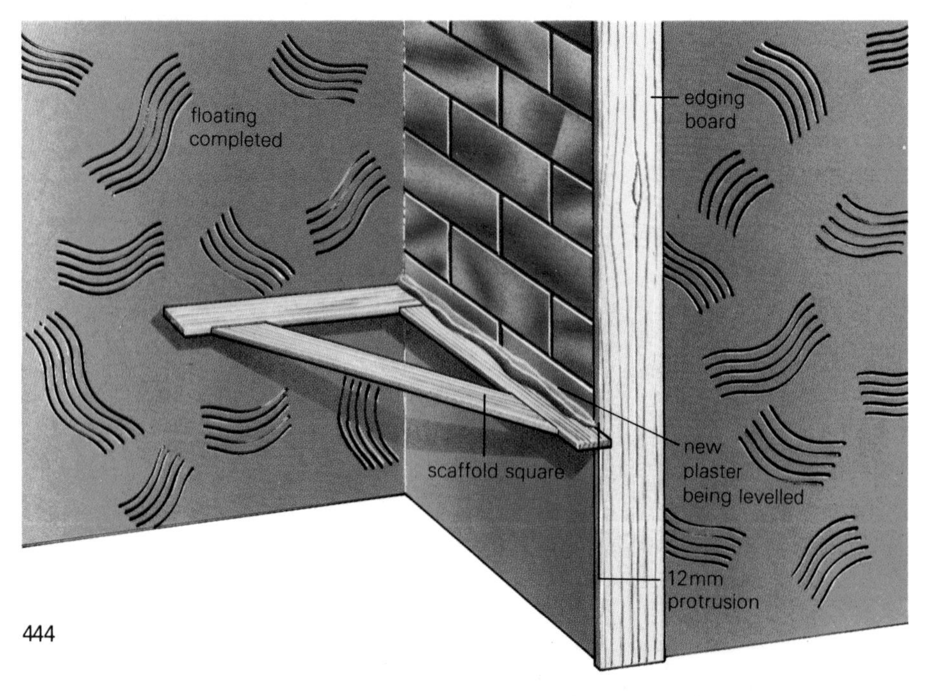

is applied, it is often difficult to achieve a neat finish around external and internal corners (the joint between a wall and ceiling is an internal corner). To do this accurately, internal and external angle trowels are available.

Scaffold square: One of the most difficult areas to finish accurately when plastering is around door and window reveals. To help with this a scaffold square, consisting of three pieces of wood formed into a right-angle, is necessary.

Setting out the wall

There are two methods of preparing the surface for its floating coat. The method favoured by experts—called dot and screed—involves fixing dots of plaster at each corner of the wall. These are used as guides for plastering the wall and achieving exactly the correct depth.

This, however, is not a method that most beginners should use—it is far easier to divide the wall into a number of bays using 12mm square wooden battens and use these as guides.

Position the battens vertically along the wall at about one metre intervals making sure that the battens extend from floor to ceiling (fig. C). If the area to be plastered extends around an external corner a board 100mm wide should be fixed to one side of the corner so that its edge is

C. Arrangement for plastering walls includes a system of battens at metre intervals, used to bring plaster to a constant level. Run a string line between outer battens to check that the horizontal plane is even. Start plastering from the bottom of each section

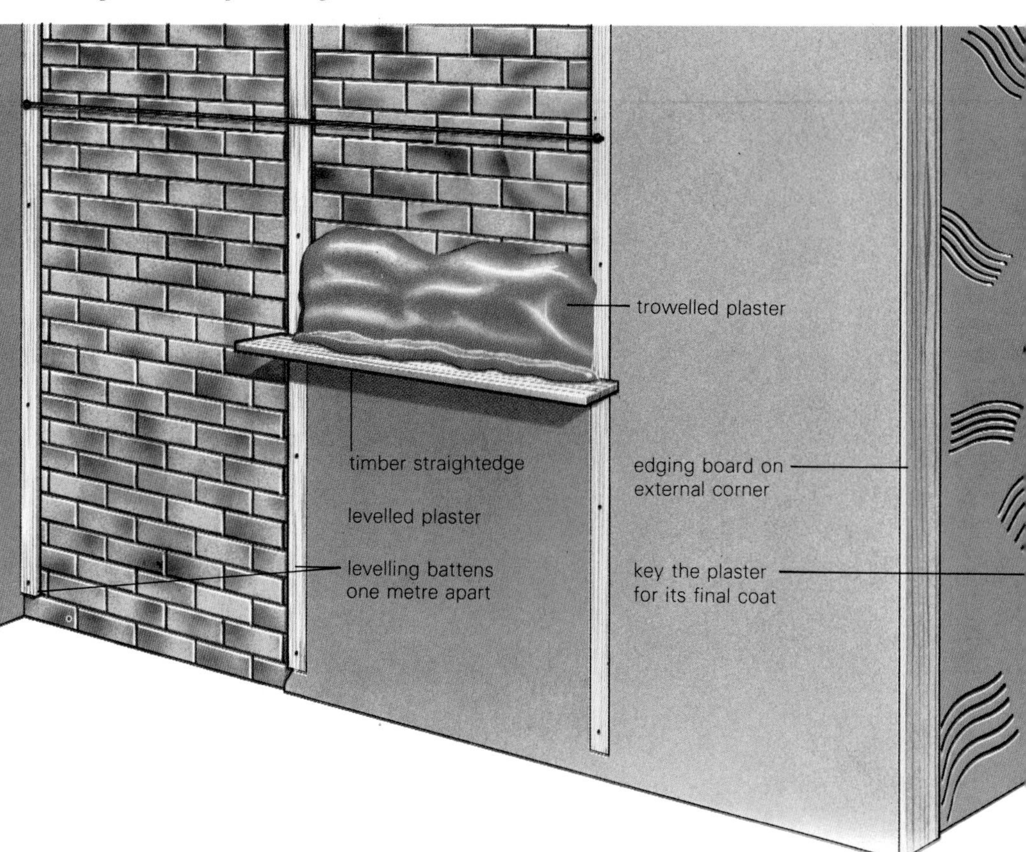

1 Strip all the old plaster from the walls and then use a wire brush to clean off the remaining residue and to expose the sound brickwork

2 Nail thin battens to the wall at no more than metre intervals but fix these in such a way that the removal is not too difficult

5 Use a stout length of timber as a straightedge, and check the run of this against the various vertical battens you have already fixed

6 Before plastering use a distemper brush to dampen the brickwork. Then use a hawk and trowel to apply undercoat plaster to the damp brickwork

9 When the floating coat has dried, use freshly made undercoat plaster to fill the batten gaps level with the surrounding area of wall

10 Before applying the skimming coat thoroughly wet the surface of the floating coat. This, again, will help to improve the adhesion of the plaster

3 Take special precautions to see that the battens are at true vertical. Pad out the battens from the wall in order to achieve this

4 A string tautly stretched between an outer set of battens can be used as an accurate check of the trueness of the fixed centre batten

7 When you have built up enough depth of plaster use the straightedge to scrape the excess from the surface level with the battens on either side

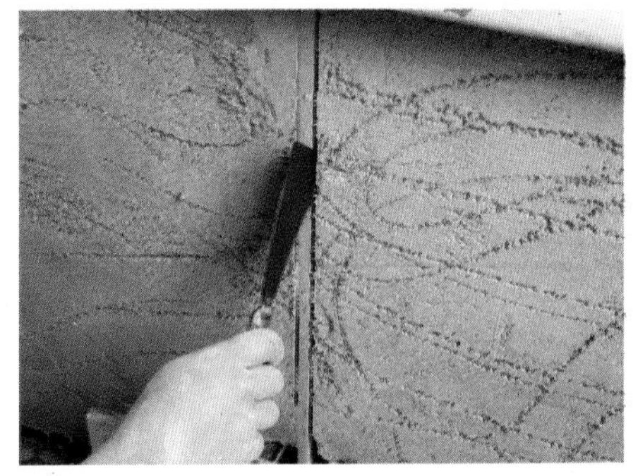

8 Before the floating coat dries use a scratcher to key the surface for the skimming coat. Then remove the battens, but do not flatten out the plaster edge

11 Prepare some finish plaster and—only dealing with a small area of wall at a time—spread this thinly using firm, long upward sweeps

12 To get a really smooth finish, keep the trowel surface clean and wet at all times and run it over the wall in a circular, polishing motion

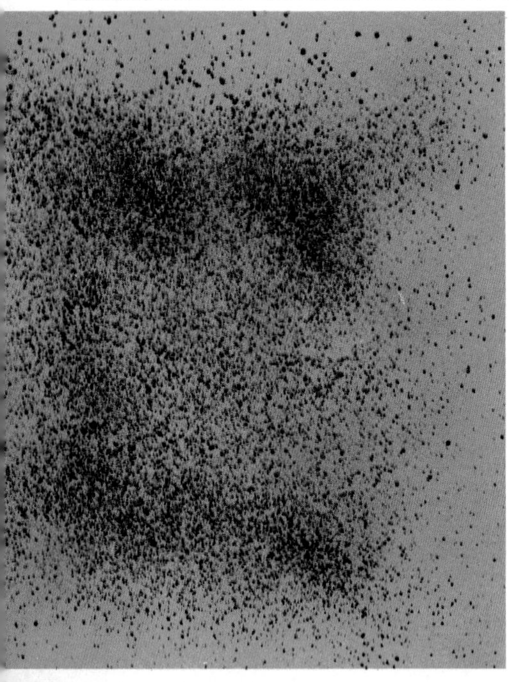

level with the other battens (fig. C). You can then use this as an accurate guide when plastering up to the corner.

Fix the setting-out boards in position using galvanized nails hammered through into the wall beneath.

Use a plumbline to check the verticals and then place a long straightedge across the face of the battens to check that they are on the same plane horizontally (fig. 5). If any of the battens are low remove them and pack a piece of thin cardboard behind to bring them up to the required level.

Great care needs to be taken to ensure that the setting out is exactly right. Once all of the boards are in position, make a final check on their alignment by stretching a line across the face of the battens. The line should just touch the face of each of the boards once it is pulled taut. Repeat this test at two or three levels and adjust the battens as necessary.

Applying the floating coat

Before the plaster is mixed the wall should be thoroughly doused with water using a distemper brush. This helps the plaster to adhere to the wall more easily as well as stabilizing chalky surfaces such as old plaster.

Always add the plaster powder to the exact amount of water held in a plastic bucket—if you try to add water to the powder the result will be a lumpy mixture. Stir it vigorously until it reaches a thick workable consistency rather like whipped cream.

Finishing awkward corners

The plastered finish around the bottom of a wall should be at right-angles to the floor, but because this is not always easy

D. (Top) Extensive mould growth may occur on new plasterwork which is subjected to persistently damp conditions.
E. (Left) Incurable shrinkage cracking on the finished coat may occur if the undercoat has not had sufficient time to completely dry out

to achieve a special internal angle trowel should be used. As the skimming coat is applied this can be run along the floor—to remove points and flatten the plaster. Be careful when doing this not to allow the trowel to dig into the surface and gouge away parts of the drying plaster.

In the same way, once a corner has been formed using retaining boards a final finish can be achieved using an external angle trowel. This should run down any external corners before the plaster dries, taking care to maintain the correct angle without damaging the corner.

Window and door reveals are also difficult to form accurately so a scaffold square is essential to guide your work. This consists of three battens of wood formed into a right-angle and can easily be constructed to your own requirements. As the reveal is plastered, push the scaffold square hard against the frame. You will then be able to see whether the reveal is correctly plastered and be able to avoid high or low points in the finish.

Once the plaster is thoroughly prepared, transfer all of it carefully to the spotboard (the mixing platform) and wash the bucket thoroughly before progressing. Then transfer about one-third of the quantity you have mixed on to the hawk by scraping it over the edge of the spotboard with the laying-on trowel.

To be useful the plaster needs to be transferred in manageable amounts from the hawk on to the trowel. To do this, stand near the wall, tilt the hawk upwards and scrape a small pat of plaster on to the trowel, holding the blade horizontally so that the load is carefully balanced on top.

When applying the plaster to the wall start near the centre of each bay and work out towards the edges. Use the blade of the trowel to push each pat of plaster hard against the wall and draw the trowel upwards in a wide sweep to flatten it. If you keep the blade of the trowel almost parallel to the wall, with its top edge tilted slightly outwards, the plaster will be fed on to the wall as the trowel moves (fig. 6).

Slowly build up the layers of plaster until the material is level with the top edges of the battening. Try to finish off one bay at a time and then, while the plaster is still wet, level the surface by placing a straightedge across the face of the battens.

After the whole wall has been plastered, the setting-out boards can be removed. This is most easily done when the plaster is semi-dry after about one hour, but take care even then that no material is pulled away as the battens are removed. Once the floating coat dries completely fill these gaps with fresh plaster up to the level of the surrounding material (fig. 9).

Applying the skimming coat

The final skimming coat is applied directly on top of the floating coat without the use of any setting-out boards as guides. If the first coat of plaster has been applied correctly, it only needs the topcoat to be a few millimetres thick to give a level finish.

Begin by wetting the wall thoroughly using clean water and a distemper brush to aid adhesion.

Mix the finishing plaster to a creamy consistency in a clean plastic bucket and transfer this on to the spotboard. The plaster should be applied very thinly—3mm at most—using firm upward strokes of the laying-on trowel to scrape it on to the wall. Try to cover as wide an area as possible in bold sweeps (fig. 11) and gradually fuse these together to cover the wall.

As the plaster is applied, wet the laying-on trowel constantly and run it over the surface in a circular polishing movement (fig. 12).

If you are finishing a large wall you will find it difficult to complete the whole area in one go because the plaster sets too fast. To avoid this, work in sections, lightly sanding away any of the overlapping lines.

Plastering an arch

Above: The key to successful arch construction lies in building an accurate template. This is fixed across the top of the opening and finished with plasterboard and a thin skim of plaster

Plastered arches—built above door or window openings, or across alcoves—add a touch of elegance to any room. Furthermore, they are surprisingly easy to construct and can be tackled by anyone who has mastered basic plastering techniques.

Preparing and marking

The easiest way to form a plasterwork arch is to build a false arch—a template—out of timber and fit this across the top of the opening.

Before you build the template check carefully that headroom above the opening will not be restricted by the addition of an arch. Once you are satisfied, remove the door and prise or cut away the frame and the door stop.

The template is made up of an inner frame of wooden battens, surrounded by an outer skin of plywood. The outer skin is fixed to both sides of the frame.

Semi-circular arch: This is the most common type of arch and the easiest to mark and cut out.

First measure across the opening directly below where you want the arch to sit and draw a line the same length on a sheet of plywood. Mark its midpoint. With this as a centre, and half the length of the line as a radius, draw a semi-circle above using a large pair of compasses or a pencil and string (figs 2 to 3).

Complete the marking out by drawing a box shape around the semi-circle. Start from each end of the baseline and draw two vertical lines up from it.

Continue these alongside the semi-circle and stop when you are about 50mm above the top of the curve at each side.

Then connect the two with a horizontal line across the top; use a fretsaw to cut out the shape of the semi-circle and the box around it.

Segmental arch: This arch allows more headroom.

Start as you did with the semi-circular arch by measuring across the opening and then draw a line the same size on the bottom of a sheet of plywood. Find the midpoint of this line and mark it clearly.

Then draw two lines running vertically up from each end towards the top of the sheet. If you extend your compass between these lines using the midpoint as a centre, you will be able to draw a number of segmental arches.

Once you have chosen the curve you want, draw it out and complete the shape by drawing a box around its top. Then use a fretsaw to cut around the outside of the arch and the box.

Building the template

If you want to build an arch in a masonry wall, you will need a sturdy framework to appoint the plywood arch pieces. For this, construct an inner frame from 25mm square battens. Strengthen the side pieces first by cutting and nailing battens across their inside.

To finish the frame, cut and fix two cross bearers between the outside pieces. Make these shorter than the width of the soffit—the underside of the arch—so that the outside of the frame can be completely covered with plasterboard and a thin skim of plaster.

Once you have nailed the outer skin to the cross bearers, fix the template to the inside of the soffit. Drill through the cross bearers and then screw the template to the brickwork on each side using wall plugs.

To complete the frame, line the bottom of the template with a piece of 3mm flexible plywood. Cut this to size and then, starting from one end, push the board upwards; nail and glue it into place.

Finishing and plastering

With the template in position, finish by lining the outside with plasterboard and then apply a thin skim of plaster over the whole arch.

Mark the outline of the arch on the back of the plasterboard using the same tools and techniques you used to mark the outside frames of the template.

Using a handyman's knife, cut through the cardboard backing and carefully separate the cut-out piece from the rest of the sheet. Fix it to the outside of the template using galvanized plasterboard nails and make sure the heads are punched well below the surface, but not right through the cardboard.

Before plastering the arch, check the template carefully and remove rough edges with a piece of abrasive paper. Treat the edges of the plasterboard with a

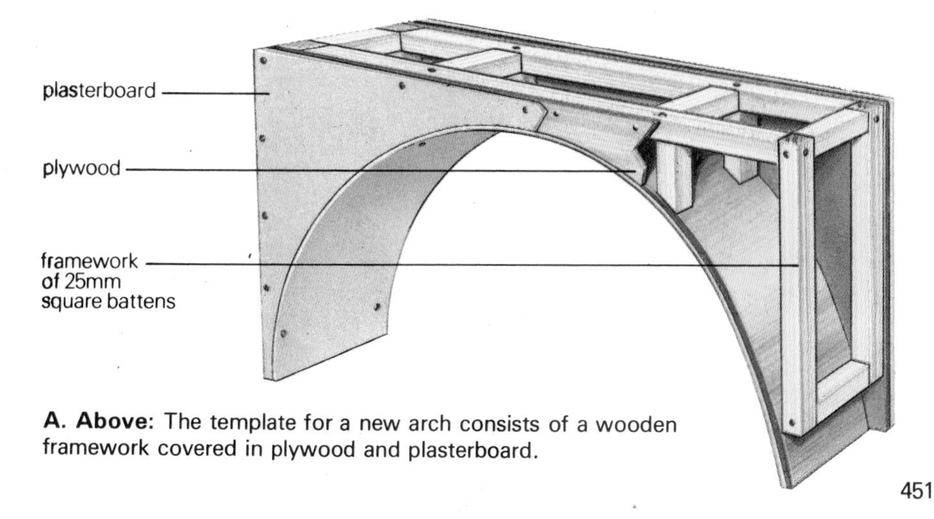

A. Above: The template for a new arch consists of a wooden framework covered in plywood and plasterboard.

1 If the arch is to be built above a doorway, the first thing to do is to remove the architrave. Neatly prise it away from its fixings with a hammer and bolster. The next task you need to do is to remove the frame and door stops. Lift these away carefully so that you do not damage the actual brickwork around the opening to the doorway

2 To construct the necessary template, you must first measure the distance across the top of the door opening at what is going to be its widest point. Then transfer this measurement to the bottom of a piece of plywood. Then you must find the midpoint of this distance and clearly mark it in pencil along the bottom of the board

5 Prefabricate each side of the template separately, then use 25mm square softwood to construct frameworks across the insides of the opening. Once you have managed to construct both frames, nail the sides together using short pieces of timber which have already been measured and then cut to the correct length so that the frame fits the opening

6 Drill holes, with a power or hand drill, for plugs in each side of the soffit and firmly screw the frame into position right across the top of the opening. The underside of the template is made from a piece of bent plywood or plasterboard. You should first wet the material thoroughly to make it much more pliable and easier to use

3 Then fix a piece of string to this midpoint and tie a pencil to the top end. You can use this to draw a semi-circular arc right across the board. Next you will need to cut along the line using a padsaw, fretsaw or electric jig saw. Remember for a through arch, you will need to mark and cut out two template sides which match identically

4 Check the template for size by holding each of the side pieces in position above the opening. If the sizes are not quite right, adjust them as necessary. If the arch is too low to allow sufficient headroom underneath, you will have to move the template further upwards to a new position and then cut it to the right size

7 When you have managed to fit the plywood or plasterboard underside of the template into position, the next thing you should do is to mark and cut out pieces of plasterboard which will then fit right across the top of the template. These should then be accurately fixed in place with galvanized nails which you should carefully hammer in

8 Finish off the new arch with two coats of plaster. Try to make sure that the top coat of plaster becomes level with the wall on each side of the arch. The angle where the soffit meets the two outside walls can be formed and then finished off smoothly and neatly with the help of a specialist corner shaping tool used by plasterers

dilute solution of PVA adhesive and cover the joints between the arch and the wall with pieces of decorator's jute scrim.

The top coat should only be thick enough to bring the arch level with the wall on each side. Apply it carefully, first to the outside face of the arch then to the underside, using a metal float. Use a corner shaping tool to finish off the external right-angled joint between the soffit and the outside wall (fig. 8). Leave to dry out for several weeks before decorating.

Arch repairs

Repairing existing arches is relatively straightforward. First check all around the arch for loose or 'blown' plaster by tapping the surface with the handle of a hammer—a hollow sound will indicate defective patches.

Use a hammer and bolster to clear away affected material.

Minor repairs: If only a small area is affected, repairs are easy because you can use the sound plaster on each side of the damage as a guide.

The only difficulty likely to arise is when you apply the first coat of plaster.

B. Below: To make repairs easy, cut two templates to match the curve of the arch but slightly proud—and mount one on each side of the wall

To help with this, make up a depth gauge from an offcut of timber long enough to span the width of the damaged patch. Cut 3mm deep rebates in each end of the gauge so that the rest of it can be slotted into the patch by this amount and the first coat of plaster applied correctly.

Mix up the plaster and push it hard against the back wall with a trowel. Rake the depth gauge across the top to level it off and remove excess material.

Leave the first coat to dry and apply the final skimming coat with care.

Large-scale repairs: If you discover that damage to the plaster around the arch is extensive, you must build a plywood template to guide your repair work.

First repair all the damaged material on the external walls with plaster, taking it as close to the edges of the soffit as you can. While this is drying, make up the template for plastering the underside.

The templates must follow the exact curve of the arch. To find this, measure the distance across the opening and cut a piece of timber slightly shorter than this length. Next, cut four wooden folding wedges and use them to hold the timber in place across the opening by driving one down from the top and one from the bottom between the soffit and the timber at each end (fig. C).

Finally, attach a piece of string to the exact midpoint of the timber using a drawing pin and tie a pencil to the other

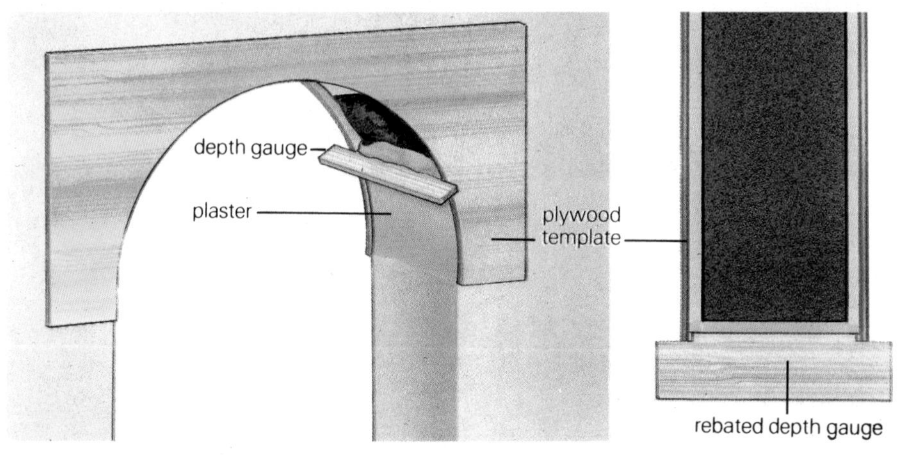

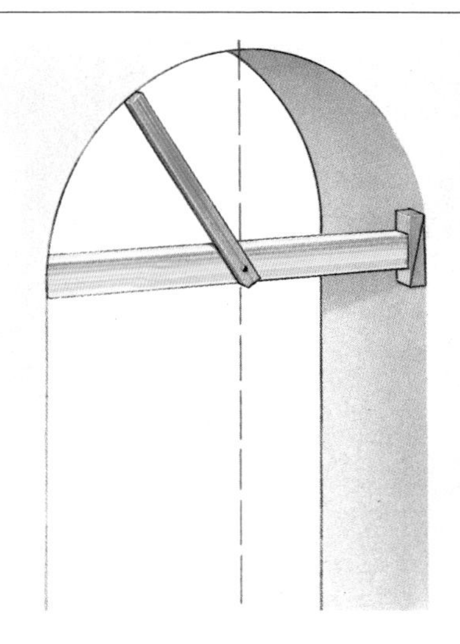

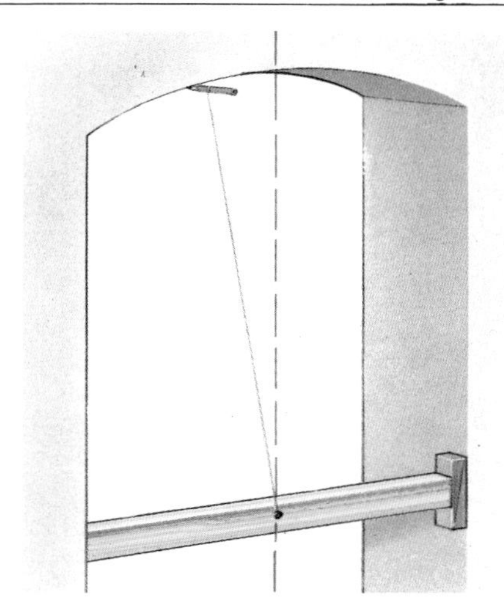

C. To reproduce the curve of an arch, fix a batten across the opening held in place with folding wedges. From the centre of the batten stretch a piece of timber or string. By adjusting the position of the cross bearer in different ways, you can then reproduce both semi-circular and segmental arches

end of the string. Extend the string upwards until the pencil touches the top of the arch and can be swung backwards and forwards to follow its curve (fig. C).

By trial and error, and adjusting the length of the string and the position of the cross bearer, you should soon be able to reproduce the exact curve of the arch along its entire length.

Once you can reproduce the arch, carefully remove the timber wedges and take away the cross bearer. Keep the string at the same length and draw the curve on a piece of plywood. Then mark a box around its outside and carefully cut out the shape you have drawn.

Fix the templates in position with masonry nails hammered into the outside walls. On timber-framed walls, nail into the studs. Level the template carefully so that the new plasterwork will finish flush with the existing plaster.

To help apply the first coat of plaster correctly, make up a depth gauge similar to the one used for the smaller repairs described above. Make this long enough so that it can span across the two templates and then cut a 3mm rebate in each side.

Apply the first coat of plaster with a trowel, pressing it hard against the brickwork across the top of the arch to help it adhere. Level it off carefully using the depth gauge, and leave it to dry for two or three hours.

Trowel this into place all along the underside of the arch so that it is level with, or just above, the templates. Then place the uncut edge of the depth gauge across the soffit and, with a sawing motion, work your way around the curve removing excess material and flattening the underside. Leave the plaster to completely dry out—this will take at least 12 hours.

Remove the templates carefully in case you damage the finished plasterwork. Fill the holes left by the fixing nails with plaster and add the finishing touches to the curve, especially around the two external angles where the soffit meets the outside walls.

Leave the completed arch as long as you can before redecorating, to give the plaster time to dry properly.

Knocking a hole in a brick wall

Home improvements can often be made just as easily by demolishing bricks and mortar as they can by building up. Knocking a small hole through a wall is a good way to master the basic techniques —and makes space for a serving hatch, window or two-way bookshelf. However, check for power cables before you start wall demolition.

Demolishing masonry normally entails using supports—temporary ones as you do the work and permanent ones afterwards, to keep the wall structurally sound.

Above: Knocking a hole in a wall is a good way of learning building techniques

External walls, and most internal walls, take the weight of the structure above them. When a hole is knocked through, this weight can bear down on the space and cause the structure to collapse.

This is prevented by installing a lintel—

a beam of concrete, galvanized steel or wood—over the hole.

Checking the wall

To find out if the wall in question is masonry or timber framed, tap it sharply with your fist. A brick wall gives out a dull, solid sound whereas a stud wall sounds loud and hollow.

If the wall is a non-loadbearing one, it usually ends slightly above the ceiling level. However, if it continues on an upstairs floor, it is loadbearing. It is also loadbearing if struts which help support the roof rest on it, or if the wall supports the ceiling joists of the room itself.

Choice of lintels

Lintels come in a variety of types. If you are knocking through an exterior wall in a house with a solid wall of standard 225mm brickwork, the easiest to use is a pre-stressed concrete lintel 220mm wide and at least 65mm thick. You set it flush with the outside edge of the opening so that the concrete is visible.

In newer houses with a cavity wall—two layers of leaves of 112mm brickwork with an air space between—a proprietary steel lintel is better.

For an interior wall of single skin brickwork, a timber or concrete lintel 100mm × 75mm thick will suffice for small openings.

Only an engineer can calculate the loadings accurately but your building inspector will advise you on the safest lintel to use if you show him an accurate drawing of the wall.

Whichever size you buy, the lintel must be at least 305mm longer than the opening you wish to span, so that it has an adequate grip or bearing on either side.

Temporary supports

A brick wall is exceptionally stable within certain limits—even with a hole in it. If you go carefully, you can cut an opening up to 1m wide in sound brickwork without any temporary support at all. Most of the bricks over the opening will just hang there during the time it takes to insert the lintel.

However, for a wider opening you should start by cutting only the slot for the lintel (fig. A), at the same time supporting the wall above with lengths of timber known as needles. When the lintel is in place and the mortar around it has hardened, you can cut away the brickwork below it (fig. A).

Needles are made from lengths of 100mm × 75mm timber and for a 1–1.5m hole, two only will be needed. The needles are inserted through holes in the wall immediately above the proposed position of the lintel and then propped on either side with suitable Acrow props to carry the weight of the whole wall down to the floor or ground. Lengths of timber—at least 200mm × 50mm—are placed between the supports and the ground to spread the weight over a greater area.

Cut the 100mm × 75mm holes for the needles with a club hammer and plugging chisel or cold chisel. Work from both sides of the wall if necessary and keep the holes as rectangular in section as possible, so the needles lie flat. Having wedged them through the wall, erect supports on both sides (fig. A).

Marking the cutting area

Having selected the approximate position of the hole, take its overall measurements and transfer these to the wall (fig. 1).

Assuming that the wall is still plastered or rendered, you must now chip away this layer, with a club hammer and bolster, to reveal the brickwork underneath (fig. 2).

When the brickwork in the centre of the cutting area is exposed, you can tell —without removing all the plaster— whether or not your proposed cutting edges correspond with vertical and horizontal joints (fig. 4). Do this by measuring from an exposed joint to the marked edge (fig. 5). If the proposed edges do not line up with any joints, move the markings of the cutting area

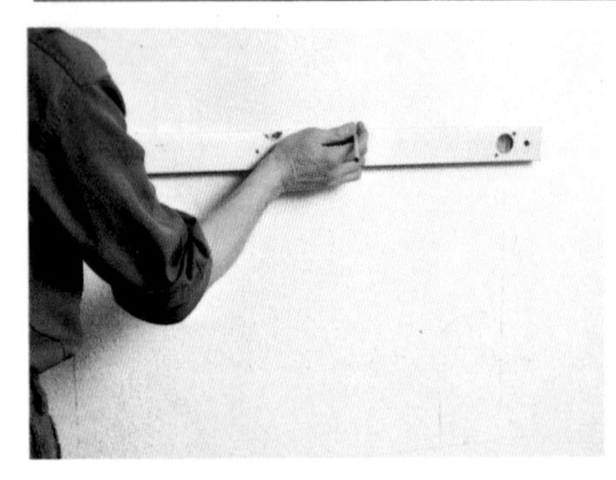

1 Mark in the measurements of the proposed opening, using a spirit level both as a straightedge and a guide that the line is completely straight

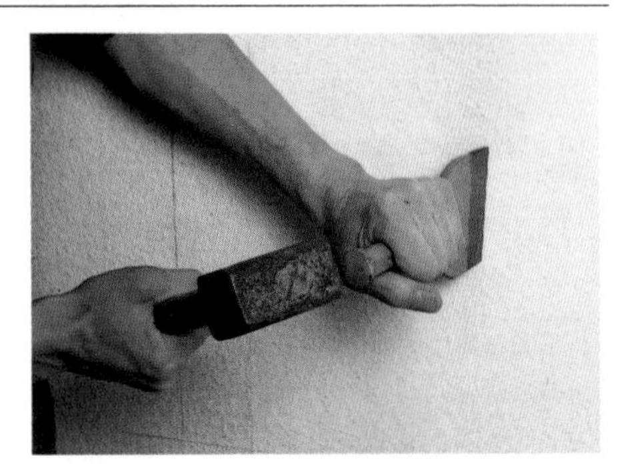

2 Plaster must be chipped away with a club hammer and bolster to expose the brickwork. Start doing this in the middle of the cutting area

5 Measure from an exposed joint to the edge. Move the cutting area over slightly if it does not correspond exactly to a vertical and horizontal joint

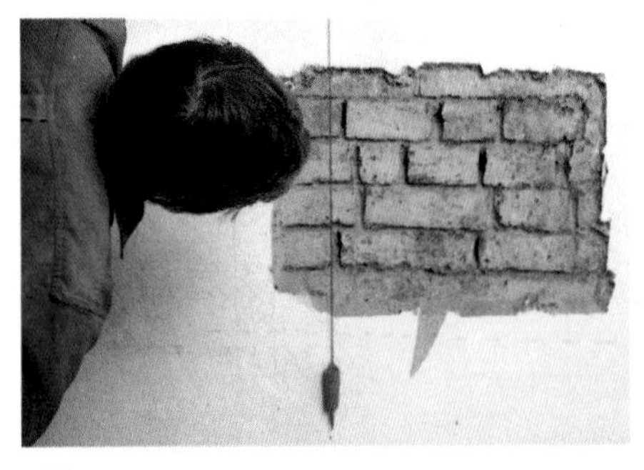

6 When the cutting edge does correspond to a mortar joint, you must use a plumbline to check that it is really level

9 When the mortar all around the brick has been loosened, try to ease it out. A stubborn brick can be easily broken up with the bolster

10 Subsequent bricks should then prove easier to remove. Next you should chip away the remaining plaster so that all the brickwork is exposed

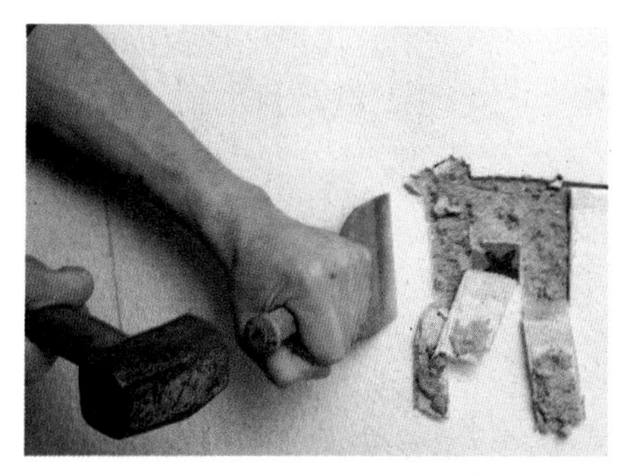

3 Use firm hammer blows and keep the bolster very steady to cut out neat areas of plaster. Always keep half a brick's length inside the markings

4 At this stage, enough brickwork is exposed to judge whether or not the proposed cutting edge will line up with any of the mortar joints

7 Mark in the position of the lintel directly above the top cutting line. Again, you should use a spirit level to keep the line even and straight

8 Using a club hammer, drive a plugging chisel into the vertical joint in the centre of the cutting area to gradually loosen it up

11 Using a club hammer and bolster, knock out the brickwork at the top of the proposed opening ready for the lintel to be inserted in the hole

12 Then lay down bedding mortar for the lintel and slide it into place. Before packing it into place, use a spirit level to check its position

13 The remaining bricks can now be carefully cut out of the opening—this time using the club hammer and a bolster chisel

14 Big gaps between the lintel and its supporting brickwork must be packed with bits of slate. Trim them to size when the mortar has set

over until they do. This keeps the number of bricks to be cut from the opening to a minimum. Check the joints for level and plumb (fig. 6).

The position of the lintel must also be marked, directly above the top cutting line (fig. 7).

Cutting out the opening

The secret of demolishing brickwork is to work carefully and steadily, removing only a little at a time. Start with a vertical joint in the middle of the cutting area and drive in a plugging chisel with a mallet (fig. 8). Loosen the mortar around one brick and try to ease it out.

After you have removed one or two bricks in this way, you can exchange the plugging chisel for the bolster. By driving it into the mortar joints, you should be able to lever bricks away rather than have to smash them out.

Enlarging the opening is a gradual, careful process and only small sections should be knocked out at a time.

Chisel cuts about 20mm apart should be completed step-by-step fashion (fig. 10). By angling the chisel blows into the line of the wall outside the cutting area, the blows are absorbed by the wall bulk and the vibration shock is lessened.

You should continue chiselling until you have cut the slot for the lintel.

Inserting the lintel

Make the bedding mortar for your lintel from three parts of soft sand to one of Portland cement with just enough water to make it workable. Slide the lintel into place and let the mortar under it harden overnight before you proceed. Check that the lintel is plumb and level (fig. 12), before the mortar dries—then you can cut the rest of the opening (fig. 13).

If the space is deeper than a normal joint (10–15mm), reinforce it by driving in bits of slate, knocking off the projecting pieces with a hammer when the mortar has dried (fig. 14). Fill the space above the lintel with the same mortar, pushed well into the gap.

Cutting the main hole

The plaster must be gradually stripped back to the line of the final cut and cut neatly with the bolster. A neat job at this stage reduces the amount of making-good needed when the framework is installed (fig. 16).

In a solid wall you must cut off all the half- and quarter-bricks that project into the opening. Tap them firmly on top with the hammer and bolster, then a bit harder from the face side to cut them off squarely.

In an outside cavity wall, the procedure is slightly different. Square off the

15 Use the same type of mortar as that for bedding the lintel to fill the space around it. Pack the mortar well in with the edge of a trowel

16 The opening is complete and ready to receive whatever finish has been decided on. However, leave the mortar to dry for about a day

opening in the outside leaf as you would for a solid wall. But do not cut off the protruding bricks or blocks on the inner leaf—they will be needed to close the cavity later.

Openings in stud partition walls

The first step in making an opening in a stud partition wall is to find the studs. Bang on the wall with your fist; where you hear a 'solid' sound there will be a stud.

The next step is to site the opening so that you will do as little damage as possible to the existing plasterboard. You will anyway have to cut the opening over-depth so that you can nail the timber lintel to the studs on either side. Try, by siting the opening neatly between two existing studs, to avoid having to cut over-width as well.

Mark out the proposed opening, plus the depth of the lintel and bottom bearer, in the same way as for a masonry wall. Cut the plasterboard on one side with a handyman's knife and steel rule. Then poke a nail through the wall, at each of the four corners, to show where to cut the other side.

Next, saw through the middle stud or studs at the top and bottom. To help keep your saw cut straight, use a pencil and try square to mark right round the studs, and saw alternately from each of the four edges.

Skew-nail the lintel to the studs on either side of the opening, and nail in the bottom bearer.

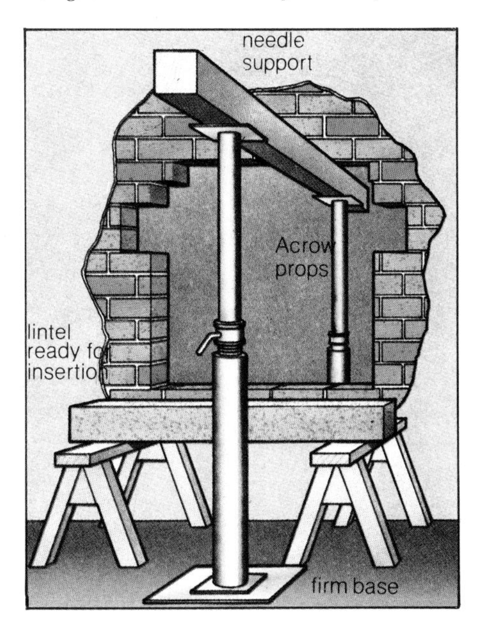

A. Walls with openings of more than 1m must be supported temporarily with Acrow props and a stout timber beam until the lintel is fitted in place

Building a serving hatch

A hole in the wall can be easily and cheaply converted into a practical and attractive serving hatch between the kitchen area and the adjacent dining room.

After knocking a suitable hole through the wall and inserting the necessary lintel, make up an open box, or frame, which is a loose fit within the opening. Then level this frame in the hole using wooden wedges. Check with a spirit level that it is true, then screw through the sides only—do not do the top and bottom as well, or you may, by doing so, pull the box completely out of the desired shape.

Fit a hardwood surround to the opening so that you give a neat appearance to the hatch and then hang the doors you have chosen.

There are many alternatives and variations to the basic design. For example, the hatch can be made without any doors or, for extra privacy, doors on each side of the opening can be incorporated. You can also fit a recessed fluorescent light into the wall above the hatchway to particularly highlight this area at other times in the day when you are not having meals.

The dimensions and details given in the plans are suitable for a small kitchen hatch through a single brick wall. If your wall turns out to be thicker or thinner than the type shown, the width of the boards forming the main carcase should be carefully modified to suit your own particular requirements. Otherwise all the other dimensions should remain exactly the same.

Removing a fireplace

An open fireplace with an ugly surround is an unsightly and draughty liability, particularly in a house where fires are rarely lit or central heating has been installed. By removing the hearth and surround and blocking up the opening you can create a more spacious and attractive room.

However, some old fireplace surrounds—in brick, timber or cast-iron—make an attractive feature which you might not want to destroy. In this case the decorative surround can be retained while the opening is sealed with building blocks or boarding.

Above: Seal the opening neatly using either bricks or building blocks. Check that they are correctly and evenly aligned with the adjoining brickwork using a spirit level or straightedge

Fireplace construction

Most fireplaces consist of a surround, a fireback and grate, and a front hearth. The surround serves a purely decorative function while the fireback, grate and hearth ensure that the fire burns efficiently without risk of accident.

Tiled surround: A number of fireplaces consist of a concrete surround and hearth which is then covered in decorative tiles. The surround is held in place by two metal plugs, bonded to the concrete backing and screwed firmly into the chimney breast or wall behind the fire.

Timber surround: Many fires have a wooden surround, usually with a stone or concrete front hearth protruding beneath the fire opening. The surround is screwed in position on top of a framework of wooden battens fixed to the chimney breast or wall.

Stone or brick surround: This type consists of a number of stone or brickwork courses built up from the hearth against the wall or chimney breast. The gap above the fire is often bridged by a 'soldier' arch of bricks placed on end, held up by a steel support underneath. Although stone or brickwork surrounds are usually built without being tied into the wall behind, occasionally steel wall ties are inserted between courses to help strengthen the structure.

Cast-iron surround: These are held in place in a similar fashion to tiled surrounds: plugs bonded to the back of the cast-iron frame are held tight against the wall with screws. Most cast-iron surrounds also have an inner cast-iron grate frame fitted around the sides and top of the fireplace and held in position either with nuts and bolts or countersunk screws.

Front hearth: Some fires have a front hearth which protrudes into the room below the fireplace opening and is made of the same material as the surround.

Planning the work

Removing a fireplace and blocking up the opening is a relatively straightforward job providing you plan the work carefully.

To remove the surround, hearth and fireback use a crowbar, club hammer and a bolster, safety glasses or goggles.

Where the surround is screwed to the wall or chimney breast you also need a large screwdriver, plus a hacksaw to cut through any fixings which cannot easily be shifted.

Sheet polythene can be bought in large rolls to completely cover the floor and protect it while the work is going on.

Removing the surround

Since the surround is likely to be resting on top of the hearth it is best to start by removing this.

Tiled surrounds: Here the first task is to remove the plaster covering the two fixing lugs. To do this start at the top right hand corner of the fire and chip away the plaster using a hammer and bolster. When you have uncovered the fixing lugs, ask a helper to steady the fire surround while you undo them. Sometimes they will simply unscrew from the wall; if not, cut them off at or near their junction with the wall using a bolster or hacksaw.

With your helper still steadying the far end of the surround, use your left hand to steady the other end and hold the crowbar in your right hand. Insert this between the surround and the chimney breast, somewhere near the base. If the surround moves by even a few millimetres there are no more fixing lugs. If not, there may be fixing lugs at the bottom edges which should be removed before you proceed.

Once you are sure that all the lugs are free, slowly lower the surround to the ground in front of the fire. Two people can usually carry the surround outside to be disposed of.

Removing a timber surround: The procedure used to remove a wooden surround is much the same as for a tiled one except that the fixing lugs usually face towards the fire opening rather than outwards away from it.

Start by taking the crowbar and driving it between the wooden part of the surround and the brickwork behind it. By levering with the crowbar and using your

1 If the fireplace surround has a mantelpiece, start by working this loose with a club hammer and bolster, then lift it away from the wall

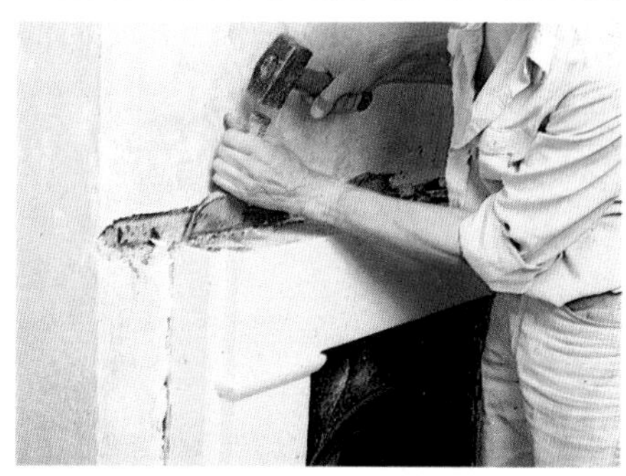

2 Remove the plaster down both sides of the surround and, if you uncover the fixing lugs, unscrew them or, if necessary, cut them loose

3 Once the surround has been removed, pull the fireback away from its fixing mortar or break it loose with the club hammer

4 The inside of the fireplace is lined with brick. Break this loose with the hammer and bolster and then load all the material into strong bags

5 Do the same with the bricks along the bottom of the fireplace. Then use a small shovel to transfer the pieces into the waste bags

6 Then clean the brickwork around the outside of the opening. Remove all the loose mortar and plaster with a hammer and bolster

7 To help cut down the inevitable dust, dampen the brickwork behind the opening. A small garden spray makes this job a lot easier and much cleaner

8 Once the brickwork has been damped down, use a small brush and dustpan to sweep away loose soot and other material which has gathered

11 As you progress, hold a straightedge against the face of the blockwork to check that the vertical and horizontal alignment is correct

12 Once the opening is completely sealed up you must remove the remaining lengths of skirting board on each side of the chimney breast

15 Now apply the first coat of plaster in wide, upward sweeps. Push the float hard against the wall so that you fill in any deep gaps

16 Finish off with a thin topcoat of plaster. Make this as smooth as possible and try to level it off smoothly with the existing wall surface

9 Fill the opening with bricks or, if more suitable, lightweight building blocks. Cut blocks to the correct size with a hammer and bolster

10 Lay a thick bed of mortar across the floor just inside the opening. Then build upwards, leaving a small gap for the necessary ventilation grille

13 Next, damp down all of the brickwork around the opening. This stabilizes the wall area and helps the plaster finish to adhere correctly

14 Once the mortar between the blocks has set, run the blade of the bolster along each joint to even them out and remove any high spots

17 Fix the ventilation grille into position using either screws and wall plugs or just a thin skim of plaster all around the outside

18 When the plaster has completely dried, cut a piece of skirting board to length and secure it across the front of the chimney breast

hands to pull the surround away from the wall you should be able to open a gap between the surround and the wall big enough to look down.

Check whether the timber is held in place by any other fixings—either metal studs or bars. If not, simply lever the facing away from the wall.

If there are other fixings, work your way around the edges of the facing, gently levering it away from the wall; do this a small amount at a time to avoid damaging the wall and brickwork.

Removing a brick surround: A stone or brickwork surround is easily removed with a hammer and bolster one course at a time. Starting from the top, insert the bolster into each of the layers of mortar. Then gently tap each brick free and remove it.

You may come across steel ties bridging the two walls, in which case work these loose by knocking them gently backwards and forwards with the hammer then pull them free with your hand. Continue downwards, removing the soldier arch and steel support as you go until you reach the fire hearth.

Levelling the hearth

Most hearths consist of a slab of concrete—usually covered in tiles—which sits below the opening and is bedded into place on a weak lime-mortar mix. If the bottom of the hearth is level with the surrounding floor loosen the bedding mortar by chopping around it with a hammer and bolster. Then insert the crowbar under one end of the hearth and raise it high enough to push a thin batten of wood underneath. Do the same with the other side and you should be able to lift the whole hearth away with the help of another person and dispose of it outside.

Removing the fireback

The fireback is usually held in place by a bed of mortar laid against the edges of the opening. It is usually old and crumbly so if it does not immediately pull free, use the hammer and bolster to break it into more easily handled pieces. The cavity above will be full of soot and rubble and you should make sure that this is removed and the opening brushed clean before you continue. Then remove and dispose of the fireback.

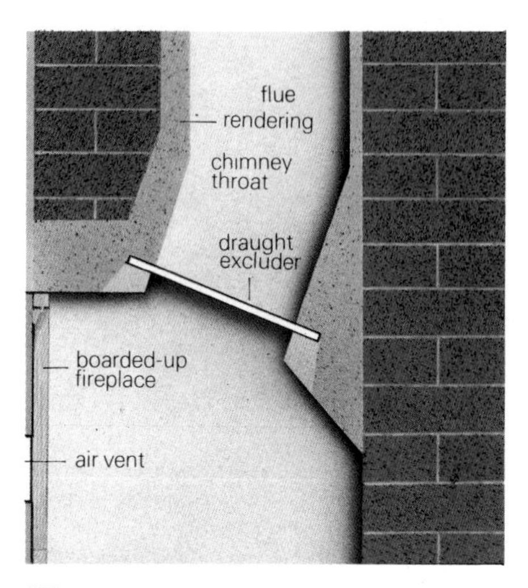

A. Below: Cement a draught excluder across the chimney throat to prevent any draughts and unwanted falls of soot

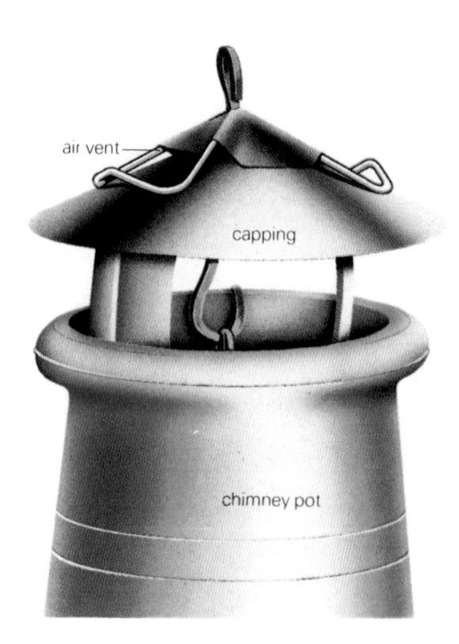

B. Below: Fit a rain bonnet to the chimney pot. This ventilates the flue, but effectively stops penetrating damp

Blocking up the opening

Once the fireplace has been knocked down and the area cleaned, the opening should be blocked off to prevent draughts and to stop dust falling down the chimney into the room. For this you can use bricks, lightweight building blocks or more lightweight materials such as hardboard, chipboard or asbestos.

In order to bed the blocking material into place and allow a neat plastered finish, you need to cut away some of the existing plaster around the opening with the hammer and bolster. If you decide to retain the present surround, first carefully break out the fireback and then cut away the plaster around the opening to a distance of about 200mm on each side.

What you do next depends on whether you block up the opening with bricks or some type of sheeting. But whatever method you use, the blocked opening must contain a ventilation grille, fitted at a distance of about 100mm from the floor.

Bricking in: Bricks and lightweight building blocks are both perfectly adequate where you want to block up an opening permanently.

First prepare a mix of 1:4 mortar and lay a bed of it on the floor between the existing wall. Then build up each course of bricks; remember to leave a gap 100mm from the floor to accommodate the vent.

As the wall is built upwards, hold a straightedge against the face of the brickwork to check vertical and horizontal alignment.

Build up successive courses until you fill the cavity. You may have to ease the last brick into position.

Finally, look over the new brickwork and fill all gaps to create a smooth and flat surface. Leave it to dry out for 12 hours before plastering.

Boarding up: For this use 6mm oil-tempered hardboard, chipboard or, if you intend to fit a gas fire in front of the wall, asbestos sheeting. Measure and cut the sheeting to size, and make an internal hole to take the ventilator using a drill and a padsaw. When cutting and drilling asbestos, make sure you wear a mask to avoid breathing in the dust.

Fix the sheeting into place by marking and drilling holes along its edge and using wall plugs to secure it to the wall beneath. Make sure that the board is just below the surface of the surrounding plasterwork. The surface can then be neatly plastered and finished level.

Replastering

Before plastering make sure that the surface is prepared properly and that old and flaking plaster is stabilized.

Once both coats of plaster have been applied and allowed to dry thoroughly, the ventilation grille can be fitted and fixed firmly in place with bolts or self-tapping screws (fig. 17).

Although the plaster may dry hard after about 20 minutes, it often takes months to settle on the brickwork below; consequently, redecorating—especially with wallpaper—should not be undertaken straight away. Two or three months should be allowed to elapse.

Sealing

Disused fireplaces often run the risk of penetrating damp as a result of rain falling down the chimney. The simplest way of avoiding this is to fit a rain bonnet—a blocking piece which is cemented into the chimney pot. The bonnet effectively stops rain entering the chimney, but allows air to circulate freely (fig. B).

Alternatively, you could remove the chimney pot, cover the opening with slate and then seal it with mortar flaunching. In this case, though, ventilation must be provided in the form of an airbrick in the chimney stack.

Note that in the UK, sealing a chimney constitutes a structural alteration and you will need building permission from your local Building Control office or District Surveyor. He will want to know how the sealed chimney is to be ventilated and also what alternative methods of heating are being used.

Stone fireplace kits

Modern living rooms can all too easily look soulless without a welcoming focal point and it is not difficult to see why the traditional open fire is coming back into vogue. But the actual fireplace and accompanying chimney are only half the secret of a fire's appeal. Equally important is the fire surround, which blends a fire with its room and offers all sorts of decorative potential. But whether you are starting from scratch or dressing up an old fireplace, a highly practical and relatively inexpensive alternative to the conventional surrounds is a stone fireplace kit of the type featured here.

The choice of kits

The kits are available in a wide variety of designs, each of which comes in a number of sizes to fit standard grate and hearth sizes. The kit manufacturers will also supply the necessary components to any design that you require.

A. Below: The attraction of stone fireplace kits as opposed to other fire surrounds is the flexibility in the style of design that is now offered

The kits are supplied with 'interiors' or 'insert panels'. These are stones, usually of the same material as the surround, which fit around the actual fire recess opening to accommodate heating appliances of different types and sizes. In some cases—for example in the absence of a solid fuel fire—they are not necessary.

None of the manufacturers supply bedding mortar materials, although in some cases the colouring agent for the final pointing, where required, is included.

Equipment

Apart from the kit itself you must obtain approximately 50kg of mortar ingredients. Most kits recommend one part Portland cement to three parts soft sand; some suggest that you add lime or plasticizer or a few squirts of washing-up liquid to make it spread more easily.

Tools: The mortar is mixed and laid with a bricklayer's trowel, and the blocks are tapped into place with a heavy hammer. A spirit level is vital for checking that the courses are horizontal. A large builder's

level is best, as this also allows you to check that the construction is plumb. It is useful to have a true straightedge for extending the breadth of your levelling.

The blocks must be wetted before they are positioned, so it is a good idea to have a large bowl of water to hand. Keep another bowl of water and a stiff brush for cleaning any spilt mortar off the stones. The recommended mortar joint varies slightly from kit to kit, but 10mm is the average.

The body blocks must be tied to the wall during construction. A simple way to do this is by driving 150mm masonry nails into the wall at various levels, leaving about 50mm to be held firm in the mortar joints of the surround. About ten such nails, inserted at approximately 300mm and 600mm heights, will be adequate for a small fire surround.

Planning the fire surround

The planning must begin with the heating appliance you intend to use. It is relatively easy to accommodate gas or electric fires, and most solid fuel fires are also manufactured in standard sizes.

However, if you wish to install a more sophisticated solid fuel system, using either enclosed room heater fires which stand proud of the recess opening, or perhaps incorporating a back boiler for central heating, you must make sure that the design can be modified to accommodate the appliance and any interior modifications necessary to the fireplace.

Do not build the fireplace first, and similarly do not plan it around an appliance which you may later want to replace. Sophisticated solid fuel fires may require quite elaborate chimney modifications which will be much more difficult to construct after your fire surround is in place. Solid fuel fires of all kinds also require asbestos rope-lined expansion joints to accommodate the expansion caused by the intense heat.

Whatever installation you are planning it makes sense to incorporate expansion joints in the hearth and between the fireback and the fire surround or any inset panels. Similarly you should make sure that there is a throat-forming lintel across the fireplace opening to protect the surround from excessive heat.

A fireplace hearth must be built on top of a constructional hearth. This is the sub-hearth of stone or concrete which is designed to protect the house timbers from the fire.

Where the fireplace has been covered in, you may find such a hearth under the carpet, or even under hardboard placed over the original floorboards. In most cases, however, the constructional hearth will still be covered by the old tiled or brick hearth. In either case

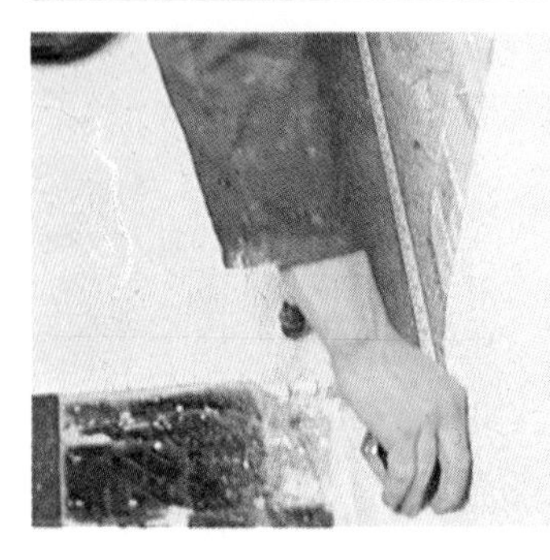

1 Prepare the fireplace by stripping away the existing surround and exposing the constructional hearth, then check the size of the opening

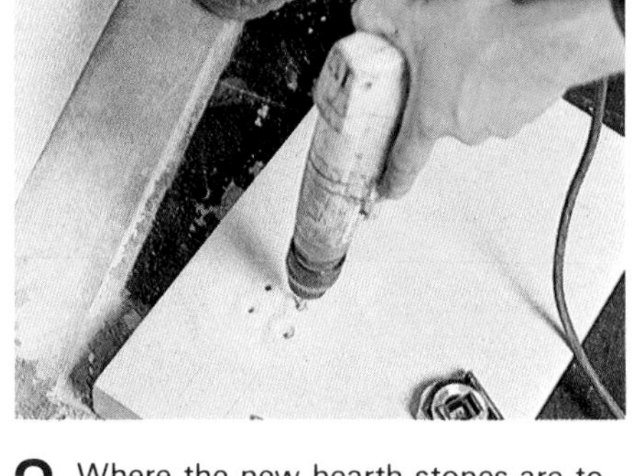

2 Where the new hearth stones are to cover existing gas pipes, drill a series of holes in the relevant stone in order to form one hole of the correct size

5 Once the hearth stones have been fixed in place, 'butter' each stone as you lay it with a generous amount of mortar and tap it down into place

6 Lay each body block with careful reference to a spirit level and double check across corresponding lines of stones for absolute accuracy

9 Continuing to follow the plan, start laying the body blocks to the side of the surround. Be sure to keep checking the level as you go along

10 If your initial measurements were accurate, the stones will fit your room perfectly—but take care not to stain any existing decorations while working

3 Lay the hearth stones in a dry run to check that they fit snugly against the wall and that any obstructions such as pipes are easily accommodated

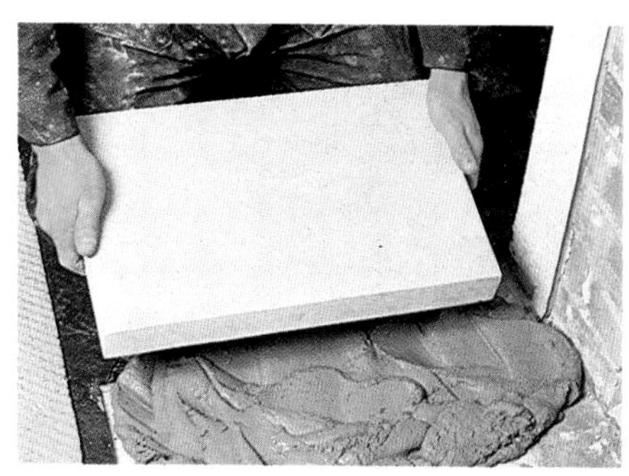

4 Mix up the mortar for the hearth stones, then lay them in place. Allow at least one and a half hours for the mortar to set before continuing

7 Take special care to check that the mantel stones are level; in this case you should bring the mortar infill right up to the surface of the mantel

8 Where a particular design continues the hearth, prepare the floor and wall, then bed the stone in mortar. Finally, check that the level is true

11 Once the body blocks comprising the extension have been laid, lay the mantel stones; however, as before, do not fill the back of the stones

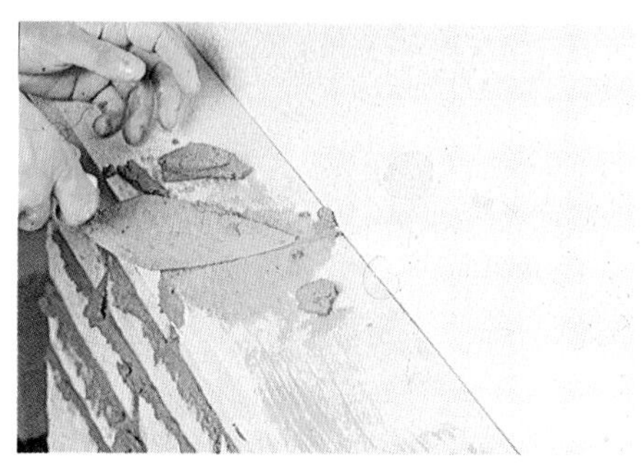

12 When the entire surround is completed, you can start paying attention to the pointing. To begin with, fill all the gaps with mortar

13 Make a dry mortar mix and trowel it well into the spaces that exist between all the hearth stones, the body blocks and the mantel stones

14 Having filled all the joints that show, scrape off the excess mortar with your trowel taking care not to damage the pointing as you go along

remove the covering and clean the constructional hearth so that it will readily accept the new hearth. If there is no constructional hearth you must build one.

Most types of hearth can easily be prised up. Of course, you may well have to remove the fireplace surround first. This is detailed in the last section and is a simple, but heavy, job. Most types of fire surround are screwed to the wall through concealed lugs. Chip away the plaster in a 25mm band all the way round the surround to reveal the lugs and remove their fixing screws. Then, with the help of an assistant, prise the surround from the wall and remove it from the hearth.

To remove the hearth, first chip around the base with a hammer and bolster to break the mortar bond underneath, and create an opening for a larger lever. Use a spade to lever up the hearth, then knock wooden wedges into the gap. Drive the wedges under the hearth to lift it up, then get an assistant to help you remove it.

If the back hearth is in particularly bad condition, it may have to be replaced. Remove it using a spade as described above. Not all fireplace kits include a new back hearth, and it may be necessary to order one specially tailored to the dimensions required.

Before you start the actual installation of a fireplace kit, pay some further thought to whether the existing fire back is adequate, whether the chimney needs modification to accommodate a new type of appliance and in the case of a back boiler system whether the existing boiler is sound.

In most cases the new fire surround will be larger than the original, and considerably heavier. Because of this you must also examine the floor and determine whether the surround will be resting on joists or merely on floorboards. If the floor is not suitable for the considerable extra weight you must shore it up either with props to support sagging joists, or additional joists or rafters.

Finally, if the chimney has not been swept recently, this must be attended to. Make sure that it draws properly and is not blocked by any obstructions.

Constructing the fireplace kit

Different kits use different methods of construction, but the basic procedures remain the same. The majority of kit manufacturers recommend that the body blocks are placed first, these being supported at their base up to the level of the hearth. They advise adding the hearth later in order to prevent the hearth block from being accidentally stained by a spillage of mortar.

On the other hand, laying the hearth

15 Then use a damp sponge to wash off any mortar stains on the stones, taking care not to damage the still wet pointing you have just done

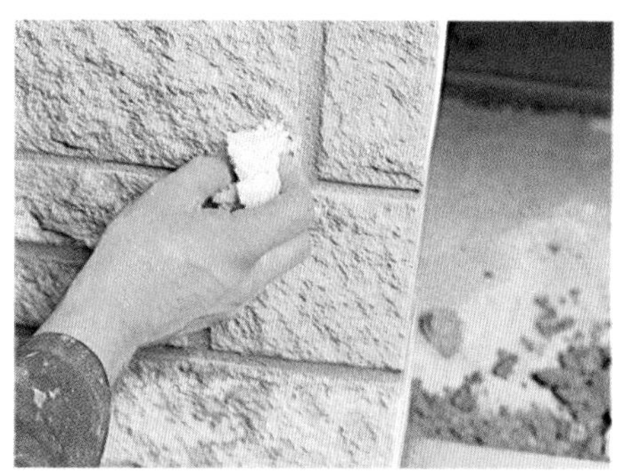

16 Allow the pointing to dry, then brush off any mortar. Finally clean any spilt mortar from the fireplace with a small sponge and water

first provides a firm, clean base upon which to build and so some manufacturers recommend this approach. In this case the mortar bed under the base must be allowed at least one and a half hours to set otherwise the weight of the blocks may move the hearth out of place.

Brush away any dust or loose fragments from the receiving surfaces, then dampen them to reduce premature drying of the mortar. Similarly, soak the blocks in water for two minutes, and wet the mantel slabs with a brush.

Laying the body blocks: Place joint thickness gauging wedges at the back of the work, and the joint thickness straightedge along the front. Leave room for decorative pointing at the fire opening, and make the necessary expansion joints as the construction proceeds.

Using generous portions of mortar, tap each block home until it meets resistance from the spacers (fig. 5). Check that the blocks are both level and vertical with the spirit level. Any excess mortar will be squeezed out at the back of the joint so, when each block is bedded in, loosely fill with mortar behind it.

On each course start at the fire opening and work outwards. Then return to the other side of the opening and complete the course before building upwards.

Take particular care to insert the lintel stone correctly. In some cases this must be reinforced with a flat steel bar as specified by the manufacturers. Continue upwards until the mantel is reached then lay the stone mantels in the same way as the blocks. In this case, there is usually an overhang.

While the bodywork mortar is setting you can lay the hearth. First, put down a generous bed of mortar, stopping just short of the edge to give a neat appearance. If you are installing a new back hearth, lay this first and make an expansion joint of asbestos rope between the two slabs. Tap the hearth home so that it is perfectly level, checking it with the spirit level. Cover it to protect the smooth surface from pointing spillages.

Finishing off: When the main body of mortar has set, remove the straightedge to allow for pointing. Then carefully insert small slices of mortar—plain or coloured—into all the joints that show. The joints may be finished off in a number of ways, according to taste. For a rubbed joint, run a piece of pipe or your thumb wrapped with a wet cloth along each joint.

Finally, clean up the work before any mortar sets. Allow the whole construction to dry out for a week before lighting the fire, and burn only small fires for the first few days. During this time, make good the plaster around the fireplace and redecorate to enhance the effect.

Interior stone cladding

Traditional stone or brick wall surfaces are now enjoying a revival of interest. Despite increasingly sophisticated interior designs, few modern methods of wallcladding can match the texture and appearance of a well-constructed stone or brickwork surface.

Reconstituted stone walls

The most authentic and popular material for interior stonework is reconstituted stone. It is produced by several manufacturers both in block form for building, and in tile form for wall facing. The process reproduces as closely as possible the feel, shape and colour of stone and can be purchased in kit form or separately to harmonize with any existing home furnishings or colour scheme.

Wall facing tiles are between 10mm and 30mm thick and are available in a variety of sizes to ensure the widest possible choice of designs.

Kits are available in random or coursed sizes, and can be purchased in a single colour or in mixed shades. Normally each pack covers an area of around $0.5m^2$, with adhesive and grout included.

Hand-made brick tiles

An alternative to stone tiles is the hand-made brick tiling similar to real bricks but only 16mm thick.

Tiles are available in packs of 29, with ten corner tiles per pack. The corner tiles include right-angled returns for external corners, giving the appearance of solid brickwork. Each pack of 29 tiles covers an area of $0.5m^2$, allowing 9mm for each mortar course, and manufacturers also supply adhesives and grout.

Mortar and pointing compounds

You should choose the colour of the pointing compound as carefully as you choose the shade of the stone or brick tiles. Best results are normally achieved by using a sand which gives the mortar a colour close to that of the tiles. Use cement, lime and sand in a 1:2:8 ratio to make up a fairly stiff mix.

Planning and preparation

Like any other household job, make sure that you have all the tools you need before beginning work. These will include a trowel, a tape measure or ruler, a marking pencil, spirit level, wiping rags or sponges, bolster and hammer (or a power tool with a stone cutting attachment), an old hacksaw, dust sheets or old newspapers, and a supply of 10mm wooden 'spacers'.

Spacers are thin pieces of timber which are placed between the tiles as they are applied to the surface. They ensure that the spacing of the tiles and the thickness of the mortar joints remain constant, and also support the tiles themselves until the adhesive has set.

Your first step is to calculate the area you wish to cover.

Give special consideration to corners—both internal and external. For a more attractive appearance, you should make sure that the joints show at the side of external corners rather than at the front. Consequently, the front surface will be approximately 35mm wider than the existing wall surface (2 × 16mm width of tile, with allowance for adhesive).

Internal angles, in either brick or stone, offer a choice of jointing; you can either butt the tiles on the side wall against those on the back wall, or butt the back surface against the side. But because using one method exclusively forms a continuous vertical joint which is not particularly attractive, it is better to stagger the joints on alternate courses; at the first internal corner joint, butt the back surface against that of the side (or

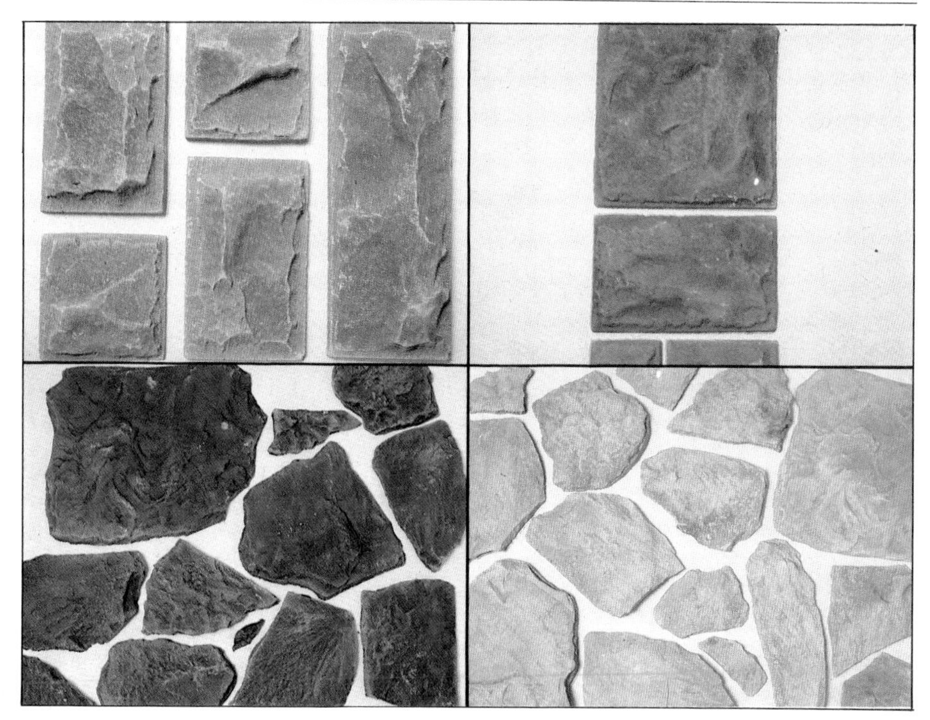

A. Above: Stone cladding is available from builders' merchants or from the manufacturers in many different finishes and colours. **Top left and right**: Stone blocks. **Bottom**: Random pattern stone blocks

the soffit), but on the next course, butt the side surface against that of the back wall. In this way you can offset the effect of an unsightly corner, and create the appearance of authentic bonding.

Measure the area carefully, systematically recording the dimensions. Divide irregular wall surfaces first of all into the largest flat surfaces, then measure each remaining area before adding all the dimensions together.

Make sure you order enough tiles, allowing some spares, and adhesive.

Preparing the surface

Make sure that all existing surfaces are sound, clean and free from loose dust and grease. Prime sound timber and plaster surfaces with a PVA bonding agent. Where damp has attacked plaster, chip it off and replace it with a sand/cement render—even if the cause has been remedied. If the plaster is newly laid, wait four weeks before fixing the tiles to it; surfaces must be perfectly dry and not liable to subside or move.

Tiles can be fixed to ordinary timber-framed walls covered in plasterboard. But certain conditions apply in this case. Once the tiles are set they will be non-flexible; consequently, the surface to which they are attached should be the same. Provide enough support to partition walls to prevent movement which may result in the failure of the bonding. In the case of timber walls, bear in mind that the timber must be ventilated and that you should allow air to flow behind it.

Remove wallpaper from any surface you wish to cover and, in the case of painted surfaces, check that the paint is in good condition. Scrape off any flaking

1 Before you start work, divide up the tiles according to size and shape. Then lay them out on sheets of newspaper equal to the area you want to cover. This allows you to establish the most pleasing pattern. As you do this mark out those tiles that need to be cut to complete the design using a try square and a felt-tipped marker

2 Most manufacturers supply bags of fixative suitable for use with their tiles, but in some cases, if they do not, you can just use ordinary mortar. Add the contents of each bag of mortar to the recommended amount of water and then stir it together thoroughly until you have achieved a rich creamy consistency which will be easy to work with

5 For a particularly clean cut, you should score the actual edges of the tiles as well. Make sure that the marks are at right-angles to the face and back. Once the tile has been scored on all four sides, place it on a completely flat surface and strike it firmly and accurately with a hammer and bolster along the scored line. The tile will split neatly in two

6 If any of the adhesive strays on to the tiles by mistake, do not leave it to dry out but wipe it off immediately with a sponge that is clean and damp. For a more attractive appearance to the tiles, try to ensure that the joints show at the sides of external corners rather than being particularly noticeable from the front of the finished wall

3 Apply the fixative in dabs on the back corners and centres of each tile. Start at one of the bottom corners and work upwards. Keep to your same planned design as much as possible. Once each tile is positioned, place a 10mm spacer between it and the adjoining tile so that you always maintain a consistent width of joint

4 Tiles can be cut to size using an angle grinder which has been fitted with a stone cutting wheel—this is particularly useful if you need to cut tiles lengthways. Alternatively, score both the face and the back of each tile with a large hacksaw—taking great care as you do it to follow the marked out cutting lines on each tile

7 Leave the mortar to set for at least 24 hours minimum. Then carefully remove each of the wooden spacers, which are giving the necessary gap, with the aid of a tool like a screwdriver. Then use a stiff—it must not be too liquid—mixture of 1:2:8 cement/lime/sand for the actual pointing between all the tiles. Point carefully with a trowel

8 Carefully smooth out the joints with either a finger covered in a cloth or by using a small section of rubber tubing. When the mortar has virtually dried, sweep the surface of the tiles firmly with a soft brush. This really cleans the stone thoroughly and also helps the pointing to blend into the joints properly. Finally touch up any small defects in the pointing

paintwork and use a bonding agent to secure what is left. Roughen gloss paint using glasspaper to provide an adequate key for the wall-cladding adhesive.

Planning features

Lay out the tiles on the sheets of newspaper to establish the most pleasing pattern. When doing so, avoid creating unsightly cross-joints—such as when four tiles meet at their corners. Also, try to avoid the necessity of cutting too many tiles as this is time-consuming and wasteful. Where tiles must be cut, simply mark them clearly to fit the appropriate space. Avoid using cut tiles at the edges of the tiled area because this would look unauthentic and flimsy. Instead, lay out the pattern, beginning at the edges, then fill in the centre. Carefully mark each tile for cutting.

Fixing the stonework

When you have laid out the tiles in the most pleasing pattern, and to the correct dimensions, either number the tiles from the bottom course upwards and stack them for use, or apply them directly to the wall from their pattern on the floor. Mix the recommended adhesive in quantities sufficient to fix only one square metre at a time as this will reduce wastage.

There are three different methods for applying the adhesive and these largely depend upon the surface with which you are working. Generally, the adhesive is best applied in 'dabs' on the back corners and centres of the tile so that the tile can then gently be slid into position. Alternatively, you can apply a thin layer all over the back of the tile. But where the existing wall surface is uneven, trowel the adhesive on to the wall rather than the tile.

Spacing

Start at the bottom course with a corner tile. Bear in mind, however, that the tile should be placed so that it overlaps tiles on any side walls: if this is necessary, place a tile against the side wall to establish the exact size of the overlap.

Lay the tiles one course at a time, checking the vertical and horizontal positioning against a known square edge of a spirit level. Between each tile, place a 6mm spacer to maintain a consistent mortar course. Some manufacturers supply their own spacers with the kit, but you can just as easily make up your own from some timber offcuts which are all the same width.

Tile cutting

Your ability to cut tiles will largely depend on your tools and the type of tile you are using, but usually there is a choice of two methods; either cut the tiles with a stone cutting power drill attachment, or use a hammer and bolster. In both cases, mark the cutting line clearly and squarely using a clear marker and a try or combination square.

Pointing

A variety of mortar colouring additives is available to bring out the best shades in the stone you have used. Whatever the colour, leave the adhesive to set for 24 hours before removing the spacers and attempting to point the gaps.

Unless you are using a pointing compound recommended by the manufacturer, make up a stiff cement/lime/sand in a ratio of 1:2:8. Try to use a sand which matches the colour of the stone, and add only enough water to hold the mortar together.

Mix only enough mortar to complete a square metre at a time: the job is time-consuming and dry mortar quickly becomes unusable.

Use a piece of rubber tube or a cloth-covered finger to create a consistent recess in the mortar. Brush off any excess with a soft-headed brush before the mortar sets, but avoid smearing it over the face of the tile.

Brick tiles

The procedure for setting brick tiles is exactly the same as for stone tiles, except that corner tiles are provided.

Drystone walling

It is not difficult to see why drystone walls are so widely used in many country areas and why they also have an instant appeal to the home improver. Although sometimes difficult to erect, they last for literally hundreds of years and still retain their natural attractiveness when other types of walls and fences need to be replaced or repaired.

A drystone wall uses no mortar in its construction and depends instead for its strength and durability on the correct choice and placement of uncut stones of various sizes.

Component parts

Most free-standing drystone walls are made up of five basic stones which vary in size and shape. Once in place, each stone binds on others to strengthen the whole structure and help waterproof the wall.

To give the wall a solid base on which to sit, a shallow trench is dug just below the proposed site. This is then filled with two or three layers of flat stones.

Above this the wall is built using a combination of medium-sized edging stones, and larger stones—*throughs*—which span the whole width of the wall at random intervals to help strengthen it. Between the edging stones, the centre of the wall is packed with smaller stones—the *infill*—to stop the whole structure collapsing inwards (fig. A).

After a final course consisting entirely of throughs the wall is given a topping of rounded *coping* stones set on edge.

Planning the work

Before you order any materials, go to the site of the proposed wall and carefully plan its exact length, height and width. Bear in mind that only very rarely should you need to exceed the dimensions of an average farm wall—1.3m high with a 650mm wide base. Nor should any absolute beginner attempt to build a wall more than 6m long.

From these dimensions you can

A. Below: A drystone wall uses five basic stones, which are carefully positioned for strength and rigidity

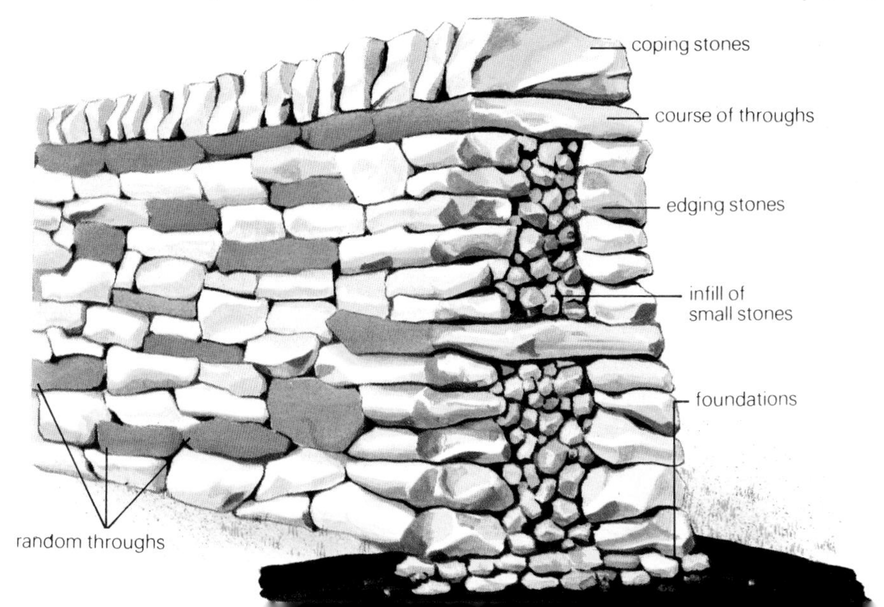

1 Divide your stones into neat piles according to size. Make the foundations 100mm wider than the wall base. Mark these dimensions with stakes and string

2 Using the lines as a guide, dig a 150mm plot for the foundations. Make sure it is square, then compact any loose earth in the bottom of the plot by trampling it or tamping it down

5 Put the batter frames into the ground at each end of the foundations, then tie pieces of string to the uprights. Extend them along both sides, about 50mm above ground level

6 Use these strings as guides to place the outer edging stones and move them as the wall progresses. Then pack the centre with small infill stones and a number of large throughs at random

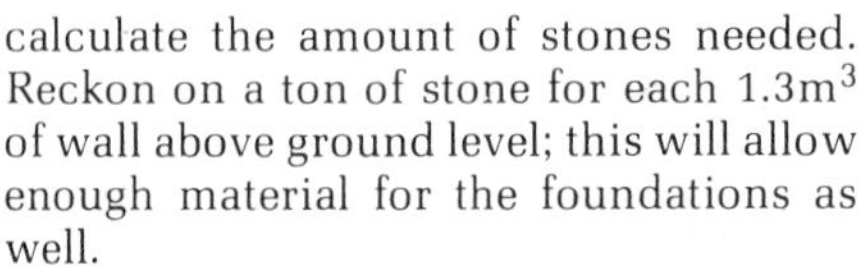

calculate the amount of stones needed. Reckon on a ton of stone for each $1.3m^3$ of wall above ground level; this will allow enough material for the foundations as well.

Almost any type of stone can be used but the best are hard rocks such as granite, basalt or sandstone.

So that you have a variety of stones from which to choose, order a range of different sizes—from small stones 50–100mm square for the infill, to the large throughs long enough to span the width of the wall.

3 Lay large rectangular-shaped stones side by side as the basic foundations. Then, as you build upwards, fill the gaps in the middle with small loosely packed stones which slot neatly into place

4 With the foundations completed, build a pair of batter frames to act as guides. Then nail two smaller timber battens across the uprights so that it looks like a cross-section of the wall

7 Place throughs along and across the wall as you approach the end of each section so that you leave a neat, flat vertical face. Then select some throughs for the top

8 Lay large, flat throughs, slightly longer then the wall span, along the top. On top of the throughs lay a course of round-topped coping stones, set on edge and all leaning in the same direction

Building the foundations

Make the foundations the same length as the proposed wall and about 100mm wider than its base. Mark these dimensions by driving four wooden stakes into the ground at each of the outside corners. Tie marking strings between the stakes and lay them along the ground to mark the outside of the plot (fig. 1).

Using the inside of the lines as a guide, dig a shallow trench 150mm deep all around the outside of the area. Then shovel out the earth in the middle to the same depth.

Select a number of large, regular-shaped stones to line the outside of the plot.

Complete the bottom layer by filling in the gaps in the middle of the plot.

Lay further layers of stone in the same way until you are nearly level with the ground. Then run a long straightedge across the top of the hole to check that the top layer of stones is level.

Building the wall

Before you start building, construct a pair of 'batter frames' to act as a guide to the correct placement of the outer stones. Make each of these from four pieces of lightweight timber—two side and two crosspieces—shaped like a cross-section of the wall.

Position the two outer timbers so that they slope gently inwards towards the top of the proposed wall at an angle of roughly 10° and sharpen the bottom ends so that you can drive them into the ground. Then nail the other two pieces across the side pieces to complete the frame. Check that both frames are tall enough to accommodate the wall you want to build, and that their batter is correct, before continuing.

Push the frames into the ground at either end of your foundations and tie string between them, on both sides, about 50mm from the ground (fig. 5).

Lay the bottom course 50mm in from the sides of the foundations using medium-sized edging stones.

Once the bottom course is in position, fill the gap down the centre with small infill stones. Next, move the guiding strings upwards and start work on the second course.

On each course from the second upwards, insert a number of large 'throughs' at random intervals.

Lay courses of stone until you reach a position about 500mm lower than where you want the wall to end. Then add a double course of finishing stones.

Topping the wall

Finish the wall with a complete course of throughs capped by a row of rounded coping stones set on edge.

On top of the throughs, at both ends of the wall, place two medium-sized edging stones to act as 'stops'. Then lay flat, round-topped stones on edge.

Below: You can add a special feature to any drystone wall by building a small section of the top as a planter for flowers. The wall shown also has a bay at the end to form a pier flanking an entrance way. Construct the wall using the techniques described up to the top course of through stones. Then continue with two courses of edging stones set in mortar

INDEX

The numbers in **bold** indicate projects and the *italic* numbers refer to pictures.

Picture Credits
Barnaby's Picture Library: 442
Barbara Bellingham: 298
BMV: 55, 56, 57, 58, 59
Simon Butcher: 6, 8, 9, 152, 153, 154, 155, 201, 202, 306, 307, 390, 396, 397, 450, 452, 453, 478, 479
Gavin Cochrane: 120, 121, 122, 245, 292, 293, 311, 314, 338, 411, 412, 424/5, 456, 458, 459, 460, 461
Design Council: 387
Dolly Mixtures: 35
Peter Dazeley: 436/7
Ray Duns: 11, 12, 13, 14/15, 16, 17, 18, 19, 26, 28, 29, 30, 32, 33, 34, 48, 49, 50, 52, 53, 54, 63, 64, 68, 71, 92, 95, 103, 104, 106, 107, 111, 112, 113, 144, 145, 146, 147, 164, 179, 180, 181, 182, 183, 194, 198, 199, 218/19, 222, 223, 225, 226, 229, 230, 232, 233, 253, 255, 256, 257, 259, 261, 278, 279, 289, 291, 327, 328, 329, 330, 349, 352, 353, 354, 356, 357, 358, 360, 361, 362, 364, 366, 375, 377, 378, 380, 381, 382, 383, 407, 410, 417, 420, 421, 426, 427, 428, 446, 447, 463, 465, 466, 467, 472, 473, 474, 477, 478, 482, 483, 484
Chris Fairclough: 130, 133, 134, 135
Nelson Hargreaves: 430, 434
Clive Helm: 244
J. A. Hewetson & Co.: 84
James Johnson: 85, 159, 160, 161, 162, 163, 316, 317, 318
David Jordan: 462
Nigel MacIntyre: 343
Bill McLaughlin: 237, 240, 402, 422
Nigel Messett: 98, 99, 100, 127, 128, 138, 140, 141, 142
Martin Palmer: 67, 404
Rotoflex Home Lighting: 241, 242
Sandersons Collection: 40
Harry Smith Collection: 398
Solid Fuel Advisory Service: 265, 266, 267, 268, 270
John Ward: 21, 22, 23, 276, 277, 319, 322, 323
Gary Warren: 116
Michael Warren: 401, 403
Elizabeth Whiting: 5, 62, 82/3, 165, 238, 239, 243, 325, 384/5, 386, 388, 399, 400

Artwork Credits
Advertising Arts: 66/7, 72/3, 234, 235, 236, 265, 266, 267, 268, 282, 332, 337, 350, 415, 416, 429, 451, 454, 455, 481
Creative Group Aim: 308/9
Bernard Fallon: 20, 24, 25, 46/7, 60, 65, 79, 93, 108/9, 123, 124, 125, 126, 150/1, 156/7, 174, 197, 203, 204, 205, 220, 221, 294, 313, 315, 359, 365, 418/19, 431, 432, 433, 435, 443, 444, 445, 448
John Harwood: 86/7, 90, 273, 275
Trevor Lawrence: 139, 340
Nigel Osborne: 207, 208, 209, 210, 211, 468
Sue Rodger: 339
Colin Salmon: 166, 167, 168/9, 170, 171
Ian Stephen: 392, 394, 395
Venner Artists: 31, 94, 114, 128, 129, 132, 136, 137, 172, 185, 186/7, 190, 194/5, 227, 248/9, 250/1, 252, 262/3, 300, 301, 302/3, 318, 321, 341, 342, 343, 369, 370/1, 374
Gary Warren: 118/19
David Watson: 345
Edward Williams Arts: 297
Paul Williams: 470/1
Ted Williams: 214, 217